Statutory Instruments 1987

PART II

SECTION 1

Published by Authority

LONDON

HER MAJESTY'S STATIONERY OFFICE

1989

ISBN 0 11 840284 6

HMSO publications are available from:

HMSO Publications Centre
(Mail and telephone orders only)
PO Box 276, London, SW8 5DT
Telephone orders 01-873 9090
General enquiries 01-873 0011
(queuing system in operation for both numbers)

HMSO Bookshops
49 High Holborn, London, WC1V 6HB   01-873 0011 (Counter service only)
258 Broad Street, Birmingham, B1 2HE   021-643 3740
Southey House, 33 Wine Street, Bristol, BS1 2BQ   (0272) 264306
9-21 Princess Street, Manchester, M60 8AS   061-834 7201
80 Chichester Street, Belfast, BT1 4JY   (0232) 238451
71 Lothian Road, Edinburgh, EH3 9AZ   031-228 4181

HMSO's Accredited Agents
(see Yellow Pages)

and through good booksellers

Price for two sections £128 net

Printed in the United Kingdom for Her Majesty's Stationery Office
Dd8051772 6/89 C7 G409 10170

Contents of the Edition

PART I

SECTION 1

SECTION 2

PART II

SECTION 1

SECTION 2

PART III

List of Instruments in Part II

STATUTORY INSTRUMENTS

OTHER INSTRUMENTS

STATUTORY INSTRUMENTS

1987 No. 783

PUBLIC HEALTH, ENGLAND AND WALES
PUBLIC HEALTH, SCOTLAND
PUBLIC HEALTH, NORTHERN IRELAND

The Control of Pollution (Anti-Fouling Paints and Treatments) Regulations 1987

Made - - - -	*30th April 1987*
Laid before Parliament	*7th May 1987*
Coming into force	*28th May 1987*

The Secretary of State for the Environment, as respects England, the Secretary of State for Wales, as respects Wales, the Secretary of State for Scotland, as respects Scotland, and the Secretary of State for Northern Ireland, as respects Northern Ireland–

(1) having consulted persons appearing to them to represent persons whose activities are likely to be prohibited or restricted by these Regulations;

(2) having published on 13th March 1987 in the London Gazette, the Belfast Gazette and the Edinburgh Gazette a notice indicating the effect of these Regulations, if made, and specifying–

(a) the date on which it is proposed they should come into force;

(b) places where a draft of them might be inspected free of charge by members of the public in office hours; and

(c) a period of 21 days beginning with the date on which the notice was first published as the period in which written representations might be made to the Secretaries of State;

(3) having considered the representations made to them in accordance with the notice; and

(4) considering it appropriate to make these Regulations to prevent the substances to which they apply causing damage to freshwater, estuarial and marine animals and plants,

in exercise of the powers conferred on them by sections 100 and 104(1) of the Control of Pollution Act 1974(**a**) and of all other powers enabling them in that behalf, hereby make the following Regulations in the form of the draft mentioned in paragraph (2)(b) above:

Citation and commencement

1. These Regulations may be cited as the Control of Pollution (Anti-Fouling Paints and Treatments) Regulations 1987 and shall come into force on 28th May 1987.

(**a**) 1974 c.40.

Interpretation

2. In these Regulations–

"anti-fouling paint" means any surface coating containing one or more chemical compounds which have the effect of inhibiting the growth of or having other detrimental effects on freshwater, estuarial or marine life and which is intended to be applied in a liquid or semi-liquid form to the hull of a ship or boat;

"anti-fouling treatment" means any treatment containing one or more chemical compounds which have the effect of inhibiting the growth of or having other detrimental effects on freshwater, estuarial or marine life and which is intended for application in a liquid or semi-liquid form to any net, cage, float or other apparatus used in connection with the propagation or cultivation of fish or shellfish;

"tri-organotin compound" means a chemical compound in which tin is chemically bound directly to three alkyl or aryl radicals by a carbon linkage;

"retail sale" means sale by way of business to a person who does not buy, or hold himself out as buying, in the course of a business;

"wholesale" means supply by way of business to a person who buys, or holds himself out as buying, in the course of a business.

Anti-fouling paints and treatments to which the Regulations apply

3. These Regulations apply to any anti-fouling paint or treatment containing a tri-organotin compound.

Prohibition of supply of paints and treatments

4.—(1) No person shall supply, whether for retail sale or by way of retail sale, an anti-fouling paint to which these Regulations apply.

(2) No person shall supply, whether by way of retail sale or wholesale, an anti-fouling treatment to which these Regulations apply.

Offences

5.—(1) A person who contravenes regulation 4 shall be guilty of an offence and shall be liable on summary conviction to a fine not exceeding £2000, and on conviction on indictment to a fine.

(2) Where a person is charged with an offence under these Regulations it shall be a defence for him to prove that he took all reasonable steps and exercised all due diligence to avoid committing the offence.

Revocations

6. The Control of Pollution (Anti-Fouling Paints) Regulations 1985(**a**) and the Control of Pollution (Anti-Fouling Paints) (Amendment) Regulations 1986(**b**) are hereby revoked.

29th April 1987	*Nicholas Ridley* Secretary of State for the Environment
30th April 1987	*Nicholas Edwards* Secretary of State for Wales
30th April 1987	*Malcolm Rifkind* Secretary of State for Scotland
30th April 1987	*Tom King* Secretary of State for Northern Ireland

(**a**) S.I. 1985/2011.   (**b**) S.I. 1986/2300.

EXPLANATORY NOTE

(This note is not part of the Regulations)

These Regulations, which apply throughout the United Kingdom, prohibit the retail sale and the supply for retail sale of anti-fouling paints containing a tri-organotin compound as well as the wholesale and retail sale of anti-fouling treatments containing such a compound.

The Control of Pollution (Anti-Fouling Paints) Regulations 1985 and the Control of Pollution (Anti-Fouling Paints) (Amendment) Regulations 1986, which prohibited the retail sale and the supply for retail sale of anti-fouling paints containing organo-tin compounds above a certain concentration, are revoked.

S T A T U T O R Y   I N S T R U M E N T S

1987 No. 784

PUBLIC PASSENGER TRANSPORT

The Heathrow Taxi Sharing Scheme Order 1987

Made - - - -	*30th April 1987*
Laid before Parliament	*8th May 1987*
Coming into force -	*1st June 1987*

The Secretary of State for Transport, in exercise of the powers conferred by section 10(4), (5), (6) and (10) of the Transport Act 1985**(a)**, and of all other enabling powers, hereby makes the following Order:

1. This Order may be cited as the Heathrow Taxi Sharing Scheme Order 1987 and shall come into force on 1st June 1987.

2. The Secretary of State hereby makes the Heathrow Taxi Sharing Scheme as set out in the Annex to this Order.

Signed by authority of the Secretary of State

D. B. Mitchell
Minister of State,
Department of Transport

30th April 1987

ANNEX

THE HEATHROW TAXI SHARING SCHEME 1987

Interpretation

1. In this Scheme, unless the context otherwise requires:

"authorised destination" means any destination of a journey within the zones described in paragraph 1 of the Schedule to this Scheme;

"authorised place" means the hackney carriage stand at Terminal 1 at Heathrow Airport;

"exclusive service" means a service other than at separate fares;

"shared service" means a service at separate fares;

"taxi" means a vehicle licensed under section 6 of the Metropolitan Public Carriage Act 1869**(b)**.

(a) 1985 c.67.
(b) 1869 c.115.

Application

2.—(1) The requirements of this Scheme shall apply to taxis standing for hire or hired at separate fares under the terms of this Scheme for a journey from the authorised place to an authorised destination.

(2) Any taxi may at the option of the holder of the licence for that vehicle be used for the carriage of passengers at separate fares under the terms of this Scheme.

Authorised place and availability

3.—(1) The authorised place is designated as the place from which taxis may be hired under this scheme.

(2) A taxi shall be available for hire under this Scheme when it is standing at the authorised place and displaying a notice containing the words specified in paragraph 4 of this Scheme.

Signs on vehicles

4. There shall be displayed on any taxi standing for hire under the terms of this Scheme (in addition to any other sign, mark or notice which is required to be displayed on the taxi) a notice containing the words "Shared Taxi".

Arrangements for a shared service

5. If a person seeks to hire a shared service a taxi available for hire under this Scheme and the driver is unable to find at least one other person to share the hiring within a reasonable time, then no fare shall be payable and the driver shall be free to seek an alternative hiring provided that the driver and the first mentioned person may continue to wait for another person to offer to share the taxi for so long as they both agree to do so.

Fares, meters and signs

6.—(1) The maximum fare payable by each passenger for a journey shall be the appropriate amount indicated in paragraph 2 of the Schedule to this Scheme.

(2) No fare shall be charged for any child under the age of two years, and no such child shall be counted when calculating the number of people sharing the vehicle.

(3) For the purpose of computing fares, each child over the age of two years but under the age of ten years shall be charged at half fare and when calculating the number of people sharing the vehicle–
   (a) if an even number of such children are being carried, one half of that number shall be counted; and
   (b) if an odd number of such children are being carried, one half of the even number immediately following that odd number shall be counted.

(4) A charge shall be made for each article of luggage equal to the charge that would be made if the taxi were hired by a single passenger for an exclusive service(a), and this charge shall be payable by the passenger whose luggage it is.

(5) Before the commencement of any journey from the authorised place by a taxi for the purpose of a shared service, any person may (notwithstanding any earlier agreement) decide not to be carried as a passenger and no fare or other charge shall be payable by that person.

(6) The taxi meter shall not be operated and the roof sign shall not be illuminated during the hiring.

Obligatory hirings

7. The driver of a taxi available for hire under this Scheme shall not, without reasonable excuse, refuse a hiring to two or more persons seeking a shared service to any authorised destination or destinations; but he may, with the agreement of those persons, wait for a reasonable period for further passengers to share the hiring.

(a) *See* para. 41 of the London Cab Order 1934 (S.R. & O. 1934/1346); the relevant amending instruments are S.I. 1980/588 and 1984/707.

Luggage

8. The driver shall not refuse to carry in his taxi the luggage of a passenger if the luggage can be accommodated safely within the luggage compartment of the taxi with the luggage of other passengers already accepted by him.

Route

9. The route taken by the taxi and the order in which passengers are set down shall be determined by the driver, but he shall not unreasonably prolong the journey of any passenger.

Paragraphs 1 and 6

SCHEDULE

ZONES AND FARES

1. (a) In this Schedule–
"the West Zone" means Paddington and Victoria stations and the area within a boundary formed by the following roads:

> Holland Road; Addison Crescent; Addison Road; Warwick Gardens; Pembroke Road; Earls Court Road; Redcliffe Gardens; Redcliffe Square; Redcliffe Gardens; Edith Grove; Cremorne Road; Cheyne Walk; Chelsea Embankment; Grosvenor Road; Besborough Gardens; Vauxhall Bridge Road; Victoria Street; Bressendon Place; Lower Grosvenor Place; Grosvenor Place; Hyde Park Corner; Park Lane; Marble Arch; Edgware Road; Harrow Road; Bishopsbridge Road; Westbourne Grove; Pembroke Villas; Pembroke Road; Notting Hill Gate; Holland Park Avenue.

"the East Zone" means Marylebone, Euston, Kings Cross and St Pancras Stations and the area within a boundary formed by the following roads:

> Vauxhall Bridge Road; Victoria Street; Bressendon Place; Lower Grosvenor Place; Grosvenor Place; Hyde Park Corner; Park Lane; Marble Arch; Edgware Road; Marylebone Road; Euston Road; Pentonville Road; Kings Cross Road; Farringdon Road; Farringdon Street; New Bridge Street; Victoria Embankment; Bridge Street; Parliament Square; St Margaret's Street; Old Palace Yard; Abingdon Street; Millbank; Bessborough Gardens.

(b) Each Zone mentioned in sub-paragraph (a) shall include all those parts of roads which form the zone boundary except that any part of a road that forms the boundary of both zones shall be in the East, and not the West, Zone.

2. The maximum fare payable by each person for a journey in a taxi to which the Scheme applies shall be the sum of the amount indicated in the Table and the charge for luggage (if any) under paragraph 6(4) of the Scheme.

Table

Column 1 Number of people sharing at commencement of the hiring	Column 2 Fare per person West Zone destination	Column 3 Fare per person East Zone destination
2	£10	£12
3	£8	£10
4	£7	£8
5	£6	£7

EXPLANATORY NOTE

(This note is not part of the Order)

This Order contains in its Annex the Heathrow Taxi Sharing Scheme.

The Scheme applies to taxis standing for hire or hired at the authorised place (namely, the hackney carriage stand at Terminal 1, Heathrow Airport) for a journey to an authorised destination (being any destination within the zones described in paragraph 1 of the Schedule to the Scheme)—see paragraphs 1, 2 and 3(1) of the Annex.

Taxis available for hire under the Scheme are to display a sign containing the words "Shared Taxi"—see paragraphs 3(2) and 4. The fares payable are specified in paragraph 6 of the Annex, read with paragraph 2 of the Schedule.

Paragraphs 5 and 7 to 9 contain supplementary provisions relating to the arrangements for shared services, obligatory hirings, luggage and the route to be followed.

1987 No. 785

LOCAL GOVERNMENT, ENGLAND AND WALES

The Rate Limitation (Designation of Authorities) (Exemption) Order 1987

Made - - - -	*30th April 1987*
Laid before the House of Commons	*8th May 1987*
Coming into force	*29th May 1987*

Whereas the total of relevant expenditure for local authorities in England as estimated for the purposes of the Rate Support Grant Report (England) 1987/88**(a)** was greater than that total as estimated for the purposes of the Rate Support Grant Report (England) 1986/87**(b)** by 9.542%:

Now, therefore, the Secretary of State in exercise of the powers conferred on him by section 2(3) and (8) of the Rates Act 1984**(c)**, and of all other powers enabling him in that behalf, hereby makes the following Order:–

Citation, commencement and application

1.—(1) This Order may be cited as the Rate Limitation (Designation of Authorities) (Exemption) Order 1987, and shall come into force on 29th May 1987.

(2) This Order applies to England only.

Exemption from designation

2. The amount of £12.2 million is hereby substituted for the amount of £11.1 million specified in section 2(2)(a) of the Rates Act 1984.

3. The Rate Limitation (Designation of Authorities) (Exemption) Order 1986**(d)**, which specifies the amount of £11.1 million, is revoked.

Nicholas Ridley
Secretary of State for the Environment

30th April 1987

(a) 1987 HC-253.
(b) 1985 HC-140.
(c) 1984 c.33.
(d) S.I. 1986/344.

EXPLANATORY NOTE

(This note is not part of the Order)

Section 2(1) of the Rates Act 1984 provides that an authority in whose case a maximum rate or precept is to be prescribed in any financial year is to be designated by the Secretary of State in the preceding financial year.

Section 2(2)(a) of the Act exempts an authority from designation in any financial year if its total expenditure for that financial year does not appear to the Secretary of State to be likely to exceed its grant-related expenditure, or £11.1 million, whichever is the greater.

Section 2(3) of the Act provides that, if the total of relevant expenditure (as estimated for the purposes of the Rate Support Grant Report for each financial year) changes from one year to the next, the Secretary of State shall substitute for the amount for the time being specified in section 2(2)(a) of the Act a proportionately greater or smaller amount, rounded to the nearest hundred thousand pounds.

The total of relevant expenditure for local authorities in England, as estimated for the purposes of the Rate Support Grant Report (England) 1987/88, is 9.542% greater than the corresponding figure estimated for the purposes of the Rate Support Grant Report (England) 1986/87.

This order, which applies to England only, substitutes an amount of £12.2 million for the amount of £11.1 million currently specified. It comes into force on 29th May 1987.

STATUTORY INSTRUMENTS

1987 No. 786

LOCAL GOVERNMENT, ENGLAND AND WALES

The Rate Limitation (Designation of Authorities) (Exemption) (Wales) Order 1987

Made - - - -	*22nd April 1987*
Laid before the House of Commons	*5th May 1987*
Coming into force	*26th May 1987*

Whereas the total of relevant expenditure for local authorities in Wales as estimated for the purposes of the Welsh Rate Support Grant Report 1986/87(**a**) was greater than that total as estimated for the purposes of the Welsh Rate Support Grant Report 1985/86(**b**) by 5·48%;

Now, therefore, the Secretary of State in exercise of the powers conferred on him by section 2(3) and (8) of the Rates Act 1984(**c**), and of all other powers enabling him in that behalf, hereby makes the following order:

Title, commencement and application

1. This order may be cited as the Rate Limitation (Designation of Authorities) (Exemption) (Wales) Order 1987, and shall come into force on 26th May 1987. It applies to Wales only.

Exemption from Designation

2. The amount of £11·1 million is hereby substituted for the amount of £10·5 million specified in section 2(2)(a) of the Rates Act 1984.

3. The Rate Limitation (Designation of Authorities) (Exemption) (Wales) Order 1985(**d**), which specifies the amount of £10·5 million, is revoked.

Nicholas Edwards
Secretary of State for Wales

22nd April 1987

(**a**) 1985–86 Sess. HC-100.
(**b**) 1984–85 Sess. HC-100.
(**c**) 1984 c.33.
(**d**) S.I. 1985/823.

EXPLANATORY NOTE

(This note is not part of the Order)

Section 2(1) of the Rates Act 1984 provides that an authority in whose case a maximum rate or precept is to be prescribed in any financial year is to be designated by the Secretary of State in the preceding financial year.

Section 2(2)(a) of the Act exempts an authority in Wales from designation in any financial year if its total expenditure for that financial year does not appear to the Secretary of State to be likely to exceed its grant-related expenditure, or £10.5 million, whichever is the greater.

Section 2(3) of the Act provides that, if the total of relevant expenditure (as estimated for the purposes of the Rate Support Grant Report for each financial year) changes from one year to the next, the Secretary of State shall substitute for the amount for the time being specified in section 2(2)(a) of the Act a proportionately greater or smaller amount, rounded to the nearest hundred thousand pounds.

The total of relevant expenditure for local authorities in Wales, as estimated for the purposes of the Welsh Rate Support Grant Report 1986/87, is 5·48% greater than the corresponding figure estimated for the purposes of the Welsh Rate Support Grant Report 1985/86.

This order, which applies to Wales only, substitutes an amount of £11.1 million for the amount of £10.5 million currently specified in section 2(2)(a) of the Act. It comes into force on 26th May 1987.

1988

STATUTORY INSTRUMENTS

1987 No. 787 (C.21)

LICENSED CONVEYANCING

The Administration of Justice Act 1985 (Commencement No.4) Order 1987

Made - - - - *30th April 1987*

The Lord Chancellor, in exercise of the powers conferred on him by section 69(2) of the Administration of Justice Act 1985(**a**), hereby makes the following Order:–

1. This Order may be cited as the Administration of Justice Act 1985 (Commencement No. 4) Order 1987.

2. The provisions of the Administration of Justice Act 1985 specified in Part I of the Schedule to this Order shall come into force on 11th May 1987 and the provision of that Act specified in Part II of the Schedule shall come into force on 1st December 1987.

Dated 30th April 1987   *Hailsham of St Marylebone*, C.

(**a**) 1985 c. 61.

SCHEDULE

Article 2

PART I

PROVISIONS COMING INTO FORCE ON 11TH MAY 1987

Provisions of the Act	Subject matter
Sections 6(1), 6(2), 6(3) and 6(5)	Preparation of conveyancing documents by unqualified persons.
Section 11	Provision of conveyancing services by licensed conveyancers.
Section 14	Applications for licences
Section 15	Issue of licences by the Council of Licensed Conveyancers.
Section 16	Conditional licences.
Section 17	Imposition of conditions during currency of licence.
Section 18	Suspension or termination of licences.
Section 19	Register of licensed conveyancers.
Section 20	Rules as to professional practice, conduct and discipline.
Section 21	Professional indemnity and compensation.
Section 24	Preliminary investigation of disciplinary cases.
Section 25	The Discipline and Appeals Committee.
Section 26	Proceedings on disciplinary cases.
Section 27	Removal of disqualification from holding a licence.
Section 28	Revocation of licence on grounds of fraud or error.
Section 29	Appeals from decisions of Council in relation to licences.
Section 30 (and Schedule 4)	Supplementary provisions relating to disciplinary and other proceedings.
Section 31 (and Schedule 5)	Intervention in licensed conveyancer's practice and examination of files.
Section 32 (and Schedule 6)	Provision of conveyancing services by recognised bodies.
Section 33	Legal professional privilege.
Sections 34(1) and 34(2)	Modification of existing enactments relating to conveyancing, etc.
Section 35	Penalty for pretending to be a licensed conveyancer or recognised body.
Section 36	Offences by bodies corporate.
Section 37	Service of documents.
Section 39	Interpretation.

PART II

PROVISIONS COMING INTO FORCE ON 1ST DECEMBER 1987

Provisions of the Act	Subject matter
Section 6(4)	Preparation of conveyancing documents by unqualified persons.

EXPLANATORY NOTE

(This note is not part of the Order)

This Order brings into operation on 11th May 1987 the following provisions of the Administration of Justice Act 1985 and their consequential amendments and repeals–

(a) Sections 6(1), 6(2), 6(3), 6(5): providing for the preparation of certain conveyancing documents by unqualified persons if they are employees of qualified persons, and for the institution of proceedings under s.22 of the Solicitors Act 1974 (c. 47) by local weights and measures authorities;

(b) Sections 11, 14, 15, 16, 17, 18, 19, 20 and 21: providing for the provision of conveyancing services by licensed conveyancers, and providing rule making powers exercisable by the Council of Licensed Conveyancers to govern the granting of licences to persons seeking to practise as licensed conveyancers, and to govern the professional conduct and financial requirements to be observed by licensed conveyancers in practice;

(c) Sections 24, 25, 26, 27, 28, 29, 30 (and Schedule 4), 31 (and Schedule 5), 32 (and Schedule 6), 33, 34, 35, 36, 37 and 39: providing rule making powers exercisable by the Council of Licensed Conveyancers to govern the disciplinary procedure to be followed in cases in which complaints or allegations are made concerning the conduct or convictions of a licensed conveyancer, and to govern the recognition by the Council of bodies corporate seeking to provide conveyancing services, and various consequential provisions.

and on 1st December 1987 the following provision of the Administration of Justice Act 1985 and its consequential amendments and repeals–

(a) Section 6(4): providing that contracts for the sale or other disposition of land (except contracts to grant certain short leases) shall be included within the class of document which unqualified persons are prohibited from preparing by s.22 of the Solicitors Act 1974.

NOTE TO EARLIER COMMENCEMENT ORDERS

(This note is not part of the Order)

Provision	Date of commencement	S.I. No.
Section 2, except insofar as it relates to the investigation of any complaint made to the Law Society relating to the quality of any professional services provided by a solicitor		
Sections 4, 5, 7, 8, 12, 46		
Section 67(2), so far as it relates to the provisions of the Solicitors Act 1974 mentioned in Part III of Schedule 8	12th March 1986	1986/364
Schedule 1		
Schedule 3		
Section 50	28th April 1986	
Sections 13, 22, 23, 38, 47, 51, 55		
Section 67(1), so far as it relates to paragraph 7 of Schedule 7		
Section 67(2), so far as it relates to so much of Part III of Schedule 8 as refers to the Supreme Court Act 1981 (c. 54) and the County Courts Act 1984 (c. 28)	1st October 1986	1986/1503
Sections 1 and 3		
Section 2, so far as it relates to the investigation of any complaint made to the Law Society relating to the quality of any professional services provided by a solicitor	1st January 1987	1986/2260
Section 48	12th January 1987	

STATUTORY INSTRUMENTS

1987 No. 788

LICENSED CONVEYANCING

The Licensed Conveyancers' Discipline and Appeals Committee (Legal Assessor) Rules 1987

Made - - - -	*30th April 1987*
Coming into force	*26th May 1987*

The Lord Chancellor, in exercise of the powers conferred on him by paragraph 3(2) of Schedule 4 to the Administration of Justice Act 1985(**a**), hereby makes the following Rules:

Citation and Commencement

1. These Rules may be cited as the Licensed Conveyancers' Discipline and Appeals Committee (Legal Assessor) Rules 1987 and shall come into force on 26th May 1987.

Interpretation

2. In these Rules, unless the context otherwise requires:–

"The Act" means the Administration of Justice Act 1985;

"The Committee" means the Discipline and Appeals Committee established under section 25(1) of the Act;

"The Legal Assessor" means the assessor appointed by the Council for Licensed Conveyancers under paragraph 3(1) of Schedule 4 to the Act.

Duties

3. It shall be the duty of the Legal Assessor to:

(a) be present at all proceedings under section 26 of the Act and advise the Committee on any questions of law and the admission of evidence arising from the proceedings which they may refer to him;

(b) inform the Committee forthwith of any irregularity in the conduct of proceedings before them which may come to his knowledge and to advise them of his own motion where it appears to him that, but for such advice, there is a possibility of a mistake of law being made.

Advice to be tendered in public

4. Where the Legal Assessor advises the Committee on any question of law as to evidence, procedure or any other matter specified in the rules, he shall do so in the presence of every party to the proceedings, or every person representing such a party, who appears at the proceedings or, if the advice is tendered after the Committee have begun to deliberate as to their findings, every such party or person shall be informed what advice the assessor tendered.

Where advice not accepted

5. If on any occasion the Committee do not accept the advice of the Legal Assessor, a record shall be made of the question referred to him, of the advice given and of the refusal

---

(**a**) 1985 c. 61.

to accept it (together with the reasons for such a refusal), and a copy of the record shall be given to every party, or person representing a party, to the proceedings who appears thereat.

Advice to be available to all parties

6. Copies of written advice made for the purposes of either of the last two foregoing Rules shall be available on application to every party to the proceedings who does not appear thereat.

Dated 30th April 1987   *Hailsham of St Marylebone,* C.

EXPLANATORY NOTE

(This note is not part of the Rules)

These Rules regulate the functions of the assessor appointed by the Council for Licensed Conveyancers under paragraph 3(1) of Schedule 4 to the Administration of Justice Act 1985 to assist the deliberations of the Council's Discipline and Appeals Committee.

STATUTORY INSTRUMENTS

1987 No. 789

LICENSED CONVEYANCING

The Licensed Conveyancers' Discipline and Appeals Committee (Procedure) Rules Approval Order 1987

Made - - - -	*30th April 1987*
Laid before Parliament	*5th May 1987*
Coming into force -	*26th May 1987*

Whereas the Council for Licensed Conveyancers have, in exercise of their powers under paragraph 1 of Schedule 4 of the Administration of Justice Act 1985(a), made rules of procedure and submitted them to the Lord Chancellor for his approval.

Now, therefore, the Lord Chancellor, in exercise of the powers conferred on him by paragraph 1 of the said Schedule, hereby approves the rules in the form set out in the Schedule to this Order.

This Order may be cited as the Licensed Conveyancers' Discipline and Appeals Committee (Procedure) Rules Approval Order 1987 and shall come into force on 26th May 1987.

Dated 30th April 1987   *Hailsham of St Marylebone, C.*

SCHEDULE

PART I

PRELIMINARY

Citation and commencement

1. These Rules may be cited as the Licensed Conveyancers' Discipline and Appeals Committee (Procedure) Rules 1987 and shall come into operation on 26th May 1987.

(a) 1985 c. 61.

Interpretation

2. In these Rules, unless the context otherwise requires:–

"The Act" means the Administration of Justice Act 1985;

"case relating to conduct" means:–

    (a) a case where an allegation under Section 24(1)(a)(ii) or (iii) or where a complaint under Section 24(1)(b) of the Act is made against a licensed conveyancer; or

    (b) a case where an allegation under paragraph 3(1)(a)(ii) or where a complaint under paragraph 3(1)(b) of Schedule 6 to the Act is made against a recognised body;

"case relating to conviction" means:–

    (a) a case where an allegation under Section 24(1)(a)(i) of the Act is made against a licensed conveyancer: or

    (b) a case where an allegation under paragraph 3(1)(a)(i) of Schedule 6 to the Act is made against a recognised body;

"the Chairman" means the Chairman or the acting Chairman of the Discipline and Appeals Committee;

"the Committee" means the Discipline and Appeals Committee established under Section 25(1) of the Act and includes a quorum of that Committee as provided for in the Licensed Conveyancers' Investigating Committee and Discipline and Appeals Committee Rules 1987;

"the Complainant" means the body or person by whom a complaint has been made to the Council against a licensed conveyancer or recognised body.

"the Legal Assessor" means an assessor appointed to the Council under paragraph 3 of Schedule 4 to the Act;

"party" means any complainant or respondent or the Solicitor;

"the respondent" means any licensed conveyancer or recognised body against whom an allegation or complaint under Section 24(1) of or paragraph 3(1) of Schedule 6 to the Act is referred to the Discipline and Appeals Committee;

"the Secretary" means the Secretary of the Council and includes any deputy or assistant or person appointed temporarily to perform the duties of that office;

"the Solicitor" means a solicitor nominated by the Council to act as their solicitor for the purposes of these rules, and in relation to a hearing includes counsel instructed by the Solicitor to act on behalf of the Council.

PART II

CASES RELATING TO CONVICTION AND RELATING TO CONDUCT AND CASES RELATING TO LICENCES OBTAINED THROUGH FRAUD

Application of Part II

3. Where, in accordance with the provisions of Section 24 of the Act, the Investigating Committee decide to refer a case to the Discipline and Appeals Committee, the provisions contained in this part of these Rules shall have effect.

Notice of Hearing

4.—(1) As soon as possible after the case has been referred to the Committee the Solicitor shall send to the respondent a "notice of hearing" as nearly as possible in the form set out in the Appendix to these Rules specifying the matters alleged against the respondent in the form of a charge or charges, and stating the day, time and place at which the Committee will hold a hearing into these matters, together with a copy of these Rules, in a registered letter addressed to the respondent at his registered or last known address.

(2) In any case in which there is a complainant, the Solicitor shall send him a copy of the notice of hearing and a copy of these Rules.

(3) The Committee shall not hold a hearing unless a notice of hearing has been served on the respondent or unless the Committee are satisfied that all reasonable efforts have been taken to serve the notice and that the substance of the matters alleged therein against the respondent and the likelihood of a hearing resulting therefrom are well known to him.

(4) Except with the agreement of the respondent, the hearing shall not be held on any day earlier than twenty eight days after the date of posting the notice of hearing.

Postponement or cancellation of hearing

5.—(1) The Chairman of his own motion or upon the application of any party, may postpone the hearing.

(2) Where, before the hearing opens, it appears to the Chairman or, at any stage of the

proceedings, it appears to the Committee that a notice of hearing is defective, he or they shall cause the notice to be amended unless it appears that the required amendment cannot be made without injustice; or, if he or they consider that the circumstances in which an amendment is made require it, shall direct that the hearing shall be postponed or shall not be held.

(3) The solicitor shall, as soon as possible, give to all parties to whom a notice of hearing has been sent notification of any decision to postpone or not to hold a hearing, informing them of the date fixed for a postponed hearing.

Access to documents

6. Upon application by any party to the hearing the Solicitor shall send to that party copies of any statutory declaration, explanation, answer, admission or other statement or communication sent to the Council by any party to the hearing, provided that nothing in this Rule shall compel the Solicitor to produce copies of any written advice sent by himself to the Council which would be privileged from discovery in any legal proceedings to which the Council was a party.

Procedure at hearing

7. The procedure at any hearing held by the Committee under Section 25 of the Act shall be that set out in the following provisions contained in this part and in Part V of these Rules.

Appearance and representation

8. Any party (including an applicant to whom Part III of these Rules applies) may appear either in person, or by counsel or solicitor, or by an officer or member of any professional organisation of which he is a member, or by a professional colleague, or by any member of his family, or, where the respondent is a recognised body, by an officer or employee of that body.

The reading of the charge

9.—(1) The charge shall be read in the presence of the parties provided that if the respondent does not appear but the Committee nevertheless decide that the hearing shall proceed the charge shall be read in his absence.

(2) As soon as the charge has been read the respondent may, if he so desires, object to the charge, or to any part of it, on a point of law, and any other party may reply to any such objection; and, if any such objection is upheld, no further proceedings shall be taken on that charge or on that part of the charge.

Proof of Conviction in a case relating to conviction

10.—(1) In cases arising out of a complaint or information from which it appears that a licensed conveyancer or recognised body has been convicted of a criminal offence the following order of proceedings shall be observed concerning proof of the convictions alleged in the charge:–

     (a) the complainant, or, if no complainant appears, the Solicitor shall adduce evidence of the convictions;

     (b) if no evidence is adduced concerning any particular conviction, the Chairman shall thereupon announce that that conviction has not been proved;

     (c) if the respondent appears, then the Chairman shall ask him concerning each conviction of which evidence is so adduced whether he admits the conviction; and if he admits it the Chairman shall thereupon announce that the conviction has been proved.

   (2)(a) Where the respondent appears, the following further order of proceedings shall be observed:–

       (i) if the respondent submits that a conviction elsewhere than in the United Kingdom was for an offence which, if committed in England and Wales would not have constituted a criminal offence, he may adduce evidence and may address the Committee in that behalf;

       (ii) if the respondent does not admit all the convictions, he may then adduce evidence concerning any conviction which he has not admitted on the question whether he was convicted as alleged, and may address the Committee on that question;

     Provided that only one address may be made under either of the aforementioned sub-paragraphs and, where the respondent adduces evidence, that address shall be made either before that evidence is begun or after it is concluded;

     (b) on the conclusion of proceedings under the last foregoing paragraph, the Committee shall consider every conviction of which evidence has been adduced and shall determine whether or not it has been proved; and the Chairman shall announce their determination in such terms as they may approve.

Proof of the facts alleged in cases relating to conduct

11.—(1) In cases relating to conduct the following order of proceedings shall be observed as respects proof of the charge or charges:–

(a) the case against the respondent shall be opened by the complainant (if any appears) or else by the Solicitor;

(b) thereafter evidence shall be adduced of the facts alleged in the charge or charges;

(c) if no evidence is adduced concerning any particular charge the Committee shall announce a finding that the respondent is not guilty in respect of the matters to which that charge relates.

(2) Where the respondent appears the following further order of proceedings shall be observed:–

(a) at the close of the case against him the respondent may, if he so desires, make either or both of the following submissions relating to any charge concerning which evidence has been adduced, namely–

(i) that no sufficient evidence has been adduced upon which the Committee could find that the facts alleged in the charge have been proved;

(ii) that the facts alleged in the charge are not such as to justify the charge;

and where such a submission is made, any other party may reply thereto.

(b) If a submission is made under the last foregoing sub-paragraph, the Committee shall consider and determine whether it should be upheld. If the Committee determine to uphold it they shall record, and the Chairman shall announce, their finding that, in relation to the matters to which that charge relates, the respondent is not guilty.

(c) The respondent may adduce evidence in answer to any charge concerning which evidence has been adduced and, whether he adduces evidence or not, may address the Committee. Except with the leave of the Committee only one address may be made under this paragraph and, where the respondent adduces evidence, shall be made either before that evidence is begun or after it is concluded.

(d) At the close of the case for the respondent, the complainant or the Solicitor, as the case may be, may, with the leave of the Committee, adduce evidence to rebut any evidence adduced by the respondent; and if he does so, the respondent may make a further address limited to the rebutting evidence.

(e) The complainant or the Solicitor, as the case may be, may address the Committee by way of reply to the respondent's case–

(i) if oral evidence (not being evidence as to character) other than that of the respondent himself has been given on the respondent's behalf; or

(ii) with the leave of the Committee, where no such evidence has been given.

(f) Without prejudice to that last foregoing sub-paragraph, if the respondent has made a submission to the Committee on a point of law any other party shall have a right of reply limited to that submission.

(3) On the conclusion of the aforesaid proceedings, the Committee shall consider and determine as respects each charge which remains outstanding which, if any, of the facts alleged in the charge have been proved to their satisfaction.

(4) If under the last foregoing paragraph the Committee determine as respects any charge, either that none of the facts alleged in the charge has been proved to their satisfaction, or that such facts as have been so proved would be insufficient to justify the charge, the Committee shall record a finding that the respondent is not guilty in respect of the matters to which that charge relates.

Procedure upon proof of conviction or of the facts alleged

12.—(1) Where in a case relating to conviction the Committee have found that a conviction has been proved the following order of proceedings shall be observed:–

(a) the Chairman shall invite the complainant or the Solicitor, as the case may be, to address the Committee, and to adduce evidence as to the circumstances leading up to the conviction and as to the character and previous history of the respondent;

(b) the Chairman shall then invite the respondent to address the Committee by way of mitigation and to adduce evidence as aforesaid.

(2) Where in a case relating to conduct the Committee have found that the facts or any of them alleged in any charge have been proved to their satisfaction (and have not on those facts recorded a finding of not guilty) the following order of proceedings shall be observed:–

(a) the Chairman shall invite the complainant or the Solicitor, as the case may be, to address the Committee and to adduce evidence as to the circumstances leading up to the facts in question, the extent to which such facts support the charge against the respondent, and as to the character and pevious history of the respondent;

(b) the Chairman shall then invite the respondent to address the Committeee by way of mitigation and to adduce evidence as aforesaid.

(3) The Committee shall next consider and determine whether it shall be sufficient to conclude the case. If the Committee determine not to conclude the case, they shall next consider and determine whether to postpone judgment.

(4) If the Committee determine to postpone judgment, the judgment of the Committee shall stand postponed until such future meeting of the Committee as they may determine.

(5) If the Committee determine not to postpone judgment, they may make one or more of the orders referred to in Section 26(2) of or paragraph 4(2) of Schedule 6 to the Act.

Announcement of determination

13. The Chairman shall announce the determination or determinations of the Committee under the foregoing Rules in such terms as the Committee may approve.

Revocation of order for interim suspension

14. If in any case an order has been made by the Investigating Committee under Section 24(5) of the Act for interim suspension the Discipline and Appeals Committee shall, when they have determined the case, revoke such order if it has not previously expired.

Procedure in cases relating both to conviction and to conduct

15. Where in any case allegations are made against the respondent which relate both to conviction and to conduct, the Committee shall proceed upon the charge or charges of each kind separately under Rule 10 or Rule 11 of these Rules according as the charge relates to conviction or to conduct and shall then proceed under so much of Rule 12 of these Rules as may be applicable either upon the charge or charges of each kind separately or upon the charges of both kinds concurrently, according as the circumstances of the case may require.

Procedure upon postponement of judgment

16.—(1) Where under any of the foregoing provisions of these Rules the judgment of the Committee in any case stands postponed, the following shall be the procedure.

(2) The Solicitor shall, not later than forty two days before the day fixed for the resumption of the proceedings, send to the respondent a notice, which shall:

    (a) specify the day, time and place at which the proceedings are to be resumed and invite him to appear thereat;

    (b) unless the Chairman otherwise directs, invite the respondent to furnish the Secretary with the names and addresses of persons to whom reference may be made confidentially or otherwise concerning his character and conduct; and

    (c) invite the respondent to send to the Solicitor not less than twenty one days before the day fixed for the resumption of the proceedings a copy of any statement or statutory declaration, whether made by the respondent or not, relating to his conduct since the hearing of his case or setting out any material facts which have arisen since that hearing.

(3) A copy of the notice and of any statement or statutory declaration sent in accordance with the provisions of the last foregoing sub-paragraph shall be sent to the complainant, if any, if he is a party to the proceedings, and he may in turn, if he so desires, send to the Solicitor a statement or statutory declaration, whether made by himself or not, concerning any matter raised by the respondent.

(4) At the meeting at which the proceedings are resumed the Chairman shall first invite the Solicitor to recall, for the information of the Committee, the position in which the case stands and the Committee may then receive further oral or documentary evidence in relation to the conduct or the respondent since the hearing and evidence of any conviction recorded against the respondent which has not been the subject of a charge under these Rules, and shall hear any other party to the proceedings who desires to be heard.

(5) The Committee shall then consider and determine whether it shall be sufficient to conclude the case.

(6) If the Committee determine not to conclude the case, they shall next consider and determine whether they should further postpone their judgment on the charges on which their judgment was previously postponed; and if the Committee determine further to postpone judgment, the judgment of the Committee shall stand postponed until such future meeting of the Committee as they may determine; and the Chairman shall announce their determination in such terms as the Committee may approve.

(7) The provisions of this Rule shall apply to any case in which judgment is further postponed.

(8) If the Committee determine that judgment shall not be further postponed paragraph (5) of Rule 12 of these Rules shall apply.

(9) At any resumed proceedings any new charge alleged against the respondent in accordance with these Rules shall first be dealt with in accordance with such of Rules 9 and 11 and so much of Rule 12 as may be applicable and if the Committee determine neither to conclude the case nor to postpone judgment in respect of any such new charge, the Committee may apply paragraph (5) of Rule 12 simultaneously to the new charge and the charge in respect of which they had postponed judgment.

Cases where it is alleged that a licence or recognition was obtained through fraud

17.—(1) Where it is alleged that a respondent was issued a licence or granted recognition as a result of fraud on his part, the Solicitor shall send to the respondent a notice of hearing:

(a) specifying the nature of the fraud alleged, stating the day, time and place at which the Committee will hold a hearing on the question;

(b) inviting his attendance at such hearing; and

(c) containing such further information as the nature of the case may require.

(2) The provisions of Rule 4 shall apply as though such notice were a notice of hearing such as is mentioned in that rule.

(3) A copy of the notice shall be sent to any person who is alleged to have been a party to the fraud alleged and to such other persons (if any) as the Chairman may direct, and any such person may with the leave of the Chairman appear at the hearing as an additional party thereto.

(4) The hearing shall proceed as though the question were a charge contained in a notice of hearing in a case relating to conduct and the provisions of Rule 11 shall accordingly apply thereto.

(5) If the Committee are satisfied that the licence has been issued or recognition granted as a result of fraud, they shall make an order in writing, under the hand of the Chairman, that the licence or recognition, having been proved to the satisfaction of the Committee to have been issued or granted as a result of fraud, shall be revoked and the Chairman shall announce the determination in such terms as the Committee may approve.

(6) Whether or not the Committee proceed to determine that a licence or recognition has been proved to their satisfaction to have been issued or granted as a result of fraud, they may, if they are satisfied that the licence or recognition has been issued or granted as a result of error, recommend the Council to revoke or amend the licence or grant of recognition in accordance with their conclusions.

(7) Where a hearing relates to two or more licences or recognition of bodies, the Committee may proceed under the foregoing provisions of this rule in respect of those licences or recognitions either separately or taken together, as the Committee think fit.

Procedure where there is more than one respondent

18. Nothing in this part of these Rules shall prevent one hearing being held into charges against two or more respondents; and where such a hearing is held the foregoing Rules shall apply with the necessary adaptations and subject to any directions given by the Committee as to the order in which proceedings shall be taken under any of those Rules by or in relation to the several respondents, so however that any of the rights ensured to a respondent under those Rules shall be exercised separately by each of the respondents who desires to invoke that right.

PART III

REMOVAL OF DISQUALIFICATION FROM HOLDING A LICENCE

Procedure

19.—(1) Where in accordance with the provisions of Section 27 of the Act an application for the removal of a disqualification has been made to the Committee, the following provisions shall have effect:-

(a) the Committee shall afford to the applicant an opportunity of being heard by the Committee, subject to the provisions of Rule 8, and of adducing evicence;

(b) the Committee may require such evidence as they think necessary concerning the identity or character of the applicant or his conduct since he was disqualified and for this purpose may receive written or oral evidence.

(2) Subject to the foregoing provisions of this Rule, the procedure of the Committee in connection with the application shall be such as they may determine.

PART IV

APPEALS FROM THE DECISIONS OF COUNCIL IN RELATION TO LICENCES OR GRANTS OF RECOGNITION

Procedure

20. In the case of an appeal against an order of the Council under Section 29(1) of or paragraph 8(1) of Schedule 6 to the Act, the following procedure shall apply:-

    (a) within twenty eight days of the order the appellant shall lodge notice of appeal with the Committee in such form as the Council may prescribe;

    (b) the Committee shall afford to the appellant an opportunity of being heard by the Committee, subject to the provisions of Rule 8, and of adducing evidence;

    (c) the Committee may require such evidence as they think fit including:-

        (i) in the case of an appeal under Section 29(1) evidence of the character or conduct of the appellant; and

        (ii) in the case of an appeal under paragraph 8(1) of Schedule 6 evidence of the character or conduct of officers or employees of the appellant.

21. For the purposes of this Part, where an application for recognition under Section 32 of the Act has not been granted or refused by the Council within forty two days, the applicant may bring an appeal under paragraph 8(1) of Schedule 6 aforesaid as if the application had been refused on the forty second day after the application was lodged with the Council.

PART V

GENERAL

Hearing and adjournment

22.—(1) Subject to the provisions of paragraph 3 of Schedule 4 to the Act and any Rules made thereunder the Committee may deliberate in camera (with or without the Legal Assessor) at any time and for any purpose during or after the hearing of any proceedings.

(2) Subject to paragraph (1) all proceedings before the Committee shall take place in the presence of all parties thereto who appear therein and shall be held in public except as provided by the following paragraph hereof.

(3) Where in the interests of justice or for any other special reason it appears to the Committee that the public should be excluded from any proceedings or part thereof, the Committee may direct that the public shall be so excluded: but a direction under this paragraph shall not apply to the announcement in pursuance of any of these Rules of a determination of the Committee.

(4) The Committee may adjourn their proceedings from time to time as they think fit.

Evidence

23.—(1) Where any respondent or applicant has supplied to the Committee or the Secretary on their behalf the name of any person to whom reference may be made confidentially as to his character or conduct the Committee may consider any information received from such person in consequence of such reference without disclosing the same to the respondent or applicant.

(2) The Committee may receive oral, documentary, or other evidence of any fact which appears to them relevant to the hearing of the case before them:

Provided that where a fact which it is sought to prove or the form in which any evidence is tendered is such that it would not be admissible in criminal proceedings in an English court, the Committee shall not receive evidence of that fact or in that form, unless after consultation with the Legal Assessor they are satisfied that it is desirable in the interests of justice to receive it having regard to the difficulty and expense of obtaining evidence which would be so admissible.

(3) The Committee may cause any person to be called as a witness in any proceedings before them whether or not the parties consent thereto.

(4) Questions may be put to any witness by the Committee through the Chairman or by the Legal Assessor with the leave of the Chairman.

Voting

24.—(1) Any question put to the vote shall be put in the form of a motion. The Chairman shall call upon the members present to vote for or against the motion by raising their hands and shall declare that the motion appears to him to have been carried or not carried as the case may be.

(2) Where on any of the questions the votes are equal, the question shall be deemed to have been

resolved in favour of the respondent or applicant, as the case may be, and for the purpose of this paragraph a decision to postpone judgment shall be taken to be in favour of the respondent or applicant unless he has indicated to the Committee that he is opposed to postponement.

Notes and transcript of proceedings

25. A shorthand writer shall be appointed by the Committee to take notes of their proceedings and any party to proceedings of the Committee shall, on application to the Solicitor and on payment of the proper charges, be furnished by the Solicitor with a transcript of the shorthand notes of any part of the proceedings at which the parties were entitled to be present.

Absence of Chairman

26. Anything authorised or required by these Rules to be done by the Chairman may, if he is absent or unable to act, be done:–

    (i) by any other eligible member of the Committee authorised in that behalf by the Chairman; or

    (ii) where the Chairman fails or is unable to give such authorisation, by any eligible member nominated by the other members present.

APPENDIX

COUNCIL FOR LICENSED CONVEYANCERS FORM OF NOTICE OF THE PROPOSED HEARING

Sir/Madam,

On behalf of the Council for Licensed Conveyancers notice is hereby given to you that in consequence of [a complaint made against you to the Council] [information received by the Council] there will be a hearing into the following charge[s] against you:–

[If the charge relates to conviction] that you were on the   day of [specify Court recording the conviction] convicted of [set out particulars of the conviction in sufficient detail to identify the case].

[If the charge relates to conduct] that you [set out briefly the facts alleged], and that in relation to the facts alleged you have [failed to comply with any condition to which that licence was subject] [failed to comply with any Rules made by the Council].

[Where there is more than one charge, the charges are to be numbered consecutively, the charges relating to conviction being set out before charges relating to conduct].

Notice is further given to you that on [day of the week], the   day of   , 19 , a meeting of the Discipline and Appeals Committee of the Council will be held at   , at   , to consider the above mentioned charge[s] against you, and to determine whether or not to make an order under Section 26(2) of or paragraph 4(2) of Schedule 6 to the Administration of Justice Act 1985.

You are hereby invited to answer in writing the above mentioned charges[s] and also to appear before the Committee at the place and time specified above, for the purpose of answering it[them]. You may appear in person or by Counsel or solicitor, or by any officer or member of any professional organisation of which you are a member, or by a professional colleague, or by any member of your family [or where one of the respondents is a recognised body, by an officer or employee of that body]. The Committee have power if you do not appear, to hear and decide upon the said charge[s] in your absence.

If you desire to make any application that the hearing should be postponed, you should send the application to the Solicitor to the Council as soon as possible, stating the grounds on which you desire a postponement. Any such application will be considered by the Chairman of the Discipline and Appeals Committee in accordance with Rule 5 of the Council for Licensed Conveyancers' Discipline and Appeals Committee (Procedure) Rules 1987 (S I 1987, No   ) a copy of which is sent herewith.

                        Yours faithfully,

                        Solicitor to the Council for Licensed Conveyancers

EXPLANATORY NOTE

(This note is not part of the Order)

By this Order the Lord Chancellor approves Rules made by the Council for Licensed Conveyancers which provide the procedure for hearing disciplinary cases against licensed conveyancers or recognised bodies or cases where it is alleged that a licence was issued on grounds of fraud (Part II), for the removal of a disqualification from holding a licence (Part III) and for appeals from the decisions of Council in relation to licences or grants of recognition (Part IV). Part V contains general provisions as to the conduct of hearings, the admissability of evidence and the method of voting at hearings.

1987 No. 790

ANIMALS

ANIMAL HEALTH

The Infectious Diseases of Horses Order 1987

Made - - - -	*29th April 1987*
Coming into force	*20th May 1987*

The Minister of Agriculture, Fisheries and Food, the Secretary of State for Scotland and the Secretary of State for Wales, acting jointly, in exercise of the powers conferred on them by sections 1, 7(1), 8(1), 15(4), 17(1), 17(2), 23, 28, 35(3), 72, 87(2) and 88(2) of the Animal Health Act 1981(a), and of all other powers enabling them in that behalf, hereby Order as follows:–

Title and commencement

1. This Order may be cited as the Infectious Diseases of Horses Order 1987 and shall come into force on 20th May 1987.

Extension of definitions of "animals" and "disease"

2. For the purposes of the Act in its application to this Order–

(a) the definition of "animals" in section 87(1) of the Act is hereby extended so as to comprise horses, asses, jennets, mules, rhinoceroses, tapirs and zebras; and

(b) the definition of "disease" in section 88(1) of the Act is hereby extended so as to comprise African horse sickness, contagious equine metritis, dourine, epizootic lymphangitis, equine infectious anaemia, equine viral encephalomyelitis and glanders (including the form of glanders commonly known as farcy).

Interpretation

3.—(1) In this Order, unless the context otherwise requires–

"the Act" means the Animal Health Act 1981;

"the appropriate Minister" means, in relation to England, the Minister, and in relation to Scotland or to Wales, the Secretary of State;

"approved disinfectant" means a disinfectant for the time being listed in Schedule 1 or Schedule 2 to the Diseases of Animals (Approved Disinfectants) Order 1978(b) as approved for use under a general order;

"bedding" means any material used for the bedding of horses;

"carcase" means the carcase of a horse, and includes any part of a carcase, and the meat, bones, blood, hide, skin, hooves, offal or other part of a horse, separately or otherwise, or any portion thereof;

"Chief Veterinary Officer" means the Chief Veterinary Officer of the Ministry;

"disease" means African horse sickness, contagious equine metritis, dourine, epizootic lymphangitis, equine infectious anaemia, equine viral encephalomyelitis and glanders (including the form of glanders commonly known as farcy);

(a) 1981 c.22.
(b) S.I. 1978/32; relevant amending instrument is S.I. 1987/74.

"Divisional Veterinary Officer" means the veterinary inspector appointed for the time being by the Minister to receive information about horses and carcases affected or suspected of being affected with disease for the area in which such horses or carcases are;

"horse" means a horse, ass, jennet, mule, rhinoceros, tapir or zebra;

"infected place" means a place declared to be an infected place by a notice in Form A served under article 5;

"inspector" means a person appointed to be an inspector for the purposes of the Act by the Minister or by a local authority, and, when used in relation to an officer of the Ministry, includes a veterinary inspector;

"the Minister" and "the Ministry" means respectively the Minister and the Ministry of Agriculture, Fisheries and Food;

"premises" includes land;

"veterinary inspector" means a veterinary inspector appointed by the Minister;

"veterinary surgeon" means a person registered in the register of veterinary surgeons or in the supplementary veterinary register.

(2) Any reference in this Order–

    (a) to a numbered article or Schedule, is a reference to the article or Schedule bearing that number in this Order, and

    (b) to a lettered Form, is a reference to the Form bearing that letter in Schedule 1 to this Order.

Notification of disease

4.—(1) A person who has in his possession or under his charge any horse or carcase which is affected or suspected of being affected with disease (other than contagious equine metritis), and any veterinary surgeon or other person who in the course of his duties examines or inspects any such horse or carcase shall, with all practicable speed, notify the fact to a member of the police force for the area in which the horse or carcase is, or to an inspector, or to the Divisional Veterinary Officer.

(2) Where notification under paragraph (1) above is given to a member of a police force or to an inspector of the local authority he shall immediately transmit the information contained in the notification by the most expeditious means–

    (a) in the case of a member of a police force to the Divisional Veterinary Officer and to an inspector of the local authority; and

    (b) in the case of an inspector of the local authority, to the Divisional Veterinary Officer.

(3) Any person who, in the course of examining at a laboratory a sample of any kind originating from a horse or carcase, isolates an organism which he knows or suspects to be an organism which causes contagious equine metritis shall–

    (a) with all practicable speed notify the fact to the Divisional Veterinary Officer;

    (b) when giving such notice provide the Divisional Veterinary Officer (in so far as he is able to do so) with the following information–

        (i) his name and address,

        (ii) the name and address of the laboratory at which the organism, or suspected organism, was isolated,

        (iii) the identity of the horse and the name and address of the person in possession or charge of the horse,

        (iv) the date on which the sample was taken from the horse,

        (v) the date on which the organism, or suspected organism, was isolated,

        (vi) such further information as the veterinary inspector may reasonably require; and

    (c) make available to the Divisional Veterinary Officer a culture of the organism.

Declaration of infected place

5.—(1) If an inspector has reasonable grounds for supposing that disease exists, or has within 56 days existed, on any premises he may serve a notice in Form A on the occupier or the person in charge of the premises declaring them to be an infected place.

(2) On the service of a notice in Form A under paragraph (1) above the premises shall become an infected place and be subject to such of the rules contained in article 7 as are set out in the notice and to any other rules set out in the notice for the purpose of preventing the spread of disease.

(3) The rules applied to an infected place by a notice in Form A served under paragraph (1) above shall continue in force until the notice in Form A is withdrawn by a notice in Form B served by an inspector of the Ministry on the occupier or person in charge of the premises in respect of which the notice in Form A was served.

(4) A veterinary inspector may at any time alter the limits of an infected place by the service of a further notice on the occupier or person in charge of such place.

Veterinary enquiry as to the existence of disease

6.—(1) If a veterinary inspector has reasonable grounds for supposing that disease exists or has within 56 days existed on any premises he shall, with all practicable speed, take such steps as may be necessary to establish the correctness of that supposition.

(2) For the purposes of such an enquiry a veterinary inspector may–

(a) examine any horse or carcase on the premises;

(b) make such tests and take such samples from any horse or carcase on the premises as he may consider necessary for the purpose of diagnosis; and

(c) mark for identification purposes any horse or carcase on the premises.

(3) The occupier of the premises and his employees, and any person who is or has been in possession or charge of any horse or carcase which is or has been on the premises, shall–

(a) provide such reasonable facilities and comply with such reasonable requirements as are necessary for the purposes of the enquiry; and

(b) if so required by an inspector or by an officer of the appropriate Minister, give such information as he possesses as to–

(i) any horse or carcase which is or has been on the premises, and

(ii) any other horse or carcase with which any horse or carcase which is or has been on the premises may have come into contact.

(4) If, on completion of the enquiry, the veterinary inspector is of the opinion that disease exists, or has within 56 days existed, on the premises his opinion to that effect shall be subject to confirmation by or on behalf of the Chief Veterinary Officer.

(5) If, on completion of the enquiry, the veterinary inspector is of the opinion that disease does not exist, and has not within 56 days existed, on the premises, or if his opinion as to the existence of disease on the premises is not confirmed by or on behalf of the Chief Veterinary Officer in accordance with paragraph (4) above, then any notice in Form A declaring the premises to be an infected place shall immediately be withdrawn by a notice in Form B served by an inspector of the Ministry on the occupier or the person in charge of the premises.

Rules to be observed in an infected place

7.—(1) Any premises declared to be an infected place shall be subject to such of the following rules as are set out in the notice declaring them to be an infected place, namely–

Rule 1. Any horse or carcase which is affected or suspected of being affected with disease shall be isolated from all other horses in the infected place and detained there in such manner as may be directed by a veterinary inspector.

Rule 2. No person shall move a horse or carcase into or out of the infected place, or cause or permit a horse or carcase to be so moved, except under the authority of a licence issued by a veterinary inspector and in accordance with any conditions subject to which the licence is issued.

Rule 3. No person shall move out of the infected place, or cause or permit to be so moved, any fodder, manure, bedding, vehicle, equipment or other thing used or intended to be used for or in connection with horses except under the authority of a licence issued by an officer of the appropriate Minister and in accordance with any conditions subject to which the licence is issued.

Rule 4. No person shall–

    (a) enter any part of the infected place except under the authority of a licence issued by an officer of the appropriate Minister and in accordance with any conditions subject to which the licence is issued, and unless he is wearing overall clothing and boots which are capable of being disinfected or which are disposable; or

    (b) leave any part of the infected place without first washing his hands and either thoroughly cleansing and disinfecting with an approved disinfectant his overall clothing and boots or removing them and leaving them on the infected place.

Rule 5. The occupier or person in charge of the infected place shall maintain a footbath containing such disinfectant as shall be specified by an inspector in a convenient position at every exit from the infected place, and shall renew the disinfectant daily and whenever so directed by an inspector.

Rule 6. The occupier of the infected place shall, if so required by a veterinary inspector, erect and maintain to the satisfaction of a veterinary inspector fly-proof screens at any place in which any horse or carcase is isolated in accordance with Rule 1 above.

Rule 7. The owner or person in charge of any horse in an infected place shall take all such steps as may be necessary to prevent it from straying from that place.

Rule 8. Notice of the death or slaughter of any horse in an infected place shall be given, with all practicable speed, to the Divisional Veterinary Officer. The carcase of any such horse shall be disposed of only with the consent, and under the direction, of the Divisional Veterinary Officer.

Rule 9. No person, other than a veterinary surgeon acting in accordance with an approval given by the Divisional Veterinary Officer, shall cut the skin of any carcase in an infected place.

Rule 10.—(1) A notice supplied by the appropriate Minister stating that the premises are an infected place shall be exhibited at every entrance to the infected place.

    (2) No person shall alter, remove or deface such a notice.

(2) A veterinary inspector may by notice in writing served on the occupier or the person in charge of the infected place direct that–

    (a) such additional rules as may be specified in the notice shall apply to the infected place; or

    (b) any of the rules set out in the notice in Form A shall cease to apply to the infected place, or shall be modified to the extent or in the manner specified in the notice.

Disinfection or destruction of infected articles or materials

8. An inspector of the Ministry may, by notice in writing served on the owner or person in charge of any thing which is derived from or which has been used in connection with any horse or carcase in an infected place, require him to disinfect the thing with an approved disinfectant and to the inspector's satisfaction, or to destroy it, or to surrender it to the inspector who shall arrange for its disposal.

Disposal of carcases

9. If so required by the Divisional Veterinary Officer, an inspector of the local authority shall, where there is on any premises a carcase which is affected or suspected of being affected with disease, immediately dispose of that carcase at the local authority's expense in such manner as the Divisional Veterinary Officer shall direct.

Restrictions on premises exposed to infection

10.—(1) If an inspector has reasonable grounds for supposing–

  (a) that disease may spread to any premises; or

  (b) that there is or has within 56 days been on any premises a horse which has been exposed to disease, he may serve a notice in Form C on the occupier or person in charge of those premises.

(2) on the service of a notice in Form C and until the notice expires or is withdrawn in accordance with paragraph (3) below–

    (a) no person shall move, or cause or permit to be moved, any horse or carcase on to or out of the premises to which the notice relates, except under the authority of a licence issued by an inspector of the Ministry and in accordance with any conditions subject to which the licence is issued;

    (b) no person shall move out of the premises to which the notice relates, or cause or permit to be so moved, any fodder, manure, bedding, vehicle, equipment or other thing used for or about any horse except under the authority of a licence granted by an inspector of the Ministry and in accordance with any conditions subject to which the licence is issued;

    (c) no person shall allow any horse to stray from the premises to which the notice relates; and

    (d) the premises shall be subject to such other restrictions, specified in the notice, as the inspector may consider necessary for the purpose of preventing the spread of disease.

(3) A notice in Form C shall remain in force for such period as may be specified therein or until it is withdrawn by a notice in Form D served by an inspector on the occupier or person in charge of the premises to which the notice in Form C relates.

Cleansing and disinfection

11.—(1) A veterinary inspector may, by notice in writing served on the occupier of any premises in which there is or has been within 56 days been a horse or carcase which is affected or suspected of being affected with disease, require him to cleanse and disinfect with an approved disinfectant those premises at his own expense, in accordance with the provisions of paragraphs 1 and 2 of Schedule 2 to this Order, and within such period as may be specified in the notice.

(2) A veterinary inspector may by notice in writing served on the owner or person in charge of any vehicle which is used or has at any time during the previous 56 days been used for the carriage of a horse or carcase which is affected or suspected of being affected with disease, require him to cleanse and disinfect with an approved disinfectant at his own expense,–

    (a) the vehicle; and

    (b) any apparatus or other thing used in connection with the carriage of any such horse or carcase in the vehicle,

in accordance with the provisions of paragraph 3 of Schedule 2 to this Order, and within such period as may be specified in the notice.

(3) If any person on whom a notice is served under paragraph (1) or (2) above fails to comply with the requirements of the notice, an inspector or other officer of the Ministry or an inspector of the local authority may, without prejudice to any proceedings for an offence arising out of such default, carry out or cause to be carried out the requirements of the notice, and the amount of any reasonable expenses incurred by an inspector or other officer of the Ministry or by an inspector of the local authority shall be recoverable as a civil debt by the Minister, or, as the case may be, by the local authority from the person in default.

Marking of horses

12. An inspector may, for the purposes of this Order, mark, or cause to be marked, any horse.

Power of Ministry inspectors to prohibit or control movement

13.—(1) If an inspector of the Ministry has reasonable grounds for supposing that the movement of any horse, carcase or other thing on to or out of any premises would give rise to the risk of the spread of disease he may–

    (a) by notice served on the occupier or person in charge of the premises, prohibit the movement of any horse, carcase or other thing on to or out of the premises; or

    (b) by notice served on the owner of the horse, carcase or other thing, impose such conditions in respect of its movement as he considers necessary.

(2) A notice served under paragraph (1) above shall remain in force for such period as may be specified therein or until it is withdrawn by a further notice served by an inspector of the Ministry on the person on whom the notice was served.

Offences

14. Any person who, without lawful authority or excuse, proof of which shall lie on him–

    (a) defaces, obliterates or removes any mark applied to any horse by or under any provision of this Order; or

    (b) contravenes any provision of this Order or any provision of a licence, approval or notice issued, granted or served under this Order; or

    (c) fails to comply with any such provision or with any condition of such a licence, approval or notice; or

    (d) knowingly causes or permits any such contravention or non-compliance, commits an offence against the Act.

Local authority to enforce Order

15. The provisions of this Order shall, except where otherwise provided, be executed and enforced by the local authority.

Revocation

16. The Orders listed in Schedule 3 are revoked.

In Witness whereof the Official Seal of the Minister of Agriculture, Fisheries and Food is hereunto affixed on 29th April 1987.

Michael Jopling
Minister of Agriculture, Fisheries and Food

23rd April 1987

John J. Mackay
Parliamentary Under-Secretary of State, Scottish Office

23rd April 1987

Nicholas Edwards
Secretary of State for Wales

SCHEDULE 1

FORMS

FORM A

ANIMAL HEALTH ACT 1981

THE INFECTIOUS DISEASES OF HORSES ORDER 1987
(Articles 5, 6 and 7)

NOTICE DECLARING INFECTED PLACE

To...

of...

....

I, the undersigned, being an inspector of the Ministry of Agriculture, Fisheries and Food/*of the local authority for the .... of.................................hereby give you notice as the occupier/*person in charge of the premises described below that, in accordance with the provisions of the above Order, the premises are hereby declared to be an infected place for the purposes of the said Order and that the premises shall become subject to the Rules set out on the back of this notice.

Any infringement of these Rules may constitute an offence against the Animal Health Act 1981 and render a person liable to penalties on conviction.

This notice remains in force until it is withdrawn by a subsequent notice (Form B) served by an inspector of the Ministry.

Description of infected place, stating full postal address

Premises ....

Full postal address...

....

Signed... Dated...

Name in block letters..

Official address..

....

Note:—The inspector is with all practicable speed to send copies of this notice to the Divisional Veterinary Officer, to the local authority, to the police officer in charge of the nearest police station of the police force for the area and to the Secretary, Ministry of Agriculture, Fisheries and Food, Government Buildings, Block B, Hook Rise South, Surbiton, Surrey KT6 7NF.

---

*delete as appropriate.

RULES TO BE OBSERVED ON THE INFECTED PLACE (Article 7)

Rule 1. Any horse or carcase which is affected or suspected of being affected with disease shall be isolated from all other horses in the infected place and detained there in such manner as may be directed by a veterinary inspector.

Rule 2. No person shall move a horse or carcase into or out of the infected place, or cause or permit a horse or carcase to be so moved, except under the authority of a licence issued by a veterinary inspector and in accordance with any conditions subject to which the licence is issued.

Rule 3. No person shall move out of the infected place, or cause or permit to be so moved, any fodder, manure, bedding, vehicle, equipment or other thing used or intended to be used for or in connection with horses except under the authority of a licence issued by an officer of the appropriate Minister and in accordance with any conditions subject to which the licence is issued.

Rule 4. No person shall–
   (a) enter any part of the infected place except under the authority of a licence issued by an officer of the appropriate Minister and in accordance with any conditions subject to which the licence is issued, and unless he is wearing overall clothing and boots which are capable of being disinfected or which are disposable; or
   (b) leave any part of the infected place without first washing his hands and either thoroughly cleansing and disinfecting with an approved disinfectant his overall clothing and boots or removing them and leaving them on the infected place.

Rule 5. The occupier or person in charge of the infected place shall maintain a footbath containing such disinfectant as shall be specified by an inspector in a convenient position at every exit from the infected place, and shall renew the disinfectant daily and whenever so directed by an inspector.

Rule 6. The occupier of the infected place shall, if so required by a veterinary inspector, erect and maintain to the satisfaction of a veterinary inspector, fly-proof screens around at any place in which any horse or carcase is isolated in accordance with Rule 1 above.

Rule 7. The owner or person in charge of any horse in an infected place shall take all such steps as may be necessary to prevent it from straying from that place.

Rule 8. Notice of the death or slaughter of any horse in an infected place shall be given, with all practicable speed, to the Divisional Veterinary Officer. The carcase of any such horse shall be disposed of only with the consent, and under the direction, of the Divisional Veterinary Officer.

Rule 9. No person, other than a veterinary surgeon acting in accordance with an approval given by the Divisional Veterinary Officer, shall cut the skin of any carcase in an infected place.

Rule 10.–(1) A notice supplied by the appropriate Minister stating that the premises are an infected place shall be exhibited at every entrance to the infected place.

   (2) No person shall alter, remove or deface such a notice.

[ADDITIONAL RULES]

FORM B

ANIMAL HEALTH ACT 1981

THE INFECTIOUS DISEASES OF HORSES ORDER 1987

(Articles 5 and 6)

WITHDRAWAL OF NOTICE DECLARING INFECTED PLACE (FORM A)

To ....

of ....

....

I, the undersigned, being an inspector of the Ministry of Agriculture, Fisheries and Food hereby withdraw, as from the date of this notice, the Infected Place Notice (Form A) signed by .... and served on you on the .... day of 19

Signed...   Dated ....

Name in block letters...

Official address ....

....

Note:—The inspector is with all practicable speed to send copies of this notice to the Divisional Veterinary Officer, to the local authority, to the police officer in charge of the nearest police station of the police force for the area and to the Secretary, Ministry of Agriculture, Fisheries and Food, Government Buildings, Block B, Hook Rise South, Surbiton, Surrey KT6 7NF.

FORM C

ANIMAL HEALTH ACT 1981

THE INFECTIOUS DISEASES OF HORSES ORDER 1987

(Article 10)

NOTICE IMPOSING RESTRICTIONS ON PREMISES EXPOSED TO INFECTION

To ....

of ....

....

I, the undersigned, being an inspector of the Ministry of Agriculture, Fisheries and Food/*of the local authority for the ....

of .... hereby give you notice as the occupier or person in charge of the premises described below that, in accordance with the provisions of the above Order,–

    (a)   no person shall move, or cause or permit to be moved, any horse or carcase into or out of the premises to which the notice relates, except under the authority of a licence issued by an inspector of the Ministry and in accordance with any conditions subject to which the licence is issued;

    (b)   no person shall move out of the premises to which the notice relates, or cause or permit to be so moved, any fodder, manure, bedding, vehicle, equipment or other thing used for or about any horse, except under the authority of a licence granted by an inspector of the Ministry and in accordance with any conditions subject to which the licence is issued;

    (c)   no person shall allow any horse to stray from the premises to which the notice relates; and

    (d)   (other restrictions).

These restrictions imposed by this notice apply until–

    (a)   *midnight on .... 19 .

    (b)   *this notice is withdrawn by a further notice (Form D) served on you by an inspector of the Ministry or of the local authority.

Description of premises, stating full postal address

Premises ....

Full postal address...

....

Signed... Dated...

Name in block letters...

Official address..

....

Note:—The inspector is with all practicable speed to send copies of this notice to the Divisional Veterinary Officer, to the local authority, to the police officer in charge of the nearest police station of the police force for the area and to the Secretary, Ministry of Agriculture, Fisheries and Food, Government Buildings, Block B, Hook Rise South, Surbiton, Surrey KT6 7NF; in these copies there should be added the name and address of any person (as specified below) whose premises have been declared an infected place and from which there is or has been a risk of spread of infection to the premises described in this notice.

Name..

Address ....

....

*delete as appropriate.

FORM D

THE ANIMAL HEALTH ACT 1981

THE INFECTIOUS DISEASES OF HORSES ORDER 1987

(Article 10)

NOTICE WITHDRAWING RESTRICTIONS ON PREMISES EXPOSED TO INFECTION

To ....

of ....

....

I, the undersigned, being an inspector of the Ministry of Agriculture, Fisheries and Food/*of the local authority for the ....
of .... hereby withdraw as from the date of this notice the notice (Form C) signed by .... and served on you on the
.... day of 19

Signed.. Dated ....

Name in block letters...

Official address...

....

Note:—The inspector is with all practicable speed to send copies of this notice to the Divisional Veterinary Officer, to the local authority, to the police officer in charge of the nearest police station of the police force for the area and to the Secretary, Ministry of Agriculture, Fisheries and Food, Government Buildings, Block B, Hook Rise South, Surbiton, Surrey KT6 7NF.

*delete as appropriate.

SCHEDULE 2

CLEANSING AND DISINFECTION

(Article 11)

Cleansing and disinfection of premises

1.   Where any premises are required to be cleansed and disinfected under article 11(1) of this Order, such cleansing and disinfection shall be carried out in the following manner, that is to say–

(a)   the floor and all parts of the premises which have been in contact with any horse or carcase shall first be thoroughly saturated with an approved disinfectant;

(b)   the floor and all other such parts of the premises shall be swept or scraped and the sweepings and scrapings shall be removed from the premises and forthwith be buried or destroyed;

(c)   any thing on the premises which has been in contact with any horse or carcase on the premises shall be thoroughly saturated with an approved disinfectant;

(d)   the floor and all other such parts of the premises shall again be thoroughly saturated with an approved disinfectant.

2.   In the case of a field or other open space which is not capable of being treated in the manner described in paragraph 1 above, cleansing and disinfection shall be carried out so far as is practicable and to the satisfaction of an inspector of the Ministry.

Cleansing and disinfection of vehicles

3.   When a vehicle is required to be cleansed and disinfected under article 11(2) of this Order, such cleansing and disinfection shall be carried out in the following manner, that is to say–

(a)   the whole of the interior of the vehicle and such parts of the outside of the vehicle as a veterinary inspector may direct shall first be thoroughly saturated with an approved disinfectant;

(b)   the whole of the interior of the vehicle shall be swept or scraped and the sweepings and scrapings, and any manure, litter or dung in the vehicle, shall be removed from the vehicle and forthwith be buried or destroyed;

(c)   those parts of the vehicle described in sub-paragraph (a) above shall again be thoroughly saturated with an approved disinfectant;

(d)   any apparatus, equipment or other thing used in connection with the carriage of any horse or carcase in the vehicle shall be thoroughly saturated with disinfectant, effectively cleansed and then again saturated with an approved disinfectant.

SCHEDULE 3

REVOCATION

Article 16

Orders revoked	References
The Epizootic Lymphangitis Order of 1938	S.R. and O. 1938/193.
The Glanders or Farcy Order of 1938	S.R. and O. 1938/228.
The Infectious Diseases of Horses Order 1975	S.I. 1975/888.
The Dourine Order 1975	S.I. 1975/889.

EXPLANATORY NOTE

(This note is not part of the Order)

This Order consolidates, with amendments, the provisions of various orders relating to diseases of horses listed in Schedule 3 to the Order, which are revoked.

The Order continues to provide for–

(a) the compulsory notification of diseases of horses (as defined in article 3(1)) (article 4);

(b) the declaration as an infected place of premises where diseases of horses are suspected to exist (article 5) and rules to be observed in respect of an infected place (article 7);

(c) the investigation by a veterinary inspector into the existence of diseases of horses and the examination by him of horses or carcases for this purpose (article 6);

(d) the prohibition of the movement of horses, carcases and other things on to or out of premises exposed to infection (article 10); and

(e) the cleansing and disinfection of premises and vehicles (article 11).

The only changes of substance are that the provisions of this Order apply to the disease known as contagious equine metritis in addition to the diseases of horses referred to in the Orders listed in Schedule 3 and that there is no longer any provision relating to the compulsory slaughter of horses suspected of being affected with glanders.

STATUTORY INSTRUMENTS

1987 No. 794 (S. 62)

RATING AND VALUATION

The Valuation Timetable (Scotland) Amendment (No. 2) Order 1987

Made - - - -	*30th April 1987*
Coming into force	*8th May 1987*

The Secretary of State, in exercise of the powers conferred on him by sections 13(1) and 42(1) of the Valuation and Rating (Scotland) Act 1956(**a**), and of all other powers enabling him in that behalf, hereby makes the following Order:

1. This Order may be cited as the Valuation Timetable (Scotland) Amendment (No. 2) Order 1987 and shall come into force on 8th May 1987.

2. The entry in column 2 of the Schedule to the Valuation Timetable (Scotland) Order 1984(**b**) relating to the date for making valuations (in respect of the prevailing level of rents) mentioned in column 1 of that Schedule shall be amended by substituting for the words "1st July" the words "1st April".

Michael Ancram
New St. Andrew's House, Edinburgh
Parliamentary Under Secretary of State,
30th April 1987
Scottish Office

EXPLANATORY NOTE

(This note is not part of the Order)

This Order amends the entry in the Schedule to the Valuation Timetable (Scotland) Order 1984 containing the timetable for making valuations (in respect of the prevailing level of rents).

The Order amends the date for making such valuations from 1st July to 1st April in the year 2 years prior to a year of revaluation.

(**a**) 1956 c.60; section 13(1) was amended by the Local Government (Scotland) Act 1975 (c.30), Schedule 6, Part II, paragraph 20(a) and was extended by the Local Government (Financial Provisions) (Scotland) Act 1963 (c.12), section 22(d).
(**b**) S.I. 1984/1504, as amended by S.I. 1987/432.

STATUTORY INSTRUMENTS

1987 No. 798

BUILDING AND BUILDINGS

The Building (Inner London) Regulations 1987

Made - - - -	*5th May 1987*
Laid before Parliament	*11th May 1987*
Coming into force	*1st July 1987*

The Secretary of State, in exercise of the powers conferred on him by the provisions of the Building Act 1984(a) specified in Schedule 1 to these Regulations and of all other powers enabling him in that behalf, after consulting the Building Regulations Advisory Committee, any local authority who appear to him to be concerned and such other bodies as appear to him to be representative of the interests concerned in accordance with section 14(3) of and paragraph 4 of Schedule 3 to that Act, hereby makes the following Regulations:

Citation and commencement

1. These Regulations may be cited as the Building (Inner London) Regulations 1987 and shall come into force on 1st July 1987.

Further application of building regulations and the Building Act 1984 to inner London

2.—(1) The Building Regulations 1985(b) and the Building (Approved Inspectors etc.) Regulations 1985(c) shall be amended as provided in Part I of Schedule 2 to these Regulations, being amendments to apply further provisions of those Regulations to inner London.

(2) The following provisions of the Building Act 1984 apply in relation to a local authority in inner London as they apply to a local authority outside inner London—

section 18 (building over sewer etc.);

section 21 (provision of drainage);

section 22 (drainage of buildings in combination);

section 23 (provision of facilities for refuse).

(3) Paragraph 5 of Schedule 3 to the Building Act 1984 shall have effect with the insertion after "71" of ", 72(1) to (4), (6) and (7), 73".

Consequential modifications and repeals

3.—(1) The Building (Prescribed Fees etc.) Regulations 1985(d) and the Building (Inner London) Regulations 1985(e) shall be amended as provided in Part II of Schedule 2 to these Regulations.

(a) 1984 c.55.
(b) S.I. 1985/1065; relevant amending instrument is S.I. 1985/1936.
(c) S.I. 1985/1066, amended by S.I. 1985/1936.
(d) S.I. 1985/1576; relevant amending instrument is S.I. 1985/1936.
(e) S.I. 1985/1936, to which there are amendments not relevant to these Regulations.

(2) The enactments mentioned in Schedule 3 shall have effect subject to the modifications specified in that Schedule.

(3) The enactments and instruments mentioned in Schedule 4 are repealed or revoked to the extent specified in the third column of that Schedule.

Transitional Provisions

4.—(1) Subject to paragraph (2) below, these Regulations do not apply to any building, structure or work if on 1st July 1987 the Building (Inner London) Regulations 1985 do not apply to that building, structure or work, or if, before that date—

(a) a contract was entered into for the erection of the building, construction of the structure or execution of the work; or

(b) the erection of the building, construction of the structure or execution of the work was commenced; or

(c) plans were deposited or notice was given in respect of the building, structure or work under any of the enactments and instruments which would be repealed or revoked if these Regulations applied; or

(d) in respect of the building, structure or work, a building notice was given or full plans were deposited under regulation 11 of the Building Regulations 1985 or an initial notice or a public body's notice was given,

until that building, structure or work has been completed.

(2) Notwithstanding paragraph (1) above, these Regulations shall apply to any building, structure or work if, on or after 1st July 1987–

(a) in respect of that building, structure or work, a building notice is given or full plans are deposited under regulation 11 of the Building Regulations 1985 or an initial notice or a public body's notice is given, and

(b) those plans or that notice includes work in respect of which any of the enactments or instruments repealed or revoked by these Regulations requires the deposit of plans or the giving of notice; and

(c) at the time that those plans are deposited or that notice is given the building work to which those plans or that notice relate has not been commenced.

Preamble

SCHEDULE 1

ENABLING POWERS

Sections 1(1), 3, 8(2), 16(9) and (10), 17(1) and (6), 35, 47(1) to (5), 49(1) and (5), 50(1), (3), (4), (6) and (7), 51(1) and (2), 52(1), (2), (3) and (5), 53(2) and (4), 54(1) to (3) and (5) and 56(1) and (2) of, and paragraphs 1, 2, 3, 5, 7, 8, 10 and 11 of Schedule 1, paragraphs 2 and 3 of Schedule 3 and paragraphs 1, 2(1), (2), (4) and (5), 3(1) and (2), 4(2) and (4), and 5 of Schedule 4 to, the Building Act 1984(a).

(a) 1984 c.55.

SCHEDULE 2   Regulations 2(1) and 3(1)

AMENDMENTS TO BUILDING REGULATIONS

PART I

1. The Building Regulations 1985**(a)** shall be amended as follows–

(a) in regulation 12(2)(c)(i) omit the words "if Part H (drainage and waste disposal) of Schedule 1 applies,",

(b) in regulation 14–

(i) in paragraph (1) omit the words "Subject to paragraph (1A),"; and

(ii) omit paragraph (1A),

(c) in regulation 15 for the words "A local authority outside inner London" substitute the words "The local authority",

(d) in Schedule 1 (Requirements) in the third column (Limits on application)–

(i) omit the words "This requirement does not apply in inner London." opposite paragraph G4 (sanitary conveniences); and

(ii) omit the words "The requirements of this Part do not apply in inner London." in Part H (drainage and waste disposal).

2. The Building (Approved Inspectors etc.) Regulations 1985**(b)** shall be amended as follows—

in regulation 10–

(i) for the words "paragraphs (1A) and" substitute the word "paragraph"; and

(ii) omit paragraph (1A).

PART II

3. The Building (Prescribed Fees etc.) Regulations 1985**(c)** shall be amended as follows:–

(a) in regulation 5 omit the words "Subject to regulation 6A" in the three places where they occur;

(b) in regulation 6 omit the words "Subject to regulation 6A"; and

(c) omit regulation 6A.

4. Schedule 2 to the Building (Inner London) Regulations 1985**(d)** shall be amended by the omission of paragraphs 1(2), (3), (4), and (6), 2(2) and 3(2), (3) and (4).

SCHEDULE 3   Regulation 3(2)

MODIFICATION OF ENACTMENTS

1. The London Building Acts (Amendment) Act 1939**(e)** shall have effect–

(a) in section 4, in the definition of "domestic building", with the omission of the words from "and for the purposes of Part V" to the end of that definition;

(b) in section 21, with the substitution for subsections (4A) and (4B)**(f)** of the following:–

"(4A) Subsection (4) of this section shall not apply if:

(a) the width of any opening in any wall of a storey (or if there is more than one opening in any such wall, the width of all such openings taken together) does not exceed one-half of the length of the wall, and

(b) each opening is closed by two steel plate doors, metal covered doors or steel rolling shutters, one on each side of the wall, and

(c) those doors or shutters are–

(i) constructed in accordance with specification 1 or 2 or 3 or 4, and

(ii) installed in accordance with the general installation requirements

---

(a) S.I. 1985/1065; relevant amending instrument is S.I. 1985/1936.
(b) S.I. 1985/1066, amended by S.I. 1985/1936.
(c) S.I. 1985/1576; relevant amending instrument is S.I. 1985/1936.
(d) S.I. 1985/1936, to which there are amendments not relevant to these Regulations.
(e) 1939 c.xcvii.
(f) Inserted by the Building (Inner London) Regulations 1985 (S.I. 1985/1936).

of the Rules for the Construction and Installation of Firebreak Doors and Shutters of the Fire Offices' Committee, dated February 1985.";

(c) in section 34(1), with the insertion, after proviso (ii)(B), of the following–

"or (C) a building to which section 4(1)(a) of the Building Act 1984 applies.";

(d) in section 35(1), with the insertion, before paragraph (iii) of the proviso, of the following paragraph–

"(ii) the provisions of this subsection shall not apply to any building to which section 4(1)(a) of the Building Act 1984 applies; and";

(e) in section 145, with the omission of subsection (4)**(a)**.

2. The London Government Act 1963**(b)** shall have effect with the insertion at the end of paragraph 18 of Part III of Schedule 9 of the following sub-paragraph–

"(3) Nothing in this paragraph applies to the erection of a building or extension of a building if section 18 of the Building Act 1984 would apply if plans of that building or extension were, in accordance with building regulations, deposited with a local authority.".

3. The Greater London Council (General Powers) Act 1969**(c)** shall have effect, in section 26 (Building control)–

(a) with the omission of "and any byelaws made thereunder" from subsection (1); and

(b) with the substitution of "the Building Regulations 1985" for "any such byelaws as aforesaid" in subsection (2)(b).

4. The City of London (Various Powers) Act 1973**(d)** shall have effect, in section 7 (Sanitation byelaws: dispensation and increase of penalties) with the substitution of the following for subsection (8)–

"(8) This section applies to byelaws in force from time to time made by the Corporation under section 5 (Byelaws as to pipes conveying acids) of the City of London (Various Powers) Act 1926.".

5. The Building Act 1984 shall have effect, in section 18–

(a) with the substitution, in subsection (2), of "a local authority" for the words from "the council" to "1939";

(b) with the substitution, in subsection (3), of "local authority" for "council of a district or outer London borough" and of "authority" for "council"; and

(c) with the insertion, after subsection (5), of the following subsection–

"(6) This section does not apply to the Inner Temple or the Middle Temple.".

(a) Inserted by the Building (Inner London) Regulations 1985 (S.I. 1985/1936).
(b) 1963 c.33.
(c) 1969 c.lii.
(d) 1973 c.xx.

SCHEDULE 4

Regulation 3(3)

REPEALS

PART I

GENERAL

Chapter	Short Title	Extent of repeal
1939 c.xcvii.	The London Building Acts (Amendment) Act 1939.	In section 4, in the definition of "domestic building", the words from "and for the purposes of Part V" to the end of that definition.
		Section 19.
1963 c.33.	The London Government Act 1963.	In Part III of Schedule 9, paragraph 6.
1969 c.lii.	The Greater London Council (General Powers) Act 1969.	In section 26(1), the words "and any byelaws made thereunder".
1971 c.xxviii.	The Greater London Council (General Powers) Act 1971.	In section 4(1), paragraphs (a)(ii) and (iii) and (b).
1984 c.55.	The Building Act 1984.	In Schedule 3– in paragraph 1, the words "8 to 10, 16, 18, 21 to 23," and the words "to 29, 32, 36, 37, 39 and 40"; paragraphs 7, 8, 9 and 11; and in paragraph 13, the words from "save that" to the end of that paragraph.
1984 c.xxvii.	The Greater London Council (General Powers) Act 1984.	Section 36.
	The by-laws made by the London County Council and confirmed on 21st August 1930 with respect to water closets, urinals, earth closets, privies and cesspools, and the proper accessories thereof in connection with buildings.	All the by-laws.
	The by-laws made by the London County Council and confirmed on 12th March 1962 with respect to drainage.	All the by-laws.
	The by-laws made by the London County Council on 11th December 1962 for the removal, etc., of refuse.	Part II.

PART II

THE CITY OF LONDON

Chapter	Short Title	Extent of repeal
11 & 12 Vict. c. clxiii.	The City of London Sewers Act 1848.	Sections 63 and 72.
14 & 15 Vict. c. xci.	The City of London Sewers Act 1851.	Section 39.
63 & 64 Vict. c. ccxxviii.	The City of London (Various Powers) Act 1900.	Section 54.
16 & 17 Geo.5 c. vii.	The City of London (Various Powers) Act 1926.	Section 6.
23 & 24 Geo.5 c. xxiii.	The City of London (Various Powers) Act 1933.	Section 5.
9 & 10 Eliz.2 c. xxviii.	The City of London (Various Powers) Act 1961.	Section 32(3)(a).
	The byelaws made by the Mayor and Commonalty and Citizens of the City of London and confirmed on 1st February 1984 with respect to water closets, soil appliances, discharge pipes and traps, etc.	The whole byelaws except insofar as they relate to conveying acids from premises where chemicals are used.

5th May 1987

Nicholas Ridley
Secretary of State for the Environment

EXPLANATORY NOTE

(This note is not part of the Regulations)

These Regulations bring into force for inner London–
    (1) sections 18, 21–23 and 72(5) of the Building Act 1984 (regulations 2(2) and (3)), and
    (2) parts G4 (sanitary conveniences) and H (drainage and waste disposal) of the Building Regulations 1985 (regulation 2(1) and Schedule 2),
thus completing the application of the national system of building control to inner London.

Regulation 3 and Schedule 2 repeal earlier amendments made by the Building (Inner London) Regulations 1985 to the Building (Approved Inspectors, etc) Regulations 1985 and the Building (Prescribed Fees, etc) Regulations 1985. The two latter instruments therefore apply fully in inner London.

Schedule 4 repeals superseded enactments and instruments. These include the LCC's byelaws for sanitary conveniences and drainage (and the power to charge fees in respect of applications under them) and Part II of the LCC's byelaws for the removal, etc of refuse. Part II of the Schedule repeals the corresponding City legislation and the City Corporation's sanitation byelaws (except for the byelaws relating to the discharge of acids).

Regulation 4 contains transitional provisions to permit work in progress at the date of coming into force of the Regulations to be completed under the existing procedures.

The Regulations also make certain minor modifications to the London Building Acts (Amendment) Act 1939 in respect of fire precautions and means of escape and to the London Government Act 1963 in respect of building over sewers and make some consequential amendments to the Building Act 1984 (Schedule 3).

"Inner London" means the area comprising the inner London boroughs, the City of London, the Inner Temple and the Middle Temple.

The Rules for the Construction and Installation of Firebreak Doors and Shutters of the Fire Offices' Committee dated February 1985, referred to in paragraph 1 of Schedule 3, may be obtained from the Loss Prevention Council Limited at 140 Aldersgate Street, London EC1A 4HY.

STATUTORY INSTRUMENTS

1987 No. 799

FAMILY PROVISION

The Family Provision (Intestate Succession) Order 1987

Made - - - -	*1st May 1987*
Coming into force	*1st June 1987*

Whereas a draft of this Order has been laid before Parliament and a period of forty days beginning with the day of laying has expired:

Now therefore, the Lord Chancellor, in exercise of the powers conferred on him by section 1(1)(a) and (b) of the Family Provision Act 1966**(a)**, hereby makes the following Order:–

1. This Order may be cited as the Family Provision (Intestate Succession) Order 1987 and shall come into force on 1st June 1987.

2. In the case of a person dying after the coming into force of this Order, section 46(1) of the Administration of Estates Act 1925**(b)** shall apply as if the net sums charged by paragraph (i) on the residuary estate were:–

(a) under paragraph (2) of the Table, the sum of £75,000; and

(b) under paragraph (3) of the Table, the sum of £125,000.

Dated 1st May 1987

Hailsham of St. Marylebone, C.

EXPLANATORY NOTE

(This note is not part of the Order)

The estate of a person dying intestate is charged with a fixed sum (the statutory legacy) in favour of the surviving spouse. This Order increases the statutory legacy from £40,000 to £75,000 where the intestate is survived by issue, and from £85,000 to £125,000 where there is no surviving issue but the intestate is survived by certain close relatives.

By virtue of section 1(3) of the Family Provision Act 1966, this Order supersedes the Family Provision (Intestate Succession) Order 1981 (S.I. 1981/255) in relation to the estate of a person dying on or after 1st June 1987.

(a) 1966 c.35.

(b) 1925 c.23; section 46(1) was, so far as is relevant, amended by section 1 of the Intestates' Estates Act 1952 (c.64) and section 1 of the Family Provision Act 1966.

STATUTORY INSTRUMENTS

1987 No. 800 (S. 63)

FOOD

FOOD HYGIENE

The Fresh Meat Export (Hygiene and Inspection) (Scotland) Regulations 1987

Made - - - -	*29th April 1987*
Laid before Parliament	*14th May 1987*
Coming into force	*11th June 1987*

ARRANGEMENT OF REGULATIONS

SCHEDULES

The Secretary of State, in exercise of the powers conferred on him by section 2(2) of the European Communities Act 1972(a) (being one of the Ministers designated(b) for the purposes of that section in relation to the common agricultural policy of the European Economic Community), and by sections 13, 26(3) and 56 of the Food and Drugs (Scotland) Act 1956(c), and of all other powers enabling him in that behalf, having in accordance with section 56(6) of the said Act of 1956 consulted with such organisations as appear to him to be representative of interests substantially affected by the Regulations, hereby makes the following Regulations:

Citation, extent and commencement

1. These Regulations, which may be cited as the Fresh Meat Export (Hygiene and Inspection) (Scotland) Regulations 1987, shall apply to Scotland and shall come into force on 11th June 1987.

(a) 1972 c.68; section 2 is subject to Schedule 2 to that Act and is to be read with sections 289F and 289G of the Criminal Procedure (Scotland) Act 1975 (c.21) (as inserted by section 54 of the Criminal Justice Act 1982 (c.48)), and S.I. 1984/526.
(b) S.I. 1972/1811.
(c) 1956 c.30; section 26(3) was amended by paragraph 123 of Schedule 27 to the Local Government (Scotland) Act 1973 (c.65) and by section 22(a) of the Local Government and Planning (Scotland) Act 1982 (c.43); section 56(8) was amended by, and section 56(8A) inserted by, paragraph 8 of Schedule 15 to the Criminal Justice Act 1982 (c.48); section 56(8A) was amended by the Law Reform (Miscellaneous Provisions) (Scotland) Act 1985 (c.73), section 41 and is to be read with section 289G of the Criminal Procedure (Scotland) Act 1975 and S.I. 1984/526.

Interpretation

2.—(1) In these Regulations, unless the context otherwise requires –

"the Act" means the Food and Drugs (Scotland) Act 1956;

"animals" means domestic animals of the following species: bovine animals (including buffalo), swine, sheep, goats and solipeds;

"ante-mortem health inspection" means inspection of live animals in a slaughterhouse in accordance with the requirements of regulation 8 and Schedule 6;

"carcase" means the whole body of a slaughtered animal after bleeding and dressing in accordance with the requirements of Schedule 7;

"cold store" means premises, not forming part of a slaughterhouse or cutting premises, used for the cold storage of meat intended for sale for human consumption;

"country of destination" means the Member State to which fresh meat is sent;

"cutting premises" means premises used for the purpose of cutting up meat intended for sale for human consumption, whether or not they form part of a slaughterhouse;

"cutting up" means cutting meat into cuts smaller than half carcases cut into three wholesale cuts or boning meat;

"disinfect" means to apply hygienically satisfactory chemical or physical agents or processes with the intention of eliminating micro-organisms;

"examine in detail" means to examine by making multiple deep incisions into lymph nodes;

"export" means to send to a Member State;

"export cold store" means a cold store currently approved by the Secretary of State under these Regulations for the cold storage of fresh meat for export;

"export cutting premises" means cutting premises currently approved by the Secretary of State under these Regulations for the purpose of cutting up fresh meat for export;

"export slaughterhouse" means a slaughterhouse currently approved by the Secretary of State under these Regulations for the purpose of producing fresh meat for export;

"fresh" as applied to meat means all meat which has not undergone any preserving process and which includes meat vacuum wrapped or wrapped in a controlled atmosphere; however chilled and frozen meat shall be considered to be fresh meat;

"health mark" means a mark made by or under the supervision and responsibility of an official veterinary surgeon in accordance with regulation 8 and of a kind and in the manner set out in Schedule 11;

"inspector" means a person who is qualified in accordance with regulation 18 of the Food (Meat Inspection) (Scotland) Regulations 1961(**a**) and who is appointed in accordance with regulation 12(2);

"lairage" means that part of a slaughterhouse used for the confinement of animals awaiting slaughter there;

"local authority" means the council of an islands area or district and in relation to any land or premises means the local authority within whose area the land or premises is or are situated;

"meat" means the flesh or other edible part of animals;

"occupier" means any person carrying on the business of an export slaughterhouse, export cutting premises or export cold store, either together or separately;

"offal" means meat other than that of the carcase whether or not naturally connected to the carcase;

"official veterinary surgeon" means a veterinary surgeon designated by the Secretary of State;

"packing", in relation to meat, means placing wrapped meat into a carton or similar receptacle, and "package" shall be construed accordingly;

"post-mortem health inspection" means inspection of slaughtered animals in a slaughter-house in accordance with the requirements of regulation 8 and Schedule 8;

"sell" includes offer or expose for sale or have in possession for sale;

(**a**) S.I. 1961/243, amended by S.I. 1963/1231, 1979/1563, 1981/996, 1983/702 and 1985/1068.

"slaughterhouse" means any premises used for slaughtering animals, the flesh of which is intended for sale for human consumption, and includes any place used in connection therewith but does not include any place used in connection with a slaughterhouse solely for the manufacture of bacon and ham, sausages, meat pies or other manufactured meat products, or for the storage of meat used in such manufacture;

"transhipment centre" means an export slaughterhouse or export cutting premises currently approved by the Secretary of State under these Regulations for the purpose of unloading, assembling, inspecting and loading consignments of fresh meat for export where such meat bears the health mark of other premises approved by the Secretary of State under these Regulations or the meat comes from outside Scotland and satisfies the requirements of the European Economic Community;

"veterinary officer" means a veterinary officer of the Secretary of State;

"viscera" means offal from the thoracic, abdominal and pelvic cavities, including the trachea and oesophagus;

"workroom" means any part of a slaughterhouse (other than a slaughterhall), or cutting premises, in which meat is handled, hung or stored;

"wrapping", in relation to meat, means placing in a material which comes into direct contact with the meat.

(2) Except insofar as the context otherwise requires, any reference in these Regulations to a numbered regulation or Schedule shall be construed as a reference to the regulation or Schedule bearing that number in these Regulations.

Exemption

3.   These Regulations shall not apply to fresh meat which is exported with the authority of the country of destination and intended exclusively as supplies for international organisations and military forces stationed on its territory but serving under another flag.

Approval of premises

4.—(1) The Secretary of State on an application made to him under this regulation –

(a) shall approve the premises to which the application relates as –

  (i) an export slaughterhouse if he is satisfied that the premises comply with the requirements of Schedule 1 and that the method of operation in those premises complies with the requirements of Part I of Schedule 5 and Schedules 6, 7 and 8;

  (ii) export cutting premises if he is satisfied that –

    (aa) in the case of premises to which the Slaughterhouse Hygiene (Scotland) Regulations 1978(a) apply, the premises comply with the requirements of Part I of Schedule 2 and the method of operation in those premises complies with the requirements of Part I of Schedule 5 and Schedule 9, and

    (ab) in the case of premises to which the Slaughterhouse Hygiene (Scotland) Regulations 1978 do not apply, the premises comply with the requirements of Schedule 2 and the method of operation in those premises complies with the requirements of Parts I and II of Schedule 5 and Schedule 9, save that such premises shall not be approved if they are situated within the curtilage of a slaughterhouse which is not approved for export;

  (iii) an export cold store if he is satisfied that the premises comply with the requirements of Schedule 3 and that the method of operation in those premises can comply with the requirements of Part III of Schedule 5 and Schedule 13, and such approval may relate to particular categories of meat;

  (iv) a transhipment centre if he is satisfied that the premises, being an export slaughterhouse or export cutting premises, comply with the requirements of Schedule 4; and

(b) shall refuse so to approve those premises if he is not so satisfied.

(a) S.I. 1978/1273, amended by S.I. 1984/842, 1985/1068, 1856 and 1986/1808.

(2) Each application for the approval of any premises under this regulation shall be made in writing to the Secretary of State by the occupier of, or a person proposing to occupy, those premises.

(3) The Secretary of State shall notify the local authority in writing of each such application and shall arrange for a veterinary officer to inspect the premises named in the application and to make a report on those premises.

(4) Where a local authority have been notified under paragraph (3) of this regulation of an application for the approval of any premises, they may submit written representations relating to that application to the Secretary of State within 21 days after the receipt of such notification and shall send a copy of any representations to the applicant.

(5) Within 21 days after the receipt of a copy of any representations submitted by the local authority under paragraph (4) of this regulation the applicant may submit written observations on those representations to the Secretary of State.

(6) In determining whether or not to approve any premises under paragraph (1) of this regulation the Secretary of State shall have regard to –
  (a) the report made on the premises by the veterinary officer under paragraph (3) of this regulation;
  (b) any representations submitted by the local authority under paragraph (4) of this regulation; and
  (c) any observations submitted by the applicant under paragraph (5) of this regulation.

(7) The Secretary of State shall notify the applicant and the local authority in writing of his decision on each application for the approval of premises under this regulation and of the reasons for any refusal to approve such premises.

(8) Any approval of any premises under this regulation shall be subject to the condition that no significant alteration shall be made to –
  (a) the premises or the equipment in those premises otherwise than by way of repairs and maintenance; or
  (b) the method of operation in those premises;
without the prior agreement in writing of the Secretary of State who shall have regard to any views expressed by the local authority.

(9) Following the approval of any premises as an export slaughterhouse or as export cutting premises the Secretary of State shall issue to the local authority the necessary equipment for application of the health mark.

Premises approved prior to 11th June 1987

5.   Any slaughterhouse, cutting premises, cold store or transhipment centre in respect of which approval granted by the Secretary of State for the purpose of the export of fresh meat is in force immediately prior to 11th June 1987 shall be deemed to be approved in accordance with regulation 4.

Suspension and revocation of approval

6.—(1) The Secretary of State may suspend or revoke his approval of any export slaughterhouse, export cutting premises, export cold store or transhipment centre and require the withdrawal of the equipment for the application of the health mark if after an inspection of or an enquiry into, and a report on, the premises by a veterinary officer and, in the case of revocation of approval, after consultation with the local authority and the occupier, he is satisfied in respect of these premises that the requirements of these Regulations are no longer or have not been complied with, and no action has been taken to ensure that a similar breach does not recur or that the condition attached to the approval of those premises referred to in regulation 4(8) has not been observed.

(2) The Secretary of State shall forthwith notify the occupier and the local authority of his decision under paragraph (1) of this regulation to suspend or revoke his approval of any premises, of the date on which the suspension or revocation is to take effect and of the reasons for such suspension or revocation.

(3) Any notification under paragraph (2) of this regulation shall be given in writing in the case of any revocation of approval and may be given orally or in writing in the case of any

suspension of approval, and where any such notification is given orally it shall be confirmed in writing.

(4) Where the Secretary of State has suspended approval of any premises under this regulation, those premises shall be treated throughout the period of suspension as if approval had not been granted under regulation 4.

(5) Where the suspension of approval of any premises under this regulation is not expressed to end on a specified date it may, if the Secretary of State thinks fit, be ended by notice given by him to the occupier, and the Secretary of State shall notify the local authority in writing that the suspension of approval of the premises has been ended.

Use of premises for production, cutting up, storage and loading of fresh meat for export

7.—(1) No person shall use any premises as a slaughterhouse for the production of fresh meat for export unless at the time of such use those premises are currently approved by the Secretary of State as an export slaughterhouse in accordance with regulation 4(1)(a)(i).

(2) No person shall use any premises, whether or not they comprise a part of a slaughterhouse, for the purpose of cutting up fresh meat for export unless at the time of such use those premises are currently approved by the Secretary of State as export cutting premises in accordance with regulation 4(1)(a)(ii).

(3) No person shall use any premises for the cold storage of fresh meat for export where those premises do not form part of an export slaughterhouse or export cutting premises unless at the time of such use those premises are currently approved by the Secretary of State as an export cold store in accordance with regulation 4(1)(a)(iii).

(4) No person shall use any premises for the purpose of unloading, assembling, inspecting and loading consignments of fresh meat for export where such meat bears the health mark of other premises approved by the Secretary of State under these Regulations or the meat comes from outside Scotland and satisfies the requirements of the European Economic Community unless at the time of such use the first mentioned premises are an export cold store or are currently approved by the Secretary of State as a transhipment centre in accordance with regulation 4(1)(a)(iv).

(5) In any export slaughterhouse, without prejudice to the requirements of the Slaughterhouse Hygiene (Scotland) Regulations 1978, the Slaughter of Animals (Prevention of Cruelty) (Scotland) Regulations 1955(a) and the Slaughter of Animals (Stunning Pens) (Scotland) Regulations 1963(b), the requirements of Part I of Schedule 5 and Schedules 6, 7 and 8 shall be complied with at all times and the requirements of Schedules 11 and 14 shall be complied with whenever fresh meat for export is being produced.

(6) In any export cutting premises, without prejudice to the requirements of the Slaughterhouse Hygiene (Scotland) Regulations 1978 or the Food Hygiene (Scotland) Regulations 1959(c), as appropriate, the requirements of Part I of Schedule 5 and Schedules 9, 10, 11, 12 and 14 shall be complied with whenever fresh meat for export is being cut up, and in the case of premises to which the Slaughterhouse Hygiene (Scotland) Regulations 1978 do not apply Part II of Schedule 5 shall also be complied with whenever fresh meat for export is being cut up.

(7) In any export cold store the requirements of Part III of Schedule 5 and Schedule 13 shall be complied with whenever fresh meat for export is in cold storage.

(8) Any area which is not approved for export purposes and is within the curtilage of an export slaughterhouse, export cutting premises or export cold store shall not be operated in such a way as to affect adversely the hygiene standards required by these Regulations.

Inspection and health marking

8.—(1) Subject to paragraph (2) of this regulation, every animal which is to be slaughtered in an export slaughterhouse shall be subjected to an ante-mortem health inspection in accordance with Schedule 6.

(a) S.I. 1955/1993, amended by S.I. 1963/1888, 1983/874 and 1984/1205.
(b) S.I. 1963/1888, to which there are amendments not relevant to these Regulations.
(c) S.I. 1959/413, amended by S.I. 1959/1153, 1961/622, 1966/967, 1978/173 and 1985/1068.

(2) In the case of an animal to which the provisions of regulation 14 of the Slaughter of Animals (Prevention of Cruelty) (Scotland) Regulations 1955 apply, such animal may be slaughtered in an export slaughterhouse without having been subjected to an ante-mortem health inspection if, after taking all reasonable steps to that end, the occupier is unable to secure such inspection before it is necessary in compliance with the said regulation 14 for the animal to be slaughtered.

(3) Every animal slaughtered in an export slaughterhouse shall be subjected to a post-mortem health inspection in accordance with the appropriate provisions of Schedule 8.

(4) Where fresh meat intended for export has been passed as fit for human consumption following ante- and post-mortem health inspections and is eligible for export in accordance with these Regulations, it shall be marked in accordance with the requirements of Schedule 11 and, subject to paragraph (5) of this regulation, no other meat shall be so marked.

(5) Where fresh meat is not intended for export but has been passed as fit for human consumption following ante- and post-mortem inspection and is eligible for export in accordance with these Regulations, it shall be marked in accordance with regulation 9A of, and Schedule 6 to, the Food (Meat Inspection) (Scotland) Regulations 1961(a) except that where the owner of the meat so requests it shall be marked in accordance with the requirements of Schedule 11.

(6) Where fresh meat has been passed as fit for human consumption following ante- and post-mortem health inspections but is not eligible for export in accordance with these Regulations, it shall be marked in accordance with regulation 9A of, and Schedule 6 to, the Food (Meat Inspection) (Scotland) Regulations 1961.

(7) No person shall remove, or cause or permit to be removed, from an export slaughterhouse any blood intended for human consumption or any carcase or part of a carcase or any offal until it has been inspected in accordance with these Regulations and, in the case of fresh meat passed as fit for human consumption after inspection, until it has been marked in accordance with paragraphs (4) to (6) of this regulation.

(8) The occupier shall give the local authority not less than 24 hours' notice of the day and time on and at which fresh meat intended for export is to be cut up on, or despatched from, any export cutting premises or admitted to, or despatched from, any export cold store.

(9) Where a local authority have been given notice under paragraph (8) of this regulation they shall arrange for fresh meat intended for export to be supervised –

    (a) during cutting up on, and despatch from, any export cutting premises in accordance with the requirements of Schedule 10; and

    (b) during admission to, and despatch from, any export cold store in accordance with the requirements of Schedule 13.

(10) No person shall apply the health mark described in Schedule 11 except in premises currently approved by the Secretary of State as an export slaughterhouse or export cutting premises.

Health certificate

9. The official veterinary surgeon shall sign the health certificate referred to in Schedule 14 only if he is satisfied that the fresh meat has been produced, inspected, prepared, stored and handled in accordance with the requirements of these Regulations.

Conditions for export of fresh meat

10.—(1) No person shall export or sell for export for human consumption any fresh meat being carcases, half carcases, quarter carcases, half carcases cut into three wholesale cuts or offal unless –

    (a) it has been obtained from an export slaughterhouse which is supervised in accordance with regulation 12;

    (b) it comes from an animal which has been subjected to an ante-mortem health inspection and following such inspection has been passed as fit for slaughter for human consumption;

(a) S.I. 1961/243, amended by S.I. 1983/702.

(c) it has been prepared under hygienic conditions in accordance with the requirements of Schedule 5;

(d) it comes from an animal which has been subjected to a post-mortem health inspection and which has shown no evidence of disease or other abnormal condition except for traumatic lesions incurred shortly before slaughter or localised malformations or pathological changes and it is established that these do not render unfit for human consumption those parts of the carcase or offal not affected by such lesions, malformations or changes;

(e) it has been given a health mark in accordance with the requirements of Schedule 11;

(f) if it has been stored after the post-mortem health inspection, this has been done under hygienic conditions in an export slaughterhouse, export cutting premises or an export cold store which in each case is supervised in accordance with regulation 12;

(g) it is accompanied by a health certificate in accordance with the requirements of Schedule 14; and

(h) if it has been transported, this has been done under hygienic conditions in accordance with the requirements of Schedule 15.

(2) No person shall export or sell for export for human consumption any fresh meat which has been cut up unless –

(a) it has been obtained from export cutting premises which are supervised in accordance with regulation 12;

(b) it has been cut up and obtained in accordance with the requirements of Schedule 9;

(c) it comes from –

(i) fresh meat from animals slaughtered in Scotland which satisfies the requirements of paragraph 1(a), (b), (c), (d), (e), (f) and (h) of this regulation; or

(ii) fresh meat from animals slaughtered in England or Wales or Northern Ireland which satisfies the requirements of the European Economic Community; or

(iii) fresh meat imported in accordance with the requirements of the European Economic Community;

(d) it has been prepared under hygienic conditions in accordance with the requirements of Schedule 5;

(e) it has been given a health mark in accordance with the requirements of Schedule 11;

(f) if it has been stored, this has been done under hygienic conditions in an export slaughterhouse, export cutting premises or an export cold store which in each case is supervised in accordance with regulation 12;

(g) it has been subjected to supervision in accordance with the requirements of Schedule 10;

(h) if it is wrapped or packed, this has been done under hygienic conditions in accordance with the requirements of Schedule 12;

(i) it is accompanied by a health certificate in accordance with the requirements of Schedule 14; and

(j) if it has been transported, this has been done under hygienic conditions in accordance with the requirements of Schedule 15.

(3) No person shall export or sell for export for human consumption -

(a) fresh meat of animals in which any form of tuberculosis or any living or dead cysticercus bovis or cysticercus cellulosae have been found;

(b) those parts of carcases or offal showing the traumatic lesions, malformations or changes referred to in paragraph (1)(d) of this regulation;

(c) those parts of carcases or offal which have been contaminated;

(d) fresh meat which has been treated with natural or artificial colouring matters;

(e) fresh meat which has been treated with ionizing or ultra-violet radiation.

(4) Except where the country of destination has granted a general authorisation or an authorisation restricted to a specific case, no person shall export or sell for export for human consumption –

   (a) fresh meat from cryptorchid or hermaphrodite swine or from boars (unless it is to undergo one of the treatments provided for in Council Directive 77/99/EEC(**a**) and it bears a special mark in accordance with the requirements of Schedule 11);

   (b) heads of bovine animals and fresh meat from the heads of bovine animals excluding tongues and brains;

   (c) fresh meat from animals to which tenderisers have been administered;

   (d) blood;

   (e) fresh meat in pieces each weighing less than 100g;

   (f) minced meat or meat which is similarly finely divided and mechanically recovered meat.

Admission of animals and carcases to an export slaughterhouse

11.—(1) Without prejudice to regulations 10 to 12 of the Food (Meat Inspection) (Scotland) Regulations 1961, an official veterinary surgeon may require that the accommodation or alternative method of operation and facilities referred to in paragraph 2(b) of Schedule 1 shall be used for –

   (a) the slaughtering and dressing of any animal which is brought into an export slaughterhouse and which is known or suspected to be diseased or injured;

   (b) the carrying out of any necessary examination performed under regulation 32(2) of the Slaughterhouse Hygiene (Scotland) Regulations 1978 on any undressed and unbled carcase which is brought into an export slaughterhouse;

   (c) the dressing of any undressed and bled carcase which is brought into an export slaughterhouse.

(2) Fresh meat from any carcase which has been examined or dressed in accordance with sub-paragraphs 1(b) or (c) of this regulation shall not be eligible for export.

Supervision of approved premises

12.—(1) Each local authority shall, in relation to any export slaughterhouse, export cutting premises or export cold store, appoint for each such establishment one or more official veterinary surgeon or surgeons to provide the health certification of fresh meat intended for export in accordance with the provisions of Schedule 14 and to be responsible for the carrying out of the following functions in relation to those premises –

   (a) the ante-mortem health inspection of animals;

   (b) the post-mortem health inspection of slaughtered animals;

   (c) the health marking of fresh meat;

   (d) securing the observance of the requirements of regulation 7 and Schedules 5, 7, 9 and 12;

   (e) the supervision of export cutting premises with particular reference to the functions set out in Schedule 10;

   (f) securing the observance of the requirements of Schedule 15 relating to the transport of fresh meat intended for export;

   (g) the supervision of export cold stores in accordance with the requirements of Schedule 13;

   (h) the supervision at transhipment centres of the unloading, assembly and inspection of fresh meat and the loading of fresh meat into the vehicle in which it is to be exported.

(2) Each local authority shall, in relation to any export slaughterhouse, export cutting premises or export cold store, appoint a sufficient number of other persons to act as inspectors under the supervision and responsibility of the official veterinary surgeon in relation to the functions specified in paragraph 1(a) to (h) of this regulation.

Charges by local authorities

13.—(1) Subject to the provisions of this regulation, a local authority may make charges in respect of the function of providing health certification of fresh meat intended for export and

(**a**) O.J. No. L26, 31.1.77, p.85.

the other functions specified in regulation 12(1)(a) to (h) of such amounts as are determined by them from time to time.

(2) Charges made in pursuance of this regulation shall relate to functions exercised in respect of individual premises within the local authority area.

(3) In determining such charges as aforesaid, the local authority shall ensure that from time to time the charges are reasonably sufficient to meet the costs of the authority which are –

  (a) specified in paragraph (5) of this regulation; and

  (b) necessarily incurred in exercise of the functions referred to in paragraph (1) of this regulation.

(4) In determining such charges as aforesaid a local authority shall consult with such persons or organisations as appear to them to be representative of interests substantially affected by the charges and shall provide to any such person or organisation at his or their written request a breakdown in writing of the calculation of the charges against the costs specified in paragraph (5) of this regulation.

(5) The costs referred to in paragraph (3)(a) of this regulation are –

  (a) the remuneration paid to any official veterinary surgeon or inspector engaged in exercising the functions referred to in paragraph (1) of this regulation in the premises concerned, together with related costs being employer's National Insurance and superannuation contributions. Where an official veterinary surgeon or inspector is engaged part-time in the premises concerned, such remuneration and costs shall relate to the proportion of time actually spent in exercise of the said functions in the premises;

  (b) the cost of protective clothing and equipment, including the cleaning, maintenance and repair of these items, used by an official veterinary surgeon or inspector in exercise of the said functions in the premises concerned. Where such items are not used exclusively in the premises concerned, such costs shall be apportioned according to usage;

  (c) the cost of travel and subsistence incurred by an official veterinary surgeon or inspector in respect of his exercise of the said functions in relation to the premises concerned. Where such travel and subsistence does not relate exclusively to the performance of the said functions in the premises concerned, such costs shall be apportioned accordingly;

  (d) the administrative costs incurred by the local authority in respect of the exercise of the said functions in the premises concerned.

Powers of entry

14. Any person authorised in that behalf either by the Secretary of State or the local authority on producing, if so required, a duly authenticated document showing his authority, shall have a right to enter, at any reasonable time, any premises which he has reasonable cause to believe to be premises on which animals are slaughtered for export for human consumption or on which fresh meat is prepared, stored or sold for export for human consumption, for the purpose of –

  (a) performing his functions under these Regulations, and

  (b) ascertaining whether there is or has been on, or in connection with, the premises any contravention of the provisions of these Regulations:

Provided that admission to any premises ostensibly used only as a private dwelling-house shall not be demanded as of right unless 24 hours' notice of the intended entry has been given to the occupant of such premises.

Obstruction

15. No person shall wilfully obstruct a person authorised under regulation 14 who is acting in the execution of these Regulations.

Information to be provided by local authorities

16. Each local authority shall provide the Secretary of State with such information relating to the execution of their duties under these Regulations as he may from time to time require.

Enforcement by local authorities

17.   Each local authority shall execute and enforce the provisions of these Regulations in their area with the exception of regulations 4 and 6 which shall be executed and enforced by the Secretary of State.

Offences and penalties

18.   Any person who contravenes or fails to comply with any requirement of these Regulations shall be guilty of an offence and shall be liable –
  (a) on summary conviction to a fine not exceeding £2,000;
  (b) on conviction on indictment to a fine or to imprisonment for a term not exceeding one year, or both.

Application of the Food (Meat Inspection) (Scotland) Regulations 1961 to export slaughterhouses

19.   The provisions of these Regulations are without prejudice to the application in relation to any export slaughterhouse of the Food (Meat Inspection) (Scotland) Regulations 1961, except that the provisions of regulations 4 to 9, 16, 17, 22 and 23 of, and Schedules 1, 2 and 4 to, the 1961 Regulations shall not apply in relation to any such slaughterhouse.

Application of enactments

20.—(1) Section 45 (which relates to contravention due to act or default of some other person), section 46 (which relates to conditions under which warranty may be pleaded as a defence) and section 47 (which relates to offences in relation to warranties and certificates of analysis) of the Act shall apply for the purposes of these Regulations as if references therein to proceedings taken or brought under that Act included references to proceedings taken or brought for an offence under these Regulations.

(2) Section 64(3) of the Local Government (Scotland) Act 1973(**a**) (which relates to protection for local government officers acting in good faith) shall have effect for the purposes of these Regulations as if references therein to that Act were references to these Regulations.

Revocations

21.   The Regulations specified in Schedule 16 are revoked to the extent stated in that Schedule.

New St. Andrew's House, Edinburgh
29th April 1987

John J. MacKay
Parliamentary Under Secretary of State,
Scottish Office

(**a**) 1973 c.65.

SCHEDULE 1

CONDITIONS FOR THE APPROVAL OF EXPORT SLAUGHTERHOUSES

1. The slaughterhouse shall comply with the requirements of Parts II and III (and without taking into account the provisions of regulation 57 in Part IV) of the Slaughterhouse Hygiene (Scotland) Regulations 1978.

2. In addition the slaughterhouse shall have –
  (a) a suitable, sufficient and separate room or rooms exclusively reserved for the storage of hides, skins, horns, hooves, swine bristles and fat not intended for human consumption;
  (b) suitable, sufficient and separate accommodation capable of being securely locked for the slaughter and dressing of any animal which is diseased or injured or suspected of being diseased or injured, save that such accommodation need not be provided if –
      (i) such diseased animals are slaughtered after completion of the slaughter of animals whose meat is intended for export;
      (ii) steps are taken to prevent contamination of such meat;
      (iii) the premises are cleaned and disinfected under official supervision before being used again for the slaughtering of animals intended for export; and
      (iv) suitable and sufficient facilities are provided for the introduction of the carcase of an injured animal into the slaughterhall in a manner which will not prejudice the hygienic operation of the slaughterhouse;
  (c) a suitable and sufficiently large refrigerated room for the cooling of and for the exclusive storage of meat prepared in an export approved slaughterhouse; the room shall be equipped with corrosion resistant fittings capable of preventing meat coming into contact with the floors and walls and, where a room is used to store meat already cooled, it shall also have a recording thermometer or recording telethermometer;
  (d) a suitable, sufficiently large and adequately equipped room or rooms capable of being securely locked for the exclusive use of the official veterinary surgeon and inspectors, having regard to the number of such persons employed;
  (e) sufficient and adequately equipped showers which are for the use of persons working in the slaughterhouse and are situated near the accommodation where such persons may change their clothes;
  (f) facilities which will enable the inspections provided for in these Regulations to be carried out efficiently;
  (g) means of controlling access to and exit from the slaughterhouse;
  (h) where necessary, adequate means of steam extraction in rooms where work on meat is undertaken;
  (i) a place and adequate equipment for cleansing and disinfecting vehicles;
  (j) doors and door frames made of a hard wearing, non-corrodible material or, if made of wood, faced on both sides with a smooth, impermeable covering;
  (k) facilities for the hygienic handling and protection of meat during loading and unloading;
  (l) insulation materials which are rotproof and odourless;
  (m) a separate room or rooms capable of being securely locked for the retention of meat rejected as being unfit for human consumption; except that where such meat is removed as often as may be necessary and at least daily and the quantities are not sufficient to require the provision of a separate room or rooms, then suitable and sufficient receptacles shall be provided which are capable of being securely locked; such receptacles shall be used only for holding meat rejected as being unfit for human consumption and shall be clearly marked to that effect; and any chutes used to transport meat to such receptacles shall be so constructed and installed as to enable them to be kept clean and avoid the risk of contamination of the fresh meat;
  (n) suitable refrigeration equipment which will enable the internal temperature of the meat to be maintained at the level prescribed in Schedule 7; such equipment shall include drainage which must present no risk of contamination of the meat;
  (o) in the accommodation where persons working in the slaughterhouse may change their clothes, surfaces of walls and floors which are smooth, washable and impermeable;
  (p) on all hand washing facilities in changing rooms and rooms associated with the sanitary conveniences, taps which are not operable by hand or arm;
  (q) in the lairage, walls and floors which are durable, impermeable, and easy to clean and disinfect;
  (r) a suitable, sufficient and separate room exclusively reserved for the preparation and cleaning of offal other than the emptying and cleaning of stomachs and intestines and the dressing of guts and tripe and which includes a separate area for heads at a sufficient distance from

other offal where these operations are carried out in the slaughterhouse other than on the slaughterline;

(s) a suitable and separate place for the packaging of offal in accordance with the requirements of Part II of Schedule 12.

3. Water which is required to be clean and wholesome shall meet the requirements of Council Directive 80/778/EEC(**a**) and records of the results of water tests and any consequent action shall be available at all times to an official veterinary surgeon or to a veterinary officer and shall be kept for a period of not less than three years. Water which is not clean and wholesome may only be used in the slaughterhouse for the purpose of fire fighting or the operation of refrigerators or steam boilers, and pipes carrying such water shall be arranged so as not to allow any such water to be used for any other purpose; and all such pipes shall clearly be distinguished from those used for potable water and shall present no risk of contamination of the fresh meat.

4. In the case of a slaughterhouse where both swine and other animals are slaughtered, and no separate accommodation for the slaughter of swine exists, the slaughterhouse shall contain suitable and sufficient accommodation for the scalding, depilation, scraping and singeing of swine. Where such operations take place such accommodation shall be separated from the slaughter line for other species either by an open space of at least 5 metres or by a partition at least 3 metres high.

SCHEDULE 2   Regulation 4(1)(a)(ii)

CONDITIONS FOR THE APPROVAL OF EXPORT CUTTING PREMISES

PART I

REQUIREMENTS APPLICABLE IN ALL EXPORT CUTTING PREMISES

1. Without prejudice to the requirements of the Slaughterhouse Hygiene (Scotland) Regulations 1978 or the Food Hygiene (Scotland) Regulations 1959, as the case may be, the cutting premises shall have –

(a) suitable and sufficient refrigerated accommodation for –

    (i) the reception and storage of meat; and

    (ii) the separate storage of wrapped or packed meat;

(b) a room for cutting up meat in accordance with the requirements of Schedule 9 and for wrapping meat in accordance with the requirements of Part I of Schedule 12;

(c) a separate room for packing meat in accordance with the requirements of Part II of Schedule 12 except that cutting, boning, wrapping and packaging of meat may take place in the same room provided that the room is sufficiently large and so arranged that the hygiene of the operation is assured, that the rooms in which packaging and wrapping material are stored are free from dust and vermin and are not connected in any way with rooms containing substances which might contaminate fresh meat, and the requirements of paragraph 1(k) of Schedule 9 are observed;

(d) a suitable, sufficiently large and adequately equipped room or rooms capable of being securely locked for the exclusive use of the official veterinary surgeon and inspectors, having regard to the number of such persons employed;

(e) suitable storage accommodation under hygienic conditions for packaging and wrapping material;

(f) suitable, sufficient and adequately equipped rooms, not being any part of the premises which at any time contain meat, where persons working in the cutting premises may change their clothes; the surfaces of the walls and floors of such rooms shall be smooth, washable and impermeable;

(g) sufficient and adequately equipped showers which are for the use of persons working in the cutting premises and are situated near the rooms referred to in sub-paragraph (f) of this paragraph;

(h) a separate room or rooms capable of being securely locked for the retention of meat not intended for human consumption; except that where such meat is removed as often as may be necessary and at least daily and the quantities are not sufficient to require the provision of a separate room or rooms, then suitable and sufficient receptacles shall be provided which

---

(**a**) O.J. No. L229, 30.8.80, p.11.

are capable of being securely locked; such receptacles shall be used only for holding meat not intended for human consumption and clearly marked to that effect and any chutes used to transport meat to such receptacles shall be so constructed and installed as to enable them to be kept clean and avoid the risk of contamination of the fresh meat;

(i) in the room referred to in sub-paragraph (b) of this paragraph, a recording thermometer or recording telethermometer;

(j) facilities which will enable the inspections and supervision provided for in these Regulations to be carried out efficiently;

(k) means of controlling access to and exit from the premises;

(l) doors and door frames made of a hard wearing, non-corrodible material or, if made of wood, faced on both sides with a smooth, impermeable covering;

(m) insulation materials which are rotproof and odourless;

(n) facilities for the hygienic handling and protection of meat during loading and unloading;

(o) suitable refrigeration equipment which will enable the internal temperature of the meat to be maintained at the level prescribed in Schedule 9; such equipment shall include satisfactory drainage which presents no risk of contamination of the meat;

(p) on all hand washing facilities in work rooms, changing rooms and rooms associated with the sanitary conveniences, taps which are not operable by hand or arm;

(q) a place and adequate equipment for cleansing and disinfecting vehicles;

(r) suitable and sufficient means of ventilation to the external air and where necessary adequate means of steam extraction.

2. Water which is required to be clean and wholesome shall meet the requirements of Council Directive 80/778/EEC and records of the results of water tests and any consequent action shall be available at all times to an official veterinary surgeon or to a veterinary officer and shall be kept for a period of not less than three years. Water which is not clean and wholesome may only be used in the cutting premises for the purposes of fire fighting or the operation of refrigerators or steam boilers, and pipes carrying such water shall be arranged so as not to allow any such water to be used for any other purpose and all such pipes shall clearly be distinguished from those used for potable water and shall present no risk of contamination of the fresh meat.

PART II

ADDITIONAL REQUIREMENTS APPLICABLE IN EXPORT CUTTING PREMISES NOT SUBJECT TO THE SLAUGHTERHOUSE HYGIENE (SCOTLAND) REGULATIONS 1978

Without prejudice to the requirements of the Food Hygiene (Scotland) Regulations 1959, the cutting premises shall have –

(a) a sufficient, clean and wholesome supply of water within the meaning of Council Directive 80/778/EEC available at an adequate pressure throughout the premises;

(b) a sufficient, clean, constant and wholesome supply of hot water within the meaning of Council Directive 80/778/EEC under adequate pressure available in the workrooms during working hours;

(c) satisfactory drainage, with traps for solids, which shall be maintained in proper working order;

(d) at places readily accessible to the work stations, suitable facilities adequately equipped with hot and cold or warm running water at a suitable temperature for the washing of hands by persons working in the cutting premises; any taps supplying these facilities shall not be operable by hand and disposable towels, which shall only be used once, shall be provided in a suitable container and a receptacle shall be provided for used towels;

(e) at places readily accessible to the sanitary conveniences, suitable facilities adequately equipped with hot and cold or warm running water at a suitable temperature for the washing of hands by persons working in the cutting premises; disposable towels, which shall only be used once, shall be provided in a suitable container and a receptacle shall be provided for used towels;

(f) in rooms where work on meat is undertaken, suitable and sufficient facilities, situated as close as possible to the work stations, for the cleaning and disinfection of knives and other hand tools, such facilities to be adequately supplied with water which shall be maintained at a temperature of not less than +82C;

(g) adequate protection against the entry of insects, vermin and birds;

(h) in rooms where work on meat is undertaken, adequate lighting which does not distort colours and is of an overall intensity of not less than 220 lux, save that at places where inspection of meat is normally carried out the overall intensity shall be not less than 540 lux;

(i) in the accommodation referred to in sub-paragraphs (a) and (b) of paragraph 1 of Part I of this Schedule–

(i) floors of impervious non-slip material, so constructed and kept in such good order, repair and condition as to enable them to be thoroughly cleaned; and floors in workrooms shall be laid so as to have a fall of not less than 5 centimetres in every 3 metres (i.e. a gradient of 1 in 60);

(ii) interior wall surfaces faced with smooth, durable, impervious and washable material, which shall be of a light colour, up to a height of not less than 2 metres from the floor;

(iii) rounded angles between floor and wall surfaces and between adjacent wall surfaces;

(j) equipment and fittings of a durable and impervious material other than wood, resistant to corrosion and of such construction as to enable them to be kept clean; all equipment for handling meat and for storing receptacles containing or intended to contain meat shall be so constructed that meat and the receptacles are not permitted to come into contact with the floor.

SCHEDULE 3   Regulation 4(1)(a)(iii)

CONDITIONS FOR THE APPROVAL OF EXPORT COLD STORES

1. The cold store shall have –

(a) adequate facilities for the hygienic reception, handling, storage, inspection and despatch of meat;

(b) adequate means and procedures, including fixed apparatus for mechanical or electrical recording of temperatures, for ensuring that each storage chamber is maintained at the temperatures required by paragraph 3 of Schedule 13;

(c) adequate artificial lighting in all storage chambers;

(d) adequate changing, washing and toilet facilities; the surfaces of the walls and floors of such rooms shall be smooth, washable and impermeable;

(e) adequate facilities to ensure that meat and receptacles containing or intended to contain meat are not permitted to come into contact with the floor;

(f) adequate protection against the entry of insects, vermin and birds;

(g) interior wall surfaces faced with smooth, durable, impervious and washable material, which shall be of a light colour, up to a height of not less than the usable storage height;

(h) floor surfaces which are waterproof and rotproof;

(i) doors and door frames made of a hard wearing, non-corrodible material and, if made of wood, faced on both sides with a smooth, impermeable covering;

(j) insulation materials which are rotproof and odourless;

(k) if applicable, at places readily accessible to the work stations, suitable facilities adequately equipped with hot and cold or warm running water at a suitable temperature for the washing of hands by persons handling meat; disposable towels, which shall only be used once, shall be provided in a suitable container and a receptacle shall be provided for used towels;

(l) in rooms were unwrapped fresh meat is handled or stored, equipment and fittings must be constructed of a durable and impervious material other than wood, resistant to corrosion and capable of being kept clean;

(m) suitable refrigeration equipment which will enable the internal temperature of meat to be maintained at the level prescribed in Schedule 13; such equipment shall include satisfactory drainage which presents no risk of contamination of the meat;

(n) suitable facilities for the exclusive use of the veterinary service;

(o) an adequate number of changing rooms with smooth, waterproof, washable walls and floors, wash basins and flush lavatories, not opening directly on to the work rooms; a sufficient number of wash basins shall be provided close to the lavatories; the wash basins shall have hot and cold running water or water premixed to a suitable temperature; sufficient materials for cleaning and disinfecting hands, and disposable hand towels which can be used once only shall be provided;

(p) on all hand washing facilities in work rooms, changing rooms and rooms associated with the sanitary conveniences, taps which are not operable by hand or arm;

(q) a sufficient, clean and wholesome supply of water available at an adequate pressure throughout the premises, and a sufficient, clean, constant and wholesome supply of hot water under adequate pressure available in the work rooms during working hours; such water shall meet the requirements of Council Directive 80/778/EEC and records of the results of water tests and any consequent action shall be available at all times to an official veterinary surgeon or to a veterinary officer and shall be kept for a period of not less than three years.

2. Water which is not clean and wholesome may be used only for the purpose of firefighting or the operation of refrigeration equipment or steam boilers, and pipes carrying such water shall be so arranged

as not to allow any such water to be used for any other purpose, and all such pipes shall be clearly distinguished from those used for carrying potable water and shall present no risk of contamination of the fresh meat.

Regulation 4(1)(a)(iv)

SCHEDULE 4

CONDITIONS FOR THE APPROVAL OF TRANSHIPMENT CENTRES

The transhipment centre shall have suitable and sufficient facilities for the hygienic unloading, assembly, inspection and loading of meat, including –

(a) a suitable loading bay; and

(b) suitable and sufficient refrigerated accommodation readily accessible to the loading bay.

Regulations 4(1)(a)(i),
(ii) and (iii), 7(5),
(6) and (7), 10(1)(c) and
(2)(d) and 12(1)(d)

SCHEDULE 5

HYGIENE REQUIREMENTS IN RELATION TO STAFF, PREMISES, EQUIPMENT AND IMPLEMENTS IN EXPORT SLAUGHTERHOUSES, EXPORT CUTTING PREMISES AND EXPORT COLD STORES

PART I

REQUIREMENTS APPLICABLE IN ALL EXPORT SLAUGHTERHOUSES AND EXPORT CUTTING PREMISES

1. No person shall engage in the handling of meat if he is likely to contaminate such meat. In particular, and without prejudice to the generality of the foregoing, no person shall engage in the handling of meat if he is suffering from or suspected of suffering from, or is the carrier of, typhoid fever, paratyphoid fever or any other salmonella infection, or dysentery, infectious hepatitis, scarlet fever or any staphylococcal infection likely to cause food poisoning, or is suffering from or suspected of suffering from infectious tuberculosis or any infectious skin disease.

2. No person shall engage in the handling of meat if he is –

(a) undertaking any other activity which may involve any risk of contamination of meat; or

(b) wearing a bandage on the hands or forearms, other than a waterproof dressing protecting a non-infected wound.

3.—(1) Every person engaged in the handling of meat shall obtain a certificate signed by a registered medical practitioner certifying that there is no objection on public health grounds to his engagement in the handling of meat, and every such medical certificate shall be produced on request to an official veterinary surgeon or to a veterinary officer.

(2) Every medical certificate referred to in sub-paragraph (1) of this paragraph shall be renewed annually unless an official veterinary surgeon requires its renewal at any other time.

4. Every person engaged in slaughtering animals or working on or handling meat shall wash his hands with hot water and soap or other detergent frequently during the working day and each time work is started and resumed.

5. The occupier shall ensure that all equipment and implements which come into contact with meat are kept in a good state of repair.

6. Smoking shall be prohibited in work rooms and store rooms.

7. The occupier shall ensure that no sawdust or any similar substance is spread on floors.

PART II

ADDITIONAL REQUIREMENTS APPLICABLE IN EXPORT CUTTING PREMISES NOT SUBJECT TO THE SLAUGHTERHOUSE HYGIENE (SCOTLAND) REGULATIONS 1978

1. Every person engaged in handling meat shall –

(a) wear rubber boots or other footwear affording similar protection and overalls of washable material including a washable covering for the hair of the head, which must be kept as clean as is reasonably practicable; and any person liable to come into contact with any meat shall wear similar and adequate protective clothing;

(b) wash his hands and arms with hot water and soap or other detergent immediately after contact with meat which he knows or suspects to be diseased;

(c) ensure that all equipment and implements which come into contact with meat are cleansed and disinfected and then rinsed in clean water -

    (i) prior to commencement of work;

    (ii) frequently during the course of each working day;

    (iii) immediately after any contact with meat known or suspected to be diseased;

    (iv) before re-use after any break in work; and

    (v) at the end of each working day.

2. No person shall –

(a) urinate, defecate or spit except in a sanitary convenience;

(b) bring into or keep in any part of export cutting premises containing meat any article liable to prejudice the maintenance of hygiene or the proper performance of the functions reserved to that part of the export cutting premises.

3. The occupier of the export cutting premises shall –

(a) take all reasonable steps to prevent the entry into the premises of dogs, cats, birds, vermin and insects, and take immediate steps to remove any which may be present;

(b) ensure that the premises and any plant, equipment, machinery or implements contained therein are not used for any purpose which is not properly connected with the preparation and storage of meat, and that instruments for cutting meat are used solely for that purpose;

(c) ensure that meat and receptacles which contain or may at any time contain meat are not allowed to come into contact with the floor;

(d) cause the floor and wall surfaces of the room or rooms provided in accordance with paragraph 1(a) and 1(b) of Part I of Schedule 2 to be cleaned and disinfected as often as may be necessary to maintain them at all times in a satisfactory state of cleanliness and in any event to be thoroughly cleaned when cutting up is completed for the day;

(e) where the premises are supplied with water which is not clean and wholesome for the purpose of fire fighting or the operation of refrigerators or steam boilers, ensure that any such water is not used for any other purpose;

(f) ensure that all detergents, disinfectants and pesticides used in the premises are of such a kind and are used in such a manner as not to affect the fitness of any meat.

PART III

REQUIREMENTS APPLICABLE IN EXPORT COLD STORES

1. Every person engaged in the handling of meat or packages of meat shall –

(a) keep himself clean;

(b) wear clean and appropriate protective clothing to permit the hygienic handling of meat including, where necessary, headgear and neck protection;

(c) refrain from smoking or engaging in unhygienic practices;

(d) take precautions to avoid contamination of meat;

(e) wash his hands with hot water and soap or other detergent frequently during the working day and each time work is started and resumed;

(f) wash his hands and arms with hot water and soap or other detergent immediately after contact with meat which he knows or suspects to be diseased.

2. Every person engaged in the handling of unwrapped meat and meat wrapped only in stockinette shall obtain an annual certificate signed by a registered medical practitioner certifying that there is no objection on public health grounds to his engagement in the handling of meat, and every such medical certificate shall be produced on request to an official veterinary surgeon or to a veterinary officer.

3. The occupier shall –

(a) ensure that all detergents, disinfectants and pesticides used in the premises are of such a kind and are used in such a manner as not to affect the fitness of any meat;

(b) ensure that sawdust or any similar substance is not spread on floors;

(c) take all reasonable steps to prevent the entry into the premises of dogs, cats, birds, vermin and insects, and take immediate steps to remove any which may be present;

(d) ensure that meat and receptacles which contain or may at any time contain meat are not allowed to come into contact with the floor;

(e) ensure that all equipment and instruments which come into contact with meat and which are cleansed and disinfected are then rinsed in clean water.

Regulations 2(1), 4(1)(a)(i),   SCHEDULE 6
7(5) and 8(1)

ANTE-MORTEM HEALTH INSPECTION

REQUIREMENTS APPLICABLE IN EXPORT SLAUGHTERHOUSES

1. Animals intended for slaughter shall undergo ante-mortem health inspection on the day of their arrival at the slaughterhouse or before the beginning of daily slaughtering. The inspection shall be repeated immediately before slaughter if the animal has been kept in the lairage overnight and at any time if required by the official veterinary surgeon.

2. The occupier of the slaughterhouse or his agent shall provide adequate facilities and assistance to enable ante-mortem health inspections to be undertaken.

3. The ante-mortem health inspection shall be made under adequate natural or artificial lighting.

4. The ante-mortem health inspection shall determine –
(a) whether the animals are showing symptoms of a disease which can be transmitted through the meat to humans or animals or whether there are any indications that such a disease may occur;
(b) whether they are showing symptoms of a disease or disorder which would be likely to make the meat unfit for human consumption;
(c) whether they are injured, fatigued or stressed;
(d) where there is visible evidence that they have had substances with pharmacological effects administered to them or have consumed any other substances which may make the meat unfit for human consumption.

5. Animals shall not be slaughtered for production of meat for human consumption if they –
(a) show any of the conditions mentioned in paragraph 4(a) and (b) of this Schedule;
(b) have not been rested for an adequate period of time, which for fatigued or stressed animals must not, unless the official veterinary surgeon determines otherwise, be less than 24 hours;
(c) have been found to have any form of clinical tuberculosis.

6. An animal which shows any of the conditions mentioned in paragraph 4(a) and (b) of this Schedule shall be taken to and kept in that part of the lairage provided for the isolation of animals which are diseased or injured or suspected of being diseased or injured and shall be examined by the official veterinary surgeon. Unless the official veterinary surgeon passes the animal as fit for slaughter for human consumption, he shall require either –
(a) that it shall be slaughtered and dressed in the accommodation referred to in paragraph 2(b) of Schedule 1, or
(b) that it shall be slaughtered and dressed at a time other than that at which the slaughter of other animals is taking place and that, immediately following slaughtering and dressing of the animal and before the slaughtering of other animals takes place, the premises shall be fully cleaned and disinfected in such manner as he shall determine.

Regulations 2(1), 4(1)(a)(i),   SCHEDULE 7
7(5) and 12(1)(d)

SLAUGHTER AND DRESSING PRACTICES

REQUIREMENTS APPLICABLE IN EXPORT SLAUGHTERHOUSES

The occupier and persons engaged in the handling of meat shall ensure that –
(a) animals brought into the slaughterhall are slaughtered without delay;

(b) bleeding is completed without delay and any blood intended for human consumption is collected in a clean receptacle provided for that purpose and is so kept as to remain readily identifiable with the carcases from which it was collected until those carcases have been inspected in accordance with Schedule 8;

(c) slaughtered animals are dressed in the following manner:–

    (i) in the case of bovine animals and solipeds, the following shall be removed: the hide or skin, the head (save that where retention of the ears on carcases of bovine animals is necessary for any certification purpose the ears need be removed only after completion of that certification), the tonsils (save that, in the case of bovine animals and solipeds not intended for export, the removal of the tonsils shall not be compulsory), the viscera (save that the lungs, the heart, the liver, the spleen, the mediastinum and the kidneys may remain attached to the carcase by their natural connections save that the kidneys shall be removed from their fatty and perirenal coverings), the genital organs, the urinary bladder, the feet up to the carpal and tarsal joints, and, in the case of lactating animals, animals that have given birth or are in advanced pregnancy, the udder;

    (ii) in the case of swine, the following shall be removed: the tonsils (save that, in the case of swine not intended for export, removal of the tonsils shall not be compulsory), the hair and bristles (which may be removed by use of a debristling agent provided that the carcase is then rinsed by means of a spray system in running water which is clean and wholesome) or the skin, the claws, the viscera (save that the lungs, the heart, the liver, the spleen, the mediastinum and the kidneys may remain attached to the carcase by their natural connections save that the kidneys shall be removed from their fatty and perirenal coverings, save that, in the case of swine not intended for export, exposure of the kidneys shall not be compulsory), the genital organs, the urinary bladder, the feet up to the carpal and tarsal joints (save that in the case of swine not intended for export removal of the feet shall not be compulsory), and, in the case of lactating animals, animals that have given birth or are in advanced pregnancy, the udder;

    (iii) in the case of sheep and goats, the following shall be removed: the skin (including that of the head save that, where the head is not to be examined in accordance with the requirements of Schedule 8, Part V, removal of the skin of the head shall not be compulsory), the head (save that where retention of the ears on carcases of sheep is necessary for any certification purpose the ears need be removed only after completion of that certification), the viscera (save that the lungs, the heart, the liver, the spleen, the mediastinum and the kidneys may remain attached to the carcase by their natural connections save that the kidneys shall be removed from their fatty coverings), the genital organs, the urinary bladder, the feet up to the carpal and tarsal joints and, in the case of lactating animals, animals that have given birth or are in advanced pregnancy, the udder;

(d) evisceration must be carried out immediately and completed not later than 45 minutes after stunning or, in the case of ritual slaughter, half an hour after bleeding;

(e) the following are discarded at the time of skinning the carcase –

    (i) the head of a sheep or a goat, including the tongue and the brains, if the head, including the tongue and the brains, is excluded from human consumption;

    (ii) the penis, provided that it shows no evidence of pathological condition;

(f) subject to paragraph (e) of this Schedule, the offal (other than the feet) of any animal are so kept as to remain readily identifiable with the carcase until that carcase has been inspected in accordance with Schedule 8 or confirmed as not to be required for the execution of such checks as are required by Council Directive 86/469/EEC(a), and the feet of any animal are kept available for inspection in the slaughterhouse until an official veterinary surgeon or inspector authorises their removal;

(g) carcases of solipeds, bovine animals over six months old and swine over four weeks old are split lengthwise through the spinal column before being submitted for inspection in accordance with Schedule 8 (save that in the case of swine over four weeks old not intended for export the carcase need not be so split); heads of solipeds shall be split; an official veterinary surgeon or inspector may require any carcase or head to be split lengthwise if he considers it necessary for the purpose of carrying out the inspections prescribed in Schedule 8;

(h) slaughtered animals are dressed and treated in such a manner as not to prevent or hinder inspection in accordance with Schedule 8 or checks required to be carried out in accordance with the provisions of Council Directive 86/469/EEC and in particular no carcase is cut up and, subject to paragraph (e) of this Schedule, no part other than the hide or skin of any slaughtered animal is removed from the slaughterhouse until the inspection prescribed in Schedule 8 has been completed, and no action is taken which might alter or destroy any evidence of disease before inspection;

(a) O.J. No. L275, 26.9.86, p.36.

(i) where the blood or offal of several animals is collected in one receptacle, the entire contents of that receptacle are regarded as unfit for human consumption if the meat of any of the animals from which the blood or offal was collected is declared unfit for human consumption;

(j) fresh meat intended for export is placed without undue delay in refrigerated accommodation and is brought progressively to an internal temperature of not more than +7C for carcases, half carcases, quarter carcases and half carcases cut into three wholesale cuts, and +3C for offal, and is subsequently kept constantly at or below that temperature;

(k) meat which is brought into an export slaughterhouse and which is not eligible for export in accordance with these Regulations is stored and handled apart from or at other times than meat which is eligible for export;

(l) bleeding, flaying or removing bristles, dressing and evisceration is carried out in such a way as to avoid contamination of the carcase or offal;

(m) no implement is left in the meat;

(n) fresh meat intended for freezing is only frozen by a rapid method and is stored at a temperature of not more than -12C.

Regulations 2(1), 4(1)(a)(i), 7(5) and 8(3)	SCHEDULE 8

POST-MORTEM HEALTH INSPECTION

REQUIREMENTS APPLICABLE IN EXPORT SLAUGHTERHOUSES

PART I

GENERAL INSTRUCTIONS

1.   The carcase and offal and the blood of each slaughtered animal shall be examined without delay by an official veterinary surgeon or inspector. He shall have regard to –

(a) the age and sex of the animal;

(b) the state of nutrition of the animal;

(c) any evidence of bruising or haemorrhage;

(d) any local or general oedema;

(e) the efficiency of bleeding;

(f) any swelling, deformity or other abnormality of bones, joints, musculature or umbilicus;

(g) any abnormality in consistency, colour, odour and, where appropriate, taste;

(h) the condition of the pleura and peritoneum;

(i)   any other evidence of abnormality.

2.   The inspection shall include -

(a) palpation of certain organs, in particular the lungs, liver, spleen and tongue and, where considered necessary by the official veterinary surgeon, the uterus and udder;

(b) incisions of organs and lymph nodes as specified in Parts II, III, IV, V and VI of this Schedule.

3.   Where the official veterinary surgeon considers it necessary, incisions and inspection of meat other than those specified in Parts II, III, IV, V and VI of this Schedule shall be undertaken.

4.   Where necessary the official veterinary surgeon shall arrange for laboratory investigations to be carried out.

5.—(1) Any carcase, offal or blood which shows evidence of the diseases or conditions mentioned in the Annex to this Part of this Schedule, or which may for any reason be suspected of being unfit for human consumption, shall be isolated and shall not be removed from the place of isolation until it has been inspected by the official veterinary surgeon.

(2) Subject to sub-paragraph (3) of this paragraph, if the official veterinary surgeon is satisfied that the carcase or offal, or any part of the carcase or offal, or the blood is unfit for human consumption he shall give instructions, save in the case to which sub-paragraph (4) applies, that the carcase or offal, or such part of the carcase or offal, or the blood shall not be disposed of for human consumption but shall be disposed of in accordance with the provisions of any regulations providing for the disposal of an unfit carcase, offal or blood.

(3) If the official veterinary surgeon is satisfied that the carcase or offal, or any part of the carcase or offal, or the blood is derived from an animal which was suffering from any of the diseases specified in the Annex to this Part of this Schedule, he shall, after having made any assessment required by the Annex to this Part of this Schedule, give instructions, save in the case to which sub-pargraph (4) applies, that the carcase or offal, or such part of the carcase or offal as he is by the Annex in relation to that condition directed to give such instructions, or the blood shall not be disposed of for human consumption but shall be disposed of in accordance with the provisions of any regulations providing for the disposal of an unfit carcase, offal or blood.

(4) If the official veterinary surgeon has given instructions under sub-paragraphs (2) or (3) that the carcase or offal, or any part of the carcase or offal, or the blood derived from an animal is unfit for human consumption, the provisions of section 9 of the Food and Drugs (Scotland) Act 1956 (which relates to the examination and seizure of unsound food) shall apply in the case of the carcase or offal, or any part of the carcase or offal, or the blood.

ANNEX

INDICATIONS OF UNFITNESS FOR HUMAN CONSUMPTION

1. The official veterinary surgeon shall direct that no part of the carcase, offal or blood of any animal shall be sold for human consumption if he is satisfied from his examination of the carcase or offal that the animal was suffering from any of the following diseases or conditions, namely –

actinobacillosis (generalised) or actinomycosis (generalised),
anaemia (advanced),
anthrax,
blackleg,
bruising, extensive and severe,
caseous lymphadenitis associated with emaciation,
caseous lymphadenitis (generalised),
cysticercus bovis (generalised),
cysticercus cellulosae,
cysticercus ovis (generalised),
decomposition (generalised),
emaciation (pathological),
fever,
foot and mouth disease,
glanders,
immaturity,
      (a) stillborn or unborn carcases,
      (b) oedematous carcases, and carcases in poor physical condition,
jaundice,
malignant catarrhal fever,
mastitis (acute septic),
melanosis (generalised),
metritis (acute septic),
odour (abnormal) associated with disease or otherwise prejudicial to health,
oedema (generalised),
pericarditis (acute septic),
peritonitis (acute diffuse septic),
pleurisy (acute diffuse septic),
pneumonia (acute septic),
pyaemia (including joint-ill),
sarcocysts (generalised),
septicaemia or toxaemia,
swine erysipelas (acute),
swine fever,
tetanus,
trichinosis,
tuberculosis (generalised),
tuberculosis with emaciation,

tumours,

  (a) malignant with secondary growths,

  (b) multiple,

uraemia.

2. The official veterinary surgeon shall direct that the blood of any animal shall not be sold for human consumption if he is satisfied -

  (a) that the carcase or offal of that animal are affected with any infectious conditions, or

  (b) that the blood is contaminated by stomach contents or other extraneous matter.

3.—(1) An official veterinary surgeon shall in determining for the purpose of this Schedule whether tuberculosis is generalised take into account the sum of the evidence of disease and the character of the lesions throughout the entire carcase and, for the purposes of this paragraph, shall accept the existence of tuberculosis in the associated lymph node of an organ or viscera as evidence of the disease in the organ or viscera.

(2) If the official veterinary surgeon is satisfied that any of the following conditions exist in the carcase or offal of an animal, namely –

  (a) miliary tuberculosis of both lungs with evidence of tuberculosis elsewhere;

  (b) multiple and actively progressive lesions of tuberculosis;

  (c) widespread tuberculosis infection of the lymph nodes of the carcase;

  (d) diffuse acute lesions of tuberculosis of both the pleura and peritoneum associated with an enlarged or tuberculous lymph node of the carcase;

  (e) active or recent lesions present in the substance of any two of the following:–

   the spleen, kidney, udder, uterus, ovary, testicle, brain or its membranes, spinal cord or its membranes, in addition to tuberculous lesions in the respiratory and digestive tracts;

  (f) in the case of a calf, congenital tuberculosis;

he shall determine the tuberculosis to be generalised.

(3) When, as the result of his examination, the official veterinary surgeon is satisfied that a carcase or offal of an animal is affected with tuberculosis other than of the kinds mentioned in paragraph 1 of this Annex he shall direct that –

  (a) any part of the carcase in relation to which he is satisfied that it is so infected;

  (b) any part of the carcase, contiguous to any such part;

  (c) the head including the tongue, when tuberculosis exists in any lymph node associated with the head or tongue; and

  (d) any organ when tuberculosis exists on the capsule or in the substance of the organ, or the viscera when tuberculosis exists on the surfaces or substances of the viscera or in any lymphatic glands associated with the organ or the viscera as the case may be;

shall not be sold for human consumption.

(4) An official veterinary surgeon shall direct that any part of a carcase or offal contaminated with tuberculous material shall not be sold for human consumption.

4.—(1) In any case in which the official veterinary surgeon, in the course of his examination, is satisfied that any part of the carcase or any offal is affected with a localised infestation of cysticercus bovis he shall direct that that part of the carcase or offal shall not be sold for human consumption.

(2) Where in any such case as aforesaid an official veterinary surgeon has directed that any part of the carcase of an animal or any offal of an animal shall not be sold for human consumption, the remainder of the meat of the animal shall also be subject to the like direction unless it is forthwith placed in cold storage at a temperature not exceeding -7C for a period of not less than three weeks or at a temperature not exceeding -10C for a period of not less than two weeks or is treated by such other method as may be approved by the Secretary of State:

  Provided that the alimentary tract in any such case shall not be placed in cold storage or be sold for human consumption.

(3) Any person who causes any part of a carcase or any offal to be placed in cold storage for the purposes of the last foregoing sub-paragraph shall, at the same time as he causes it to be so placed, give notice to the local authority within whose district the cold store is situated, in such form as the local authority may require, of the date of the placing and the period for which it is intended that the part of a carcase or offal, as the case may be, will remain in cold storage.

5.—(1) If, as a result of his inspection of a carcase and offal of an animal, an official veterinary surgeon is satisfied that the following conditions exist therein, namely –

  (a) caseous lymphadenitis associated with emaciation;

  (b) multiple, acute and actively progressive lesions of caseous lymphadenitis; or

(c) multiple lesions of caseous lymphadenitis which are inactive but widespread;

he shall direct that no part of the carcase and offal shall be sold for human consumption.

(2) If an official veterinary surgeon is satisfied that caseous lymphadenitis exists on the surface or substance of an organ or in its associated lymph node he shall direct that the organ and its associated lymph node shall not be sold for human consumption.

(3) If an official veterinary surgeon is satisfied that caseous lymphadenitis exists otherwise than as described in sub-paragraphs (1) and (2) of this paragraph he shall direct that the lesion and such of the surrounding parts as he may think proper, having regard to the age and degree of activity of the lesion, shall not be sold for human consumption.

6. Where, as a result of his examination, the official veterinary surgeon is satisfied that the whole or any part of the carcase or any offal derived from an animal is affected by any disease or condition other than one mentioned in the foregoing paragraphs of this Annex or is contaminated, he shall direct that the whole of the carcase and all offal or the part of the carcase and the parts adjacent thereto or the offal, as he may think proper, shall not be sold for human consumption.

7. Where, as a result of his examination, the official veterinary surgeon is satisfied that a part of the carcase or offal derived from an animal is affected by a slight localised infestation by a parasite not transmissible to man but that the remainder of the carcase or offal as the case may be is fit for human consumption, an official veterinary surgeon or an inspector may, if he thinks fit, remove the parasite and trim the surrounding part and shall direct that the trimmings shall not be sold for human consumption.

PART II

DETAILED INSTRUCTIONS

BOVINE ANIMALS OVER 6 WEEKS

1. In the case of bovine animals over 6 weeks old the inspection shall include in particular an examination of –
  (a) the head and the throat; the surface of the tongue after it has been freed to permit a detailed inspection of the mouth and the fauces; the retro-pharyngeal, submaxillary and parotid lymph nodes shall be examined in detail; the external (masseter) cheek muscles in which at least two deep incisions shall be made and internal (pterygoid) cheek muscles in which at least one deep incision shall be made; all incisions shall be made parallel to the mandible from its upper muscular insertion;
  (b) the lungs, the trachea and oesophagus; the oesophagus shall be palpated; the trachea and the main branches of the bronchi shall be opened lengthwise and the lungs shall be incised in their posterior third, at right angles to their main axes; save that these incisions are not necessary where the lungs are excluded from human consumption; the bronchial and mediastinal lymph nodes shall be examined in detail;
  (c) the pericardium, which shall be opened, and the heart; the latter shall be incised lengthwise so as to open the ventricles and to cut through the intra-ventricular septum;
  (d) the diaphragm;
  (e) the surfaces and substance of the liver and the hepatic lymph nodes; an examination of the bile ducts shall be carried out by means of incisions into the gastric surface of the liver and at the base of the caudate lobe; the hepatic lymph nodes shall be palpated;
  (f) the alimentary tract, the mesentery and the gastric, pancreatic and mesenteric lymph nodes; these lymph nodes shall be palpated and, if an official veterinary surgeon or inspector considers it necessary, the gastric and mesenteric lymph nodes shall be examined in detail;
  (g) the surface of the spleen;
  (h) the kidneys which, if an official veterinary surgeon or inspector considers it necessary, shall be incised and the renal lymph nodes examined in detail;
  (i) the pleura and the peritoneum;
  (j) the genital organs;
  (k) the udder which, if an official veterinary surgeon or inspector considers it necessary, shall be incised; in the case of a cow the udder must be opened by a long deep incision as far as the lactiferous sinuses unless it is to be excluded from human consumption; if an official veterinary surgeon or inspector considers it necessary the supramammary lymph nodes shall be palpated and examined in detail;
  (l) the feet, if an official veterinary surgeon or inspector considers it necessary.

2. Where evidence of tuberculosis is found, an official veterinary surgeon or inspector shall –

(a) split the carcase, examine the vertebrae, ribs, sternum, spinal cord and brain, incise the kidneys;

(b) examine in detail such of the following lymph nodes as he has not already so examined: superficial inguinal, prescapular, prepectoral, presternal, suprasternal, xiphoid, subdorsal, intercostal, iliac, sublumbar, ischiatic, precrural and popliteal, the lymph nodes least likely in the particular case to show evidence of infection being examined first.

PART III

DETAILED INSTRUCTIONS

BOVINE ANIMALS LESS THAN 6 WEEKS

1. In the case of bovines less than 6 weeks old the inspection shall include in particular an examination of –

(a) the head, the throat, the surface of the tongue, the mouth and the fauces; the retro-pharyngeal lymph nodes shall be examined in detail;

(b) the lungs, the trachea and oesophagus; the trachea and the main branches of the bronchi shall be opened lengthwise and the lungs shall be incised in their posterior third, at right angles to their main axes; save that these incisions are not necessary where the lungs are to be excluded from human consumption; the bronchial and mediastinal lymph nodes shall be examined in detail;

(c) the pericardium, which shall be opened, and the heart; the latter shall be incised lengthwise so as to open the ventricles and to cut through the intra-ventricular septum;

(d) the diaphragm;

(e) the surfaces and substance of the liver and the hepatic lymph nodes; the liver shall be incised if an official veterinary surgeon or inspector considers it necessary; the hepatic lymph nodes shall be palpated and, if an official veterinary surgeon or inspector considers it necessary, examined in detail;

(f) the alimentary tract, the mesentery and the gastric, pancreatic and mesenteric lymph nodes; the gastric and mesenteric lymph nodes shall be palpated and, if an official veterinary surgeon or inspector considers it necessary, examined in detail;

(g) the surface of the spleen;

(h) the kidneys which, if an official veterinary surgeon or inspector considers it necessary, shall be incised and the renal lymph nodes examined in detail;

(i) the pleura and the peritoneum;

(j) the umbilical region and joints which shall be palpated; where an official veterinary surgeon or inspector considers it necessary the umbilical region shall be incised, the joints shall be opened and the synovial fluid examined;

(k) the feet, if an official veterinary surgeon or inspector considers it necessary.

2. Where evidence of tuberculosis is found, an offical veterinary surgeon or inspector shall –

(a) split the carcase, examine the vertebrae, ribs, sternum, spinal cord and brain, incise the kidneys;

(b) examine in detail such of the following lymph nodes as he has not already so examined: superficial inguinal, prescapular, prepectoral, presternal, suprasternal, xiphoid, subdorsal, intercostal, iliac, sublumbar, ischiatic, precrural and popliteal, the lymph nodes least likely in the particular case to show evidence of infection being examined first.

PART IV

DETAILED INSTRUCTIONS

SWINE

1. In the case of swine the inspection shall include in particular an examination of –

(a) the head, the throat, the surface of the tongue, the mouth and the fauces; the submaxillary lymph nodes shall be examined in detail;

(b) the lungs, the trachea and oesophagus; the trachea and the main branches of the bronchi shall be opened lengthwise and the lungs shall be incised in their posterior third, at right angles to their main axes (save that the lungs need not be incised if they are to be excluded from human consumption); the bronchial and mediastinal lymph nodes shall be examined and palpated;

(c) the pericardium, which shall be opened, and the heart; the latter shall be incised lengthwise so as to open the ventricles and to cut through the intra-ventricular septum;

(d) the diaphragm;

(e) the surfaces and substance of the liver and the hepatic lymph nodes; the hepatic lymph nodes shall be palpated;

(f) the alimentary tract, the mesentery and the gastric, pancreatic and mesenteric lymph nodes; the gastric and mesenteric lymph nodes shall be palpated and, if an official veterinary surgeon or inspector considers it necessary, examined in detail;

(g) the surface of the spleen;

(h) the kidneys (save that in the case of swine not intended for export examination of the kidneys shall not be compulsory); if an official veterinary surgeon or inspector considers it necessary the kidneys shall be incised and the renal lymph nodes examined in detail;

(i) the pleura and the peritoneum;

(j) the genital organs;

(k) the udder and the supramammary lymph nodes; in the case of sows the supramammary lymph nodes shall be examined in detail;

(l) the umbilical region and joints of young animals which shall be palpated; where an official veterinary surgeon or inspector considers it necessary the umbilical region shall be incised and the joints shall be opened;

(m) the feet, if an official veterinary surgeon or inspector considers it necessary.

2. An investigation for cysticercus cellulosae shall be carried out which shall include examination of the directly visible muscular surfaces, in particular the thigh muscles, the pillars of the diaphragm, the intercostal muscles, the heart, tongue and larynx; if an official veterinary surgeon or inspector considers it necessary, both the abdominal wall and the psoas muscles, freed from fatty tissue, shall be examined.

3. If an abscess is found in the carcase or in any organ of any swine, or if an official veterinary surgeon or inspector has reason to suspect the presence of any such abscess, he shall require the carcase to be split through the spinal column if it has not already been so split and shall examine in detail such of the following lymph nodes as he has not already so examined: superficial inguinal, supramammary, cervical, prepectoral, prescapular, presternal, sublumbar, iliac, precrural and, if he considers it necessary, the popliteal.

4. Where evidence of tuberculosis is found, an official veterinary surgeon or inspector shall –

(a) split the carcase, examine the vertebrae, ribs, sternum, spinal cord and brain, expose and incise the kidneys;

(b) examine in detail such of the following lymph nodes as he has not already so examined: superficial inguinal, cervical, prepectoral, prescapular, subdorsal, sublumbar, iliac, precrural and, if he considers it necessary, the popliteal.

PART V

DETAILED INSTRUCTIONS

SHEEP AND GOATS

1. In the case of sheep and goats the inspection shall include in particular an examination of –

(a) the head after flaying with, if an official veterinary surgeon or inspector considers it necessary, the surface of the tongue, the mouth, throat, retro-pharyngeal and parotid lymph nodes (save that these examinations and the flaying are not required if the local authority ensures that the head, including the tongue and brains, is excluded from human consumption);

(b) the lungs, the trachea and oesophagus; if an official veterinary surgeon or inspector considers it necessary the trachea and the main branches of the bronchi shall be opened lengthwise and the lungs shall be incised in their posterior third, at right angles to their main axes; the bronchial and mediastinal lymph nodes shall be palpated and, if an official veterinary surgeon or inspector considers it necessary, examined in detail;

(c) the pericardium, which shall be opened, and the heart; where an official veterinary surgeon or inspector considers it necessary the heart shall be incised lengthwise so as to open the ventricles and to cut through the intra-ventricular septum;

(d) the diaphragm;

(e) the surfaces and substance of the liver which shall be incised on the gastric surface to examine the bile ducts; the hepatic lymph nodes shall be examined and palpated;

(f) the alimentary tract and the mesentery; the gastric, pancreatic and mesenteric lymph nodes shall be examined;

(g) the surface of the spleen;

(h) the kidneys which if an official veterinary surgeon or inspector considers it necessary shall be incised and the renal lymph nodes examined in detail;

(i) the pleura and the peritoneum;

(j) the genital organs;

(k) the udder; the supramammary lymph nodes shall be examined;

(l) the umbilical region and the joints of young animals which shall be palpated; where an official veterinary surgeon or inspector considers it necessary the umbilical region shall be incised and the joints shall be opened;

(m) the feet, if an official veterinary surgeon or inspector considers it necessary.

2.　Where an official veterinary surgeon or inspector has reason to suspect that a suppurative condition exists in the carcase of any sheep or lamb he shall –

(a) examine by palpation as well as by observation such of the lymph nodes as are readily accessible; and

(b) in the case of a sheep, examine in detail such of the following lymph nodes as he has not already so examined: prescapular, superficial inguinal, precrural; and, in the case of a lamb, examine in detail such lymph nodes if he has found evidence of disease in the course of visual examination or palpation.

3.　Where evidence of tuberculosis is found, an official veterinary surgeon or inspector shall split the carcase, examine the vertebrae, ribs, sternum, spinal cord and brain, expose and incise the kidneys.

PART VI

DETAILED INSTRUCTIONS

DOMESTIC SOLIPEDS

1.　In the case of domestic solipeds the inspection shall include in particular an examination of –

(a) the head and the throat; the surface of the tongue after it has been freed to permit a detailed inspection of the mouth and the fauces; the retro-pharyngeal, submaxillary and parotid lymph nodes shall be palpated and, if an official veterinary surgeon or inspector considers it necessary, examined in detail;

(b) the lungs, the trachea and oesophagus; the trachea and the main branches of the bronchi shall be opened lengthwise and the lungs shall be incised in their posterior third, at right angles to their main axes (save that these incisions are not necessary where the lungs are excluded from human consumption); the bronchial and mediastinal lymph nodes shall be palpated and, if an official veterinary surgeon or inspector considers it necessary, examined in detail;

(c) the pericardium, which shall be opened, and the heart; the latter shall be incised lengthwise so as to open the ventricles and to cut through the intra-ventricular septum;

(d) the diaphragm;

(e) the surfaces and substance of the liver and the hepatic lymph nodes; the liver shall be incised if an official veterinary surgeon or inspector considers it necessary; the hepatic lymph nodes shall be palpated and, if an official veterinary surgeon or inspector considers it necessary, the hepatic lymph nodes shall be examined in detail;

(f) the alimentary tract, the mesentery and the gastric, pancreatic and mesenteric lymph nodes; if an official veterinary surgeon or inspector considers it necessary the lymph nodes shall be examined in detail;

(g) the surface of the spleen;

(h) the kidneys, which shall be palpated and, if an official veterinary surgeon or inspector considers it necessary, incised; if an official veterinary surgeon or inspector considers it necessary the renal lymph nodes shall be examined in detail;

(i) the pleura and the peritoneum;

(j) the genital organs of stallions and mares;

(k) the udder and the supramammary lymph nodes shall be examined and, if an official veterinary surgeon or inspector considers it necessary, the supramammary lymph nodes shall be examined in detail;

(l) the umbilical region and joints of young animals which shall be palpated; where an official veterinary surgeon or inspector considers it necessary the umbilical region shall be incised and the joints shall be opened;

(m) all grey or white horses must be examined for melanosis and melanomata; in particular the muscles of one shoulder and the prescapular lymph node shall be examined; this lymph node shall be exposed beneath the scapular cartilage by loosening the attachment of one shoulder;

in addition the kidneys shall be examined after splitting by a longitudinal incision which exposes both cortex and medulla.

2.   An investigation for glanders shall be carried out by means of careful examination of mucous membranes of the trachea, larynx, nasal cavities, sinuses and their ramifications, after splitting the head in the median plane and excision of the nasal septum.

3.   Where evidence of tuberculosis is found, an official veterinary surgeon or inspector shall –

  (a) split the carcase, examine the vertebrae, ribs, sternum, spinal cord and brain, incise the kidneys;

  (b) examine in detail such of the following lymph nodes as he has not already so examined: superficial inguinal, prescapular, prepectoral, presternal, suprasternal, xiphoid, subdorsal, intercostal, iliac, sublumbar, ischiatic, precrural and popliteal, the lymph nodes least likely in the particular case to show evidence of infection being examined first.

SCHEDULE 9   Regulations 4(1)(a)(ii),
                                7(6), 10(2)(b) and 12(1)(d)

CUTTING PRACTICES

REQUIREMENTS APPLICABLE IN EXPORT CUTTING PREMISES

The occupier of the cutting premises shall –

  (a) make available to an official veterinary surgeon or inspector all necessary facilities for the supervision of the premises in accordance with the requirements of Schedule 10 and in particular allow him unimpeded access at all times to all parts of the premises where meat is cut up or stored;

  (b) make available to an official veterinary surgeon or inspector, when required to do so, evidence of the origin of any meat brought into the cutting premises;

  (c) ensure that any meat which is not eligible for export in accordance with these regulations is stored and cut up apart from or at other times than meat which is eligible for export;

  (d) ensure that as soon as fresh meat intended for cutting up enters the cutting premises it is placed in the refrigerated accommodation provided for the reception and storage of meat awaiting cutting and there maintained at an internal temperature of not more than +7C for carcases, half carcases, quarter carcases and half carcases cut into three wholesale cuts, and +3C for offal:

  Provided that meat transferred directly and without risk of contamination from an export slaughterhouse to export cutting premises within the same site complex by means of an extension of the overhead rail system employed in that slaughterhouse or other hygienic transport system may, notwithstanding the requirements of this sub-paragraph, of sub-paragraph (f) of this Schedule and of sub-paragraph (j) of Schedule 7, but subject to the two following conditions, be cut up without first being chilled.

  The conditions referred to in the foregoing proviso are that –

    (i) cutting up shall take place without delay, and

    (ii) as soon as cutting up, wrapping and packing are completed the meat shall be placed immediately in the refrigerated accommodation referred to in paragraph 1(a)(ii) of Part I of Schedule 2 and be brought progressively to an internal temperature of not more than +7C for cut meat and +3C for offal;

  (e) ensure that meat is brought into the room provided in accordance with paragraph 1(b) of Part I of Schedule 2 as and when required, that it remains in that room only for the minimum time required to carry out the necessary cutting up operations, and that on completion of cutting up, wrapping and packing the meat is transferred without undue delay to the refrigerated accommodation referred to in paragraph 1(a)(ii) of Part I of Schedule 2 and there maintained at an internal temperature of not more than +7C for cut meat and +3C for offal;

  (f) ensure that the cutting up does not take place until the meat has reached an internal temperature of not more than +7C for carcases, half carcases, quarter carcases and half carcases cut into three wholesale cuts, and +3C for offal, that during cutting up, wrapping and packing the meat is kept at an internal temperature of not more than +7C for carcases and cuts and +3C for offal, and that while cutting up is taking place the temperature of the room does not exceed +12C;

  (g) ensure that any splinters of bone and clots of blood are removed from meat during cutting up;

  (h) ensure that no carcase, offal or cut meat is wiped down;

  (i) ensure that meat obtained from cutting up and not intended for human consumption is collected in the receptacles referred to in paragraph 1(h) of Part I of Schedule 2 as it is cut;

(j) ensure that no implement is left in the meat;

(k) ensure that when cutting, boning, wrapping and packing operations take place in the same room, the following conditions are observed:-

    (i) packaging and wrapping material shall during storage be contained in a sealed and undamaged protective cover under hygienic conditions in a separate room;

    (ii) packaging and wrapping material shall not be stored on the floor;

    (iii) packaging material shall be assembled under hygienic conditions before being brought into the cutting room;

    (iv) packaging material shall be hygienically brought into the room and shall be used without delay: it shall not be handled by persons who handle fresh meat;

    (v) immediately after packing and wrapping the meat shall be placed in the storage rooms referred to in paragraph 1(a)(ii) of Part I of Schedule 2;

(l) ensure that fresh meat intended for freezing is only frozen by a rapid method and is stored at a temperature of not more than -12C.

Regulations 7(6), 8(9)(a),   **SCHEDULE 10**
10(2)(g) and 12(1)(e)

HEALTH CONTROL OF CUT MEAT

REQUIREMENTS APPLICABLE IN EXPORT CUTTING PREMISES

1. The official veterinary surgeon shall be responsible for the supervision of cutting premises while meat intended for export is being cut up and shall ensure that the requirements of these Regulations are observed. In particular he shall –

(a) supervise the maintenance of a register for fresh meat entering and leaving the premises;

(b) be responsible for the inspection of fresh meat intended for export held in the premises and at the time of its despatch;

(c) issue the certificate provided for in Schedule 14;

(d) be responsible for the maintenance of hygiene standards in the premises, with particular reference to the requirements of Schedule 5;

(e) be responsible for the taking of all samples necessary for any laboratory tests which may be required and the recording of the results of such tests in a register; these results shall be made available to the owner of the meat on request.

2. The official veterinary surgeon may be assisted by inspectors in the discharge of the responsibilities set out in paragraph 1(a), (b), (d) and (e) of this Schedule.

Regulations 2(1),   **SCHEDULE 11**
7(5) and (6), 8(4) and (10),
and 10(1)(e), (2)(e) and (4)(a)

HEALTH MARKING

REQUIREMENTS APPLICABLE IN EXPORT SLAUGHTERHOUSES AND EXPORT CUTTING PREMISES

1. The health mark shall be applied by or under the supervision and responsibility of the official veterinary surgeon.

2. The health mark shall consist of an oval mark 6.5 cm wide by 4.5 cm high containing in legible form in letters 0.8 cm high and figures 1 cm high the following information –

(a) on the upper part, the letters "UK" or the letters "UNITED KINGDOM";

(b) in the centre, the approval number of the export slaughterhouse or export cutting premises;

(c) on the lower part, the letters "EEC";

(d) in addition, for fresh meat from boars and cryptorchid or hermaphrodite swine, the oval mark shall be covered along the main diameter by 2 parallel straight lines being as evident as the external edge of the mark with a distance apart of at least 1.0cm.

3.   Carcases weighing more than 65 kg shall have the health mark applied in ink or hot-branded on each half carcase in at least the following places - external surface of the thigh, loins, back, breast and shoulder. Other carcases shall have the health mark applied in ink or hot-branded in at least four places - on the shoulders and on the external surface of the thighs.

4.   Livers of bovine animals, swine and solipeds shall be hot-branded with the health mark.

5.   All the offal unless they are wrapped or packed in accordance with the requirements of Schedule 12 shall have the health mark applied in ink or hot-branded, but in the case of bovine animals under 3 months old, and swine, sheep and goats, health marking of tongues and hearts shall not be compulsory.

6.   Cuts, other than cuts weighing less than 100g each and cuts of fat, obtained in export cutting premises from carcases marked with the health mark and which do not bear a health mark shall, unless they are wrapped or packed in accordance with the requirements of Schedule 12, have that mark applied in ink or hot-branded.

7.   Cuts of swine belly and back fat from which the rind has been removed may be grouped into lots containing not more than five cuts; each lot and each piece, if it is separate, shall be sealed under the supervision of the official veterinary surgeon and be provided with a label which meets the requirements of paragraph 3 of Part II of Schedule 12.

8.   Only methyl violet shall be used for marking meat in ink in accordance with this Schedule.

SCHEDULE 12

Regulations 7(6),
10(2)(h) and 12(1)(d)

WRAPPING AND PACKING OF CUT MEAT AND OFFAL

PART I

WRAPPING

1.   The occupier shall ensure that any material used for wrapping meat is strong enough to protect the meat during the course of handling and transport and does not cause a deterioration in the organoleptic characteristics of the meat or transmit to it any substance harmful to human health and that only transparent and uncoloured wrapping material is used, except where the wrapping material used conforms to the requirements of paragraph 6 of this Part of this Schedule.

2.   The occupier shall ensure that the wrapping operation is carried out immediately after cutting and in a hygienic manner and that wrapping material is not re-used for wrapping meat. The wrapping material shall not be handled by persons who handle fresh meat.

3.   The occupier shall ensure that cut meat, other than cuts of pig belly and pork fat, is wrapped in accordance with paragraphs 1 and 2 of this Part of this Schedule unless it is transported hanging up.

4.   The occupier shall ensure that wrappings contain meat of only one animal species.

5.   The occupier shall ensure that all wrapped meat intended for sale bears a reproduction of the health mark bearing the letters "UK" on the wrapping material or on a label affixed to the wrapping material. The health mark shall include the approval number of the export cutting premises except that in the case of offal wrapped in an export approved slaughterhouse it shall bear the approval number of that slaughterhouse.

6.   The occupier shall ensure that wrapped meat is packed in accordance with the requirements of Part II of this Schedule, save that where the wrapping material used fulfills the requirement of packaging material in accordance with the provisions of paragraph 1 of Part II of this Schedule it does not in addition require to be packed.

PART II

PACKING

1.   The occupier shall ensure that any material used for packing meat is strong enough to protect the meat during the course of handling and transport and does not cause a deterioration in the organoleptic characteristics of the meat or transmit to it any substance harmful to human health.

2. The occupier shall ensure that any material used for packing meat is not re-used for this purpose unless it is made of a non-corrodible and impervious substance which is easy to clean and has been cleaned and disinfected prior to re-use for packing meat.

3. The occupier shall ensure that –
  (a) every package bears the health mark either on the package itself or on a label affixed to wrapping material which fulfills the requirements of paragraph 6 of Part I of this Schedule;
  (b) such label is serially numbered; and
  (c) such label is affixed in such a way that it is torn when the package is opened.

4. The occupier shall ensure that packages contain meat of only one animal species.

Regulations 4(1)(a)(iii),
7(7), 8(9)(b) and 12(1)(g)

SCHEDULE 13

STORAGE OF MEAT

REQUIREMENTS APPLICABLE IN EXPORT COLD STORES

1. The occupier of the cold store shall facilitate supervision of the store, and of the handling and inspection of the meat, and shall place the necessary facilities at the disposal of an official veterinary surgeon or inspector.

2. The owner of the meat and the occupier of the cold store shall secure arrangements for supervision of meat during movement into the store and during storage as follows –
  (a) unwrapped meat, meat wrapped in stockinette and all Intervention meat owned by the Intervention Board for Agricultural Produce shall be supervised during movement into the store and during storage by an official veterinary surgeon or inspector; however, for privately-owned, packed and wrapped meat supervision during movement into the store and during storage may be waived at the owner's discretion;
  (b) for all meat there shall be maintained at the store adequate records including the accompanying veterinary health certificate in the form prescribed in the Annex to Schedule 14, and thermographs (identified and validated) to record the time and date when the meat was taken into store, its location in the store and the storage conditions; these records shall be made available on request to an official veterinary surgeon or inspector and shall be sufficient to provide the information necessary to enable the official veterinary surgeon to issue the health certificate provided for in Schedule 14.

3. The occupier shall ensure that fresh meat intended for export is –
  (a) kept at an internal temperature of not more than +7C for carcase and cuts and +3C for offal and, if frozen, maintained at a temperature of not more than -12C;
  (b) supervised by an official veterinary surgeon or inspector at the time of loading for despatch;
  (c) handled, loaded and unloaded, stored and, if freezing is carried out, frozen in a hygienic manner, and in particular that it is handled, loaded and unloaded under cover;
  (d) adequately protected during storage from the risk of contamination including taint;
  (e) stored separately from meat which is not eligible for export in accordance with these Regulations;
  (f) identifiable as to origin while it is being stored;
  (g) made available for inspection on request by an official veterinary surgeon or inspector.

4. The occupier shall ensure that where meat that is not packed is brought into the cold store for freezing it is not stored on wooden pallets and that during freezing it is suspended from either a rail system or suitable frames of a material resistant to corrosion.

Regulations 7(5)
and (6), 9, 10(1)(g)
and (2)(i), and 12(1)

SCHEDULE 14

HEALTH CERTIFICATE

1. Where meat is to be exported directly the official veterinary surgeon shall sign a health certificate which is to accompany the meat to the country of destination at the time the meat is loaded into the means of transport in which it is to travel.

2. The health certificate shall be provided by the Secretary of State and shall correspond in form to, and contain the information specified in, the model in the Annex to this Schedule. It shall be expressed at least in English and in the language of the country of destination.

3. Where meat is not intended for immediate export the official veterinary surgeon shall sign a health certificate which will accompany the meat to other export premises or to premises approved under the provisions of Council Directive 77/99/EEC(**a**) at the time the meat is loaded into the means of transport in which it is to travel.

4. A health certificate under paragraph 3 above shall be provided by the Secretary of State and shall contain the information specified in the model in the Annex to this Schedule.

ANNEX

HEALTH CERTIFICATE FOR FRESH MEAT INTENDED FOR CONSIGNMENT TO A MEMBER STATE(**1**) OF THE EEC

No ....(**2**)

Exporting country ....

Ministry...

Department..

Ref(**2**) ....

I. Identification of meat:

Meat of...

(animal species)

Nature of cuts...

Nature of packaging...

Number of cuts or packages ....

Month(s) and year(s) when frozen...

Net weight ....

II. Origin of meat:

Address(es) and veterinary approval number(s) of the approved slaughterhouse(s)

....

....

Address(es) and veterinary approval number(s) of the approved cutting plant(s)

....

....

Address(es) and veterinary approval number(s) of the approved store(s)

....

....

III. Destination of meat:

The meat will be sent from ....

....

(place of loading)

to...

(**a**) O.J. No. L26, 31.1.77, p.85.

(country and place of destination)

....

by the following means of transport(3)..

....

Name and address of consignor...

....

Name and address of consignee...

....

IV. Health attestation:

I, the undersigned, official veterinarian, certify that the meat described above was obtained under the conditions governing production and control laid down in Directive 64/433/EEC on health problems affecting intra-Community trade in fresh meat and that it is, therefore, considered as such to be fit for human consumption.

Done at...

on ....

Signature of the Official Veterinarian

....

....

Notes

(1) Fresh meat: in accordance with the directive referred to in IV of this certificate, all edible parts of domestic bovine animals (including buffalo), swine, sheep and goats and solipeds which have not undergone any preserving process and including meat vacuum wrapped or wrapped in a controlled atmosphere; however, chilled and frozen meat shall be considered to be fresh meat.

(2) Optional.

(3) In the case of trucks and lorries state the registration number, in the case of aircraft the flight number, and in the case of boats the name and, where necessary, the number of the container.

<table>
<tr><td>Regulations 10(1)(h)
and (2)(j), and 12(1)(f)</td><td>SCHEDULE 15</td></tr>
</table>

TRANSPORT OF FRESH MEAT INTENDED FOR EXPORT

REQUIREMENTS APPLICABLE TO OCCUPIERS OR PERSONS RESPONSIBLE FOR THE CONTROL AND MANAGEMENT OF TRANSPORT

1. Fresh meat shall be loaded at a temperature of not more than +7C for carcases and cuts and +3C for offal and shall be transported in sealed vehicles so designed and equipped that the meat is maintained at a temperature of not more than +7C for carcases and cuts and +3C for offal and, if frozen, maintained at not more than -12C throughout the period of transport; however when fresh meat is transported from an export slaughterhouse to export cutting premises in the United Kingdom sealing of vehicles shall not be required.

2. The interior surfaces of vehicles used for the transport of fresh meat and any other parts of the vehicle which may come into contact with the meat shall be so finished as to enable them effectively to be kept clean and disinfected and shall be constructed of material resistant to corrosion which does not cause a deterioration in the organoleptic characteristics of the meat or render it harmful to human health.

3.   Vehicles used for the transport of fresh meat shall be provided with efficient devices for protecting the meat against the entry of insects and dust and shall be watertight; where such vehicles are used for the transport of carcases, half carcases, quarter carcases and unpacked cut meat they shall be equipped with fittings of material resistant to corrosion for hanging the meat fixed at such a height that the meat cannot come into contact with the floor, except that fittings for hanging such meat shall not be required where the meat is transported by aircraft in which suitable facilities resistant to corrosion have been provided for hygienically loading, holding and unloading the meat.

4.   Vehicles used for the transport of fresh meat shall not be used for conveying live animals or any substance which may be detrimental to, or contaminate, the meat so conveyed.

5.   Fresh meat shall not be transported in the same vehicle at the same time as any other product likely to affect the hygiene of the meat or to contaminate it unless it is transported in such a manner that it will not contaminate the fresh meat.

6.   Stomachs shall be scalded or cleaned and feet and heads skinned or scalded and depilated before being transported in a vehicle containing other fresh meat.

7.   Fresh meat shall not be transported in vehicles which are not properly cleaned and disinfected.

8.   Carcases, half carcases and quarter carcases, other than frozen meat packed in a hygienic manner, shall be suspended throughout the period of transport except where such meat is transported by aircraft in which suitable facilities resistant to corrosion have been provided for hygienically loading, holding and unloading the meat. Other cuts and offal, other than the viscera, shall be hung or placed on supports if not placed in packages of material resistant to corrosion. The supports and packages shall be hygienically satisfactory and where appropriate shall meet the requirements of Schedule 12.

9.   The viscera may only be transported in strong, clean and impervious packages which may only be re-used after being cleaned and disinfected.

10.   The official veterinary surgeon shall be satisfied before despatch that the loading bay is clean and that transport vehicles comply with the requirements of this Schedule.

SCHEDULE 16   Regulation 21

Column 1 *References*	Column 2 *Regulations revoked*	Column 3 *Extent of revocation*
S.I. 1981/1034	The Fresh Meat Export (Hygiene and Inspection) (Scotland) Regulations 1981	The whole Regulations
S.I. 1983/703	The Fresh Meat Export (Hygiene and Inspection) (Scotland) Amendment Regulations 1983	The whole Regulations
S.I. 1984/1885	The Fresh Meat Export (Hygiene and Inspection) (Scotland) Amendment Regulations 1984	The whole Regulations
S.I. 1985/1068	The Food (Revision of Penalties and Mode of Trial) (Scotland) Regulations 1985	In Schedule 1 the item relating to S.I. 1981/1034

EXPLANATORY NOTE

(This note is not part of the Regulations)

These Regulations apply to Scotland only and come into force on 11th June 1987.

The Regulations revoke and re-enact the provisions of the Fresh Meat Export (Hygiene and Inspection) (Scotland) Regulations 1981 and subsequent amending instruments, which implemented in part the provisions of Council Directive No. 64/433/EEC (OJ No. 121, 29.7.1964, p. 2012/64; OJ/SE 1963-64, p. 185) on health problems affecting intra-Community trade in fresh meat, as amended by Council Directive No. 66/601/EEC (OJ No. 192, 27.10.1966, p. 3302/66; OJ/SE 1965-66, p. 244), Council Directive No. 69/349/EEC (OJ No. L256, 11.10.1969, p. 5; OJ/SE 1969 (II), p. 432), Council Directive No. 83/90/EEC (OJ No. L59, 5.3.1983, p.10) and the Act annexed to the Treaty of Accession to the European Economic Community (Annex I(II)(F) - Cmnd 5179 I). These Regulations in addition implement Council Directive No. 86/587/EEC (OJ No. L399, 2.12.86, p.26).

The Regulations apply to fresh meat of domestic bovine animals (including buffalo), swine, sheep, goats and solipeds. They prescribe conditions which must be satisfied for the production, cutting up, storage and transport of such meat when it is intended for export, or for sale for export, to a Member State of the EEC for human consumption.

In particular, the Regulations –

(a) provide that only premises which are approved by the Secretary of State may be used for the production, cutting up, storage and loading of fresh meat for intra-Community trade, and that such premises must comply with prescribed requirements as to structure and hygiene (regulations 4 to 7 and 10 and Schedules 1 to 4); and

(b) lay down requirements as to slaughter, dressing and cutting practices, ante- and post-mortem inspection, hygiene, health control of cut meat, health marking, certification, storage, wrapping, packing and transport of such meat (regulations 8 to 11 and Schedules 5 to 15).

Apart from the approval, suspension and revocation of approval of premises for intra-Community trade (regulations 4 to 6), which are functions of the Secretary of State, enforcement of the Regulations is the responsibility of local authorities (regulation 17). They are required to provide the necessary supervision and inspection resources at approved premises (regulation 12), for which they may make charges (regulation 13).

The Regulations also make provision for powers of entry by persons authorised by the Secretary of State or local authorities (regulation 14) and concerning offences and penalties (regulation 18).

The Regulations do not affect the application as appropriate to export-approved premises of the provisions of the Slaughter of Animals (Prevention of Cruelty) (Scotland) Regulations 1955, the Food Hygiene (Scotland) Regulations 1959, the Food (Meat Inspection) (Scotland) Regulations 1961, the Slaughter of Animals (Stunning Pens) (Scotland) Regulations 1963 or the Slaughterhouse Hygiene (Scotland) Regulations 1978, except that they disapply (in regulation 19 of these Regulations) certain provisions of the said Food (Meat Inspection) (Scotland) Regulations 1961.

1987 No. 801

WAGES COUNCILS

The Unlicensed Place of Refreshment Wages Council (Variation) Order 1987

Made	-	-	-	-	*6th May 1987*
Laid before Parliament					*15th May 1987*
Coming into force					*13th June 1987*

Whereas the Secretary of State has had regard to the matters referred to in section 13(2)(a) and (b) of the Wages Act 1986(**a**) and has in accordance with the said section 13(2) consulted such persons and organisations as appear to him to be appropriate;

Now, therefore, the Secretary of State in exercise of the powers conferred on him by section 13(1) of the Wages Act 1986 and of all other powers enabling him in that behalf, hereby makes the following Order:–

1. This Order may be cited as the Unlicensed Place of Refreshment Wages Council (Variation) Order 1987 and shall come into force on the 13th June 1987.

2. The scope of operation of the Unlicensed Place of Refreshment Wages Council shall be varied by the exclusion therefrom of–

(a) workers who are employed in a central catering establishment;

(b) workers who are employed by a local authority; and

(c) workers who are employed in an industrial or staff canteen undertaking;

which exclusion is set out in paragraphs 2(8), (9) and (10) of the Schedule to this Order, and accordingly the said Wages Council shall operate only in relation to workers to whom the said Schedule applies and their employers.

3. The Schedule to the Wages Board (Unlicensed Place of Refreshment) Order 1944(**b**), as amended by the Wages Board (Unlicensed Place of Refreshment) (Amendment) Order 1946(**c**) and the Wages Board (Unlicensed Place of Refreshment) (Amendment) Order 1947(**d**), shall have effect as if for the Schedule thereto there were substituted the Schedule to this Order.

4. The Wages Board (Unlicensed Place of Refreshment) (Amendment) Order 1946 and the Wages Board (Unlicensed Place of Refreshment) (Amendment) Order 1947 are hereby revoked.

Signed by order of the Secretary of State.

David Trippier
Parliamentary Under Secretary of State,
Department of Employment

6th May 1987

(**a**) 1986 c.48.
(**b**) S.R. & O. 1944/1399.
(**c**) S.R. & O. 1946/743.
(**d**) S.R. & O. 1947/1731.

SCHEDULE

(WORKERS TO WHOM THE ORDER APPLIES)

1. Subject to the provisions of paragraph 2 hereof the workers to whom this Schedule applies are all workers employed in Great Britain in a catering undertaking who are employed by the person or body of persons carrying on that undertaking and who are so employed either:–

(1) for the purposes of such of the activities of the undertaking as are carried on at an unlicensed place of refreshment or a central catering establishment or in the course of a catering contracting business; or

(2) in connection with the provision of food or drink or living accommodation provided wholly or mainly for workers employed for the purposes of any of the activities specified in sub-paragraph (1) of this paragraph;

and who are engaged on any of the following work, that is to say:–

(a) the preparation of food or drink;

(b) the service of food or drink;

(c) work incidental to such preparation or service;

(d) work connected with the provision of living accommodation for workers employed for the purposes of any of the activities specified in sub-paragraph (1) of this paragraph;

(e) work in connection with any retail sale of goods on premises where the main activity is the supply of food or drink for immediate consumption;

(f) transport work;

(g) work performed at any office or at any store or warehouse or similar place or at any garage or stable or similar place;

(h) any work other than that specified in sub-paragraphs (a) to (g) hereof performed on or about the premises or place where food or drink is prepared or served including work in connection with any service or amenity provided on or about such premises or place.

2. This Schedule does not apply to any of the following workers in respect of their employment in any of the following circumstances, that is to say:–

(1) workers who are employed by the same employer partly in a catering undertaking and partly in some other undertaking, if their employment in the catering undertaking is confined to work specified either in sub-paragraph (f) or sub-paragraph (g) of paragraph 1 hereof or partly to work specified in the said sub-paragraph (f) and partly to work specified in the said sub-paragraph (g), and they are mainly employed on work in or in connection with that other undertaking;

(2) workers who are employed for the purposes of any of the activities carried on at a hotel, inn, boarding house, guest house, hostel, holiday camp, club or other similar establishment and who are so employed by the person or body of persons carrying on such establishment, unless the establishment is either:–

(a) an establishment which is not a residential establishment within the meaning of this Schedule and the worker is employed for the purposes of the activities carried on at a place of refreshment where food or drink is supplied mainly for persons who do not reside at the establishment; or

(b) carried on by the person or persons carrying on a catering undertaking such as is referred to in paragraph 1 hereof for the purpose of providing accommodation wholly or mainly for the workers mentioned in that paragraph;

(3) workers who are employed for the purposes of any of the activities carried on at any of the following establishments, that is to say:–

(a) any hospital, nursing home or convalescent home or similar establishment providing accommodation for the sick, infirm or mentally defective;

(b) any orphanage, children's home or similar establishment;

(c) any institution or home where living accommodation is provided for the aged or indigent;

(d) any university, college, school or similar establishment;

and who are employed by the person or body of persons carrying on the establishment, or, in the case of any of the establishments specified in sub-paragraph (d) hereof by such person or body of persons aforesaid or by the person or body of persons carrying on any boarding house which forms part of the establishment;

(4) workers who are employed by a railway company for the purposes of any of the activities carried on at a railway station or in a railway train;

(5) workers who are employed for the purposes of any of the activities carried on at a theatre, music-hall or other similar place of entertainment ordinarily used for the public performance of stage plays or variety entertainments, unless the worker is so employed in the course of a catering contracting business;

(6) workers who are employed for the purposes of any of the activities carried on at a travelling stall, barrow or other similar vehicle from which food or drink is sold by an itinerant salesman;

(7) workers who are employed by the Crown;

(8) workers who are employed in a central catering establishment;

(9) workers who are employed by a local authority;

(10) workers who are employed in an industrial or staff canteen undertaking.

3. In this Schedule the following expressions have the meanings hereby assigned to them:–
"catering contracting business" means a business or part of a business wholly or mainly engaged in supplying food or drink for immediate consumption:–

   (a) on premises not ordinarily occupied by the person or body of persons carrying on the business; or

   (b) in a railway train where the business is carried on otherwise than by a railway company;
   and any activities incidental or ancillary thereto;

"catering undertaking" means any undertaking or any part of an undertaking which consists wholly or mainly in the carrying on (whether for profit or not) of one or more of the following activities, that is to say, the supply of food or drink for immediate consumption, the provision of living accommodation for guests or lodgers or for persons employed in the undertaking and any other activity so far as it is incidental or ancillary to any such activity as aforesaid of the undertaking;
"central catering establishment" means an establishment wholly or mainly engaged in the preparation of food or drink for immediate consumption at two or more places of refreshment carried on by the person or body of persons carrying on the establishment but does not include an establishment wholly or mainly engaged on the preparation of food or drink for consumption on the same premises or in the same building as those on which or as that in which the establishment itself is carried on;
"industrial or staff canteen undertaking" means an undertaking or any part of an undertaking which is wholly or mainly engaged in supplying food or drink for immediate consumption and activities incidental or ancillary thereto, and which is carried on for the use of employed persons in connection with their employment:–

   (a) by their employer or employers; or

   (b) by the employed persons themselves; or

   (c) by the employed persons and their employer or employers jointly; or

   (d) by any other person or body of persons in pursuance of an arrangement or arrangements with the employer or employers of the employed persons, or with the employed persons themselves, or with the employed persons and their employer or employers jointly; or

   (e) by a dock authority or by a person or body of persons under an arrangement with a dock authority;

but excluding any such undertaking carried on:–

   (a) directly by the Crown; or

   (b) by an employer or by workers and their employer jointly, wholly or mainly for the use of workers employed by the employer:–

      (i) in the business of supplying food or drink for immediate consumption by the general public; or

      (ii) at or in connection with a shop, if the shop includes a restaurant, cafe or similar place where meals are served to the general public; or

      (iii) at or in connection with an hotel, boarding house, hostel or other similar establishment; or

      (iv) at or in connection with any hospital, nursing home or other similar establishment; or

      (v) at or in connection with any university, college, school or other similar establishment; or

   (c) directly by the British Railways Board (not being an undertaking carried on by a committee of management of employees of the British Railways Board).

For the purpose of this definition "dock authority" means any person or body of persons whether incorporated or not who are authorised to construct or are owners or lessees of any dock authorised by or under any Act, and "dock" includes a wharf or quay.

"place of refreshment" means any place which is used either regularly or occasionally as or for the purposes of a restaurant, dining room, cafe, tea shop, buffet or similar place, or a coffee stall, snack bar, or other similar stall or bar;

"residential establishment" means an establishment which either contains four or more rooms ordinarily available as sleeping accommodation for guests or lodgers or, if it contains less than four such rooms, which contains sleeping accommodation ordinarily available for not less than eight guests or lodgers;

"unlicensed place of refreshment" means any place of refreshment where intoxicating liquor:–

(a) cannot legally be sold (or supplied in the case of a restaurant, dining room, buffet or bar at a club) for consumption on the premises; or

(b) can legally be so sold or supplied by reason only of the fact that an occasional licence in relation to that place is for the time being in force, being a licence granted to some person other than the person carrying on, or a person in the employment of the person carrying on, the activities (other than the supply of intoxicating liquor) of a catering undertaking at that place.

EXPLANATORY NOTE

(This note is not part of the Order)

The Unlicensed Place of Refreshment Wages Board was established in 1944 under the Catering Wages Act 1943 (c.24). It became a Wages Council under the Terms and Conditions of Employment Act 1959 (c.26) and was continued in existence under the Wages Councils Act 1959 (c.69), the Wages Councils Act 1979 (c.12) and the Wages Act 1986. The said Wages Council did not apply wages orders made by it under section 14 of the Wages Councils Act 1979 to certain workers. These workers (except for part-time managers) are excluded from the scope of the Wages Council by this Order.

This Order, which comes into force on the 13th June 1987, varies the scope of operation of the said Wages Council by excluding therefrom:–

(a) workers employed in a central catering establishment;

(b) workers employed by a local authority;

(c) workers employed in an industrial or staff canteen undertaking.

This Order also revokes the Wages Board (Unlicensed Place of Refreshment) (Amendment) Order 1946 and the Wages Board (Unlicensed Place of Refreshment) (Amendment) Order 1947.

STATUTORY INSTRUMENTS

1987 No. 802

FEES AND CHARGES

The Measuring Instruments (EEC Initial Verification Requirements) (Fees) (Amendment) Regulations 1987

Made - - - -	*1st May 1987*
Laid before Parliament	*11th May 1987*
Coming into force	*1st June 1987*

The Secretary of State for Trade and Industry, with the consent of the Treasury, in exercise of the powers conferred on him by section 56(1) and (2) of the Finance Act 1973**(a)**, and of all other powers enabling him in that behalf, hereby makes the following Regulations:–

1.—(1) These Regulations may be cited as the Measuring Instruments (EEC Initial Verification Requirements) (Fees) (Amendment) Regulations 1987 and shall come into force on 1st June 1987.

(2) The Measuring Instruments (EEC Initial Verification Requirements) (Fees) (Amendment) Regulations 1986**(b)** are hereby revoked.

2. The Measuring Instruments (EEC Initial Verification Requirements) (Fees) Regulations 1982**(c)** are hereby amended as follows:–

    (a) in regulation 4, by omitting the figures "£21.00" and "£16.80" and substituting therefor respectively the figures "£23.20" and "£18.40"; and

    (b) in paragraph (a) of the Schedule, by omitting the figure "£36.00" and substituting therefor the figure "£39.60".

Lucas of Chilworth
Parliamentary Under-Secretary of State,
Department of Trade and Industry

27th April 1987

We consent.

Michael Neubert
Tony Durant
Two of the Lords Commissioners
of Her Majesty's Treasury

1st May 1987

(a) 1973 c.51.
(b) S.I. 1986/1043.
(c) S.I. 1982/811, amended by S.I. 1985/386.

EXPLANATORY NOTE

(This note is not part of the Regulations)

These Regulations further amend the Measuring Instruments (EEC Initial Verification Requirements) (Fees) Regulations 1982. They increase the fees payable in connection with services provided by the Department of Trade and Industry in respect of EEC initial verification of certain measuring instruments and systems (from £36.00 per hour to £39.60 per hour).

They also increase the single fee for services provided by the Department of Trade and Industry in respect of EEC initial verification of all classes of alcoholometers and alcohol hydrometers. The increase is from £21.00 to £23.20, except that, when submitted in a batch of 10 or more applications, the increase is from £16.80 to £18.40 per application.

STATUTORY INSTRUMENTS

1987 No. 803

FEES AND CHARGES

The Measuring Instruments (EEC Pattern Approval Requirements) (Fees) Regulations 1987

Made - - - -	*1st May 1987*
Laid before Parliament	*11th May 1987*
Coming into force	*1st June 1987*

The Secretary of State for Trade and Industry, with the consent of the Treasury, in exercise of the powers conferred on him by section 56(1) and (2) of the Finance Act 1973(**a**), and of all other powers enabling him in that behalf, hereby makes the following Regulations:

1.—(1) These Regulations may be cited as the Measuring Instruments (EEC Pattern Approval Requirements) (Fees) Regulations 1987 and shall come into force on 1st June 1987.

(2) The Measuring Instruments (EEC Pattern Approval Requirements) (Fees) (No. 2) Regulations 1981(**b**), the Measuring Instruments (EEC Pattern Approval Requirements) (Fees) (Amendment) Regulations 1985(**c**) and the Measuring Instruments (EEC Pattern Approval Requirements) (Fees) (Amendment) Regulations 1986(**d**) are hereby revoked.

2.   In these Regulations –

"the principal Regulations" means the Measuring Instruments (EEC Requirements) Regulations 1980(**e**);

"the relevant Community obligations" means the Community obligations of the United Kingdom under Council Directive No. 71/316/EEC(**f**) (which relates to measuring instruments in general) and the following Council Directives:–

Council Directive No.	*Subject Matter*
71/319/EEC(**g**)	meters for liquids other than water
71/348/EEC(**h**) as amended(**i**)	ancillary equipment for meters for liquids other than water
73/360/EEC(**j**) as amended(**k**)	non-automatic weighing machines

---

(**a**) 1973 c.51.   (**b**) S.I. 1981/1825.   (**c**) S.I. 1985/852.   (**d**) S.I. 1986/831.   (**e**) S.I. 1980/1058, amended by S.I. 1981/1727, 1983/530, 1984/1618, 1985/306, 1871.   (**f**) OJ No.L202,6.9.1971,p.1 (OJ/SE 1971 (II)p.707), as amended by Council Directive No. 72/427/EEC (OJ No. L291,28.12.1972,p.156, OJ/SE 1972, 28–30 Dec,p.71), Cmnd.7463,p.174, and Council Directive No. 83/575/EEC (OJ No. L332, 28.11.1983, p.43).   (**g**) OJ No.L202, 6.9.1971,p.32 (OJ/SE 1971 (III)p.740).   (**h**) OJ No.L239,25.10.1971, p.9 (OJ/SE 1971(III)p.860).   (**i**) Cmnd.7463, p.175.   (**j**) OJ No.L335,5.12.1973,p.1.   (**k**) OJ No.L236,27.8.1976,p.26.

Council Directive No.	Subject Matter
73/362/EEC(**a**) as amended(**b**)	material measures of length
75/33/EEC(**c**)	cold-water meters
75/410/EEC(**d**)	continuous totalising weighing machines
76/765/EEC(**e**)	alcoholometers and alcohol hydrometers
77/95/EEC(**f**)	taximeters
77/313/EEC(**g**) as amended(**h**)	measuring systems for liquids other than water
78/1031/EEC(**i**)	automatic checkweighing and weight grading machines
79/830/EEC(**j**)	hot-water meters

3.—(1) The fees payable in connection with the services provided by the Department of Trade and Industry in pursuance of the relevant Community obligations relating to the grant and extension of EEC pattern approval and modifications or additions to EEC approved patterns, implemented by regulation 7 of, and Schedule 2 to, the principal Regulations, shall be determined and payable in accordance with the Schedule hereto, whether or not EEC pattern approval is granted or extended as the case may be.

(2) In the case of alcoholometers and alcohol hydrometers and taximeters, in respect of which regulation 7 of and Schedule 2 to the principal Regulations are applied by regulation 5 of the Alcoholometers and Alcohol Hydrometers (EEC Requirements) Regulations 1977(**k**) and regulation 6 of the Taximeters (EEC Requirements) Regulations 1979(**l**) respectively, the fees shall be determined and payable as in paragraph (1) above.

4. All fees received under these Regulations shall be paid into the Consolidated Fund.

Lucas of Chilworth
Parliamentary Under Secretary of State,
Department of Trade and Industry

27th April 1987

We consent,

Michael Neubert
Tony Durant
Two of the Lords Commissioners of Her Majesty's Treasury

1st May 1987

(**a**) OJ No. L335, 5.12.1973, p.56.   (**b**) OJ No. L206, 29.7.1978, p.8.   (**c**) OJ No. L14, 20.1.1975, p.1.
(**d**) OJ No. L183, 14.7.1975, p.25.   (**e**) OJ No. L262, 27.9.1976, p.143.   (**f**) OJ No. L26, 31.1.1977, p.59.
(**g**) OJ No. L105, 28.4.1977, p.18.   (**h**) OJ No. L252, 27.8.1982, p.10.   (**i**) OJ No. L364, 27.12.1978, p.1.
(**j**) OJ No. L259, 15.10.1979, p.1.   (**k**) S.I. 1977/1753, to which there are amendments not relevant to these Regulations.   (**l**) S.I. 1979/1379, to which there are amendments not relevant to these Regulations.

SCHEDULE   Regulation 3

FEES FOR EEC PATTERN APPROVAL

1.—(1) Where regulation 7(1) or (5) of the principal Regulations applies (application for grant or extension of EEC pattern approval), the fees shall be–

    (a) an amount calculated to the nearest quarter of an hour in respect of any time taken by examination staff conducting the examination at the rate of £33.00 per hour and by equipment test unit staff in testing the pattern at the rate of £27.00 per hour, including any time spent in travelling, and any time during which the pattern is tested in an environmental testing chamber at the rate of £10.00 per hour, due and payable as indicated in sub-paragraphs (2) and (3) below; and

    (b) the amount of additional expenses, if any, incurred by or occasioned to the Secretary of State, by reason of any part of the examination taking place at a place other than the National Weights and Measures Laboratory of the Department of Trade and Industry, due and payable as indicated in sub-paragraphs (2) and (3) below.

(2) Subject to sub-paragraph (3) below, the amounts referred to in sub-paragraphs (1)(a) and (b) above shall be due and payable on the service on the applicant of an invoice from the Secretary of State quarterly in arrears.

(3) On completion of the examination, the Secretary of State shall serve an invoice on the applicant for the final amount of the fees, together with the notification of such completion, and the final amount shall thereupon, and before notification of the result, be due and payable to the Secretary of State.

2.—(1) Where regulation 7(2) of the principal Regulations applies (application for approval of modifications or additions to an EEC approved pattern), the fees shall be–

    (a) an amount calculated as indicated in paragraph 1(1)(a) above, due and payable as indicated in sub-paragraphs (2) and (3) below; and

    (b) the amount of additional expenses, if any, incurred by or occasioned to the Secretary of State, by reason of any part of the examination taking place at a place other than the National Weights and Measures Laboratory of the Department of Trade and Industry, due and payable as indicated in sub-paragraph (3) below.

(2) The Secretary of State shall, on receipt of an application for approval of modifications or additions to an EEC approved pattern, estimate to the nearest hour the time to be taken in conducting the examination and testing the pattern and thereby estimate the amount to be payable in accordance with sub-paragraph (1)(a) above, and shall serve an invoice on the applicant for the amount so estimated, which shall thereupon be due and payable to the Secretary of State.

(3) On completion of the examination, the Secretary of State shall–

    (a) serve an invoice on the applicant for the final amount of the fees, together with the notification of such completion, and the final amount, after deducting the amount received under sub-paragraph (2) above, shall thereupon, and before notification of the result, be due and payable to the Secretary of State; or

    (b) if the amount received under sub-paragraph (2) above exceeds the final amount, repay the balance to the applicant.

EXPLANATORY NOTE

(This note is not part of the Regulations)

These Regulations replace the Measuring Instruments (EEC Pattern Approval Requirements) (Fees) (No. 2) Regulations 1981 (S.I. 1981/1825), the Measuring Instruments (EEC Pattern Approval Requirements) (Fees) (Amendment) Regulations 1985 (S.I. 1985/852) and the Measuring Instruments (EEC Pattern Approval Requirements) (Fees) (Amendment) Regulations 1986 (S.I. 1986/831). They increase the fees payable in connection with services provided by the Department of Trade and Industry in respect of an application for grant of an EEC pattern approval, including approval of modifications or additions to an EEC approved pattern, and provide a fee on an application for extension of an EEC pattern approval, of the following measuring instruments–

(a) meters for liquids other than water;

(b) ancillary equipment for meters for liquids other than water;

(c) non-automatic weighing machines;

(d) material measures of length;

(e) cold-water meters;

(f) continuous totalising weighing machines;

(g) alcoholometers and alcohol hydrometers;

(h) taximeters;

(i) measuring systems for liquids other than water;

(j) automatic checkweighing and weight grading machines;

(k) hot-water meters.

The increased fees for examiner staff time are £33.00 per hour (from £30.80 per hour), for equipment test unit staff time £27.00 per hour (from £24.20 per hour) and for use of an environmental testing chamber £10.00 per hour (from £4.00 per hour).

1987 No. 804

TOWN AND COUNTRY PLANNING, ENGLAND AND WALES

The Town and Country Planning (Control of Advertisements) (Amendment) Regulations 1987

Made - - - -	*5th May 1987*
Laid before Parliament	*8th May 1987*
Coming into force	*1st July 1987*

The Secretary of State for the Environment, in exercise of the powers conferred by sections 63, 109 and 287 of the Town and Country Planning Act 1971(**a**) and of all other powers enabling him in that behalf, hereby makes the following regulations:–

Citation and commencement

1. These Regulations may be cited as the Town and Country Planning (Control of Advertisements) (Amendment) Regulations 1987 and shall come into force on 1st July 1987.

Amendment of the Town and Country Planning (Control of Advertisements) Regulations 1984

2. The Town and Country Planning (Control of Advertisements) Regulations 1984(**b**) are hereby amended as follows–

(1) in regulation 8 (contravention of regulations), for "£200" substitute "£400" and for "£20" substitute "£40";

(2) at the end of regulation 14(1) insert the following–

"Class VIII—Directional advertisements for tourist attractions and facilities in experimental areas.

An advertisement described in Schedule 2A displayed in an experimental area as defined in that Schedule, during the period there described and subject to the conditions and limitations there specified and to the provisions of paragraph (2)(b) and (c) of this regulation.";

(3) in regulation 15(1) after "regulation 14" insert "(other than Class VIII)",

(4) after Schedule 2 to those Regulations insert the Schedule to these Regulations as Schedule 2A to those Regulations.

(**a**) 1971 c.78; section 63 was amended by section 45 of the Housing and Planning Act 1986 (c.63); and section 109 was amended by section 46 of the Criminal Justice Act 1982 (c.48) and by paragraph 13 of Schedule 11 to the Housing and Planning Act 1986.
(**b**) S.I. 1984/421.

SCHEDULE

DIRECTIONAL ADVERTISEMENTS FOR TOURIST ATTRACTIONS AND FACILITIES IN EXPERIMENTAL AREAS.
(Regulation 14, Class VIII).

Interpretation

1. In this Schedule–
"existing directional advertisement" means a directional advertisement which is being displayed with express consent or with consent deemed to be granted under these Regulations;

"traffic sign" means a sign (whether or not it is a directional advertisement) employed wholly for the control, guidance or safety of traffic, and displayed by, or with the permission of, a local highway, traffic or police authority in accordance with regulations and general directions made by the Secretary of State or in accordance with an authorisation and any relevant direction given by him.

Description of advertisement

2. An advertisement (in this Schedule called a "directional advertisement") which is displayed for the purpose of directing visitors to the locality to a tourist attraction or a tourist facility specified thereon.

Definition of experimental areas and prescription of period

3. For the purpose of assessing the effect on amenity or public safety of advertisements of the description prescribed by paragraph 2 above, an area comprising the area of the Borough of Ashford, and the Districts of Dover and Shepway, is hereby defined as an experimental area for a period of two years beginning with 1st July 1987.

Conditions and limitations

4. The display of a directional advertisement is subject to the following limitations and conditions in addition to the standard conditions–

(1) the advertiser shall, not later than twenty one days beginning with the date on which the advertisement is first displayed,–

    (a) notify the local planning authority in writing of–

        (i) the date on which the advertisement was so displayed;

        (ii) the precise location of the advertisement; and

        (iii) the tourist attraction or tourist facility specified in the advertisement; and

    (b) provide the local planning authority, by means of a scale drawing, or a plan, or a coloured photograph, with a description of the advertisement from which it may be readily identified;

(2) the advertisement shall not exceed 0.5 square metre in area and shall consist of white letters, figures, symbols, emblems or devices on a brown background;

(3) such letters, figures, symbols, emblems or devices shall be of a height of not less than 40 millimetres nor more than 250 millimetres, and neither they nor the background on which they are displayed shall consist of reflective material;

(4) the advertisement shall not be displayed on land forming part of a highway but shall be displayed on land adjacent to a highway by which the specified tourist attraction or facility may be approached;

(5) the advertisement shall be single sided and shall be displayed so as to be reasonably visible to the driver of a vehicle approaching it;

(6) an advertisement shall not be displayed–

    (a) within 50 metres of an existing traffic sign if it faces in the same direction as that traffic sign;

    (b) within 25 metres of an existing directional advertisement for any tourist attraction or tourist facility;

    (c) if there is already an existing directional advertisement for the specified tourist attraction or tourist facility on the same approach route to that attraction or facility;

    (d) outside a radius of two miles from the main entrance to the specified tourist attraction or facility;

(7) sub-paragraphs (5) and (6) above do not apply to one advertisement for a tourist attraction or tourist facility which is displayed at or immediately opposite the main entrance to such attraction or facility, and such advertisement may be double-sided.

Nicholas Ridley
Secretary of State for the Environment

5th May 1987

EXPLANATORY NOTE

(This note is not part of the Regulations)

These Regulations, made by the Secretary of State for the Environment after consultation (as respects regulation 2(1)) with the Secretary of State for Wales, amend the Town and Country Planning (Control of Advertisements) Regulations 1984.

Regulation 2(1) amends regulation 8 (contravention of regulations) of the 1984 Regulations. The fine of £200 specified in that regulation is increased to £400 to follow an increase to the standard scale by the Criminal Penalties etc. (Increase) Order 1984 (S.I. 1984/447). The daily fine of £20 for a continuing offence is increased to £40. These amendments apply throughout England and Wales.

The other amendments follow from section 45 of the Housing and Planning Act 1986 which amended section 63 of the Town and Country Planning Act 1971 (control of advertisements) and gave the Secretary of State powers to make regulations for experimental areas. During the period for which these areas are prescribed, certain advertisements can be displayed without express consent in order to assess their effect on amenity and public safety.

Regulation 2(2) and (4) of, and the Schedule to, these Regulations accordingly insert into the 1984 Regulations a new class (VIII) in regulation 14 (which specifies classes of advertisements which may be displayed without the grant of express consent) and a new Schedule (2A). These provide for the display, during an experimental period of two years from the coming into force of these Regulations, of advertisements which direct visitors to tourist attractions or tourist facilities in the areas of Ashford, Dover and Shepway in Kent.

Regulation 15 of the 1984 Regulations (which empowers the Secretary of State to exclude the application of regulation 14 in any particular area or any particular case) does not apply to a Class VIII advertisement (regulation 2(3)).

S T A T U T O R Y   I N S T R U M E N T S

1987 No. 805

ROAD TRAFFIC

The Community Drivers' Hours and Recording Equipment (Exemptions and Supplementary Provisions) (Amendment) Regulations 1987

Made - - - -	*6th May 1987*
Laid before Parliament	*11th May 1987*
Coming into force	*1st June 1987*

The Secretary of State for Transport, being a Minister designated (a) for the purpose of section 2(2) of the European Communities Act 1972(b) in relation to the regulation and supervision of working conditions of persons engaged in road transport and the regulation of the type, description, construction or equipment of vehicles, in exercise of the powers conferred by that section, hereby makes the following Regulations:

1. These Regulations may be cited as the Community Drivers' Hours and Recording Equipment (Exemptions and Supplementary Provisions) (Amendment) Regulations 1987 and shall come into force on 1st June 1987.

2. The Community Drivers' Hours and Recording Equipment (Exemptions and Supplementary Provisions) Regulations 1986(c) shall be further amended as follows.

3. For regulation 2 there shall be substituted the following regulation:

"**2.**—(1) Pursuant to Article 13(1) of the Community Drivers' Hours Regulation, exemption is granted from all the provisions of that Regulation, except Article 5 (minimum ages for drivers) in respect of any vehicle falling within a description specified in Part I of the Schedule to these Regulations.

(2) Pursuant to Article 13(2) of the Community Drivers' Hours Regulation, exemption is granted from all the provision of that Regulation, except Article 5, in respect of any vehicle falling within a description specified in Part II of the Schedule to these Regulations.".

4. For regulation 4 there shall be substituted the following regulation:

"**4.**—(1) Pursuant to Article 3(2) of the Community Recording Equipment Regulation, exemption is granted from the provisions of that Regulation in respect of any vehicle falling within a description specified in Part I of the Schedule to these Regulations.

(2) Pursuant to Article 3(3) of the Community Recording Equipment Regulation, exemption is granted from the provisions of that Regulation in respect of:
- (a) any vehicle falling within a description specified in Part II of the Schedule to these Regulations; and
- (b) any vehicle which is being used for collecting sea coal.".

(a) S.I. 1975/1707 and 1972/1811.
(b) 1972 c.68.
(c) S.I. 1986/1456, to which there is an amendment not relevant to these Regulations.

5.—(1) In the heading to the Schedule for the line

"VEHICLES EXEMPTED BY REGULATIONS 2 and 4"

there shall be substituted the lines

"PART I

VEHICLES EXEMPTED BY REGULATIONS 2(1) and 4(1)"; and

(2) After paragraph 11 of the Schedule there shall be added the following heading and paragraphs:

"PART II

VEHICLES EXEMPTED BY REGULATIONS 2(2) and 4(2)

12.   Any vehicle which is being used by the Royal National Lifeboat Institution for the purpose of hauling lifeboats.

13.   Any vehicle which was manufactured before 1st January 1947.

14.   Any vehicle which is propelled by steam.".

Peter Bottomley
Signed by authority of the Secretary of State   Parliamentary Under Secretary of State,
6th May 1987   Department of Transport

EXPLANATORY NOTE

(This note is not part of the Regulations)

These Regulations amend the Community Drivers' Hours and Recording Equipment (Exemptions and Supplementary Provisions) Regulations 1986 ("the Principal Regulations") by providing for additional exemptions from the provisions (except Article 5) of Council Regulation (EEC) No. 3820/85 of 20th December 1985 (O.J. No. L370, 31.12.85, p.1) on the harmonisation of certain social legislation relating to road transport ("the Community Drivers Hours Regulation") and from the provisions of Council Regulation (EEC) No. 3821/85 of 20th December 1985 (O.J. No. L370, 31.12.85 p.8) on recording equipment in road transport ("the Community Recording Equipment Regulation").

The additional exemptions are contained in the new regulations 2(2) and 4(2) of and the new Part II of the Schedule to the Principal Regulations inserted by regulations 3, 4 and 5 respectively of these Regulations. They are granted after authorisation by the Commission of the European Communities given in a decision which has been taken under the provisions of Article 13(2) of the Community Drivers' Hours Regulation and Article 3(3) of the Community Recording Equipment Regulation on 6th April 1987.

These Regulations contain certain provisions which were included in a draft of Regulations bearing the title "The Community Drivers' Hours and Recording Equipment (Exemptions and Supplementary Provisions) Regulations 1986" which was laid before Parliament on 11th June 1986 and approved by both Houses of Parliament but not made.

STATUTORY INSTRUMENTS

1987 No. 806

VALUE ADDED TAX

The Value Added Tax (Terminal Markets) (Amendment) Order 1987

Made - - - -	*5th May 1987*
Laid before the *House of Commons*	*7th May 1987*
Coming into force	*1st June 1987*

The Treasury, in exercise of the powers conferred on them by section 34 of the Value Added Tax Act 1983(**a**) and of all other powers enabling them in that behalf, hereby make the following Order:

1. This Order may be cited as the Value Added Tax (Terminal Markets) (Amendment) Order 1987 and shall come into force on 1st June 1987.

2. Paragraph (2) of article 2 of the Value Added Tax (Terminal Markets) Order 1973(**b**) shall be amended by adding the words "and the London Platinum and Palladium Market.".

Tim Sainsbury
Peter Lloyd
Two of the Lords Commissioners
of Her Majesty's Treasury

5th May 1987

EXPLANATORY NOTE

(This note is not part of the Order)

This Order amends the Value Added Tax (Terminal Markets) Order 1973 and extends the zero-rating contained in that Order to supplies in the course of dealings on the London Platinum and Palladium Market, which is now added to the list of markets in that Order.

(**a**) 1983 c.55.
(**b**) S.I. 1973/173, as amended by S.I. 1975/385, 1980/304, 1981/338, 955, 1984/202, 1985/1046.

1987 No. 808

NATIONAL HEALTH SERVICE, ENGLAND AND WALES

The Disablement Services Authority (Establishment and Constitution) Order 1987

Made - - - -	*6th May 1987*
Laid before Parliament	*7th May 1987*
Coming into force	*1st July 1987*

The Secretary of State for Social Services, in exercise of powers conferred upon him by section 11 of the National Health Service Act 1977(a) and of all other powers enabling him in that behalf, hereby makes the following Order:–

Citation and commencement

1.—(1) This Order may be cited as the Disablement Services Authority (Establishment and Constitution) Order 1987 and shall come into force on 1st July 1987.

(2) This Order shall cease to have effect on 31st March 1991.

Establishment of the Disablement Services Authority

2. There is hereby established for a period ending on 31st March 1991 (hereinafter in this Order referred to as "the interim period") a special health authority which shall be known as the Disablement Services Authority (hereinafter in this Order referred to as "the Authority").

Functions of the Authority

3.—(1) Subject to paragraphs (2) and (3) below, and in accordance with such directions as the Secretary of State may give to the Authority, the Authority shall have the functions specified in this paragraph and such other functions as the Secretary of State may direct the Authority to perform on his behalf–

    (a) the provision (including fitting and repair) of artificial limbs, limb appurtenances and arm appliances;

    (b) the provision (including repair and maintenance) of non-powered and powered wheelchairs and of wheelchair accessories including the provision of special seating;

    (c) the provision of other facilities, being articles or appliances for use in the aftercare of disabled persons, as the Secretary of State may direct;

    (d) the payment, in accordance with regulations, of travelling expenses incurred by persons availing themselves of any services provided by the Authority;

    (e) the formulation and development of long-term policies designed to secure the efficient management of the artificial limb service and the wheelchair service;

(a) 1977 c.49; section 11 was amended by the Health Services Act 1980 (c.53) Schedule 1, paragraph 31.

(f) the implementation of the policies referred to at sub-paragraph (e) above during the interim period and the submission of recommendations to the Secretary of State as to the implementation after the interim period of the said policies.

(2) In performing any function conferred upon the Authority by this Order the Authority shall have regard to the following–

(a) the relationship between its responsibilities and any responsibilities for the provision of related services for disabled persons falling to other health authorities in accordance with functions exercised by them on behalf of the Secretary of State;

(b) the terms of any agreements approved by the Secretary of State relating to the remuneration and conditions of employment of officers of the Department of Health and Social Security whose services have been made available to the Authority.

(3) Nothing in this Order shall enable the Authority to carry out any research or development.

Constitution of the Authority

4. The Authority shall consist of not more than 10 members of whom one shall be the chairman and one the vice-chairman.

Enforceability of right and liability

5. Any right or liability which was enforceable by or against the Department of Health and Social Security before the date of the coming into force of this Order in connection with the artificial limb and appliance services, shall be enforceable by or against the Authority.

Admission to meetings

6. The Public Bodies (Admission to Meetings) Act 1960**(a)** shall apply to the Authority.

Signed by authority of the Secretary of State for Social Services.

John Major
Minister of State,
Department of Health and Social Security

6th May 1987

EXPLANATORY NOTE

(This note is not part of the Order)

This Order provides for the establishment and constitution of a special health authority to be known as the Disablement Services Authority for the purpose of carrying out certain specified functions relating to the artificial limb and appliance service and such other functions as the Secretary of State may direct.

(a) 1960 c.67; paragraph 1 of Schedule 1 was amended by the National Health Service Reorganisation Act 1973 (c.32), Schedule 4, paragraph 99.

STATUTORY INSTRUMENTS

1987 No. 809

NATIONAL HEALTH SERVICE, ENGLAND AND WALES

The Disablement Services Authority Regulations 1987

Made - - - -	*6th May 1987*
Laid before Parliament	*7th May 1987*
Coming into force	*1st July 1987*

The Secretary of State for Social Services, in exercise of powers conferred by paragraphs 12 and 16 of Schedule 5 to the National Health Service Act 1977(a) and of all other powers enabling him in that behalf, hereby makes the following Regulations:-

Citation, commencement and interpretation

1.—(1) These Regulations may be cited as the Disablement Services Authority Regulations 1987 and shall come into force on 1st July 1987.

(2) In these Regulations, unless the context otherwise requires–
"the Authority" means the Disablement Services Authority established by the Disablement Services Authority (Establishment and Constitution) Order 1987(b);
"member" means the chairman or other member of the Authority.

Appointment of members

2. The chairman and the other members of the Authority shall be appointed by the Secretary of State.

Tenure of office of members

3. Subject to the following provisions of these Regulations, the term of office of members shall be for such period, expiring on or before 31st March 1991, as the Secretary of State shall specify on making the appointment.

Termination of tenure of office

4.—(1) A member may resign his office at any time during the period for which he was appointed by giving notice in writing to the Secretary of State.

(2) Where the Secretary of State is satisfied that it is not in the interest of the Authority or the health service that a person whom he has appointed as a member should continue to hold that office, he may forthwith terminate that member's tenure of office.

(a) 1977 c.49; *see* section 128(1) for the definition of *regulations*.
(b) S.I. 1987/808.

Vice-chairman

5.—(1) The Secretary of State may appoint a member of the Authority to be vice-chairman for such period as the Secretary of State may specify on making the appointment.

(2) Where no such appointment is made, the chairman and members of the Authority shall elect one of their number, other than the chairman, to be vice-chairman for a period of one year or, where the period of his membership during which he is elected has less than a year to run, for the remainder of such period.

(3) Any member so appointed or elected may at any time resign from the office of vice-chairman by giving notice in writing–

    (a) if he was appointed by the Secretary of State, to the Secretary of State;

    (b) in any other case, to the chairman,

and the Secretary of State may thereupon appoint another member, or failing such appointment, the chairman and members shall thereupon elect another member as vice-chairman in accordance with paragraph (1), or as the case may be, paragraph (2) of this regulation.

Application of regulations relating to membership and procedure

6. The provisions of regulation 5(4), (6) and (7) (termination of tenure of office), regulation 7 (disqualification for appointment), regulation 8 (cessation of disqualification), regulation 10 (powers of vice-chairman), regulation 11 (appointment of committees and sub-committees), regulation 12 (arrangements for exercise of functions), regulation 13 (meetings and proceedings), regulation 14 (disability of chairman and members in proceedings on account of pecuniary interests) of, and Schedule 1 (rules as to meetings and proceedings) to the National Health Service (Regional and District Health Authorities: Membership and Procedure) Regulations 1983(**a**) shall apply in relation to the Authority as if any reference therein to an Authority were a reference to the Authority and as if there were omitted any reference therein to a joint committee.

Reports and papers by the Authority

7. The Authority shall make reports to the Secretary of State in such manner and at such time, being at least once each year, as the Secretary of State may direct and shall furnish to the Secretary of State such information as he may from time to time require.

Signed by authority of the Secretary of State for Social Services.

John Major
Minister of State,
Department of Health and Social Security

6th May 1987

EXPLANATORY NOTE

(This note is not part of the Regulations)

These Regulations provide for the appointment and tenure of office of the chairman, and other members of the special health authority known as the Disablement Services Authority. They also provide for the procedure of, and report to the Secretary of State by, that Authority.

(**a**) S.I. 1983/315.

STATUTORY INSTRUMENTS

1987 No. 812

OFFSHORE INSTALLATIONS

The Offshore Installations (Safety Zones) (No. 28) Order 1987

Made - - - -		*6th May 1987*
Coming into force		*8th May 1987*

The Secretary of State, in exercise of the powers conferred on him by section 21(1), (2) and (3) of the Oil and Gas (Enterprise) Act 1982(a) (hereinafter referred to as "the Act"), and of all other powers enabling him in that behalf, hereby makes the following Order:–

1. This Order may be cited as the Offshore Installations (Safety Zones) (No. 28) Order 1987 and shall come into force on 8th May 1987.

2.—(1) A safety zone is hereby established around the installation specified in Column 1 of the Schedule hereto (being an installation maintained in waters to which section 21 of the Act(b) applies) having a radius of five hundred metres from the point as respects that installation which has the co-ordinates of latitude and longitude according to European Datum (1950) specified in Columns 2 and 3 of the Schedule.

(2) The prohibition under section 21(3) of the Act on a vessel entering or remaining in a safety zone without the consent of the Secretary of State shall not apply to a vessel entering or remaining in the safety zone established under paragraph (1) above –

    (a) in connection with the laying, inspection, testing, repair, alteration, renewal or removal of any submarine cable or pipe-line in or near that safety zone;

    (b) to provide services for, to transport persons or goods to or from, or under the authority of a government department to inspect, any installation in that safety zone;

    (c) if it is a vessel belonging to a general lighthouse authority performing duties relating to the safety of navigation;

    (d) in connection with the saving or attempted saving of life or property;

    (e) owing to stress of weather; or

    (f) when in distress.

Alick Buchanan-Smith
Minister of State, Department of Energy

6th May 1987

(a) 1982 c.23.   (b) *See* section 21(9).

Article 2(1)

SCHEDULE

SAFETY ZONE

(1) *Name or other designation of the offshore installation*	(2) *Latitude North*	(3) *Longitude East*
Brae B 16/7A	58° 47′ 32.44″	01° 20′ 50.72″

EXPLANATORY NOTE

(This note is not part of the Order)

This Order establishes, under section 21 of the Oil and Gas (Enterprise) Act 1982, a safety zone, having a radius of 500 metres from a specified point, around the installation specified in the Schedule to this Order and maintained in waters to which the section applies (these include territorial waters and waters in areas designated under section 1(7) of the Continental Shelf Act 1964 (c.29)).

Vessels (which for this purpose include hovercraft, submersible apparatus and installations in transit) are prohibited from entering or remaining in the safety zone except with the consent of the Secretary of State or in the circumstances mentioned in article 2(2) of the Order.

STATUTORY INSTRUMENTS

1987 No. 813

OFFSHORE INSTALLATIONS

The Offshore Installations (Safety Zones) (No. 29) Order 1987

Made - - - -	*6th May 1987*
Coming into force	*8th May 1987*

The Secretary of State, in exercise of the powers conferred on him by section 21(1), (2) and (3) of the Oil and Gas (Enterprise) Act 1982(a) (hereinafter referred to as "the Act"), and of all other powers enabling him in that behalf, hereby makes the following Order:–

1. This Order may be cited as the Offshore Installations (Safety Zones) (No. 29) Order 1987 and shall come into force on 8th May 1987.

2.—(1) A safety zone is hereby established around the installation specified in Column 1 of the Schedule hereto (being an installation maintained in waters to which section 21 of the Act(b) applies) having a radius of five hundred metres from the point as respects that installation which has the co-ordinates of latitude and longitude according to European Datum (1950) specified in Columns 2 and 3 of the Schedule.

(2) The prohibition under section 21(3) of the Act on a vessel entering or remaining in a safety zone without the consent of the Secretary of State shall not apply to a vessel entering or remaining in the safety zone established under paragraph (1) above –

    (a) in connection with the laying, inspection, testing, repair, alteration, renewal or removal of any submarine cable or pipe-line in or near that safety zone;

    (b) to provide services for, to transport persons or goods to or from, or under the authority of a government department to inspect, any installation in that safety zone;

    (c) if it is a vessel belonging to a general lighthouse authority performing duties relating to the safety of navigation;

    (d) in connection with the saving or attempted saving of life or property;

    (e) owing to stress of weather; or

    (f) when in distress.

Alick Buchanan-Smith
Minister of State, Department of Energy

6th May 1987

(a) 1982 c.23. (b) *See* section 21(9).

Article 2(1)

SCHEDULE

SAFETY ZONE

(1) Name or other designation of the offshore installation	(2) Latitude North	(3) Longitude East
Conoco Valiant 49/21 PTD	53° 19′ 06.08″	02° 05′ 44.88″

EXPLANATORY NOTE

(This note is not part of the Order)

This Order establishes, under section 21 of the Oil and Gas (Enterprise) Act 1982, a safety zone, having a radius of 500 metres from a specified point, around the installation specified in the Schedule to this Order and maintained in waters to which the section applies (these include territorial waters and waters in areas designated under section 1(7) of the Continental Shelf Act 1964 (c.29)).

Vessels (which for this purpose include hovercraft, submersible apparatus and installations in transit) are prohibited from entering or remaining in the safety zone except with the consent of the Secretary of State or in the circumstances mentioned in article 2(2) of the Order.

1987 No. 814

OFFSHORE INSTALLATIONS

The Offshore Installations (Safety Zones) (No. 30) Order 1987

Made	-	-	-	*6th May 1987*
Coming into force				*8th May 1987*

The Secretary of State, in exercise of the powers conferred on him by section 21(1), (2) and (3) of the Oil and Gas (Enterprise) Act 1982(a) (hereinafter referred to as "the Act"), and of all other powers enabling him in that behalf, hereby makes the following Order:–

1. This Order may be cited as the Offshore Installations (Safety Zones) (No. 30) Order 1987 and shall come into force on 8th May 1987.

2.—(1) A safety zone is hereby established around the installation specified in Column 1 of the Schedule hereto (being an installation maintained in waters to which section 21 of the Act(b) applies) having a radius of five hundred metres from the point as respects that installation which has the co-ordinates of latitude and longitude according to European Datum (1950) specified in Columns 2 and 3 of the Schedule.

(2) The prohibition under section 21(3) of the Act on a vessel entering or remaining in a safety zone without the consent of the Secretary of State shall not apply to a vessel entering or remaining in the safety zone established under paragraph (1) above –

> (a) in connection with the laying, inspection, testing, repair, alteration, renewal or removal of any submarine cable or pipe-line in or near that safety zone;

> (b) to provide services for, to transport persons or goods to or from, or under the authority of a government department to inspect, any installation in that safety zone;

> (c) if it is a vessel belonging to a general lighthouse authority performing duties relating to the safety of navigation;

> (d) in connection with the saving or attempted saving of life or property;

> (e) owing to stress of weather; or

> (f) when in distress.

Alick Buchanan-Smith
Minister of State, Department of Energy

6th May 1987

(a) 1982 c.23. (b) *See* section 21(9).

Article 2(1)   **SCHEDULE**

                                      SAFETY ZONE

| (1) | (2) | (3) |
Name or other designation of the offshore installation	*Latitude North*	*Longitude East*
Conoco/Britoil Loggs 49/16 P	53° 23′ 24.00″	02° 00′ 19.50″

EXPLANATORY NOTE

(This note is not part of the Order)

This Order establishes, under section 21 of the Oil and Gas (Enterprise) Act 1982, a safety zone, having a radius of 500 metres from a specified point, around the installation specified in the Schedule to this Order and maintained in waters to which the section applies (these include territorial waters and waters in areas designated under section 1(7) of the Continental Shelf Act 1964 (c.29)).

Vessels (which for this purpose include hovercraft, submersible apparatus and installations in transit) are prohibited from entering or remaining in the safety zone except with the consent of the Secretary of State or in the circumstances mentioned in article 2(2) of the Order.

STATUTORY INSTRUMENTS

1987 No. 820 (C.22)

PETROLEUM

The Petroleum Act 1987 (Commencement No. 1) Order 1987

Made - - - - 6th May 1987

The Secretary of State, in exercise of his powers under section 31(2) of the Petroleum Act 1987**(a)**, and of all other powers enabling him in that behalf, hereby makes the following Order:–

1. This Order may be cited as the Petroleum Act 1987 (Commencement No. 1) Order 1987.

2. The provisions of the Petroleum Act 1987 specified in the Schedule hereto shall come into force on 30th June 1987.

Alick Buchanan-Smith
Minister of State, Department of Energy

6th May 1987

SCHEDULE   Article 2

PROVISIONS OF THE PETROLEUM ACT 1987 COMING INTO FORCE ON 30th JUNE 1987

Provisions of the Act	Subject matter of provisions
Section 17	Amendment of model clauses incorporated in existing licences.
Section 18	Amendment of model clauses for incorporation in future licences.
Schedule 1	Amendment of existing licences.
Schedule 2	Amendment of model clauses.

(a) 1987 c.12.

EXPLANATORY NOTE

(This note is not part of the Order)

This Order brings into force those provisions of the Petroleum Act 1987 which amend the model clauses of existing and future petroleum licences. The amendments will therefore apply in relation to the chargeable period for petroleum royalties which commences on 1st July 1987, and subsequent chargeable periods.

STATUTORY INSTRUMENTS

1987 No. 821 (L.3)

COUNTY COURTS
SUPREME COURT OF ENGLAND AND WALES

FUNDS

The Court Funds Rules 1987

Made - - - -		*7th May 1987*
Laid before Parliament		*11th May 1987*
Coming into force		*1st June 1987*

COURT FUNDS RULES 1987

ARRANGEMENT OF RULES

Preliminary (rules 1–5)

TABLE OF CONTENTS

PART V

Range of Investments

PART VI

Dealings with Foreign Currencies

PART VII

Payment, Transfer and Delivery of Funds out of Court

PART VIII

Conversion, Allotment and Write-off of Securities

PART IX

National Debt Commissioners

PART X

Unclaimed Funds in Court

PART XI

Certificates in Respect of Funds in Court

COURT FUNDS RULES 1987

The Lord Chancellor, in exercise of the powers conferred on him by section 38(7) of the Administration of Justice Act 1982**(a)** and with the concurrence of the Treasury, hereby makes the following Rules.

PRELIMINARY

Citation, commencement and revocation

1.—(1) These Rules may be cited as the Court Funds Rules 1987 and shall come into force on 1st June 1987.

(2) The Rules specified in the schedule to these Rules are hereby revoked, except that those Rules shall continue to apply to such extent as may be necessary for giving effect to any order or request made before 1st June 1987.

Interpretation

2.—(1) Unless the context otherwise requires, expressions used in these Rules shall have the same meaning as in the Rules of the Supreme Court 1965**(b)**, or the County Court Rules 1981**(c)**, as the case may be, and those Rules shall be referred to in these Rules as the "RSC" and the "CCR" respectively.

(2) The following expressions shall have the following meanings:

"Accountant General" means the Accountant General of the Supreme Court or an officer appointed by him under rule 4;

"Appointed Officer" means an officer appointed by the Accountant General under rule 4(1);

"Authenticated" means authenticated with the impression of a stamp issued by the Accountant General;

"Authorised Officer" means an officer authorised by the Accountant General under rule 4(2);

"The Bank" means the Bank of England or such bank or banks as may be designated by the Lord Chancellor with the concurrence of the Treasury;

(a) 1982 c.53.
(b) S.I. 1965/1776, as amended.
(c) S.I. 1981/1687, as amended.

"Basic Account" means a deposit account bearing interest as established under rule 26;

"Capital Fund" means the common investment fund of that name established by the Common Investment Fund Scheme 1965(a);

"Carry over" means to transfer a fund in Court or any part thereof from one account to another in the books of the Court Funds Office;

"Central Investment Branch" means the central investment branch of the Public Trust Office;

"Common Investment Fund" means a fund established by a scheme made under section 42 of the Administration of Justice Act 1982;

"Court" includes, unless otherwise specified, the following:–

The Supreme Court
Any county court
The Employment Appeal Tribunal
The Lands Tribunal;

"Any county court" means a judge or registrar exercising the powers of a county court in chambers as well as in open court;

"Court Funds Office" means the Court Funds Division of the Public Trust Office;

"Court Funds Office account" means the cash account of the Accountant General at the Bank;

"Duty" means inheritance tax, or capital transfer tax, or estate, succession or legacy duty;

"Employment Appeal Tribunal" means the tribunal established under section 87 of the Employment Protection Act 1975(b);

"Foreign Currency" means currency other than sterling;

"Fund" or "Fund in Court" has the meaning assigned by section 47 of the Administration of Justice Act 1982;

"Holding" means the units in any one common investment fund purchased on any one valuation day and held in respect of a particular long-term investment account;

"Interest" means interest accruing on funds and includes dividends;

"Interest bearing account" means an account of funds established under rule 26;

"Lodge in court" means pay or transfer into court or deposit in court;

"Lodgment Schedule" means a schedule to an order directing funds to be lodged to the account of the Accountant General;

"Master" means a Master of the Supreme Court or Master of the Court of Protection and includes the Admiralty Registrar, a Registrar of the Family Division, a Registrar in Bankruptcy, a District Registrar, a county court Registrar and the Registrar of the Employment Appeal Tribunal;

"Master of the Court of Protection" means the Master of the Court of Protection, the Public Trustee or any other officer nominated by the Lord Chancellor to act for the purposes of Part VII of the Mental Health Act 1983(c);

"National Savings Stock" means stock registered on the National Savings Stock Register;

"Order" means an order or judgment of the High Court or Court of Appeal or a county court, an order, certificate or direction under the seal of the Court of Protection, an order under the seal of the Employment Appeal Tribunal or an order under the seal of the Lands Tribunal;

"Patient" means a person who, by reason of mental disorder within the meaning of Part VII of the Mental Health Act 1983 is incapable of managing and administering his property and affairs;

"Payment Schedule" means a schedule to an order directing the payment of funds from the account of the Accountant General;

"Person under disability" means a person who is a minor or a patient;

"Proper Officer" means the Registrar of the Employment Appeal Tribunal or of the Lands Tribunal and the Chief Clerk of a Supreme Court Office, a county court,

(a) S.I. 1965/1467.
(b) 1975 c.71.
(c) 1983 c.20.

a District Registry, the Principal Registry of the Family Division or a district probate Registry, an officer appointed by the Public Trustee, the Secretary of the Principal Registry of the Family Division and any other officer of the Court acting on behalf of a Chief Clerk or the Secretary of the Principal Registry of the Family Division as the case may be, in accordance with directions given by the Lord Chancellor;

"Securities" includes units purchased and investments effected by placing money to special accounts;

"Special Account" means an investment account bearing interest as established under rule 26;

"Suitors' money" means money in a county court or to be brought into a county court other than a fund;

"Taxing Officer" means any person who by virtue of RSC Order 62, rule 19 or CCR Order 38, rule 2(2) has power to tax costs;

"Unit" means one of the shares into which a common investment fund is treated as being divided.

(3) Unless the context otherwise requires, a rule or Part referred to by number means the rule or Part so numbered in these Rules.

Court Funds Office

3. The office of the Accountant General shall continue to be known as the Court Funds Office.

Discharge of Accountant General's functions

4.—(1) The functions of the Accountant General under these Rules may be discharged, to such extent as he may direct, by any officer appointed by him.

(2) The Accountant General, with the approval of the Treasury, may from time to time authorise in writing any officer to authenticate on his behalf any direction issued by him for the purpose of giving effect to these Rules and such authorisation may be either general or in respect of any particular class or classes of transaction.

Power to authorise use of forms

5. Nothing in these Rules shall prejudice the power of the Accountant General to authorise and require the use of such forms as he may consider appropriate for any purpose.

PART I

AUTHORITIES FOR LODGMENT, PAYMENT OUT, TRANSFER ETC

Lodgment Schedule

6.—(1) Where lodgment of funds in court is directed by an order or authorised by a Master, the Accountant General shall not make such lodgment until he has received:–

    (i) in proceedings in the Chancery Division or in the Court of Protection, a lodgment schedule; or

    (ii) in proceedings in the Queen's Bench Division, Family Division, or any other court or tribunal, a copy of the order

but in the case of proceedings mentioned in sub-paragraph (ii) he may refuse to make such lodgment until he has received a lodgment schedule.

(2) Where proceedings in which money has been lodged in court are ordered to be transferred to another court, the proper officer of the transferring court shall so advise the Accountant General in writing.

Payment Schedule

7.—(1) Where an order directs the manner in which any fund in court is to be dealt with by the Accountant General, a payment schedule shall be lodged with him.

(2) Subject to paragraph (3) a payment schedule signed and authenticated by a proper officer shall be sufficient authority to the Accountant General to deal with a fund in accordance with the schedule.

(3) Where money is lodged in court in proceedings under section 84 of the Law of Property Act 1925(a) and directions are given by the Lands Tribunal instructing the Accountant General to deal with that fund, such directions shall be sufficient authority to the Accountant General to deal with the fund accordingly.

Preparation and amendment of Schedules

8.—(1) In any proceedings other than proceedings in the Court of Protection, the Lands Tribunal or the Employment Appeal Tribunal, where an order is made for the lodgment of or dealing with funds in court, the party having carriage of the order shall prepare and submit the lodgment or payment schedule to the appropriate court office for authentication.

(2) Without prejudice to paragraph (1), the proper officer of a court in which an order has been made for the lodgment of or dealing with funds in court, may prepare the lodgment or payment schedule where he considers it appropriate to do so.

(3) The proper officer of the court in question shall sign and authenticate the lodgment or payment schedule and forward it to the Accountant General.

(4) Any amendment to a schedule needed to correct a clerical or accidental error or omission shall be signed by the proper officer.

Certificate of a Master or Taxing Master

9.—(1) Where a payment schedule directs a Master to ascertain and certify a sum to be dealt with by the Accountant General or directs that costs shall be taxed and paid out of funds in court, the Master or Taxing Officer shall certify:—

    (i) the amount ascertained or the amount of the taxed costs (including the fees of taxation); and

    (ii) the name and address of the person to whom payment is to be made;

and shall send the certificate to the Accountant General in the approved form.

(2) A certificate issued by a Master or Taxing Officer following a taxation shall, unless described as an interim certificate, be deemed to include all the costs directed to be taxed and paid out of funds in court.

Particulars of interest ordered to be paid as directed in judgment or order

10.—(1) Where interest is directed by an order to be paid on any sum in court, the payment schedule shall state:—

    (i) the rate per cent at which interest is payable;

    (ii) the date from which and, if known, the date to which interest is to be calculated;

    (iii) whether the interest should be paid with or without deduction of income tax; and

    (iv) the amount of such interest, if ascertainable when the payment schedule is drawn up.

(2) If the amount of interest cannot be stated in the payment schedule, then either:—

    (i) the schedule shall direct that the amount be ascertained and certified by a Master; or

    (ii) the party having carriage of the order shall agree in writing with the Accountant General the amount of interest.

(a) 1925 c.20.

(3) Whenever interest is required to be calculated for a period which is, or includes, a period of less than a year, the interest shall be calculated on a daily basis in respect of that period.

Regular payments

11. Where a payment schedule directs that regular payments (not being interest payable as it accrues due) are to be made by the Accountant General, the schedule shall state the dates on which payments are to be made and whether the payments are to be made with or without deduction of income tax at the basic rate.

Funds on which duty is payable

12. Where a fund in court is subject to payment of duty but the order relating to it does not provide for such payment, the payment schedule shall state that the fund is subject to duty; and if the payment schedule directs the carry over of any part of a fund subject to duty, the words "subject to duty" shall be written boldly at the top of the first page of the schedule relating to the account to which the fund is to be carried over.

PART II

LODGMENT OF FUNDS IN COURT

Accountant General's directions for payment to the Bank

13. Money shall not be paid directly to the Bank save on the direction of the Accountant General.

Lodgment on receipt of a Lodgment Schedule

14.—(1) Approval for the lodgment of funds in court shall be given by the Accountant General on receipt of a lodgment schedule in proceedings:–

    (i) in the Court of Protection and in the Employment Appeal Tribunal;

    (ii) in the Chancery Division of the High Court, where the lodgment is:–

        (a) directed by a lodgment schedule; or

        (b) made under the Life Assurance Companies (Payment into Court) Act 1896**(a)** or the Trustee Act 1925**(b)**, and the lodgment schedule is accompanied by a copy of an affidavit filed in accordance with RSC Order 92; or

    (iii) in a county court where money is paid into court under the Trustee Act 1925 in accordance with CCR Order 49, rule 20, and the lodgment schedule has been authenticated by the proper officer.

(2) Where the Accountant General receives from a company a notice of claim after the making of the affidavit required under RSC Order 92, rule 1, he shall note the account accordingly.

Lodgment on receipt of a written request

15.—(1) Approval for the lodgment of funds in court shall be given by the Accountant General on receipt of a written request in proceedings:–

    (i) in the Queen's Bench or Family Divisions of the High Court where the request is accompanied by a sealed copy order directing the lodgment, or where in Admiralty proceedings the lodgment is made under RSC Order 75, rule 24, and the request is made by the Admiralty Marshal;

    (ii) in the Chancery Division of the High Court where the lodgment is made in proceedings:–

(a) 1896 c.8.
(b) 1925 c.19.

(a) under section 84 of the Law of Property Act 1925; or
(b) under the Trustee Act 1925 where the written request is signed by or on behalf of the personal representative; or
(c) under any enactment other than those mentioned in rule 14(1)(ii) or in this paragraph where it is accompanied by the appropriate document authorising lodgment where specific authority to lodge is required by the relevant enactment;

(iii) in any Division of the High Court where the lodgment is made under RSC Order 22, rule 1:—

(a) in satisfaction of a claim and the request is accompanied by a copy of the writ and the notice of payment into court; or
(b) a defence of tender is pleaded and the request is accompanied by a copy of the writ and a copy of the defence;

(iv) in the Admiralty Registry if the request is sealed by the Registry.

(2) The Accountant General may give approval for lodgment of funds in court notwithstanding that a request is not accompanied by a sealed copy order directing lodgment in accordance with paragraph (1)(i), provided that he is satisfied that such an order has been made and the reason why a copy of the order does not accompany the request is stated in the request.

Lodgment of money in Court

16.—(1) Money to be lodged in court in accordance with rules 14 or 15, save money representing the proceeds of sale or redemption of National Savings Stock, shall be paid into the Court Funds Office, either directly or in accordance with paragraph (2).

(2) Where money is paid into a District Registry it shall be forwarded within one working day of the date of receipt to the Court Funds Office, together with a request in the approved form giving the full circumstances under which the lodgment has been made.

(3) Where money is paid under paragraphs (1) or (2), cheques or other instruments shall be made payable to the Accountant General of the Supreme Court.

(4) Money received in the Court Funds Office shall be paid into the Bank for the credit of the Accountant General's account as soon as practicable.

(5) Lodgments of money which are not required to be paid into the Court Funds Office under this rule shall be made directly to the Bank to the credit of the Accountant General's account.

(6) The effective date of lodgment shall be:—

(i) in the case of cash or a banker's draft, the date of its receipt in the Court Funds Office or, where paragraph (2) applies, in the District Registry;
(ii) in the case of a cheque or instrument other than one subject to sub-paragraph (1) the date of its receipt in the Court Funds Office or District Registry as the case may be or such later date as the Accountant General may determine;
(iii) in the case of a lodgment to which paragraph (5) applies, the date certified by the Bank as that on which the money was placed to an account for the credit of the Accountant General.

(7) Any person who desires or is directed to pay money into a county court under any statute and has complied with the requirements of the relevant County Court Rules shall pay the money into the appropriate court office, by a cheque or other instrument made payable to the Accountant General of the Supreme Court which shall be forwarded to the Accountant General within one working day of the date of receipt.

Securities transferable by delivery and deposit of effects

17.—(1) The lodgment in the Supreme Court of securities transferable by delivery and the deposit of effects shall be made either by delivery to the Court Funds Office or, if the Accountant General so directs, by delivery to the Bank.

(2) Where lodgment under paragraph (1) is made by delivery to the Bank:–

    (i) effects so delivered shall be secured in locked boxes or otherwise to the satisfaction of the Bank, and any person delivering effects shall, if the Bank so requires, permit them to be inspected in his presence by an officer of the Bank; and

    (ii) the Bank shall give a written receipt for the delivery of any securities or effects.

(3) Any person who deposits effects in court in accordance with these Rules shall provide the Accountant General with an inventory of those effects signed and certified by him as a true and accurate record.

(4) Any person who desires or is directed to deposit securities in a county court under any statute, and has complied with the requirements of the relevant County Court Rules, shall deposit the securities with the proper officer who shall give the depositor a receipt of the deposit and shall forward the security certificate or certificates to the Accountant General.

Return of Lodgment directions

18.   Where:–

    (i) money lodged directly with the Bank has been received and credited to the Accountant General's account; or

    (ii) securities transferable by delivery or effects have been delivered to the Bank; or

    (iii) securities (other than those transferable by delivery) have been transferred into the Accountant General's name in the books of the Bank or in the books of a company,

the Bank or company, as the case may be, shall certify on the lodgment direction issued under rule 14 that funds have been lodged and shall send it to the Court Funds Office.

Payment of suitors' money into a county court

19.   Suitors' money to be paid into a county court may be paid by post or otherwise into the court office, and payment may be made during office hours on any day on which the office is open and the proper officer shall give a receipt for it.

20.—(1) Subject to paragraph (2), all monies payable under a judgment or order of a county court shall be paid into court.

(2) Paragraph (1) shall not apply to costs payable under any order or where the order made in a matrimonial cause as defined by section 32 of the Matrimonial and Family Proceedings Act 1984**(a)**, otherwise provides.

21.   Money received under rule 19 which is not required for making authorised payments shall be paid by the proper officer into the cash account within one working day of the day of receipt.

22.   An officer of a county court who receives money under the process of the court shall give a written receipt for every sum so received in the form prescribed.

23.   Money transmitted from one court to another pursuant to County Court Rules shall be transmitted to the proper officer of the receiving court by crossed payable order drawn in favour of Her Majesty's Paymaster General.

24.   Where money has been paid into court in an action or matter proceeding in the High Court, and the action or matter is transferred to a county court, the proper officer of the county court shall notify the Accountant General accordingly and, on receipt of such a notice, the Accountant General shall deal with it as if it had been transferred to him under rule 31.

(a) 1984 c.42.

PART III

APPROPRIATION

25.—(1) Where a defendant has lodged money in court in accordance with RSC Order 14 as a condition of liberty to defend and he desires to appropriate the whole or any part of such money in satisfaction of the whole or any part of the plaintiff's claim pursuant to RSC Order 22, rule 8, he shall lodge with the Accountant General a notice of appropriation in the approved form.

(2) Where a defendant wishes to appropriate money which has been paid into a county court and placed to a basic account under rule 31(4) he shall notify the proper officer and the Accountant General accordingly in the approved form.

(3) On receipt of a notice of appropriation the Accountant General shall note the relevant account accordingly and shall withdraw the sum mentioned in the notice from the basic account.

(4) If the plaintiff does not give notice of acceptance within the time limited by the RSC or the CCR, as the case may be, the Accountant General shall place the money in the basic account 21 days after he has received the notice of appropriation.

(5) Where, before appropriation, interest has accrued on the money in question the interest may be included in the appropriation, and this rule shall apply to the interest in the same way as it applies to the money lodged.

PART IV

PLACING OF MONEY OTHER THAN FOREIGN CURRENCY TO AN INTEREST BEARING ACCOUNT

Establishment of interest bearing accounts

26. There shall be established the following two interest bearing accounts, namely a basic account (that is to say, a deposit account) and a special account (that is to say, an investment account) to which shall accrue, in accordance with these Rules, interest derived from the transfer to, and investment by, the National Debt Commissioners of the money placed to all the accounts of those kinds.

Interest on money placed to an interest bearing account

27.—(1) The rate at which interest on money placed to a basic account or a special account is to accrue shall be as prescribed from time to time by a direction made by the Lord Chancellor with the concurrence of the Treasury.

(2) Interest on money placed to a basic account or a special account shall accrue from day to day from the day on which the money is placed to the account until the day preceding its withdrawal from the account.

(3) Accrued interest shall be credited:–
>   (i) on the capital sum when it is withdrawn from the account; or
>   (ii) on transfer of the capital sum from a basic account to a special account; and
>   (iii) on 31st March and 30th September each year in respect of money placed to a basic account and on 31st May and 30th November each year in respect of money placed to a special account.

(4) Accrued interest shall be credited without deduction of income tax.

Time for placing money to an interest bearing account

28.—(1) Subject to the provisions of this part of the Rules and to any direction of the court, all money (including interest) shall be placed to a basic account or, in the case of a person under disability, to a special account, on the day on which the schedule or other authority is received in the Courts Fund Office or on the effective date of lodgment of the money, whichever is the later.

(2) Where judgment is given in favour of a person under disability, or settlement of his claim is approved by the court, the money to which he is entitled shall, subject to any directions of the court, be placed to a special account in his name as at the date of the judgment or on the effective date of lodgment of the money, whichever is the later, without further authority.

(3) Interest shall not accrue from a date earlier than that on which the money is placed to an interest bearing account in accordance with this rule.

Money not to be placed to a basic account

29. Money, including interest, shall not be placed to a basic account where the money:–

> (i) has been directed by an order or other authority to be dealt with other than by being placed to a basic account; or
>
> (ii) has been carried over to an account of unclaimed balances under rule 57; or
>
> (iii) stood to the credit of a fund in court before 1st October 1965, without a request that it be placed on deposit; or
>
> (iv) was paid into court in satisfaction of a claim before 1st April 1983, without a direction that it be placed on deposit; or
>
> (v) amounts to a sum which is less than £10.

Money to be placed to a special account

30. Money, including interest, shall only be placed to a special account where the person entitled to it is under a disability and it amounts to a sum which is not less than £10.

Money paid in satisfaction, etc.

31.—(1) Where money is lodged in the Supreme Court under RSC Order 22, rule 1 or is appropriated under RSC Order 22, rule 8 in satisfaction of a claim and is not accepted within the time limited by RSC Order 22, rule 3(1), it shall be placed to a basic account 21 days after the effective date of lodgment or appropriation.

(2) Where money is paid into a county court in satisfaction of a claim and the plaintiff has not given notice of acceptance of the payment within the time limited by the CCR, the proper officer shall remit the amount of the payment to the Court Funds Office 22 days after the effective date of payment into that court.

(3) Where money is paid into a county court in such circumstances that it is to await the outcome of an order of court, whether it is paid into court as a condition of obtaining relief or otherwise, the proper officer shall remit the amount of the payment to the Court Funds Office on, or as soon as practicable after, the effective date of payment into that court.

(4) Where money is remitted under paragraphs (2) or (3) the remittance shall be accompanied by a notice stating the date and the reason why the money was paid into court, and on receipt of such a remittance and notice in the Court Funds Office, the Accountant General shall place the money to a basic account.

(5) Where the plaintiff is under a disability money lodged or paid into court under paragraphs (1) or (2) shall be placed to a basic account in any event, whether or not he has accepted it, until the claim is determined or settlement is reached, unless the court otherwise directs.

Interest on money paid in satisfaction

32.—(1) Subject to paragraphs (4) and (5), interest on money remitted to the Court Funds Office under rule 31(2) shall start to accrue 21 days after the effective date of payment into the county court.

(2) Subject to paragraphs (4) and (5), interest on money remitted to the Court Funds Office under rule 31(3) shall start to accrue from the effective date of payment into the county court.

(3) Where a court determines a claim, or, as the case may be, approves a settlement on behalf of a person under a disability, any interest which has accrued on the money in court shall be dealt with as the court orders.

(4) Where money placed to a basic account under rule 31(1) is accepted within the time limited by RSC Order 22, rule 3(1), no interest shall be payable in respect of the period between lodgment or appropriation, or where there has been more than one lodgment or appropriation between the latest lodgment or appropriation, and the date of acceptance.

(5) Where money has been placed to a basic account under rule 31(4) but it appears that the plaintiff, having accepted the money within the time limited by the CCR, has become entitled to have it paid out to him, no interest shall be payable on that money in respect of the period between lodgment, or where there has been more than one lodgment, between the last lodgment and the date of acceptance.

(6) Where money appropriated under the CCR in satisfaction of a claim is accepted within the time limit, no interest shall be payable in respect of the period between appropriation, or where there has been more than one appropriation between the latest appropriation, and the date of acceptance.

Withdrawal of money from an interest bearing account

33. Money shall only be withdrawn from an interest bearing account where the money, including any interest which has accrued at the time of withdrawal, is required to be withdrawn for the purpose of giving effect to a direction of the court or these Rules; provided that such interest shall not be used if directed by the court to be otherwise dealt with.

PART V

RANGE OF INVESTMENTS

Range of investments

34.—(1) Subject to paragraph (3), money under the control of, or subject to an order of the court, may be invested or reinvested by the Accountant General in accordance with these Rules, in the following ways:–

    (i) it may be placed to a basic account or, in the case of a person under a disability, to a special account;

   (ii) it may be transferred to such of the funds established by common investment schemes as may be specified;

  (iii) it may be invested in any manner specified in Part I, paragraphs 1 to 10 and 12 of Part II and paragraphs 2 and 3 of Part III of Schedule 1 to the Trustee Investment Act 1961(a), as supplemented by the provisions of Part IV of that Schedule.

(2) Money subject to an order of the court may be invested or reinvested by the Accountant General in accordance with instructions received by him from the Central Investment Branch.

(3) Money under the control of or subject to an order of the Court of Protection may be invested or reinvested by the Accountant General in such investments as that court may direct.

(a) 1961 c.62.

Time for investment

35. Subject to the provisions of Part IV and this Part of the Rules and to any directions of the court, money, including interest, shall be invested as soon as it is available.

Amount for investment

36.—(1) Notwithstanding rule 34, no sum of money or interest shall be invested in any case where in the view of the Accountant General the cost of investment, by way of commission or otherwise, would be disproportionate to the amount of money involved.

(2) Any money which is not invested shall be placed, in the case of a person under a disability, to a special account and in all other cases to a basic account and shall be drawn from the account and invested when it, together with the interest credited to it, and further sums of money or interest credited to the account which are required to be invested in the same manner, amount to a sum in respect of which the cost of investment is not disproportionate.

Investment in Common Investment Fund

37.—(1) Where funds are required to be invested in Common Investment Fund units or such units are required to be realised, the purchases and sales shall be effected on the first available valuation day.

(2) Funds shall not be directed to be invested in Capital Fund Units unless the authority giving the direction is satisfied that the funds are likely to remain so invested for at least five years: provided that this paragraph shall not apply in any case where there is an express request for investment in Capital Fund Units by or on behalf of one or more of the persons interested in the fund, or, if no such person is ascertained or traceable, by the person who pays the funds into court.

PART VI

DEALINGS WITH FOREIGN CURRENCIES

38.—(1) Foreign currency may only be lodged in court when:–
    (i) it is lodged under RSC Order 22, rule 1 in satisfaction of a claim for a debt or liquidated demand, and is in the currency in which the claim is made; or
    (ii) the court so directs or permits.

(2) Foreign currency lodged in accordance with paragraph (1) shall be paid into court in the manner approved by the Accountant General.

39.—(1) Where foreign currency is lodged in court, the court may direct that it shall be placed in an interest bearing account in that currency or any other currency, and any interest shall accrue from the date of the order or the date of placing it in the account, whichever is the later; and the Accountant General shall deal with the interest as the court may direct.

(2) Any charges incurred by placing foreign currency to an account shall be deducted from the currency so placed or from the accrued interest, as may be appropriate.

(3) Where income from a security in court is received in a foreign currency, the court may give such direction as it thinks fit, and in the absence of such direction the foreign currency shall be converted into sterling and invested in accordance with the provisions of Part IV.

PART VII

PAYMENT, TRANSFER AND DELIVERY OF FUNDS OUT OF COURT

Payments out of money by post and identification of payees

40.—(1) In this rule the person entitled to the payment out of money lodged in court is referred to as the payee.

(2) Subject to paragraphs (3) and (4) below, the payment out of money lodged in court shall be made by the Accountant General, by a cheque crossed generally, by post as follows:–

    (i) where the address of the payee is stated in the Payment Schedule or supplementary authority and that schedule or authority is dated not more than one year prior to the date on which the Accountant General is able to make payment, he shall make payment to the payee at the address so stated;

    (ii) where the Payment Schedule or supplementary authority is dated more than one year prior to the date on which the Accountant General is able to make payment, he shall make payment on receipt of a written request from the payee in the approved form.

(3) On receipt of a written request from the payee or a donee under a power of attorney given by the payee the Accountant General may make payment to a bank in the United Kingdom for the credit of the account of the payee at that bank or at a bank in the country in which he resides.

(4) The Accountant General may, if he thinks fit, refuse to make a payment until he is satisfied as to the identity and entitlement of any person claiming to be the payee and the Accountant General may refuse to make a remittance by post in any individual case and may require the personal attendance of the payee at the Court Funds Office or a court office as a condition of payment.

Payment etc. after a change of name or style

41. Where a person entitled to payment of a fund in court changes his name or style before the fund is paid, transferred or delivered to him, the Accountant General shall, except where payment is to be made to the person as Receiver under Part VII of the Mental Health Act 1983, require evidence of the change before dealing with the fund.

Payment pursuant to direction of the Court of Protection

42. Where a patient is entitled to a fund in court (other than pursuant to an order made under Part VII of the Mental Health Act 1983) the Accountant General shall, on receipt of a direction from the Master of the Court of Protection, either pay the money to the patient's Receiver or carry it over to such account as the Master may direct.

Payment etc. to representatives of deceased persons

43.—(1) Where a person entitled to a fund in court either in his own right or as sole or sole surviving executor dies, the Accountant General may, where the fund exceeds £5,000, pay it to the personal representative of the deceased on production of a grant of probate or office copy thereof, or, where the deceased was entitled to the fund in his own right, letters of administration in respect of the deceased's estate.

(2) Where a person entitled to a fund in court in his own right dies intestate and no grant of administration has been issued, the Accountant General may, where the assets of the deceased (including the fund in court and after deduction of debts and funeral expenses) do not exceed £5,000, pay the fund to the person who appears to him to have the prior right to a grant of administration of the estate, on lodgment in the Court Funds Office of a written declaration of kinship.

(3) Where two or more persons were entitled to payment of a fund in court as personal representatives and any of them dies before the fund is dealt with, the Accountant General may pay the fund to the surviving personal representatives on proof of the

death of the deceased personal representative; and where the fund does not exceed £5,000 the Accountant General may, unless a court otherwise directs, pay the fund to any one of them.

Payment out without order of money lodged in satisfaction

44.—(1) In this rule and in rule 45 a person in respect of whose cause of action a sum has been paid into court in satisfaction, whether by way of claim or counterclaim, is referred to as a plaintiff and a person against whom such a cause of action lies is referred to as a defendant.

(2) The Accountant General shall, on receipt of a written request, pay by cheque to the plaintiff money lodged in court in satisfaction of a claim, or appropriated in accordance with rule 25, and accepted by him in accordance with Rules of Court: provided that where a solicitor is acting for the plaintiff in the proceedings in which the money was lodged or appropriated by virtue of a legal aid certificate issued in accordance with the Legal Aid (General) Regulations 1980**(a)**, the Accountant General shall pay the money to that solicitor, or to the Law Society if there is no longer a solicitor acting.

(3) In the case of proceedings in a District Registry, the plaintiff shall, when he sends the written request to the Court Funds Office, send a copy of it to the District Registry in question.

(4) The Accountant General shall not make any payment under paragraph (1) where:–

    (i) money has been lodged by one, or some, only off several defendants sued jointly or in the alternative, unless the plaintiff discontinues the action against all the other defendants and those defendants consent in writing to the payment, and a copy of the notice of discontinuance and the written consent of each consenting defendant required by RSC Order 22, rule 4 or CCR Order 11, rule 4(3), as the case may be, is lodged with the Accountant General; or

    (ii) a defence of tender before action has been pleaded; or

    (iii) the claim is made by, or on behalf of, a minor or a patient; or

    (iv) money has been lodged in proceedings under the Fatal Accidents Act 1976**(b)** and the Law Reform (Miscellaneous Provisions) Act 1934**(c)**, or under the first mentioned Act alone where more than one person is entitled to the money; or

    (v) money has been lodged in court, or money in court has been increased by a further lodgment, and has been accepted after the hearing of the action has begun, except in circumstances provided for under RSC Order 22, rule 3.

Payment out to defendant without order

45. Where money lodged or appropriated by the defendant in satisfaction of the whole of the plaintiff's claim has been accepted and paid to the plaintiff in accordance with rule 44, the Accountant General shall forthwith pay any accrued interest remaining in court in respect of that claim to the defendant but no interest shall be payable to the defendant after the date on which the plaintiff serves notice of acceptance.

Payment out of interest on securities

46. Where securities are lodged in court under rule 15 or money lodged under that rule is invested, any interest which accrues shall (subject to any contrary provision contained in the relevant enactment) be paid by the Accountant General to the person in whose name the lodgment was made.

Transfer or delivery of securities

47.—(1) Subject to paragraph (2) where pursuant to directions of the court or under these Rules the Accountant General is required to transfer or deliver any securities or

(a) S.I. 1980/1894, as amended.
(b) 1976 c.30.
(c) 1934 c.41.

effects held in his name he shall issue directions accordingly which shall be sufficient authority for the transfer or delivery and, in the case of a transfer of securities on sale, for the Bank to receive the proceeds of sale.

(2) The directions of the Accountant General shall not be required for the transfer of National Savings Stock, on sale or otherwise.

Charges on purchase or sale of securities

48. Except where rule 34 applies and subject to any directions of the court:–

(i) where money in court is invested in the purchase of securities, the payment for the purchase shall include all applicable charges; and

(ii) where securities in court are sold, all applicable charges shall be deducted from the proceeds of sale:

provided that, if the schedule directing a purchase or sale also directs that charges are not to be deducted from the fund in court, the transaction shall not be completed until such charges have been paid either to the stockbroker or to the Accountant General, as the case may be.

Application of funds dealt with before receipt of Payment Schedule

49. Unless otherwise directed by the court, where an order has been made dealing with a fund and, after the date of the order but before the Payment Schedule relating to it is received in the Court Funds Office, interest has accrued or money and interest have been dealt with in accordance with a previous direction of the court or under these Rules, the part of the fund attributable to accrued interest or to money or interest shall be treated as follows:–

(i) interest on securities directed to be transferred, delivered or carried over shall be dealt with as the securities are directed to be dealt with under the Payment Schedule;

(ii) interest which has accrued on securities directed to be sold shall be dealt with as the proceeds of sale are directed to be dealt with under the Payment Schedule, except where the sale is to raise a specified sum of money, when the interest is included with the capital;

(iii) where interest which has accrued on securities directed to be transferred, delivered or carried over has been invested in the purchase of further securities, the securities so purchased and any interest on them shall be dealt with as the original securities are directed to be dealt with;

(iv) where interest which has accrued on securities directed to be sold has been invested in the purchase of further securities, the securities so purchased shall be sold and the proceeds of sale added to the proceeds of the original securities;

(v) money or accrued interest which has been placed to a basic or special account shall be withdrawn and, together with any interest credited on withdrawal, applied as directed by the Payment Schedule: provided that where such money is directed to be invested, any interest credited on withdrawal shall be applied as interest accruing on the investment is directed to be applied.

Payment of suitors' money out of a county court

50.—(1) Subject to the provisions of this rule, the proper officer of each county court shall appoint a day in the week on which all payments out of court shall be made, and may appoint a different day from time to time.

(2) In each week on the appointed day the proper officer shall, without demand, pay to each entitled person all money to which that person has become entitled since the appointed day in the previous week.

(3) Money paid out of court under paragraph (2) shall be paid by crossed payable order to the person entitled to it or to his solicitor and the proper officer shall, at the same time, furnish him with a statement of the money so paid.

(4) Notwithstanding anything in this rule, the proper officer may, on request, pay money out of court to the person who he is satisfied is entitled to it on a day other than the appointed day.

Specially created account

51.—(1) In apportioning to any account the interest received in respect of securities the Accountant General shall exclude all fractions of one penny and shall carry over the aggregate of such fractions to a specially created account.

(2) The Accountant General shall from time to time transfer to the cash account of Her Majesty's Paymaster General, for the credit of the Administration of Justice: England and Wales (Lord Chancellor's Department) Vote all sums standing to the specially created account.

PART VIII

CONVERSION, ALLOTMENT AND WRITE-OFF OF SECURITIES

Application to the court concerning conversion and allotment

52.   Where a question has arisen as to an allotment or conversion of securities which have been paid into court under section 63 of the Trustee Act 1925, or in any other case in which he considers it appropriate because no application will otherwise be made, the Accountant General may apply to the court for directions as to how the securities should be dealt with.

Conversion and allotment of securities

53.—(1) Where a security in court has been converted into another security the Accountant General shall write-off the original security from the account to which it is standing and shall place to that account the whole, or where appropriate a proportionate part, of the substituted security and shall, so far as practicable and unless otherwise directed by the court, deal with the substituted security and any interest on it in the same manner as the original security and interest.

(2) Where a security in court is paid off and the money received is invested or placed to an interest bearing account, the security purchased or money in the account and any interest on it shall, unless the court otherwise directs, be dealt with by the Accountant General in the same manner as the original security and interest.

(3) Where an allotment is made in respect of a security in court the Accountant General may:-

> (i) credit the whole, or where appropriate a proportionate part, of the allotment to the account of the original security if the allotment is fully paid; or
>
> (ii) sell the allotment and credit the whole, or a proportionate part, of the proceeds of sale to that account or otherwise as the court may direct if the allotment is not fully paid;
>
> (iii) sell any non-apportionable shares and apportion such proceeds as nearly as practicable to the appropriate account.

Arrangements with the Bank over paid off securities, etc.

54.—(1) Where bearer or similar bonds or securities deposited at the Bank to the credit of the Accountant General are being paid off, the Bank shall take the necessary steps to receive the principal money and interest due and shall inform the Accountant General in writing of the amounts of the securities paid off and of the principal money and interest received.

(2) Where the interest on securities in court is payable on the presentation of coupons in a series and the last coupon of any such series has been presented and paid, the Bank shall take the necessary steps to obtain a new series of coupons.

Securities of dissolved companies

55. Where a company has been wound up and the Accountant General has received:–

(i) written notice from the liquidator or from the Department of Trade that no assets are or will be distributable in respect of the securities of the company; and

(ii) written notice from the Registrar of the Companies Registration Office that the company has been dissolved;

he shall withdraw from the Bank the certificate representing any security in that company and shall write-off any such security from the account to which it stands.

PART IX

NATIONAL DEBT COMMISSIONERS

National Debt Commissioners

56.—(1) Where, in the opinion of the Accountant General, the cash balance in his account at the Bank exceeds the amount that he requires to satisfy current demands, he shall remit the excess to the National Debt Commissioners; and where, in his opinion the balance is insufficient to meet such demands, the Commissioners shall remit to that account such amount as the Accountant General may in writing request.

(2) As soon as practicable after half-yearly interest accruing on money placed to an interest bearing account has been credited to the appropriate account in accordance with these Rules, the Accountant General shall certify to the National Debt Commissioners the amount of the interest and the Commissioners shall credit that amount to the account kept by them of money received from the Accountant General.

PART X

UNCLAIMED FUNDS IN COURT

Unclaimed funds

57.—(1) Subject to the provisions of this rule, the Accountant General may carry over an unclaimed fund in court to an account of unclaimed balances when five years have elapsed since an account was opened for the fund.

(2) Subject to paragraph (3), a fund shall be treated as unclaimed if:–

(i) it stands to the credit of an account which has not been dealt with for a period of five years otherwise than by the continuous investment or placing on deposit of accrued interest, the compulsory conversion, redemption or acquisition of securities or the placing on deposit of any money arising therefrom; and

(ii) the Accountant General is satisfied that all reasonable steps have been taken to trace the person entitled to it and to pay it to him.

(3) Where a fund was lodged in court for the benefit of a minor, the period of five years mentioned in paragraph 2(i) shall not begin to run until the minor's 18th birthday, or, if his date of birth is not known, until 18 years have elapsed since the account was opened.

(4) Where the person entitled to a fund was a patient, the Accountant General may at any time, if so requested by the proper officer of the Court of Protection, and provided he is satisfied that all reasonable steps have been taken to trace the person entitled to the fund and to pay it to him, carry the fund over to an account of unclaimed balances.

(5) In the case of a fund paid into court by the Public Trustee under the Trustee Act 1925, the Accountant General may at any time, provided he is satisfied that all reasonable

steps have been taken to trace the person entitled to the fund and to pay it to him, carry the fund over to an account of unclaimed balances.

(6) On receipt of a Payment Schedule directing a dealing with a fund carried over in accordance with this rule, the Accountant General shall carry back the unclaimed balance to the appropriate account.

(7) Where a fund is carried back under paragraph (6) simple interest shall be credited to the fund in respect of the whole period during which the fund stood to an account of unclaimed balances at the rate of interest prescribed at the date when the fund is carried back, for money placed in a basic account.

Lists of unclaimed funds

58.—(1) The Accountant General shall maintain a list of the accounts in respect of which funds have been carried over to an account of unclaimed balances under rule 57, which may be inspected at the Court Funds Office during normal office hours.

(2) The proper officer of each county court shall maintain a list of unclaimed funds in the custody of that court, which may be inspected at the court office; and he shall send to the Accountant General a copy of the list from time to time.

Disposal of unclaimed effects in court

59.—(1) Where effects have been deposited in court on or after 3rd July 1978 and have been carried over to an account of unclaimed balances under rule 57, the Accountant General may send to the court a copy of any inventory provided to him in accordance with rule 17(3) in respect of such effects when 25 years have elapsed since he received the authority for such lodgment.

(2) On receipt of an inventory sent in accordance with paragraph (1) the court may:–

(i) cause enquiries to be made whether any party to the proceedings in which the effects were deposited wishes to make any application in respect of them, or whether any other person who may have an interest in the effects can be found; and

(ii) of its own motion and without reference to any party or person (other than a party or person who may have an interest and whose whereabouts or the whereabouts of whose personal representatives are known), order the final disposal of the effects by sale, realisation or otherwise; provided that the court shall not order the destruction of any effects unless it is satisfied that they have no realisable value.

(3) For the purpose of any reference to a party or other person who may have an interest in the effects in question it shall not be necessary to revive any proceedings which may have abated or to issue any summons unless the court so directs and an order for such final disposal may be made after oral or written communication with such party or person.

(4) The amount of the net proceeds of any sale or realisation under paragraph (2) should be certified by the proper officer and placed to the credit of the unclaimed balance account in which the effects were held prior to the sale or realisation.

Disposal of unclaimed securities in court

60.—(1) Where any securities (including Common Investment Fund units) are carried over under rule 57, or are standing to an account of unclaimed balances on 1st June 1987 the Accountant General shall sell the securities and pay the proceeds into the account of unclaimed balances.

(2) The Accountant General shall write-off any securities carried over under rule 57 or standing to an account of unclaimed balances on 1st June 1987 which have no value.

(3) Where any sum carried over under rule 57 stands to an interest bearing account the Accountant General shall withdraw the sum and place it to the account of unclaimed balances.

Repayment of closed county court funds

61.—(1) Where a fund in a county court has been closed a person may apply to the court at which the funds account was kept for repayment of all or part of the fund to him.

(2) Where the court is satisfied that the claimant is entitled to the whole or part of the fund, it may order the payment to him of money standing to the credit of the account as at the date of its closure or of a sum of money representing the value of the fund at the date of its closure.

(3) Where the court makes an order under paragraph (2) the proper officer shall send a sealed copy of the court's order to the Accountant General.

(4) On receipt of the order the Accountant General shall take such steps as may be necessary to give effect to it, and shall forward a remittance for the amount of the fund to the claimant.

Unclaimed money in county court

62. This part of these Rules shall apply, with such modifications as may be necessary, to unclaimed moneys which have not been dealt with for a period of one year immediately before the preceding 1st March.

PART XI

CERTIFICATES IN RESPECT OF FUNDS IN COURT

Certificates of funds in court, copies of accounts etc.

63.—(1) The Accountant General may, on receipt of a written request from a person appearing to him to be interested in a fund in court, issue to him a certificate as to lodgment in court, non-payment into court under an order, carry over of the fund to an account of unclaimed balances or any other dealing with the fund; and the certificate shall, where appropriate, state the account to which the fund has been placed, the amount standing to its credit, and particulars of any charges or restraints on the fund of which the Accountant General is aware.

(2) On receipt of a written request the Accountant General may issue to a person appearing to him to be interested in a fund in court a copy of the account relating to the fund, which shall be authenticated by the National Audit Office if that person so requires.

(3) The Accountant General shall supply an annual statement of any fund in court for the benefit of a minor to that person or to his representative.

Hailsham of St. Marylebone, C.

Dated 5th May 1987

We concur,

Michael Neubert
Mark Lennox-Boyd
Two of the Lords Commissioners
of Her Majesty's Treasury

Dated 7th May 1987

SCHEDULE

Rules Revoked

Title			*Reference*
Supreme Court Funds		Rules 1975	S.I. 1975/1803
Supreme Court Funds (Amendment)		Rules 1976	S.I. 1976/2235
Supreme Court Funds (Amendment)		Rules 1979	S.I. 1979/106
Supreme Court Funds (Amendment No. 2)		Rules 1979	S.I. 1979/1620
Supreme Court Funds (Amendment)		Rules 1980	S.I. 1980/1858
Supreme Court Funds (Amendment)		Rules 1981	S.I. 1981/1589
Supreme Court Funds (Amendment)		Rules 1982	S.I. 1982/123
Supreme Court Funds (Amendment No. 2)		Rules 1982	**S.I. 1982/787**
Supreme Court Funds (Amendment)		Rules 1983	S.I. 1983/290
Supreme Court Funds (Amendment)		Rules 1984	S.I. 1984/285
Supreme Court Funds (Amendment)		Rules 1986	S.I. 1986/1142
Supreme Court Funds (Amendment No. 2)		Rules 1986	S.I. 1986/2115
County Court Funds		Rules 1965	S.I. 1965/1500
County Court Funds	(Amendment No. 2)	Rules 1969	S.I. 1969/1547
County Court Funds	(Amendment)	Rules 1971	S.I. 1971/260
County Court Funds	(Amendment)	Rules 1972	S.I. 1972/334
County Court Funds	(Amendment)	Rules 1976	S.I. 1976/2234
County Court Funds	(Amendment)	Rules 1978	S.I. 1978/750
County Court Funds	(Amendment No. 2)	Rules 1982	S.I. 1982/786
County Court Funds	(Amendment)	Rules 1983	S.I. 1983/291

EXPLANATORY NOTE

(This note is not part of the Rules)

These Rules amalgamate, with corrections and detailed changes, the Supreme Court Funds Rules and the County Court Funds Rules. The main changes of detail which they make are:–

(a) the allocation of day to day interest on the Special Investment Account (formerly called the Short Term Investment Account) instead of in respect of whole months only (rules 26 and 27(2));

(b) the crediting of interest on sums held to the account of unclaimed balances which are eventually paid out of court (rule 57(7)).

STATUTORY INSTRUMENTS

1987 No. 822

LANDLORD AND TENANT

The Assured Tenancies (Approved Bodies) (No.2) Order 1987

Made - - - -	*6th May 1987*
Laid before Parliament	*11th May 1987*
Coming into force	*1st June 1987*

The Secretary of State for the Environment, as respects England, and the Secretary of State for Wales, as respects Wales, in exercise of the powers conferred upon them by section 56(4) of the Housing Act 1980(a), and of all other powers enabling them in that behalf, hereby make the following Order:–

1. This Order may be cited as the Assured Tenancies (Approved Bodies) (No.2) Order 1987 and shall come into force on 1st June 1987.

2. The bodies named in the Schedule to this Order are hereby specified for the purposes of Part II of the Housing Act 1980.

SCHEDULE

BODIES SPECIFIED FOR THE PURPOSES OF PART II OF THE HOUSING ACT 1980

1. Abbey National Building Society.
2. Addison Housing Association Limited.
3. Airways Housing Society Limited.
4. Aldwyck Housing Association Limited.
5. Boleyn and Forest Housing Society Limited.
6. Bridge Housing Society Limited.
7. Brook Street Housing Association Limited.
8. Cheltenham and District Housing Association Limited.
9. Cherwell Homes Limited.
10. Cherwell Housing Trust.
11. Clwyd Alyn Housing Association Limited.
12. Coastal Counties Housing Association Limited.
13. Colombo Estates Limited.
14. Copec Housing Trust.
15. Copec Three Housing Association Limited.

(a) 1980 c.51.

16. Copec Two Housing Association Limited.
17. Corlan Housing Association Limited.
18. Fairlake Second Housing Association Limited.
19. Family Care Housing Association Limited.
20. Harewood Housing Society Limited.
21. Harry Arthur Bookbinder, Margaret Bookbinder, Nicholas Bookbinder, and Penelope Luiten trading as Abco Homes.
22. Headrow Housing Group Limited.
23. Jephson Second Housing Association Limited.
24. Metropolitan Housing Trust Limited.
25. MHT Services Limited.
26. MIH Special Projects Housing Association Limited.
27. Muir Group Housing Association Limited.
28. Nene Housing Society Limited.
29. Notting Hill Housing Trust.
30. Secondary Housing Association for Wales Limited.
31. Secondary Housing Association for Wales (Co-operative) Limited.
32. South East Lancashire Housing Association Limited.
33. South West Housing Society Limited.
34. S.R.J. Properties Limited.
35. The St. Pancras Housing Association in Camden.
36. Third Caldmore Housing Association Limited.
37. United Kingdom Housing Trust Limited.
38. Wales & West Housing Association Limited.
39. Western Permanent Housing Society Limited.
40. R W Willan (Estates) Limited.
41. Yorkshire Metropolitan Housing Association Limited.

Signed by authority of the Secretary of State   *Richard Tracey*
5th May 1987   Parliamentary Under Secretary of State,
                                                      Department of the Environment

                                                          Nicholas Edwards
6th May 1987   Secretary of State for Wales

EXPLANATORY NOTE

(This note is not part of the Order)

Assured tenancies are tenancies which would otherwise have been protected tenancies or housing association tenancies under the Rent Act 1977 (c.42), and which meet certain other conditions. Such tenancies are subject to Part II of the Landlord and Tenant Act 1954 (c.56), as modified by Schedule 5 to the Housing Act 1980. They can only be granted by bodies approved under section 56 of the 1980 Act.

This Order approves forty-one bodies for the purposes of section 56.

STATUTORY INSTRUMENTS

1987 No. 823 (S.64)

LEGAL AID AND ADVICE, SCOTLAND

The Civil Legal Aid (Scotland) (Fees) Amendment Regulations 1987

Made - - - -	*8th May 1987*
Laid before Parliament	*11th May 1987*
Coming into force	*1st June 1987*

The Secretary of State, in exercise of the powers conferred upon him by section 33 of the Legal Aid (Scotland) Act 1986(**a**), and of all other powers enabling him in that behalf, hereby makes the following Regulations:

1.—(1) These Regulations may be cited as the Civil Legal Aid (Scotland) (Fees) Amendment Regulations 1987 and shall come into force on 1st June 1987.

(2) In these Regulations "the principal Regulations" means the Civil Legal Aid (Scotland) (Fees) Regulations 1987(**b**).

2. For the Table of Fees set out in Schedule 3 to the principal Regulations (Fees of Counsel for Proceedings in the Court of Session) there shall be substituted the Table of Fees set out in the Schedule to these Regulations.

3. The amendments to the principal Regulations made in regulation 2 of these Regulations shall apply only to fees for work done on or after 1st June 1987.

Ian Lang
New St. Andrew's House, Edinburgh   Parliamentary Under Secretary of State,
8th May 1987   Scottish Office

(**a**) 1986 c.47.
(**b**) S.I. 1987/366.

Regulation 2

SCHEDULE

TABLE OF FEES

CHAPTER I – JUNIOR COUNSEL

PART I – UNDEFENDED ACTIONS OF DIVORCE OR SEPARATION-AFFIDAVIT PROCEDURE

1.	*Summons or other initiating writ*	
	(a) Subject to sub-paragraph (b) below the fees shall be–	
	(i) Where the facts set out in section 1(2)(b) (unreasonable behaviour) of the Divorce (Scotland) Act 1976(**a**) are relied on	£22.00
	(ii) Where the facts set out in section 1(2)(a) (adultery) or section 1(2)(c) (desertion) of the said Act are relied on and the action is not straightforward	£22.00
	(iii) Where the facts set out in the said section 1(2)(a) (adultery) or section 1(2)(c) (desertion) are relied on and the action is straightforward	£18.00
	(iv) Where the facts set out in section 1(2)(d) (2 years' non-cohabitation and consent) or 1(2)(e) (5 years' non-cohabitation) of the said Act are relied on	£18.00
	(b) Where common law interdict and/or any order under the Matrimonial Homes (Family Protection) (Scotland) Act 1981(**b**) or any other ancillary order is also sought, the fee shall be within the following range:–	
	From	£22.00
	To	£41.50
2.	*Minute*	
	(a) Minute involving arrangements for a child or children and/or financial provision	£16.50
	(b) Any other minute	£12.50
3.	*By Order Roll appearance*	£12.50
4.	*All other work*	
	The fees specified in Part IV shall apply.	

PART II – CONSISTORIAL ACTIONS OTHER THAN THOSE TO WHICH PART I APPLIES

1.	*Summons or other initiating writ*	
	The fees specified in Part I shall apply.	
2.	*Minute for pursuer relating to custody, aliment or access*	£18.50
3.	*Defences or answers*	
	(a) Defences or answers in purely skeleton form to preserve rights of parties	£10.50
	(b) Answers to minute	£16.50
	(c) The fee for defences or answers to which sub-paragraphs (a) or (b) do not apply shall be within the following range:–	
	From	£18.00
	To	£37.00
4.	*Joint minute regulating custody, aliment or access*	
	Framing or adjusting the minute	£16.00
5.	*By Order Roll appearance*	£12.50
6.	*All other work*	
	The fees specified in Part IV shall apply.	

(**a**) 1976 c.39.
(**b**) 1981 c.59.

PART III – PETITIONS

1. *Petition (including any revisals thereto)*

    (a) Petition for interdict £47.00

    (b) Other Outer House petitions £31.00

    (c) Inner House petition: such fee shall be allowed as appears to the auditor to provide reasonable remuneration for the work.

2. *Answers (including any revisals thereto)*

    (a) Petition for interdict £47.00

    (b) Other Outer House petitions £28.50

    (c) Inner House petitions: such fee shall be allowed as appears to the auditor to provide reasonable remuneration for the work.

3. *All other work*

    The fees specified in Part IV shall apply.

PART IV - ORDINARY ACTIONS

1. *Summons (including any revisals thereto)*

    (a) Straightforward cases £39.00

    (b) Other cases £51.50

2. *Defences (including any revisals thereto)*

    (a) Where in purely skeleton form to preserve rights of parties £10.50

    (b) Otherwise the fee shall be within the following range, having regard to nature of summons:-

    From £39.00

    To £51.50

3. *Adjustment of record*

    (a) Adjustment fee (each occasion) £16.50

    (b) Additional adjustment fee, where skeleton defences require to be amplified, where additional parties are introduced, etc. £39.00

4. *Specification of documents*

    Standard calls only £16.50

5. *Minutes, etc.*

    (a) Formal amendments or answers £15.00

    (b) Amendments or answers other than formal £26.50

    (c) Revising and signing tender or acceptance £6.50

    (d) Note of exceptions £16.50

    (e) Abandonment, sist, restriction, etc. £8.00

    (f) Issue or counter issue £8.00

6. *Notes*

    (a) Note on quantum only £41.50

    (b) Note advising on tender or extra-judicial offer, where not merely confirming advice at consultation £47.00

    (c) Note on line of evidence £47.00

    (d) The fee for other types of note shall be within the following range:-

    From £16.00

    To £47.00

7. *Consultations*

    (a) Before proof or trial, or otherwise involving a significant degree of preparation or lengthy discussion–

        (i) Junior alone £57.50

        (ii) Junior with Senior £31.00

    (b) Other consultations–

        (i) Junior alone £47.00

        (ii) Junior with Senior £26.50

8. *Motions*

    (a) Unopposed motions on By Order (Adjustment) Roll, etc.   £8.00

    (b) Opposed motions:–

    Attendance for up to half hour   £16.50

    Attendance for each subsequent half hour or part thereof   £12.50

    (c) Motions on By Order Roll (including advice)   £15.00

9. *Procedure Roll, proof or jury trial*

    (a) Junior alone – per day   £171.00

    (b) Junior with Senior – per day   £129.50

10. *Inner House*

    (a) Single Bills

        (i) Unopposed   £12.50

        (ii) Opposed–

    Attendance for each half hour or part thereof   £18.50

    (b) Reclaiming motion

        (i) Junior opening or appearing alone – per day   £181.50

        (ii) Junior otherwise – per day   £140.00

    (c) Motion for new trial

        (i) Junior alone – per day   £181.50

        (ii) Junior with Senior – per day   £140.00

11. *Attendance at judgement*

    (a) Outer House   £15.00

    (b) Inner House   £18.50

CHAPTER II – SENIOR COUNSEL

CONSISTORIAL ACTIONS, PETITIONS AND ORDINARY ACTIONS

1. *Revisal of pleadings*

    (a) Revisal of summons, defences, petition or answers   £68.00

    (b) Adjustment fee (open record) (each occasion)   £26.50

2. *Minutes, etc. – revisal fees*

    (a) Amendments (other than formal) or answers   £28.50

    (b) Admissions, tender or acceptance (in appropriate cases)   £8.00

    (c) Note of exceptions   £8.00

3. *Notes*

    (a) Note on quantum only   £62.00

    (b) Advice on tender or extra-judicial offer where not merely confirming advice at consultation   £68.00

    (c) Note on line of evidence (revisal)   £68.00

    (d) The fee for other notes shall be within the following range:-

    From   £21.00

    To   £68.00

4. *Consultations*

    (a) Before proof or trial, or otherwise involving a significant degree of preparation or lengthy discussion   £82.50

    (b) Other consultations   £68.00

5. *Day in court*

    (a) Inner House – per day   £243.50

    (b) Outer House – per day   £227.50

EXPLANATORY NOTE

(This note is not part of the Regulations)

These Regulations amend the Civil Legal Aid (Scotland) (Fees) Regulations 1987 so as to increase the fees allowable to Counsel for civil legal aid (and for legal aid in certain proceedings relating to children) given under the Legal Aid (Scotland) Act 1986. The increase will apply to fees for work done on or after 1st June 1987. The overall increase is around 4½%.

STATUTORY INSTRUMENTS

1987 No. 824 (S. 65)

LEGAL AID AND ADVICE, SCOTLAND

The Criminal Legal Aid (Scotland) (Fees) Amendment Regulations 1987

Made - - - -	*8th May 1987*
Laid before Parliament	*11th May 1987*
Coming into force	*1st June 1987*

The Secretary of State, in exercise of the powers conferred upon him by section 33 of the Legal Aid (Scotland) Act 1986(**a**), and of all other powers enabling him in that behalf, hereby makes the following Regulations:

1.—(1) These Regulations may be cited as the Criminal Legal Aid (Scotland) (Fees) Amendment Regulations 1987 and shall come into force on 1st June 1987.

(2) In these Regulations "the principal Regulations" means the Criminal Legal Aid (Scotland) (Fees) Regulations 1987(**b**).

2. For the Table of Fees set out in Schedule 3 to the principal Regulations (Fees of Counsel) there shall be substituted the Table of Fees set out in the Schedule to these Regulations.

3. The amendments to the principal Regulations made by regulation 2 of these Regulations shall apply only to fees in relation to proceedings concluded on or after 1st June 1987.

Ian Lang
New Andrew's House, Edinburgh
8th May 1987

Parliamentary Under Secretary of State,
Scottish Office

(**a**) 1986 c.47.
(**b**) S.I. 1987/365.

SCHEDULE

Regulation 2

TABLE OF FEES

CHAPTER 1 – JUNIOR COUNSEL

	Junior with Senior	Junior alone
1. *Trial per day*		
(a) In Edinburgh	£126.00	£177.50
(b) In Glasgow	£149.00	£218.00
(c) Elsewhere within 60 miles journey by road from Edinburgh	£154.50	£223.50
(d) In Aberdeen, Inverness or Dumfries	£212.00	£298.50
(e) Elsewhere beyond 60 miles journey by road from Edinburgh: Such fee as the auditor considers appropriate with regard to the journey involved and the level of fees prescribed in this paragraph.		
2. *Appeals, etc.*		
(a) Drafting grounds of appeal against conviction, including any note of appeal	£ 32.50	£ 46.00
(b) Hearing in appeal against conviction - per day	£126.00	£177.50
(c) Note of adjustments to stated case	£ 32.50	£ 46.00
(d) Hearing on stated case or bill of suspension relating to conviction or conviction and sentence	£ 57.50	£ 74.50
(e) Any appeal against sentence including fee for drafting note of appeal	£ 23.00	£ 51.50
(f) Appeal relating to granting of bail	£ 17.00	£ 17.00
3. *Consultations*		
(a) In Edinburgh Additional fee if held in prison	£ 40.00 £ 6.00	£ 57.50 £ 6.00
(b) Elsewhere within 60 miles journey by road from Edinburgh	£ 74.50	£ 97.50
(c) In Aberdeen, Inverness or Dumfries	£149.00	£177.50
(d) Elsewhere beyond 60 miles journey by road from Edinburgh: Such fee as the auditor considers appropriate with regard to the journey involved and the level of fees prescribed in this paragraph.		
4. Opinion on appeal, etc.		£ 34.50
5. Revisal of stated case		£ 34.50
6. Drafting bill of suspension		£ 34.50
7. Remits for sentence and pleas in mitigation		£ 34.50

CHAPTER 2 - SENIOR COUNSEL

1. *Trial - per day*

(a) In Edinburgh	£229.50
(b) In Glasgow	£269.50
(c) Elsewhere within 60 miles journey by road from Edinburgh	£275.50
(d) In Aberdeen, Inverness or Dumfries	£372.50

(e) Elsewhere beyond 60 miles journey by road from Edinburgh:
Such fee as the auditor considers appropriate with regard to the journey involved and the level of fees prescribed in this paragraph.

2. *Appeals, etc.*

(a) Revising grounds of appeal against conviction, including any note of appeal	£ 63.00
(b) Hearing in appeal against conviction - per day	£229.50
(c) Note of adjustments to stated case	£ 63.00
(d) Hearing on stated case or bill of suspension relating to conviction or conviction and sentence	£114.50
(e) Any appeal against sentence including revisal of note of appeal	£ 74.50
(f) Appeal relating to granting of bail	£ 23.00

3. *Consultations*

(a) In Edinburgh	£ 86.00
Additional fee if held in prison	£ 6.00
(b) Elsewhere within 60 miles journey by road from Edinburgh	£137.50
(c) In Aberdeen, Inverness or Dumfries	£264.00

(d) Elsewhere beyond 60 miles journey by road from Edinburgh:
Such fee as the auditor considers appropriate with regard to the journey involved and the level of fees prescribed in this paragraph.

4. Opinion on appeal	£ 51.50
5. Revisal of stated case	£ 51.50
6. Revisal of bill of suspension	£ 51.50
7. Remits for sentence and pleas in mitigation	£ 51.50

EXPLANATORY NOTE

(This note is not part of the Regulations)

These Regulations amend the Criminal Legal Aid (Scotland) (Fees) Regulations 1987 so as to increase the fees allowable to Counsel for criminal legal aid given under the Legal Aid (Scotland) Act 1986. The increased fees will apply to proceedings concluded on or after 1st June 1987. The overall increase is around 4½%.

STATUTORY INSTRUMENTS

1987 No. 825 (S. 66)

LEGAL AID AND ADVICE, SCOTLAND

The Legal Aid (Scotland) (Fees in Civil Proceedings) Amendment Regulations 1987

Made - - - -	*8th May 1987*
Laid before Parliament	*11th May 1987*
Coming into force	*1st June 1987*

The Secretary of State, in exercise of the powers conferred on him by sections 14A and 15 of the Legal Aid (Scotland) Act 1967(**a**) as read with section 45 of, and paragraph 3(1) of Schedule 4 to, the Legal Aid (Scotland) Act 1986(**b**), and of all other powers enabling him in that behalf, hereby makes the following Regulations:

1.—(1) These Regulations may be cited as the Legal Aid (Scotland) (Fees in Civil Proceedings) Amendment Regulations 1987 and shall come into force on 1st June 1987.

(2) In these Regulations "the principal Regulations" means the Legal Aid (Scotland) (Fees in Civil Proceedings) Regulations 1984(**c**).

2. For the Table of Fees in Schedule 3 to the principal Regulations there shall be substituted the Table of Fees set out in the Schedule to these Regulations.

3. The amendments to the principal Regulations made by regulation 2 of these Regulations shall apply only to fees in relation to work done on or after 1st June 1987.

Ian Lang
Parliamentary Under Secretary of State,
Scottish Office

New St Andrew's House, Edinburgh
8th May 1987

(**a**) 1967 c.43; section 14A was inserted by section 3 of the Divorce Jurisdiction, Court Fees and Legal Aid (Scotland) Act 1983 (c.12).
(**b**) 1986 c.47.
(**c**) S.I. 1984/519; the relevant amending instruments are S.I. 1985/557 and 1986/681.

Regulation 2   **SCHEDULE**

TABLE OF FEES

CHAPTER I – JUNIOR COUNSEL

PART I – UNDEFENDED ACTIONS OF DIVORCE OR SEPARATION-AFFIDAVIT PROCEDURE

1.	*Summons or other initiating writ*	
	(a) Subject to sub-paragraph (b) below the fees shall be–	
	(i) Where the facts set out in section 1(2)(b) (unreasonable behaviour) of the Divorce (Scotland) Act 1976(**a**) are relied on	£22.00
	(ii) Where the facts set out in section 1(2)(a) (adultery) or section 1(2)(c) (desertion) of the said Act are relied on and the action is not straightforward	£22.00
	(iii) Where the facts set out in the said section 1(2)(a) (adultery) or section 1(2)(c) (desertion) are relied on and the action is straightforward	£18.00
	(iv) Where the facts set out in section 1(2)(d) (2 years' non-cohabitation and consent) or 1(2)(e) (5 years' non-cohabitation) of the said Act are relied on	£18.00
	(b) Where common law interdict and/or any order under the Matrimonial Homes (Family Protection) (Scotland) Act 1981(**b**) or any other ancillary order is also sought, the fee shall be within the following range:–	
	From	£22.00
	To	£41.50
2.	*Minute*	
	(a) Minute involving arrangements for a child or children and/or financial provision	£16.50
	(b) Any other minute	£12.50
3.	*By Order Roll appearance*	£12.50
4.	*All other work*	
	The fees specified in Part IV shall apply.	

PART II – CONSISTORIAL ACTIONS OTHER THAN THOSE TO WHICH PART I APPLIES

1.	*Summons or other initiating writ*	
	The fees specified in Part I shall apply.	
2.	*Minute for pursuer relating to custody, aliment or access*	£18.50
3.	*Defences or answers*	
	(a) Defences or answers in purely skeleton form to preserve rights of parties	£10.50
	(b) Answers to minute	£16.50
	(c) The fee for defences or answers to which sub-paragraphs (a) or (b) do not apply shall be within the following range:–	
	From	£18.00
	To	£37.00
4.	*Joint minute regulating custody, aliment or access*	
	Framing or adjusting the minute	£16.00
5.	*By Order Roll appearance*	£12.50
6.	*All other work*	
	The fees specified in Part IV shall apply.	

(**a**) 1976 c.39.
(**b**) 1981 c.59.

PART III – PETITIONS

1.	*Petition (including any revisals thereto)*	
	(a) Petition for interdict	£47.00
	(b) Other Outer House petitions	£31.00
	(c) Inner House petition: such fee shall be allowed as appears to the auditor to provide reasonable remuneration for the work.	
2.	*Answers (including any revisals thereto)*	
	(a) Petition for interdict	£47.00
	(b) Other Outer House petitions	£28.50
	(c) Inner House petitions: such fee shall be allowed as appears to the auditor to provide reasonable remuneration for the work.	
3.	*All other work*	
	The fees specified in Part IV shall apply.	

PART IV – ORDINARY ACTIONS

1.	*Summons (including any revisals thereto)*	
	(a) Straightforward cases	£39.00
	(b) Other cases	£51.50
2.	*Defences (including any revisals thereto)*	
	(a) Where in purely skeleton form to preserve rights of parties	£10.50
	(b) Otherwise the fee shall be within the following range, having regard to nature of summons:–	
	From	£39.00
	To	£51.50
3.	*Adjustment of record*	
	(a) Adjustment fee (each occasion)	£16.50
	(b) Additional adjustment fee, where skeleton defences require to be amplified, where additional parties are introduced, etc.	£39.00
4.	*Specification of documents*	
	Standard calls only	£16.50
5.	*Minutes, etc.*	
	(a) Formal amendments or answers	£15.00
	(b) Amendments or answers other than formal	£26.50
	(c) Revising and signing tender or acceptance	£6.50
	(d) Note of exceptions	£16.50
	(e) Abandonment, sist, restriction, etc.	£8.00
	(f) Issue or counter issue	£8.00
6.	*Notes*	
	(a) Note on quantum only	£41.50
	(b) Note advising on tender or extra-judicial offer, where not merely confirming advice at consultation	£47.00
	(c) Note on line of evidence	£47.00
	(d) The fee for other types of note shall be within the following range:–	
	From	£16.00
	To	£47.00
7.	*Consultations*	
	(a) Before proof or trial, or otherwise involving a significant degree of preparation or lengthy discussion–	
	(i) Junior alone	£57.50
	(ii) Junior with Senior	£31.00
	(b) Other consultations–	
	(i) Junior alone	£47.00
	(ii) Junior with Senior	£26.50

8.	*Motions*	
	(a) Unopposed motions on By Order (Adjustment) Roll, etc.	£8.00
	(b) Opposed motions:–	
	Attendance for up to half hour	£16.50
	Attendance for each subsequent half hour or part thereof	£12.50
	(c) Motions on By Order Roll (including advice)	£15.00
9.	*Procedure Roll, proof or jury trial*	
	(a) Junior alone – per day	£171.00
	(b) Junior with Senior – per day	£129.50
10.	*Inner House*	
	(a) Single Bills	
	(i) Unopposed	£12.50
	(ii) Opposed–	
	Attendance for each half hour or part thereof	£18.50
	(b) Reclaiming motion	
	(i) Junior opening or appearing alone – per day	£181.50
	(ii) Junior otherwise – per day	£140.00
	(c) Motion for new trial	
	(i) Junior alone – per day	£181.50
	(ii) Junior with Senior – per day	£140.00
11.	*Attendance at judgement*	
	(a) Outer House	£15.00
	(b) Inner House	£18.50

CHAPTER II – SENIOR COUNSEL
CONSISTORIAL ACTIONS, PETITIONS AND ORDINARY ACTIONS

1.	*Revisal of pleadings*	
	(a) Revisal of summons, defences, petition or answers	£68.00
	(b) Adjustment fee (open record) (each occasion)	£26.50
2.	*Minutes, etc. – revisal fees*	
	(a) Amendments (other than formal) or answers	£28.50
	(b) Admissions, tender or acceptance (in appropriate cases)	£8.00
	(c) Note of exceptions	£8.00
3.	*Notes*	
	(a) Note on quantum only	£62.00
	(b) Advice on tender or extra-judicial offer where not merely confirming advice at consultation	£68.00
	(c) Note on line of evidence (revisal)	£68.00
	(d) The fee for other notes shall be within the following range:–	
	From	£21.00
	To	£68.00
4.	*Consultations*	
	(a) Before proof or trial, or otherwise involving a significant degree of preparation or lengthy discussion	£82.50
	(b) Other consultations	£68.00
5.	*Day in court*	
	(a) Inner House – per day	£243.50
	(b) Outer House – per day	£227.50

EXPLANATORY NOTE

(This note is not part of the Regulations)

These Regulations amend the Legal Aid (Scotland) (Fees in Civil Proceedings) Regulations 1984 so as to increase the fees allowable to counsel for legal aid in civil proceedings given under the Legal Aid (Scotland) Act 1967. The increased fees will apply to fees for work done on or after 1st June 1987.

The Legal Aid (Scotland) Act 1967 continues in effect, despite its general repeal by the Legal Aid (Scotland) Act 1986, in respect of legal aid applications which were granted before commencement of the 1986 Act on 1st April 1987. (See paragraph 3(1) of Schedule 4 to the 1986 Act.) It is thus only in respect of work done following upon such applications that these Regulations increase the fees.

The overall increase is around $4\frac{1}{2}$ per cent.

STATUTORY INSTRUMENTS

1987 No. 826 (S. 67)

LEGAL AID AND ADVICE, SCOTLAND

The Legal Aid (Scotland) (Fees in Criminal Proceedings) Amendment Regulations 1987

Made - - - -	*8th May 1987*
Laid before Parliament	*11th May 1987*
Coming into force	*1st June 1987*

The Secretary of State, in exercise of the powers conferred on him by sections 14A and 15 of the Legal Aid (Scotland) Act 1967(**a**) as read with section 45 of, and paragraph 3(1) of Schedule 4 to, the Legal Aid (Scotland) Act 1986(**b**), and of all other powers enabling him in that behalf, hereby makes the following Regulations:

1.—(1) These Regulations may be cited as the Legal Aid (Scotland) (Fees in Criminal Proceedings) Amendment Regulations 1987 and shall come into force on 1st June 1987.

(2) In these Regulations "the principal Regulations" means the Legal Aid (Scotland) (Fees in Criminal Proceedings) Regulations 1984(**c**).

2. For the Table of Fees in Schedule 3 to the principal Regulations there shall be substituted the Table of Fees set out in the Schedule to these Regulations.

3. The amendments to the principal Regulations made by regulation 2 of these Regulations shall apply only to fees in relation to proceedings concluded on or after 1st June 1987.

Ian Lang
Parliamentary Under Secretary of State,
Scottish Office

New St Andrew's House, Edinburgh
8th May 1987

(**a**) 1967 c.43; section 14A was inserted by section 3 of the Divorce Jurisdiction, Court Fees and Legal Aid (Scotland) Act 1983 (c.12).
(**b**) 1986 c.47.
(**c**) S.I. 1984/520; the relevant amending instruments are S.I. 1985/554 and 1986/674.

SCHEDULE

Regulation 2

TABLE OF FEES

CHAPTER 1 - JUNIOR COUNSEL

	Junior with Senior	*Junior alone*
1. *Trial per day*		
(a) In Edinburgh	£126.00	£177.50
(b) In Glasgow	£149.00	£218.00
(c) Elsewhere within 60 miles journey by road from Edinburgh	£154.50	£223.50
(d) In Aberdeen, Inverness or Dumfries	£212.00	£298.50
(e) Elsewhere beyond 60 miles journey by road from Edinburgh: Such fee as the auditor considers appropriate with regard to the journey involved and the level of fees prescribed in this paragraph.		
2. *Appeals, etc.*		
(a) Drafting grounds of appeal against conviction, including any note of appeal	£ 32.50	£ 46.00
(b) Hearing in appeal against conviction - per day	£126.00	£177.50
(c) Note of adjustments to stated case	£ 32.50	£ 46.00
(d) Hearing on stated case or bill of suspension relating to conviction or conviction and sentence	£ 57.50	£ 74.50
(e) Any appeal against sentence including fee for drafting note of appeal	£ 23.00	£ 51.50
(f) Appeal relating to granting of bail	£ 17.00	£ 17.00
3. *Consultations*		
(a) In Edinburgh Additional fee if held in prison	£ 40.00 £ 6.00	£ 57.50 £ 6.00
(b) Elsewhere within 60 miles journey by road from Edinburgh	£ 74.50	£ 97.50
(c) In Aberdeen, Inverness or Dumfries	£149.00	£177.50
(d) Elsewhere beyond 60 miles journey by road from Edinburgh: Such fee as the auditor considers appropriate with regard to the journey involved and the level of fees prescribed in this paragraph.		
4. Opinion on appeal, etc.		£ 34.50
5. Revisal of stated case		£ 34.50
6. Drafting bill of suspension		£ 34.50
7. Remits for sentence and pleas in mitigation		£ 34.50

CHAPTER 2 - SENIOR COUNSEL

1. *Trial - per day*

(a) In Edinburgh	£229.50
(b) In Glasgow	£269.50
(c) Elsewhere within 60 miles journey by road from Edinburgh	£275.50
(d) In Aberdeen, Inverness or Dumfries	£372.50

(e) Elsewhere beyond 60 miles journey by road from Edinburgh:
Such fee as the auditor considers appropriate with regard to the journey involved and the level of fees prescribed in this paragraph.

2. *Appeals, etc.*

(a) Revising grounds of appeal against conviction, including any note of appeal	£ 63.00
(b) Hearing in appeal against conviction - per day	£229.50
(c) Note of adjustments to stated case	£ 63.00
(d) Hearing on stated case or bill of suspension relating to conviction or conviction and sentence	£114.50
(e) Any appeal against sentence including revisal of note of appeal	£ 74.50
(f) Appeal relating to granting of bail	£ 23.00

3. *Consultations*

(a) In Edinburgh	£ 86.00
Additional fee if held in prison	£ 6.00
(b) Elsewhere within 60 miles journey by road from Edinburgh	£137.50
(c) In Aberdeen, Inverness or Dumfries	£264.00

(d) Elsewhere beyond 60 miles journey by road from Edinburgh:
Such fee as the auditor considers appropriate with regard to the journey involved and the level of fees prescribed in this paragraph.

4. Opinion on appeal	£ 51.50
5. Revisal of stated case	£ 51.50
6. Revisal of bill of suspension	£ 51.50
7. Remits for sentence and pleas in mitigation	£ 51.50

EXPLANATORY NOTE

(This note is not part of the Regulations)

These Regulations amend the Legal Aid (Scotland) (Fees in Criminal Proceedings) Regulations 1984 so as to increase the fees allowable to counsel for legal aid in criminal proceedings given under the Legal Aid (Scotland) Act 1967. The increased fees will apply to proceedings concluded on or after 1st June 1987.

The Legal Aid (Scotland) Act 1967 continues in effect, despite its general repeal by the Legal Aid (Scotland) Act 1986, in respect of legal aid applications which were granted before commencement of the 1986 Act on 1st April 1987. (See paragraph 3(1) of Schedule 4 to the 1986 Act.) It is thus only in respect of proceedings following upon such applications that these Regulations increase the fees.

The overall increase is around $4\frac{1}{2}$ per cent.

STATUTORY INSTRUMENTS

1987 No. 827

TELECOMMUNICATIONS

The Public Telecommunication System Designation (British Cable Services Limited) Order 1987

Made - - - -	*8th May 1987*
Laid before Parliament	*11th May 1987*
Coming into force	*9th June 1987*

Whereas the Secretary of State has granted to British Cable Services Limited a licence ("the Licence") under section 7 of the Telecommunications Act 1984(**a**) ("the Act"), to which section 8 of the Act applies, for the running of the telecommunication systems specified in Annex A to the Licence ("the Applicable Cabled Systems");

Now, therefore, the Secretary of State, in exercise of the powers conferred on him by section 9 of the Act, hereby makes the following Order:

1. This Order may be cited as the Public Telecommunication System Designation (British Cable Services Limited) Order 1987 and shall come into force on 9th June 1987.

2. Each of the Applicable Cabled Systems is hereby designated as a public telecommunication system.

Geoffrey Pattie
Minister of State,
Department of Trade and Industry

8th May 1987

EXPLANATORY NOTE

(This note is not part of the Order)

The Secretary of State granted to British Cable Services Limited on 8th May 1987 a licence under section 7 of the Telecommunications Act 1984 to run the telecommunication systems specified in Annex A to that licence, in the West Surrey and East Hampshire area. A copy of the licence was laid before Parliament on 11th May 1987. This Order designates those telecommunication systems as public telecommunication systems. Consequently, by virtue of section 9(3) of that Act, British Cable Services Limited will be a public telecommunications operator when the Order comes into force.

A copy of the licence may be obtained from the Office of Telecommunications, Atlantic House, Holborn Viaduct, London EC1N 2HQ.

(**a**) 1984 c.12.

STATUTORY INSTRUMENTS

1987 No. 836

ANIMALS

ANIMAL HEALTH

The Sheep Scab (Amendment) Order 1987

Made - - - -	*6th May 1987*
Coming into force	*27th May 1987*

The Minister of Agriculture, Fisheries and Food and the Secretary of State for Scotland and the Secretary of State for Wales, acting jointly, in exercise of the powers conferred on them by sections 1, 7(1), 8(1), 14(1) and (2), 15(4), 17(1), 23 and 25 of the Animal Health Act 1981(a) and of all other powers enabling them in that behalf, order as follows:–

Title and commencement

1. This Order may be cited as the Sheep Scab (Amendment) Order 1987 and shall come into force on 27th May 1987.

Amendment

2.—(1) The Sheep Scab Order 1986(b) shall be amended in accordance with the provisions of this article.

(2) In paragraph (3)(a)(ii) of article 15 (declaration to be made in respect of the movement of any sheep out of an infected area) after the words "from which" there shall be inserted the words ", and to which,".

(3) For paragraph (4) of article 17 (issue by the local authority of licences for the holding of markets) there shall be substituted the following paragraph–

"(4) A licence to hold a market issued by the local authority under paragraph (3) above may permit the holding of a market for–

(a) dipped sheep, on the condition that no sheep other than dipped sheep are present in, or admitted to, the same market on the same day;

(b) slaughter sheep, on the condition that no sheep other than slaughter sheep are present in, or admitted to, the market on the same day; or

(c) both dipped and slaughter sheep, on the condition that adequate provision is made (to the local authority's satisfaction) to ensure that slaughter sheep and dipped sheep are kept separate from each other whilst they are in the market,

and, in each case, on the condition that adequate facilities for the cleansing and disinfection of vehicles in which sheep have been carried to the market are available at, or in the immediate vicinity of, the market".

(4) In paragraph (2)(a) and (b) of article 24 (movement of any sheep on to or out of approved holding premises under licence) for the words "in Form H1" there shall be substituted the words "in Form H2" and consequently in Form H1 the reference to article 24 shall be omitted.

(a) 1981 c.22.
(b) S.I. 1986/862.

(5) In paragraphs (1)(a) and (2) of article 27 (record keeping by sheep dealers) after the words "in Form P" there shall be inserted the words "or in a form substantially to the like effect".

(6) At the end of paragraph (2) of article 30 (sampling of fleeces) there shall be added the words "and shall comply with all reasonable requirements of the inspector with a view to facilitating the taking of such samples".

(7) In Schedule 1 (forms)–

    (a) in Form H1, in the Table, after column (4) there shall be inserted the following column–

"

5 Date of dipping, address of premises where dipped and name of dip used

"; and

    (b) in Form J, in the first and second Tables–

      (i) for the second column there shall be substituted the following column–

"

Address of premises where dipped

", and

(ii) for the fourth column there shall be substituted the following column—

"
Name of dip used
"

In Witness whereof the Official Seal of the Minister of Agriculture, Fisheries and Food is hereunto affixed on 6th May 1987.

Michael Jopling
Minister of Agriculture, Fisheries and Food

5th May 1987

John J. Mackay
Parliamentary Under-Secretary of State,
Scottish Office

5th May 1987

Nicholas Edwards
Secretary of State for Wales

EXPLANATORY NOTE

(This note is not part of the Order)

This Order amends the Sheep Scab Order 1986. The changes of substance made by this Order are the inclusion of provisions in the 1986 Order which—

(1) permit a sheep dealer to keep records of sales of sheep for the purposes of article 27 of the 1986 Order in a form which is in effect substantially the same as Form P set out in Schedule 1 to the 1986 Order (article 2(5)); and

(2) require the occupier of any premises on which there are sheep and the owner or person in charge of the sheep to comply with all reasonable requirements of an inspector with a view to facilitating the taking of samples of the fleece of those sheep by the inspector under article 30(2) of the 1986 Order (article 2(6)).

STATUTORY INSTRUMENTS

1987 No. 839

PUBLIC PASSENGER TRANSPORT

The London (British Rail) Taxi Sharing Scheme Order 1987

Made - - - -	*8th May 1987*
Laid before Parliament	*12th May 1987*
Coming into force -	*1st July 1987*

The Secretary of State for Transport, in exercise of the powers conferred by section 10(4), (5), (6) and (10) of the Transport Act 1985(a), and of all other enabling powers, hereby makes the following Order:

1. This Order may be cited as the London (British Rail) Taxi Sharing Scheme Order 1987 and shall come into force on 1st July 1987.

2. The Secretary of State hereby makes the London (British Rail) Taxi Sharing Scheme as set out in the Annex to this Order.

Signed by authority of the Secretary of State

David Mitchell
Minister of State,
Department of Transport

8th May 1987

ANNEX

The London (British Rail) Taxi Sharing Scheme 1987

Interpretation

1. In this Scheme, unless the context otherwise requires:–
"authorised destination" means any destination indicated in the Schedule to this Scheme of a journey which may be made under the Scheme from a particular authorised place;
"authorised place" means a place designated in the Schedule to this Scheme from which taxis may be hired under the terms of the Scheme;
"exclusive service" means a service other than at separate fares;
"shared service" means a service at separate fares;
"taxi" means a vehicle licensed under section 6 of the Metropolitan Public Carriage Act 1869(b).

(a) 1985 c.67.
(b) 1869 c.115.

Application

2.—(1) The requirements of this Scheme shall apply to taxis standing for hire or hired at separate fares under the terms of this Scheme for a journey from an authorised place to an authorised destination.

(2) Any taxi may at the option of the holder of the licence for that vehicle be used for the carriage of passengers at separate fares under the terms of this Scheme.

Availability

3. A taxi shall be available for hire under this Scheme when it is standing at an authorised place and displaying a notice containing the words specified in paragraph 4 of this Scheme.

Signs on vehicles

4. There shall be displayed on any taxi standing for hire under the terms of this Scheme (in addition to any other sign, mark or notice which is required to be displayed on the taxi) a notice containing the words "Shared Taxi".

Arrangements for a shared service

5. If a person seeks to hire for a shared service a taxi available for hire under this Scheme and the driver is unable to find at least one other person to share the hiring within a reasonable time, then no fare shall be payable and the driver shall be free to seek an alternative hiring provided that the driver and the first mentioned person may continue to wait for another person to offer to share the taxi for so long as they both agree to do so.

Fares and meters

6.—(1) The maximum fare payable by each passenger for a journey shall be the appropriate amount indicated in the Schedule to this Scheme.

(2) No fare shall be charged for any child under the age of two years.

(3) Each child over the age of two years but under the age of ten years shall be charged at half fare.

(4) A charge shall be made for each article of luggage equal to the charge that would be made if the taxi were hired by a single passenger for an exclusive service**(a)**, and this charge shall be payable by the passenger whose luggage it is.

(5) Before the commencement of any journey from an authorised place by a taxi for the purpose of a shared service, any person may (notwithstanding any earlier agreement) decide not to be carried as a passenger and no fare or other charge shall be payable by that person.

(6) The taxi meter shall not be operated and the roof sign shall not be illuminated during the hiring.

Obligatory hirings

7. The driver of a taxi available, for hire under this Scheme shall not, without reasonable excuse, refuse a hiring to two or more persons seeking a shared service to any single authorised destination; but he may wait for a reasonable period for further passengers to share the hiring.

Luggage

8. The driver shall not refuse to carry in his taxi the luggage of a passenger if the luggage can be accommodated safely within the luggage compartment of the taxi with the luggage of other passengers already accepted by him.

(a) *See* paragraph 41 of the London Cab Order 1934 (S.R. & O. 1934/1346); the relevant amending instruments are S.I. 1980/588 and 1984/707.

Route

9. The route taken by the taxi and the order in which passengers are set down shall be determined by the driver, but he shall not unreasonably prolong the journey of any passenger.

Touting

10.—(1) The driver may tout for passengers to share the taxi with a passenger who has already requested a service at separate fares only from the part of an authorised place where his taxi is standing for hire or from any place within 6 metres of his taxi.

(2) The driver may tout by word of mouth only and when touting shall conduct himself in an orderly manner.

SCHEDULE   Paragraphs 1 and 6

RANKS AND FARES

The places listed in column 1 of the Table are designated as authorised places. Passengers may be carried at separate fares to the corresponding places listed in column 2 in relation to a particular authorised place. The maximum fare paid by each passenger for a journey shall be the sum of the amount shown in column 3 opposite the destination and the corresponding authorised place and the charge of luggage (if any) under paragraph 6(4) of the Scheme.

Table

Column 1	Column 2	Column 3
Authorised places	*Authorised destinations*	*Maximum fares*
Waterloo Station forecourt	Kings Cross Station	£1.80
	St Pancras Station	£1.80
	Euston Station	£1.80
	Paddington Station	£1.80
Paddington Station forecourt	King's Cross Station	£1.80
	St Pancras Station	£1.80
	Euston Station	£1.80
	Waterloo Station	£1.80

EXPLANATORY NOTE

(This note is not part of the Order)

This Order contains in its Annex the London (British Rail) Taxi Sharing Scheme.

The Scheme applies to taxis standing for hire or hired at the authorised places designated in the Schedule – the forecourts of Waterloo and Paddington stations – for journeys to the other stations indicated in the Schedule (paragraphs 1 and 2 of the Annex).

Taxis available for hire under the Scheme are to display a sign containing the words "Shared Taxi" (paragraphs 3 and 4). The fares payable are specified in paragraph 6 and the Schedule.

Paragraphs 5 and 7 to 10 contain supplementary provisions relating to the arrangements for shared services, obligatory hirings, luggage, the route to be followed and touting.

1987 No. 841

ROAD TRAFFIC

The Goods Vehicles (Operators' Licences, Qualifications and Fees) (Amendment) Regulations 1987

Made - - - -	*8th May 1987*
Laid before Parliament	*13th May 1987*
Coming into force	*1st July 1987*

The Secretary of State for Transport–

(a) in exercise of the powers conferred by sections 60(2), 85(1) and (2), 89(1) and 91(1) of the Transport Act 1968(**a**), now vested in him(**b**), and of all other enabling powers; and

(b) being a Minister designated(**c**) for the purposes of section 2(2) of the European Communities Act 1972(**d**) in relation to the regulation and supervision of qualifications of persons engaged in road transport, in exercise of the powers conferred by that section, after consultation with representative organisations in accordance with section 91(8) of the Transport Act 1968(**e**), and with the Council on Tribunals in accordance with section 10 of the Tribunals and Inquiries Act 1971(**f**), hereby makes the following Regulations:

Citation, commencement and interpretation

1. These Regulations may be cited as the Goods Vehicles (Operators' Licences, Qualifications and Fees) (Amendment) Regulations 1987 and shall come into force on 1st July 1987.

2. In these Regulations, "the principal Regulations" means the Goods Vehicles (Operators' Licences, Qualifications and Fees) Regulations 1984(**g**).

Amendment of regulations

3. The principal Regulations are hereby further amended in accordance with the following provisions of these Regulations.

4.—(1) In paragraph (2) of regulation 3–

(a) in the definition of "company", "holding company" and "subsidiary", for the words "section 154 of the Companies Act 1948" there shall be substituted the words "respectively sections 735 and 736 of the Companies Act 1985(**h**)";

(b) in the definition of "dual purpose vehicle", for the words "Regulation 3(1) of

(**a**) 1968 c.73; sections 85(1), 89(1) and 91(1) were amended by the Transport Act 1980 (c.34), Schedule 9, Part II.
(**b**) S.I. 1970/1681, 1979/571 and 1981/238.
(**c**) S.I. 1975/1707.
(**d**) 1972 c.68.
(**e**) Section 91(8) was amended by the Transport Act 1982 (c.49), Schedule 6.
(**f**) 1971 c.62.
(**g**) S.I. 1984/176, as amended by S.I. 1986/666 and 1391.
(**h**) 1985 c.6.

the Motor Vehicles (Construction and Use) Regulations 1978" there shall be substituted the words "column 2 of the Table in regulation 3(2) of the Road Vehicles (Construction and Use) Regulations 1986(**a**)";

(c) in the definition of "tower wagon", for the words "Schedule 4 to" there shall be substituted the words "section 4(2) of"(**b**); and

(d) the definitions of "hackney carriage" and "public service vehicle" shall be omitted.

(2) In paragraph (5) of regulation 3–

(a) for the words "Regulation 3(1) of the Motor Vehicles (Construction and Use) Regulations 1978" there shall be substituted the words "column 2 of the Table in regulation 3(2) of the Road Vehicles (Construction and Use) Regulations 1986"; and

(b) for the words "Regulation 42 of the said Regulations of 1978" there shall be substituted the words "regulation 66 of those Regulations".

5. In regulation 9, for paragraph (4) there shall be substituted the following paragraph–

"(4) A direction given by a licensing authority under paragraph (1) shall, for the purposes of Part V, be regarded as having been given under section 69(1), but subsection (3) of that section shall not apply in relation to any such direction.".

6.—(1) In paragraph (5) of regulation 10, for sub-paragraph (b) there shall be substituted the following sub-paragraph–

"(b) where a licence is held, or an application is made, by a body corporate–

(i) the making of a winding up order;

(ii) the passing of a resolution for voluntary winding up; or

(iii) the requirement of professional competence ceases to be satisfied,

so, however, that parts (i) and (ii) of this sub-paragraph do not apply in the case of a voluntary liquidation for the purpose of reconstruction.".

(2) In paragraphs (2) and (4) of regulation 10, for the words "(i) to (iv)" in both places where they occur there shall be substituted the words "(i) and (ii)".

7. In regulation 18, for paragraph (b)(**c**) there shall be substituted the following paragraph–

"(b) be signed–

(i) if made by an individual, by that person;

(ii) if made by persons in partnership, by all of the partners or by one of them with the authority of the others;

(iii) if made by any other body or group of persons, by one or more individual persons authorised for that purpose by the body or group;

or, in any of the above cases, by a solicitor acting on behalf of (as the case may be) the person, body or group; and".

8. In paragraph (3) of regulation 30–

(a) after the word "revoked" there shall be inserted the word "surrendered"; and

(b) for the words "within 7 days after a notice to that effect has been" there shall be substituted the words "on or before the date specified in a notice to that effect".

9. In paragraph (1) of regulation 32, for the word "or" where it appears after the word "granted" there shall be substituted the word "of".

10. For paragraph (2) of regulation 35(**d**), there shall be substituted the following paragraphs–

(**a**) S.I. 1986/1078, to which there are no relevant amending instruments.

(**b**) Section 4(2) of the Vehicles (Excise) Act 1971 (c.10) was amended by the Finance Act 1986 (c.41), Schedule 2, Part I, paragraph 2.

(**c**) Paragraph (b) was substituted by regulation 5 of the Goods Vehicles (Operators' Licences, Qualifications and Fees) (Amendment) Regulations 1986 (S.I. 1986/666).

(**d**) Paragraphs (1) and (2) of regulation 35 were substituted by regulation 7 of S.I. 1986/666.

"(2) If a licence is suspended, revoked, surrendered, terminated prematurely or curtailed the licensing authority shall refund to the person to whom the licence was granted or (if appropriate) who is the last person to have been deemed, pursuant to regulation 10(6)(a), to be the holder of the licence any fee paid pursuant to paragraph (1A)(b) or (1B)(a) above–

(a) in the case of a suspended licence, in respect of each period of 12 months during which the licence is suspended;

(b) in the case of a revoked, surrendered or prematurely terminated licence, in respect of each period of 12 months during which the licence would, but for the revocation, surrender or termination, have remained in force; or

(c) in the case of a curtailed licence, only when the curtailment involves a reduction in the number of authorised vehicles and then only in respect of the number of such vehicles by which the licence is curtailed and further only in respect of each period of 12 months during which the licence (assuming it is not revoked, surrendered or prematurely terminated) will remain in force.

(3) Any period of less than 12 months shall be disregarded for the purpose of any refund under paragraph (2) above.".

11. In Schedule 5–

(a) for paragraphs 4, 5 and 6 there shall be substituted the following paragraph–

"4. A motor vehicle constructed or adapted primarily for the carriage of passengers and their effects, and any trailer drawn by it, while being so used.";

(b) for paragraph 13 there shall be substituted the following paragraph–

"13. A vehicle used by or under the control of Her Majesty's United Kingdom forces."; and

(c) for paragraph 21 there shall be substituted the following paragraph–

"21. A tower wagon or trailer drawn thereby, provided that the only goods carried on the trailer are goods required for use in connection with the work on which the tower wagon is ordinarily used as such.".

Modification of Part V of Transport Act 1968

12. In subsection (6) of section 69 of the Transport Act 1968(**a**), as having effect subject to the modifications specified in Schedule 4 to the principal Regulations in accordance with regulation 32(3), for sub-paragraph (iii)(**b**) there shall be substituted the following sub-paragraph–

"(iii) a company which is a subsidiary of such a company; or".

Signed by authority of the Secretary of State.

Peter Bottomley
8th May 1987   Parliamentary Under Secretary of State, Department of Transport

---

(**a**) 1968 c.73.
(**b**) Sub-paragraph (iii) was inserted by paragraph 2(p) of Schedule 4 to the principal Regulations.

EXPLANATORY NOTE

(This note is not part of the Regulations)

These Regulations further amend the Goods Vehicles (Operators' Licences, Qualifications and Fees) Regulations 1984, as follows–

    (a) regulation 4 amends a number of definitions, to reflect changes in other legislation;

    (b) regulation 5 substitutes a new paragraph (4) in regulation 9, so that a decision of a licensing authority under regulation 9 to revoke a licence is treated for the purposes of Part V of the Transport Act 1968 as having been given under section 69(1) of that Act;

    (c) regulation 6 amends regulation 10(5), so that a licence will not automatically cease to have effect on the appointment of a receiver or manager of the holder, or on a debenture-holder taking possession of any of the property of that holder;

    (d) regulation 7 amends regulation 18, so that environmental representations may be signed by a solicitor on behalf of (as well as by) the representor or representors. Also, the requirement for sealing when such representations are made by a body or group with a common seal is removed;

    (e) regulation 8 amends regulation 30, to ensure that vehicle discs are returned when a licence is surrendered, and to enable the licensing authority to state in a notice when such discs are to be returned;

    (f) regulation 10 substitutes a new paragraph (2) in regulation 35, and provides for a partial refund of fees when a licence is suspended, revoked, terminated prematurely or curtailed (as well as when it is surrendered); and

    (g) regulation 11 amends Schedule 5 (cases in which a licence is not required) to reflect changes in other legislation.

Regulations 9 and 12 correct errors in the 1984 Regulations.

STATUTORY INSTRUMENTS

1987 No. 844

INCOME TAX

The Income Tax (Building Societies) (Amendment) Regulations 1987

Made - - - -	*8th May 1987*
Laid before the House of Commons	*11th May 1987*
Coming into force	*1st June 1987*

The Commissioners of Inland Revenue, in exercise of the powers conferred on them by section 343 (1A) of the Income and Corporation Taxes Act 1970(**a**), hereby make the following Regulations:

Citation and commencement

1. These Regulations may be cited as the Income Tax (Building Societies) (Amendment) Regulations 1987 and shall come into force on 1st June 1987.

Interpretation

2. In these Regulations "the 1986 Regulations" means the Income Tax (Building Societies) Regulations 1986(**b**).

Amendments to the 1986 Regulations

3. In regulation 2(1) of the 1986 Regulations–
   - (a) in paragraph (*a*) of the definition of "qualifying certificate of deposit" after "£50,000" there shall be inserted "(or, for a deposit denominated in foreign currency, not less than the equivalent of £50,000 at the time when the deposit is made)";
   - (b) in paragraph (*b*) of the definition of "qualifying certificate of deposit"–
     - (i) the words "before the expiry of the period of twelve months" shall be omitted, and
     - (ii) after the word "arises" there shall be inserted "not later than the end of the period of five years";
   - (c) in paragraph (*a*) of the definition of "qualifying time deposit"–
     - (i) the words "in sterling and" shall be omitted, and
     - (ii) after "£50,000" there shall be inserted "(or, for a deposit denominated in foreign currency, not less than the equivalent of £50,000 at the time when the deposit is made)".

(**a**) 1970 c.10; subsection (1A) was inserted in section 343 by section 40(3) of the Finance Act 1985 (c.54) and amended by section 47(1) of the Finance Act 1986 (c.41). Other relevant amendments to section 343 were made by sections 37 and 38 of, and paragraph 40 of Schedule 6 and Part II of Schedule 14 to, the Finance Act 1971 (c.68), section 111 of, and paragraph 22 of Schedule 24 to, the Finance Act 1972 (c.41), section 14 of, and paragraph 5(a) of Schedule 2 to the Finance Act 1978 (c.42), sections 26(5) and 128 of, and Part V of Schedule 23 to, the Finance Act 1984 (c.43), by sections 40 and 98(6) of, and Part V of Schedule 27 to, the Finance Act 1985 (c.54) and by section 47(2) and (3) of the Finance Act 1986. (**b**) S.I. 1986/482.

4. In regulation 6(1) of the 1986 Regulations after paragraph (*f*) there shall be inserted–

"(*ff*) a payment to a company resident in the United Kingdom, which company is a 51 per cent. subsidiary of the building society making the payment, where the building society and the company have jointly elected that any such payments shall be made gross and the election is in force at the time of the payment;".

5. After regulation 6(2) of the 1986 Regulations there shall be inserted–

"(3) Section 257 of the Taxes Act 1970 shall apply to an election under paragraph (1) (ff) as it applies to an election under subsection (1) or subsection (2) of section 256 of that Act but as if–

(a) subsection (2) were omitted, and

(b) the references in subsections (1), (3) and (4) to "the companies" were references to "the building society and the company" and the reference in subsection (3) to "each company" were a reference to "both the building society and the company".

(4) For the purposes of paragraph (1) (ff)–

(a) a company shall be treated as a 51 per cent subsidiary of a building society if and so long as more than 50 per cent. of its ordinary share capital is owned directly or indirectly by the building society,

(b) subject to paragraph (c), a building society shall be treated as owning share capital directly or indirectly in a company if it would be so treated for the purposes of section 532 of the Taxes Act, and

(c) in determining whether a building society owns more than 50 per cent. of the ordinary share capital of a company, it shall be treated as not being the owner–

(i) of any share capital which it owns directly or indirectly in a company which is not resident in the United Kingdom, or

(ii) of any share capital which it owns indirectly and which is owned directly by a company for which a profit on the sale of the shares would be a trading receipt."

A. J. G. Isaac
B. Pollard
Two of the Commissioners of Inland Revenue

8th May 1987

EXPLANATORY NOTE

(This note is not part of the Regulations)

These Regulations, which come into force on 1st June 1987, amend the Income Tax (Building Societies) Regulations 1986 ("the 1986 Regulations").

Regulation 1 provides for citation and commencement.

Regulation 2 provides for interpretation.

Regulation 3(a) amends the definition of "qualifying certificate of deposit" in regulation 2(1) of the 1986 Regulations in relation to deposits denominated in a foreign currency.

Regulation 3(b) further amends the definition of "qualifying certificate of deposit" in regulation 2(1) of the 1986 Regulations by increasing the period, within which the obligation of a building society to pay the amount payable by it must arise, from less than twelve months beginning on the date of issue of the certificate to five years beginning on that date.

Regulation 3(c) amends the definition of "qualifying time deposit" in regulation 2(1) of the 1986 Regulations, by removing the requirement that the deposit must be in sterling.

Regulation 4 amends regulation 6(1) of the 1986 Regulations (gross payments) so that a payment to a 51 per cent. subsidiary company of a building society may be made gross where the building society and the subsidiary company jointly elect that the payment should be so made.

Regulation 5 makes procedural amendments to Regulation 6 of the 1986 Regulations consequent on the power to make gross payments to subsidiary companies.

STATUTORY INSTRUMENTS

1987 No. 851

POLICE

The Police Regulations 1987

Made - - - - *7th May 1987*

Laid before Parliament *13th May 1987*

Coming into force - *15th June 1987*

ARRANGEMENT OF REGULATIONS

Schedule   3—Annual leave.

Schedule   4—University scholars.

Schedule   5—Scales of pay.

Schedule   6—Effect of disciplinary action on pay and allowances.

Schedule   7—Subsistence, refreshment and lodging allowances.

Schedule   8—Motor vehicle allowances.

Schedule   9—Bicycle allowance.

Schedule 10—Typewriter allowance.

Schedule 11—Dog handler's allowance.

Schedule 12—Issue of uniform and equipment.

In exercise of the powers conferred upon me by section 33 of the Police Act 1964(a), and after satisfying the requirements of section 46(3) of that Act(b) and section 2(1) of the Police Negotiating Board Act 1980(c) as to the furnishing of drafts of the Regulations to the Police Advisory Board for England and Wales and to the Police Negotiating Board for the United Kingdom, and taking into consideration any representations or recommendations made by them respectively, I hereby make the following Regulations:-

PART I

GENERAL

Citation and operation

1. These Regulations may be cited as the Police Regulations 1987 and shall come into force on 15th June 1987.

Revocations

2. The Regulations set out in Schedule 1 are hereby revoked.

References to transfers

3.—(1) Except where the context otherwise requires, a reference in these Regulations to a member of a police force voluntarily transferring from one force to another shall be construed as a reference to such a member leaving a force for the purpose of joining another force and joining that other force, where-

  (a) he left the force first mentioned in this regulation on or after 1st January 1963 for the purposes aforesaid with, in the case of the chief officer of police, the consent of the police authority;

  (b) he left the force first mentioned in this regulation before 1st January 1963 for the purposes aforesaid with the written consent of the chief officer of police.

(2) Except where the context otherwise requires, a reference in these Regulations to a member of a police force being statutorily transferred from one force to another shall be construed as a reference to such a member being transferred-

---

(a) 1964 c.48.

(b) Section 46(3), as amended by s.4(6) of the Police Act 1969 (c.63), was amended by s.2(4) of the Police Negotiating Board Act 1980 (c.10).

(c) 1980 c.10.

(a) by or under the Local Government Act 1933(**a**), the Police Act 1946(**b**), the Local Government Act 1958(**c**), the London Government Act 1963(**d**), the Police Act 1964, or the Local Government Act 1972(**e**),

(b) in the case of a person who was a member of the River Tyne police force, under the Harbours Act 1964(**f**).

(3) Except where the context otherwise requires, a reference in these Regulations to a member of a police force transferring from one force to another shall be construed as a reference to his either voluntarily so transferring or being statutorily so transferred.

References to provisions of these Regulations

4. In these Regulations, unless the context otherwise requires, a reference to a regulation shall be construed as a reference to a regulation contained in these Regulations, a reference to a Schedule shall be construed as a reference to a Schedule to these Regulations, a reference to a paragraph shall be construed as a reference to a paragraph in the same regulation or, as the case may be, the same Part of the same Schedule and a reference to a sub-paragraph shall be construed as a reference to a sub-paragraph contained in the same paragraph.

Meanings assigned to certain expressions, etc.

5.—(1) In these Regulations, unless the context otherwise requires, the following expressions have the meanings hereby respectively assigned to them, that is to say:–

"central police officer" has the same meaning as in the Police Pensions Regulations;

"Discipline Regulations" means the regulations relating to discipline from time to time in force under section 33 of the Police Act 1964 and sections 94(5), 101 and 102 of the Police and Criminal Evidence Act 1984(**g**);

"inspector" includes chief inspector;

"overseas policeman" has the same meaning as in the Police Pensions Regulations;

"pensionable service" has the same meaning as in the Police Pensions Regulations;

"Police Pensions Regulations" means the regulations from time to time in force under the Police Pensions Act 1976(**h**);

"Promotion Regulations" means the regulations relating to qualification and selection for promotion from time to time in force under section 33 of the Police Act 1964;

"public holiday" means Christmas Day, Good Friday or a bank holiday;

"reversionary member of a home police force" has the same meaning as in the Police Pensions Regulations;

"rostered rest day" has the meaning assigned thereto by regulation 27(1);

"superintendent" includes chief superintendent;

"university scholar" and, in relation to such a scholar, "course" and "study" have the meanings respectively assigned to them in paragraph 1 of Schedule 4.

(2) In these Regulations, unless the context otherwise requires, a reference to a police force shall include a reference to the Royal Ulster Constabulary and a police force maintained under the Police (Scotland) Act 1967(**i**), so however that nothing in these Regulations shall be construed as relating to the government, administration or conditions of service of the Royal Ulster Constabulary or such a force.

(3) In these Regulations a reference to an aerodrome constabulary is a reference to such a constabulary within the meaning of the Aviation Security Act 1982(**j**); and a

---

(**a**) 1933 c.51. (**b**) 1946 c.46. (**c**) 1958 c.55.
(**d**) 1963 c.33. (**e**) 1972 c.70. (**f**) 1964 c.40.
(**g**) 1984 c.60. (**h**) 1976 c.35. (**i**) 1967 c.77.
(**j**) 1982 c.36.

reference to a rank in such a constabulary corresponding to a rank in a police force is a reference to a rank in that constabulary designated for the purposes hereof by the Secretary of State as the rank corresponding to the rank in question.

(4) Nothing in these Regulations shall be construed as authorising pay or allowances payable to any person to be reduced retrospectively.

Modification of Regulations in relation to metropolitan police force

6.—(1) All payments required to be made under these Regulations by the Secretary of State as police authority for the metropolitan police district shall be paid out of the metropolitan police fund.

(2) Any reference to a police authority in a provision of these Regulations concerned with property shall in relation to the metropolitan police force be construed as including a reference to the Receiver for the metropolitan police district.

PART II
GOVERNMENT

ORGANISATION

Authorised establishment

7. The authorised establishment of the several ranks of a police force and any changes thereto shall be subject to the approval of the Secretary of State and shall be sufficient to provide for the carrying out of police duties under responsible supervision in each tour of duty.

Ranks

8.—(1) The ranks of a police force shall be known by the following designations:-
Chief Constable.
Deputy Chief Constable.
Assistant Chief Constable or Commander.
Chief Superintendent.
Superintendent.
Chief Inspector.
Inspector.
Sergeant.
Constable.

(2) Notwithstanding anything in paragraph (1), in the metropolitan police force ranks other than those specified in that paragraph may be adopted with the approval of the Secretary of State.

Beats, sections, sub-divisions and divisions

9. The area to which a constable is assigned for duty either generally or for a particular period of hours shall be known as a beat; a number of beats grouped for supervision by a sergeant or an inspector shall be known as a section; a number of sections grouped for supervision by an inspector, chief inspector or superintendent shall be known as a sub-division; a number of sections or sub-divisions grouped for supervision by a chief superintendent shall be known as a division.

Restrictions on the private life of members

10. The restrictions on private life contained in Schedule 2 shall apply to all members of a police force; and no restrictions other than those designed to secure the proper exercise of the functions of a constable shall be imposed by the police authority or the chief officer of police on the private life of members of a police force except such as may temporarily be necessary or such as may be approved by the Secretary of State after

consultation with the Police Advisory Board for England and Wales, and any such restriction temporarily imposed shall be reported forthwith to the Secretary of State.

Business interests incompatible with membership of a police force

11.—(1) If a member of a police force or a relative included in his family proposes to have, or has, a business interest within the meaning of this regulation, the member shall forthwith give written notice of that interest to the chief officer of police unless that business interest was disclosed at the time of his appointment as a member of the force.

(2) On receipt of a notice given under paragraph (1), the chief officer of police shall determine whether or not the interest in question is compatible with the member concerned remaining a member of the force and shall notify the member in writing of his decision.

(3) Within 10 days of being notified of the chief officer's decision as aforesaid, or within such longer period as the police authority may in all the circumstances allow, the member concerned may appeal to the police authority against that decision by sending written notice of his appeal to the police authority.

(4) Upon receipt of such notice, the police authority shall send to the member concerned copies of any documents submitted to them by the chief officer of police setting out the matters on which he relies in support of his decision and shall afford the member concerned a reasonable opportunity to comment thereon.

(5) Where a member of a police force has appealed to the police authority under paragraph (3) the police authority shall give him written notice of their determination of the appeal but, where they have upheld the decision of the chief officer of police and, within 10 days of being so notified or within such longer period as the police authority may in all the circumstances allow, the member makes written request to the police authority for the reference of the matter to the Secretary of State, the matter shall be so referred and, unless and until the determination of the police authority is confirmed by the Secretary of State, it shall be of no effect and in particular, no action in pursuance thereof shall be taken under paragraph (6).

(6) Where a member of a police force, or a relative included in his family, has a business interest within the meaning of this regulation which the chief officer of police has determined, under paragraph (2), to be incompatible with his remaining a member of the force and either the member has not appealed against that decision under paragraph (3) or, subject to paragraph (5), on such appeal, the police authority has upheld that decision, then, the chief officer of police may, subject to the approval of the police authority, dispense with the services of that member; and before giving such approval, the police authority shall give the member concerned an opportunity to make representations and shall consider any representations so made.

(7) For the purposes of this regulation, a member of a police force or, as the case may be, a relative included in his family, shall have a business interest if–

    (a) the member holds any office or employment for hire or gain (otherwise than as a member of a police force) or carries on any business;

    (b) a shop is kept or a like business carried on by the member's spouse (not being separated from him) at any premises in the area of the police force in question or by any relative included in his family at the premises at which he resides; or

    (c) the member, his spouse (not being separated from him) or any relative included in his family living with him holds, or possesses a pecuniary interest in, any such licence or permit as is mentioned in paragraph (8);

and a reference to a relative included in a member's family shall include a reference to his spouse, parent, son, daughter, brother or sister.

(8) The licence or permit referred to in paragraph (7)(c) is a licence or permit granted in pursuance of the law relating to liquor licensing, refreshment houses or betting and gaming or regulating places of entertainment in the area of the police force in question.

(9) If a member of a police force or a relative included in his family has a business interest within the meaning of this regulation and, on that interest being notified or disclosed as mentioned in paragraph (1), the chief officer of police has, by written notice,

required the member to furnish particulars of such changes in that interest, as respects its nature, extent or otherwise, as may be mentioned in the notice then, in the event of any such change in that interest being proposed or occurring, this regulation shall have effect as though the changed interest were a newly proposed, or newly acquired, interest which has not been notified or disclosed as aforesaid.

(10) In its application to a chief constable, deputy chief constable or assistant chief constable, this regulation shall have effect as if–

(a) for any reference therein to the chief officer of police there were substituted a reference to the police authority;

(b) for any reference in paragraph (3), (5) or (6) to an appeal there were substituted a reference to a request for reconsideration; and

(c) the references in paragraph (6) to the approval of the police authority were omitted;

but a police authority shall not dispense with the services of a chief constable, deputy chief constable or assistant chief constable under this regulation without giving him an opportunity of making representations and shall consider any representations so made.

(11) In its application to a member of the metropolitan police force, this regulation shall have effect as if–

(a) for any reference to the chief officer of police there were substituted a reference to an assistant commissioner of police of the metropolis; and

(b) for any reference to the police authority there were substituted a reference to the commissioner of police of the metropolis;

except that nothing in this paragraph shall affect the power of the commissioner of police, subject to the approval of the police authority, to dispense with the services of a member of the metropolitan police force in pursuance of paragraph (6).

APPOINTMENT, PROBATION AND RETIREMENT

Business interests precluding appointment to a police force

12.—(1) Save in so far as the chief officer of police may allow at the request of the candidate concerned, a person shall not be eligible for appointment to a police force if he or a relative included in his family has a business interest within the meaning of regulation 11, and paragraphs (7) and (8) thereof shall apply for the purposes of the interpretation of this regulation as they apply for the purposes of that regulation.

(2) In its application to a candidate for appointment as chief officer of police or in the rank of deputy chief constable or assistant chief constable, paragraph (1) shall have effect as if for any reference to the chief officer of police there were substituted a reference to the police authority.

Qualifications for appointment to a police force

13.—(1) A candidate for appointment to a police force–

(a) must produce satisfactory references as to character, and, if he has served in any police force, in the armed forces, in the civil service or as a seaman, produce satisfactory proof of his good conduct while so serving;

(b) must have attained the age of 18 years 6 months and, unless he has previous service as a member of a police force or by reason of other experience or his personal qualities is specially suitable for appointment, must not have attained the age of 30 years or, if he has previous wholetime service in the armed forces or previous service as a seaman, 40 years;

(c) must be certified by a registered medical practitioner approved by the police authority to be in good health, of sound constitution and fitted both physically and mentally to perform the duties on which he will be employed after appointment;

(d) must, if a candidate for appointment in the rank of constable–

(i) unless the chief officer of police otherwise decides, be not less in height than, in the case of a man, 172 cms, or in the case of a woman, 162 cms, and

(ii) satisfy the chief officer of police that he is sufficiently educated by passing a written or oral examination in reading, writing and simple arithmetic, or an examination of a higher standard, as may be prescribed by the chief officer of police;

(e) must, if a candidate for appointment in the rank of sergeant or inspector, be qualified for promotion to such rank in accordance with the provisions of the Promotion Regulations;

(f) must give such information as may be required as to his previous history or employment or any other matter relating to his appointment to the police force;

(g) shall be given a notice in terms approved by the Secretary of State drawing attention to the conditions of service contained therein.

(2) For the purposes of this regulation–

(a) the expression "armed forces" means the naval, military or air forces of the Crown including any women's service administered by the Defence Council, and

(b) the expression "seaman" has the same meaning as in the Merchant Shipping Act 1894**(a)**.

Appointment of chief constable

14. Every appointment to the office of chief constable shall be subject to the approval of the Secretary of State, and, without prejudice to regulations 12 and 13, no person shall be appointed to such a post in a police force unless he has at least 2 years' experience in some other force in the rank of superintendent or a higher rank.

Appointment of deputy chief constable

15. Every appointment to the rank of deputy chief constable shall be subject to the approval of the Secretary of State, and, without prejudice to regulations 12 and 13, no person shall be appointed to such a rank in a police force unless he has at least 2 years' experience in some other force in the rank of superintendent or a higher rank.

Probationary service in the rank of constable

16.—(1) This regulation shall apply to a member of a police force appointed in the rank of constable other than such a member who transferred to the force from another police force, having completed the required period of probation therein.

(2) A member of a police force to whom this regulation applies shall, unless paragraph (3) applies to his case, be on probation for the first 2 years of his service as a constable in that police force following his last appointment thereto or for such longer period as the chief officer of police, with the approval of the Secretary of State, determines in the circumstances of a particular case:

Provided that where, in the opinion of the chief officer of police, the said period of probation was seriously interrupted by a period of absence from duty by reason of injury or illness, the chief officer of police may at his discretion extend the period of probation for such longer period not exceeding 12 months as he determines in the circumstances of that particular case.

(3) A member of a police force to whom this regulation applies who has served on probation for a period of not less than a year following a previous appointment to that or any other police force shall be on probation for the first year of his service as a constable in the police force first mentioned in this paragraph following his last appointment thereto or for such longer period as the chief officer of police, with the approval of the Secretary of State, determines in the circumstances of a particular case:

Provided that the chief officer of police may at his discretion–

(a) reduce the period of probation, so however that the reduced period, when aggregated with the previous period of probation, shall not be less than 2 years, or

(a) 1894 c.60.

(b) dispense with the period of probation, if the member, following his previous appointment, completed the required period of probation in the force in question.

(4) For the purposes of this regulation–

    (a) in reckoning service, any period of unpaid leave shall be disregarded;

    (b) in the case of a university scholar, in reckoning service his period of study shall be disregarded;

    (c) in the case of a member who has been statutorily transferred from one force to some other force, his service in those two forces shall be treated as if it were service in the same police force;

    (d) in the case of a member of a police force who has been transferred thereto from an aerodrome constabulary by an order under section 30 of the Aviation Security Act 1982, his service in that constabulary shall be treated as if it were service in that police force.

Discharge of probationer

17.—(1) Subject to the provisions of this regulation, during his period of probation in the force the services of a constable may be dispensed with at any time if the chief officer of police considers that he is not fitted, physically or mentally, to perform the duties of his office, or that he is not likely to become an efficient or well conducted constable.

(2) A constable whose services are dispensed with under this regulation shall be entitled to receive a month's notice or a month's pay in lieu thereof.

(3) A constable's services shall not be dispensed with in accordance with this regulation and any notice given for the purposes thereof shall cease to have effect if he gives written notice to the police authority of his intention to retire and retires in pursuance of the said notice on or before the date on which his services would otherwise be dispensed with; and such a notice taking effect on that date shall be accepted by the police authority notwithstanding that less than a month's notice is given.

(4) Where a constable has received a notice under this regulation that his services are to be dispensed with and he gives written notice of his intention to retire and retires under paragraph (3), he shall nevertheless be entitled to receive pay up to and until the date on which the month's notice he has received would have expired or where he has received or is due to receive a month's pay in lieu of notice he shall remain entitled to that pay notwithstanding the notice he has given under paragraph (3).

Retirement

18.—(1) Without prejudice to the provisions mentioned in paragraph (3), a member of a police force may retire only if he has given to the police authority a month's written notice of his intention to retire or such shorter notice as may have been accepted by that authority:

Provided that, while suspended under the Discipline Regulations, a member may not, without the consent of the chief officer of police, give notice for the purposes of this regulation or retire in pursuance of a notice previously given.

(2) In the case of a chief officer of police, deputy chief constable or assistant chief constable, the preceding paragraph shall have effect as if for the reference to the chief officer of police there were substituted a reference to the police authority.

(3) The provisions referred to in paragraph (1) are–

    (a) the provisions of sections 5 and 6 of the Police Act 1964 relating to retirement in the interests of efficiency;

    (b) the provisions of section 58(3) of the Police Act 1964 relating to the retirement of chief constables affected by amalgamations or local government reorganisation;

    (c) the provisions of the Police Pensions Regulations relating to compulsory retirement, and

    (d) the provisions of the Discipline Regulations relating to resignation as an alternative to dismissal.

PERSONAL RECORDS

Contents of personal records

19.—(1) The chief officer of police shall cause a personal record of each member of the police force to be kept.

(2) The personal record shall contain—

  (a) a personal description of the member;

  (b) particulars of the member's place and date of birth;

  (c) particulars of his marriage (if any) and of his children (if any);

  (d) a record of his service (if any) in any branch of Her Majesty's naval, military or air forces or in the civil service;

  (e) a record of his service (if any) in any other police force and of his transfers (if any) from one police force to another;

  (f) a record of whether he passed or failed to pass any qualifying examination at which he was a candidate;

  (g) a record of his service in the police force including particulars of all promotions, postings, removals, injuries received, periods of illness, commendations, rewards, punishments other than cautions, and the date of his ceasing to be a member of the police force with the reason, cause or manner thereof:

Provided that, if the member so requests–

  (i) a punishment of a fine or of a reprimand shall be expunged after 3 years free from punishment other than a caution;

  (ii) any other punishment shall be expunged after 5 years free from punishment other than a caution.

(3) A member of a police force shall, if he so requests, be entitled to inspect his personal record.

Transfer of personal records

20. Where a member of a police force transfers to another police force his personal record shall be transferred to the chief officer of police of that other police force.

Personal record of member leaving force

21.—(1) Where a member of a police force ceases to be a member of that police force the member shall, unless he transfers to another police force, be given a certificate showing his rank and setting out the period of his service in that police force and in any other police force and the reason, cause or manner of his leaving the force:

Provided that, where the member was required to resign or was dismissed, the certificate shall not contain any description of the circumstances in which he was required to resign or was dismissed.

(2) The chief officer of police may append to the certificate any recommendation which he feels justified in giving, such as that–

  his conduct was exemplary;

  his conduct was very good;

  his conduct was good.

(3) Where a member of a police force ceases to be a member of that police force, otherwise than by transferring to another police force, his personal record shall be kept for such time as the chief of police may think fit and shall then be destroyed.

Fingerprints

22.—(1) Every member of a police force shall in accordance with the directions of the chief officer of police have his fingerprints taken.

(2) Fingerprints of members of a police force taken in accordance with paragraph (1) shall be kept separate from the fingerprints of persons whose fingerprints have been taken otherwise than in accordance with that paragraph.

(3) The fingerprints of a member of a police force taken in accordance with paragraph (1) and all copies and records thereof shall be destroyed on his ceasing to be a member of that force, except that, where by reason of a statutory transfer he becomes a member of another force, his fingerprints and all copies and records thereof shall be transferred to the chief officer of police of that other police force.

PART III

DUTY, OVERTIME AND LEAVE

Duty to carry out lawful orders

23. Every member of a police force shall carry out all lawful orders and shall at all times punctually and promptly perform all appointed duties and attend to all matters within the scope of his office as a constable.

Limitations on duties to be assigned to members statutorily transferred

24.—(1) Where a member of a police force has previously served in a police force for an area comprised in whole or in part in the area for which his present force is maintained and he ceased to be a member of his former force and became a member of his present force by reason only of one or more such statutory transfers as are mentioned in paragraph (2), then, subject to paragraph (3), he shall not be assigned to duties which, in the opinion of the Secretary of State, make it necessary for him to move his home to a place which is outside the area for which his former force was maintained.

(2) In paragraph (1) the reference to a statutory transfer is a reference to a statutory transfer being–

    (a) a transfer in accordance with the provisions of an amalgamation scheme under the Police Act 1964, or

    (b) a transfer taking effect on 1st April 1974,

except that where the former force was a police force for a borough, the said reference is to any statutory transfer.

(3) Paragraph (1) shall not apply to a person by reason of his previous service in a particular police force if–

    (a) since he became a member of that police force he has been a chief officer of police, or

    (b) after he was statutorily transferred from that police force he has given written notice to the chief officer of the police force of which he was at the time a member that the protection accorded by paragraph (1) should cease to apply to him, or

    (c) that force was a county or combined police force and after he was statutorily transferred therefrom but before 1st February 1968 he was assigned to such duties as are mentioned in paragraph (1),

without prejudice, however, to the application of paragraph (1) to him by reason of service in another police force after his statutory transfer from the force first mentioned in this paragraph and before his statutory transfer to his present force.

(4) Paragraph (1) shall apply in the case of a member of a police force who ceased to be such and became a serviceman, a reversionary member of a home police force or a central police officer–

    (a) where on ceasing to be such, he resumed service in, or, as the case may be, exercised his right of reversion to, his former force, as if he had not ceased to be a member of that force, or

    (b) where on ceasing to be such, he resumed service in, or, as the case may be, exercised his right of reversion to some other force to which members of his former force had been transferred as mentioned in paragraph (2), as if he had been so transferred from his former force to that other force.

(5) In this regulation the expressions "present force" and "former force" mean, respectively, the force first mentioned and that secondly mentioned in paragraph (1).

Work not required to be performed

25. A member of a police force shall not be required to perform–

    (a) the regular duty of cleaning or any part of the cleaning of a particular police station which the Secretary of State has directed is not a duty which the police may be required to perform;

    (b) any other work not connected with police duty which, in the opinion of the Secretary of State, the police may not properly be required to perform.

Normal daily period of duty

26.—(1) This regulation shall apply to every member of a police force below the rank of superintendent who is not assigned to duties which the Secretary of State has specially excepted from the provisions of this regulation.

(2) The normal daily period of duty (including the period of refreshment referred to in paragraph (3)) of a member of a police force to whom this regulation applies shall be 8 hours.

(3) As far as the exigencies of duty permit–

    (a) the normal daily period of duty shall be performed in one tour of duty; and

    (b) subject to paragraph 4 of Schedule 3, an interval of 45 minutes shall be allowed for refreshment.

(4) Where a member is required to perform his normal daily period of duty in more than one tour of duty and does not travel to and from his home between tours, an interval for refreshment and rest shall normally be included at the beginning or end of one of those tours.

(5) In this Part of these Regulations, the expression "day", in relation to members of a police force, means a period of 24 hours commencing at such time or times as the chief officer shall fix and the chief officer may fix different times in relation to different groups of members.

(6) In discharging his functions under paragraph (5), the chief officer shall have regard to the wishes of the joint branch board.

Rostering of duties

27.—(1) A chief officer shall cause to be published, in accordance with this regulation, annual duty rosters for members of his force below the rank of superintendent and in these Regulations–

    (a) a reference to a rostered rest day is to be construed, in relation to a member of a police force who is required to do duty on that day, as a reference to a day which according to the duty roster was, immediately before he was so required to do duty, to have been a rest day for the member; and

    (b) a day off granted in lieu of a rostered rest day shall be treated as a rostered rest day.

(2) Each such roster shall be published at intervals not exceeding 12 months and not later than one month before the date on which it is to come into force.

(3) Each such roster shall set out, for the 12 months following the date on which it comes into force, in relation to each member of the force to which it relates–

    (a) his rest days;

    (b) those days, being public holidays, on which he may be required to do duty; and

    (c) the times at which his scheduled daily periods of duty are to begin and end.

(4) Subject to paragraph (5), a duty roster shall make provision for–

    (a) an interval of not less than 8 hours between the ending of each of a member's daily periods of duty and the beginning of the next; and

    (b) an interval between each of his rostered rest days not exceeding 7 days;

unless the joint branch board agrees otherwise.

(5) Where, owing to the exigencies of duty, it is necessary to alter a duty roster, the officer responsible for making the alteration shall endeavour, so far as practicable, to avoid thereby requiring a member to do an additional daily period of duty such that the condition in paragraph (4)(a) would not be satisfied in relation thereto.

Overtime

28.—(1) Subject to, and in accordance with, the provisions of this regulation a member of a police force shall be compensated in respect of time for which he remains on duty after his tour of duty ends or is recalled between two tours of duty (hereafter in these Regulations referred to as "overtime").

(2) Such a member shall not be compensated under this regulation for overtime for which he receives an allowance or time off under regulation 29 or 67.

(3) A member of a police force to whom regulation 26 applies shall, subject to paragraph (6), be granted an allowance in respect of each week at the rate of a twenty-fourth of a day's pay for each completed period of 15 minutes of overtime worked by him on any occasion during that week.

(4) Where such a member, before the expiry of any pay period, elects in respect of specified overtime worked by him during the weeks ending within that period, to be granted in lieu of an allowance time off subject to and in accordance with paragraph (5), and in accordance therewith receives time off in respect of any overtime, no allowance in respect thereof shall be payable under paragraph (3).

(5) Subject to the exigencies of duty, where by virtue of an election under the foregoing paragraphs time off falls to be granted to a member in respect of any overtime worked by him in any week then, within such time (not exceeding 3 months) after that week as the chief officer of police may fix, he shall grant to the member time off equal, subject to paragraph (6), to the period of that overtime worked by him during that week and, in addition, for each completed 45 minutes of such overtime, an additional 15 minutes off.

(6) For the purposes of paragraphs (3) and (5), no account shall be taken of any period of less than 30 minutes of overtime worked on any occasion other than a period of 15 minutes of overtime in respect of which the member was informed at the commencement of his tour that he would be required to remain on duty after his tour ended.

(7) In computing any period of overtime for the purposes of this regulation–
   (a) where the member is engaged in casual escort duty, account shall be taken only of–
      (i) time during which he is in charge of the person under escort,
      (ii) such other time as is necessarily spent in travelling to or from the place where the member is to take charge of, or hand over, the person under escort, as the case may be, and
      (iii) any other time that may be allowed by the chief officer of police, so however that, if the member is so engaged overnight and has proper sleeping accommodation, whether in a train or otherwise, the chief officer of police may exclude such period not exceeding eight hours, during which the member is not in charge of the person under escort as he considers appropriate in the circumstances;
   (b) where the tour or tours of duty does not or do not amount in the aggregate to more than the normal daily period of duty, no account shall be taken of any overtime except so much as together with the tour or tours of duty exceeds the normal daily period of duty; and
   (c) where a member is recalled to duty between two rostered tours of duty and is entitled to reckon less than 4 hours of overtime in respect of any period for which he is recalled, disregarding any overtime reckonable by virtue of regulation 31 (travelling time treated as duty), he shall be deemed to have worked for such period 4 hours overtime in addition to any overtime reckonable by virtue of regulation 31.

(8) For the purposes of this regulation the following expressions have the meanings hereby respectively assigned to them, that is to say:–

"a day's pay" means the member's pay for the week in question divided by 5;

"member recalled to duty" does not include a member who is only warned to be in readiness for duty if required;

"pay period" means the period for which, in pursuance of regulation 46, a member is paid;

"week" means the period of 7 days beginning with such day as is fixed by the chief officer of police.

Public holidays and rest days for lower ranks

29.—(1) This regulation shall apply to every member of a police force below the rank of superintendent.

(2) Subject to the following provisions of this regulation, a member shall, so far as the exigencies of duty permit, be allowed a day's leave on each public holiday and be granted rest days at the rate of two rest days in respect of each week.

(3) A member shall, if required to do duty on a day which is a rostered rest day, be granted–

(a) where he receives less than 8 days' notice of the requirement, an allowance at the appropriate rate and, in addition, another rest day in lieu thereof, which shall be notified to him within 4 days of notification of the requirement;

(b) where he receives at least 8 but less than 29 days' notice of the requirement, an allowance at the appropriate rate;

(c) in any other case, another rest day in lieu thereof, which shall be notified to him within 4 days of notification of the requirement.

(4) A member shall, if required to do duty on a day which is a public holiday, be granted–

(a) where he receives less than 8 days' notice of the requirement–

(i) an allowance at the appropriate rate and, in addition,

(ii) another day off in lieu thereof, which shall be notified to him within 4 days of notification of the requirement, and which shall be treated for the purposes of this regulation as a public holiday;

(b) in any other case, an allowance at the appropriate rate.

(5) A member who is required to do duty on a day which is a public holiday or a rostered rest day may, within 28 days of the day in question, elect to receive, in lieu of an allowance as mentioned in paragraph (3)*(a)* or *(b)* or paragraph (4)*(a) or (b)*, time off equal–

(a) in the case of a day which is a public holiday, to double, and

(b) in the case of a rostered rest day, to one and a half times,

the period of completed quarters of an hour of duty on the day in question.

(6) Where such a member who is required to do duty on a day which is a public holiday or a rostered rest day has elected to receive time off as mentioned in paragraph (5), the chief officer of police shall, subject to the exigencies of duty, grant such time off within such time (not exceeding 3 months) as he may fix; and subject to such time off being taken, no allowance in respect of the day in question shall be payable under paragraph (3)*(a)* or *(b)* or, as the case may be, paragraph (4)*(a)* or *(b)*.

(7) Subject to paragraph (8), for the purposes of this regulation–

(a) a member of a police force who is paid a dog handler's allowance shall not be treated as required to do duty by reason only of his being required to care for the dog;

(b) "a day's pay" means a week's pay at the rate at which the member was paid on the day in question divided by five;

(c) "the appropriate rate" means a sixteenth of a day's pay for each completed 15 minutes of duty done on a public holiday, and three sixty-fourths of a day's pay for each such period of duty done on a rostered rest day;

(d) a reference to a day which is a public holiday is to be construed, in relation to the member concerned, as a reference to a day within the meaning of regulation 26(5) commencing at any time on the calendar date of the public holiday in question;

(e) in paragraph (2) the expression "week" means a period of 7 days beginning with such day as is fixed by the chief officer of police;

(f) a period of less than 4 completed hours of duty on a day which is a public holiday or on a rostered rest day shall be treated as though it were a period of 4 completed hours of duty; and

(g) where a member is required to do duty on a day which is a public holiday or on a rostered rest day, his period of duty shall include (save for the purposes of sub-paragraph (f)) the time occupied by him in going to, and returning from, his place of duty, not exceeding such reasonable limit as may be fixed by the chief officer of police, save that, for the purposes of this sub-paragraph, there shall be disregarded any period of time so occupied–

  (i) which together with the member's period of duty exceeds 6 hours, or

  (ii) which is treated as a period of duty under regulation 31.

(8) Where it is at his own request that a member works on a day which is a public holiday or a rostered rest day he shall not be treated for the purposes of this regulation as having been required to do duty on that day but shall be granted another day off in lieu thereof, which shall be treated as a public holiday or a rostered rest day as the case may be.

Public holidays and monthly leave days for higher ranks

30.—(1) This regulation shall apply to every member of a police force of, or above, the rank of superintendent.

(2) Such a member shall, so far as the exigencies of duty permit, be allowed a day's leave on each public holiday and be granted in each month–

  (a) in the case of a superintendent, 8 monthly leave days;

  (b) in any other case, $1\frac{1}{2}$ monthly leave days.

(3) Such a member who is required to do duty on a public holiday shall be granted a day's leave in lieu of each such day unless the exigencies of duty do not permit such grant within 12 months in the case of a superintendent or 3 months in any other case.

(4) Where the exigencies of duty have precluded the grant to a superintendent, in any month, of 8 monthly leave days, then, during the next following twelve months he shall, so far as the exigencies of duty permit, be granted the number of days not granted as additional monthly leave days.

(5) For the purposes of this regulation the expression "month" means that period of 28 days beginning with such day as is fixed by the chief officer of police.

Travelling time treated as duty

31.—(1) This regulation shall apply where a member of a police force is–

  (a) required to perform his normal daily period of duty in more than one tour of duty, or

  (b) recalled to duty between two tours of duty,

and travels to and from his home between tours or, as the case may be, in consequence of his recall (in this regulation referred to as "relevant travelling").

(2) In computing any period of overtime for the purposes of regulation 28 or any period of duty for the purposes of regulation 29 (save for the purposes of paragraph 7(f) thereof) the time occupied by such a member in relevant travelling, not exceeding such reasonable limit as may be fixed by the chief officer of police, shall be treated as a period of duty.

(3) For the purposes of regulation 60, the use of a motor vehicle for relevant travelling shall be treated as such use for the purpose of duties performed by the member concerned.

(4) Relevant travelling expenses shall be treated as expenses incurred in the execution of duty and, unless they are expenses in respect of which an allowance is payable under these Regulations, the member concerned shall be reimbursed those expenses to the extent that they do not exceed such reasonable limit as the police authority may fix.

Meetings of Police Federation treated as police duty

32.—(1) The attendance of a member of a police force at one of the following meetings of the Police Federation, that is to say, a quarterly meeting of a branch board, an ordinary meeting of a central committee, a meeting of the conferences arrangements committee, the annual meeting of the joint central committee with the joint central committee of the Scottish Police Federation and the central committee of the Police Federation for Northern Ireland, the annual meeting of a central conference or a women's regional conference shall be treated as an occasion of police duty.

(2) Subject to the approval of the chief officer of police, the attendance of a member of a police force at an additional meeting of a branch board of the Police Federation or at a meeting of a committee of a branch board shall be treated as an occasion of police duty.

(3) Subject to the approval of the Secretary of State, the attendance of a member of a police force at a meeting of the Police Federation, other than such a meeting as is mentioned in paragraph (1) or (2), shall be treated as an occasion of police duty.

Annual leave

33.—(1) Every member of a police force shall, so far as the exigencies of duty permit, be granted annual leave in accordance with Schedule 3.

(2) The annual leave of a member of a police force shall be additional to the days upon which he is not required to perform police duties in accordance with–

  (a) regulation 29, in the case of a member below the rank of superintendent, or

  (b) regulation 30, in the case of a member of, or above, the rank of superintendent;

and a member below the rank of superintendent shall, so far as the exigencies of duty permit, be allowed to take his annual leave in one period continuous with such days as aforesaid falling within the period in which he desires to take annual leave.

Sick leave

34.—(1) A member of a police force shall not be entitled to be absent from duty on account of injury or illness unless a registered medical practitioner has certified him to be unfit for duty:

Provided that–

  (a) with the consent of the police authority, a member may be so absent without such certificate of unfitness where the period of unfitness for duty does not exceed 7 days, including any day on which, even if he were fit to do so, he would not have been required to perform police duty;

  (b) if, notwithstanding such certificate of unfitness for duty, a registered medical practitioner appointed or approved by the police authority has examined the member and certified him to be fit for duty he shall no longer be entitled to be absent from duty.

(2) This regulation shall apply to a member who is in quarantine as it applies to a member who is ill and any reference to fitness or unfitness for duty shall be construed accordingly.

Maternity leave

35.—(1) During the maternity period a woman member of a police force shall not be entitled to any sick leave in respect of any injury, illness or incapacity for duty which is solely or mainly due to pregnancy or childbirth or their after effects but shall be entitled to take maternity leave for the whole or any part or parts of the period.

(2) The maternity leave granted in respect of any particular maternity period shall be paid maternity leave, as respects 3 months thereof, and unpaid maternity leave, as respects the remainder:

Provided that a member shall not be entitled to more than 3 months' paid maternity leave during any period of 12 months or, in the case of a constable, to any paid maternity leave before the end of her period of probation in the force.

(3) In this regulation the maternity period means, in relation to a woman member of a police force who is certified by a registered medical practitioner approved by the police authority to be pregnant, the period beginning 6 months before the date which is estimated by the said medical practitioner as being the probable date of birth and ending 9 months after the birth of the child.

University scholars

36. This Part of these Regulations shall have effect in relation to a university scholar subject to the provisions of paragraph 2 of Schedule 4.

PART IV
PAY

Rate of pay

37.—(1) The rate of pay of a member of a police force shall be in accordance with the appropriate scale mentioned in Schedule 5.

(2) Subject to regulations 41, 42 and 43, section 2(1) of the Police (Overseas Service) Act 1945(a) and section 43(1) of the Police Act 1964, in reckoning the service of a member of a police force in any rank for the purposes of any of the aforesaid scales of pay, account shall be taken of all his service in that rank, whether in that or another police force; and service in a higher rank, on temporary promotion thereto or otherwise, shall be treated as if it had been service in that rank:

Provided that in reckoning a member's service in any rank–
   (a) that service shall be treated as unbroken by, and including, any period of service in Her Majesty's forces which he is entitled to reckon as pensionable service;
   (b) except where the police authority in the circumstances of a particular case otherwise determine with the approval of the Secretary of State, no account shall be taken of any previous service in that rank which terminated in his reduction in rank as a punishment but any previous service in a higher rank which so terminated shall be treated as if it had been service in the rank to which the member was reduced;
   (c) no account shall be taken of any performance of the duties of that rank in respect of which a temporary salary is payable under regulation 38;
   (d) any period of unpaid leave shall be disregarded;
and, in the case of a member of a police force of a rank higher than that of inspector, this paragraph shall have effect subject to any contrary agreement so far as it relates to the reckoning of previous service in that or another force, not being a force from which he was statutorily transferred to his present force.

(3) Where a member of a combined police force has been a member of a police force for an area comprised in whole or in part in the combined area (hereafter in this paragraph referred to as "the former force") and–
   (a) he ceased to be a member of the former force and became a member of the combined force by reason only of the provisions of one or more amalgamation schemes under the Police Act 1964, and
   (b) immediately before he ceased to be a member of the former force he held the rank of deputy chief constable,

---

(a) 1945 c.17 (9 & 10 Geo. 6), as read with s.11 of the Overseas Development and Co-operation Act 1980 (c.63).

then, notwithstanding anything in paragraph (1), his pay may be increased by such amount as may be approved by the Secretary of State.

(4) Nothing in this regulation shall affect the operation of any provisions of the Discipline Regulations and, in relation to a member of a police force suspended or fined thereunder, the provisions of paragraphs 1 and 3 of Schedule 6 or of paragraph 4 thereof shall have effect.

(5) Paragraph (1) and Schedule 5 shall have effect in relation to a university scholar subject to the provisions of paragraph 3 of Schedule 4.

Temporary salary

38.—(1) A member of a police force of the rank of superintendent who is required for a continuous period exceeding 7 days to perform duties normally performed by a member of the force of a higher rank than his own, otherwise (subject to paragraph (2)) than as the direct or indirect result of the absence of any member of the force on a monthly or other leave day granted under regulation 30, shall be paid in respect of that period, other than the first 7 days thereof, at a rate equal to the lowest rate of pay for that higher rank.

(2) Where any member of the force is absent for a continuous period comprising both–

(a) monthly or other leave days granted under regulation 30, and

(b) one or more annual leave days granted under regulation 33,

paragraph (1) shall have effect as if the entire continuous period of absence were a period of annual leave.

(3) A member of a police force below the rank of superintendent who, in any year, has been required to perform duties normally performed by a member of the force of a higher rank than his own for 14 complete days shall be paid in respect of each further complete day in that year on which he is required to perform such duties at a rate equal to the lowest rate of pay to which he would be entitled on promotion to the higher rank:

Provided that where a member is entitled to be paid under this paragraph and the higher rank is that of superintendent or above there shall be no entitlement to an allowance, or time off, under regulation 28 or 29 in respect of such duties; but where in such a case the member is required to do duty on a public holiday or rostered rest day, he shall be granted a day's leave for each such day.

(4) For the purposes of this regulation the expression "year" means a period of 12 months beginning on 1st April.

(5) For the purposes of this regulation, the expression "day" means, in relation to a member of a police force below the rank of superintendent, his normal daily period of duty.

London weighting

39. The annual pay of a member of the City of London or metropolitan police force shall be increased by £885, but any allowance under these Regulations calculated by reference to a member's pay, shall be calculated as if this regulation had not been made.

Reckoning of service in the Royal Ulster Constabulary

40.—(1) Where a member of a police force joined or rejoined that force having left the Royal Ulster Constabulary, on or after 17th December 1969, for that purpose or on exercising the right of reversion conferred by section 2(1) of the Police Act 1969 then, for the purposes of regulation 37, his service in any rank in the Royal Ulster Constabulary shall be treated as if it were service in the corresponding rank in the police force he joined or rejoined as aforesaid:

Provided that in the case of a member of a police force of a rank higher than that of inspector this paragraph shall have effect subject to any contrary agreement.

(2) A member of a police force of the rank of constable shall be entitled to reckon, for the purposes of the scale of pay for that rank, any period of service in the Royal Ulster Constabulary not reckonable under paragraph (1).

(3) In this regulation, any reference to a rank corresponding to a rank in a police force is a reference to a rank in the Royal Ulster Constabulary designated by the Secretary of State for the purposes hereof as the rank corresponding to the rank in question.

Reckoning by constables of service in certain constabularies

41.—(1) A member of a police force of the rank of constable shall be entitled to reckon for the purposes of the scale of pay for that rank any period of service in a constabulary mentioned in paragraph (2).

(2) The constabularies referred to in paragraph (1) are–
 (a) the Ministry of Defence Police, that is to say the force established by section 1 of the Ministry of Defence Police Act 1987**(a)**;
 (b) the Port of London Authority's police force, that is to say the force of constables appointed under section 154 of the Port of London Act 1968**(b)**.

Reckoning of service in an airport constabulary

42. Where a member of an aerodrome constabulary has been transferred to a police force by an order under section 30 of the Aviation Security Act 1982 then, for the purposes of regulation 37, his service in any rank in that constabulary shall be treated as if it were service in the corresponding rank in a police force.

Reckoning by constables of overseas police service

43.—(1) A member of a police force of the rank of constable shall be entitled to reckon for the purposes of the scale of pay for that rank the following periods of service, that is to say, any period of–
 (a) certified overseas police service such as is mentioned in paragraph (2);
 (b) certified service in the British South Africa Police such as is mentioned in paragraph (3),
 (c) such service in a police force in the Channel Islands or the Isle of Man as is mentioned in paragraph (4),
notwithstanding that such service is not service in the rank of constable in a police force in Great Britain.

(2) The reference in paragraph (1) to certified overseas police service is a reference to–
 (a) continuous service as a member of a police force in any territory or country outside the United Kingdom, being a colony, protectorate or protected state within the meaning of the British Nationality Act 1948**(c)**, a dependent territory within the meaning of the British Nationality Act 1981**(d)** or, where appropriate, the territory or country wherein the colony, protectorate, protected state or dependent territory was incorporated after the inception of the service, subject to it having been certified by or on behalf of the Secretary of State that–
  (i) the service was, at its inception, pensionable, and
  (ii) in his opinion the person concerned ceased so to serve for reasons connected with constitutional developments in the territory or country in question, or
 (b) continuous service for 6 years or more as a member of a police force outside the United Kingdom, subject to it having been certified by or on behalf of the Secretary of State that–
  (i) the person concerned so served under a contract of service,
  (ii) immediately before he ceased so to serve, the person concerned was, for the purposes of section 12 of the Overseas Development and Co-operation Act 1980**(e)**, a person designated in accordance with such an agreement as is therein mentioned, and

---

(a) 1987 c.4.   **(b)** 1968 c.xxxii.   **(c)** 1948 c.56.
(d) 1981 c.61.   **(e)** 1980 c.63.

(iii) in his opinion the person concerned ceased so to serve for reasons connected with constitutional developments in the territory or country in question,

except that the said reference in paragraph (1) does not include a reference to service as a reversionary member of a home police force.

(3) The reference in paragraph (1) to certified service in the British South Africa Police is a reference to continuous service as a member thereof, for a period which included 11th November 1965, up to such time, on or after that date, as the person concerned ceased to perform duties therein, subject to his having ceased to perform those duties before 2nd March 1970 and subject to it having been certified by or on behalf of the Secretary of State that he approves the application of this regulation in the case of the person concerned.

(4) The reference in paragraph (1) to service in a police force in the Channel Islands or the Isle of Man is a reference to service in–

(a) the Island police force maintained under the Guernsey Law of 1919 entitled Loi Ayant Rapport à la Police Salariée pour l'Ile Entière.

(b) the States of Jersey police force maintained under the Jersey Laws entitled the Police Force (Jersey) Law 1974, or

(c) the Isle of Man Constabulary maintained under the Police (Isle of Man) Act 1962 (an Act of Tynwald).

Deductions from pay of social security benefits and statutory sick pay

44.—(1) There shall be deducted from the pay of a member of a police force–

(a) the amount of any sickness benefit, invalidity pension or invalidity allowance to which he is entitled under the Social Security Acts 1975–1982, and

(b) any statutory sick pay to which he is entitled under the Social Security and Housing Benefits Act 1982**(a)**,

and for the purposes of sub-paragraph *(a)* above any increase for adult and child dependants shall be treated as forming part of the benefit or allowance to which it relates.

(2) For the purposes of this regulation, a policewoman who as a married woman or widow has elected to pay contributions under Part I of the Social Security Act 1975 at the reduced rate, shall be deemed to be entitled to any social security benefits mentioned in paragraph (1) to which she would have been entitled had she not elected to contribute at the reduced rate.

Calculation of monthly, weekly and daily pay

45.—(1) A month's pay shall be calculated, for all purposes, at a monthly rate of pay determined by dividing by 12 the annual rate.

(2) A week's pay shall be calculated, for all purposes, at a weekly rate of pay determined by dividing by $52\frac{1}{6}$ the annual rate.

(3) A day's pay shall be calculated, except for the purposes of regulations 28 and 29, at a daily rate determined by dividing by 7 the weekly rate, determined as aforesaid.

Pay day

46.—(1) Members of a police force shall be paid at such intervals as the police authority may fix and the police authority may fix different intervals for different classes of members.

(2) In fixing the interval for any class the police authority shall have regard to the wishes of the members of that class.

(a) 1982 c.24.

PART V

ALLOWANCES AND OTHER EMOLUMENTS

Restriction on payment of allowances

47.—(1) No allowances shall be paid to a member of a police force except as provided by these Regulations or approved by the Secretary of State, and the amounts and conditions of payment of such allowances shall be as so provided or approved.

(2) Nothing in this regulation shall apply to the reimbursement of expenses incurred by a member of a police force in the execution of his duty, being expenses authorised either generally or specifically by the police authority in respect of which no allowance is payable under these Regulations.

Restriction on payments for private employment of police

48. Without prejudice to the generality of regulation 47, a member of a police force who is engaged on duty at the request of any person who has agreed to pay the police authority or, in the case of a member of the metropolitan police force, the Receiver for the metropolitan police district for the member's services shall not be entitled to any payment for those services except as provided by these Regulations; and any payments made in pursuance of that agreement shall be made by that person to the police authority or to the Receiver for the metropolitan police district, as the case may be.

Rent allowance

49.—(1) A member of a police force who is not provided with a house or quarters free of rent and rates shall be paid a rent allowance which shall be either a maximum limit allowance or a flat-rate allowance:

Provided that–

    (a) a member to whom regulation 50 applies who is so provided with quarters shall be paid a rent allowance in addition;

    (b) a member of a police force shall not be paid a rent allowance if he is on unpaid leave.

(2) Subject to paragraph (3), a maximum limit allowance–

    (a) shall be paid to a member married to (but not separated from) a person who either–

      (i) is not a member of a police force, or

      (ii) is such a member but is on unpaid leave;

    (b) shall be paid to an unmarried member, or a member separated from his spouse, who–

      (i) has attained the age of 30 years,

      (ii) has served for 5 years as a member of that or any other police force and

      (iii) occupies as owner or tenant the accommodation in which he is living;

    (c) may, if the police authority think fit, be paid to a member, not being a member to whom sub-paragraph (a) or (b) applies who–

      (i) has a dependent relative living with him, or

      (ii) is separated from, or has divorced or been divorced by, his spouse, or

      (iii) is a widower or widow;

and in all other cases a flat-rate allowance shall be paid.

(3) A maximum limit allowance shall not be payable–

    (a) to a member who lives in accommodation in respect of which he makes no payment (by way of rent, rates or otherwise), or

    (b) to a member who shares with another member accommodation of which they are joint owners or tenants so, however, that this sub-paragraph shall not preclude the payment of a maximum limit allowance by virtue of sub-paragraph (ii) of paragraph (2)(a).

(4)(a) A maximum limit allowance payable to a member shall not be less than a half of, nor more than, the maximum limit for his rank but, subject as aforesaid shall be the aggregate of the amount paid in rates and the amount of any rate rebate granted to him together with–

    (i) where the member owns the house he occupies, the amount which in the opinion of the District Valuer would be paid in rent therefor if the house were let unfurnished,

    (ii) where the member is living in unfurnished accommodation, the amount paid in rent therefor, or

    (iii) subject to sub-paragraph (a)(i), where the member is living in furnished accommodation, an amount which in the opinion of the police authority would have been paid in rent therefor had the accommodation been unfurnished:

Provided that where part of the said house or part of the said accommodation is let to or occupied by a tenant or lodger, as the case may be, who is not a member of a police force, the police authority may make a deduction from the said aggregate in respect of such part.

    (b) The maximum limit shall be fixed by the police authority with the approval of the Secretary of State for each rank.

(5) A flat-rate allowance shall be an allowance equal to half the amount fixed as the maximum limit for members of the same rank.

(6) Except where the member's spouse or former spouse is a member of a police force, a married member who is separated from his spouse or a member who is divorced, or been divorced by, his spouse, may, if he regularly makes periodic payments to or for the benefit of his spouse or former spouse, be granted–

    (a) where he is in receipt of a rent allowance under paragraph (1), an addition to that rent allowance, or

    (b) where he is provided with a house or quarters free of rent and rates, a rent allowance,

equal to whichever is the lesser of the two following amounts, namely, the amount by which his former allowance exceeds his present allowance or the amount paid by him to or for the benefit of his spouse or former spouse.

(7) In this regulation–

    (a) the expression "his former allowance" means–

        (i) in relation to a member who, immediately before his spouse commenced to live apart from him, was being provided with a house or quarters free of rent and rates, a sum fixed as the value for the time being of that house or those quarters;

        (ii) in relation to any other member, the maximum limit allowance which would for the time being be payable to him if he were still entitled to such an allowance and the aggregate referred to in paragraph (4)(a) were unchanged since immediately before his spouse commenced to live apart from him;

    (b) the expression "his present allowance" means the rent allowance which is being paid to the member under paragraph (1) or, as the case may be, a sum fixed as the value for the time being of the house or quarters with which he is provided;

    (c) the expression "rates" includes–

        (i) any general rate within the meaning of the General Rate Act 1967**(a)** and in addition any rate mentioned in paragraphs (a), (b) and (c) of the definition of "excepted rate" in section 115(1) of that Act (drainage, tithe, common and other rates of a similar character),

        (ii) any rate or charge for a supply of water for domestic purposes, and

        (iii) the reasonable costs of emptying a cess-pit where the premises do not have main drainage;

    (d) the expression "rate rebate" means a rate rebate granted under a statutory or

---

(a) 1967 c.9.

local rate rebate scheme within the meaning of section 22 of the Local Government Act 1974(a);

(e) a reference to the provision of a house or quarters free of rent and rates is a reference to such provision by a police authority.

Supplementary rent allowance

50.—(1) This regulation shall apply to–

(a) a member of a police force who–

(i) is a widower or widow with a child or children or is married,

(ii) is not living with his family, and

(iii) satisfies the chief officer of police that the only reason why he is not so living is that he is unable to find suitable accommodation for his family at a reasonable cost within a reasonable distance of his place of duty;

(b) a member of a police force, other than such a member as is mentioned in sub-paragraph (a), who is temporarily assigned to duties which, in the opinion of the chief officer of police, require him to live otherwise than in his former accommodation,

except that this regulation shall not apply to such a member as is mentioned in sub-paragraph (b) for a continuous period exceeding 30 months unless the police authority, in the circumstances of the case, so determine, or in respect of any period for which he has not retained, or has let or sub-let, his former accommodation.

(2) Notwithstanding the provisions of regulation 49, the rent allowance to be paid to a member to whom this regulation applies shall be that which would be payable under the said regulation 49–

(a) in the case of such a member as is mentioned in paragraph (1)(a), if he were a member of the force of the police area in which his family are for the time being living and he were living with his family;

(b) in the case of such a member as is mentioned in paragraph (1)(b), if he had not been assigned to such duties as are there mentioned and had continued to occupy his former accommodation.

(3) A member to whom this regulation applies shall be paid a supplementary rent allowance–

(a) if he is living in quarters provided free of rent and rates, at the weekly rate of £8.33;

(b) if he is not so living, at the weekly rate £8.33 higher than that of a flat-rate allowance payable under regulation 49 to a member of the force of the police area in which he is for the time being serving.

(4) A supplementary rent allowance payable under paragraph (3) may be reduced or withdrawn by the police authority in respect of any period consisting of one or more complete weeks throughout which the member in question is absent from his usual or temporary normal place of duty and is either–

(a) on leave of absence; or

(b) provided with board and lodging free of charge or an allowance in lieu.

Application of regulations 49 and 50 to members of regional crime squads and motorway patrol groups

51.—(1) This regulation shall apply to a member of a police force who is assigned to duty with a regional crime squad or a motorway patrol group established in pursuance of a collaboration agreement made under section 13 of the Police Act 1964.

(2) Where a member of a police force to whom this regulation applies moves his home and the removal is in the opinion of the appropriate committee of chief officers of police due to the exigencies of police duty or is made at the request of that committee and is, in their opinion, in the interest of the efficiency of the crime squad or patrol group concerned, then notwithstanding the provisions of regulation 49, the rent allowance to

(a) 1974 c.7.

be paid to him shall be that which would be payable to him under that regulation if he was a member of the force of the police area in which his home is for the time being situate.

(3) Where a member of a police force to whom this regulation applies does not move his home, then, regulation 50 shall have effect in relation to him-

(a) as if for paragraph (1)(a)(iii) there were substituted the following provision:-

"(iii) in the opinion of the appropriate committee of chief officers of police, is not so living for the sole reason that he could not conveniently return daily to the family home;";

(b) as if in paragraph (1)(b) for the words "chief officer" there were substituted the words "appropriate committee of chief officers";

(c) as if in paragraph (1) for the words "30 months" there were substituted the words "24 months";

(d) as if for paragraph (2)(a) and (b) there were substituted the following provision:-

"if he were living with his family, or, as the case may be, in his former accommodation";

(e) as if in paragraph (3)(b) for the word "serving" there were substituted the word "living".

(4) In this regulation any reference to the appropriate committee of chief officers of police is a reference to the chief officers of police who are parties to the collaboration agreement referred to in paragraph (1) or such one or more of their number as they may have designated to act on their behalf for the purposes of this regulation.

Compensatory grant

52.—(1) In each financial year a member of a police force who, during the preceding financial year, has paid income tax for any year attributable to the inclusion of a rent allowance or compensatory grant in his emoluments in respect of service as a member of that force shall be paid a compensatory grant.

(2) The amount of the compensatory grant made to a member of a police force in any year shall be the amount by which the income tax in fact deducted from his emoluments in respect of service as a member of that force during the preceding year, according to the tax tables prepared or prescribed by the Commissioners of Inland Revenue, is increased by the inclusion in such emoluments of a rent allowance or any compensatory grant.

(3) The compensatory grant may, except in the circumstances described in paragraph (4), be paid by such instalments throughout the year in which it is payable as the police authority may determine.

(4) Where in the course of a financial year, a member of a police force leaves the force or dies whilst serving therein, he or his personal representative, as the case may be, shall be paid the whole of the compensatory grant due to the member during that year and, in addition, shall be paid a further compensatory grant determined in accordance with paragraph (5) by reference to the compensatory grant (hereafter referred to as the notional grant) which, had he not left the force or died, would have been due to him in a subsequent year by reason of income tax deducted from his emoluments, while in fact a member of the police force.

(5) A further compensatory grant shall be of the amount which the member or his personal representative, as the case may be, satisfies the police authority is equal, after deduction of income tax payable by him and attributable thereto, to the amount of the notional grant; and, for the purposes hereof, the attributable income tax shall be the tax which would not have been payable but for the inclusion of the further compensatory grant in the member's income except that, where the member's total income in the financial year in question exceeds his emoluments as a member of a police force during the period of 12 months preceding his retirement or death, the attributable tax shall be calculated as if it was not payable at a rate in excess of the basic rate save in so far as it would have been so payable had the member's total income in that financial year equalled his emoluments as a member of a police force in that period of 12 months.

II/1g*

(6) For the purposes of the preceding provisions of this regulation–

   (a) the expression "year" or "financial year" means a year commencing on 6th April and ending on the following 5th April;

   (b) the expression "income tax" includes all income tax whether payable at the basic rate or a higher rate; and

   (c) where a member of a police force has served more than once in the same force, references in this regulation to service in the force shall be construed as references to his service therein since his last appointment thereto.

Removal allowance

53.—(1) Where a member of the police force moves his home in circumstances to which this paragraph applies, the police authority–

   (a) shall either reimburse the reasonably incurred cost of removal or carry out the removal;

   (b) shall, where the member was the owner of his former home, reimburse expenses reasonably incurred by him in connection with the disposal thereof;

   (c) shall, where the member is the owner of his new home, reimburse expenses reasonably incurred by him in connection with the acquisition thereof if–

   (i) he was the owner of his former home, or

   (ii) the police authority, after consulting the chief officer of police, are satisfied that he could neither have been provided with a suitable house or quarters nor have been reasonably expected to find suitable rented accommodation within a reasonable distance of his normal place of duty,

   so, however, that where the police authority are of opinion that the member could have acquired a suitable home for a consideration less than that actually paid, they may restrict the reimbursement of expenses directly related to the consideration paid by him to expenses which would have been reasonably incurred had he paid that lesser consideration;

   (d) shall reimburse the member his payments in connection with his former home by way of mortgage interest, rent or rates (within the meaning of regulation 49(7)) payable in respect of the first 13 weeks following the move and may, if they think fit, reimburse him such payments in respect of a further period not exceeding 13 weeks up to an amount equal to that which would have been payable to him by way of rent allowance in respect of the period in question had he not moved but had continued to be entitled to a rent allowance payable at the rate at which such an allowance was payable immediately before the move so, however, that where the police authority are of opinion that the member has not taken all reasonable steps to reduce or terminate his liability to make such payments as aforesaid they may restrict the reimbursement to payments which the member would have been liable to make had he taken all such steps.

(2) Paragraph (1) applies where the member moves his home–

   (a) on joining the force in the rank of assistant chief constable or a higher rank; or

   (b) except as a consequence of joining the force otherwise than on being statutorily transferred thereto, and the removal is, in the opinion of the chief officer of police, due to the exigencies of police duty or is made at the request of the chief officer of police and is, in his opinion, in the interests of the efficiency of the force.

(3) Where a member of a police force moves his home in consequence of his voluntarily transferring from one force to another otherwise than in circumstances to which paragraph (2) applies, the police authority of the force to which he transfers–

   (a) may either reimburse the reasonable cost of removal or carry out the removal;

   (b) may, in the circumstances mentioned in paragraph (1)(b), reimburse the expenses there mentioned;

   (c) may, in the circumstances and subject to the conditions mentioned in paragraph (1)(c), reimburse the expenses there mentioned;

   (d) may, subject to the conditions mentioned in paragraph (1)(d), reimburse the expenses there mentioned.

(4) Where the cost of removal is reimbursed or the removal is carried out by the police authority under paragraph (1) or (2), then, subject to paragraph (5), in respect of expenditure incidental to the move the police authority shall pay the member an allowance of the amount hereinafter provided.

(5) An allowance under paragraph (4)–

    (a) shall not be payable, where a member who has never been married moves from furnished accommodation;

    (b) shall only be payable if the chief officer of police so decides, where a member moves from unfurnished into furnished accommodation.

(6) In the case of a member who–

    (a) moves into furnished accommodation; or

    (b) moves into unfurnished accommodation but has not previously, while a member of a police force, lived in such accommodation,

the amount of the allowance under paragraph (4) shall be £20.

(7) In the case of any other member the amount of the allowance under paragraph (4) shall not exceed £600 nor be less than the minimum amount mentioned in paragraph (8) but, subject as aforesaid, shall equal the aggregate of the following amounts–

    (a) the amount of the expenditure incidental to the move reasonably incurred by the member, and

    (b) where he satisfies the police authority that, in consequence of the move, he has failed to benefit, in whole or in part, from expenditure reasonably incurred by him prior to the move (other than such payments as are referred to in paragraph (1)(d)), the whole or the proportionate part of that expenditure so far as it is not recoverable by him.

(8) The minimum amount referred to in paragraph (7) shall be–

    (a) where the member holds, or is transferring to be appointed in, a rank higher than that of chief superintendent, such amount as may be determined by the police authority;

    (b) where he holds, or is transferring to be appointed in, the rank of superintendent, £129;

    (c) where he holds, or is transferring to be appointed in, the rank of inspector, £102;

    (d) where he holds, or is transferring to be appointed in, any rank lower than inspector, £82.

(9) Where a member of a police force has been requested by the chief officer of police, in the interests of the efficiency of the force, to move his home, and–

    (a) the member has, in consequence, in connection with the contemplated disposal of his home and acquisition of a new home, incurred any expenses; and

    (b) he would, if he had moved his home, have been reimbursed those expenses by the police authority in pursuance of paragraph (1)(b) or (c); but

    (c) in consequence of a subsequent decision of the chief officer of police, the member does not in fact move his home,

he shall be entitled, notwithstanding that he has not moved his home, to be reimbursed those expenses by the police authority.

(10) In this regulation–

    (a) any reference to an owner of any property is a reference to an occupier thereof whose interest therein is either a freehold interest or a leasehold interest which is neither a yearly or shorter tenancy nor a furnished tenancy, and

    (b) any reference to expenses incurred in connection with the disposal or acquisition of any property shall be construed as including, in particular, estate agent's, auctioneer's and solicitor's fees and expenses in connection with the redemption, transfer or taking out of a mortgage.

Uniform allowance

54. A member of a police force of or above the rank of inspector who does duty in uniform but is not supplied with uniform by the police authority shall be paid in lieu a uniform allowance at a rate calculated to cover the cost of supplying and maintaining the required uniform.

Women's stocking allowance

55. A woman member of a police force who is not provided with stockings or tights by the police authority shall be paid in lieu an allowance at such annual rate as shall be determined by the Secretary of State unless she is being paid either a uniform allowance under regulation 54 or a plain clothes allowance under regulation 56(1).

Plain clothes allowances

56.—(1) A member of a police force below the rank of assistant chief constable who is required for a continuous period of not less than a week to do duty in plain clothes shall be paid a plain clothes allowance at such annual rate as shall be determined by the Secretary of State.

(2) A member of a police force below the rank of superintendent who is required to perform duties in plain clothes for not less than 40 hours in the aggregate in any period of 6 months shall, subject to paragraph (3), be paid a plain clothes allowance in respect of such duties at such hourly rate as shall be determined by the Secretary of State.

(3) For the purposes of paragraph (2) and the calculation of the aggregate duration of the duties there referred to–

    (a) where the duties were performed on an occasion falling within such a continuous period of plain clothes duty as is mentioned in paragraph (1), no account shall be taken of those duties;

    (b) where the duties performed on any occasion lasted less than 4 complete hours, no account shall be taken of those duties;

    (c) where the duties performed on any occasion lasted for a completed number of hours and a fraction of an hour, no account shall be taken of that fraction.

(4) Notwithstanding anything in paragraph (1) or (2), where a member of a police force is provided with overalls when doing duty in plain clothes or for any other reason is, in the opinion of the Secretary of State, put to substantially less or substantially more than the normal expense caused by wearing his own clothes, a plain clothes allowance payable to him under paragraph (1) or (2) shall be payable not at the rate determined under the paragraph in question but at such rate as may be approved by the Secretary of State having regard to the circumstances of the case.

Detective duty and detective expenses allowances

57.—(1) This regulation shall apply in the case of a member of a police force who is assigned, for a period of not less than a week, to detective duty and, while so assigned, is, in the opinion of the chief officer of police, usually engaged in outside duty.

(2) Such a member of the rank of superintendent shall be paid a detective duty allowance at the rate of £518 a year.

(3) Such a member below the rank of superintendent shall be paid a detective expenses allowance at the rate of £1 a week.

(4) Regulation 45 shall apply to the calculation of detective duty allowance as it applies to the calculation of pay.

Subsistence, refreshment and lodging allowances

58.—(1) A member of a police force of or below the rank of superintendent who, being retained on duty beyond his normal daily period of duty or being engaged on duty away from his usual place of duty, necessarily incurs additional expense to obtain food or lodging, shall–

    (a) if the period for which he is so retained or engaged exceeds an hour but does not exceed 5 hours, be paid a refreshment allowance;

    (b) if the period for which he is so retained or engaged exceeds 5 hours, be paid a subsistence allowance;

(c) if the said expense includes the expense of obtaining lodging, be paid a lodging allowance.

(2) A member of a police force of or below the rank of superintendent who satisfies the chief officer of police that during his normal daily period of duty he was, although not away from his usual place of duty, unable by reason of the exigencies of duty to obtain his meals in his usual way and that he necessarily incurred additional expense for the purpose may be paid a refreshment allowance.

(3) Where the place of duty of a member of a police force has been temporarily changed the expression in this regulation "usual place of duty" shall, after such period from the date of change as the chief officer of police may determine, mean the temporary place of duty.

(4) A subsistence, refreshment or lodging allowance payable under the foregoing provisions of this regulation shall be of an amount determined in accordance with Schedule 7.

(5) A member of a police force above the rank of superintendent may be paid an allowance, at such annual rate as is determined by the police authority, to cover additional expenditure incurred by him in obtaining food and lodging by reason of the exigencies of duty.

Advances to cover expenses when away on duty

59. Where a member of a police force of or below the rank of inspector is required to do duty away from his usual place of duty he shall, if he so requests, be given an advance to cover, as far as practicable, any expenses which he will probably incur.

Motor vehicle allowances

60.—(1) Where the chief officer of police is of opinion that the duties normally performed by a member of a police force are of such a nature that it is–

    (a) essential, or

    (b) desirable,

that the member in question should, at all material times, have a motor vehicle at his disposal, he may authorise that member to use (subject to his directions) a motor vehicle owned by the member for the purposes of duties performed by him and, subject as hereinafter provided, in respect of such use the member shall be paid a motor vehicle allowance.

(2) A motor vehicle allowance shall not be payable in respect of the authorised use of a motor vehicle unless there was in force in relation thereto a policy of insurance in terms approved by the police authority, in relation to the use in question, for the purposes thereof.

(3) A motor vehicle allowance shall not be payable in respect of the authorised use of a motor car of a cylinder capacity exceeding 500 c.c. unless the member concerned was willing to carry passengers for the purposes of the duties performed by him or, in the case of passengers being members of a police force, by those members.

(4) A motor vehicle allowance in respect of the authorised use of a motor car of a cylinder capacity exceeding 500 c.c. shall, subject as aforesaid, be payable–

    (a) where the chief officer of police is of the opinion mentioned in paragraph (1)(a), at the essential user's rate;

    (b) where the chief officer of police is of the opinion mentioned in paragraph (1)(b), at the casual user's rate,

as provided in Schedule 8:

Provided that where the member concerned holds a rank above that of superintendent he may instead be paid a flat-rate motor vehicle allowance at such annual rate as is determined by the police authority on such basis as is approved by the Secretary of State.

(5) A motor vehicle allowance in respect of the authorised use of–

    (a) a motor car of a cylinder capacity not exceeding 500 c.c., or

    (b) a motor bicycle,

shall, subject as aforesaid, be payable on such conditions and at such rate as is approved by the Secretary of State.

(6) In its application to a chief officer of police this regulation shall have effect as if any reference therein to that officer were a reference to the police authority.

(7) Paragraph 1 of Schedule 8 shall have effect for the purposes of the interpretation of this regulation.

Bicycle allowance

61.—(1) Where a member of a police force is authorised by the chief officer of police to use a bicycle owned by him for the purposes of duties normally and from time to time performed by him, he shall in respect of such use be paid a bicycle allowance of an amount determined in accordance with Schedule 9.

(2) In this regulation the expression "bicycle" does not include a motor bicycle, that is to say a mechanically propelled bicycle (including a motor scooter and a bicycle with an attachment for propelling it by mechanical power) and a reference to a bicycle owned by a member of a police force is a reference to a bicycle kept and used by him.

Typewriter allowance

62.—(1) Where, immediately before the coming into effect of these Regulations a member of a police force was in receipt of a typewriter allowance in respect of the use of a typewriter owned by him which he is authorised by the chief officer of police to use for the purposes of duties normally and from time to time performed by him, he shall, in respect of such use, continue to be paid such an allowance in accordance with Schedule 10, and the police authority shall continue to supply him with typewriter ribbons free of charge.

(2) In this regulation a reference to a typewriter owned by a member of a police force is a reference to a typewriter kept and used by him.

Dog handler's allowance

63.—(1) Where a dog owned by the police authority is kept and cared for by a member of a police force at his home, the member shall be paid a dog handler's allowance in respect of the care accorded to the dog on the member's rest days and on public holidays.

(2) A dog handler's allowance shall be of an amount determined in accordance with Schedule 11.

(3) For the purposes of this regulation and of Schedule 11 a member of a police force shall be treated as keeping and caring for a dog at his home if he would be so doing but for his being on annual leave.

Allowance in respect of medical charges

64. A member of a police force shall be reimbursed any charges incurred in his case under section 77, 78 or 79 of the National Health Service Act 1977**(a)** (which sections relate to charges for certain drugs, medicines and appliances and for dental treatment).

London allowance

65. A member of the City of London or metropolitan police force shall be paid a London allowance at the rate of £1,011 a year.

Promotion examination allowances

66.—(1) A constable who has taken an examination or paper in consequence of which he obtains a pass in the qualifying examination for promotion to the rank of sergeant shall, subject to paragraph (3), be paid a promotion examination allowance of £45.

(2) A constable or sergeant who has taken an examination or paper in consequence of which he obtains a pass in the qualifying examination for promotion to the rank of

---

(a) 1977 c.49.

inspector shall, subject to paragraph (3), be paid a promotion examination allowance of £45.

(3) A constable's promotion examination allowance shall not be payable to a member of a police force who previously–

    (a) has obtained, or been deemed to have obtained, a pass in the corresponding qualifying examination held under any Promotion Regulations made on or after 17th September 1952, or

    (b) while serving in a police force in Scotland or in such a constabulary as is mentioned in paragraph (4), has received a payment for passing the examination which qualified him, in that force or constabulary, for promotion from constable to sergeant or, as the case may be, from sergeant to inspector.

(4) The reference in paragraph (3) to a constabulary is a reference to any force of constables outside Great Britain previous service in which a member of a police force may reckon as pensionable service; and where the rank in such a constabulary which appears to the Secretary of State to correspond to that of constable, sergeant or, as the case may be, inspector is not so styled, paragraph (3)(b) shall have effect in relation to that constabulary as if for any reference therein to that rank there were substituted a reference to such a rank as the Secretary of State determines to be the corresponding rank.

(5) Where an overseas policeman, a central police officer or a member of the Royal Ulster Constabulary enjoying a right of reversion to a home police force has, while serving as such, qualified for a promotion examination allowance under paragraph (1) or (2), he shall, subject to paragraph (3), be paid such an allowance on exercising his right of reversion to his police force under section 2(1) of the Police (Overseas Service) Act 1945, section 43(1) of the Police Act 1964 or, as the case may be, section 2(1) of the Police Act 1969.

(6) An allowance payable under paragraph (1) or (2) shall be payable by the police authority maintaining the force of which the person concerned was a member when he took the examination or paper referred to in the paragraph in question, and an allowance payble under paragraph (5) shall be payable by the police authority maintaining the force to which the person concerned reverts.

(7) In this regulation any reference to the qualifying examination for promotion to the rank of sergeant or to the qualifying examination for promotion to the rank of inspector shall be construed as a reference to the qualifying examination or, in relation to a period before 1st June 1967, both the qualifying examinations, held under the Promotion Regulations, for promotion from constable to sergeant or, as the case may be, from sergeant to inspector.

Allowance for recurring escort duty, etc.

67. An allowance may be paid, of such amount and under such conditions as may be approved by the Secretary of State on the recommendation of the police authority, in respect of recurring escort duty or other specific duties involving recurring retention on duty beyond the normal daily period and not covered by any other payment.

Continuance of allowances when member ill

68. If a member of a police force who is regularly in receipt of a plain clothes allowance, detective duty allowance, detective expenses allowance or any allowance to meet an expense which ceases during his or her absence from duty is placed upon the sick list or is on maternity leave, the allowance shall be payable during his or her absence from duty up to a period of a month, but thereafter, during the remainder of his or her absence from duty, payment may be suspended at the discretion of the chief officer of police.

Allowances in respect of periods of suspension

69. This part of these Regulations shall have effect in relation to a member of a police force suspended under the Discipline Regulations, subject to the provisions of paragraphs 2 and 3 of Schedule 6.

University scholars

70. This Part of these Regulations shall have effect in relation to a university scholar subject to the provisions of paragraph 4 of Schedule 4.

Allowance under regulation 59 of the Police Regulations 1971

71. Where immediately before 1st September 1978 a member of a police force, other than the City of London or metropolitan police force, was entitled to an allowance under regulation 59 of the Police Regulations 1971**(a)** he shall be entitled to an allowance as follows–

    (a) in the case of an inspector, at the rate of £50 a year;

    (b) in the case of a sergeant or constable, at the rate of £72 a year;

while he remains a member of that force.

PART VI
HOUSING, UNIFORM AND EQUIPMENT

Provision of house or quarters

72.—(1) A member of a police force who is not paid a rent allowance under regulation 49(1) shall be provided with a house or quarters free of rent and rates:

Provided that–

    (a) a member to whom regulation 50 applies may be provided with quarters as aforesaid notwithstanding that he is paid a rent allowance under regulation 49(1) as modified by regulation 50(2);

    (b) a member shall not be provided with a house or quarters if that member is on unpaid leave.

(2) Where 2 members of a police force are married to each other (and not separated) the provision made in their case in pursuance of paragraph (1) may comprise the provision to them jointly of a house or married quarters free of rent and rates.

Issue of uniform and equipment

73.—(1) Uniform and equipment shall be issued by the police authority free of charge to sergeants and constables in accordance with the provisions of Schedule 12.

(2) Uniform and equipment may, if the police authority so determine, be issued as required to a member of the police force of or above the rank of inspector.

Re-issue of uniform and equipment

74. Uniform and equipment handed back to the police authority shall not be re-issued to another member of the police force until it has received any necessary cleaning or renovation and is in serviceable condition.

Ownership of uniform and equipment

75. Subject to regulation 76 the uniform and equipment issued by the police authority shall not become the property of the member of the police force to whom they are issued and shall be handed back by him to the police authority on his leaving the force.

(a) S.I. 1971/156; the relevant amending instrument is S.I. 1977/1988 (regulation 59 was revoked, subject to transitional provisions (preserved by regulation 2(2) of S.I. 1979/1470), by regulation 6 of S.I. 1978/1169).

Replacement of uniform and equipment

76. On any article of uniform or equipment being replaced by the police authority the article shall be handed back to the police authority unless the member, with the consent of the police authority, buys such article at a price to be fixed by the police authority or, with such consent, retains it without payment.

Home Office
7th May 1987

Douglas Hurd
One of Her Majesty's Principal Secretaries of State

SCHEDULE 1   Regulation 2

REVOCATIONS

Regulations	*References*
The Police Regulations 1979	S.I. 1979/1470.
The Police (Amendment) Regulations 1980	S.I. 1980/405.
The Police (Amendment) (No. 2) Regulations 1980	S.I. 1980/803.
The Police (Amendment) (No. 3) Regulations 1980	S.I. 1980/1455.
The Police (Amendment) Regulations 1981	S.I. 1981/41.
The Police (Amendment) (No. 2) Regulations 1981	S.I. 1981/1371.
The Police (Amendment) Regulations 1982	S.I. 1982/271.
The Police (Amendment) (No. 2) Regulations 1982	S.I. 1982/1486.
The Police (Amendment) Regulations 1983	S.I. 1983/160.
The Police (Amendment) (No. 2) Regulations 1983	S.I. 1983/1349.
The Police (Amendment) (No. 3) Regulations 1983	S.I. 1983/1812.
The Police (Amendment) Regulations 1984	S.I. 1984/1590.
The Police (Amendment) (No. 2) Regulations 1984	S.I. 1984/1808.
The Police (Amendment) Regulations 1985	S.I. 1985/130.
The Police (Amendment) (No. 2) Regulations 1985	**S.I. 1985/885**
The Police (Amendment) (No. 3) Regulations 1985	S.I. 1985/1045.
The Police (Amendment) (No. 4) Regulations 1985	S.I. 1985/1577.
The Police (Amendment) Regulations 1986	S.I. 1986/784.
The Police (Amendment) (No. 2) Regulations 1986	S.I. 1986/2032.
The Police (Amendment) (No. 3) Regulations 1986	S.I. 1986/2241.

SCHEDULE 2   Regulation 10

RESTRICTIONS ON THE PRIVATE LIFE OF MEMBERS OF POLICE FORCES

1. A member of a police force shall at all times abstain from any activity which is likely to interfere with the impartial discharge of his duties or which is likely to give rise to the impression amongst members of the public that it may so interfere; and in particular a member of a police force shall not take any active part in politics.

2. A member of a police force shall not reside at premises which are not for the time being approved by the chief officer of police.

3.—(1) A member of a police force shall not, without the previous consent of the chief officer of police, receive a lodger in a house or quarters with which he is provided by the police authority or sub-let any part of the house or quarters.

(2) A member of a police force shall not, unless he has previously given written notice to the chief officer of police, receive a lodger in a house in which he resides and in respect of which he receives a rent allowance or sub-let any part of such a house.

4. A member of a police force shall not wilfully refuse or neglect to discharge any lawful debt.

Regulation 33

SCHEDULE 3

ANNUAL LEAVE

1.—(1) Subject to regulation 33, and the provisions of this Schedule, every member of a police force of or above the rank of superintendent shall be granted in each leave year the following period of annual leave, namely–

    (a) in the case of a member of the rank of superintendent, 31 days;

    (b) in the case of a member of a rank higher than that of superintendent who has not completed 10 years' relevant service, not less than 42 days; and

    (c) in any other case, not less than 48 days.

(2) Subject as aforesaid and to paragraph (3) below every member of a police force holding a rank below that of superintendent shall be granted in each leave year commencing after 31st December 1986 the period of leave set out opposite his relevant service as a member of a police force in the Table below:–

Table

Relevant service	Annual leave
Under 5 years' relevant service	20 days
5 or more years' relevant service	22 days
10 or more years' relevant service	25 days
15 or more years' relevant service	26 days
20 or more years' relevant service	28 days

(3) Where the annual leave entitlement of a member of a police force immediately before the coming into effect of this paragraph, in respect of the first leave year commencing after 31st December 1986, exceeded the period prescribed in his case in respect of that year by the foregoing provisions of this paragraph he shall continue to be entitled to be granted such greater period of leave until such time as he shall have completed such number of years' relevant service as, by virtue of the said provisions, entitle him to an increased period of leave.

2. In the leave year in which a member of a police force is appointed to, is promoted in, or retires from the force or completes such number of years' relevant service as will entitle him to an increased period of annual leave, his annual leave shall be calculated at the rate of a twelfth of the period of annual leave appropriate, under paragraph 1, to the rank held by him for each complete month of service in that rank in the leave year in question, a fraction of a day being reckoned as a day:

Provided that where a member of a police force is promoted or completes the said number of years' relevant service while completing a month's service in the leave year in question, he shall be treated for the purposes of this paragraph as if he had been promoted or, as the case may be, completed the said number of years' relevant service at the beginning of that month's service.

3.—(1) In the case of a member of a police force of a rank not higher than that of superintendent, the chief officer of police may, in his discretion and subject to the exigencies of duty–

    (a) notwithstanding anything in paragraphs 1 and 2, where he is satisfied that, in any leave year, the member has not taken the full period of annual leave specified in those paragraphs, grant the member, during the following leave year, additional days of annual leave not exceeding the number of days not taken, so, however, that he shall not exercise his discretion so as to grant more than 5 additional days of annual leave to a member unless he is satisfied that there are exceptional circumstances and that it is in the interests of efficiency to do so;

(b) grant the member not more than 5 additional days of annual leave, to be taken in the last month of the leave year, subject to a corresponding reduction being effected in the member's period of annual leave under paragraph 1 for the following year.

4.—(1) Subject to sub-paragraph (2), days of annual leave granted under this Schedule may be taken, in the discretion of the chief officer of police and subject to the exigencies of duty, as a single period, or as single days, or in periods of more than one day or as half days.

(2) In the case of a member below the rank of superintendent, not more than 3 days of annual leave shall be taken as half days, and where annual leave is so taken, the member–

(a) shall do duty on that day for 4 hours, and

(b) shall not be entitled to be allowed an interval for refreshment such as is mentioned in regulation 26(3).

5.—(1) Where a member of a police force has been recalled to duty from a period of absence from duty to which this paragraph applies, he shall be granted, in compensation for being recalled to duty on any day during that period which is a day of annual leave or a day taken off in lieu of overtime–

(a) if he was so recalled to duty for 1 or 2 days (whether or not in the latter case those days formed a single period), 2 days' annual leave in lieu of each such day for which he was so recalled; or

(b) if he was so recalled to duty for 3 or more days (whether or not forming a single period), 2 days' annual leave in lieu of each of the first 2 such days for which he was so recalled, and $1\frac{1}{2}$ days' annual leave in lieu of each such day for which he was so recalled thereafter.

(2) This paragraph applies to a period of absence from duty of 3 or more days, where at least one of those days is a day of annual leave and the other days, if not days of annual leave, are rostered rest days, days taken off in lieu of overtime, public holidays (or days taken off in lieu thereof) or monthly leave days, or any combination thereof.

6.—(1) For the purposes of this Schedule, the following expressions have the meanings hereby respectively assigned to them, that is to say:–

"leave year" means that period of 12 months beginning on such date as may from time to time be determined by the police authority;

"relevant service" means any service which the member concerned is entitled to reckon for the purposes of his scale of pay together with any service which he was previously so entitled to reckon–

(a) in the case of a member below the rank of superintendent, in any lower rank;

(b) in any other case, in the rank of superintendent or any higher rank.

except that relevant service shall not include any such service as is mentioned in regulation 43.

(2) Where a member of an aerodrome constabulary has been transferred to a police force by an order under section 30 of the Aviation Security Act 1982**(a)** then, for the purposes of this paragraph, his service in any rank in that constabulary shall be treated as if it were service in the corresponding rank in a police force.

SCHEDULE 4 Regulations 5, 36, 37 and 70

UNIVERSITY SCHOLARS

1.—(1) In this Schedule a reference to a university scholar is a reference to a member of a police force nominated for a course of university study by the Secretary of State or by the police authority maintaining the force of which he is a member in pursuance of arrangements in that behalf

---

(a) 1982 c.36.

approved by the Secretary of State and, in relation to such a member, the expression "course" means the course for which he has been nominated and which he has undertaken and "study" means study for the purposes of that course.

(2) For the purposes of this paragraph a full-time course leading to a degree awarded by the Council for National Academic Awards shall be treated as a course of university study notwithstanding that the course is provided otherwise than at a university.

2. Regulations 26, 28 and 29 shall not apply to a university scholar for the duration of his course except for such period or periods, if any, as he is engaged otherwise than in study.

3.—(1) This paragraph shall apply to a university scholar, not being a member of the City of London or of the metropolitan police force, who has undertaken a course of study given wholly or mainly at an institution within the City of London or the metropolitan police district.

(2) Where such a university scholar takes up residence within the City of London or the metropolitan police district and the taking up of such residence is, in the opinion of the police authority, due to his having undertaken his course, then, for the duration of the course (whether or not he is so resident throughout that period), he shall be entitled to supplementary pay at the rate of £885 a year and his rate of pay, determined in accordance with Part IV of these Regulations, shall be increased accordingly.

4.—(1) Where a university scholar moves his home and the removal is in the opinion of the police authority due to his having undertaken his course, then, notwithstanding the provisions of regulation 49, the rent allowance to be paid to him shall be that which would be payable to him under that regulation if he was a member of the force of the police area in which his home is for the time being situate.

(2) Where a university scholar does not move his home, then, regulation 50 shall have effect in relation to him for the duration of his course–
  (a) as if for paragraph (1)(a)(iii) there were substituted the following provision:–
        "(iii) satisfies the police authority that the only reason he is not so living is that he could not, without detriment to his studies, return daily to the family home,";
  (b) as if for paragraph (1)(b) there were substituted the following provision:–
        "(b) a member of a police force, other than such a member as is mentioned in sub-paragraph (a), who satisfies the police authority that the only reason why he is not living in his former accommodation is that he could not, without detriment to his studies, return daily thereto,"; and
  (c) as if for paragraph (2)(a) and (b) there were substituted the following provision:–
        "if he were living with his family or, as the case may be, in his former accommodation.".

(3) Where a university scholar moves his home and the removal is, in the opinion of the police authority, due to his having undertaken or completed his course of study and is, in their opinion, reasonable in all the circumstances of his case, regulation 53 shall have effect in his case as if the removal were such as is mentioned in paragraph (1) thereof.

Regulation 37   **SCHEDULE 5**

                                    SCALES OF PAY

1.—(1) The annual pay of a member holding a rank referred to in the first column of the following Table A shall, subject as hereinafter provided, be determined by reference to his service in that rank in accordance with the scale set opposite to his rank–
  (a) in the case of a member of the City of London or metropolitan police force, in the second and third columns of the said Table;

  (b) in any other case, in the second and fourth columns.

Table A

Rank	Service in Rank	Annual pay	
		London	Provinces
		£	£
Chief Superintendent	Less than 1 year	24,372	24,372
	After 1 year	24,720	24,720
	After 2 years	25,275	25,275
	After 3 years	25,878	25,878
Superintendent	Less than 1 year	22,482	21,924
	After 1 year	22,923	22,482
	After 2 years	23,361	23,040
	After 3 years	23,805	23,805
Chief Inspector	Less than 1 year	16,887	16,116
	After 1 year	17,304	16,566
	After 2 years	17,748	17,016
	After 3 years	18,222	17,472
	After 4 years	18,693	17,928
Inspector	Less than 1 year	14,958	14,193
	After 1 year	15,375	14,637
	After 2 years	15,918	15,213
	After 3 years	16,407	15,660
	After 4 years	16,887	16,116
Sergeant	Less than 1 year	12,372	12,372
	After 1 year	12,936	12,936
	After 2 years	13,389	13,389
	After 3 years	13,836	13,836
	After 4 years	14,193	14,193

(2) Except in the case of a member of the City of London or metropolitan police force, where immediately before 1st September 1978 the annual pay of a chief superintendent was greater than £8,703, his annual pay determined in accordance with Table A above shall be increased by £147.

(3) Except in the case of a member of the City of London or metropolitan police force, where immediately before 1st September 1978 the annual pay of a superintendent was greater than £7,839, his annual pay determined in accordance with Table A above shall be increased by £42.

(4) Where a member of the City of London or metropolitan police force holding the rank of chief superintendent has held that rank or the rank of superintendent in one or other of those forces at all times since 1st September 1985, his annual pay determined in accordance with Table A shall be increased by £474.

(5) Where a member of the City of London or metropolitan police force holding the rank of superintendent has held that rank in one or other of those forces at all times since 1st September 1985, his annual pay determined in accordance with Table A shall be increased–

    (a) where he has, or is to be treated as having, more than two years' reckonable service in that rank, by £474;

    (b) where he has, or is to be treated as having, more than one but less than two years' such service, by £624; and

    (c) in any other case, by £855.

(6) Where a member of the City of London police force holding the rank of chief inspector held that rank immediately before 1st September 1978, his annual pay determined in accordance with Table A above shall be increased by £450.

(7) Where a member is promoted to or appointed in the rank of superintendent and the aggregate amount of his pay and of his allowances under regulations 28, 29, 57 and 67 in respect of his period of service in the rank of chief inspector during the year immediately before the date of his promotion or appointment exceeded the amount which would have been the aggregate of his pay and of any allowance under regulation 57 in respect of that period of service had he been a superintendent with less than a year's reckonable service in that rank, his annual pay shall be determined as if he had an additional year's service in the rank of superintendent.

(8) Where a member promoted to or appointed in the rank of chief inspector or inspector last served before his promotion or appointment–

    (a) in the case of a chief inspector, in the rank of inspector;

(b) in the case of an inspector, in the rank of sergeant,

and had 4 or more years' reckonable service in the rank of inspector or, as the case may be, of sergeant, then his annual pay for the rank he holds shall be determined as if he had an additional year's service therein.

(9) Where a member promoted to or appointed in the rank of sergeant last served before his promotion or appointment in the rank of constable, then his annual pay for the rank of sergeant shall be determined–

(a) if he had 12 or more (but less than 14) years' reckonable service as a constable, as if he had an additional year's service as a sergeant;

(b) if he had 14 or more years' service as a constable, as if he had an additional 2 years' service as a sergeant.

(10) In sub-paragraphs (7) to (9) any reference to a member's reckonable service in any rank is a reference to the service reckonable for the purposes of his scale of pay in the rank including any additional service reckonable by virtue of this paragraph or otherwise.

2.—(1) The annual pay of a member holding the rank of constable shall, subject as hereinafter provided, be determined by reference to his reckonable service in accordance with the scale in the following Table B.

Table B

Annual pay of constables

Reckonable service	Annual Pay
	£
Before completing 1 year of service	7,752
After 1 year of service	8,289
After 2 years of service	9,756
After 3 years of service	9,987
After 4 years of service	10,317
After 5 years of service	10,671
After 6 years of service	11,013
After 7 years of service	11,355
After 8 years of service	11,691
After 12 years of service	12,372
After 15 years of service	12,936

(2) In the case of a constable who first became a member of a police force after he had attained the age of 22 years, his annual pay during the period before he completes 2 years' reckonable service shall be determined in accordance with Table B as if at all times during that period he had two years' reckonable service.

(3) For the purposes of this paragraph–

(a) any reference to a member's reckonable service is a reference to the service reckonable for the purposes of his scale of pay; and

(b) in determining whether or not a person has served continuously as a member of a police force there shall be disregarded any break in service occurring on transfer from one police force to another or which ends with the man exercising a statutory right of reversion to his police force.

3. The scale of pay of a member holding a rank above that of constable, not being a rank mentioned in Table A in paragraph 1, shall be such as shall be determined by the Secretary of State.

Regulation 37   SCHEDULE 6

EFFECT OF DISCIPLINARY ACTION ON PAY AND ALLOWANCES

1.—(1) Subject to paragraph 3, a member of a police force suspended under the Discipline Regulations who–

(a) is detained in pursuance of a sentence of a court in a prison or other institution to which the Prison Act 1952**(a)** applies, or is in custody (whether in prison or elsewhere) between conviction by a court and sentence, or

    (b)   has absented himself from duty and whose whereabouts are unknown to the chief officer of police (or a deputy chief officer acting as chief officer),

shall not, by virtue of regulation 37, be entitled to pay in respect of his period in detention or custody or, as the case may be, in respect of the period during which his whereabouts are unknown as aforesaid.

(2) Where the member suspended is a chief constable or other senior officer within the meaning of the Police (Discipline) (Senior Officers) Regulations 1985**(b)**, sub-paragraph (1) shall have effect as if for the reference therein to the chief officer of police (or a deputy chief officer acting as chief officer) there were substituted a reference to the police authority.

2. Subject to paragraph 3, a member of a police force suspended under the Discipline Regulations shall not, by virtue of Part V of these Regulations, be entitled to any allowance, in respect of the period of suspension, other than–

    (a)   a rent allowance, supplementary rent allowance, or compensatory grant; or

    (b)   in the case of a member to whom paragraph 1(1) does not apply, a London allowance or an allowance under regulation 71.

3. Where a member of a police force returns to duty when the period of suspension comes to an end and–

    (a)   it has been decided that he shall not be charged with a disciplinary offence, or

    (b)   he has been so charged and all the charges have been dismissed, or

    (c)   he has been so charged and has been punished by a reduction in his rate of pay, fine, reprimand or caution.

he shall receive, as from the date of his suspension, the pay to which, but for paragraph 1, and the allowances to which, but for paragraph 2, he would have been entitled by virtue of these Regulations.

4. Where a member of a police force is fined under the Discipline Regulations, the fine shall, without prejudice to any other method of recovery, be recoverable by way of deductions from the member's pay during the period of 13 weeks following the imposition of the fine so, however, that the aggregate sum which may be deducted in pursuance of this paragraph in respect of any one week (whether on account of one or more fines) shall not exceed a seventh of his weekly pay:

Provided that in the event of the member leaving the police force, the whole amount of any fine unpaid may be deducted from any pay then due.

SCHEDULE 7   Regulation 58

SUBSISTENCE, REFRESHMENT AND LODGING ALLOWANCES

1.—(1) Subject as hereafter in this Schedule provided, the amount of a subsistence, refreshment or lodging allowance payable under regulation 58(4) shall be in accordance with such scale appropriate to the rank of the member of a police force concerned as shall be determined by the Secretary of State; and separate scales shall be determined for members of the rank of superintendent and for members below that rank.

(2) The scales of refreshment allowances shall provide for the allowance payable in respect of one meal and that payable in respect of two meals.

(3) The scales of subsistence allowances shall provide for the allowance payable in respect of a period of retention or engagement on duty of–

    (a)   over 5 hours but not exceeding 8 hours;

    (b)   over 8 hours but not exceeding 12 hours;

    (c)   over 12 hours but not exceeding 24 hours;

    (d)   over 24 hours.

(a) 1952 c.52.   **(b)** S.I. 1985/519.

2. If a lodging allowance is payable as well as a subsistence allowance in respect of a period of retention or engagement on duty of 16 hours or less, the subsistence allowance shall be of the amount appropriate to a retention or engagement for a period exceeding 8 hours and not exceeding 12 hours.

3. If the chief officer of police is satisfied in any particular case that the amount of the allowances calculated in accordance with paragraphs 1 and 2 is not sufficient to cover the actual expenses necessarily incurred, he may authorise payment of the difference.

4. If the chief officer of police is satisfied in any particular case that the amount of the allowances calculated in accordance with paragraphs 1 and 2 would be excessive having regard to the additional expenses necessarily incurred, he may direct that the amount of the allowances shall be reduced to such an amount as he determines, not being less than the amount of such expenses.

5. If in any particular case or class of cases the period of retention or engagement on duty exceeds a week and the chief officer of police is satisfied that the amount of the allowances calculated in accordance with paragraph 1 would be excessive, he may direct that there shall be granted in lieu thereof of a weekly allowance at such lower rate as may be necessary to cover the reasonable expenses of the member concerned.

6. If a member of a police force below the rank of superintendent is required during any period to accompany a member of that or a higher rank, paragraph 1 shall apply to his case as respects that period as if he held the rank of superintendent.

Regulation 60

SCHEDULE 8

MOTOR VEHICLE ALLOWANCES

1. For the purposes of regulation 60 and this Schedule the following expressions have the meanings hereby respectively assigned to them:–

"authorised use" means the use, authorised under regulation 60, of a motor vehicle owned by the member of a police force concerned for the purposes of his duties as a member of that force or, where he has been statutorily transferred from one force to another force, as a member of either of those forces, and "period of authorised use" means the period during which such use is authorised;

"cyclinder capacity" means the cylinder capacity of the engine of a vehicle calculated in accordance with the regulations from time to time in force under the Vehicles (Excise) Act 1971**(a)**;

"motor bicycle" means a mechanically propelled bicycle (including a motor scooter, a bicycle with an attachment for propelling it by mechanical power and a mechanically propelled bicycle used for drawing a sidecar);

"motor car" means a mechanically propelled vehicle other than a motor bicycle and, accordingly, includes a mechanically propelled tricycle;

"year" means a period of twelve months beginning on such date as may be determined by the police authority;

and a reference to a motor vehicle owned by a member of a police force is a reference to such a vehicle kept and used by him.

2.—(1) Subject as hereinafter provided, the amount of a motor vehicle allowance payable at the essential user's rate shall in any year comprise a fixed element and a mileage element calculated as provided in sub-paragraphs (2) and (3).

(2) The fixed element shall be calculated by reference to the number of completed months comprised in the period of authorised use for the year in question, at such annual rate as is specified by the Secretary of State by reference to the cylinder capacity of the motor car in question.

(3) The mileage element shall be calculated in relation to authorised use at such rate as is specified by the Secretary of State by reference to the cylinder capacity of the motor car in question, and for that purpose he may so specify–

(a) a basic rate, in relation to authorised use not exceeding such mileage as is specified by him ("the basic mileage"), and

---

(a) 1971 c.10.

(b) a reduced rate in relation to authorised use in excess of the basic mileage.

(4) Where in any year a motor vehicle allowance is payable at the essential user's rate it shall be payable in such instalments, in advance or in arrears, as the police authority may determine; but when the amount of the allowance for that year is finally calculated, any over-payment shall be recoverable.

(5) Where in any year a motor vehicle allowance is payable at the essential user's rate to a member of a police force and the member is on sick leave, or maternity leave, or the motor car in question is out of order, for a continuous period of four or more weeks in that year the allowance shall be reduced by such amount as the police authority, with the approval of the Secretary of State, determines as being appropriate in all the circumstances.

(6) Where in any year a motor vehicle allowance is payable at the essential user's rate but the period of authorised use is a fraction only of that year, sub-paragraph (3) shall have effect as if for the reference to the basic mileage there were substituted a reference to the corresponding fraction of that mileage; and for the purposes of this paragraph the monthly rate of the fixed element of such an allowance so payable shall be taken to be a twelfth of the annual rate.

3. The amount of a motor vehicle allowance payable at the casual user's rate shall in any year be an amount calculated in relation to the mileage of authorised use in that year at such rate as is specified by the Secretay of State by reference to that mileage and the cylinder capacity of the motor car in question, except that where the amount of the allowance would be less if it were calculated at the essential user's rate, it shall be an amount calculated in accordance with paragraph 2.

4. The amount of a motor vehicle allowance payable to a member of a police force shall not exceed that which would be payable if the vehicle in question were of such a cylinder capacity, not being less than 1,000 c.c., as the chief officer of police, with the approval of the police authority, has determined appropriate for use for the purposes of the duties normally performed by the member concerned.

SCHEDULE 9   Regulation 61

BICYCLE ALLOWANCE

1. The amount of a bicycle allowance shall be calculated by reference to the duration of the authority given for the purposes of regulation 61 at such annual rate as is specified by the Secretary of State.

2. The allowance shall be payable quarterly or at such shorter intervals as the police authority may determine in advance or in arrears, as they may determine; but where payment is made in advance, any overpayment shall be recoverable.

SCHEDULE 10   Regulation 62

TYPEWRITER ALLOWANCE

1. The amount of a typewriter allowance shall be calculated by reference to the duration of the authority given for the purposes of regulation 62 at such annual rate as is specified by the Secretary of State.

2. The allowance shall be payable quarterly or at such shorter intervals as the police authority may determine in advance or in arrears, as they may determine; but where payment is made in advance, any overpayment shall be recoverable.

Regulation 63

SCHEDULE 11

DOG HANDLER'S ALLOWANCE

1. Subject as hereinafter provided, a dog handler's allowance shall be payable–

    (a) in the case of a constable, at the annual rate of £567,

    (b) in any other case, at the annual rate of £771.

2. Where the member keeps and cares for at his home more than one dog owned by the police authority, the annual rate of the allowance shall be multiplied by the number of such dogs so kept and cared for.

Regulation 73

SCHEDULE 12

ISSUE OF UNIFORM AND EQUIPMENT

1. The uniform specified in the following Tables for men and women respectively shall be issued in accordance with those Tables subject to any modifications approved by the Secretary of State:

Provided that where particular duties or the duties of a particular member of a police force entail greater or less wear than normal the issue of any article of uniform may be made as required:–

Tables

Men

Article	Issue	Maximum number in issue
Jacket.	1 annually (period of wear 4 years).	4
Trousers.	2 pairs annually (period of wear 2 years).	4 pairs.
Greatcoat.	If the police authority approves the issue of greatcoats to the force, as required.	1
Cape.	As required.	2
Raincoat or mackintosh.	As required.	2
Headdress.	As required.	2
Shirts (either collar attached or complete with 3 separate collars).	After an initial issue of not less than 4 nor more than 6 (as the police authority may determine) 3 annually or, in the case of shirts with separate collars, 2 annually.	—
Ties.	2 annually.	—
Long sleeved pullover or jersey.	As required.	2

Women

Article	Issue	Maximum number in issue
Jacket.	1 annually (period of wear 4 years).	4
Skirt or pair of trousers.	2 annually (period of wear 2 years).	4
Greatcoat.	As required.	1 or 2 (as the police authority may determine).
Other outer garments comprising the following items– (a) a coat being a raincoat or mackintosh, or (b) a cloak, a gaberdine coat and a fully waterproofed coat as the police authority may determine.	As required.	2
Headdress.	As required. As required.	1 of each item 2
Shirts (general issue, either collar attached or complete with 3 separate collars).	After an initial issue of not less than 4 nor more than 6 (as the police authority may determine), 2 annually.	—
Shirts (summer issue, for wear with or without ties).	After an initial issue of 3, 2 annually.	—
Ties.	2 annually.	—
Long sleeved pullover or jersey.	As required.	2

2. Uniform or equipment issued by the police authority which is lost or damaged otherwise than owing to the member's default or is faulty or is ill-fitting shall be replaced or repaired by the police authority free of charge:

Provided that this paragraph shall not apply to minor repairs or alterations which can be satisfactorily carried out by the member.

3. Clothing for particular duties such as mounted duty, cycling, driving of vehicles, or stable duty shall be issued as required.

4. Where, in the case of women members, stockings or tights are provided by the police authority for the purposes of duty the issue shall be at the rate of 24 pairs annually.

5. Issues of equipment shall be made as circumstances require.

EXPLANATORY NOTE

(This note is not part of the Regulations)

These Regulations consolidate, with amendments, the Police Regulations 1979 and the instruments amending those Regulations, namely the Regulations set out in Schedule 1. In addition to minor and drafting amendments the Regulations make the following changes of substance–

(i) in regulation 59 (Advances to cover expenses when away on duty—formerly regulation 57) an advance is to be made only if the member so requests; and

(ii) in Schedule 9, paragraph 1 (Bicycle allowance) and Schedule 10, paragraph 1 (Typewriter allowance) the annual rate is no longer prescribed but is to be specified by the Secretary of State.

S T A T U T O R Y   I N S T R U M E N T S

1987 No. 852 (C.23)

PUBLIC ORDER

The Public Order Act 1986 (Commencement No. 3) Order 1987

Made - - - - *11th May 1987*

In exercise of the powers conferred upon me by section 41 of the Public Order Act 1986(**a**), I hereby make the following Order:–

1.— (1) This Order may be cited as the Public Order Act 1986 (Commencement No. 3) Order 1987.

(2) In this Order "the 1986 Act" means the Public Order Act 1986.

2.   The provisions of the 1986 Act specified in the Schedule to this Order shall come into force on 1st August 1987.

Home Office   *Douglas Hurd*
11th May 1987   One of Her Majesty's Principal Secretaries of State

---

Article 2   SCHEDULE

PROVISIONS OF THE PUBLIC ORDER ACT 1986 COMING INTO FORCE ON 1st AUGUST 1987

Provisions of the Act	Subject matter of provisions
Section 30	Power of court to make exclusion order.
Section 31	Offences connected with football.
Section 32	Effect of exclusion order.
Section 33	Application to terminate exclusion order.
Section 34	Information about exclusion orders and terminating orders.
Section 35	Power to order photographs.
Section 36	Prescribed football matches.
Section 37	Power to extend sections 30 to 35 to other sporting events.

(**a**) 1986 c.64.

EXPLANATORY NOTE

(This note is not part of the Order)

This Order brings into force on 1st August 1987 those provisions of the Public Order Act 1986 which are not already in force.

STATUTORY INSTRUMENTS

1987 No. 853

PUBLIC ORDER

The Public Order (Football Exclusion) Order 1987

Made - - - -	*11th May 1987*
Laid before Parliament	*14th May 1987*
Coming into force	*1st August 1987*

In exercise of the powers conferred upon me by sections 34(4) and 36(1) of the Public Order Act 1986**(a)**, I hereby make the following Order:–

1.—(1) This Order may be cited as the Public Order (Football Exclusion) Order 1987 and shall come into force on 1st August 1987.

(2) In this Order "the 1986 Act" means the Public Order Act 1986.

2. The General Secretary of The Football Association Limited shall be a prescribed person for purposes of section 34 of the 1986 Act.

3. An association football match specified in the Schedule to this Order shall be a prescribed football match for purposes of section 36 of the 1986 Act.

Douglas Hurd

Home Office
11th May 1987

One of Her Majesty's Principal Secretaries of State

Article 3

SCHEDULE

PRESCRIBED FOOTBALL MATCHES

1. An association football match in which one or both of the participating teams represents a club which is for the time being a member (whether a full or associate member) of The Football League.

2. An international association football match.

3. An association football match (not already specified in paragraph 1 above) in the competition for–

    (a)   the European Champion Clubs' Cup;
    (b)   the European Cup Winners' Cup; or
    (c)   the UEFA Cup.

(a) 1986 c.64.

EXPLANATORY NOTE

(This note is not part of the Order)

Where, on convicting a person of an offence within section 31 of the Public Order Act 1986, a court makes an exclusion order prohibiting that person from entering any premises for the purpose of attending a prescribed football match there or the court subsequently makes an order terminating an exclusion order, section 34 of the Act requires the clerk of the magistrates' court or the appropriate officer of the Crown Court, as appropriate, to provide a copy of the order to the person to whom the exclusion order relates, the chief officer of police for the area in which the offence was committed and any prescribed person.

Article 2 of this Order prescribes the General Secretary of The Football Association Ltd and article 3 prescribes the association football matches for these purposes.

STATUTORY INSTRUMENTS

1987 No. 854

MERCHANT SHIPPING
MARINE POLLUTION

The Merchant Shipping (Fees) (Amendment) (No. 2) Regulations 1987

Made - - - -	*11th May 1987*
Laid before Parliament	*15th May 1987*
Coming into force	*16th May 1987*

The Secretary of State for Transport, in exercise of the powers conferred by:–

   (i) section 33 of the Merchant Shipping (Safety Convention) Act 1949(**a**);

  (ii) section 1(1)(d) of the Anchors and Chain Cables Act 1967(**b**);

 (iii) section 6 of the Fishing Vessels (Safety Provisions) Act 1970(**c**);

 (iv) section 84 of the Merchant Shipping Act 1970(**d**);

  (v) section 17 of and Schedule 5 to the Merchant Shipping Act 1974(**e**);

 (vi) section 21(1) and (3)(r) of the Merchant Shipping Act 1979(**f**);

(vii) article 3(2)(a) of the Merchant Shipping (Prevention and Control of Pollution) Order 1987(**g**);

and now vested in him(**h**) and of all other powers enabling him in that behalf, and with the consent and approval of the Treasury (except in respect of the powers conferred by the Act of 1974) hereby makes the following Regulations:–

1. These Regulations may be cited as the Merchant Shipping (Fees) (Amendment) (No. 2) Regulations 1987 and shall come into force on 16th May 1987.

2. The Merchant Shipping (Fees) (Amendment) Regulations 1987(**i**) are hereby revoked.

3. The Merchant Shipping (Fees) Regulations 1987(**j**) shall be amended as follows:

 (a) there shall be added to regulation 5 the following paragraph:–

"(3) Where a fee payable under these Regulations is for, or covers, the issue or endorsement of a certificate, the certificate need not be issued or endorsed unless that fee has been paid.".

 (b) in the Schedule, in Part I, paragraph 1(2):–

(**a**) 1949 c.43; section 33 was extended by section 2(4) of the Merchant Shipping Act 1964 (c.47), which was amended by S.I. 1980/539.   (**b**) 1967 c.64.   (**c**) 1970 c.27.   (**d**) 1970 c.36.   (**e**) 1974 c.43.   (**f**) 1979 c.39.   (**g**) S.I. 1987/470.   (**h**) *See* S.I. 1970/1537.   (**i**) S.I. 1987/548.   (**j**) S.I. 1987/63, amended by S.I. 1987/548 which is revoked by these Regulations.

    (i)   in section A (CREW), there shall be added at the end the following entries:–

Merchant Shipping (Safety Officials and Reporting of Accidents and Dangerous Occurrences) Regulations 1982	876	1984/93
Merchant Shipping (Certification of Deck Officers) Regulations 1985	1306	
Merchant Shipping (Protective Clothing and Equipment) Regulations 1985	1664	
Merchant Shipping (Certification of Marine Engineer Officers and Licensing of Marine Engine Operators) Regulations 1986	1935	

   (ii)   in section C (DANGEROUS GOODS) there shall be added the following entries:–

Merchant Shipping (Chemical Tankers) Regulations 1986	1068
Merchant Shipping (Gas Carriers) Regulations 1986	1073

  (iii)   in section E (FIRE AND LIFE SAVING), there shall be added the following entry:–

Merchant Shipping (Life-Saving Appliances) Regulations 1986	1066

   (iv)   in section I (RADIO AND NAVIGATIONAL EQUIPMENT), the entry relating to the Merchant Shipping (Navigational Equipment) Regulations 1980 shall be omitted;

    (v)   in section J (SHIPS – CONSTRUCTION AND EQUIPMENT), the entry relating to the Anchors and Chain Cables Rules 1970(a) shall be omitted;

   (vi)   in section K the title "OIL POLLUTION" shall be changed to "PREVENTION AND CONTROL OF POLLUTION", and there shall be added the following entries:–

Merchant Shipping (IBC Code) Regulations 1987	549
Merchant Shipping (BCH Code) Regulations 1987	550
Merchant Shipping (Control of Pollution by Noxious Liquid Substances in Bulk) Regulations 1987	551

(c) In the Schedule, in Part I, paragraph 2(d), for "the Merchant Shipping (Navigational Equipment) Regulations 1980" there shall be substituted "the Merchant Shipping (Navigational Equipment) Regulations 1984", and for "the Merchant Shipping (Radios) (Fishing Vessels) Rules 1984" there shall be substituted "the Merchant Shipping (Radio) (Fishing Vessels) Rules 1974";

(d) In the Schedule, in Part I, paragraph 3:–

    (i) the words "and except in relation to the services referred to in paragraph 5 below" shall be inserted after "Subject to paragraph 4 below";

   (ii) in sub-paragraph (c) "under section 76(1) of the Act of 1970" shall be added after "inspection" where it first appears and the word "on" shall be inserted after "whether or not"; and

  (iii) in sub-paragraph (e) the words "except in relation to section K of paragraph 1(2) above, consideration of" shall be inserted at the start;

(e) in the Schedule, in Part I, there shall be added the following new paragraph:–

(a) S.I. 1970/1453.

"**5.** Subject to any additional charge payable under Part X of this Schedule, the fee for supervision and inspection under the Anchors and Chain Cables Rules 1970, and the issue of Certificates under those Rules, shall be determined by the amount of work involved charged at an hourly rate of £45.50.";

(f) in the Schedule, in Part III, for "below," there shall be substituted "below)";

(g) in the Schedule, in Part V, the listed fees set out in column 1 of the Table below shall be replaced by those set out in column 2 of that Table.

Column 1	Column 2
£	£
145	150
210	215
45	47
80	83

(h) in the Schedule, in Part VI, the fees of £6 shall each be replaced by a fee of £5;

(i) in the Schedule, Part VIII shall be replaced by the following:–

"PART VIII
SEAMEN'S DOCUMENTS

Fees for the Issue of British Seamen's Cards and Discharge Books

1. In this Part "the Regulations" means the Merchant Shipping (Seamen's Documents) Regulations 1987(**a**); and the person to whom a British Seaman's Card or a discharge book has been issued is referred to as the holder of it.

Service

2.—(1) For the issue of a British Seaman's Card:–

(a) to a British Seaman under regulation 5 of the Regulations:

    (i) on postal application   £15

    (ii) other   £35

(b) to a person who would, but for the provisions of regulation 9 of the Regulations, be regarded as the holder of a British Seaman's Card:

    (i) on postal application   £15

    (ii) other   £35

(c) to a person who has ceased to be regarded as the holder of a British Seaman's Card because it has been lost, destroyed or defaced through shipwreck or fire at sea
         No fee.

(2) For the issue of a discharge book under paragraph 1 or paragraph 2 of regulation 18 of the Regulations to a seaman–

(**a**) S.I. 1987/408.

(a) who, in accordance with regulation 17(1)(b) of the Regulations, produces a Seaman's Record Book (as defined in regulation 1(2)(e) of the Regulations), which has been issued to him, or a discharge book of which he would, but for the provisions of regulation 24(b) of the Regulations, be regarded as the holder:

    (i) on postal application   £15

    (ii) other   £35

(b) to whom a Seaman's Record Book (as so defined) has been issued or who was the holder of a discharge book which in either case has been lost, destroyed or defaced through shipwreck or fire at sea.

No fee.";

(j) in the Schedule, in Part X:–

    (i) for the sub-heading and the opening paragraph there shall be substituted the following:–

"Fees in Respect of Surveys or Inspections, in or outside the United Kingdom, for Waiting Time and Attendance at Unusual Hours, Weekends and Public Holidays

        (i) When an inspector or surveyor is unable to start an inspection, survey or test at the appointed hour, unless this is for reasons over which the applicant, his agent or supplier has no control or

        (ii) where (except for similar reasons) an inspection, survey or test is disrupted; or

        (iii) where an inspector or surveyor is called upon to perform services in the United Kingdom at unusual hours, or outside the United Kingdom;

an additional fee in accordance with the following Table shall be payable:

Provided that where the inspector or surveyor is able to avoid waiting time by carrying out other available surveys or inspection work in the vicinity, for which the appropriate fees have been paid, such additional fees will not be payable.";

    (ii) in the heading to column 3 of the Table "etc" shall be deleted;

    (iii) there shall be added to the Table a fourth column with the heading "Radio Surveys" and sub-heading "£ per hour" or part thereof" with the entries set out in the table below, to be made in respect to the entries referred to on the left:–

Radio Surveys
£ per hour or part thereof

1. For waiting time prior to the commencement of and during the course of a survey or inspection:

   for periods not in excess of one hour   No fee

   for periods in excess of one hour–

   for surveys in the United Kingdom   £49.00

   for surveys abroad   £98.00

2. For abortive visits in the United Kingdom: for the time wasted in excess of one hour at the place of survey or inspection plus the time occupied in travelling to and from the place of survey   £49.00

3. When a surveyor or inspector is called upon to perform services in the United Kingdom at unusual hours:
   for work undertaken during the following hours including time occupied in travelling:

   Monday to Fridays inclusive between 6pm and 8am and all day Saturday   £24.50

   Sundays and Public Holidays   £49.00

4. When a surveyor or inspector is called upon to perform services outside the United Kingdom which involve working total hours in any one week in excess of normal weekly employment hours, for the excess hours of work   £12.30 per hour

6th May 1987

John Moore
Secretary of State for Transport

We consent to and approve the making of these Regulations,

Peter Lloyd
Mark Lennox-Boyd

11th May 1987   Two of the Lords Commissioners of Her Majesty's Treasury

EXPLANATORY NOTE

(This note is not part of the Regulations)

These Regulations replace the Merchant Shipping (Fees) (Amendment) Regulations 1987 which were made without the consent and approval of the Treasury. Those Regulations amended the Merchant Shipping (Fees) Regulations 1987. The main amendments were to increase the fees payable in respect of the registration of ships by approximately 3.6%, and to include further regulations for services in respect of which hourly fees are payable, in particular the regulations made to implement the coming into force of Annex II (Control of Pollution by Noxious Liquid Substances in Bulk) to the Convention for the Prevention of Pollution of Ships 1973 (MARPOL).

These Regulations also amend the principal Fee Regulations referred to, to provide that if a fee is for, or covers, a certificate, the certificate need not be issued or endorsed unless the fee is paid.

STATUTORY INSTRUMENTS

1987 No. 855

MERCHANT SHIPPING

The Carriage of Passengers and their Luggage by Sea (United Kingdom Carriers) Order 1987

Made - - - -	*28th April 1987*
Coming into force	*1st June 1987*

The Secretary of State for Transport, in exercise of the powers conferred upon him by sections 14 and 16 of, and by paragraphs 4 and 5 of Part II of Schedule 3 to, the Merchant Shipping Act 1979(**a**) and of all other powers enabling him in that behalf hereby makes the following Order:–

1. This Order may be cited as the Carriage of Passengers and their Luggage by Sea (United Kingdom Carriers) Order 1987 and shall come into force on 1st June 1987.

2. In relation to any carrier whose principal place of business is in the United Kingdom, paragraph 1 of Article 7 to the Convention Relating to the Carriage of Passengers and their Luggage by Sea, set out in Part I of Schedule 3 to the Merchant Shipping Act 1979, (including that paragraph as applied to domestic carriage by the Carriage of Passengers and their Luggage by Sea (Domestic Carriage) Order 1987(**b**)) shall have effect as if for the limit of 700,000 francs there specified there were substituted a limit of 1,525,000 francs.

3. The Merchant Shipping (Sterling Equivalents) (Various Enactments) Order 1986(**c**) is hereby amended by substituting, in the table in article 3, the following entry for the entry for Article 7, paragraph 1:–

"Article 7, paragraph 1 (for carriers other than UK carriers)	700,000	£38,173.40
Article 7, paragraph 1 (for UK carriers)	1,525,000	£80,009.00".

Michael Spicer
Signed by the authority of the Secretary of State   Parliamentary Under Secretary
28th April 1987   of State, Department of Transport

(**a**) 1979 c. 39.
(**b**) S.I. 1987/670.
(**c**) S.I. 1986/1777.

EXPLANATORY NOTE

(This note is not part of the Order)

This Order increases the limit of liability of carriers whose principal place of business is in the United Kingdom for death or injury of passengers carried by them by sea to the amount of 1,525,000 gold francs per passenger per carriage, and fixes the sterling equivalent of that amount at £80,009.00.

The limit for other carriers remains that specified in the Convention Relating to the Carriage of Passengers and their Luggage by Sea (set out in Schedule 3 to the Merchant Shipping Act 1979), namely 700,000 gold francs (sterling equivalent currently £38,173.40).

STATUTORY INSTRUMENTS

1987 No. 856

PEACE TREATIES

The Treaty of Peace (Bulgaria) Vesting Order 1948 Revocation Order 1987

Made - - - -	*22nd April 1987*
Coming into force	*22nd April 1987*

The Secretary of State in exercise of the powers conferred by the Treaty of Peace (Bulgaria) Order 1948(**a**) and now vested in him(**b**) hereby makes the following Order:

1. The Treaty of Peace (Bulgaria) Vesting Order 1948(**c**) is hereby revoked.

2. This Order may be cited as the Treaty of Peace (Bulgaria) Vesting Order 1948 Revocation Order 1987.

A.C. Russell
An Under Secretary in the
Department of Trade and Industry

Dated this 22nd day of April 1987

EXPLANATORY NOTE

(This note is not part of the Order)

The Treaty of Peace (Bulgaria) Vesting Order 1948 vested in the Administrator of Bulgarian Property certain property of Bulgarian nationals. That property has now been disposed of and the Order is now spent. This Order revokes it.

(**a**) S. R. & O. 1948/114.
(**b**) S.I. 1970/1537.
(**c**) S. R. & O. 1948/2092.

STATUTORY INSTRUMENTS

1987 No. 857

PEACE TREATIES

The Treaty of Peace (Hungary) Vesting Order 1948 Revocation Order 1987

Made - - - -	*22nd April 1987*
Coming into force	*22nd April 1987*

The Secretary of State in exercise of the powers conferred by the Treaty of Peace (Hungary) Order 1948(**a**) and now vested in him(**b**) hereby makes the following Order:

1.   The Treaty of Peace (Hungary) Vesting Order 1948(**c**) is hereby revoked.

2.   This Order may be cited as the Treaty of Peace (Hungary) Vesting Order 1948 Revocation Order 1987.

A.C. Russell
An Under Secretary in the
Dated this 22nd day of April 1987 Department of Trade and Industry

EXPLANATORY NOTE

(This note is not part of the Order)

The Treaty of Peace (Hungary) Vesting Order 1948 vested in the Administrator of Hungarian Property certain property of Hungarian nationals. That property has now been disposed of and the Order is now spent. This Order revokes it.

(**a**) S. R. & O. 1948/116.
(**b**) S.I. 1970/1537.
(**c**) S. R. & O. 1948/2093.

STATUTORY INSTRUMENTS

1987 No. 858

PEACE TREATIES

The Treaty of Peace (Roumania) Vesting Order 1948 Revocation Order 1987

Made - - - -	*22nd April 1987*
Coming into force	*22nd April 1987*

The Secretary of State in exercise of the powers conferred by the Treaty of Peace (Roumania) Order 1948(**a**) and now vested in him(**b**) hereby makes the following Order:

1. The Treaty of Peace (Roumania) Vesting Order 1948(**c**) is hereby revoked.

2. This Order may be cited as the Treaty of Peace (Roumania) Vesting Order 1948 Revocation Order 1987.

A.C. Russell
An Under Secretary in the
Department of Trade and Industry

Dated this 22nd day of April 1987

EXPLANATORY NOTE

(This note is not part of the Order)

The Treaty of Peace (Roumania) Vesting Order 1948 vested in the Administrator of Roumanian Property certain property of Roumanian nationals. That property has now been disposed of and the Order is now spent. This Order revokes it.

(**a**) S. R. & O. 1948/118.
(**b**) S.I. 1970/1537.
(**c**) S. R. & O. 1948/2094.

STATUTORY INSTRUMENTS

1987 No. 859

FINANCIAL SERVICES

The Financial Services (Disclosure of Information) (Designated Authorities No.2) Order 1987

Made - - - -	*11th May 1987*
Laid before Parliament	*12th May 1987*
Coming into force	*13th May 1987*

The Secretary of State, in exercise of the powers conferred by section 180(3) and (4) of the Financial Services Act 1986(**a**) and section 449 (1B) and (1C) of the Companies Act 1985(**b**), hereby makes the following Order:

Citation and Commencement

1. This Order may be cited as the Financial Services (Disclosure of Information) (Designated Authorities No.2) Order 1987 and shall come into force on the day after it is laid before Parliament.

Designation of authorities and specification of functions

2. For the purposes of section 180 of the Financial Services Act 1986 and section 449 of the Companies Act 1985–
   (a) the Insolvency Practitioners Tribunal is designated as an authority in relation to its functions under the Insolvency Act 1986(**c**);
   (b) the Occupational Pensions Board is designated as an authority in relation to its functions under the Social Security Act 1973(**d**) and the Social Security Acts 1975 to 1986; and
   (c) the body known as the Panel on Take-overs and Mergers is designated as an authority in relation to all its functions.

Michael Howard
Parliamentary Under Secretary of State,
Department of Trade and Industry

11th May 1987

(**a**) 1986 c. 60.
(**b**) 1985 c. 6; subsections (1B) and (1C) of section 449 of the Companies Act 1985 were inserted by paragraph 9 of Schedule 13 to the Financial Services Act 1986.
(**c**) 1986 c. 45.
(**d**) 1973 c. 38.

EXPLANATORY NOTE

(This note is not part of the Order)

This Order designates certain authorities as authorities for the purposes of section 180 of the Financial Services Act 1986 and section 449 of the Companies Act 1985 in relation to specified functions. The Insolvency Practitioners Tribunal to which cases may be referred under the Insolvency Act 1986 is designated in relation to its functions under that Act. The Occupational Pensions Board is designated in relation to its functions under the Social Security Act 1973 and the Social Security Acts 1975 to 1986. The Panel on Take-overs and Mergers is designated in relation to all its functions. The effect of designation is to permit the disclosure of information which would otherwise be restricted if disclosure is for the purpose of enabling or assisting the designated authority to discharge the specified functions.

STATUTORY INSTRUMENTS

1987 No. 860

VALUE ADDED TAX

The Value Added Tax (Finance) Order 1987

Made - - - -	*11th May 1987*
Laid before the House of Commons	*12th May 1987*
Coming into force	*13th May 1987*

The Treasury, in exercise of the powers conferred on them by section 17(2) of the Value Added Tax Act 1983(**a**) and of all other powers enabling them in that behalf, hereby make the following Order:

1. This Order may be cited as the Value Added Tax (Finance) Order 1987 and shall come into force on 13th May 1987.

2. Group 5 of Schedule 6 to the Value Added Tax Act 1983 shall be varied by deleting item 6 and by substituting the following:–

"**6.** The issue, transfer or receipt of, or any dealing with, any security or secondary security being:–

(a) shares, stock, bonds, notes (other than promissory notes), debentures, debenture stock or shares in an oil royalty; or

(b) any document relating to money, in any currency, which has been deposited with the issuer or some other person, being a document which recognises an obligation to pay a stated amount to bearer or to order, with or without interest, and being a document by the delivery of which, with or without endorsement, the right to receive that stated amount, with or without interest, is transferable; or

(c) any bill, note or other obligation of the Treasury or of a Government in any part of the world, being a document by the delivery of which, with or without endorsement, title is transferable, and not being an obligation which is or has been legal tender in any part of the world; or

(d) any letter of allotment or rights, any warrant conferring an option to acquire a security included in this item, any renounceable or scrip certificates, rights coupons, coupons representing dividends or interest on such a security, bond mandates or other documents conferring or containing evidence of title to or rights in respect of such a security; or

(e) units or other documents conferring rights under any trust established for the purpose, or having the effect of providing, for persons having funds available for investment, facilities for the participation by them as beneficiaries under the trust, in any profits or income arising from the acquisition, holding, management or disposal of any property whatsoever.".

Peter Lloyd
Mark Lennox-Boyd
11th May 1987   Two of the Lords Commissioners of Her Majesty's Treasury

---

(**a**) 1983 c. 55.

EXPLANATORY NOTE

(This note is not part of the Order)

This Order is concerned with the value added tax exemption for securities and secondary securities in item 6, Group 5 of Schedule 6 to the Value Added Tax Act 1983. It deletes the reference in that item to section 42 of the Exchange Control Act 1947 (c. 14) and substitutes a full definition of securities and secondary securities. The Order does not alter the coverage of the exemption.

STATUTORY INSTRUMENTS

1987 No. 861

SOCIAL SECURITY

The Social Security Revaluation of Earnings Factors Order 1987

Made - - - -	*11th May 1987*
Laid before Parliament	*12th May 1987*
Coming into force	*3rd June 1987*

The Secretary of State for Social Services, in exercise of the powers conferred upon him by section 21 of the Social Security Pensions Act 1975(**a**) and of all other powers enabling him in that behalf, having on a review under the said section 21 concluded, having had regard to earlier Orders under that section (**b**) , that earnings factors for the relevant previous tax years have not, during the period taken into account for that review, maintained their value in relation to the general level of earnings obtaining in Great Britain, hereby makes the following Order:

Citation and commencement

1. This Order may be cited as the Social Security Revaluation of Earnings Factors Order 1987 and shall come into force on 3rd June 1987.

Revaluation of earnings factors

2. The earnings factors relevant–
(a) to the calculation–
   (i) of the additional pension (**c**) in the rate of any long-term benefit; or
   (ii) of any guaranteed minimum pension; or
(b) to any other calculation required under Part III of the Social Security Pensions Act 1975 (including that Part as modified by or under any other enactment),
are directed to be increased for the tax years specified in the Schedule hereto by the percentage of their amount shown opposite the said tax years in the said Schedule.

Rounding of fractional amounts

3. Where any earnings factor as increased in accordance with this Order would not but for this article be expressed as a whole number of pounds, it shall be so expressed by the rounding down of any fraction of a pound less than one half and the rounding up of any other fraction of a pound.

(**a**) 1975 c.60; section 21 was amended by the Social Security Act 1979 (c.18), section 10, the Social Security Act 1980 (c.30), section 3(3) and Schedule 5, and the Social Security Act 1985 (c.53), section 4, Schedule 3, paragraphs 1 and 7.
(**b**) S.I. 1979/832, 1980/728, 1981/598, 1982/607, 1983/655, 1984/581, 1985/688, 1986/809.
(**c**) *See* section 18(1) of the Social Security Act 1986 (c.50).

Signed by authority of the Secretary of State for Social Services.

Nicholas Lyell
Parliamentary Under Secretary of State,
11th May 1987   Department of Health and Social Security

Article 2		SCHEDULE

Tax year	*Increase*
1978–79	158.6
1979–80	128.1
1980–81	90.6
1981–82	59.6
1982–83	45.0
1983–84	34.7
1984–85	24.7
1985–86	17.0
1986–87	7.4

EXPLANATORY NOTE

(This note is not part of the Order)

This Order is made consequent upon a review under section 21 of the Social Security Pensions Act 1975 ("the Pensions Act"), which provides for the revaluation of earnings factors so that they maintain their value in relation to the general level of earnings obtaining in Great Britain.

The Order directs that the earnings factors relevant to the calculation of the additional pension in the rate of any long-term benefit or of any guaranteed minimum pension or to any other calculation required under Part III of the Pensions Act for the tax years specified in the Schedule to the Order are to be increased by the percentage of their amount specified in that Schedule. The percentage for the tax years 1986–87 has been fixed at 7.4 per cent; those for earlier years have also been increased. The Order also provides for the rounding of fractional amounts.

For the purpose of certain occupational pension schemes which are contracted-out under Part III of the Pensions Act, the increases made by this Order are applied, by sections 35(5) and 41C(4A), to the earnings factor used in calculating an earner's guaranteed minimum pension and by sections 44(6)(a) and 45(3)(a) for the purpose of determining the amount of any state scheme premium.

In certain cases where guaranteed minimum pensions are preserved under arrangements approved by the Occupational Pensions Board under section 44 of the Pensions Act, section 35(5) has effect subject to provisions set out in section 21(1) of the Social Security (Miscellaneous Provisions) Act 1977 (c.5).

Section 21(1) of the 1977 Act and sections 44(6)(a) and 45(3)(a) of the Pensions Act were amended by section 4 of and Schedule 3 to the Social Security Act 1985 (c.53) which also added paragraph 4A to section 41C of the Pensions Act.

1987 No. 862

WAGES COUNCILS

The Wages Councils (Meetings and Procedure) Regulations 1987

Made - - - -	*12 May 1987*
Laid before Parliament	*14th May 1987*
Coming into force	*4th June 1987*

The Secretary of State, in exercise of the powers conferred on him by section 25 of, and paragraph 7 of Schedule 2 to, the Wages Act 1986(**a**) and of all other powers enabling him in that behalf, hereby makes the following Regulations:–

Citation, commencement and interpretation

1.—(1) These Regulations may be cited as the Wages Councils (Meetings and Procedure) Regulations 1987 and shall come into force on 4th June 1987.

(2) In these Regulations –

"member" means a person for the time being appointed to be a member of a wages council;

"representative member" means a member appointed to represent employers or workers;

"independent member" means a member appointed as being an independent person;

"chairman" means the independent member acting as chairman of any meeting of a wages council by virtue of an appointment made by the Secretary of State under paragraph 3 of Schedule 2 to the Wages Act 1986.

Revocation

2. The Wages Councils (Meetings and Procedure) Regulations 1975(**b**) and the Wages Councils and Central Co-ordinating Committees (Conditions of Office) Regulations 1975(**c**) are hereby revoked.

Quorum

3. In order to constitute a meeting of a wages council there shall be present at least one of the independent members and at least one third of the whole number of the representative members.

Voting

4. Subject to regulation 5, every member of a wages council present at a meeting of the council shall have one vote.

(**a**) 1986 c. 48.   (**b**) S.I. 1975/2136.   (**c**) S.I. 1975/2137.

5.—(1) If the chairman of a meeting of a wages council thinks fit, or if more than half of the representative members present who represent employers, or who represent workers, request, a vote of the representative members shall be taken by sides and the vote of the majority of representative members present on each side shall be the vote of that side.

(2) On such a vote, the independent members shall not vote but in the event of the vote resulting in a disagreement between the two sides, the question may be decided by the majority vote of the independent members present or, if the chairman is the only independent member present, by the vote of the chairman.

Notice of meetings

6. Notice of a meeting of a wages council shall be deemed to be sufficiently given to a member if sent by post to his ordinary or last known address, but the accidental omission to give notice of a meeting to, or the non-receipt of notice of a meeting by, any member shall not invalidate the proceedings at any meeting.

Signed by order of the Secretary of State

David Trippier
Parliamentary Under Secretary of State,
Department of Employment

12th May 1987

EXPLANATORY NOTE

(This note is not part of the Regulations)

These Regulations prescribe procedures which are to apply to the meetings of wages councils and relate to the quorum, the method of voting and notices of meetings. The Regulations revoke and replace the Wages Councils (Meetings and Procedure) Regulations 1975 and also revoke the Wages Councils and Central Co-ordinating Committees (Conditions of Office) Regulations 1975.

STATUTORY INSTRUMENTS

1987 No. 863

WAGES COUNCILS

The Wages Councils (Notices) Regulations 1987

Made - - - -	*12th May 1987*
Laid before Parliament	*14th May 1987*
Coming into force	*4th June 1987*

The Secretary of State, in exercise of the powers conferred on him by sections 19(2) and (3) and 25 of and paragraphs 1 and 2 of Schedule 3 to the Wages Act 1986**(a)** and of all other powers enabling him in that behalf, hereby makes the following Regulations:–

Citation, commencement and revocation

1.—(1) These Regulations may be cited as the Wages Councils (Notices) Regulations 1987 and shall come into force on 4th June 1987.

(2) The Wages Councils and Statutory Joint Industrial Councils (Notices) Regulations 1975**(b)** are hereby revoked.

Interpretation

2. In these Regulations, "the Act" means the Wages Act 1986.

Publication of notices of proposal to make an order

3.—(1) Before making an order under section 14 of the Act a wages council shall publish notice of any rate or limit which the council proposes to fix under subsection (1) of that section, and, subject to paragraph (2) that notice shall be published in the London and Edinburgh Gazettes.

(2) Where the issue of the London or Edinburgh Gazette in which the notice was expected to appear does not contain the notice, or where the council has reason to believe that the issue of the London or Edinburgh Gazette in which it wishes the notice to appear will not be published or will be published late, the council may publish the notice in an English national daily newspaper instead of the London Gazette or, as the case may be, in a Scottish national daily newspaper instead of the Edinburgh Gazette.

(3) The date to be taken for the purposes of the Act as the date of publication of a notice to which paragraph (1) refers shall be the first or only date on which the notice is published in England and Scotland or, if the notice is published on different dates in those countries, the date on which it is first published in the country in which it is published second.

(a) 1986 c.48.
(b) S.I. 1975/2138.

Notice to employers of notice of proposal

4.—(1) As soon as may be after the publication by a wages council of the notice referred to in regulation 3, the council shall send to every employer appearing to the council to be affected thereby a notice fulfilling the requirements of paragraphs (2) and (3).

(2) The notice required to be sent by paragraph (1) shall:
- (a) set out the contents of the notice referred to in regulation 3;
- (b) state the date from which the council intends its proposals to come into force;
- (c) state the place where further copies of the proposals may be obtained;
- (d) state the period, being a period of not less than 28 days beginning with the date of publication of the notice referred to in regulation 3, within which written representations with respect to the proposals may be sent to the council;
- (e) state that the order will not apply to workers under the age of 21.

(3)(a) Subject to sub-paragraph (b), the notice required to be sent by paragraph (1) shall also give short and, so far as practicable having regard to that requirement, legally accurate explanations of:
- (i) the way in which any rate or limit which will have effect (or continue to have effect) if an order implementing the proposals is made, will apply to time workers under section 14(1) and (2) of the Act and, where the council operates in relation to piece workers, to piece workers under sections 14(3) and 15(1) and (2) of the Act;
- (ii) the effect of section 14(5) of the Act and, where the council operates in relation to piece workers, of section 15(4) of the Act on the way in which any such rate will apply to time to which that section or those sections apply, specifying separately, where the council operates in relation to homeworkers who are time workers, the effect of section 14(5) in relation to those workers and, where the council operates in relation to homeworkers who are piece workers, the effect of section 15(4) in relation to those workers;
- (iii) the requirement on employers contained in regulation 6(1) to post notices and, where the council operates in relation to homeworkers, the requirement on employers under regulation 6(2) to send notices.
- (b) No explanation as required by sub-paragraph (i) of paragraph (3)(a) shall be given where:
  - (i) the council does not operate in relation to any piece workers; and
  - (ii) no limit will have effect if an order implementing the proposals is made.

Notice to employers of orders made under section 14 of the Act

5. As soon as may be after a wages council has made an order under section 14 of the Act, the council shall send to every employer appearing to the council to be affected thereby a notice which:
- (a) adequately describes the provisions of the order;
- (b) states that the order does not apply to workers under the age of 21;
- (c) contains explanations of the matters specified in paragraph (3)(a)(i), (ii) and (iii) of regulation 4 being explanations which, in relation to the matters specified in paragraph 3(a)(i), reflect where appropriate the exception in paragraph 3(b) of regulation 4, and which, in relation to the matters specified in paragraph 3(a)(i) and (ii), are framed by reference to the application of any rate or limit which has effect but otherwise comply with the requirements of paragraph 3(a);
- (d) where the order amends or partially revokes a previous order made by the council, contains particulars of the matters previously in force left unaffected by the amendment or revocation and indicates the matters amended or revoked.

Posting and sending of notices by employers

6.—(1) An employer of workers affected by any notice mentioned in regulation 4 or 5 who are not homeworkers shall, on receipt of that notice, post up and keep posted up at any place of business of his where any such workers work clear copies of the notice in such positions and numbers as will ensure that a copy can easily be seen and read by each such worker.

(2) An employer of homeworkers affected by any notice mentioned in regulation 4 or 5 shall, on receipt of that notice, send to each such homeworker, at his last known address, a clear copy of that notice.

Signed by order of the Secretary of State

David Trippier
Parliamentary Under Secretary of State,
Department of Employment

12th May 1987

EXPLANATORY NOTE

(This note is not part of the Regulations)

These Regulations require a wages council proposing to make an order under the Wages Act 1986 to publish notice of the proposals in the London and Edinburgh Gazettes and to send employers notice of the proposals and notice of the provisions of an order once it is made. The Regulations prescribe the contents of the notices and require employers to post copies of the notices sent to them at workplaces so that the notices can be read by workers affected and to send copies of the notices to homeworkers affected.

The Regulations revoke the Wages Councils and Statutory Joint Industrial Councils (Notices) Regulations 1975.

STATUTORY INSTRUMENTS

1987 No. 864 (S.68)

EDUCATION, SCOTLAND

The Students' Allowances (Scotland) Regulations 1987

Made - - - -	*11th May 1987*
Laid before Parliament	*14th May 1987*
Coming into force	*4th June 1987*

The Secretary of State, in exercise of the powers conferred on him by sections 73(f) and 74(1) of the Education (Scotland) Act 1980(**a**) and of all other powers enabling him in that behalf, hereby makes the following Regulations:

Citation and commencement

1. These Regulations may be cited as the Students' Allowances (Scotland) Regulations 1987 and shall come into force on 4th June 1987.

Interpretation

2.—(1) In these Regulations–

"allowance" means an allowance paid or to be paid under these Regulations or the Regulations revoked by these Regulations;

"British Islands" means the United Kingdom, the Channel Islands and the Isle of Man;

"employment" includes the holding of any office and any occupation for gain, and "employed" shall be construed accordingly;

"European Community" means the area consisting of the member states of the European Economic Community (including the United Kingdom) as constituted from time to time;

"National of a member state of the European Community" means a person who is a national for the purposes of the Community Treaties of any member state of the European Economic Community (including the United Kingdom) as constituted from time to time;

"qualification" includes authorisation, recognition, registration, enrolment, approval and certification;

"refugee" means–

(a) a person who is recognised by Her Majesty's Government as a refugee within the meaning of the United Nations Convention relating to the Status of Refugees done at Geneva on 28th July 1951(**b**) as extended by the Protocol thereto which entered into force on 4th October 1967(**c**), or

(b) a person who enjoys asylum in the United Kingdom in pursuance of a decision of Her Majesty's Government though not so recognised;

"vocational training establishment" means a further education establishment being a vocational school within the meaning of Article 7 of Council Regulation (EEC) No. 1612/68(**d**) on freedom of movement of workers within the Community.

(**a**) 1980 c.44.
(**b**) Cmnd. 9171.
(**c**) Cmnd. 3906. (Out of print: photocopies are available free from Awards Branch, Scottish Education Department, Haymarket House, Clifton Terrace, Edinburgh EH12.)
(**d**) O.J. No. L257, 19.10.68, p. 2. (O.J./S.E. 1968 (II), p. 475).

(2) In these Regulations any reference to a "qualifying day" in relation to a course of study means–

(a) as respects a course starting in the autumn term of any year, 30th June in that year;

(b) as respects a course starting in the spring term of any year, 31st October in the year preceding that year; and

(c) as respects a course starting in the summer term of any year, the last day of February in that year.

(3) In these Regulations any reference to a "relevant date" in relation to a course of study is–

(a) as respects a course starting in the autumn term of any year, a reference to the earlier of 31st August in that year or the first day of that term;

(b) as respects a course starting in the spring term of any year, a reference to the earlier of 31st December in the year preceding that year or the first day of that term; and

(c) as respects a course starting in the summer term of any year, a reference to the earlier of 31st March in that year or the first day of that term.

(4) In these Regulations any reference to a person being "ordinarily resident" in Scotland on the qualifying day includes–

(a) a person whom the Secretary of State is satisfied to have been not so resident only because he, his spouse, or his parent was for the time being–

(i) employed outside Scotland; or

(ii) attending a course of study or undertaking postgraduate research outside Scotland; and

(b) a person who, in accordance with paragraph 9(3)(c) of the Education (Mandatory Awards) Regulations 1986(**a**), is treated as ordinarily resident in the area in which the establishment providing his course is situated, if that establishment is in Scotland.

(5) In these Regulations any reference to a person being "ordinarily resident" in the British Islands or in the European Community for a period includes–

(a) a person whom the Secretary of State is satisfied to have been born and to have spent the greater part of his life in the British Islands or, as the case may be, the European Community; and either–

(i) his parents or either of them have been ordinarily resident in the British Islands or, as the case may be, the European Community throughout the period of 3 years immediately preceding the relevant date (as defined in paragraph (3) above) and he himself is not an independent student; or

(ii) whether or not he is an independent student, he has been ordinarily resident for at least one year of that period in the British Islands or, as the case may be, the European Community, provided that the Secretary of State is also satisfied that he has not been so resident for any part of that period wholly or mainly for the purpose of receiving full-time education; and

(b) a person whom the Secretary of State is satisfied to have been not so resident only because he, his spouse, or his parent was for the time being–

(i) employed outside the British Islands or, as the case may be, the European Community; or

(ii) attending a course of study or undertaking post graduate research outside the British Islands or, as the case may be, the European Community.

(6) In these Regulations any reference to an "independent student" means a student who prior to the relevant date (as defined in paragraph (3) above) has–

(i) attained the age of 25 years; or

(ii) been married for at least 3 years; or

(iii) supported himself out of his earnings for periods aggregating not less than 3 years; or

(iv) no parent living,

and a student will be regarded as having supported himself out of his earnings for any period or periods, for which–

(**a**) S.I. 1986/1306.

(a) the student was in receipt of training in pursuance of the Manpower Services Commission's Training Opportunities Programme, Youth Opportunities Programme, or Youth Training Scheme; or

(b) the student was in receipt of unemployment benefit under section 14(1)(a) of the Social Security Act 1975(**a**); or

(c) before 24th November 1980(**b**), the student was registered for employment; or

(d) on and after that date but before 18 October 1982, the student was registered and available for employment; or

(e) on and after 18th October 1982, the student was available for employment and, if under the age of 18 years, registered for employment; or

(f) the student held a Scottish Studentship or comparable award; or

(g) the student received sickness benefit, invalidity pension, maternity allowance or severe disablement allowance under section 14(1)(b), 15(1)(b), 22(1) or 36(1) of the Social Security Act 1975(**c**); or

(h) the student had the care of a person under the age of 18 years who was dependent on him;

and for the purposes of this definition any reference to a person registered or available for employment is a reference to his being so registered or available for the purposes of section 5 of the Supplementary Benefits Act 1976(**d**), and any reference to a provision contained in the Supplementary Benefits Act 1976 or the Social Security Act 1975 is a reference to that provision as from time to time in force.

(7) In these Regulations any reference to a person's child includes a reference to a person adopted in pursuance of adoption proceedings, a stepchild and an illegitimate child of whom the person concerned is the mother or in whose case the person has admitted paternity or has been adjudged the putative father; and "parent" shall be construed accordingly.

Revocations

3. The Regulations listed in the Schedule hereto are hereby revoked.

Payment of allowances

4. The Secretary of State may pay an allowance, in accordance with the provisions of section 73(f) of the Education (Scotland) Act 1980 and these Regulations, to or in respect of any person attending a course of education who satisfies the requirements specified in regulation 5.

Persons eligible for an allowance

5. An allowance may be paid only to or in respect of a person who satisfies one of the following requirements:–

(a) (i) he is ordinarily resident in Scotland on the qualifying day in relation to the course in respect of which he seeks an allowance, provided that his residence there on that day is not in any sense attributable to or connected with any period of residence within 3 years immediately preceding the relevant date as respects any part of which the Secretary of State is of the opinion that its purpose was wholly or mainly that of receiving full-time education; and

(ii) he has been ordinarily resident throughout the period of 3 years preceding the relevant date in the British Islands, provided that the Secretary of State is satisfied that he has not been so resident for any part of that period wholly or mainly for the purpose of receiving full-time education; or

(b) (i) he is the child of a national of a member state of the European Community, provided that the national–

(1) where employed on the qualifying day, is then in employment in the United Kingdom; or

(**a**) 1975 c.14.
(**b**) On that date Schedule 2 to the Social Security Act 1980 (c.30), which made relevant amendments to the Supplementary Benefits Act 1976 (c.71), came into force by virtue of S.I. 1980/729.
(**c**) Section 36 was substituted by section 11 of the Health and Social Security Act 1984 (c.48).
(**d**) 1976 c.71; section 5 was substituted by section 38(1) of the Social Security and Housing Benefits Act 1982 (c.24).

(2) where not employed on the qualifying day (by reason of retirement or otherwise), was last employed in such employment; or

(3) whether or not employed on the qualifying day, has been, during the 3 year period preceding that date, in such employment for an aggregate period of not less than a year; and

(ii) he is ordinarily resident in Scotland on the qualifying day in relation to the course in respect of which he seeks an allowance, provided that his residence there on that day is not in any sense attributable to or connected with any period of residence within 3 years immediately preceding the relevant date as respects any part of which the Secretary of State is of the opinion that its purpose was wholly or mainly that of receiving full-time education; and

(iii) he has been ordinarily resident throughout the period of 3 years preceding the relevant date in the European Community, provided that the Secretary of State is satisfied that he has not been so resident for any part of that period wholly or mainly for the purpose of receiving full-time education; or

(c) he is a national of a member state of the European Community who has been ordinarily resident throughout the period of 3 years preceding the relevant date in the European Community, provided that the Secretary of State is satisfied that he has not been so resident for any part of that period wholly or mainly for the purpose of receiving full-time education, and who–

(i) is ordinarily resident in Scotland on the qualifying day;

(ii) has entered the United Kingdom wholly or mainly for the purpose of taking up or of seeking employment;

(iii) during the year preceding the relevant date has been in employment in the United Kingdom for an aggregate period of not less than 9 months; and

(iv) seeks an allowance in respect of a course provided by a vocational training establishment being a course leading to a qualification which is needed for, or is designed to fit, a person for engagement in a specific profession or trade; or

(d) he is a refugee or the spouse or child of a refugee, provided that the refugee has been ordinarily resident in the British Islands and has not ceased to be so ordinarily resident since he was first recognised as a refugee or was awarded asylum; or

(e) he is a national, or the child of a national, of a member state of the European Community (the Kingdom of Spain and the Portuguese Republic being deemed for the purposes of this paragraph to have been member states of the European Community from 1st September 1983) and he–

(i) seeks an allowance in respect of a course of study at an educational establishment in Scotland, and

(ii) has been ordinarily resident in the European Community throughout the 3 years immediately preceding the relevant date, provided that the Secretary of State is satisfied that he has not been so resident for any part of that period wholly or mainly for the purpose of receiving full-time education,

in which case the allowance payable may be only that described in regulation 6(1)(a) (tuition and other fees); or

(f) a person to whom, or in respect of whom, an allowance has been paid in accordance with these Regulations or those revoked by them within the year immediately preceding the relevant date.

Allowances

6.—(1) The amount of an allowance shall be determined by the Secretary of State and may include sums in respect of–

(a) tuition and other fees payable in respect of the holder of the allowance;

(b) travelling expenses necessarily incurred, or to be incurred, by the holder in attending the course of study in respect of which the allowance is awarded;

(c) the maintenance of the holder and of any persons dependent on him during periods of full-time study and during vacations;

(d) other expenses incurred, or to be incurred, by the holder in taking advantage of educational facilities.

(2) In determining the amount of an allowance, the Secretary of State shall take account of the sums, if any, which, in accordance with principles determined by him from time to time, the holder, the holder's parents and the holder's spouse can reasonably be expected to contribute towards the holder's expenses.

(3) The amount of an allowance may be revised at any time if the Secretary of State thinks fit having regard to–
   (a) the failure of the holder to comply with the conditions of allowance, or
   (b) all the circumstances of the holder or his parents or both as the case may be, or
   (c) any error made in the computation of the amount of the allowance.

Conditions of allowance

7.—(1) Every allowance shall be held subject to the following conditions:–
   (a) the holder shall attend regularly the course of study in respect of which the allowance is awarded;
   (b) the Secretary of State shall be satisfied as to the conduct and progress of the holder; and
   (c) the holder shall provide the Secretary of State with such information and such documents as he may from time to time require to enable him to exercise his functions under these Regulations.

If these conditions are not complied with or if the holder receives from any other source any sum which in the opinion of the Secretary of State makes it unnecessary for him to be assisted by means of an allowance, the Secretary of State may suspend payment of the allowance or terminate the allowance.

(2) It shall be a condition of payment of an allowance that the applicant gives a written undertaking to pay to the Secretary of State any amount of which the Secretary of State may request repayment in the circumstances specified in paragraph (3) below:
Provided that if the applicant is a minor and has any parent or guardian, the parent or guardian shall consent to the undertaking.

(3) Where the Secretary of State is satisfied that there has been an overpayment of allowance for any reason and requests repayment of the overpayment or so much thereof as he thinks fit, and the holder of the allowance has given an undertaking under paragraph (2) above, the holder of the allowance shall be obliged to pay to the Secretary of State the amount requested.

Method of payment

8.—(1) The allowance may be paid to the holder or to another person for his behoof, or in part to the holder and in part to the said other person, and any sum in respect of fees payable to an educational institution which is included in the amount of the allowance may be paid on behalf of the holder to the institution.

(2) The allowance may be paid in a single payment or by instalments as the Secretary of State thinks fit, but no payment shall be made before the holder has been accepted for admission to the course of study in respect of which the allowance is awarded.

11th May 1987   *John J. MacKay*
New St. Andrew's House, Edinburgh   Parliamentary Under Secretary of State,
                                                                Scottish Office

SCHEDULE

Regulation 3

REVOCATIONS

Regulations revoked	References
The Students' Allowances (Scotland) Regulations 1971	S.I. 1971/124
The Students' Allowances (Scotland) Amendment Regulations 1974	S.I. 1974/1187
The Students' Allowances (Scotland) Amendment Regulations 1983	S.I. 1983/798
The Students' Allowances (Scotland) Amendment (No. 2) Regulations 1983	S.I. 1983/1536

EXPLANATORY NOTE

(This note is not part of the Regulations)

These Regulations supersede and substantially re-enact the Students' Allowances (Scotland) Regulations 1971 (as amended) and enable the Secretary of State to pay allowances to persons attending courses of education who fulfil certain requirements as to eligibility. They also prescribe the conditions subject to which an allowance is paid. The principal differences in substance from the amended 1971 Regulations are described below.

Persons attending a course of study or undertaking postgraduate research outside Scotland may be deemed to be ordinarily resident in Scotland (regulation 2(4)(a)(ii)).

Certain persons who are denied awards by local educational authorities in England and Wales because they are classified as "no area students" may be eligible for allowances if their courses are in Scotland (regulation 2(4)(b)).

Persons who have been married for at least 3 years before the relevant date relating to the beginning of their courses are classified as independent students (regulation 2(6)(ii)).

Persons who have no parent living on the relevant date relating to the beginning of their courses are classified as independent students (regulation 2(6)(iv)).

Periods in the Youth Training Scheme count towards classification as independent students (regulation 2(6)(a)).

For persons who gain eligibility for an award by virtue of their parents' employment in the United Kingdom, that employment may be anywhere in the United Kingdom (regulation 5(b)).

Nationals of member states of the European Community who gain eligibility for an award by virtue of employment in the British Islands must have been ordinarily resident in Scotland on the qualifying day, but their employment may have been anywhere in the United Kingdom (regulation 5(c)).

Refugees and asylees do not have to be ordinarily resident in Scotland on the qualifying day before their courses begin in order to qualify for an allowance (regulation 5(d)).

Provision is made to permit the payment of tuition and other fees to nationals of the European Community who undertake courses of education in Scotland and who do not otherwise satisfy the residence requirements for an award (regulation 5(e)).

Persons who have been in receipt of an allowance for another course in the year before a new course begins do not have to satisfy further conditions as to residence (regulation 5(f)).

STATUTORY INSTRUMENTS

1987 No. 865 (S. 69)

SHERIFF COURT, SCOTLAND

Act of Sederunt (Fees of Solicitors in the Sheriff Court) (Amendment) 1987

Made - - - -	*8th May 1987*
Laid before Parliament	*14th May 1987*
Coming into force	*8th June 1987*

The Lords of Council and Session, under and by virtue of the powers conferred on them by section 40 of the Sheriff Courts (Scotland) Act 1907(**a**) and of all other powers enabling them in that behalf, do hereby enact and declare:

Citation and commencement

1.—(1) This Act of Sederunt may be cited as the Act of Sederunt (Fees of Solicitors in the Sheriff Court) (Amendment) 1987 and shall come into force on 8th June 1987.

(2) This Act of Sederunt shall be inserted in the Books of Sederunt.

Amendment of solicitors' fees

2.—(1) In the Act of Sederunt (Fees of Solicitors in the Sheriff Court) 1986(**b**), in the Schedule, in Chapters I, II, III, IV and VI of the Table of Fees, for the fees specified in column 2 of the Schedule to this Act of Sederunt in relation to the paragraphs specified in column 1 of that Schedule there shall be substituted the fees specified in column 3 of that Schedule.

(2) Notwithstanding sub-paragraph (1) of this paragraph, the fees specified in column 2 of the Schedule to this Act of Sederunt shall continue to have effect in respect of work done before the coming into force of this Act of Sederunt.

Edinburgh
8th May 1987

Emslie
Lord President, I.P.D.

(**a**) 1907 c.51; section 40 was amended by the Secretaries of State Act 1926 (c.18), section 1(3), by the Schedule to the Administration of Justice (Scotland) Act 1933 (c.41), and by the Divorce Jurisdiction, Court Fees and Legal Aid (Scotland) Act 1983 (c.12), Schedule 1, paragraph 7 and Schedule 2.
(**b**) S.I. 1986/978.

SCHEDULE

(1) (Number of paragraph)	(2) (Current fee)	(3) (New Fee)
CHAPTER I:–		
PART I. 1. (a)	£ 44.80	£ 47.50
(b)	£ 38.60	£ 40.90
2. (a)	£212.10	£224.85
3.	£190.80	£202.25
PART II. 1. Table A. 1.	£148.40	£157.30
2.	£106.00	£112.40
3.	£ 31.80	£ 33.70
4.	£286.20	£303.40
2. Table B. 1.	£121.90	£129.20
2.	£ 58.30	£ 61.80
3.	£ 31.80	£ 33.70
4.	£212.00	£224.80
3. Table C. 1.	£ 57.80	£ 61.25
2.	£ 33.90	£ 35.95
3.	£ 91.70	£ 97.20
CHAPTER II:–		
1. (a)	£ 97.00	£102.80
(b)	£ 34.00	£ 36.05
2. (a)	£145.20	£153.90
(b)	£ 97.00	£102.80
(c)	£ 17.00	£ 18.00
(d)	£ 24.40	£ 25.85
3.	£ 6.20	£ 6.60
4. (a)(i)	£ 72.60	£ 76.95
(ii)	£ 17.00	£ 18.00
(iii)	£ 7.40	£ 7.85
(b)(ii)	£ 42.50	£ 45.05
(iii)	£ 7.40	£ 7.85
5.	£ 14.70	£ 15.60
6. (a)	£ 31.80	£ 33.70
(b)	£ 4.50	£ 4.80
7. (a)(i)	£ 90.70	£ 96.15
(ii)	£ 60.70	£ 64.35
(iii)	£ 18.10	£ 19.20
(iv)	£ 17.00	£ 18.00
(v)	£ 7.40	£ 7.85
(b)(i)	£ 54.40	£ 57.65
(ii)	£ 30.10	£ 31.90
(iii)	£ 17.00	£ 18.00
(iv)	£ 7.40	£ 7.85
8. (a)	£ 37.40	£ 39.65
(b)	£ 24.40	£ 25.85
(c)(i)	£ 34.00	£ 36.05
(ii)	£ 17.00	£ 18.00
(d)	£ 7.40	£ 7.85
9. (a)(i)	£ 41.40	£ 43.90
(ii)	£ 27.20	£ 28.85
(b)(i)	£ 34.00	£ 36.05
(ii)	£ 22.70	£ 24.05
(c)	£ 30.10	£ 31.90
10. (a)(i)	£ 42.50	£ 45.05
(ii)	£ 30.10	£ 31.90

(1) (Number of paragraph)	(2) (Current fee)	(3) (New Fee)
(b)(i)	£ 24.40	£ 25.85
(ii)	£ 15.30	£ 16.20
11. (a)	£ 60.70	£ 64.35
(b)	£ 36.30	£ 38.50
(c)	£ 15.30	£ 16.20
(d)	£ 7.90	£ 8.40
12. (a)	£ 17.00	£ 18.00
(b)	£ 7.40	£ 7.85
(c)	£ 7.40	£ 7.85
13. (a)	£ 30.10	£ 31.90
(b)	£ 17.00	£ 18.00
(c)	£ 7.40	£ 7.85
(d)	£ 7.40	£ 7.85
14. (a)(i)	£ 56.70	£ 60.10
(ii)	£ 17.00	£ 18.00
(iii)	£ 7.40	£ 7.85
(iv)	£ 7.40	£ 7.85
(b)	£ 28.40	£ 30.10
15. (a)(i)	£ 33.50	£ 35.50
(ii)	£ 25.00	£ 26.50
(b)	£ 56.70	£ 60.10
16. (a)	£ 44.80	£ 47.50
(b)	£ 36.30	£ 38.50
(c)	£ 11.30	£ 12.00
17. (a)	£ 0.80	£ 0.85
19. (a)	£ 18.70	£ 19.80
(b)	£ 37.40	£ 39.65
(c)	£ 37.40	£ 39.65
CHAPTER III:–		
1.	£ 17.00	£ 18.00
2. (a)	£ 7.40	£ 7.85
3.	£ 4.00	£ 4.25
4.	£ 6.20	£ 6.60
5.	£ 1.70	£ 1.80
6. (i)	£ 0.80	£ 0.85
7.	£ 1.70	£ 1.80
8.	£ 7.40	£ 7.85
9.	£ 1.70	£ 1.80
10.	£ 1.70	£ 1.80
11.	£ 7.90	£ 8.40
12. (a)	£ 0.80	£ 0.85
(b)	£ 3.40	£ 3.60
(c)	£ 1.70	£ 1.80
13.	£ 3.40	£ 3.60
14. (a)	£ 1.70	£ 1.80
(b)	£ 1.70	£ 1.80
(c)	£ 3.40	£ 3.60
(d)	£ 3.40	£ 3.60
15. (a)	£ 3.40	£ 3.60
(b)	£ 3.40	£ 3.60
(c)	£ 3.40	£ 3.60
(d)	£ 5.10	£ 5.40
16. (a)	£ 3.40	£ 3.60
(b)	£ 3.40	£ 3.60
(c)	£ 3.40	£ 3.60
(d)	£ 2.30	£ 2.45
(e)	£ 2.30	£ 2.45
(f)	£ 2.30	£ 2.45

(1)	(2)	(3)
(Number of paragraph)	(Current fee)	(New Fee)
CHAPTER IV:–		
PART I. 1.	£ 30.10	£ 31.90
2. (a)	£ 3.40	£ 3.60
(b)	£ 9.60	£ 10.20
3.	£ 9.60	£ 10.20
PART II. 1.	£ 41.40	£ 43.90
2. (a)	£ 3.40	£ 3.60
	£ 7.40	£ 7.85
(b)	£ 3.40	£ 3.60
(c)	£ 10.80	£ 11.45
3.	£ 10.80	£ 11.45
4.	£ 37.40	£ 39.65
5.	£ 18.70	£ 19.80
6. (a)	£ 15.90	£ 16.85
(b)	£ 7.40	£ 7.85
7. (a)	£ 15.90	£ 16.85
(b)	£ 7.40	£ 7.85
8. (a)	£ 22.70	£ 24.05
(b)	£ 13.60	£ 14.40
9. (a)	£ 18.70	£ 19.80
(b)	£ 10.80	£ 11.45
10. (a)	£ 10.80	£ 11.45
(b)	£ 5.70	£ 6.05
11. (a)	£ 22.70	£ 24.05
(i)	£ 15.90	£ 16.85
(ii)	£ 15.90	£ 16.85
(b)	£ 37.40	£ 39.65
12. (a)	£ 18.70	£ 19.80
(b)	£ 17.00	£ 18.00
(c)	£ 10.80	£ 11.45
(d)	£ 7.40	£ 7.85
13. (a)(i)	£ 22.70	£ 24.05
(ii)	£ 13.60	£ 14.40
(b)(i)	£ 18.70	£ 19.80
(ii)	£ 10.80	£ 11.45
(c)	£ 10.80	£ 11.45
(d)	£ 7.40	£ 7.85
(e)	£ 10.20	£ 10.80
(f)	£ 6.80	£ 7.20
14.	£ 7.40	£ 7.85
15. (a)	£ 51.00	£ 54.05
(b)	£ 10.80	£ 11.45
16. (a)	£ 22.70	£ 24.05
(b)	£ 22.70	£ 24.05
(c)	£ 10.80	£ 11.45
CHAPTER VI:–		
1.	£ 25.50	£ 27.05
3. (a)	£ 12.50	£ 13.25
(b)	£ 10.80	£ 11.45
4.	£ 25.50	£ 27.05

EXPLANATORY NOTE

(This note is not part of the Act of Sederunt)

This Act of Sederunt increases the fees payable to solicitors under Chapters I, II, III, IV and VI of the Table of Fees in the Act of Sederunt (Fees of Solicitors in the Sheriff Court) 1986 by 6 per cent (rounded to the nearest 5 pence). The increase applies to work done on or after 8th June 1987. The existing fees continue to have effect in respect of work done before the coming into force of this Act of Sederunt.

STATUTORY INSTRUMENTS

1987 No. 866

GAS

The Gas Act 1986 (Government Shareholding) Order 1987

Made - - - -	10th May 1987
Laid before Parliament	13th May 1987
Coming into force -	3rd June 1987

Whereas British Gas public limited company, being the successor company(a) to the British Gas Corporation, ceased to be wholly owned by the Crown on 8th December 1986, and whereas the Government shareholding carries 2.680 per cent of the voting rights exercisable in all circumstances at general meetings of the company:

Now, therefore, the Secretary of State, in exercise of the powers conferred on him by section 54(1) of the Gas Act 1986(b) and of all other powers enabling him in that behalf, hereby makes the following Order:–

1. This Order may be cited as the Gas Act 1986 (Government Shareholding) Order 1987 and shall come into force on 3 June 1987.

2. The target investment limit in relation to the shares for the time being held in British Gas public limited company by the Treasury and their nominees and by the Secretary of State and his nominees by virtue of any provision of Part II of the Gas Act 1986 shall be 2.680 per cent of the voting rights exercisable in all circumstances at general meetings of the company.

10th May 1987

Peter Walker
Secretary of State for Energy

EXPLANATORY NOTE

(This note is not part of the Order)

This Order sets the target investment limit for the Government shareholding in British Gas plc at 2.680 per cent of the voting rights exercisable in all circumstances at general meetings of the company, being the proportion of those rights carried by shares which, at the date this Order is made, are held by the Government in the company by virtue of Part II of the Act (section 54(3) of the Gas Act 1986).

(a) *See* S.I. 1986/1317; this Order nominated British Gas public limited company as the successor company to the British Gas Corporation for the purposes of section 49 of the Gas Act 1986 (c.44).
(b) 1986 c.44.

1987 No. 867

BEE DISEASES

The Importation of Bees (Amendment) Order 1987

Made - - - -	*12th May 1987*
Laid before Parliament	*14th May 1987*
Coming into force	*4th June 1987*

The Minister of Agriculture, Fisheries and Food, the Secretary of State for Scotland and the Secretary of State for Wales, acting jointly, in exercise of the powers conferred on them by section 1(1) and (2) of the Bees Act 1980(**a**) and of all their other enabling powers, hereby make the following Order:

Title and commencement

  1. This Order may be cited as the Importation of Bees (Amendment) Order 1987 and shall come into force on 4th June 1987.

Amendment

  2. The Importation of Bees Order 1980(**b**) shall be amended as follows–
- (a) in article 2 (interpretation) after the definition of "bees" there shall be added the following definition–
" "bee pests" means any organisms or pathogens which are injurious to bees or any cultures of any such organisms or pathogens;" and
- (b) in article 3 (prohibition of importation of bees), article 4 (general licences) and article 5 (specific licences) after the word "bees" wherever it appears in those articles there shall be added the words "or bee pests".

  In Witness whereof the Official Seal of the Minister of Agriculture, Fisheries and Food is hereunto affixed on 11th May 1987.

Michael Jopling
Minister of Agriculture, Fisheries and Food

11th May 1987

John J. Mackay
Parliamentary Under Secretary of State,
Scottish Office

12th May 1987

Nicholas Edwards
Secretary of State for Wales

(**a**) 1980 c.12.   (**b**) S.I. 1980/792.

EXPLANATORY NOTE

(This note is not part of the Order)

This Order amends the Importation of Bees Order 1980, which prohibits the importation of bees into Great Britain except under a licence issued by the responsible Minister (as defined in that Order), by prohibiting the importation of bee pests (being organisms or pathogens which are injurious to bees or any cultures of any such organisms or pathogens) except under such a licence (article 2).

STATUTORY INSTRUMENTS

1987 No. 868

TERMS AND CONDITIONS OF EMPLOYMENT

The Statutory Sick Pay (General) Amendment (No.2) Regulations 1987

Made - - - -	*12th May 1987*
Laid before Parliament	*14th May 1987*
Coming into force	*7th June 1987*

The Secretary of State for Social Services, in exercise of the powers conferred by sections 3(4A)(b) and (5), 26(1) and (3) and 47 of, and paragraph 1 of Schedule 1 to, the Social Security and Housing Benefits Act 1982(**a**), and of all other powers enabling him in that behalf, after agreement by the Social Security Advisory Committee that proposals to make these Regulations should not be referred to it(**b**), hereby makes the following Regulations:

Citation, commencement and interpretation

1.—(1) These Regulations may be cited as the Statutory Sick Pay (General) Amendment (No.2) Regulations 1987 and shall come into force on 7th June 1987.

(2) In these Regulations, "the General Regulations" means the Statutory Sick Pay (General) Regulations 1982(**c**).

Period of entitlement ending or not arising

2. In regulation 3 of the General Regulations, after paragraph (3) there shall be added the following paragraphs:

"(4) Where a period of entitlement is current as between an employee and her employer and the employee –

(a) is or was pregnant,

(b) has reached or been confined before reaching the day immediately preceding the 6th week before the expected week of confinement, and

(c) is not by virtue of that pregnancy or confinement entitled to statutory maternity pay under Part V of the Social Security Act 1986(**d**) or to maternity allowance under section 22 of the Social Security Act 1975(**e**),

the period of entitlement shall end on that day, or if earlier, on the day she was confined.

(**a**) 1982 c.24; section 3(4A)(b) was inserted by section 18(5) of the Social Security Act 1985 (c.53). Section 26(1) is cited because of the meaning ascribed to the word "prescribed" and section 47 because of the meaning ascribed to the word "regulations".   (**b**) *See* section 10(2)(b) of the Social Security Act 1980 (c.30).   (**c**) S.I.1982/894. (**d**) 1986 c.50.   (**e**) 1975 c.14.

(5) Where an employee –

(a) has been confined or has reached the beginning of the 6th week before the expected week of her confinement, and

(b) is not either by virtue of or in expectation of that confinement entitled to statutory maternity pay under Part V of the Social Security Act 1986(a) or to maternity allowance under section 22 of the Social Security Act 1975(b),

a period of entitlement as between her and her employer shall not arise in relation to a period of incapacity for work where the first day in that period falls within 18 weeks of the beginning of the 6th week before her expected week of confinement, or if earlier, of the week in which she was confined.

(6) In paragraphs (4) and (5) "confinement" and "confined" have the same meanings as in section 50 of the Social Security Act 1986.".

Statements relating to payment of statutory sick pay

3. In regulation 15A of the General Regulations(c) (statements relating to the payment of statutory sick pay) –

(a) in paragraph (1) for sub-paragraph (c), there shall be substituted the following sub-paragraph –

"(c) the employer is or was liable to make a payment of statutory sick pay to the employee in respect of any week within that period, and for this purpose a week includes any days rounded up to a week in accordance with paragraph (4),"; and

(b) in paragraph (2)(b) the words "and days" shall be omitted.

Meaning of "earnings"

4. In regulation 17 of the General Regulations (meaning of earnings) –

(a) in paragraph (2), sub-paragraph (f) is revoked, and

(b) in paragraph (3), after sub-paragraph (g) there shall be added the following sub-paragraph –

"(h) any sum payable by way of statutory maternity pay under Part V of the Social Security Act 1986, including sums payable in accordance with regulations made under section 46(8)(b) of that Act.".

Signed by authority of the Secretary of State for Social Services.

John Major
Minister of State,
Department of Health and Social Security

12th May 1987

(a) 1986 c.50.   (b) 1975 c.14.   (c) Regulation 15A was inserted by S.I. 1986/477, regulation 7.

EXPLANATORY NOTE

(This note is not part of the Regulations)

These Regulations amend the Statutory Sick Pay (General) Regulations 1982.

Section 3 of the Social Security and Housing Benefits Act 1982, as amended by the Social Security Act 1986, section 86, Schedule 10, paragraph 77, prevents a woman entitled to either statutory maternity pay or a maternity allowance from also receiving statutory sick pay. Regulation 2 makes further provision preventing a woman who is not entitled to either benefit from receiving statutory sick pay for a period of 18 weeks at the time of confinement.

Regulation 3 makes minor changes to the provisions governing statements required to be completed by employers in connection with payments of statutory sick pay.

Regulation 4 provides that for the purposes of statutory sick pay the expression "earnings" includes payments of statutory maternity pay. It also revokes a provision which is now otiose.

STATUTORY INSTRUMENTS

1987 No. 869

ROAD TRAFFIC

The International Carriage of Perishable Foodstuffs (Vehicles With Thin Side Walls) Regulations 1987

Made - - - -	*11th May 1987*
Laid before Parliament	*14th May 1987*
Coming into force	*4th June 1987*

The Secretary of State for Transport in exercise of the powers conferred by section 56(1) and (2) of the Finance Act 1973(a), and of all other enabling powers, with the consent of the Treasury, hereby makes the following Regulations:–

Commencement and citation

1. These Regulations shall come into force on 4th June 1987 and may be cited as the International Carriage of Perishable Foodstuffs (Vehicles With Thin Side Walls) Regulations 1987.

Fees

2.—(1) The fees payable in connection with the testing of units of transport equipment for conformity with the constructional requirements specified in Articles 2 and 4 of the Agreement of the 24th June 1986 shall be–

    (a) where the testing is carried out at the Refrigerated Vehicle Test Centre, a fee of £55 per unit;

    (b) where the testing is carried out at a place other than the Refrigerated Vehicle Test Centre–

        (i) a fee of £160 for each unit for up to four units presented at the same time, and

        (ii) a fee of £40 for each unit in addition.

(2) The Agreement of the 24th June 1986 referred to in the preceding paragraph is the Agreement on the rules governing the carriage of frozen and deep frozen foodstuffs by equipment with thin side walls to and from Italy made at Paris on the 24th June 1986 between the Governments of the Italian Republic, the French Republic, the Federal Republic of Germany, the Kingdom of Belgium, the Kingdom of Denmark, the United Kingdom and the Kingdom of the Netherlands.

(a) 1973 c.51.

Peter Bottomley

Signed by authority of the Secretary of   Parliamentary Under Secretary of State,
State   Department of Transport
8th May 1987

We consent to the making of these Regulations

Peter Lloyd
Mark Lennox-Boyd
11th May 1987   Two of the Lords Commissioners of
                                               Her Majesty's Treasury

EXPLANATORY NOTE

(This note is not part of the Regulations)

These Regulations prescribe the fees payable in connection with the testing of units of transport equipment with thin side walls used for the international carriage of frozen and deep frozen foodstuffs to and from Italy between 1st April and 31st October, for conformity with the constructional requirements of the Agreement of 24th June 1986 specified in Regulation 2(2). This agreement was entered into in conformity with Article 7 of the Agreement on the International Carriage of Perishable Foodstuffs and on the Special Equipment to be used for such Carriage (ATP) of the 1st September 1970 (Cmmd 8272). Copies of the Agreement of 24th June 1986 may be obtained from the Department of Transport, Room S10/13, 2 Marsham Street, London, SW1P 3EB.

The fees prescribed are–

   (a) where the testing is carried out at the Refrigerated Vehicle Test Centre, a fee of £55 per unit;

   (b) where the testing is carried out at a place other than the Refrigerated Vehicle Test Centre–

      (i) a fee of £160 for each unit for up to four units presented at the same time, and

      (ii) a fee of £40 for each unit in addition.

1987 No. 870 (S. 70)

AGRICULTURE

The Milk Quota (Calculation of Standard Quota) (Scotland) Amendment (No. 2) Order 1987

Made - - - -	*13th May 1987*
Laid before Parliament	*14th May 1987*
Coming into force	*15th May 1987*

The Secretary of State, in exercise of the powers conferred on him by paragraph 6 of Schedule 2 to the Agriculture Act 1986(**a**), and of all other powers enabling him in that behalf, hereby makes the following Order:

Application, citation and commencement

1. This Order, which applies to tenancies in Scotland, may be cited as the Milk Quota (Calculation of Standard Quota) (Scotland) Amendment (No. 2) Order 1987 and shall come into force on 15th May 1987.

Amendment of Principal Order

2. The Milk Quota (Calculation of Standard Quota) (Scotland) Order 1986(**b**) is hereby amended by substituting for the Schedule thereto the Schedule to this Order.

Revocation

3. The Milk Quota (Calculation of Standard Quota) (Scotland) Amendment Order 1987(**c**) is hereby revoked.

John J. MacKay
Parliamentary Under Secretary of State,
Scottish Office

New St. Andrew's House, Edinburgh
13th May 1987

(**a**) 1986 c.49.
(**b**) S.I. 1986/1475.
(**c**) S.I. 1987/734.

Article 2

SCHEDULE

| (1)
Breed | (2)
Severely disadvantaged land | | (3)
Disadvantaged land | | (4)
Other land | |
| | (a)
*Standard
Yield/Hectare* | (b)
*Average
Yield/Hectare* | (a)
*Standard
Yield/Hectare* | (b)
*Average
Yield/Hectare* | (a)
*Standard
Yield/Hectare* | (b)
*Average
Yield/Hectare* |
	litres	litres	litres	litres	litres	litres
Channel Is. South Devon, and breeds with similar characteristics	4,580	5,270	5,825	6,694	6,660	7,650
Ayrshire and Dairy Shorthorn, and breeds with similar characteristics	5,235	6,028	6,660	7,656	7,615	8,750
Others	5,385	6,200	6,850	7,875	7,830	9,000

EXPLANATORY NOTE

(This note is not part of the Order)

This Order amends the Milk Quota (Calculation of Standard Quota) (Scotland) Order 1986, which prescribes the "standard yield per hectare" and the "average yield per hectare" to be taken into account in determining the "standard yield" for the purposes of calculating the payment which a tenant in Scotland is entitled, by Schedule 2 to the Agriculture Act 1986, to obtain from his landlord in respect of milk quota on the termination of a lease of a tenancy.

This Order substitutes for the Schedule to that Order a new Schedule, in which the "standard yield per hectare" prescribed by article 3 of that Order is revised.

This Order also revokes the Milk Quota (Calculation of Standard Quota) (Scotland) Amendment Order 1987. After making that Order, an error was discovered and it is consequently revoked prior to its coming into force.

STATUTORY INSTRUMENTS

1987 No. 871 (S. 71)

COURT OF SESSION, SCOTLAND

Act of Sederunt (Rules of Court Amendment No. 2) (Solicitors' Fees) 1987

Made	-	-	-	-	*8th May 1987*
Coming into force					*8th June 1987*

The Lords of Council and Session, under and by virtue of the powers conferred on them by section 16 of the Administration of Justice (Scotland) Act 1933(**a**) and of all other powers enabling them in that behalf, do hereby enact and declare:

Citation and commencement

1.—(1) This Act of Sederunt may be cited as the Act of Sederunt (Rules of Court Amendment No. 2) (Solicitors' Fees) 1987 and shall come into force on 8th June 1987.

(2) This Act of Sederunt shall be inserted in the Books of Sederunt.

Amendment of solicitors' fees

2.—(1) In rule 347 of the Rules of the Court of Session (fees of solicitors)(**b**), in Chapters I and III of the Table of Fees, for the fees specified in column 2 of the Schedule to this Act of Sederunt in relation to the paragraphs specified in column 1 of that Schedule there shall be substituted the fees specified in column 3 of that Schedule.

(2) Notwithstanding sub-paragraph (1) of this paragraph, the fees specified in column 2 of the Schedule to this Act of Sederunt shall continue to have effect in respect of work done before the coming into force of this Act of Sederunt.

(3) In paragraph 6 of Chapter I of the Table of Fees in rule 347, for the last item (telegrams or telephone calls etc.), substitute the following items:–

"Telephone calls (except under the next item) £1.80
Telephone calls (lengthy) to be treated as attendances or long letters.".

Edinburgh
8th May 1987

Emslie
Lord President, I.P.D.

(**a**) 1933 c. 41; section 16 was amended by the Divorce Jurisdiction, Court Fees and Legal Aid (Scotland) Act 1983 (c. 12), Schedule 1, paragraph 8.
(**b**) S.I. 1965/321, as relevantly amended by S.I. 1986/967.

SCHEDULE

Paragraph 2(1)

(1) (Number of paragraph)			(2) (Current fee)	(3) (New fee)
CHAPTER I:–				
1.	(a)		£ 4.00	£ 4.25
	(b)		£ 1.70	£ 1.80
	(c)		£ 6.20	£ 6.60
2.			£ 0.80	£ 0.85
3.			£ 1.70	£ 1.80
4.			£ 3.40	£ 3.60
			£ 3.40	£ 3.60
			£ 3.40	£ 3.60
5.	(a)		£ 7.40	£ 7.85
	(b)		£ 7.40	£ 7.85
	(d)		£ 1.70	£ 1.80
			£ 3.40	£ 3.60
			£ 3.40	£ 3.60
CHAPTER III:–				
PART I.			£ 72.60	£ 76.95
PART II.	1.		£103.20	£109.40
	2.		£ 58.40	£ 61.90
	3.	(a)	£ 14.80	£ 15.70
		(b)	£ 21.50	£ 22.80
		(c)	£ 27.20	£ 28.85
	4A.	(a)	£ 21.50	£ 22.80
		(b)	£ 7.40	£ 7.85
		(c)	£ 4.50	£ 4.80
	4B.	(a)	£ 24.40	£ 25.85
		(b)	£ 7.40	£ 7.85
	6.		£ 72.60	£ 76.95
	7.		£ 23.25	£ 24.65
PART IIA.				
1. Table A.	1. Column 2		£148.40	£157.30
	Column 3		£169.60	£179.80
	2. Column 2		£106.00	£112.35
	Column 3		£127.20	£134.85
	3. Column 2		£ 31.80	£ 33.70
	Column 3		£ 47.70	£ 50.55
	4. Column 2		£286.20	£303.35
	Column 3		£344.50	£365.20
2. Table B.	1. Column 2		£121.90	£129.20
	Column 3		£143.00	£151.60
	2. Column 2		£ 58.30	£ 61.80
	Column 3		£ 74.20	£ 78.65
	3. Column 2		£ 31.80	£ 33.70
	Column 3		£ 47.70	£ 50.55
	4. Column 2		£212.00	£224.70
	Column 3		£264.90	£280.80
3. Table C.	1.		£ 29.70	£ 31.50
	2.		£ 33.90	£ 35.95
	3.		£ 63.60	£ 67.45
PART III.	1.		£152.00	£161.10
			£212.10	£224.85
	2.		£103.20	£109.40
	4.		£ 18.10	£ 19.20

(1) (Number of paragraph)			(2) (Current fee)	(3) (New fee)
	5.		£ 18.10	£ 19.20
PART IV.	1.	(a)	£142.90	£151.50
		(b)	£ 15.30	£ 16.20
		(c)	£ 30.10	£ 31.90
	2.	(a)	£152.00	£161.10
		(b)	£ 94.70	£100.40
		(c)(i)	£ 15.30	£ 16.20
		(ii)	£ 7.40	£ 7.85
		(d)	£ 44.80	£ 47.50
		(e)	£ 66.90	£ 70.90
	3.	(a)	£ 30.10	£ 31.90
		(b)	£ 7.40	£ 7.85
		(c)	£ 22.70	£ 24.05
	4.	(a)	£ 28.90	£ 30.65
		(b)	£ 7.90	£ 8.40
		(c)	£ 3.40	£ 3.60
		(d)	£ 28.90	£ 30.65
		(e)	£ 7.90	£ 8.40
		(f)	£ 3.40	£ 3.60
	5.		£ 14.70	£ 15.60
	6.	(a)	£ 31.80	£ 33.70
		(b)	£ 4.50	£ 4.80
	7.	(a)	£ 30.10	£ 31.90
		(b)	£ 14.70	£ 15.60
		(c)	£ 7.40	£ 7.85
		(d)	£ 11.90	£ 12.60
	8.	(a)	£ 60.70	£ 64.35
		(b)	£ 48.80	£ 51.70
		(c)	£ 18.10	£ 19.20
		(d)	£ 4.50	£ 4.80
	9.	(a)	£ 66.90	£ 70.90
		(b)	£ 30.10	£ 31.90
		(c)	£ 7.40	£ 7.85
	10.	(a)	£ 7.90	£ 8.40
		(b)	£ 22.70	£ 24.05
		(c)	£ 7.40	£ 7.85
	11.		£ 85.10	£ 90.20
	12.	(a)	£ 22.70	£ 24.05
		(b)	£ 7.90	£ 8.40
		(c)	£ 32.90	£ 34.90
		(d)	£ 15.30	£ 16.20
		(e)	£ 77.70	£ 82.35
		(f)	£ 42.50	£ 45.05
	13.	(a)	£206.40	£218.80
		(b)	£ 18.10	£ 19.20
		(c)	£ 37.40	£ 39.65
	15.	(a)	£ 44.80	£ 47.50
		(b)	£ 30.10	£ 31.90
		(c)	£ 30.10	£ 31.90
	16.		£ 77.70	£ 82.35
	17.		£ 7.40	£ 7.85
	18.		£ 54.40	£ 57.65

(1) (Number of paragraph)			(2) (Current fee)	(3) (New fee)
	19.		£ 11.30	£ 12.00
	20.	(a)	£ 60.70	£ 64.35
		(b)	£ 18.10	£ 19.20
PART V.	1.	(a)	£ 44.80	£ 47.50
		(b)	£ 22.70	£ 24.05
		(c)	£ 18.70	£ 19.80
	2.	(a)	£ 54.40	£ 57.65
		(b)	£ 26.70	£ 28.30
		(c)	£ 18.70	£ 19.20
	3.	(a)	£ 44.80	£ 47.50
		(b)	£ 7.40	£ 7.85
	6.		£ 18.10	£ 19.20

EXPLANATORY NOTE

(This note is not part of the Act of Sederunt)

This Act of Sederunt increases the fees payable to solicitors under Chapters I and III of the Table of Fees in rule 347 of the Rules of the Court of Session by 6 per cent (rounded to the nearest 5 pence). The increase applies to work done on or after 8th June 1987. The existing fees continue to have effect in respect of work done before that date. The Act of Sederunt also amends paragraph 6 of Chapter I of the Table of Fees by substituting provisions in relation to charges for telephone calls.

STATUTORY INSTRUMENTS

1987 No. 874

CIVIL AVIATION

The Stansted Airport Aircraft Movement Limit Order 1987

Approved by both Houses of Parliament

Made - - - -	*13th May 1987*
Coming into force	*1st June 1987*

Whereas it appears to the Secretary of State for Transport that the existing runway capacity of Stansted Airport is not fully utilised for a substantial proportion of the time for which its runway is available for the take-off or landing of aircraft, and whereas a draft of this Order has been laid before and approved by a resolution of each House of Parliament in accordance with section 79(3) of the Airports Act 1986**(a)**:

Now, therefore, the Secretary of State, in exercise of the powers conferred upon him by sections 32 and 79 of the Airports Act 1986, and after consultation with the Civil Aviation Authority, the airport operator and such of the other persons referred to in section 32(6) as he considered appropriate, hereby makes the following Order:—

1. This Order may be cited as the Stansted Airport Aircraft Movement Limit Order 1987 and shall come into force on 1st June 1987.

2. At Stansted Airport there shall, subject to article 3, be a limit on the number of occasions on which aircraft may take-off or land during any period of one year, taken from 1st March in each year, of 78,000.

3. Article 2 shall not apply to aircraft taking-off or landing at the airport in any of the following circumstances or cases, namely:—

(a) the aircraft is not carrying, for hire or reward, any passengers;

(b) the aircraft is engaged on non-scheduled air transport services where the passenger seating capacity of the aircraft used does not exceed ten;

(c) the aircraft is required to land at the airport because of an emergency or any other circumstances beyond the control of the operator and commander of the aircraft;

(d) the aircraft is engaged on the Queen's flight, or on a flight operated primarily for the purposes of the transport of Government Ministers or visiting Heads of State or dignitaries from abroad.

4. For the purposes of article 3(a) an aircraft is not to be taken as carrying, for hire or reward, any passengers by reason only that:

(a) it is carrying employees of the operator of the aircraft or of an associated company of the operator; or

(b) it is carrying attendants who are travelling with its cargo or are on a return flight having attended cargo on their previous flight;

(a) 1986 c.31.

and for the purposes of article 3(b) an aircraft is engaged on non-scheduled air transport services if the flight on which it is engaged is not part of a series of journeys between the same two places amounting to a systematic service.

5. For the purposes of article 4, a company shall be treated as an associated company of the operator of the aircraft if either that company or the operator of the aircraft is a body corporate of which the other is a subsidiary or if both of them are subsidiaries of one and the same body corporate.

13th May 1987

John Moore
Secretary of State for Transport

EXPLANATORY NOTE

(This note is not part of the Order)

This Order sets an aircraft movement limit at Stansted Airport of 78,000 per annum (taken from 1st March each year) and provides for the circumstances or cases in which aircraft movements are not to be counted towards this limit.

STATUTORY INSTRUMENTS

1987 No. 875

ATOMIC ENERGY AND RADIOACTIVE SUBSTANCES

The British Nuclear Fuels plc (Financial Limit) Order 1987

Made - - - -	*11th May 1987*
Coming into force	*15th May 1987*

The Secretary of State, in exercise of the powers conferred on him by section 2(1)(a) of the Nuclear Industry (Finance) Act 1977**(a)** and with the approval of the Treasury, hereby makes the following Order, a draft of which has been approved by a resolution of the Commons House of Parliament in accordance with section 2(4) of the Nuclear Industry (Finance) Act 1977:–

1. This Order may be cited as the British Nuclear Fuels plc (Financial Limit) Order 1987 and shall come into force on 15th May 1987.

2. The financial limit applicable to British Nuclear Fuels plc mentioned in the said section 2(1)(a) shall be £1,500 million.

Alastair Goodlad
Parliamentary Under Secretary of State,
11th May 1987   Department of Energy

We approve,

Peter Lloyd
Mark Lennox-Boyd
11th May 1987   Two of the Lords Commissioners of Her Majesty's Treasury

---

(a) 1977 c.7; section 2(1)(a) was amended by the Nuclear Industry (Finance) Act 1981 (c.71), section 1.

EXPLANATORY NOTE

(This note is not part of the Order)

Section 2 of the Nuclear Industry (Finance) Act 1977 as amended by section 1 of the Nuclear Industry (Finance) Act 1981 imposes a limit of £1,000 million (which may be increased to £1,500 million by order) on the total of:–

(i) amounts which the Secretary of State and the United Kingdom Atomic Energy Authority between them may subscribe for shares in British Nuclear Fuels plc (other than those which were initially issued under section 7 of the Atomic Energy Authority Act 1971 (c.11));

(ii) amounts outstanding in respect of loans made to the company by the Secretary of State under section 12 of the 1971 Act;

(iii) principal amounts of loans for the repayment of which the Secretary of State may become liable under guarantees of such loans under section 1(1) of the 1977 Act; and

(iv) amounts due from the company to the Secretary of State in respect of his repayment of any loan under such a guarantee.

This Order extends the limit to £1,500 million.

British Nuclear Fuels Limited was re-registered under the Companies Acts 1948 to 1981 as a public limited company on 3rd January 1984.

1987 No. 876

PUBLIC HEALTH, ENGLAND AND WALES
PUBLIC HEALTH, SCOTLAND

NOISE

The Lawnmowers (Harmonization of Noise Emission Standards) (Amendment) Regulations 1987

Made - - - -	*12th May 1987*
Laid before Parliament	*14th May 1987*
Coming into force -	*1st July 1987*

The Secretary of State, being a Minister designated(**a**) for the purposes of section 2(2) of the European Communities Act 1972(**b**) in relation to matters relating to the harmonization of sound power level requirements of equipment for cutting grass, in exercise of the powers conferred on him by that section and of all his other enabling powers, hereby makes the following Regulations:–

1. These Regulations, which extend to Great Britain, may be cited as the Lawnmowers (Harmonization of Noise Emission Standards) (Amendment) Regulations 1987, and shall come into force on 1st July 1987.

2. The Lawnmowers (Harmonization of Noise Emission Standards) Regulations 1986(**c**) are hereby amended as follows:–

(a) in regulation 2(1)–

(i) in the definition of "EEC mark", "and" shall be deleted; and

(ii) at the end of the definition of "the Directive" there shall be added "as amended by Commission Directive 87/252/EEC adapting it to technical progress"(**d**);

(b) in regulation 7–

(i) at the end of paragraph (1), there shall be added the following proviso:–

"Provided that such checks may only be carried out if the lawnmower is for the time being held by or on behalf of the manufacturer, importer or other supplier of the lawnmower"; and

(ii) in paragraph (2), after "a lawnmower" there shall be inserted "under paragraph (1) above";

(c) in Schedule 1–

(i) at the end of item 1.1 there shall be added "of lawnmower";

(**a**) S.I. 1985/749.
(**b**) 1972 c.68.
(**c**) S.I. 1986/1795.
(**d**) OJ No. L117, 5.5.87, pp. 22–27.

(ii) for the words in item 1.5 there shall be substituted "Identification of the series"; and

(iii) after item 1.5 there shall be added the following:-

" 1.6 Name of manufacturer of motor . . . . . .

1.7 Type of motor . . . . . .

1.8 The maximum speed of rotation of motor during the test . . . . . . rpm";

(d) in Schedule 3-

(i) for the words in item 4. there shall be substituted "Identification of the series"; and

(ii) after item 4. there shall be added the following:-

"5. Motor:

—manufacturer . . . . . .

—type . . . . . .

—speed of rotation during the test . . . . . . rpm"; and

(e) in Schedule 4, below the form of model for EEC mark there shall be added the following:-

"All the dimensions shown above may be multiplied, for example by $\frac{1}{2}$, $\frac{1}{3}$, 2, 3, 4 etc., and a tolerance of 20% shall be allowed on all the dimensions.".

Giles Shaw
Minister of State for Industry,
12th May 1987   Department of Trade and Industry

EXPLANATORY NOTE

(This note is not part of the Regulations)

These Regulations amend the Lawnmowers (Harmonization of Noise Emission Standards) Regulations 1986 ("the principal Regulations") and implement Commission Directive 87/252/EEC (OJ No. L117, 5.5.87, pp. 22–27) which amends Council Directive 84/538/EEC (OJ No. L300, 19.11.84 pp. 171–178), which relates to the permissible sound power level of certain lawnmowers. The Directive provides for indoor testing and testing on artificial surfaces and makes certain changes to the technical requirements.

The Regulations also amend Regulation 7 of the principal Regulations and make it clear that periodic checks of lawnmowers by the Secretary of State to ensure compliance with the requirements of the Directive can only be carried out if the lawnmower is for the time being held by or on behalf of the manufacturer, importer or supplier.

STATUTORY INSTRUMENTS

1987 No. 877

MEDICINES

The Medicines (Child Safety) Amendment Regulations 1987

Made - - - -	*12th May 1987*
Laid before Parliament	*14th May 1987*
Coming into force	*4th June 1987*

The Secretaries of State concerned with health in England, in Wales and in Scotland and the Department of Health and Social Services for Northern Ireland, acting jointly, in exercise of powers conferred by sections 87(1) and 129(5) of the Medicines Act 1968**(a)** and now vested in them **(b)** and of all other powers enabling them in that behalf, after consulting such organisations as appear to them to be representative of interests likely to be substantially affected by the following Regulations, pursuant to section 129(6) of that Act, and after taking into account the advice of the Medicines Commission pursuant to section 129(7) of that Act, hereby make the following Regulations:–

Citation interpretation and commencement

1. These Regulations which may be cited as the Medicines (Child Safety) Amendment Regulations 1987, shall be read as one with the Medicines (Child Safety) Regulations 1975**(c)** (hereinafter referred to as "the principal Regulations"), and shall come into force on 4th June 1987.

Amendment of regulation 2(3) of the principal Regulations

2. Regulation 2(3) is amended in accordance with the following provisions:–

(1) In regulation 2(3)(b), for the words "British Standard 5321 published on 31st October 1975 as amended by AMD 2077 published on 16th August 1976", there are substituted the words "British Standard 6652 published by the British Standards Institution on 30th September 1985".

(2) In regulation 2(3)(d) after the words "1st January 1976" there is added the word "or".

(3) After regulation 2(3)(d) there is added:–
"(e) reclosable containers which are opaque or dark-tinted, identical in all respects to containers which comply with the requirements of British Standard 5321 published on 31st October 1975 as amended by AMD 2077 published on 16th August 1976 and which–
(i) have been certified by the British Standards Institution as complying with those requirements, or

---

(a) 1968 c. 67.
(b) In the case of the Secretaries of State concerned with health in England and in Wales by virtue of article 2(2) of, and Schedule 1 to, the Transfer of Functions (Wales) Order 1969 (S.I. 1969/388) and in the case of the Department of Health and Social Services for Northern Ireland by virtue of section 40 of, and Schedule 5 to, the Northern Ireland Constitution Act 1973 (c. 36), and section 1(3) of, and paragraph 2(1)(b) of Schedule 1 to the Northern Ireland Act 1974 (c. 28).
(c) S.I. 1975/2000, amended by S.I. 1976/1643.

(ii) until 31st January 1988, are certified by the British Standards Institution as complying with those requirements, or

(iii) are part of a series of containers (referred to in the said AMD 2077 published on 16th August 1976) in respect of which the licensing authority has already been furnished with a report by the British Standards Institution, so as to enable the licensing authority to publish a notice in the Gazette to the effect that such containers comply with the requirements of British Standard 5321 as amended.''.

Signed by authority of the Secretary of State for Social Services.

12th May 1987	*Tony Newton* Minister of State, Department of Health and Social Security
12th May 1987	*Nicholas Edwards* Secretary of State for Wales
12th May 1987	*Glenarthur* Minister of State, Scottish Office

Sealed with the Official Seal of the Department of Health and Social Services for Northern Ireland this 12th day of May 1987.

Maurice N. Hayes	*Maurice N. Hayes* Permanent Secretary

EXPLANATORY NOTE

(This note is not part of the Regulations)

These Regulations further amend the Medicines (Child Safety) Regulations 1975 which prohibit the sale or supply of certain aspirin or paracetamol other than in child resistant containers. Regulation 2(1) substitutes for the reference to British Standard 5321 (published in 1975) a reference to British Standard 6652 (published in 1985). Regulations 2(2) and (3) make transitional arrangements, and make special provision for containers which form part of a series.

The British Standard referred to in the Regulations may be obtained from any of the sales outlets operated by the British Standards Institution or by post from the Institution at Linford Wood, Milton Keynes MK14 6LE.

1987 No. 878

SOCIAL SECURITY

The Social Security (Claims and Payments) Amendment Regulations 1987

Made - - - -		*13th May 1987*
Laid before Parliament		*14th May 1987*
Coming into force		*1st July 1987*

The Secretary of State for Social Services, in exercise of the powers conferred upon him by sections 17(1)(a)(ii), 79(3), 165A and 166 of, and Schedule 20(a) to, the Social Security Act 1975(b) and of all other powers enabling him that behalf, after agreement by the Social Security Advisory Committee that proposals to make these Regulations shall not be referred to it(c), hereby makes the following Regulations:–

Citation and commencement

1. These Regulations may be cited as the Social Security (Claims and Payments) Amendment Regulations 1987 and shall come into force on 1st July 1987.

Amendment of the Social Security (Claims and Payments) Regulations 1979

2. Regulation 3 of the Social Security (Claims and Payments) Regulations 1979(d) (claims not required for entitlement to benefit in certain cases) shall be amended as follows–

    (a) the regulation shall be re-numbered as paragraph (1) of regulation 3;

    (b) the following paragraphs shall be inserted after that paragraph–

> "(2) Where invalidity benefit or severe disablement allowance has been claimed and an award of benefit made on that claim, then in respect of the period beginning immediately after the period of that award and ending 26 weeks after the first day of the period of that award it shall not be a condition of entitlement to invalidity benefit or, as the case may be, severe disablement allowance that a claim be made for it.

> (3) A person in whose case paragraph (2) of this regulation applies may be deemed to be incapable of work on any day falling within the period for which, under that paragraph, no claim for benefit is required, and an award may be made for the whole or any part of that period, subject to the condition that the beneficiary shall when required to do so prove that he in

---

(a) *See* the definitions of "Prescribe" and "Regulations".
(b) 1975 c.14; section 165A was inserted by the Social Security Act 1985 (c.53), section 17.
(c) *See* section 10(2)(b) of the Social Security Act 1980 (c.30).
(d) S.I. 1979/628; the relevant amending instruments are S.I. 1985/1250 and 1986/903.

fact remains so incapable and satisfies all the other conditions of entitlement to benefit; and if he should fail to do so the award shall be reviewed and may be revised."

Signed by authority of the Secretary of State for Social Services

Nicholas Lyell
Parliamentary Under-Secretary of State,
13th May 1987   Department of Health and Social Security

EXPLANATORY NOTE

(This note is not part of the Regulations)

These Regulations amend regulation 3 of the Social Security (Claims and Payments) Regulations 1979 which provides that in certain cases a claim is not required as a condition of entitlement to benefit.

Regulation 2 amends regulation 3 of the 1979 Regulations so as to provide that entitlement to invalidity benefit or severe disablement allowance shall continue to run for up to 26 weeks following the commencement of the period for which it has been claimed and awarded, provided that the beneficiary proves continuing incapacity when required to do so and satisfies all the other conditions for entitlement to benefit.

STATUTORY INSTRUMENTS

1987 No. 879

EDUCATION, ENGLAND AND WALES

The Education (Schools and Further Education) (Amendment) Regulations 1987

Made - - - -	*13th May 1987*
Laid before Parliament	*14th May 1987*
Coming into force *for the purpose of* *regulations 1 and 2* *for all other purposes*	*8th June 1987* *1st August 1987*

In exercise of the powers conferred by sections 27(1)(e) and (7) and 35(4) of the Education Act 1980(a) the Secretary of State for Education and Science, as respects England, and the Secretary of State for Wales, as respects Wales, hereby make the following Regulations:

Citation and commencement

1. These Regulations may be cited as the Education (Schools and Further Education) (Amendment) Regulations 1987 and shall come into force for the purposes of this regulation and regulation 2 on 8th June 1987 and for all other purposes on 1st August 1987.

Duration of school year

2. In regulation 10 (Duration of school year and day) of the Education (Schools and Further Education) Regulations 1981(b) paragraph (7) shall be amended as follows–

(1) For the words "the academic year 1985/86" there shall be substituted the words "the year ending on 31st July 1987";

(2) In the proviso, for the words "four sessions" there shall be substituted the words "two sessions".

3. With effect from 1st August 1987 the said regulation 10 shall be further amended as follows–

(1) In paragraph (2), for the provision before the proviso there shall be substituted the following provision–

"(2) In each academic year a school shall meet for not less than 380 sessions which shall constitute the school year so however that nothing in this paragraph shall require a nursery class to meet for that number of sessions:";

(a) 1980 c.20, extended by paragraph 4 of Schedule 2 to the Sex Discrimination Act 1975 (c.65) (substituted by section 33(3) of the Education Act 1980) in a manner not relevant to these Regulations.
(b) S.I. 1981/1086, amended by S.I. 1983/262 and 1986/542.

(2) In paragraph (3), for the words "paragraphs (5), (6) and (7)" there shall be substituted the words "paragraphs (5) and (6)";

(3) For paragraph (7) there shall be substituted the following paragraph–

"(7) In this regulation "academic year" means a period of 12 months beginning on 1st September unless the school has a term beginning in August in which case it means a period of 12 months beginning on 1st August.".

Revocation

4. The Education (Schools and Further Education) (Amendment) Regulations 1986(a) are hereby revoked.

13th May 1987

Kenneth Baker
Secretary of State for Education and Science

13th May 1987

Nicholas Edwards
Secretary of State for Wales

EXPLANATORY NOTE

(This note is not part of the Regulations)

These Regulations amend that part of regulation 10 of the Education (Schools and Further Education) Regulations 1981 which relates to the duration of the school year.

Regulation 2, which comes into force on 8th June 1987, amends regulation 10(7), inserted by the Education (Schools and Further Education) (Amendment) Regulations 1986, to provide that where, in the year ending on 31st July 1987, a school session is devoted to the provision to teachers at the school of training related to the introduction of the General Certificate of Secondary Education (GCSE), it shall be treated for the purpose of regulation 10 as a session on which the school has met. This provision applies in relation to a maximum of two sessions in that year.

Regulation 3, which comes into force on 1st August 1987, deletes the provisions relating to training for the GCSE inserted in 1986, as so amended (which by then will be spent) and makes fresh provision for the duration of the school year.

This duration continues to be expressed as a minimum number of sessions. Regulation 10(1) of the 1981 Regulations provides that every day on which a school meets shall normally be divided into two sessions, except in cases where the school meets on six days a week. With effect from 1st August 1987 the minimum number of sessions is reduced from 400 (subject to reduction for occasional holidays granted in term-time) to 380 in each academic year, defined as a period of 12 months beginning on 1st September, unless the school has a term which begins in August, in which case the year begins on 1st August. No provision is made for occasional holidays.

Regulation 4 revokes the amending Regulations made in 1986.

(a) S.I. 1986/542.

1987 No. 880 (S. 72)

PLANT HEALTH

The Import and Export (Plant Health Fees) (Scotland) Order 1987

Made - - - -	*12th May 1987*
Laid before Parliament	*15th May 1987*
Coming into force	*1st July 1987*

The Secretary of State, in exercise of the powers conferred on him by sections 1(2)(b), 2, 3(1) and 4A of the Plant Health Act 1967(**a**), and of all other powers enabling him in that behalf, and with the consent of the Treasury, hereby makes the following Order:

Citation, commencement and extent

1.—(1) This Order may be cited as the Import and Export (Plant Health Fees) (Scotland) Order 1987 and shall come into force on 1st July 1987.

(2) This Order extends to Scotland only.

Interpretation

2.—(1) In this Order–

"certificate" means a phytosanitary certificate;

"import licence" means a licence issued by the Secretary of State under article 17 of the Import and Export (Plant Health) (Great Britain) Order 1980(**b**);

"official label" has the same meaning as in regulation 2(1) of the Seed Potatoes Regulations 1984(**c**);

"phytosanitary certificate" means a phytosanitary certificate issued by an inspector or other officer of the Secretary of State under article 9 of the Import and Export (Plant Health) (Great Britain) Order 1980;

"premises" includes any land, building, vessel, vehicle, aircraft, hovercraft or freight container;

"small consignment" means one package of a size and weight such that it is capable of being sent by post;

"soil" includes any medium used for the growing of plant material and "soil sample" shall be construed accordingly.

(2) Where a fee prescribed in this Order is prescribed in relation to an inspection, examination or test as well as the issue of a certificate, the refusal to issue a certificate by reason of the results of the inspection, examination or test being unsatisfactory, shall not affect the amount of the fee otherwise payable.

(3) Any reference in this Order to a numbered article or Schedule shall be construed as a reference to the article or Schedule bearing that number in this Order.

(**a**) 1967 c.8; sections 2(1) and 3(1) were amended by the European Communities Act 1972 (c.68), section 4(1) and Schedule 4, paragraph 8, and section 4A was inserted by the Agriculture Act 1986 (c.49), section 3.
(**b**) S.I. 1980/420; article 17 was amended by S.I. 1985/873, 1986/1135.
(**c**) S.I. 1984/412, to which there are amendments not relevant to this Order.

Fees for export certification services

3. Subject to the following provisions of this Order, there shall be paid to the Secretary of State in respect of any service described in column 1 of Schedule 1 the fee specified in column 2 of that Schedule opposite the reference to that service.

Fees for import licensing services

4. Subject to the following provisions of this Order, there shall be paid to the Secretary of State in respect of any service described in column 1 of Schedule 2 the fee specified in column 2 of that Schedule opposite the reference to that service.

Time for payment of fees

5. The fees prescribed in Schedules 1 and 2 shall be paid on demand made by the Secretary of State.

Refund of fees

6.—(1) If an application for a service described in column 1 of Schedule 2 is withdrawn by a written request made by the applicant and received by the Secretary of State within 7 days of the date of the application, the fee paid under article 4 less an amount of £5.00 shall be refunded to the applicant.

(2) If in respect of an application for official labels in connection with the issue of a certificate for the export of seed potatoes, labels are returned unused the fee paid under article 3 less an amount of 40p per tonne may be refunded to the applicant.

New St. Andrew's House, Edinburgh
11th May 1987

John J. MacKay
Parliamentary Under Secretary of State,
Scottish Office

We consent,

12th May 1987

Peter Lloyd
Tony Durant
Two of the Lords Commissioners of Her Majesty's Treasury

Article 3

SCHEDULE 1

FEES IN RESPECT OF EXPORT CERTIFICATION SERVICES

Column 1 *Service*	Column 2 *Fee £*
1. The taking of one soil sample from a field or part of a field comprising not more than 4 hectares, or from a glass-house or container–	
(a) for the first sample taken on any day, where no other chargeable visit is being made	50.00
(b) for the first sample taken on any day, where another chargeable visit is being made	25.00
(c) for the second and each subsequent sample taken on the same day as the first sample	25.00
2. Growing season inspection of–	
(a) up to 0.5 hectares of bulbs, per day	25.00
each additional 0.5 hectares of bulbs up to 14 hectares, per day	5.00
(b) up to 0.4 hectares of outdoor plants other than bulbs, per day	25.00
each additional 0.4 hectares of outdoor plants other than bulbs up to 11 hectares, per day	5.00
(c) up to 5,000 indoor plants, per day	25.00
each additional 5,000 indoor plants up to 70,000, per day	5.00
3. Consideration of an application for official labels in connection with the issue of one certificate for the export of seed potatoes, per tonne or part thereof	1.20
4. Consideration of an application for the issue of one certificate for the export of–	
(a) grain, per 100 tonnes or part thereof	10.00
(b) frozen vegetables, frozen fruit, tea and seed samples, per consignment	10.00
(c) plants or plant products, where no inspection is required	5.00
5. Pre-export inspection of and the issue of one certificate for the export of a consignment of bulbs and other plants and plant products, including seed potatoes where an official label is not required, where an inspection at the premises of the grower is necessary and where–	
(a) the value of the consignment is up to and including £50.00 whether or not the consignment comprises items for botanical research	3.00
(b) the value of the consignment is more than £50.00 but not more than £150.00 whether or not the consignment comprises items for botanical research	10.00
(c) the value of the consignment is more than £150.00 and the consignment comprises items for botanical research	15.00
(d) the value of the consignment is more than £150.00 but not more than £300.00 and the consignment does not comprise items for botanical research	20.00
(e) the value of the consignment is more than £300.00 and the consignment does not comprise items for botanical research	30.00
6. Pre-export inspection of and the issue of one certificate for the export of a small consignment of plants and plant products where no inspection at the premises of the grower is necessary and where–	
(a) the value of the consignment is up to and including £50.00 whether or not the consignment comprises items for botanical research	3.00
(b) the value of the consignment is more than £50.00 but not more than £150.00 whether or not the consignment comprises items for botanical research	10.00
(c) the value of the consignment is more than £150.00 whether or not the consignment comprises items for botanical research	15.00
7. Pre-export inspection of and the issue of one certificate for the export of used agricultural machinery (such inspection being for traces of soil or plant debris)	30.00

SCHEDULE 2   Articles 4 and 6(1)

FEES IN RESPECT OF IMPORT LICENSING SERVICES

Column 1 *Service*	Column 2 *Fee £*
1.Consideration of an application for the issue of an import licence and the performance of any connected service, including the issue of a licence for articles imported for the following purposes, whether or not an inspection is required	
(a) scientific	40.00
(b) commercial–	
(i) potato breeders' and other quarantine material	40.00
(ii) other plant material	30.00
(c) private	20.00
2. The inspection of articles for import, per day	
(a) up to and including the first 30 minutes	30.00
(b) thereafter, for each additional 30 minutes or part thereof	15.00

EXPLANATORY NOTE

(This note is not part of the Order)

This Order, which applies to Scotland only, prescribes fees in respect of the services specified in Schedules 1 and 2 to the Order (articles 3 and 4). The services are performed in connection with applications received for the issue of phytosanitary certificates or licences in accordance with the provisions of the Import and Export (Plant Health) (Great Britain) Order 1980. Phytosanitary certificates are required to accompany exports of certain plants, plant products etc. and licences are issued to permit the importation of those articles, which would otherwise be prohibited.

The fees prescribed by the Order are payable on demand made by the Secretary of State (article 5).

The Order makes provision for a refund where an application for an import licensing service is withdrawn within a specified time (article 6(1)). A refund may also be made where in respect of an application for official labels in connection with the issue of a certificate for the export of seed potatoes, labels are returned unused (article 6(2)).

1987 No. 881 (S. 73)

AGRICULTURE

The Milk (Community Outgoers' Scheme) (Scotland) Amendment (No. 2) Regulations 1987

Made - - - -	*14th May 1987*
Laid before Parliament	*15th May 1987*
Coming into force	*10th June 1987*

The Secretary of State, being a Minister designated(**a**) for the purposes of section 2(2) of the European Communities Act 1972(**b**) in relation to the common agricultural policy of the European Economic Community, in exercise of the powers conferred on him by that section and of all other powers enabling him in that behalf, hereby makes the following Regulations:

Title and commencement

1. These Regulations may be cited as the Milk (Community Outgoers' Scheme) (Scotland) Amendment (No. 2) Regulations 1987 and shall come into force on 10th June 1987.

Amendment of principal Regulations

2.—(1) The Milk (Community Outgoers' Scheme) (Scotland) Regulations 1986(**c**) (the principal Regulations) shall have effect with the following amendments.

(2) For regulation 5 there shall be substituted the following regulation:–

"**5.** For the purpose of Articles 1 and 3(2) of the Commission Regulation (Member States to make rules for the acceptance of applications) and subject to Article 1(2) 2nd indent of the Council Regulation (Member States' authority to ensure that reductions are spread equally), where the sum of valid applications throughout the United Kingdom together relate to a quantity of eligible quota which exceeds 152, 714, 910 litres, applications representing the excess quantity shall be refused according to the following rule:–

the Secretary of State shall give preference to applications in order of their receipt by him.".

(3) In regulation 6(2) for the words "13th March 1987" there shall be substituted the words "30th December 1987".

(4) In regulation 7(3) for the words "13th March 1987" there shall be substituted the words "30th December 1987".

(5) For the Schedule thereto there shall be substituted the following Schedule.

(**a**) S.I. 1972/1811.
(**b**) 1972 c.68.
(**c**) S.I. 1986/1613, as amended by S.I. 1987/425.

New St. Andrew's House, Edinburgh
14th May 1987

John J. MacKay
Parliamentary Under Secretary of State,
Scottish Office

Article 2

SCHEDULE

(1) Breed	(2) Severely disadvantaged land		(3) Disadvantaged land		(4) Other land	
	(a) Standard Yield/Hectare	(b) Average Yield/Hectare	(a) Standard Yield/Hectare	(b) Average Yield/Hectare	(a) Standard Yield/Hectare	(b) Average Yield/Hectare
	litres	litres	litres	litres	litres	litres
Channel Is. South Devon, and breeds with similar characteristics	4,580	5,270	5,825	6,694	6,660	7,650
Ayrshire and Dairy Shorthorn, and breeds with similar characteristics	5,235	6,028	6,660	7,656	7,615	8,750
Others	5,385	6,200	6,850	7,875	7,830	9,000

EXPLANATORY NOTE

(This note is not part of the Regulations)

These Regulations implement Commission Regulation (EEC) No. 261/87 (O.J. No. L26, 29.1.1987, p.18) amending Commission Regulation (EEC) No. 2321/86 (O.J. L202, 25.7.1986, p.13), and Council Regulation (EEC) No. 776/87 (O.J. L78, 20.3.1987, p.8) amending Council Regulation (EEC) No. 1336/86 (O.J. No. L119, 8.5.1986, p.21) as regards the submission of applications for compensation for the definitive discontinuation of milk production. They amend the Milk (Community Outgoers' Scheme) (Scotland) Regulations 1986 ("the principal Regulations") to provide for the 1987/88 round of applications.

The total sum of eligible quota for which valid applications shall be accepted within the United Kingdom has been reduced to 152, 714, 910 litres. Preference shall be given to applications in order of their receipt (regulation 2(2)).

The time limit (set by regulation 6 of the principal Regulations) after which an applicant may not withdraw his application is extended to 30th December 1987 (regulation 2(3)).

Where a landlord's consent is required (under regulation 7 of the principal Regulations) an application will only be valid if that consent has been given or unreasonably refused by 30th December 1987 (regulation 2(4)).

These Regulations substitute for the Schedule to the principal Regulations a new Schedule in which the "standard yield per hectare" prescribed by the principal Regulations is revised.

STATUTORY INSTRUMENTS

1987 No. 882 (S.74)

AGRICULTURE

The Milk (Cessation of Production) (Scotland) Scheme 1987

Made - - - -	*14th May 1987*
Laid before Parliament	*15th May 1987*
Coming into force	*10th June 1987*

ARRANGEMENT OF PARAGRAPHS

The Secretary of State, in exercise of the powers conferred on him by sections 1 and 5 of the Milk (Cessation of Production) Act 1985(**a**), and of all other powers enabling him in that behalf, after consultation with the Council on Tribunals under section 10 of the Tribunals and Inquiries Act 1971(**b**), hereby makes the following Scheme:

Title, extent and commencement

1.   This Scheme may be cited as the Milk (Cessation of Production) (Scotland) Scheme 1987, shall extend to Scotland only and shall come into force on 10th June 1987.

Interpretation

2.—(1) In this Scheme, unless the context otherwise requires—

"the Act" means the Milk (Cessation of Production) Act 1985;

"allocated quota" means registered quota other than transferred quota;

"applicant" means a person who applies for compensation under this Scheme and "application" shall be construed accordingly;

"arbiter" includes the Scottish Land Court;

"authorised officer" means an officer of the Department of Agriculture and Fisheries for Scotland so authorised by the Secretary of State;

"direct sales quota" has the same meaning as in the 1986 Regulations;

"farming press" means any newspaper, journal or similar publication considered by the Secretary of State to be likely to be read by interested parties;

"Gazette" means the Edinburgh Gazette;

"holding" has the same meaning as in the 1986 Regulations;

"landlord" includes a head tenant and means—

(a) in the case of an agricultural holding to which the 1949 Act applies, the landlord within the meaning of section 93(1) of that Act;

(b) in the case of a croft within the meaning of the 1955 Act, the landlord within the meaning of section 37(1) of that Act;

(c) in the case of a holding within the meaning of the 1911 Act to which the 1949 Act does not apply, the same as it means in the 1911 Act; and

(d) where the tenancy has become vested in more than one person in several parts and the rent payable by the tenant has not been apportioned with his consent or under any statute, all the persons who together constitute the landlord of the tenancy, and "landlord's interest" shall be construed accordingly;

"landlord's amount" means an amount calculated in accordance with paragraph 13;

"milk" means cows' milk;

"notice" means notice in writing;

"quota" in relation to a holding, has the meaning ascribed to it in the 1986 Regulations;

"quota year" has the meaning ascribed to it in regulation 2(1) of the 1986 Regulations;

"registered" in relation to quota, means—

(a) in the case of direct sales quota, registered in the direct sales register maintained under the 1986 Regulations; and

(b) in the case of a wholesale quota, registered in a wholesale register maintained under those Regulations;

"relevant quota" means—

(a) in a case where the tenant's holding consists only of the relevant tenancy, the quota registered in relation to that holding under the 1986 Regulations; and

(b) in any other case, such part of that quota as would fall to be apportioned under regulation 8 of the 1986 Regulations to that tenancy on a change of occupation of that tenancy;

"tenancy" means, as the case may be—

(a) the agricultural holding within the meaning of section 1 of the 1949 Act;

(**a**) 1985 c.4.
(**b**) 1971 c.62.

(b) the croft within the meaning of section 3(1) of the 1955 Act;

(c) the holding within the meaning of section 2 of the 1911 Act;

(d) the holding of a statutory small tenant under section 32 of the 1911 Act;

(e) any part of a tenancy which is treated as a separate entity for purposes of succession, assignation or sub-letting;

"tenant" means–

(a) in the case of an agricultural holding to which the 1949 Act applies, a tenant within the meaning of section 93(1) of that Act;

(b) in the case of a croft within the meaning of the 1955 Act, a crofter within the meaning of section 3(2) of that Act;

(c) in the case of a holding within the meaning of the 1911 Act to which the 1949 Act does not apply, a landholder within the meaning of section 2(2) of the 1911 Act;

"the 1911 Act" means the Small Landholders (Scotland) Act 1911(**a**);

"the 1949 Act" means the Agricultural Holdings (Scotland) Act 1949(**b**);

"the 1955 Act" means the Crofters (Scotland) Act 1955(**c**);

"the 1986 Regulations" means the Dairy Produce Quotas Regulations 1986(**d**);

"transferred quota" means quota transferred to a holding by virtue of the transfer to that holding of the whole or part of another holding;

"wholesale quota" has the same meaning as in the 1986 Regulations.

(2) In this Scheme, unless the context otherwise requires–

(a) any reference to a numbered paragraph shall be construed as a reference to the paragraph so numbered in this Scheme, and

(b) any reference in a paragraph to a numbered or lettered subparagraph shall be construed as a reference to the subparagraph so numbered or lettered in that paragraph.

Applications under this Scheme

3.—(1) The Secretary of State shall, by advertisement published in the Gazette and the farming press, announce the opening and closing dates of the period during which applications may be submitted, and the procedural requirements in respect of applications.

(2) For the purposes of an application under this paragraph, an applicant's quota shall be taken to be the amount of quota to which he is entitled at the date of the application.

Persons eligible for payments under this Scheme

4.—(1) The Secretary of State may make payments under this Scheme to any person who is or has been a registered milk producer and who–

(a) undertakes to cease producing milk for sale or for the manufacture of any milk product for sale and to surrender all his milk quota to the reserve; or

(b) (i) is entitled to a total milk quota of at least 242,790 litres, and

(ii) undertakes to reduce his production of milk for sale or for the manufacture of any milk product for sale and to surrender not less than 50% of his milk quota to the reserve.

(2) The Secretary of State shall not make any payment under subparagraph (1) in respect of milk quota against which milk has been or will at the date of surrender have been produced in the 1987/1988 quota year.

(3) No payment under subparagraph (1) shall be made to a person who has at any time received as applicant a payment under–

(a) Council Regulation (EEC) No. 1353/73(**e**) and Commission Regulation (EEC) No. 1821/73(**f**) (which together lay down a Scheme to encourage the reduction of the production of milk and milk products);

(**a**) 1911 c.49.
(**b**) 1949 c.75.
(**c**) 1955 c.21.
(**d**) S.I. 1986/470.
(**e**) O.J. No. L141, 28.5.73, p.18.
(**f**) O.J. No. L184, 6.7.73, p.24.

(b) the Farm Structures (Payments to Outgoers) Scheme 1976(**a**);

(c) Council Regulation (EEC) No. 1078/77(**b**) and Commission Regulation (EEC) No. 1307/77(**c**) (which together lay down Schemes to encourage the reduction of the production of milk and milk products);

(d) a non-statutory Scheme under which a person receiving payments undertook to give up milk production for the period specified in, and in accordance with the terms of, that Scheme; or

(e) the Milk (Community Outgoers' Scheme) (Scotland) Regulations 1986(**d**) or any other Scheme corresponding with this Scheme which applies in any other part of the United Kingdom.

Basis of claims and rates of compensation under this Scheme

5.—(1) A person may claim compensation under this Scheme in respect of either—

(a) loss of profits in the 7 years immediately following the date on which he ceases to produce milk for sale or for processing into milk products for sale by reference to the amount of milk quota he surrenders; or

(b) the value of the amount of the milk quota he surrenders.

(2) Payments made by the Secretary of State under this Scheme shall be calculated

(a) in a case falling within subparagraph (1)(a), at the rate of 3.927 pence per litre of milk on a quantity equal to the amount of milk quota surrendered for each of the 7 years immediately following the date on which the applicant ceases to produce milk for sale or for processing into milk products for sale, in relation to the amount of quota surrendered; and

(b) in a case falling within subparagraph (1)(b), at the rate of 27.489 pence per litre on that quantity, payable in 7 equal annual instalments.

Over-subscription

6.—(1) The total amount of quota by reference to which the Secretary of State may make payments under this Scheme shall not exceed 4.425 million litres.

(2) In determining whether to accept or reject an application, the Secretary of State shall give preference to applications in order of their receipt by him.

(3) The Secretary of State shall give notice of his acceptance or rejection of an application to the applicant.

(4) An applicant may withdraw an application before the end of the period of 14 days beginning with the date of service on the applicant of a notice of acceptance served on him under subparagraph (3).

Requirement for landlord's consent

7.—(1) Subject to subparagraph (2), where an application is made by a person who occupies his holding or any part thereof as a tenant, that person shall serve a copy of the application on his immediate landlord on the day on which he submits the application.

(2) A person who occupies his holding as a tenant need not comply with the provisions of subparagraph (1) if, in respect of each of the landlords of the holding in relation to which the application is made, or of each part thereof occupied by the applicant as a tenant, either—

(a) he has obtained the consent in writing of that landlord to the application; or

(b) that landlord has unreasonably refused his consent to the application.

(3) Where within 21 days of the receipt of a copy of an application served in accordance with subparagraph (1) or of a notice served in accordance with paragraph 11, a landlord objects to the application by notice served on the tenant and (where the Secretary of State is neither the landlord nor the tenant) the Secretary of State, on one or more of the grounds

---

(**a**) S.I. 1976/2126.
(**b**) O.J. No. L131, 26.5.77, p.1.
(**c**) O.J. No. L150, 18.6.77, p.24.
(**d**) S.I. 1986/1613, as amended by S.I. 1987/425 and 881.

specified in paragraph 9, the tenant shall be deemed to have withdrawn his application for compensation unless, within 14 days of receipt of that notice of objection the tenant–

    (a) by notice served on that landlord, demands that the question whether that objection should be upheld or not shall be referred to arbitration; and

    (b) (where the Secretary of State is neither the landlord nor the tenant) by notice served on the Secretary of State, informs him of that demand.

Unreasonable refusal of consent

8. For the purposes of paragraph 7, a landlord shall have unreasonably refused his consent to an application for compensation if–

    (a) having been served with a notice of the tenant's application or intention to make an application, he has not, within 21 days of receipt of that notice, served a notice objecting to that application on one or more of the grounds specified in paragraph 9, on–

        (i) the tenant,

        (ii) his immediate tenant where that tenant is not the tenant in occupation of the tenancy, and

        (iii) where the application has already been made, (and the Secretary of State is neither the landlord nor the tenant) the Secretary of State; or

    (b) he has so objected, but on arbitration under paragraph 10 an arbiter has made a determination not to uphold the objection, and the arbiter's determination has not been reversed and there is pending no appeal or other proceedings.

Landlord's objections to an application

9.—(1) Subject to paragraph (2) the grounds upon which a landlord may object to a tenant's application for compensation for the purposes of paragraphs 7 and 8 are–

    (a) where the tenant is eligible under paragraph 4(1)(a), that the payment the landlord would receive in accordance with this Scheme would not adequately recompense him for any reduction in the annual rental value of the tenancy as a result of the cessation of its use as a dairy unit;

    (b) where the tenant is eligible under paragraph 4(1)(b), that the payment the landlord would receive in accordance with this Scheme would not adequately recompense him for any reduction in the annual rental value of the tenancy as a result of the surrender of the relevant quota;

    (c) the tenant or any landlord is bound by an agreement with a superior landlord of the tenancy or with a predecessor of that landlord to the effect either that–

        (i) the tenancy or any part thereof will be farmed as a dairy farm; or

        (ii) any quota on the tenancy or any part thereof will be maintained.

(2) A landlord may not object to a tenant's application for compensation on the ground specified in subparagraph (1)(c)(ii) if the agreement concerned relates solely to commodities other than milk.

Arbitration of landlord's objection to an application

10. On a reference under paragraph 7(3) the arbiter shall determine whether or not the objection should be upheld.

Service of notices on superior landlords

11. Where a landlord is informed, by the service of a copy of an application under paragraph 7 or by a notice under paragraph 8 or under this paragraph, of a tenant's application or intention to make an application in respect of a holding, he shall, in respect of any part of that holding in which he has an interest (but in respect of which he is not the owner), within 7 days of receipt of such copy or notice, serve a notice on his immediate landlord informing him of the tenant's application or intention to make an application, and shall send a copy of such notice to the tenant and (where none of the parties is the Secretary of State) to the Secretary of State.

Landlord's right to payment

12.—(1) Subject to subparagraph (4), where a successful applicant occupies his holding or any part thereof as a tenant, each of his landlords shall be entitled to obtain from him a payment in respect of the relevant quota.

(2) The payment to which a landlord is entitled under subparagraph (1) shall be an amount agreed between the tenant and the landlord or, in default of agreement–

   (a) where the tenant has only one landlord, the landlord's amount; and

   (b) where the tenant has two or more landlords, such proportion of the landlord's amount as shall be agreed or determined by arbitration in accordance with paragraph 14.

(3) The landlord's amount, or, where subparagraph (2)(b) applies, the proportion of the landlord's amount to which a landlord is entitled, shall be payable in seven equal yearly instalments, each instalment being due–

   (a) on the day after the day the tenant receives his instalment of compensation; or

   (b) where, in respect of any quota year the tenant (by reason of his death or any default of his) does not receive an instalment of compensation, at the end of the period of 3 months after the date on which that instalment would otherwise have become due.

(4) Where

   (a) a successful applicant who is a tenant dies before he has received all his instalments of compensation, and

   (b) a successor of the deceased tenant enters into the tenant's obligations for the purposes of paragraph 4,

any landlord of the deceased tenant shall be entitled to recover from the successor such instalments of the payment referred to in subparagraph (2) as become due to that landlord on or after the date on which that successor entered into those obligations and, from that date, the landlord shall cease to be entitled to recover those instalments from the estate of the deceased tenant.

The landlord's amount

13.—(1) Where the tenant is eligible under paragraph 4(1)(a) the landlord's amount shall be such an amount as an arbiter may determine as equal to the full rate of compensation for so much of the relevant quota as consists of–

   (a) standard quota or, where it is less, allocated quota multiplied by the landlords's fraction; and

   (b) transferred quota as follows–

      (i) where the landlord bore the whole of the cost of the transaction by virtue of which the transferred quota was transferred to the tenancy, the whole of the transferred quota; and

      (ii) where the landlord bore only a part of that cost, the corresponding part of the transferred quota.

(2) For the purposes of subparagraph (1)–

   (a) "landlord's fraction" means the fraction of which–

      (i) the numerator is an amount equal to the reduction in the annual rental value of the tenancy if farmed as a non-dairy unit; and

      (ii) the denominator is an amount equal to the annual rental value of the tenancy farmed as a dairy unit;

   (b) in assessing the rental values referred to in heads (a)(i) and (ii) the notional rent determinations shall be based respectively on the use of the tenancy for such enterprises other than dairying as a reasonably competent tenant would pursue and the current use of the tenancy as a dairy unit.

(3) Where the tenant is eligible under paragraph 4(1)(b) the landlord's amount shall be such an amount as an arbiter shall determine as equal to the full rate of compensation for so much of the relevant quota as is surrendered under this Scheme and consists of–

   (a) standard quota or, where it is less, allocated quota multiplied–

      (i) firstly, by the landlord's fraction; and

      (ii) secondly, by a fraction of which the numerator is the quota surrendered and the denominator is the registered quota; and

(b) transferred quota as follows -

    (i) where the landlord bore the whole of the cost of the transaction by virtue of which the transferred quota was transferred to the tenancy, the whole of the transferred quota multiplied by a fraction of which the numerator is the quota surrendered and the denominator is the registered quota; and

    (ii) where the landlord bore only a part of that cost, the corresponding part of the transferred quota multiplied by a fraction of which the numerator is the quota surrendered and the denominator is the registered quota.

(4) For the purposes of subparagraph (3)–

(a) "landlord's fraction" means the fraction of which–

    (i) the numerator is an amount equal to the reduction in the annual rental value of the tenancy as a consequence of the surrender of the quota; and

    (ii) the denominator is an amount equal to the annual rental value of the tenancy assuming no quota is surrendered;

(b) in assessing the rental values referred to in heads (a)(i) and (ii) the notional rent determinations shall be based respectively on the use of the tenancy for such enterprises as a reasonably competent tenant would pursue and the current use of the tenancy assuming no surrender of quota.

(5) Subject to the provisions of subparagraph (6), the standard quota for any tenancy shall be calculated by multiplying the relevant number of hectares by the prescribed standard yield per hectare and for the purposes of this subparagraph and subparagraph (6)–

(a) "relevant number of hectares" means the average number of hectares of the tenancy used during the relevant period for the feeding of dairy cows kept on the tenancy or, if different, the average number of hectares of the tenancy which could reasonably be expected to have been so used (having regard to the number of grazing animals other than dairy cows kept on the tenancy during that period); and

(b) "prescribed standard yield per hectare" means, in respect of each of the breeds shown in column 1 of the Schedule to this Scheme, the number of litres shown opposite that breed in–

    (i) column 2(a), in relation to severely disadvantaged land,

    (ii) column 3(a), in relation to disadvantaged land, and

    (iii) column 4(a), in relation to any other land.

(6) Where, by virtue of the quality of the land in question or the climatic conditions in the area, the reasonable amount is greater or less than the prescribed average yield per hectare, subparagraph (5) shall not apply, and the standard quota shall be calculated by multiplying the relevant number of hectares by such proportion of the prescribed standard yield per hectare as the reasonable amount bears to the prescribed average yield per hectare, and for the purposes of this subparagraph–

(a) the amount of milk to be taken as the prescribed average yield per hectare in respect of each of the breeds shown in column 1 of the Schedule to this Scheme shall be the number of litres shown opposite that breed in–

    (i) column 2(b), in relation to severely disadvantaged land,

    (ii) column 3(b), in relation to disadvantaged land, and

    (iii) column 4(b), in relation to any other land; and

(b) "reasonable amount" means the amount of milk which could reasonably be expected to have been produced from one hectare of the tenancy during the relevant period.

(7) In the application of this paragraph–

(a) "dairy cows" means milking cows and calved heifers;

(b) "disadvantaged land" and "severely disadvantaged land" means land which has been determined to be disadvantaged or severely disadvantaged land, as the case may be, in accordance with the definitions of those expressions as they are set out in regulation 2 of the Hill Livestock (Compensatory Allowances) Regulations 1984(a);

(a) S.I. 1984/2024.

(c) references to the "area of a tenancy used for the feeding of dairy cows kept on the tenancy" do not include references to land used for the growing of cereal crops for feeding to dairy cows in the form of loose grain; and

(d) "relevant period" means–

(i) the period in relation to which the base quota was determined, or

(ii) where the base quota was determined in relation to more than one period, the period in relation to which the majority was determined or, if equal amounts were determined in relation to different periods, the later of those periods.

Apportionment of landlord's amount

14.—(1) The landlord's amount (or, where one or more landlords have agreed with the tenant the payment to which they are entitled under paragraph 12(2), such proportion of the landlord's amount as the remaining landlords shall agree or in default of agreement as an arbiter shall determine) shall be apportioned between the landlords who have not made an agreement with the tenant under paragraph 12(2) by agreement or, in default of agreement, by arbitration, and on a reference under this paragraph an arbiter shall take all relevant factors into account in making his award.

(2) Where a reference to arbitration is made under this paragraph in conjunction with a reference under another paragraph, any additional expenses of the award caused by the apportionment under this paragraph shall be paid by the landlords in such proportions as the arbiter may determine.

Arbitrations

15.—(1) Where any matter is under this Scheme to be determined by arbitration, it shall be referred–

(a) in the case of an agricultural holding within the meaning of the 1949 Act, to arbitration under that Act or, under section 78 of that Act, to the Scottish Land Court for determination by that court;

(b) in any other case, to the Scottish Land Court, for determination by that court.

(2) Subject to subparagraph (3), where subparagraph (1)(a) applies, section 75 (or where the circumstances require, sections 77 and 87) of the 1949 Act shall apply as if the matter referred to in subparagraph (1) was required by that Act to be determined by arbitration.

(3) Where subparagraph (1)(a) applies, Schedule 6 to the 1949 Act shall apply to arbitrations under this Scheme subject to the following modifications:–

(a) in paragraph 5(**a**) (particulars of claims) as if for the words "twenty eight days" in both places where they occur, there were substituted the words "twenty one days";

(b) in paragraph 8 (time for making and signing awards) as if for the words "two months" there were substituted the words "thirty five days";

(c) paragraph 13 (arbitration award to fix a day for payment of money awarded) shall apply only in relation to expenses;

(d) paragraphs 19 to 22 (stated case procedure, and setting aside award) shall not apply.

(4) Where a matter is under this paragraph to be determined by the Scottish Land Court, paragraphs 5 and 8 of Schedule 6 to the 1949 Act subject to the modifications set out in subparagraph (3) above shall apply to a reference to the Scottish Land Court as they apply to arbitrations under that Act and references in those paragraphs to the "arbiter" and the "arbitration" shall be construed accordingly.

Temporarily reallocated quota

16. For the purposes of this Scheme, quota which has been temporarily reallocated from one holding to another under the 1986 Regulations (reallocation of wholesale quota) shall be treated as if it had not been temporarily reallocated.

(**a**) Paragraph 5 was amended by the Agriculture (Miscellaneous Provisions) Act 1963 (c.11), section 20.

Service of notices or copies of applications

17.—(1) Any notice required by this Scheme to be served on any person shall be given in writing and shall be duly served on that person if it is delivered to him, or left at his proper address or sent to him by post in a registered letter or by the recorded delivery service.

(2) In the case of an incorporated company or body, any such notice or other document shall be duly served if it is served on the secretary or clerk of that company or body.

(3) Any such notice or other document to be served by or on a landlord or tenant shall be duly served if served by or on any agent of the landlord or tenant.

(4) For the purposes of this Scheme and of section 7 of the Interpretation Act 1978(**a**) (service by post), the proper address of a person is–

(a) in the case of a secretary or clerk to a company or body, that of the registered or principal office of the company or body;

(b) in any other case, the person's last known address.

(5) Unless or until the tenant or landlord of any tenancy has received–

(a) notice that the person who before that time was his immediate landlord (the "original landlord") has ceased to be such; and

(b) notice of the name and address of the person who has become his immediate landlord,

any notice served on the original landlord by the tenant or landlord shall be deemed for the purposes of this Scheme to have been properly served.

(6) Where an original landlord receives a notice in the circumstances described in subparagraph (5), he shall forthwith serve that notice on the person on whom that notice should have been served.

(7) In this paragraph, "notice" includes a copy of an application served under paragraph 7.

Loss arising from failure to comply with provisions of this Scheme

18.—(1) Where, in consequence of the failure of any person to comply with the requirements of paragraphs 7 or 11 in relation to a holding or a part of a holding, a landlord suffers loss, the landlord shall be entitled to recover the amount involved from that person.

(2) Any award or agreement under this Scheme as to compensation, expenses or otherwise may, if any sum payable thereunder is not paid within fourteen days after the date on which it becomes payable, be recorded for execution in the Books of Council and Session or in the sheriff court books, and shall be enforceable in like manner as a recorded decree arbitral.

Recovery of compensation

19.—(1) Where any person with a view to obtaining the payment of compensation to himself or any other person–

(a) makes any statement which is untrue or misleading in a material respect, or

(b) furnishes to the Secretary of State any inaccurate information,

the Secretary of State shall be entitled to recover on demand the whole or any part of any compensation paid to him or to such other person.

(2) Where any person, having given an undertaking in accordance with the provisions of paragraph 4(1)(a) or (b)(ii), fails in any way to comply with that undertaking, the Secretary of State shall be entitled to recover from him on demand the whole or any part of any compensation paid to him or to any other person in respect of quota registered in that person's name.

(3) Where any person–

(a) intentionally obstructs an authorised officer in the exercise of the powers conferred on him by section 2(1) of the Act, or

(b) fails without reasonable excuse to comply with a requirement of this Scheme,

the Secretary of State shall be entitled to recover on demand the whole or any part of any compensation paid to that person.

(**a**) 1978 c.30.

Application to Crown

20.—(1) This scheme shall apply to any holding or part of a holding which belongs to Her Majesty or to a government department, or which is held in trust for Her Majesty for the purposes of a government department.

(2) For the purposes of this Scheme—

    (a) as respects land belonging to Her Majesty in right of the Crown, the Crown Estate Commissioners or the proper officer or body having charge of the land for the time being or, if there is no such officer or body, such person as Her Majesty may appoint in writing under the Royal Sign Manual, shall represent Her Majesty, and shall be deemed to be the landlord or tenant, as the case may be;

    (b) as respects land belonging to Her Majesty privately, such person as Her Majesty may appoint in writing under the Royal Sign Manual shall represent Her Majesty and shall be deemed to be the landlord.

Revocation

21.   The Milk (Partial Cessation of Production) (Scotland) Scheme 1986(**a**) is hereby revoked.

New St. Andrew's House, Edinburgh
14th May 1987

John J. MacKay
Parliamentary Under Secretary of State,
Scottish Office

(**a**) S.I. 1986/1614.

SCHEDULE

Article 2

(1) Breed	(2) Severely disadvantaged land		(3) Disadvantaged land		(4) Other land	
	(a) Standard Yield/Hectare	(b) Average Yield/Hectare	(a) Standard Yield/Hectare	(b) Average Yield/Hectare	(a) Standard Yield/Hectare	(b) Average Yield/Hectare
	litres	litres	litres	litres	litres	litres
Channel Is. South Devon, and breeds with similar characteristics	4,580	5,270	5,825	6,694	6,660	7,650
Ayrshire and Dairy Shorthorn, and breeds with similar characteristics	5,235	6,028	6,660	7,656	7,615	8,750
Others	5,385	6,200	6,850	7,875	7,830	9,000

EXPLANATORY NOTE

(This note is not part of the Scheme)

Article 1(2)(a) of Council Regulation (EEC) No. 1343/86 (O.J. No. L119, 8.5.86, p.34) amended Article 4(1)(a) of Council Regulation (EEC) No. 857/54 (O.J. No. L90, 1.4.84, p.13) by enabling Member States to grant compensation to producers with a milk quota in excess of a level which was to be determined who undertake to surrender at least 50% of that milk quota. Until this amendment was made, producers could only obtain compensation for the surrender of the whole of their milk quota. The level of milk quota referred to above was fixed by Article 1(1) of Commission Regulation (EEC) No. 2133/86 (O.J. No. L187, 9.7.86, p.21) at 250,000 kilogrammes (242,790 litres).

This Scheme provides for the payment of compensation to certain holders of milk quota in Scotland. Under the Scheme, compensation is to be paid to any producer who holds unused quota and who must either undertake to surrender the total of the milk quota registered in his name and to discontinue milk production, or to reduce his milk production and surrender not less than 50% of his total registered quota.

Paragraph 3 provides that the time and procedural requirements for applications for compensation shall be published in the Gazette and the farming press. The methods by which payments may be made to persons under the Scheme are explained in paragraph 5. Paragraph 6 lays down the rules for the acceptance of applications in the event of over-subscription.

An applicant for compensation who does not own all the land which he occupies must attempt to obtain the consent of any person who owns or is a superior landlord of the tenancy ("the landlord"), unless consent has already been obtained or is determined as being unreasonably refused (paragraph 7).

Paragraphs 8 and 9 spell out the criteria for deciding whether or not a landlord's consent has been unreasonably refused and paragraphs 10 and 11 deal with arbitration on this matter in cases of dispute.

Paragraph 12 provides that landlords shall be entitled to obtain from the tenant a payment in respect of the relevant quota and paragraph 13 sets out the amount (the "landlord's amount") to which landlords as a whole are entitled in the absence of agreement. The amount is to be apportioned among the landlords by agreement or arbitration (paragraph 14).

Arbitrations under the Scheme are, in the case of an agricultural holding within the meaning of the Agricultural Holdings (Scotland) Act 1949, to be referred to a single arbiter (or to the Scottish Land Court) in accordance with the provisions of Schedule 6 to the 1949 Act, three of the provisions of which have been amended for the purposes of this Scheme in order to speed up proceedings. Several more provisions of that Schedule have been disapplied to arbitrations under this Scheme, in particular the stated case procedure. In any case other than an agricultural holding, reference is to be made to the Scottish Land Court for determination. The provisions of Schedule 6 to the 1949 Act as amended by this Scheme are applied to the procedures of the Scottish Land Court (paragraph 15).

Provision is made for recovery from a tenant of any loss suffered by a landlord as a result of an application for compensation by the tenant which fails to comply with paragraph 7 and for recovery of sums agreed or awarded under the Scheme (paragraph 18).

Paragraph 19 makes provision for the recovery by the Secretary of State of compensation paid in certain specified circumstances.

This Scheme applies to Crown land (paragraph 20).

This Scheme also revokes the Milk (Partial Cessation of Production) (Scotland) Scheme 1986 (paragraph 21).

Duly authorised officers of the Secretary of State have power to enter on any land occupied by any person to whom a payment of compensation has been made and to require any person who is engaged in the production of milk to furnish accounts and records in his possession or under his control by virtue of section 2 of the Milk (Cessation of Production) Act 1985.

By section 3 of the above Act it is made an offence punishable on summary conviction by a fine not exceeding £2,000 to make a false statement knowingly or recklessly which is false in a material particular for the purpose of obtaining compensation, or to intentionally obstruct an authorised officer.

1987 No. 883 (S. 75)

LEGAL AID AND ADVICE, SCOTLAND

The Advice and Assistance (Scotland) Amendment Regulations 1987

Made - - - -		*13th May 1987*
Laid before Parliament		*15th May 1987*
Coming into force		*5th June 1987*

The Secretary of State, in exercise of the powers conferred on him by sections 12(3), 33(2) and (3) and 37(1) of the Legal Aid (Scotland) Act 1986(**a**), and of all other powers enabling him in that behalf, hereby makes the following Regulations:

Citation and commencement

1. These Regulations may be cited as the Advice and Assistance (Scotland) Amendment Regulations 1987 and shall come into force on 5th June 1987.

Interpretation

2. In these Regulations, "the principal Regulations" means the Advice and Assistance (Scotland) Regulations 1987(**b**).

Amendment of principal Regulations

3. At the end of paragraph (1) of regulation 15 of the principal Regulations there shall be added the following sub-paragraphs–

"(c) to unemployment benefit, sickness benefit, invalidity benefit, retirement pension, death grant, maternity benefit, widow's benefit, child's special allowance, attendance allowance, invalid care allowance, mobility allowance, guardian's allowance, injury benefit, disablement benefit or industrial death benefit paid under the Social Security Act 1975(**c**);

(d) to child benefit paid under the Child Benefit Act 1975(**d**);

(e) to allowances and benefit paid under the Industrial Injuries and Diseases (Old Cases) Act 1975(**e**);

(f) to any rate rebate or rent rebate or rent allowance paid under Part II of the Social Security and Housing Benefits Act 1982(**f**);

(g) to one-half of any redundancy payment within the meaning of Part VI of the Employment Protection (Consolidation) Act 1978(**g**) recovered or preserved for the client;

(**a**) 1986 c.47.
(**b**) S.I. 1987/382.
(**c**) 1975 c.14.
(**d**) 1975 c.61.
(**e**) 1975 c.16.
(**f**) 1982 c.24.
(**g**) 1978 c.44.

(h) to any payment of money in accordance with an order made under section 136 of the Employment Protection (Consolidation) Act 1978 by the Employment Appeal Tribunal;

(i) to any dwelling, household furniture or tools of trade recovered or preserved for the client as a result of advice or assistance given to him by the solicitor.".

4. In Schedule 3 to the principal Regulations–

(a) in Part I for "£75.75" there shall be substituted "£78.80"; and

(b) in Part II for "£2.20", "£14.10" where it occurs twice, "£7.05" and "£28.80" there shall be substituted "£2.30", "£14.80" in each case, "£7.40" and "£29.60" respectively.

Ian Lang
New St. Andrew's House, Edinburgh
Parliamentary Under Secretary of State,
13th May 1987
Scottish Office

EXPLANATORY NOTE

(This note is not part of the Regulations)

These Regulations amend the provisions of the Advice and Assistance (Scotland) Regulations 1987 in two respects.

Firstly, they secure that a solicitor's right under section 12(3)(c) of the Legal Aid (Scotland) Act 1986 to prior payment of fees or outlays out of any property recovered or preserved for his client shall not apply to the following property so recovered or preserved–

payments made under the Social Security Act 1975, and the Child Benefit Act 1975;

payments under the Industrial Injuries and Diseases (Old Cases) Act 1975;

a rate or rent rebate or rent allowance under the Social Security and Housing Benefits Act 1982;

certain payments under the Employment Protection (Consolidation) Act 1978;

any dwelling or household furniture or tools of a trade which the client gets back or retains through advice or help given by the solicitor.

Secondly they increase by 4% the fee allowable to solicitors in respect of representation where, following a plea of guilty, one or more adjournments are ordered by the court; and by 5% the fees allowable for advice and assistance other than by way of representation.

1987 No. 884

MERCHANT SHIPPING

MASTERS AND SEAMEN

The Merchant Shipping (Certification of Deck and Marine Engineer Officers and Licensing of Marine Engine Operators) (Amendment) Regulations 1987

Made - - - -	*13th May 1987*
Laid before Parliament	*15th May 1987*
Coming into force -	*5th June 1987*

The Secretary of State for Transport, after consulting with the organisations referred to in section 99(2) of the Merchant Shipping Act 1970(a) and the persons referred to in section 22(2) of the Merchant Shipping Act 1979(b), in exercise of powers conferred by sections 43 and 92 of the said Act of 1970 and now vested in him(c) and of section 21(1)(a) and (3) to (6) of the said Act of 1979 and of all other powers enabling him in that behalf, hereby makes the following Regulations:

PART 1

GENERAL

Citation, commencement and revocation

1. These Regulations may be cited as the Merchant Shipping (Certification of Deck and Marine Engineer Officers and Licensing of Marine Engine Operators) (Amendment) Regulations 1987 and shall come into force on 5th June 1987.

2. The Merchant Shipping (Certification of Deck Officers) Regulations 1985(d) shall be amended as follows:
   (a) in regulation 2(1) there shall be inserted at the end the following definition:–
       ""United Kingdom ship" has the same meaning as in section 21(2) of the Merchant Shipping Act 1979(e)".
   (b) for regulation 3 there shall be substituted the following:–

(a) 1970 c.36; section 43 was amended by the Merchant Shipping Act 1979 (c.39), section 37(2) and (3).
(b) 1979 c.39; section 21(6) was amended by the Criminal Justice Act 1982 (c.48), section 49(3).
(c) *See* S.I. 1970/1537.
(d) S.I. 1985/1306.
(e) As to the meaning of ''Citizen of the United Kingdom and Colonies'' referred to in section 21(2), *see now* the British Nationality Act 1981 (c.61), section 51(3).

"**3.**—(1) Subject to paragraph (3) below, Parts II and III of these Regulations apply to:–

    (a) United Kingdom ships; and

    (b) ships registered outside the United Kingdom which carry passengers:–

      (i) between places in the United Kingdom or between the United Kingdom and the Isle of Man or any of the Channel Islands; or

     (ii) on a voyage which begins and ends at the same place in the United Kingdom and on which the ship calls at no place outside the United Kingdom.

(2) Subject to paragraph (3) below, Part IV of these Regulations applies to all United Kingdom ships.

    (3) These Regulations do not apply to:–

    (a) ships which do not go to sea beyond the limits of smooth or partially smooth waters;

    (b) pleasure craft of less than 80 GRT or under 24 metres in length;

    (c) fishing vessels and Government fishery research vessels.

(4) The provisions of Parts II and III of these Regulations have effect subject to any exemption from the requirements thereof given under section 44 of the Merchant Shipping Act 1970.";

(c) in regulation 4(1) for "these Regulations apply" there shall be substituted "this Part of these Regulations applies";

(d) in regulation 4(3)(b) after "Master (Restricted) Endorsement" insert "Master (Restricted) (Limited European) Endorsement";

(e) in regulation 5(2) "under regulation 6(2) of these Regulations" shall be omitted;

(f) in regulation 5(7), in Table 1, in respect of the entries for Class 4 in column 2 of the entries for "Master Home Trade" and "Mate Home Trade" respectively, for "locations in the Extended European area" there shall be substituted "any locations";

(g) in regulation 5(9) after "that Table" insert "subject to any limitation as to area of operation or description of ship endorsed thereon";

(h) regulation 6(2) shall be deleted;

(i) in regulation 6(3) for "certificate of competency, a command endorsement" there shall be substituted "certificate of competency or a command endorsement", and "or a certificate of service (deck officer)", shall be deleted;

(j) in regulation 8, in Table 4, in the entry "Class 3 or Class 4" in column 2 after "Tugmaster" there shall be inserted "(Extended European)";

(k) in regulation 9(1) for "Standy-by" substitute "Stand-by";

(l) in regulation 18 for "these Regulations apply" there shall be substituted "this Part of these Regulations applies";

(m) in regulation 19 the following shall be substituted for paragraph (3):–

    "(3) No person shall appoint any other person to act in a capacity for which he is not duly certificated in accordance with these Regulations.";

(n) in regulation 20

    (i) in paragraph (1), "or (3)" shall be inserted after "19(1)"; and

    (ii) paragraph (2) shall be omitted;

(o) in Schedule 1, in Table A, in the entry "Limited European", in the sub-entry "1000 GRT but under 1600 GRT" in column 3, after "3(B)" there shall be added "(C)".

3. The Merchant Shipping (Certification of Marine Engineer Officers and Licensing of Marine Engine Operators) Regulations 1986**(a)** shall be amended as follows:–

    (a) in regulation 2(1) there shall be inserted at the end the following definition:–

(a) S.I. 1986/1935.

""United Kingdom ship" has the same meaning as in section 21(2) of the Merchant Shipping Act 1979.";

(b) for regulation 3 there shall be substituted the following:–

"3.—(1) Subject to paragraph (4) below, Parts II to IV of these Regulations apply to ships described in paragraph (3) below which are:–

(a) United Kingdom ships or

(b) ships registered outside the United Kingdom which carry passengers:–

(i) between places in the United Kingdom or between the United Kingdom and the Isle of Man or any of the Channel Islands; or

(ii) on a voyage which begins and ends at the same place in the United Kingdom and on which the ship calls at no place outside the United Kingdom.

(2) Subject to paragraph (4) below Part V of these Regulations applies to ships described in paragraph (3) below which are United Kingdom ships.

(3) The ships referred to in paragraphs (1) and (2) above are ships having registered power of 350 kilowatts or more, and sail training ships which in either case go to sea beyond the limits of smooth or partially smooth waters.

(4) The Regulations do not apply to fishing vessels, Government fishery research vessels or pleasure craft.

(5) The provisions of Parts II to IV of these Regulations have effect subject to any exemption from the requirements thereof given under section 44 of the Merchant Shipping Act 1970.";

(c) in regulations 4(1), 11(1), 18(1), 20(1), and 21(2) for "to which these Regulations apply" there shall in each case be substituted "to which this Part of these Regulations applies";

(d) in regulation 22

(i) "or (3)" shall be inserted after "21(1)"; and

(ii) paragraph (2) shall be omitted.

4. The Merchant Shipping (Unregistered Ships) Regulations 1972(a) shall be amended by adding the following regulation 4:–

"4. It is hereby directed that sections 43, 45 and 47 of the Merchant Shipping Act 1970 shall extend to British ships which are not registered under the law of any country but are United Kingdom ships within the meaning of section 21(2)(b) of the Merchant Shipping Act 1979 and to masters and seamen employed therein.".

Michael Spicer
Signed by authority of the Secretary of State   Parliamentary Under Secretary of State,
13th May 1987   Department of Transport

_____

(a) S.I. 1972/1876.

EXPLANATORY NOTE

(This note is not part of the Regulations)

These Regulations primarily amend the Merchant Shipping (Certification of Deck Officers) Regulations 1985.

Provisions relating to the issue of certificates of service are deleted. These provisions are no longer appropriate as the issue of certificates of service is now prevented by the requirements of Article VII(3) of the International Convention on Standards of Training and Certification for Seafarers 1978. The amendments also correct certain errors and omissions.

The Regulations also amend the Merchant Shipping (Certification of Marine Engineer Officers and Licensing of Marine Engine Operators) Regulations 1986. The effect of the amendments to these 1986 Regulations, and of similar amendments made to the 1985 Regulations, is that the Watchkeeping Requirements in both Regulations are limited to United Kingdom ships. Other provisions of the two Regulations apply also to certain foreign registered, sea-going ships which carry passengers between ports in the United Kingdom.

The Merchant Shipping (Unregistered Ships) Regulations 1972 are also amended so that the provisions of sections 43, 45 and 47 of the Merchant Shipping Act 1970 apply also to unregistered United Kingdom ships.

STATUTORY INSTRUMENTS

1987 No. 885

PUBLIC HEALTH, ENGLAND AND WALES
PUBLIC HEALTH, SCOTLAND
PUBLIC HEALTH, NORTHERN IRELAND

CONTAMINATION OF FOOD

The Food Protection (Emergency Prohibitions) (Wales) (No. 2) Amendment No. 3 Order 1987

Made - - - -	*14th May 1987*
Laid before Parliament	*14th May 1987*
Coming into force -	*25th May 1987*

Whereas the Secretary of State is of the opinion, as mentioned in section 1(1)(a) of the Food and Environment Protection Act 1985**(a)**, that there has been or may have been an escape of substances of such descriptions and in such quantities and such circumstances as are likely to create a hazard to human health through human consumption of food;

And whereas the Secretary of State is of the opinion, as mentioned in section 1(1)(b) of the said Act, that in consequence of the said escape of substances food which is or may be in the future in the area described in Schedule 1 to the Food Protection (Emergency Prohibitions) (Wales) (No. 2) Order 1986**(b)**, or which is derived or may be in the future derived from anything in that area, is, or may be, or may become, unsuitable for human consumption;

Now, therefore, the Secretary of State, in exercise of the powers conferred on him by the said section 1(1) and (2) and section 24(1) and (3) of the said Act, and of all other powers enabling him in that behalf, hereby makes the following Order:–

Title and commencement

1. This Order may be cited as the Food Protection (Emergency Prohibitions) (Wales) (No. 2) Amendment No. 3 Order 1987 and shall come into force on 25th May 1987.

Partial revocation and amendment

2. The Food Protection (Emergency Prohibitions) (Wales) (No. 2) Order 1986 is revoked to the extent that it imposes prohibitions on–

    (a) the slaughter of a sheep which–

        (i) was moved from a place in accordance with a consent given under section 2(1) of the Food and Environment Act 1985 which consent was subject to the condition that the sheep to which it applies should be marked with an apricot mark; and

---

(a) 1985 c.48.
(b) S.I. 1986/1681, amended by S.I. 1986/1707, 1756, 1775, 1849, 2242 and 1987/182 and 263.

    (ii) has been examined and marked with an ear-tag by a person authorised in that behalf by one of the Ministers; and

   (b) the supply or having in possession for supply of meat, or food containing meat, derived from such a sheep,

and accordingly that Order is further amended in accordance with the following provisions of this Order.

3. In article 6, for paragraph (2) there shall be substituted the following paragraph–
  "(2) Paragraph (1) above shall not apply in the case of–

    (a) any sheep which was moved to a market in accordance with a consent given under section 2(1) of the Act which consent did not require that the sheep to which it applies should be marked in a manner specified therein;

    (b) any sheep which was moved from any place in accordance with a consent given under the said section 2(1) which consent was subject to the condition that the sheep to which it applies should be marked with a blue mark; or

    (c) any sheep which–

      (i) was moved from any place in accordance with a consent given under the said section 2(1) which consent was subject to the condition that the sheep to which it applies should be marked with red mark or with an apricot mark; and

      (ii) has been examined and marked with an ear-tag by a person authorised in that behalf by one of the Ministers.".

Nicholas Edwards
Secretary of State for Wales

14th May 1987

EXPLANATORY NOTE

(This note is not part of the Order)

The Food Protection (Emergency Prohibitions) (Wales) (No. 2) Order 1986 as amended by S.I. 1986/1707, 1756, 1775, 1849, 2242, 1987/182 and 263 contains emergency prohibitions restricting various activities in order to prevent human consumption of food which has been or which may have been rendered unsuitable for that purpose in consequence of the escape of radioative substances from a nuclear reactor situated at Chernobyl in the USSR.

This Order excepts from the prohibition on slaughter throughout the United Kingdom any sheep, and from the prohibition on supply throughout the United Kingdom any meat derived from such a sheep, identified by an apricot paint mark which have been examined and subsequently marked with an ear-tag by a person authorised by the Minister of Agriculture, Fisheries and Food or the Secretary of State for Scotland or the Secretary of State for Wales (article 3).

STATUTORY INSTRUMENTS

1987 No. 886

INCOME TAX

The Income Tax (Official Rate of Interest on Beneficial Loans) (No. 2) Order 1987

Made - - - -	*13th May 1987*
Laid before the House of Commons	*14th May 1987*
Coming into force	*6th June 1987*

The Treasury, in exercise of the powers conferred on them by section 66(9) of the Finance Act 1976**(a)**, hereby make the following Order:

1. This Order may be cited as the Income Tax (Official Rate of Interest on Beneficial Loans) (No. 2) Order 1987 and shall come into force on 6th June 1987.

2. For the purposes of section 66**(b)** of, and Schedule 8**(c)** to, the Finance Act 1976 (which impose a charge to income tax on beneficial loans) the official rate of interest is prescribed to be $10\frac{1}{2}$ per cent. per annum.

Peter Lloyd
Mark Lennox-Boyd
13th May 1987   Two of the Lords Commissioners of Her Majesty's Treasury

EXPLANATORY NOTE

(This note is not part of the Order)

By this Order the official rate of interest for the purposes of section 66 of, and Schedule 8 to, the Finance Act 1976 (charge to income tax on beneficial loans) is prescribed to be $10\frac{1}{2}$ per cent. per annum on and after 6th June 1987.

Previous Orders – S.I.1978/28, 1980/439, 1982/1273 and 1987/512 – prescribed rates of 9 per cent. per annum (on and after 6th April 1978), 15 per cent. per annum (on and after 6th May 1980), 12 per cent. per annum (on and after 6th October 1982) and $11\frac{1}{2}$ per cent. per annum (on and after 6th April 1987) respectively.

(a) 1976 c.40.   **(b)** Section 66 was amended by section 50(1) of the Finance Act 1980 (c.48) and by section 26(9) of the Finance Act 1982 (c.39).   **(c)** Schedule 8 was amended by section 26(9) of the Finance Act 1982 (c.39) and by section 4 of the Finance (No. 2) Act 1983 (c.49).

STATUTORY INSTRUMENTS

1987 No. 887

CAPITAL TRANSFER TAX

The Inheritance Tax and Capital Transfer Tax (Interest on Unpaid Tax) Order 1987

Made - - - -	*13th May 1987*
Laid before the House of Commons	*14th May 1987*
Coming into force	*6th June 1987*

The Treasury, in exercise of the powers conferred on them by section 233 of the Inheritance Tax Act 1984**(a)**, hereby make the following Order:

1. This Order may be cited as the Inheritance Tax and Capital Transfer Tax (Interest on Unpaid Tax) Order 1987 and shall come into force on 6th June 1987.

2. The rate prescribed for the purposes of section 233 of the Inheritance Tax Act 1984 (interest on unpaid tax) shall be 6 per cent. per annum and shall apply in each of the cases referred to in paragraphs (a) and (b) of section 233(2).

Peter Lloyd
Mark Lennox-Boyd
13th May 1987   Two of the Lords Commissioners of Her Majesty's Treasury

---

(a) 1984 c.51; section 233(1)(c) was amended by section 94 of, and paragraph 11 of Schedule 26 to, the Finance Act 1985 (c.54). Section 233(2) was amended by section 101(3) of, and paragraph 32 of Schedule 19 to, the Finance Act 1986 (c.41), with respect to transfers of value made and other events occurring after 17th March 1986. By virtue of section 100(1) and (2) of the Finance Act 1986, on and after 25th July 1986 the Capital Transfer Tax Act 1984 may be cited as the Inheritance Tax Act 1984, and any reference in that Act to capital transfer tax is to have effect as a reference to inheritance tax, except where the reference relates to a liability arising before 25th July 1986.

EXPLANATORY NOTE

(This note is not part of the Order)

This Order reduces with effect from 6th June 1987 the annual rate of interest on unpaid inheritance tax, or unpaid capital transfer tax where the liability to tax arose before 25th July 1986, payable under section 233 of the Inheritance Tax Act 1984 (formerly the Capital Transfer Tax Act 1984). The annual rate is reduced to 6 per cent. This reduction also has effect in relation to repayments of capital transfer tax or inheritance tax since, by virtue of section 235 of the Act, these carry interest at the rate applicable to unpaid tax under section 233. Section 236 of the Act, as amended by paragraph 33 of Schedule 19 to the Finance Act 1986, applies the provisions of section 233 to certain special cases where tax has been overpaid or underpaid.

The previous rate was 8 per cent. with effect from 16th December 1986 (S.I.1986/1944). Immediately before 16th December 1986 rates of 9 per cent. and 11 per cent. applied with respect to transfers of value made and other events occurring after 17th March 1986 by section 233(2) (as amended by paragraph 32 of Schedule 19 to the Finance Act 1986) and originally in relation to capital transfer tax by S.I. 1985/560 with effect from 1st May 1985. Prior to this date the rates were 6 per cent. and 8 per cent. respectively with effect from 1st December 1982 (S.I. 1982/1585), 9 per cent. and 12 per cent. respectively with effect from 1st January 1980 (S.I. 1979/1688), and 6 per cent. and 9 per cent. respectively prior to 1st January 1980 (paragraph 19 of Schedule 4 to the Finance Act 1975 (c.7)).

STATUTORY INSTRUMENTS

1987 No. 888

TAXES

The Stamp Duty Reserve Tax (Interest on Tax Repaid) (No. 2) Order 1987

Made - - - -	*13th May 1987*
Laid before the House of Commons	*14th May 1987*
Coming into force	*6th June 1987*

The Treasury, in exercise of the powers conferred on them by section 92(4) of the Finance Act 1986(**a**), hereby make the following Order:

1. This Order may be cited as the Stamp Duty Reserve Tax (Interest on Tax Repaid) (No. 2) Order 1987 and shall come into force on 6th June 1987.

2. The rate specified, which for the purposes of section 92 of the Finance Act 1986 is the appropriate rate, is 8.25 per cent. per annum.

Peter Lloyd
Mark Lennox-Boyd

13th May 1987   Two of the Lords Commissioners of Her Majesty's Treasury

---

EXPLANATORY NOTE

(This note is not part of the Order)

Section 92 of the Finance Act 1986 provides that, if certain conditions have been fulfilled and a claim for repayment is made within the stipulated period, stamp duty reserve tax shall be repaid. Where the tax paid is not less than £25, it shall be repaid with interest at the appropriate rate. The section defines the "appropriate rate" as 11 per cent. per annum or such other rate as the Treasury may from time to time specify by order.

This Order specifies that on and after 6th June 1987 the appropriate rate shall be 8.25 per cent. per annum. Prior to that date the rate was 9 per cent. on and after 6th April 1987 (S.I. 1987/514).

(**a**) 1986 c.41.

STATUTORY INSTRUMENTS

1987 No. 889

ACQUISITION OF LAND

COMPENSATION

The Acquisition of Land (Rate of Interest after Entry) (No. 2) Regulations 1987

Made - - - -	*13th May 1987*
Laid before Parliament	*14th May 1987*
Coming into force	*4th June 1987*

The Treasury, in exercise of the powers conferred upon them by section 32(1) of the Land Compensation Act 1961**(a)**, and of all other powers enabling them in that behalf, hereby make the following Regulations:

1. These Regulations may be cited as the Acquisition of Land (Rate of Interest after Entry) (No. 2) Regulations 1987, and shall come into force on 4th June 1987.

2. The rate of interest on any compensation in respect of the compulsory acquisition of an interest in any land on which entry has been made before the payment of the compensation shall be 10 per cent. per annum.

3. The Acquisition of Land (Rate of Interest after Entry) Regulations 1987**(b)** are hereby revoked.

13th May 1987

Mark Lennox-Boyd
Peter Lloyd
Two of the Lords Commissioners of Her Majesty's Treasury

EXPLANATORY NOTE

(This note is not part of the Regulations)

These Regulations decrease from $11\frac{1}{4}$ per cent. to 10 per cent. per annum, in respect of any period after the coming into force of these Regulations, the rate of interest payable where entry is made, before payment of compensation, on land in England and Wales which is being purchased compulsorily, and revoke the Acquisition of Land (Rate of Interest after Entry) Regulations 1987.

(a) 1961 c.33.
(b) S.I. 1987/405.

STATUTORY INSTRUMENTS

1987 No. 890

ACQUISITION OF LAND

COMPENSATION

The Acquisition of Land (Rate of Interest after Entry) (Scotland) (No. 2) Regulations 1987

Made - - - -	*13th May 1987*
Laid before Parliament	*14th May 1987*
Coming into force	*4th June 1987*

The Treasury, in exercise of the powers conferred upon them by section 40(1) of the Land Compensation (Scotland) Act 1963**(a)**, and of all other powers enabling them in that behalf, hereby make the following Regulations:

1. These Regulations may be cited as the Acquisition of Land (Rate of Interest after Entry) (Scotland) (No. 2) Regulations 1987, and shall come into force on 4th June 1987.

2. The rate of interest on any compensation in respect of the compulsory acquisition of an interest in any land on which entry has been made before the payment of the compensation shall be 10 per cent. per annum.

3. The Acquisition of Land (Rate of Interest after Entry) (Scotland) Regulations 1987**(b)** are hereby revoked.

Mark Lennox-Boyd
Peter Lloyd
13th May 1987   Two of the Lords Commissioners of Her Majesty's Treasury

EXPLANATORY NOTE

(This note is not part of the Regulations)

These Regulations decrease from $11\frac{1}{4}$ per cent. to 10 per cent. per annum, in respect of any period after the coming into force of these Regulations, the rate of interest payable where entry is made, before payment of compensation, on land in Scotland which is being purchased compulsorily, and revoke the Acquisition of Land (Rate of Interest after Entry) (Scotland) Regulations 1987.

(a) 1963 c.51.
(b) S.I. 1987/397.

STATUTORY INSTRUMENTS

1987 No. 891

BUILDING SOCIETIES

The Building Societies Appeal Tribunal Regulations 1987

Made - - - -	*13th May 1987*
Laid before Parliament	*14th May 1987*
Coming into force	*8th June 1987*

ARRANGEMENT OF REGULATIONS

The Treasury, in exercise of the powers conferred upon them by section 48(3) of the Building Societies Act 1986(a) and of all other powers enabling them in that behalf, and after consultation with the Council on Tribunals, hereby make the following Regulations:–

Citation and commencement

1.—(1) These Regulations may be cited as the Building Societies Appeal Tribunal Regulations 1987.

(2) These Regulations shall come into force on 8th June 1987.

Interpretation

2.—(1) In these Regulations, unless the context otherwise requires–

"the Act" means the Building Societies Act 1986;

"appeal" means an appeal to which these Regulations apply in accordance with regulation 3;

"appellant" means a person who under the Act is entitled to appeal or, being so entitled, has appealed, as the case may be, to the Tribunal against a decision of the Commission;

"the chairman" means the chairman of the Tribunal appointed in accordance with section 47(2) of the Act;

"the Commission" means the Building Societies Commission established by section 1 of the Act;

"preliminary hearing" means the hearing held pursuant to regulation 10.

"the secretary" means the person appointed by the Treasury to act as secretary to the Tribunal.

(2) Unless the context otherwise requires any reference in these Regulations to a numbered regulation is a reference to the regulation bearing that number in these Regulations and any reference in a regulation to a numbered paragraph is a reference to the paragraph bearing that number in that regulation.

Application of Regulations

3. These Regulations apply to appeals under section 46 of the Act against decisions of the Commission.

Time for and manner of bringing appeals

4. An appeal shall be brought by sending a notice of appeal to the Secretary of the Building Societies Appeal Tribunal, c/o Her Majesty's Treasury, Treasury Chambers, Parliament Street, London SW1P 3AG not later than–

(a) in the case of an appeal against the decision of the Commission to refuse to grant authorisation, to impose conditions or as to the conditions imposed, 28 days,

(b) in the case of an appeal against the decision of the Commission to revoke authorisation, 10 days, or

(c) in the case of an appeal under section 46(2) of the Act, 10 days where the decision of the Commission relates to the revocation of an authorisation and 28 days in any other case,

from the date on which the Commission serves notice in writing on the appellant of its decision.

Notice of appeal

5.—(1) The notice of appeal shall be signed by or on behalf of the appellant and shall contain the following particulars:–

(a) the appellant's name;

(a) 1986 c.53.

(b) his address or, where the appellant is a building society, the address of its principal office;

(c) the address within the United Kingdom to which applications, notices and other documents in connection with the appeal should be sent to the appellant, if different from the address referred to in sub-paragraph (b);

(d) the name and address of any person appointed by the appellant to represent him or it in connection with the appeal;

(e) a statement of the decision of the Commission against which the appeal is made.

(2) The appellant shall, upon sending notice of appeal to the secretary, send a copy of the notice to the Commission and, where in making its decision the Commission makes a determination that a person is not a fit and proper person to hold or, as the case may be, to remain in an office in the society or imposes a requirement that he be removed from an office in the society, the appellant shall, if it is a building society, send a copy of the notice to that person or, if the appellant is that person himself, send a copy of the notice to the building society concerned.

Establishment of the Tribunal

6. On receipt of a notice of appeal the secretary shall forthwith request the Lord Chancellor or the Lord Advocate and the Chancellor of the Exchequer respectively to appoint the Chairman and other members of the Tribunal in accordance with section 47(2) of the Act to determine the appeal.

Respondent

7. On every appeal the Commission shall be the respondent.

Grounds of Appeal

8.—(1) The appellant shall send to the secretary a notice of grounds of appeal containing sufficient particulars to show why the decision appealed against was unlawful or was not justified by the evidence on which it was based—

(a) within 28 days from the date on which the Commission served notice in writing on the appellant of its decision, in the case of an appeal against the decision of the Commission to revoke authorisation and in the case of an appeal under section 46(2) of the Act where the decision of the Commission relates to the revocation of authorisation, and

(b) within 14 days of sending the notice of appeal to the secretary, in any other case.

(2) The appellant shall, upon sending the notice of grounds of appeal referred to in paragraph (1), send a copy of the notice to the persons to whom a copy of the notice of appeal was sent pursuant to regulation 5(2).

Supply of documents by the Commission

9. Within 14 days of receiving the copy of the notice of appeal under regulation 5, the Commission shall send to the secretary four copies of the documents listed in the Schedule to these Regulations and shall send to the appellant a list of those documents together with a copy of any documents which the Commission has not already supplied to the appellant.

Preliminary hearing

10.—(1) The secretary shall send to the appellant and the Commission and, in the case of an appeal under section 46(2) of the Act, the building society concerned a notice informing them of the time and place of the preliminary hearing which, unless the appellant and the Commission otherwise agree, shall be—

(i) not earlier than 21 days and not later than 35 days after the date of receipt by the secretary of the notice of appeal; and

(ii) not earlier than 5 days after the date on which the notice is sent.

(2) The preliminary hearing shall be in private and shall be heard by the chairman.

(3) The appellant and the Commission and, in the case of an appeal under section 46(2) of the Act, the building society concerned may appear at the preliminary hearing and may be represented by counsel or solicitor or by any other person.

(4) At the preliminary hearing the chairman shall give such directions as he considers necessary or desirable for the conduct of the appeal and shall fix the date for the hearing.

(5) Notwithstanding that the preliminary hearing shall be in private, the other members of the Tribunal may attend and a member of the Council on Tribunals or the Scottish Committee of the Council on Tribunals may attend in his capacity as such.

Interim relief

11.—(1) On an application under section 47(5) of the Act for the suspension of the operation of any condition which is the subject of an appeal, the Tribunal may determine it on the basis of written representations if the parties so agree in writing or may direct the parties to appear before it.

(2) The Tribunal shall notify its determination and the reasons for it to the Commission and the building society which made the application for interim relief and may do so to any other party to the appeal or to any person to whom notice of the appeal has been given under regulation 5(2).

Amendment of grounds of appeal

12.—(1) An appellant may amend a notice of grounds of appeal at any time before the preliminary hearing and shall promptly notify any person to whom a copy of the notice was sent pursuant to regulation 5(2) of the amendment.

(2) An appellant may amend a notice of grounds of appeal in the course of the preliminary hearing with the leave of the chairman or at any time thereafter with the leave of the Tribunal.

(3) The chairman or the Tribunal shall not give such leave unless he or it has afforded the Commission an opportunity of making representations on the proposed amendment.

(4) Leave may be granted on such terms (if any), including terms as to costs or expenses, as the chairman or the Tribunal thinks fit.

(5) Where a notice of grounds of appeal is amended with leave the appellant shall promptly notify any person to whom a copy of the notice was sent pursuant to regulation 5(2) of the amendment.

Evidence and procedure at hearing

13.—(1) For the purposes of the appeal the chairman may, on the application of a party to the appeal or on his own motion, by direction given at the preliminary hearing or by notice in writing require any person, at a time and place stated in the direction or notice, to attend and give evidence or produce any document in that person's custody or under his control which relates to any matter in question at the hearing; provided that–

  (a) no person shall be required, in obedience to such direction or notice, to attend and give evidence or to produce any such document unless the necessary expenses of his attendance are paid or tendered to him; and

  (b) no person shall be compelled to give any evidence or produce any document which he could not be compelled to give or produce if the hearing were a proceeding in a court of law in that part of the United Kingdom where the appeal is to be determined; and

  (c) in exercising the power conferred by this paragraph the chairman shall take into account, in particular, the need to protect commercially sensitive information relating to a person not a party to the appeal.

(2) Except where the chairman otherwise directs, a witness shall not be obliged to attend and give evidence or produce any document in obedience to a direction of or notice from the chairman unless that direction or notice has been served on him not less than 5 days before the day appointed for the hearing.

(3) The chairman may set aside any direction or notice under this regulation on the application of the person to whom the direction was addressed but shall not do so without first notifying any person who applied for the direction and considering any representations made by that person.

(4) The secretary shall supply a copy of any documents obtained under this regulation to any party to the appeal if that party does not already have a copy of the document and it shall be a condition of such supply that the information so supplied shall be used only for the purposes of the appeal.

(5) The hearing shall, subject to section 48(2) of the Act, be in private unless, at the preliminary hearing or at any other time the chairman directs that the hearing or any part of it shall be in public, but nothing in this paragraph shall prevent a member of the Council on Tribunals or the Scottish Committee of the Council on Tribunals from attending the hearing, and (with the consent of the parties to the appeal) any deliberations of the Tribunal, in his capacity as such.

(6) The appellant and the Commission may appear at the hearing and may be represented by counsel or solicitor or by any other person.

(7) At the hearing the appellant and the Commission shall each be entitled to make an opening statement, to call witnesses to give evidence, to cross examine witnesses called by the other party and to make a final statement.

(8) Where the building society is entitled to be heard in accordance with section 48(2) of the Act, it may be represented by counsel or solicitor or by any other person or may make written representations.

(9) The Tribunal may require any witness to give evidence on oath or affirmation which may be administered for that purpose by the chairman.

(10) Subject to paragraph (1), evidence may be admitted by the Tribunal whether or not it would be admissible in a court of law.

(11) If the appellant or the Commission shall fail to appear or be represented at the time and place fixed for the hearing, the Tribunal may proceed with the hearing or adjourn it to a later date; and if it proceeds with the hearing, it shall take into consideration any written representations which may have been submitted by either party or, in the case of an appeal under section 46(2) of the Act, by the building society concerned, whether in accordance with any provision contained in these Regulations or otherwise.

(12) The Tribunal may from time to time adjourn the hearing and, if the date, time and place of the adjourned hearing are announced before the adjournment, no further notice shall be required.

Procedure after hearing

14.—(1) The Tribunal shall after the close of the hearing notify its determination and its reasons therefor in writing to the appellant and the Commission and may do so to any person who, having appeared at the hearing or having made written representations, has asked to be notified of the determination.

(2) The Tribunal may, after hearing representations from the parties, make arrangements for the publication of its determination but in doing so shall have regard to the desirability of safeguarding commercially sensitive information and the interests of investors and for that purpose may make any necessary amendments to the text of the decision to conceal the identity of the appellant.

(3) Where appeals have been consolidated pursuant to regulation 21, the Tribunal shall give its reasons for its determination–

   (a) in respect of the appeal by a building society to that society; and

   (b) in respect of the appeal brought by a person pursuant to section 46(2) of the Act to that person and to the society concerned.

Withdrawal of appeal

15.—(1) The appellant may withdraw the appeal at any time before the hearing by giving notice in writing to the Commission and to the secretary.

(2) The appellant may at the hearing give notice to the Tribunal that he or it desires to withdraw the appeal and thereupon the Tribunal shall bring the hearing to a close.

(3) The Commission may at any time withdraw its opposition to an appeal by giving notice to the appellant and the Tribunal.

(4) If an appeal is withdrawn, it shall be deemed to be dismissed and the Tribunal shall formally notify the persons referred to in regulation 14(1) accordingly.

(5) Where an appeal is withdrawn, or the Commission withdraws from an appeal, the Tribunal may give such directions as it thinks fit for the payment of costs or expenses by any party to the appeal.

Costs

16.—(1) Any costs or expenses directed to be paid under section 48(1) of the Act (which provides that the Tribunal may give such directions as it thinks fit for the payment of costs or expenses by any party to the appeal) and required to be taxed shall be taxed by a taxing master of the Supreme Court or, in Scotland, the Auditor of the Court of Session.

(2) A direction under section 48(1) of the Act in respect of the payment of costs by a party to the appeal shall, on application being made to the High Court by the party to whom costs have been directed to be paid, be enforceable as if he had obtained a judgement of that Court in his favour, and in Scotland the certificate of taxation of such expenses taxed in accordance with paragraph (1) may be enforced in like manner as an extract registered decree arbitral bearing a warrant for execution issued from the Books of Council and Session.

Time and miscellaneous powers

17.—(1) Where the time prescribed by or under these Regulations for doing any act expires on a Saturday, Sunday or public holiday and by reason thereof the act cannot be done on that day, the act shall be in time if done on the next working day.

(2) The periods referred to in regulations 8, 9 and 10 may be extended by the chairman on such terms (if any) as the chairman after consulting the parties thinks fit and any application for such extension may be granted although it is not made until after the expiration of the period.

(3) The chairman may, after consulting the parties–
  (a) postpone the date fixed for the hearing of an appeal; or
  (b) alter the place appointed for any hearing;

and, if he exercises either of the above powers, the secretary shall notify each party and any witnesses concerned and, in the case of an appeal under section 46(2) of the Act, the building society concerned of the revised arrangements.

Tribunal's power to determine its own procedure

18. Subject to the provisions of the Act and of these Regulations, the Tribunal shall have power to determine its own procedure.

Service of notices etc.

19.—(1) Any notice or other document to be sent, served or given to any person for the purposes of the appeal may be delivered or may be sent by first class recorded delivery service or registered letter–
  (a) in the case of a document directed to the Tribunal, to the address set out in regulation 4;
  (b) in the case of a document directed to the appellant or his representative, to the address provided in the notice of appeal in accordance with regulation 5 or such other address as may subsequently be notified to the Tribunal and the Commission;
  (c) in the case of a document directed to the Commission to the address shown on the notice of its decision;

(d) in any other case, to the last known address of the person to whom the document is directed;

and documents falling within (b) or (d) above, if sent, served or given to the authorised representative of any person, shall be deemed to be sent, served or given to that person.

(2) Any such notice or other document may be sent, served or given by telex or other similar means which produce a document containing the text of the communication.

Irregularities

20—(1) Any irregularity resulting from failure to comply with any provision of these Regulations before the Tribunal have reached their decision shall not of itself render the proceedings void.

(2) In any such case the Tribunal may, and shall if they consider that any person may have been prejudiced, take such steps as they think fit before reaching their decision to cure the irregularity.

(3) Clerical mistakes in any document recording a decision of the chairman or Tribunal, or errors arising in such a document from an accidental slip or omission, may be corrected by the chairman by certificate under his hand.

Consolidation of appeals

21.   Where in making its decision the Commission made a determination that a person is not a fit and proper person to hold or, as the case may be, to remain in an office in the society or imposed a requirement that he be removed from an office in the society and both the society and the person concerned appeal against the decision, the chairman may, at the preliminary hearing or at some other time, direct that the two appeals shall be consolidated provided that the chairman shall not make such a direction without giving all parties concerned an opportunity to show cause why such a direction should not be made.

Peter Lloyd
Mark Lennox-Boyd
13th May 1987   Two of the Lords Commissioners
of Her Majesty's Treasury

SCHEDULE   Regulation 9

DOCUMENTS TO BE SENT TO THE TRIBUNAL BY THE COMMISSION

1.   In the case of an appeal against a decision of the Commission to refuse to grant or renew authorisation—
   (a) a copy of the application for authorisation submitted under paragraph 2(1) of Schedule 3 to the Act,
   (b) a copy of any information submitted under paragraph 2(1) or (2) thereof,
   (c) a copy of any notice served by the Commission under paragraph 2(4) thereof,
   (d) a copy of any written representations and a record of any oral representations made in accordance with paragraph 2(4) or (5) thereof, and
   (e) a copy of the notice served under paragraph 2(7) thereof.

2.   In the case of an appeal against a decision of the Commission to revoke authorisation—
   (a) a copy of the authorisation,
   (b) a copy of the notice served under paragraph 6(1) of Schedule 3 to the Act,

(c)   a copy of any written representations and a record of any oral representations made in accordance with paragraph 6(1) or (2) thereof, and

(d)   a copy of the notice served under paragraph 6(3) thereof.

3.   In the case of an appeal against a decision of the Commission to impose conditions or as to the conditions imposed–

(a)   a copy of any notice served under paragraph 4(1), 5(2), 7(2) or 8(2) of Schedule 3 to the Act,

(b)   a copy of any written representations and a record of any oral representations made in accordance with paragraph 4(1) or (2), 5(2) or (3), 7(2) or (3) or 8(2) or (3) thereof, and

(c)   a copy of any notice served under paragraph 4(3), 5(4), 7(4) or 8(4) thereof.

4.   In the case of an appeal under section 46(2) of the Act–

(a)   a copy of any notice served under paragraph 2(5), 4(2), 5(3), 6(2), 7(3) or 8(3) of Schedule 3 to the Act,

(b)   a copy of any written representations and a record of any oral representations made by the appellant in accordance with paragraph 2(5), 4(2), 5(3), 6(2), 7(3) or 8(3) thereof, and

(c)   a copy of any notice served under paragraph 2(7), 4(3), 5(4), 7(4) or 8(4) thereof.

EXPLANATORY NOTE

(This note is not part of the Regulations)

These Regulations make provision with respect to appeals under section 46 of the Building Societies Act 1986 against decisions of the Building Societies Commission to refuse to grant authorisation, to revoke authorisation or to impose conditions or as to the conditions imposed or that a person is not a fit and proper person to be an officer of a building society. Provision is made as to the time and manner in which appeals are to be brought, the evidence and procedure at the hearing, the procedure after the hearing, the payment of costs of appeals and other miscellaneous matters connected with them.

STATUTORY INSTRUMENTS

1987 No. 892

TAXES

The Estate Duty (Interest on Unpaid Duty) Order 1987

Made - - - -	*13th May 1987*
Laid before the House of Commons	*14th May 1987*
Coming into force	*6th June 1987*

The Treasury, in exercise of the powers conferred by section 30 of the Finance Act 1970(**a**), hereby make the following Order:

1. This Order may be cited as the Estate Duty (Interest on Unpaid Duty) Order 1987 and shall come into force on 6th June 1987.

2. The rate of interest payable under the following enactments, namely:

(a) section 18 of the Finance Act 1896(**b**);

(b) section 61(5) of the Finance (1909–10) Act 1910(**c**); and

(c) section 17(3) of the Law of Property Act 1925(**d**) and section 73(6) of the Land Registration Act 1925(**e**),

shall, as regards interest accruing on or after 6th June 1987 be 6 per cent. per annum.

3. Section 8(9) of the Finance Act 1894(**f**) shall, as regards interest accruing on or after 6th June 1987, have effect with the substitution of the word "six" for the word "eight".

Peter Lloyd
Mark Lennox-Boyd
13th May 1987   Two of the Lords Commissioners of Her Majesty's Treasury

---

EXPLANATORY NOTE

(This note is not part of the Order)

Estate Duty is chargeable in relation to deaths before 13th March 1975; it was replaced for deaths on or after that date by capital transfer tax, now known as inheritance tax. Article 2 of this Order provides that interest on unpaid estate duty will run at 6 per cent. (instead of at the previous rate of 8 per cent. as imposed by S.I. 1986/1942) under the various provisions which impose a fixed rate of interest. By Article 3 the limit on the discretionary rate of interest which may be charged where payment of estate duty is postponed on grounds of hardship is correspondingly altered by substituting 6 per cent. for 8 per cent. The effect of this Order in conjunction with section 48(1) of the Finance Act 1975 (c.7) is that from 6th June 1987 interest will also run at 6 per cent. when overpaid estate duty is repaid.

(**a**) 1970 c.24.   (**b**) 1896 c.28.   (**c**) 1910 c.8; section 61(5) was amended by section 9 of the Finance Act 1912 (c.8).   (**d**) 1925 c.20.   (**e**) 1925 c.21.   (**f**) 1894 c.30.

STATUTORY INSTRUMENTS

1987 No. 893

NORTHERN IRELAND

The Estate Duty (Northern Ireland) (Interest on Unpaid Duty) Order 1987

Made - - - -	*13th May 1987*
Laid before Parliament	*15th May 1987*
Coming into force	*6th June 1987*

The Treasury, in exercise of the powers conferred by section 1(2) of the Finance Act (Northern Ireland) 1970 (**a**) now vested in them (**b**) hereby make the following Order:

1. This Order may be cited as the Estate Duty (Northern Ireland) (Interest on Unpaid Duty) Order 1987 and shall come into force on 6th June 1987.

2. The rate of interest payable under the following enactments, namely–
(a) section 18 of the Finance Act 1896(**c**) ;
(b) section 61(5) of the Finance (1909–10) Act 1910(**d**),
shall, as regards interest accruing on or after 6th June 1987 be 6 per cent. per annum.

3. Section 8(9) of the Finance Act 1894(**e**) shall, as regards interest accruing on or after 6th June 1987 have effect with the substitution of the word "six" for the word "eight".

Peter Lloyd
Mark Lennox-Boyd
13th May 1987   Two of the Lords Commissioners of Her Majesty's Treasury

---

(**a**) 1970 c.21 (N.I.).   (**b**) The Northern Ireland (Modification of Enactments—No. 1) Order 1973 (S.I. 1973/2163), article 5(3) and Schedule 3 transferred this function from the Ministry of Finance to the Treasury. Article 9 of the same Order provides that the powers conferred by section 1(2) of the 1970 Act shall be exercisable by Statutory Instrument.   (**c**) 1896 c.28.   (**d**) 1910 c.8; section 61(5) was amended by section 9 of the Finance Act 1912 (c.8).   (**d**) 1894 c.30.

EXPLANATORY NOTE

(This note is not part of the Order)

Estate Duty is chargeable in relation to deaths before 13th March 1975; it was replaced for deaths on or after that date by capital transfer tax, now known as inheritance tax. Article 2 of this Order provides that interest on unpaid estate duty will run at 6 per cent. (instead of at the previous rate of 8 per cent. as imposed by S.I. 1986/1943) under the various provisions which impose a fixed rate of interest. By Article 3 the limit on the discretionary rate of interest which may be charged where payment of estate duty is postponed on grounds of hardship is correspondingly altered by substituting 6 per cent. for 8 per cent. The effect of this Order in conjunction with section 48(1) of the Finance Act 1975 (c.7) is that from 6th June 1987 interest will also run at 6 per cent. when overpaid estate duty is repaid.

STATUTORY INSTRUMENTS

1987 No. 894 (S.76)

LEGAL AID AND ADVICE, SCOTLAND

The Legal Aid (Scotland) (Fees in Civil Proceedings) Amendment (No.2) Regulations 1987

Made - - - -	*14th May 1987*
Laid before Parliament	*15th May 1987*
Coming into force	*5th June 1987*

The Secretary of State, in exercise of the powers conferred upon him by sections 14A and 15 of the Legal Aid (Scotland) Act 1967(**a**) as read with section 45, of and paragraph 3(1) of Schedule 4 to, the Legal Aid (Scotland) Act 1986(**b**), and of all other powers enabling him in that behalf, hereby makes the following Regulations:

1.—(1) These Regulations may be cited as the Legal Aid (Scotland) (Fees in Civil Proceedings) Amendment (No. 2) Regulations 1987 and shall come into force on 5th June 1987.

(2) In these Regulations "the principal Regulations" means the Legal Aid (Scotland) (Fees in Civil Proceedings) Regulations 1984(**c**).

2. For the Table of Fees in Schedule 1 to the principal Regulations (fees of solicitors for proceedings in the Court of Session) there shall be substituted the Table of Fees set out in Schedule 1 to these Regulations.

3. For the Table of Fees in Schedule 2 to the principal Regulations (fees of solicitors for proceedings in the Sheriff Court) there shall be substituted the Table of Fees set out in Schedule 2 to these Regulations.

4. The amendments to the principal Regulations made by regulations 2 and 3 of these Regulations shall apply only to fees for work done on or after 5th June 1987.

New St. Andrew's House, Edinburgh
14th May 1987

Ian Lang
Parliamentary Under Secretary of State,
Scottish Office

(**a**) 1967 c.43; section 14A was inserted by section 3 of the Divorce Jurisdiction, Court Fees and Legal Aid (Scotland) Act 1983 (c.12).
(**b**) 1986 c.47.
(**c**) S.I. 1984/519; relevant amending instruments are S.I. 1985/557 and 1986/681.

SCHEDULE 1   Regulation 2

TABLE OF FEES

CHAPTER 1

DETAILED FEES

1.	(a) Framing precognitions and other papers (not affidavits), not drawn by counsel – per sheet	£3.70
	(b) Framing formal documents such as inventories, title pages and accounts of expenses etc. – per sheet	£1.60
	(c) Framing affidavits – per sheet	£5.80

Note: (i) The sheet throughout this Table of Fees shall consist of 250 words or numbers.

(ii) The solicitor shall be entitled to charge for copies of the precognitions for the use of counsel and himself.

(iii) Where a skilled witness prepares his own precognition or report the solicitor shall be allowed half drawing fees for revising and adjusting it.

(iv) Where the business can properly be performed by a local solicitor the auditor in taxing an account shall allow such expenses as would have been incurred if it had been done by the nearest local solicitor, including reasonable fees for instructing and corresponding with him, unless the auditor is satisfied that it was in the interests of the client that the solicitor in charge of the case should attend personally.

2.	*Copying papers by any means*	
	First copy – per sheet	£0.71
	Additional copies – per sheet	£0.30

Note: When copied by photostatic or similar process each page shall be charged as one sheet.

3.	*Revising papers drawn by counsel, open and closed records etc.*	
	For each five sheets or part thereof.	£1.60
4.	*Citation of parties, witnesses, havers, instructions to messengers-at-arms*	
	Each party	£3.15
	Each witness or haver	£3.15
	Instructing messenger-at-arms including examining execution and settling fee	£3.15
5.	*Time charges*	
	(a) Attendance at meetings, preparation for proof, trial or debate, attendance at court, consultation with counsel, etc.–	
	Per half hour	£11.45
	or such other sum as in the opinion of the auditor is justified.	
	(b) Perusal of documents–	
	Per half hour	£6.25
	or such other sum as in the opinion of the auditor is justified.	
	(c) Allowance for time of clerk – one half of the fee in sub-paragraph (a) or (b) above.	
	(d) Attendance at court offices for performance of formal work (other than lodging process or first step of process).	£1.60
	Lodging first step of process	£3.15
	Additional fee for making up and lodging process	£1.60

Note: (i) Time necessarily occupied in travelling to be regarded as if occupied on business.

(ii) In the event of a party in a trial or proof being represented by one counsel only, allowance may be made to the solicitor should the case warrant it for the attendance of a clerk at one-half the rate chargeable for the solicitor's attendance.

6.   *Correspondence*

Letters (save as provided below) including instructions to counsel – each page of 125 words	£3.15
Formal letters	£0.75
Telegrams or telephone calls, including letters confirming	£1.60

CHAPTER II

PART I – UNDEFENDED ACTIONS

(OTHER THAN CONSISTORIAL ACTIONS)

1.	Inclusive fee to pursuer's solicitor in all undefended cases where no proof is led, to cover all work from taking instructions up to and including obtaining extract decree	£66.70

PART II – UNDEFENDED CONSISTORIAL ACTIONS

(OTHER THAN ACTIONS TO WHICH PART III APPLIES)

1.	Fee for all work (other than precognitions) up to and including the calling of summons in court	£94.80
Note:	Precognitions to be charged as in Part V, paragraph 5 of this Chapter	
2.	*Incidental procedures*	
	Fixing diet, enrolling action, preparation for proof, citing witnesses, etc.	£53.65
3.	*Amendment*	
	(a) Where summons amended, where re-service is not ordered, and motion is not starred	£13.55
	(b) Where summons amended, where re-service is not ordered and motion is starred	£19.80
	(c) Where summons amended and re-service is ordered	£25.05
4.	*Commissions to take evidence on interrogatories*	
	(a) Basic fee to cover all work up to and including lodging completed interrogatories	£19.80
	(b) Additional fee for completed interrogatories, including all copies – per sheet	£4.15
5.	*Commissions to take evidence on open commission*	
	(a) Basic fee to solicitor applying for commission but excluding attendance at execution thereof	£22.35
	(b) Attendance at execution of commission – per half hour	£11.45
6.	Where applicable the fees set out in paragraphs 6, 7, 10, 14, 16 and 21 of Part V of this Chapter may be charged.	
7.	*Proof and completion fee* – excluding accounts of expenses but including instructing counsel for proof, attendance at proof, settling with witnesses, borrowing and returning productions, procuring interlocutor, and obtaining extract decree of divorce	£66.70
8.	*Accounts*	
	Framing and lodging account and attending taxation	£21.35

PART III – UNDEFENDED CONSISTORIAL ACTIONS: AFFIDAVIT PROCEDURE

1.   In any undefended action of divorce or separation where–

       (a) the facts set out in section 1(2)(b) (unreasonable behaviour) of the Divorce (Scotland) Act 1976(**a**) are relied upon; and

---

(**a**) 1976 c.39.

(b) the pursuer seeks to prove those facts by means of affidavits–

the pursuer's solicitor may in respect of the work specified in column 1 of
Table A in this paragraph charge, in a case where he is an Edinburgh
solicitor acting alone, the inclusive fee specified in respect of that work in
column 2 of that Table, and, in any other case, the inclusive fee specified
in respect of that work in column 3 of that Table.

TABLE A

Column 1	Column 2	Column 3
Work done	*Inclusive fee Edinburgh solicitor acting alone*	*Inclusive fee any other case*
1. All work to and including calling of the summons	£138.25	£158.05
2. All work from calling to and including swearing affidavits	£98.75	£118.50
3. All work from swearing affidavits to and including sending extract decree	£29.60	£44.40
4. All work to and including sending extract decree	£266.65	£320.95
Add session fee to item 4	of 7½%	of 10%

2.   In any undefended action of divorce or separation where–

(a) the facts set out in section 1(2)(a) (adultery), 1(2)(c) (desertion), 1(2)(d)
(two years' non-cohabitation and consent) or 1(2)(e) (five years' non-
cohabitation) of the Divorce (Scotland) Act 1976 are relied on; and

(b) the pursuer seeks to prove these facts by means of affidavits–

the pursuer's solicitor may in respect of the work specified in column 1 of
Table B in this paragraph charge, in a case where he is an Edinburgh
solicitor acting alone, the inclusive fee specified in respect of that work in
column 2 of that Table, and, in any other case, the inclusive fee specified
in respect of that work in column 3 of that Table.

TABLE B

Column 1	Column 2	Column 3
Work done	*Inclusive fee Edinburgh solicitor acting alone*	*Inclusive fee any other case*
1. All work to and including calling of the summons	£113.55	£133.30
2. All work from calling to and including swearing affidavits	£54.35	£69.15
3. All work from swearing affidavits to and including sending extract decree	£29.60	£44.40
4. All work to and including sending extract decree	£197.50	£246.90
Add session fee to item 4	of 7½%	of 10%

3.   If–

(a) the pursuer's solicitor charges an inclusive fee under either paragraph 1
or paragraph 2 of this Part, and

(b) the action to which the charge relates includes a conclusion relating to
an ancillary matter–

in addition to that fee, he may charge in respect of the work specified in
column 1 of Table C in this paragraph the inclusive fee specified in
respect of that work in column 2 of that Table.

TABLE C

Column 1	Column 2
Work done	*Inclusive fee*
1. All work to and including calling of the summons	£27.65
2. All work from calling to and including swearing affidavits	£31.60
3. All work under items 1 and 2	£59.25

Add session fee to item 3 of 7½% in the case of an Edinburgh solicitor acting alone and 10% in any other case.

PART IV – OUTER HOUSE PETITIONS

A. Unopposed petitions

1. Fee for all work, including precognitions and all copyings, up to and obtaining extract decree–

    (a) in the case of an Edinburgh solicitor acting alone — £139.65

    (b) in any other case — £194.90

Note: Outlays including duplicating charges to be allowed in addition.

B. Opposed petitions

2. Fee for all work (other than precognitions) up to and including lodging petition, obtaining and executing warrant for service — £94.80

Note: Outlays including duplicating charges to be allowed in addition.

3. Where applicable, the fees set out in paragraphs 5, 6, 7, 10, 12, 14, 18, 19, 20 and 21 of Part V of this Chapter may be charged.

4. Reports–

    (a) For each report by Accountant of Court — £16.70

    (b) For any other report as under Part V, paragraph 6 of this Chapter.

5. Obtaining Bond of Caution — £16.70

PART V – DEFENDED ACTIONS

1. *Instruction fee*

    (a) To cover all work (apart from precognitions) until lodgement of open record — £131.30

    (b) Instructing re-service where necessary — £14.05

    (c) If counter-claim lodged, additional fee for solicitor for each party — £27.65

2. *Record fee*

    (a) To cover all work in connection with adjustment and closing of record including subsequent work in connection with By Order Adjustment Roll — £139.65

    (b) To cover all work as above, so far as applicable, where action settled or disposed of before record closed — £87.00

    (c) If consultation held before record closed, additional fees may be allowed as follows:–

    (i) Arranging consultation — £14.05

    (ii) Attendance at consultation – per half hour — £11.45

    (d) Additional fee (to include necessary amendments) to the solicitors for the existing pursuer and each existing defender, to be allowed for each pursuer, defender or third party brought in before the record is closed, each of — £41.15

    (e) Additional fee to the solicitors for existing pursuer and each existing defender, to be allowed for each pursuer, defender, or third party brought in after the record is closed, each of — £61.45

3. *Procedure Roll or Debate Roll*

    (a) Preparing for discussion and all work incidental thereto including instruction of counsel — £27.65

	(b) Attendance at court – per half-hour	£11.45
	(c) Advising and work incidental thereto	£20.85
4.	*Adjustment of issues and counter-issues*	
	(a) Fee to solicitor for pursuer to include all work in connection with and incidental to the lodging of an issue, and adjustment and approval thereof	£26.60
	(b) If one counter-issue, additional fee to solicitor for pursuer	£7.30
	(c) If more than one counter-issue, additional fee to solicitor for pursuer for each additional counter-issue	£3.15
	(d) Fee to solicitor for defender or third party for all work in connection with lodging of counter-issue and adjustment and approval thereof	£26.60
	(e) Fee to solicitor for defender or third party for considering issue where no counter-issue lodged	£7.30
	(f) Fee to solicitor for defender or third party for considering each additional counter-issue	£3.15
5.	*Precognitions*	
	Taking and drawing precognitions – per sheet	£13.55
Note:	(i) In addition each solicitor shall be entitled to charge for copies of the precognitions for the use of counsel and himself.	
	(ii) Where a skilled witness prepares his own precognition or report the solicitor shall be allowed, for revising and adjusting it, half of the taking and drawing fee per sheet.	
6.	*Reports obtained under order of court excluding auditor's report*	
	(a) Fee for all work incidental thereto	£29.20
	(b) Additional fee per sheet of report to include all copies required (maximum £27.60)	£4.15
7.	*Specification of documents*	
	(a) Basic fee to cover instructing counsel, revising and lodging and all incidental procedures to obtain a diligence up to and including obtaining interlocutor	£27.65
	(b) Fee to opponent's solicitor	£13.55
	(c) If commission executed, additional fee – per half hour	£11.45
	(d) If alternative procedure adopted, fee per person upon whom order served	£10.95
8.	*Commission to take evidence on interrogatories*	
	(a) Basic fee to solicitor applying for commission to cover all work up to and including lodging report of commission with completed interrogatories and cross-interrogatories	£55.75
	(b) Basic fee to opposing solicitor if cross-interrogatories lodged	£44.85
	(c) Fee to opposing solicitor if no cross-interrogatories lodged	£16.70
	(d) Additional fee to solicitor for each party for completed interrogatories or cross-interrogatories, including all copies – per sheet	£4.15
9.	*Commission to take evidence on open commission*	
	(a) Basic fee to solicitor applying for commission up to and including lodging report of commission, but excluding attendance at execution thereof	£61.45
	(b) Basic fee to opposing solicitor	£27.65
	(c) Attendance at execution of commission – per half hour	£11.45
10.	*Miscellaneous motions where not otherwise covered by this Chapter*	
	(a) Where attendance of counsel or solicitor or both not required	£7.30
	(b) Where attendance of counsel or solicitor or both required, inclusive of instruction of counsel – not exceeding half hour	£20.85
	(c) Thereafter attendance fee – per additional half hour	£11.45
11.	*Incidental procedure (not chargeable prior to approval of issue or allowance of proof)*	
	Fixing diet, obtaining note on the line of evidence, etc., borrowing and returning process, lodging productions, considering opponent's productions, and all other work prior to the consultation on the sufficiency of evidence	£78.20

12.   *Amendment of record*

   (a) Amendment of conclusions only – fee to solicitor for pursuer   £20.85

   (b) Amendment of conclusions only – fee to solicitor for opponent   £7.30

   (c) Amendment of pleadings after record closed, where no answers to the   £30.25
       amendment are lodged – fee to solicitor for proposer

   (d) In same circumstances – fee to solicitor for opponent   £14.05

   (e) Amendment of pleadings after record closed where answers are lodged –   £71.35
       fee for solicitor for each party lodging answers

   (f) Fee for adjustment of minute and answers, where applicable, to be   £39.10
       allowed in addition to solicitor for each party

13.   *Preparation for trial or proof to include fixing consultation on the sufficiency
       of evidence and attendance thereat, fee-funding precept, adjusting minute
       of admissions, citing witnesses, all work checking and writing up process,
       and preparing for trial or proof*

   (a) If action settled before trial or proof, or the trial or proof lasts only one   £189.65
       day, to include, where applicable, instruction of counsel

   (b) For each day or part of a day after the first, including instruction of   £16.70
       counsel

   (c) To cover preparing for adjourned diet and all work incidental as in (a),   £34.40
       if diet postponed more than 5 days

14.   *Copying*

   Productions, reports of commissions, duplicate inventory, jury list, list of
       witnesses, Lord Ordinary's opinion, etc. – as per Chapter I, paragraph 2.

15.   *Settlement by tender – fees for solicitor for either party*

   (a) Basic fee for lodging, or for considering, first tender   £41.15

   (b) Fee for lodging, or for considering, each further tender   £27.65

   (c) Additional fee if tender accepted   £27.65

16.   *Extra-judicial settlement*

   Fee inclusive of joint minute (not based on a judicial tender)   £71.35

17.   *Proof or trial*

   Attendance fee – per half-hour   £11.45

18.   *Accounts* – to include framing and lodging account, intimating diet, and   £50.05
       attending taxation, uplifting account and noting and intimating taxations

19.   *Ordering and obtaining extract*   £10.45

20.   *Final procedure*

   (a) If case goes to trial or proof, to include all work to close of litigation, so   £55.75
       far as not otherwise provided for, including in particular settling with
       witnesses and procuring and booking verdict, or attendance at judgement

   (b) If case disposed of before trial or proof   £16.70

21.   *Session fee – to cover communications with client and counsel*

   (a) Where no correspondent – 7½% of total fees (including copying fees)
       allowed on taxation

   (b) Where correspondent involved – 10% of total fees (including copying
       fees) allowed on taxation.

PART VI – INNER HOUSE BUSINESS

1.   *Reclaiming motions*

   (a) Fee for solicitor for appellant for all work up to interlocutor sending   £41.15
       case to roll

   (b) Fee for solicitor for respondent   £20.85

   (c) Additional fee for solicitor for each party for every 50 pages of appendix   £17.20

2.   *Appeals from inferior courts*

   (a) Fee for solicitor for appellant   £50.05

   (b) Fee for solicitor for respondent   £24.50

   (c) Additional fee for solicitor for each party for every 50 pages of appendix   £17.20

3.   *Summar or Short Roll*

     (a) Preparing for discussion, instructing counsel, and preparing appendix   £41.15

     (b) Attendance fee – per half-hour   £11.45

4.   Where applicable the fees set out in Part V of this Chapter may be charged.

5.   *Special cases and Inner House petitions*

     According to circumstances of the case.

6.   Obtaining Bond of Caution   £16.70

PART VII – ADMIRALTY AND COMMERCIAL CASES, SEQUESTRATIONS IN BANKRUPTCY, APPLICATIONS FOR SUMMARY TRIAL UNDER SECTION 10 OF THE ADMINISTRATION OF JUSTICE (SCOTLAND) ACT 1933(a) AND CASES REMITTED FROM THE SHERIFF COURT

The fees shall be based on this Table of Fees according to the circumstances.

SCHEDULE 2   Regulation 3

TABLE OF FEES

CHAPTER I – UNDEFENDED ACTIONS (OTHER THAN ACTIONS TO WHICH CHAPTER IV OR V APPLIES)

Part I – All actions except those actions of divorce or separation and aliment to which Part II applies

1.   Actions (other than those specified in paragraph 2 of this Part) in which decree is granted without proof–

     Inclusive fee to cover all work from taking instructions up to and including obtaining extract decree   £41.15

     In cases where settlement is effected after service of a writ but before the expiry of the period of notice   £35.45

2.   Actions of separation and aliment (not being actions to which Part II of this Chapter applies), adherence and aliment or custody and aliment where proof takes place–

     Inclusive fee to cover all work from taking instructions up to and including obtaining extract decree   £194.90

Part II – Actions of divorce or separation and aliment where proof is by means of affidavits

1.   In any undefended action of divorce or of separation and aliment where–

     (a) the facts set out in section 1(2)(b) (unreasonable behaviour) of the Divorce (Scotland) Act 1976 are relied upon; and

     (b) the pursuer seeks to prove those facts by means of affidavits–

     the pursuer's solicitor may in respect of the work specified in column 1 of Table A in this paragraph charge the inclusive fee specified in respect of that work in column 2 of that Table.

TABLE A

Column 1	Column 2
Work done	*Inclusive fee*
1. All work to and including the period of notice	£138.25
2. All work from the period of notice to and including swearing affidavits	£98.75
3. All work from swearing affidavits to and including sending extract decree	£29.60
4. All work to and including sending extract decree	£266.65
Add process fee to item 4	of 10%

(a) 1933 c.41.

2.   In any undefended action of divorce or separation and aliment where–

(a) the facts set out in section 1(2)(a) (adultery), 1(2)(c) (desertion), 1(2)(d) (two years' non-cohabitation and consent) or 1(2)(e) (five years' non-cohabitation) of the Divorce (Scotland) Act 1976 are relied on; and

(b) the pursuer seeks to prove those facts by means of affidavits–

the pursuer's solicitor may in respect of the work specified in column 1 of Table B in this paragraph charge the inclusive fee specified in respect of that work in column 2 of that Table.

TABLE B

Column 1	Column 2
Work done	*Inclusive fee*
1. All work to and including the period of notice	£113.55
2. All work from the period of notice to and including swearing affidavits	£54.35
3. All work from swearing affidavits to and including sending extract decree	£29.60
4. All work to and including sending extract decree	£197.50
Add process fee to item 4	of 10%

3.   If–

(a) the pursuer's solicitor charges an inclusive fee under either paragraph 1 or paragraph 2 of this Part; and

(b) the action to which the charge relates includes a crave relating to an ancillary matter–

in addition to that fee, he may charge in respect of the work specified in column 1 of Table C in this paragraph the inclusive fee specified in respect of that work in column 2 of that Table.

TABLE C

Column 1	Column 2
Work done	*Inclusive fee*
1. All work to and including the period of notice	£53.80
2. All work from the period of notice to and including swearing affidavits	£31.60
3. All work under items 1 and 2	£85.40

CHAPTER II – DEFENDED ACTIONS (OTHER THAN ACTIONS TO WHICH CHAPTER IV OR V APPLIES)

1. *Instruction fee* – to cover all work (except as hereinafter otherwise specially provided for in this Chapter) to the lodging of defences including copyings	£89.10
Additional fee where separate statement of facts and counter claim answers lodged	£31.30
2. *Adjustment fee* – to cover all work (except as hereinafter otherwise specially provided for in this Chapter) in connection with the adjustment of the record including (when appropriate) closing thereof, making up and lodging closed record and copyings–	
(a) See to solicitor for any party	£133.35
(b) See to each original party's solicitor if action settled before record is closed	£89.10
(c) Additional fee to each original party's solicitor if additional defender brought in before closing of record	£15.65
(d) Additional fee to each original party's solicitor if additional defender brought in after closing of record	£22.40
3. *Fee for framing affidavits* – per sheet	£5.80

4. (a) *Debate fee* – to include preparation for and conduct of any hearing or debate other than on evidence, enquiring for cause at avizandum and noting interlocutor–

    When debate does not exceed 1 hour £66.75

    For every half hour engaged after the first hour £15.65

    (b) *Interim interdict hearings*–

    Pursuer's solicitor – the same fees as for debate fee above, but to include both the appearance at lodging of writ and the hearing at second diet.

    Defender's solicitor's fee where the debate does not exceed 1 hour £39.05

5. *Precognitions* – taking and drawing – per sheet £13.55

    Note: Where a skilled witness prepares his own precognition or report, the solicitor shall be allowed half of above drawing fee for revising and adjusting it.

5A. *Reports obtained under order of court, excluding auditor's report*

    (a) Fee for all work incidental thereto £29.20

    (b) Additional fee per sheet of report to include all copies required (maximum £29.00) £4.15

6. *Commissions to take evidence*

    (a) On interrogatories

    Fee to solicitor applying for commission to include drawing, intimating and lodging motion, drawing and lodging interrogatories, instructing commissioner and all incidental work (except as otherwise specially provided for in this Chaper) but excluding attendance at execution of commission £83.35

    Fee to opposing solicitor if cross-interrogatories prepared and lodged £55.75

    If no cross-interrogatories lodged £16.70

    (b) Open commissions

    Fee to solicitor applying for commission to include all work (except as otherwise specially provided for in this Chapter) up to lodging report of commission but excluding attendance thereat £50.05

    Fee to solicitor for opposing party £27.65

    Fee for attendance at execution of commission – per half hour £15.65

    Travelling time – per half hour £11.45

7. *Specification of documents*

    Fee to cover drawing, intimating and lodging specification and relative motion and attendance at court debating specification £34.40

    Inclusive fee to opposing solicitor £22.35

    Fee for citation of havers, preparation for and attendance before commissioner at execution of commission–

    Where attendance before commissioner does not exceed 1 hour £31.30

    For each additional half hour after the first hour £15.65

    If commission not executed – fee for serving each party with a copy of specification to include recovering and examining documents or productions referred to therein £6.85

8. *Amendment of record*

    Fee to cover drawing, intimating and lodging minute of amendment and relative motion and relative attendance at court

    (a) Where answers lodged £38.05

    (b) Where no answers lodged £25.05

    Inclusive fee to opposing solicitor–

    (a) Where answers lodged £31.30

    (b) Where no answers lodged £20.85

    Additional fee to solicitor for each party for adjustment of minute and answers, where applicable £27.65

9. *Motions and minutes*

Fee to cover drawing, intimating and lodging any written motion or minute, including a reponing note, and relative attendances at court (except as otherwise provided for in this Chapter)–

(a) Where opposed   £39.05

(b) Where unopposed (including for each party a joint minute other than under paragraph 14(b))   £27.65

Fee to cover considering opponent's written motion, minute or reponing note and relative attendances at court–

(a) Where motion, minute or reponing note opposed   £22.35

(b) Where motion, minute or reponing note unopposed   £14.10

10. *Procedure preliminary to proof*

(a) Fee to cover fixing diet of proof, citation of witnesses, and generally preparing for proof and if necessary instructing shorthand writer   £55.75

(b) Fee to cover preparing for adjourned diet and all incidental work as in subparagraph (a) above if diet postponed for more than 6 days – for each additional diet   £33.35

(c) Drawing and lodging an inventory of productions, lodging the productions specified therein, and considering opponent's productions (to be charged once only in each process)   £14.10

Where only one party lodges productions, opponent's solicitor's fee for considering same   £7.30

11. *Conduct of proof*

Fee to cover conduct of proof and debate on evidence if taken at close of proof – per half hour   £15.65

If counsel employed, fee to solicitor appearing with counsel – per half hour   £11.45

12. *Debate on evidence*

Where debate on evidence not taken at conclusion of proof, fee for preparing for debate   £27.65

Fee for conduct of debate – per half hour   £15.65

If counsel employed, fee to solicitor appearing with counsel – per half hour   £11.45

13. *Appeals*

(a) To sheriff principal

Fee to cover instructions, marking of appeal or noting that appeal marked, noting diet of hearing thereof and preparation for hearing   £52.15

Fee to cover conduct of hearing – per half hour   £15.65

If counsel employed, fee to solicitor appearing with counsel – per half hour   £11.45

(b) To Court of Session

Fee to cover instructions, marking appeal or noting that appeal marked and instructing Edinburgh correspondents   £26.05

14. *Settlements*

(a) Judicial tender

Fee for preparation and lodging or for consideration of minute of tender   £30.70

Fee on acceptance of tender, to include preparation and lodging or consideration of minute of acceptance and attendance at court when decree granted in terms thereof   £22.95

(b) Extra-judicial settlements

Fee to cover negotiations resulting in settlement, framing or revising joint minute and attendance at court when authority interponed thereto   £52.15

15. *Final procedure*

Fee to cover settling with witnesses, enquiries for cause at avizandum, noting final interlocutor   £41.15

Fee to cover drawing account of expenses, arranging, intimating and attending diet of taxation and obtaining approval of auditor's report and adjusting account with opponent where necessary, ordering, procuring and examining extract decree   £33.35

Fee to cover considering opponent's account of expenses and attending diet of taxation or adjusting account with opponent   £10.45

16.	*Copying fees*	
	Copying all necessary papers by any means–	
	First copy – per sheet	£0.71
	Additional copies – per sheet	£0.30
Note:	A sheet shall be 250 words. When copied by photostatic or similar process, each page shall be charged as one sheet.	
17.	*Process fee*	
	Fee to cover all consultations between solicitor and client during the progress of the cause and all communications, written or verbal, passing between them:	
	10% on total fees (including copying fees) allowed on taxation.	
18.	*Fee for instruction of counsel*	
	Fee for instructing counsel to revise record	£17.15
	Fee for instructing counsel to conduct debate or proof	£34.40
	Fee for instructing counsel to conduct appeal to sheriff principal	£34.40
Note:	In each case to cover all consultations, revisal of papers and all incidental work.	

CHAPTER III – CHARGES FOR TIME, DRAWING OF PAPERS, CORRESPONDENCE, ETC.

1.	Attendance at court conducting proof or formal debate or hearing - per half hour	£15.65
2.	Time occupied in the performance of all other work including attendances with client and others and attendances at court in all circumstances, except as otherwise specifically provided–	
	(a) Solicitor – per half hour	£11.45
	(b) Allowance for time of clerk – one half of above.	
Note:	Time necessarily occupied in travelling to such to be chargeable at these rates.	
3.	Drawing all necessary papers other than affidavits (the sheet throughout this Chapter to consist of 250 words or numbers) – per sheet	£3.70
4.	Framing affidavits – per sheet	£5.80
5.	Revising papers where revisal ordered – for each five sheets	£1.60
6.	Copying all necessary papers by any means–	
	First copy – per sheet	£0.71
	Additional copies – per sheet	£0.30
Note:	When copied by photostatic or similar process each page shall be charged as one sheet.	
7.	Certifying or signing a document	£1.60
8.	Perusing any document (other than a letter) not exceeding 2 sheets in length	£3.15
	For each 2 sheets thereafter	£3.15
9.	*Lodging in process*	
	Each necessary lodging in or uplifting from process or each necessary enquiry for documents due to be lodged	£1.60
10.	*Borrowing process*	
	Each necessary borrowing of process to include return of same	£1.60
11.	*Extracts*	
	Ordering, procuring and examining extracts, interim or otherwise	£7.30
12.	*Correspondence, intimations, etc.*	
	(a) Formal letters and intimations	£0.75
	(b) Letters other than above – per page of 125 words	£3.15
	(c) Telephone calls except those to which subparagraph (d) below applies	£1.60
	(d) Telephone calls (lengthy) to be treated as attendances or long letters.	
13.	*Citations*	
	Each citation of party or witness including execution thereof	£3.15

14.	*Instructions to officers*	
	Instructing officer to serve, execute or intimate various kinds of writs or diligence including the examination of executions	£1.60
	For each party after the first on whom service or intimation is simultaneously made	£1.60
	Agency accepting service of any writ	£3.15
	Reporting diligence	£3.15
15.	*Personal diligence*	
	(a) Recording execution of charge	£3.15
	(b) Procuring fiat	£3.15
	(c) Instructing apprehension	£3.15
	(d) Framing state of debt and attendance at settlement	£4.75
16.	*Sales*	
	(a) Obtaining warrant to sell	£3.15
	(b) Instructing auctioneer or officer to conduct sale	£3.15
	(c) Perusing report of sale	£3.15
	(d) Reporting sales under poindings or sequestrations or any other judicial sales	£2.10
	(e) Noting approval of roup roll	£2.10
	(f) Obtaining warrant to pay	£2.10

CHAPTER IV – SUMMARY CAUSE

Part I – Undefended actions

1.	Fee, to include taking instructions, framing summons and statement of claim, obtaining warrant for service, serving, instructing service as necessary by sheriff officer (where appropriate), attendance endorsing minute for and obtaining decree in absence and extract decree and including posts and incidents	£30.70
2.	*Service*	
	(a) Citation by post wheresoever after the first citation for each party	£3.50
	(b) Framing and instructing service by advertisement – for each party	£9.85
3.	Attendance at court	£9.85

Part II – Defended actions

1.	(a) Instruction fee for pursuer's solicitor, to include taking instructions, framing summons and statement of claim, obtaining warrant for service, enquiring for notice of intention to defend, attendance at first calling, noting defence	£42.25
	(b) Instruction fee for defender's solicitor, to include taking instructions (including instructions for a counter-claim) and all work up to and including attendance at first calling and stating a defence–	
	Such fee as appears to the auditor to provide reasonable remuneration for the work done but not to exceed the fee prescribed in sub-paragraph (a) above.	
2.	*Service*	
	(a) Citation by post within the United Kingdom, Isle of Man, Channel Islands, or the Republic of Ireland – for each party	£3.50
	Citation by post elsewhere – for each party	£7.50
	(b) Instructing service or reservice by sheriff officer including perusing execution of citation and settling sheriff officer's fee – for each party	£3.50
	(c) Framing and instructing service by advertisement – for each party	£10.95
3.	*Attendance at court*	
	Attendance at any diet except as otherwise specifically provided	£10.95
4.	Preparing for proof, to include all work in connection with proof not otherwise provided for	£38.15

5.	Fee to cover preparing for adjourned diet and all incidental work if diet postponed for more than 6 days – for each adjourned diet	£19.10
6.	Drawing and lodging inventory of productions, lodging the productions specified therein and considering opponents' productions (to be charged once only in each process)	£16.20
	Where only one party lodges productions, opponent's solicitor's fee for considering same	£7.50
7.	*Precognitions*	
	Drawing precognitions, including instructions, attendances with witnesses and all relative meetings and correspondence – per witness	£16.20
	Where precognition exceeds 2 sheets – for each additional sheet	£7.50
8.	*Motions and minutes*	
	Fee to cover drawing, intimating and lodging of any written motion or minute, excluding a minute or motion to recall decree, and relative attendance at court (except as otherwise provided in this Chapter)–	
	(a) Where opposed	£23.15
	(b) Where unopposed (including for each party a joint minute or joint motion)	£13.90
9.	Fee to cover considering opponent's written motion or minute, excluding a minute or motion to recall decree, and relative attendance at court–	
	(a) Where motion or minute opposed	£19.10
	(b) Where motion or minute unopposed	£10.95
10.	*Conduct of proof*	
	Fee to cover conduct of proof and debate on evidence taken at close of proof – per half hour	£10.95
	Waiting time – per half hour	£5.85
11.	*Settlements*	
	Judicial tender–	
	Fee for consideration of, preparing and lodging minute of tender	£23.15
	Fee for consideration and rejection of tenders	£16.20
	Fee on acceptance of tender – to include preparing and lodging, or consideration of, minute of acceptance and attendance at court when decree granted in terms thereof	£16.20
	Extra-judicial settlement – fee to cover negotiations resulting in settlement, framing or revising joint minute and attendance at court when authority interponed thereto	£38.15
12.	*Specification of documents*	
	(a) Fee to cover drawing, intimating and lodging specification of documents and relative motion and attendance at court	£19.10
	(b) Inclusive fee to opposing solicitor	£17.40
	(c) Fee to solicitor for each party for citation of havers, preparation for and attendance before commissioner – for each half hour	£10.95
	(d) If alternative procedure adopted, fee per person upon whom order served	£7.50
13.	*Commissions to take evidence*	
	(a) Fee to cover drawing, lodging and intimating motion and attendance at court–	
	(i) Where opposed	£23.15
	(ii) Where unopposed	£13.90
	(b) Fee to cover considering such motion and attendance at court–	
	(i) Where opposed	£19.10
	(ii) Where unopposed	£10.95
	(c) Fee to cover instructing commissioner and citing witness	£10.95
	(d) Fee to cover drawing and lodging interrogatories and cross-interrogatories – per sheet	£7.50
	(e) Attendance before commissioner – per hour	£10.45
	Travelling time – per hour	£7.00

14.	Supplementary note of defence (when leave granted to lodge)	£7.50
15.	*Appeals*	
	Fee to cover instructions, marking of appeal or noting that appeal marked, noting of diet of hearing thereof and preparations for hearing	£52.15
	Fee to cover conduct of hearing – per half hour	£10.95
16.	*Final Procedure*	
	Fee to cover settling with witnesses, enquiries at avizandum, noting final interlocutor	£23.15
	Fee to cover drawing account of expenses, arranging, intimating and attending hearing on expenses, and obtaining approval of sheriff clerk's report	£23.15
	Fee to cover considering opponent's account of expenses and attendance at hearing on expenses	£10.95

EXECUTRY BUSINESS

CHAPTER V

1.	*Petition for decree dative*	
	Inclusive fee for taking instructions to present petition, drawing petition and making necessary copies, lodging and directing publication, attendance at Court, moving for decree-dative, extracting decree where necessary and all matters incidental to petition	£23.45
2.	*Restriction of Caution*	
	Inclusive fee for taking instructions to prepare petition, drawing petition and making necessary copies, lodging, instructing advertisement and all matters incidental to petition	£23.45
3.	Fees for other work shall be chargeable according to Chapter III.	

EXPLANATORY NOTE

(This note is not part of the Regulations)

These Regulations further amend the Legal Aid (Scotland) (Fees in Civil Proceedings) Regulations 1984 so as to increase the fees allowable to solicitors for legal aid in civil proceedings. The overall increase is around 5% and will apply to work done on or after 5th June 1987.

Regulation 2 and Schedule 1 substitute a new Table of Fees for the Table of Fees in Schedule 1 to the 1984 Regulations. (This Table of Fees regulates solicitors' fees for legal aid in the Court of Session, and Chapter 1 of the Table also regulates solicitors' fees for legal aid in the House of Lords, Restrictive Practices Court and Employment Appeal Tribunal, and in certain circumstances the Lands Tribunal for Scotland.)

Regulation 3 and Schedule 2 substitute a new Table of Fees for the Table of Fees in Schedule 2 to the 1984 Regulations. (This Table of Fees regulates solicitors' fees for legal aid in the sheriff court. Chapter III of the Table of Fees also regulates solicitors' fees for legal aid in the Scottish Land Court and in certain circumstances the Lands Tribunal for Scotland.)

The Legal Aid (Scotland) Act 1967 continues in effect, despite its general repeal by the Legal Aid (Scotland) Act 1986, in respect of legal aid applications which were granted before commencement of the 1986 Act on 1st April 1987 (see paragraph 3(1) of Schedule 4 to the 1986 Act). It is thus only in respect of work done following upon such applications that these Regulations increase the fees.

STATUTORY INSTRUMENTS

1987 No. 895 (S.77)

LEGAL AID AND ADVICE, SCOTLAND

The Civil Legal Aid (Scotland) (Fees) Amendment (No.2) Regulations 1987

Made - - - -	*14th May 1987*
Laid before Parliament	*15th May 1987*
Coming into force	*5th June 1987*

The Secretary of State, in exercise of the powers conferred upon him by section 33 of the Legal Aid (Scotland) Act 1986(**a**), and of all other powers enabling him in that behalf, hereby makes the following Regulations:

1.—(1) These Regulations may be cited as the Civil Legal Aid (Scotland) (Fees) Amendment (No.2) Regulations 1987 and shall come into force on 5th June 1987.

(2) In these Regulations "the principal Regulations" means the Civil Legal Aid (Scotland) (Fees) Regulations 1987(**b**).

Amendment of pricipal Regulations

2. After regulation 8 of the principal Regulations there shall be inserted the following Regulations–

"Fees or outlays in relation to solicitor's place of business

8A. Where a solicitor acts for a client in an area in which that solicitor has not a place of business he shall be entitled, when acting for that client in that area, to receive only such fees and outlays as would be payable if he had a place of business in that area.

Accounts in respect of solicitors' fees and outlays

8B.—(1) Subject to paragraph (2) below, accounts prepared in respect of fees and outlays allowable to solicitors shall be submitted to the Board not later than 6 months after the date of completion of the proceedings in respect of which that legal aid was granted.

(2) The Board may accept accounts submitted in respect of fees and outlays later than the 6 months referred to in paragraph (1) if they consider that there is a special reason for late submission.".

3. For the Table of Fees set out in Schedule 1 to the principal Regulations (Fees of Solicitors for Proceedings in the Court of Session) there shall be substituted the Table of Fees set out in Schedule 1 to these Regulations.

4. For the Table of Fees set out in Schedule 2 to the principal Regulations (Fees of Solicitors for Proceedings in the Sheriff Court) there shall be substituted the Table of Fees set out in Schedule 2 to these Regulations.

(**a**) 1986 c.47.
(**b**) S.I. 1987/366, to which there are amendments not relevant to these Regulations.

5.   The amendments to the principal Regulations contained in regulations 3 and 4 of these Regulations shall apply only to fees for work done on or after 5th June 1987.

New St. Andrew's House, Edinburgh
14th May 1987

Ian Lang
Parliamentary Under Secretary of State,
Scottish Office

Regulation 3

SCHEDULE 1

TABLE OF FEES

CHAPTER 1

DETAILED FEES

1.	(a) Framing precognitions and other papers (not affidavits), not drawn by counsel - per sheet	£3.70
	(b) Framing formal documents such as inventories, title pages and accounts of expenses etc. - per sheet	£1.60
	(c) Framing affidavits - per sheet	£5.80

Note: (i) The sheet throughout this Table of Fees shall consist of 250 words or numbers.

(ii) The solicitor shall be entitled to charge for copies of the precognitions for the use of counsel and himself.

(iii) Where a skilled witness prepares his own precognition or report the solicitor shall be allowed half drawing fees for revising and adjusting it.

(iv) Where the business can properly be performed by a local solicitor the auditor in taxing an account shall allow such expenses as would have been incurred if it had been done by the nearest local solicitor, including reasonable fees for instructing and corresponding with him, unless the auditor is satisfied that it was in the interests of the client that the solicitor in charge of the case should attend personally.

2.	*Copying papers by any means*	
	First copy – per sheet	£0.71
	Additional copies – per sheet	£0.30

Note: When copied by photostatic or similar process each page shall be charged as one sheet.

3.	*Revising papers drawn by counsel, open and closed records etc.*	
	For each five sheets or part thereof.	£1.60
4.	*Citation of parties, witnesses, havers, instructions to messengers-at-arms*	
	Each party	£3.15
	Each witness or haver	£3.15
	Instructing messenger-at-arms including examining execution and settling fee	£3.15
5.	*Time charges*	
	(a) Attendance at meetings, preparation for proof, trial or debate, attendance at court, consultation with counsel, etc.–	
	Per half hour	£11.45
	or such other sum as in the opinion of the auditor is justified.	
	(b) Perusal of documents–	
	Per half hour	£6.25
	or such other sum as in the opinion of the auditor is justified.	

(c) Allowance for time of clerk – one half of the fee in sub-paragraph (a) or (b) above.

(d) Attendance at court offices for performance of formal work (other than lodging process or first step of process). £1.60

Lodging first step of process £3.15

Additional fee for making up and lodging process £1.60

Note: (i) Time necessarily occupied in travelling to be regarded as if occupied on business.

(ii) In the event of a party in a trial or proof being represented by one counsel only, allowance may be made to the solicitor should the case warrant it for the attendance of a clerk at one-half the rate chargeable for the solicitor's attendance.

6. *Correspondence*

Letters (save as provided below) including instructions to counsel – each page of 125 words £3.15

Formal letters £0.75

Telegrams or telephone calls, including letters confirming £1.60

CHAPTER II

PART I – UNDEFENDED ACTIONS

(OTHER THAN CONSISTORIAL ACTIONS)

1. Inclusive fee to pursuer's solicitor in all undefended cases where no proof is led, to cover all work from taking instructions up to and including obtaining extract decree £66.70

PART II – UNDEFENDED CONSISTORIAL ACTIONS

(OTHER THAN ACTIONS TO WHICH PART III APPLIES)

1. Fee for all work (other than precognitions) up to and including the calling of summons in court £94.80

Note: Precognitions to be charged as in Part V, paragraph 5 of this Chapter

2. *Incidental procedures*

Fixing diet, enrolling action, preparation for proof, citing witnesses, etc. £53.65

3. *Amendment*

(a) Where summons amended, where re-service is not ordered, and motion is not starred £13.55

(b) Where summons amended, where re-service is not ordered and motion is starred £19.80

(c) Where summons amended and re-service is ordered £25.05

4. *Commissions to take evidence on interrogatories*

(a) Basic fee to cover all work up to and including lodging completed interrogatories £19.80

(b) Additional fee for completed interrogatories, including all copies – per sheet £4.15

5. *Commissions to take evidence on open commission*

(a) Basic fee to solicitor applying for commission but excluding attendance at execution thereof £22.35

(b) Attendance at execution of commission – per half hour £11.45

6. Where applicable the fees set out in paragraphs 6, 7, 10, 14, 16 and 21 of Part V of this Chapter may be charged.

7. *Proof and completion fee* – excluding accounts of expenses but including instructing counsel for proof, attendance at proof, settling with witnesses, borrowing and returning productions, procuring interlocutor, and obtaining extract decree of divorce £66.70

8. *Accounts*

Framing and lodging account and attending taxation £21.35

PART III – UNDEFENDED CONSISTORIAL ACTIONS: AFFIDAVIT PROCEDURE

1. In any undefended action of divorce or separation where–

   (a) the facts set out in section 1(2)(b) (unreasonable behaviour) of the
   Divorce (Scotland) Act 1976(a) are relied upon; and

   (b) the pursuer seeks to prove those facts by means of affidavits–

   the pursuer's solicitor may in respect of the work specified in column 1 of
   Table A in this paragraph charge, in a case where he is an Edinburgh
   solicitor acting alone, the inclusive fee specified in respect of that work in
   column 2 of that Table, and, in any other case, the inclusive fee specified
   in respect of that work in column 3 of that Table.

TABLE A

Column 1 Work done	Column 2 *Inclusive fee Edinburgh solicitor acting alone*	Column 3 *Inclusive fee any other case*
1. All work to and including calling of the summons	£138.25	£158.05
2. All work from calling to and including swearing affidavits	£98.75	£118.50
3. All work from swearing affidavits to and including sending extract decree	£29.60	£44.40
4. All work to and including sending extract decree	£266.65	£320.95
Add session fee to item 4	of 7½%	of 10%

2. In any undefended action of divorce or separation where

   (a) the facts set out in section 1(2)(a) (adultery), 1(2)(c) (desertion), 1(2)(d)
   (two years' non-cohabitation and consent) or 1(2)(e) (five years' non-
   cohabitation) of the Divorce (Scotland) Act 1976 are relied on; and

   (b) the pursuer seeks to prove these facts by means of affidavits–

   the pursuer's solicitor may in respect of the work specified in column 1 of
   Table B in this paragraph charge, in a case where he is an Edinburgh
   solicitor acting alone, the inclusive fee specified in respect of that work in
   column 2 of that Table, and, in any other case, the inclusive fee specified
   in respect of that work in column 3 of that Table.

TABLE B

Column 1 Work done	Column 2 *Inclusive fee Edinburgh solicitor acting alone*	Column 3 *Inclusive fee any other case*
1. All work to and including calling of the summons	£113.55	£133.30
2. All work from calling to and including swearing affidavits	£54.35	£69.15
3. All work from swearing affidavits to and including sending extract decree	£29.60	£44.40
4. All work to and including sending extract decree	£197.50	£246.90
Add session fee to item 4	of 7½%	of 10%

3. If–

   (a) the pursuer's solicitor charges an inclusive fee under either paragraph 1
   or paragraph 2 of this Part, and

   (b) the action to which the charge relates includes a conclusion relating to
   an ancillary matter–

   in addition to that fee, he may charge in respect of the work specified in
   column 1 of Table C in this paragraph the inclusive fee specified in
   respect of that work in column 2 of that Table.

(a) 1976 c.39.

TABLE C

Column 1 *Work done*	Column 2 *Inclusive fee*
1. All work to and including calling of the summons	£27.65
2. All work from calling to and including swearing affidavits	£31.60
3. All work under items 1 and 2	£59.25

Add session fee to item 3 of 7½% in the case of an Edinburgh solicitor acting alone and 10% in any other case.

PART IV – OUTER HOUSE PETITIONS

A. Unopposed petitions

1.   Fee for all work, including precognitions and all copyings, up to and
         obtaining extract decree–

      (a) in the case of an Edinburgh solicitor acting alone   £139.65

      (b) in any other case   £194.90

Note: Outlays including duplicating charges to be allowed in addition.

B. Opposed petitions

2.   Fee for all work (other than precognitions)up to and including lodging   £94.80
         petition, obtaining and executing warrant for service

Note: Outlays including duplicating charges to be allowed in addition.

3.   Where applicable, the fees set out in paragraphs 5, 6, 7, 10, 12, 14, 18, 19,
         20 and 21 of Part V of this Chapter may be charged.

4.   Reports–

      (a) For each report by Accountant of Court   £16.70

      (b) For any other report as under Part V, paragraph 6 of this Chapter.

5.   Obtaining Bond of Caution   £16.70

PART V – DEFENDED ACTIONS

1.   *Instruction fee*

      (a) To cover all work (apart from precognitions) until lodgement of open   £131.30
         record

      (b) Instructing re-service where necessary   £14.05

      (c) If counter-claim lodged, additional fee for solicitor for each party   £27.65

2.   *Record fee*

      (a) To cover all work in connection with adjustment and closing of record   £139.65
         including subsequent work in connection with By Order Adjustment Roll

      (b) To cover all work as above, so far as applicable, where action settled or   £87.00
         disposed of before record closed

      (c) If consultation held before record closed, additional fees may be allowed
         as follows:–

          (i) Arranging consultation   £14.05

          (ii) Attendance at consultation – per half hour   £11.45

      (d) Additional fee (to include necessary amendments) to the solicitors for   £41.15
         the existing pursuer and each existing defender, to be allowed for each
         pursuer, defender or third party brought in before the record is closed,
         each of

	(e) Additional fee to the solicitors for existing pursuer and each existing defender, to be allowed for each pursuer, defender, or third party brought in after the record is closed, each of	£61.45
3.	*Procedure Roll or Debate Roll*	
	(a) Preparing for discussion and all work incidental thereto including instruction of counsel	£27.65
	(b) Attendance at court – per half-hour	£11.45
	(c) Advising and work incidental thereto	£20.85
4.	*Adjustment of issues and counter-issues*	
	(a) Fee to solicitor for pursuer to include all work in connection with and incidental to the lodging of an issue, and adjustment and approval thereof	£26.60
	(b) If one counter-issue, additional fee to solicitor for pursuer	£7.30
	(c) If more than one counter-issue, additional fee to solicitor for pursuer for each additional counter-issue	£3.15
	(d) Fee to solicitor for defender or third party for all work in connection with lodging of counter-issue and adjustment and approval thereof	£26.60
	(e) Fee to solicitor for defender or third party for considering issue where no counter-issue lodged	£7.30
	(f) Fee to solicitor for defender or third party for considering each additional counter-issue	£3.15
5.	*Precognitions*	
	Taking and drawing precognitions - per sheet	£13.55
Note:	(i) In addition each solicitor shall be entitled to charge for copies of the precognitions for the use of counsel and himself.	
	(ii) Where a skilled witness prepares his own precognition or report the solicitor shall be allowed, for revising and adjusting it, half of the taking and drawing fee per sheet.	
6.	*Reports obtained under order of court excluding auditor's report*	
	(a) Fee for all work incidental thereto	£29.20
	(b) Additional fee per sheet of report to include all copies required (maximum £27.60)	£4.15
7.	*Specification of documents*	
	(a) Basic fee to cover instructing counsel, revising and lodging and all incidental procedures to obtain a diligence up to and including obtaining interlocutor	£27.65
	(b) Fee to opponent's solicitor	£13.55
	(c) If commission executed, additional fee – per half hour	£11.45
	(d) If alternative procedure adopted, fee per person upon whom order served	£10.95
8.	*Commission to take evidence on interrogatories*	
	(a) Basic fee to solicitor applying for commission to cover all work up to and including lodging report of commission with completed interrogatories and cross-interrogatories	£55.75
	(b) Basic fee to opposing solicitor if cross-interrogatories lodged	£44.85
	(c) Fee to opposing solicitor if no cross-interrogatories lodged	£16.70
	(d) Additional fee to solicitor for each party for completed interrogatories or cross-interrogatories, including all copies – per sheet	£4.15
9.	*Commission to take evidence on open commission*	
	(a) Basic fee to solicitor applying for commission up to and including lodging report of commission, but excluding attendance at execution thereof	£61.45
	(b) Basic fee to opposing solicitor	£27.65
	(c) Attendance at execution of commission - per half hour	£11.45
10.	*Miscellaneous motions where not otherwise covered by this Chapter*	
	(a) Where attendance of counsel or solicitor or both not required	£7.30
	(b) Where attendance of counsel or solicitor or both required, inclusive of instruction of counsel – not exceeding half hour	£20.85

	(c) Thereafter attendance fee – per additional half hour	£11.45
11.	*Incidental procedure (not chargeable prior to approval of issue or allowance of proof)*	
	Fixing diet, obtaining note on the line of evidence, etc., borrowing and returning process, lodging productions, considering opponent's productions, and all other work prior to the consultation on the sufficiency of evidence	£78.20
12.	*Amendment of record*	
	(a) Amendment of conclusions only – fee to solicitor for pursuer	£20.85
	(b) Amendment of conclusions only – fee to solicitor for opponent	£7.30
	(c) Amendment of pleadings after record closed, where no answers to the amendment are lodged – fee to solicitor for proposer	£30.25
	(d) In same circumstances – fee to solicitor for opponent	£14.05
	(e) Amendment of pleadings after record closed where answers are lodged – fee for solicitor for each party lodging answers	£71.35
	(f) Fee for adjustment of minute and answers, where applicable, to be allowed in addition to solicitor for each party	£39.10
13.	*Preparation for trial or proof to include fixing consultation on the sufficiency of evidence and attendance thereat, fee-funding precept, adjusting minute of admissions, citing witnesses, all work checking and writing up process, and preparing for trial or proof*	
	(a) If action settled before trial or proof, or the trial or proof lasts only one day, to include, where applicable, instruction of counsel	£189.65
	(b) For each day or part of a day after the first, including instruction of counsel	£16.70
	(c) To cover preparing for adjourned diet and all work incidental as in (a), if diet postponed more than 5 days	£34.40
14.	*Copying*	
	Productions, reports of commissions, duplicate inventory, jury list, list of witnesses, Lord Ordinary's opinion, etc. – as per Chapter I, paragraph 2.	
15.	*Settlement by tender – fees for solicitor for either party*	
	(a) Basic fee for lodging, or for considering, first tender	£41.15
	(b) Fee for lodging, or for considering, each further tender	£27.65
	(c) Additional fee if tender accepted	£27.65
16.	*Extra-judicial settlement*	
	Fee inclusive of joint minute (not based on a judicial tender)	£71.35
17.	*Proof or trial*	
	Attendance fee – per half-hour	£11.45
18.	*Accounts* – to include framing and lodging account, intimating diet, and attending taxation, uplifting account and noting and intimating taxations	£50.05
19.	*Ordering and obtaining extract*	£10.45
20.	*Final procedure*	
	(a) If case goes to trial or proof, to include all work to close of litigation, so far as not otherwise provided for, including in particular settling with witnesses and procuring and booking verdict, or attendance at judgement	£55.75
	(b) If case disposed of before trial or proof	£16.70
21.	*Session fee – to cover communications with client and counsel*	
	(a) Where no correspondent – 7½% of total fees (including copying fees) allowed on taxation	
	(b) Where correspondent involved – 10% of total fees (including copying fees) allowed on taxation.	

PART VI – INNER HOUSE BUSINESS

1.	*Reclaiming motions*	
	(a) Fee for solicitor for appellant for all work up to interlocutor sending case to roll	£41.15

	(b) Fee for solicitor for respondent	£20.85
	(c) Additional fee for solicitor for each party for every 50 pages of appendix	£17.20
2.	*Appeals from inferior courts*	
	(a) Fee for solicitor for appellant	£50.05
	(b) Fee for solicitor for respondent	£24.50
	(c) Additional fee for solicitor for each party for every 50 pages of appendix	£17.20
3.	*Summar or Short Roll*	
	(a) Preparing for discussion, instructing counsel, and preparing appendix	£41.15
	(b) Attendance fee – per half-hour	£11.45
4.	Where applicable the fees set out in Part V of this Chapter may be charged.	
5.	*Special cases and Inner House petitions*	
	According to circumstances of the case.	
6.	Obtaining Bond of Caution	£16.70

PART VII – ADMIRALTY AND COMMERCIAL CASES, SEQUESTRATIONS IN BANKRUPTCY, APPLICATIONS FOR SUMMARY TRIAL UNDER SECTION 10 OF THE ADMINISTRATION OF JUSTICE (SCOTLAND) ACT 1933(a) AND CASES REMITTED FROM THE SHERIFF COURT

The fees shall be based on this Table of Fees according to the circumstances.

Regulation 4

SCHEDULE 2

TABLE OF FEES

CHAPTER I – UNDEFENDED ACTIONS (OTHER THAN ACTIONS TO WHICH CHAPTER IV OR V APPLIES)

Part I – All actions except those actions of divorce or separation and aliment to which Part II applies

1.	Actions (other than those specified in paragraph 2 of this Part) in which decree is granted without proof–	
	Inclusive fee to cover all work from taking instructions up to and including obtaining extract decree	£41.15
	In cases where settlement is effected after service of a writ but before the expiry of the period of notice	£35.45
2.	Actions of separation and aliment (not being actions to which Part II of this Chapter applies), adherence and aliment or custody and aliment where proof takes place–	
	Inclusive fee to cover all work from taking instructions up to and including obtaining extract decree	£194.90

Part II – Actions of divorce or separation and aliment where proof is by means of affidavits

1.   In any undefended action of divorce or of separation and aliment where–

    (a) the facts set out in section 1(2)(b) (unreasonable behaviour) of the Divorce (Scotland) Act 1976 are relied upon; and

    (b) the pursuer seeks to prove those facts by means of affidavits–

the pursuer's solicitor may in respect of the work specified in column 1 of Table A in this paragraph charge the inclusive fee specified in respect of that work in column 2 of that Table.

(a) 1933 c.41.

TABLE A

Column 1	Column 2
Work done	*Inclusive fee*
1. All work to and including the period of notice	£138.25
2. All work from the period of notice to and including swearing affidavits	£98.75
3. All work from swearing affidavits to and including sending extract decree	£29.60
4. All work to and including sending extract decree	£266.65
Add process fee to item 4	of 10%

2.   In any undefended action of divorce or separation and aliment where–

(a) the facts set out in section 1(2)(a) (adultery), 1(2)(c) (desertion), 1(2)(d) (two years' non-cohabitation and consent) or 1(2)(e) (five years' non-cohabitation) of the Divorce (Scotland) Act 1976 are relied on; and

(b) the pursuer seeks to prove those facts by means of affidavits–

the pursuer's solicitor may in respect of the work specified in column 1 of Table B in this paragraph charge the inclusive fee specified in respect of that work in column 2 of that Table.

TABLE B

Column 1	Column 2
Work done	*Inclusive fee*
1. All work to and including the period of notice	£113.55
2. All work from the period of notice to and including swearing affidavits	£54.35
3. All work from swearing affidavits to and including sending extract decree	£29.60
4. All work to and including sending extract decree	£197.50
Add process fee to item 4	of 10%

3.   If–

(a) the pursuer's solicitor charges an inclusive fee under either paragraph 1 or paragraph 2 of this Part; and

(b) the action to which the charge relates includes a crave relating to an ancillary matter–

in addition to that fee, he may charge in respect of the work specified in column 1 of Table C in this paragraph the inclusive fee specified in respect of that work in column 2 of that Table.

TABLE C

Column 1	Column 2
Work done	*Inclusive fee*
1. All work to and including the period of notice	£53.80
2. All work from the period of notice to and including swearing affidavits	£31.60
3. All work under items 1 and 2	£85.40

CHAPTER II – DEFENDED ACTIONS (OTHER THAN ACTIONS TO WHICH CHAPTER IV OR V APPLIES)

1.	*Instruction fee* – to cover all work (except as hereinafter otherwise specially provided for in this Chapter) to the lodging of defences including copyings	£89.10
	Additional fee where separate statement of facts and counter claim answers lodged	£31.30
2.	*Adjustment fee* – to cover all work (except as hereinafter otherwise specially provided for in this Chapter) in connection with the adjustment of the record including (when appropriate) closing thereof, making up and lodging closed record and copyings–	
	(a) Fee to solicitor for any party	£133.35
	(b) Fee to each original party's solicitor if action settled before record is closed	£89.10

(c)	Additional fee to each original party's solicitor if additional defender brought in before closing of record	£15.65
(d)	Additional fee to each original party's solicitor if additional defender brought in after closing of record	£22.40
3.	*Fee for framing affidavits* – per sheet	£5.80
4.	(a) *Debate fee* – to include preparation for and conduct of any hearing or debate other than on evidence, enquiring for cause at avizandum and noting interlocutor–	
	When debate does not exceed 1 hour	£66.75
	For every half hour engaged after the first hour	£15.65
	(b) *Interim interdict hearings*–	
	Pursuer's solicitor – the same fees as for debate fee above, but to include both the appearance at lodging of writ and the hearing at second diet.	
	Defender's solicitor's fee where the debate does not exceed 1 hour	£39.05
5.	*Precognitions* – taking and drawing – per sheet	£13.55
Note:	Where a skilled witness prepares his own precognition or report, the solicitor shall be allowed half of above drawing fee for revising and adjusting it.	
5A.	*Reports obtained under order of court, excluding auditor's report*	
	(a) Fee for all work incidental thereto	£29.20
	(b) Additional fee per sheet of report to include all copies required (maximum £29.00)	£4.15
6.	*Commissions to take evidence*	
	(a) On interrogatories	
	Fee to solicitor applying for commission to include drawing, intimating and lodging motion, drawing and lodging interrogatories, instructing commissioner and all incidental work (except as otherwise specially provided for in this Chaper) but excluding attendance at execution of commission	£83.35
	Fee to opposing solicitor if cross-interrogatories prepared and lodged	£55.75
	If no cross-interrogatories lodged	£16.70
	(b) Open commissions	
	Fee to solicitor applying for commission to include all work (except as otherwise specially provided for in this Chapter) up to lodging report of commission but excluding attendance thereat	£50.05
	Fee to solicitor for opposing party	£27.65
	Fee for attendance at execution of commission – per half hour	£15.65
	Travelling time – per half hour	£11.45
7.	*Specification of documents*	
	Fee to cover drawing, intimating and lodging specification and relative motion and attendance at court debating specification	£34.40
	Inclusive fee to opposing solicitor	£22.35
	Fee for citation of havers, preparation for and attendance before commissioner at execution of commission–	
	Where attendance before commissioner does not exceed 1 hour	£31.30
	For each additional half hour after the first hour	£15.65
	If commission not executed – fee for serving each party with a copy of specification to include recovering and examining documents or productions referred to therein	£6.85
8.	*Amendment of record*	
	Fee to cover drawing, intimating and lodging minute of amendment and relative motion and relative attendance at court–	
	(a) Where answers lodged	£38.05
	(b) Where no answers lodged	£25.05
	Inclusive fee to opposing solicitor–	
	(a) Where answers lodged	£31.30
	(b) Where no answers lodged	£20.85

	Additional fee to solicitor for each party for adjustment of minute and answers, where applicable	£27.65
9.	*Motions and minutes*	
	Fee to cover drawing, intimating and lodging any written motion or minute, including a reponing note, and relative attendances at court (except as otherwise provided for in this Chapter)–	
	(a) Where opposed	£39.05
	(b) Where unopposed (including for each party a joint minute other than under paragraph 14(b))	£27.65
	Fee to cover considering opponent's written motion, minute or reponing note and relative attendances at court–	
	(a) Where motion, minute or reponing note opposed	£22.35
	(b) Where motion, minute or reponing note unopposed	£14.10
10.	*Procedure preliminary to proof*	
	(a) Fee to cover fixing diet of proof, citation of witnesses, and generally preparing for proof and if necessary instructing shorthand writer	£55.75
	(b) Fee to cover preparing for adjourned diet and all incidental work as in subparagraph (a) above if diet postponed for more than 6 days – for each additional diet	£33.35
	(c) Drawing and lodging an inventory of productions, lodging the productions specified therein, and considering opponent's productions (to be charged once only in each process)	£14.10
	Where only one party lodges productions, opponent's solicitor's fee for considering same	£7.30
11.	*Conduct of proof*	
	Fee to cover conduct of proof and debate on evidence if taken at close of proof – per half hour	£15.65
	If counsel employed, fee to solicitor appearing with counsel - per half hour	£11.45
12.	*Debate on evidence*	
	Where debate on evidence not taken at conclusion of proof, fee for preparing for debate	£27.65
	Fee for conduct of debate – per half hour	£15.65
	If counsel employed, fee to solicitor appearing with counsel – per half hour	£11.45
13.	*Appeals*	
	(a) To sheriff principal	
	Fee to cover instructions, marking of appeal or noting that appeal marked, noting diet of hearing thereof and preparation for hearing	£52.15
	Fee to cover conduct of hearing – per half hour	£15.65
	If counsel employed, fee to solicitor appearing with counsel – per half hour	£11.45
	(b) To Court of Session	
	Fee to cover instructions, marking appeal or noting that appeal marked and instructing Edinburgh correspondents	£26.05
14.	*Settlements*	
	(a) Judicial tender	
	Fee for preparation and lodging or for consideration of minute of tender	£30.70
	Fee on acceptance of tender, to include preparation and lodging or consideration of minute of acceptance and attendance at court when decree granted in terms thereof	£22.95
	(b) Extra-judicial settlements	
	Fee to cover negotiations resulting in settlement, framing or revising joint minute and attendance at court when authority interponed thereto	£52.15
15.	*Final procedure*	
	Fee to cover settling with witnesses, enquiries for cause at avizandum, noting final interlocutor	£41.15
	Fee to cover drawing account of expenses, arranging, intimating and attending diet of taxation and obtaining approval of auditor's report and adjusting account with opponent where necessary, ordering, procuring and examining extract decree	£33.35

Fee to cover considering opponent's account of expenses and attending diet of taxation or adjusting account with opponent		£10.45

16. *Copying fees*

Copying all necessary papers by any means–

First copy – per sheet £0.71

Additional copies – per sheet £0.30

Note: A sheet shall be 250 words. When copied by photostatic or similar process, each page shall be charged as one sheet.

17. *Process fee*

Fee to cover all consultations between solicitor and client during the progress of the cause and all communications, written or verbal, passing between them:

10% on total fees (including copying fees) allowed on taxation.

18. *Fee for instruction of counsel*

Fee for instructing counsel to revise record £17.15

Fee for instructing counsel to conduct debate or proof £34.40

Fee for instructing counsel to conduct appeal to sheriff principal £34.40

Note: In each case to cover all consultations, revisal of papers and all incidental work.

CHAPTER III – CHARGES FOR TIME, DRAWING OF PAPERS, CORRESPONDENCE, ETC.

1. Attendance at court conducting proof or formal debate or hearing–per half hour £15.65

2. Time occupied in the performance of all other work including attendances with client and others and attendances at court in all circumstances, except as otherwise specifically provided–

   (a) Solicitor – per half hour £11.45

   (b) Allowance for time of clerk – one half of above.

Note: Time necessarily occupied in travelling to such to be chargeable at these rates.

3. Drawing all necessary papers other than affidavits (the sheet throughout this Chapter to consist of 250 words or numbers) – per sheet £3.70

4. Framing affidavits – per sheet £5.80

5. Revising papers where revisal ordered – for each five sheets £1.60

6. Copying all necessary papers by any means–

First copy – per sheet £0.71

Additional copies – per sheet £0.30

Note: When copied by photostatic or similar process each page shall be charged as one sheet.

7. Certifying or signing a document £1.60

8. Perusing any document (other than a letter) not exceeding 2 sheets in length £3.15

For each 2 sheets thereafter £3.15

9. *Lodging in process*

Each necessary lodging in or uplifting from process or each necessary enquiry for documents due to be lodged £1.60

10. *Borrowing process*

Each necessary borrowing of process to include return of same £1.60

11. *Extracts*

Ordering, procuring and examining extracts, interim or otherwise £7.30

12. *Correspondence, intimations, etc.*

   (a) Formal letters and intimations £0.75

   (b) Letters other than above – per page of 125 words £3.15

   (c) Telephone calls except those to which subparagraph (d) below applies £1.60

   (d) Telephone calls (lengthy) to be treated as attendances or long letters.

13.	*Citations*	
	Each citation of party or witness including execution thereof	£3.15
14.	*Instructions to officers*	
	Instructing officer to serve, execute or intimate various kinds of writs or diligence including the examination of executions	£1.60
	For each party after the first on whom service or intimation is simultaneously made	£1.60
	Agency accepting service of any writ	£3.15
	Reporting diligence	£3.15
15.	*Personal diligence*	
	(a) Recording execution of charge	£3.15
	(b) Procuring fiat	£3.15
	(c) Instructing apprehension	£3.15
	(d) Framing state of debt and attendance at settlement	£4.75
16.	*Sales*	
	(a) Obtaining warrant to sell	£3.15
	(b) Instructing auctioneer or officer to conduct sale	£3.15
	(c) Perusing report of sale	£3.15
	(d) Reporting sales under poindings or sequestrations or any other judicial sales	£2.10
	(e) Noting approval of roup roll	£2.10
	(f) Obtaining warrant to pay	£2.10

CHAPTER IV – SUMMARY CAUSE

Part I – Undefended actions

1.	Fee, to include taking instructions, framing summons and statement of claim, obtaining warrant for service, serving, instructing service as necessary by sheriff officer (where appropriate), attendance endorsing minute for and obtaining decree in absence and extract decree and including posts and incidents	£30.70
2.	*Service*	
	(a) Citation by post wheresoever after the first citation for each party	£3.50
	(b) Framing and instructing service by advertisement – for each party	£9.85
3.	Attendance at court	£9.85

Part II – Defended actions

1.	(a) Instruction fee for pursuer's solicitor, to include taking instructions, framing summons and statement of claim, obtaining warrant for service, enquiring for notice of intention to defend, attendance at first calling, noting defence	£42.25
	(b) Instruction fee for defender's solicitor, to include taking instructions (including instructions for a counter-claim) and all work up to and including attendance at first calling and stating a defence–	
	Such fee as appears to the auditor to provide reasonable remuneration for the work done but not to exceed the fee prescribed in sub-paragraph (a) above.	
2.	*Service*	
	(a) Citation by post within the United Kingdom, Isle of Man, Channel Islands, or the Republic of Ireland – for each party	£3.50
	Citation by post elsewhere – for each party	£7.50
	(b) Instructing service or reservice by sheriff officer including perusing execution of citation and settling sheriff officer's fee – for each party	£3.50
	(c) Framing and instructing service by advertisement – for each party	£10.95
3.	*Attendance at court*	
	Attendance at any diet except as otherwise specifically provided	£10.95

4.	Preparing for proof, to include all work in connection with proof not otherwise provided for	£38.15
5.	Fee to cover preparing for adjourned diet and all incidental work if diet postponed for more than 6 days – for each adjourned diet	£19.10
6.	Drawing and lodging inventory of productions, lodging the productions specified therein and considering opponents' productions (to be charged once only in each process)	£16.20
	Where only one party lodges productions, opponent's solicitor's fee for considering same	£7.50
7.	*Precognitions*	
	Drawing precognitions, including instructions, attendances with witnesses and all relative meetings and correspondence – per witness	£16.20
	Where precognition exceeds 2 sheets – for each additional sheet	£7.50
8.	*Motions and minutes*	
	Fee to cover drawing, intimating and lodging of any written motion or minute, excluding a minute or motion to recall decree, and relative attendance at court (except as otherwise provided in this Chapter)–	
	(a) Where opposed	£23.15
	(b) Where unopposed (including for each party a joint minute or joint motion)	£13.90
9.	Fee to cover considering opponent's written motion or minute, excluding a minute or motion to recall decree, and relative attendance at court–	
	(a) Where motion or minute opposed	£19.10
	(b) Where motion or minute unopposed	£10.95
10.	*Conduct of proof*	
	Fee to cover conduct of proof and debate on evidence taken at close of proof – per half hour	£10.95
	Waiting time – per half hour	£5.85
11.	*Settlements*	
	Judicial tender–	
	Fee for consideration of, preparing and lodging minute of tender	£23.15
	Fee for consideration and rejection of tenders	£16.20
	Fee on acceptance of tender – to include preparing and lodging, or consideration of, minute of acceptance and attendance at court when decree granted in terms thereof	£16.20
	Extra-judicial settlement – fee to cover negotiations resulting in settlement, framing or revising joint minute and attendance at court when authority interponed thereto	£38.15
12.	*Specification of documents*	
	(a) Fee to cover drawing, intimating and lodging specification of documents and relative motion and attendance at court	£19.10
	(b) Inclusive fee to opposing solicitor	£17.40
	(c) Fee to solicitor for each party for citation of havers, preparation for and attendance before commissioner – for each half hour	£10.95
	(d) If alternative procedure adopted, fee per person upon whom order served	£7.50
13.	*Commissions to take evidence*	
	(a) Fee to cover drawing, lodging and intimating motion and attendance at court–	
	(i) Where opposed	£23.15
	(ii) Where unopposed	£13.90
	(b) Fee to cover considering such motion and attendance at court–	
	(i) Where opposed	£19.10
	(ii) Where unopposed	£10.95
	(c) Fee to cover instructing commissioner and citing witness	£10.95
	(d) Fee to cover drawing and lodging interrogatories and cross-interrogatories – per sheet	£7.50
	(e) Attendance before commissioner – per hour	£10.45

	Travelling time – per hour	£7.00
14.	Supplementary note of defence (when leave granted to lodge)	£7.50
15.	*Appeals*	
	Fee to cover instructions, marking of appeal or noting that appeal marked, noting of diet of hearing thereof and preparations for hearing	£52.15
	Fee to cover conduct of hearing – per half hour	£10.95
16.	*Final Procedure*	
	Fee to cover settling with witnesses, enquiries at avizandum, noting final interlocutor	£23.15
	Fee to cover drawing account of expenses, arranging, intimating and attending hearing on expenses, and obtaining approval of sheriff clerk's report	£23.15
	Fee to cover considering opponent's account of expenses and attendance at hearing on expenses	£10.95

EXECUTRY BUSINESS

CHAPTER V

1.	*Petition for decree dative*	
	Inclusive fee for taking instructions to present petition, drawing petition and making necessary copies, lodging and directing publication, attendance at Court, moving for decree-dative, extracting decree where necessary and all matters incidental to petition	£23.45
2.	*Restriction of Caution*	
	Inclusive fee for taking instructions to prepare petition, drawing petition and making necessary copies, lodging, instructing advertisement and all matters incidental to petition	£23.45
3.	Fees for other work shall be chargeable according to Chapter III.	

EXPLANATORY NOTE

(This note is not part of the Regulations)

These Regulations further amend the Civil Legal Aid (Scotland) (Fees) Regulations 1987 for a number of purposes, but principally so as to increase the fees allowable to solicitors for civil legal aid (and for legal aid in certain proceedings relating to children). The overall increase is around 5% and applies to work done on or after 5th June 1987.

Regulation 2 provides that where a solicitor acts for a legally aided person in an area outwith the area within which he has his place of business, his fees and outlays will be calculated as if his place of business were in that area outwith the area of his place of business.

Regulation 2 also introduces a requirement on a solicitor to submit accounts to the Scottish Legal Aid Board within 6 months from the date of completion of the proceedings in respect of which the legal aid was granted. An exception is made which allows the Board to waive this time bar where it considers that a special reason exists for the late submission of accounts.

Regulation 3 and Schedule 1 substitute a new Table of Fees for the Table of Fees in Schedule 1 to the principal Regulations. (This Table of Fees regulates solicitors' fees for legal aid in the Court of Session, and chapter I of the Table also regulates solicitors' fees for legal aid in the House of Lords, Restrictive Practices Court and Employment Appeal Tribunal, and in certain circumstances the Lands Tribunal for Scotland.)

Regulation 4 and Schedule 2 substitute a new Table of Fees for the Table of Fees in Schedule 2 to the principal Regulations. (This Table of Fees regulates solicitors' fees for legal aid in the sheriff court. Chapter III of the Table of Fees also regulates solicitors' fees for legal aid in the Scottish Land Court and in certain circumstances the Lands Tribunal for Scotland.)

STATUTORY INSTRUMENTS

1987 No. 896

INDUSTRIAL TRAINING

The Industrial Training Levy (Hotel and Catering) Order 1987

Made - - - -	*14th May 1987*
Laid before Parliament	*15th May 1987*
Coming into force	*29th May 1987*

Whereas proposals made by the Hotel and Catering Industry Training Board for the raising and collection of a levy have been submitted to, and approved by, the Manpower Services Commission under section 11(1) of the Industrial Training Act 1982(**a**) ("the 1982 Act") and have thereafter been submitted by the said Commission to the Secretary of State under that subsection;

And whereas in pursuance of section 11(3) of the 1982 Act the said proposals include provision for the exemption from the levy of employers who, in view of the small number of their employees, ought in the opinion of the Secretary of State to be exempted from it;

And whereas the Secretary of State estimates that the amount which, disregarding any exemptions, will be payable by virtue of this Order by any employer in the hotel and catering industry, does not exceed an amount which the Secretary of State estimates is equal to one per cent. of the relevant emoluments being the aggregate of the emoluments and payments intended to be disbursed as emoluments which have been paid or are payable by any such employer to or in respect of persons employed in the industry, in respect of the period specified in the said proposals as relevant, that is to say the period hereafter referred to in this Order as "the twenty-first base period";

And whereas the Secretary of State is satisfied that the proposals published by the said Board in pursuance of section 13 of the 1982 Act provide for exemption certificates relating to the levy in such cases as he considers appropriate;

Now, therefore, the Secretary of State in exercise of the powers conferred on him by sections 11(2), 12(3) and 12(4) of the 1982 Act and of all other powers enabling him in that behalf hereby makes the following Order:–

Citation and commencement

1. This Order may be cited as the Industrial Training Levy (Hotel and Catering) Order 1987 and shall come into force on 29th May 1987.

Interpretation

2.—(1) In this Order unless the context otherwise requires:–
   (a) "agriculture" has the same meaning as in section 109(3) of the Agriculture Act 1947(**b**) or, in relation to Scotland, as in section 86(3) of the Agriculture (Scotland) Act 1948(**c**)

(**a**) 1982 c. 10.   (**b**) 1947 c. 48.   (**c**) 1948 c. 45.

(b) "assessment" means an assessment of an employer to the levy;

(c) "the Board" means the Hotel and Catering Industry Training Board;

(d) "charity" has the same meaning as in section 360 of the Income and Corporation Taxes Act 1970(**a**);

(e) "emoluments" means all emoluments assessable to income tax under Schedule E of the Income and Corporation Taxes Act 1970 (other than pensions), being emoluments from which tax under that Schedule is deductible, whether or not tax in fact falls to be deducted from any particular payment thereof;

(f) "employer" means a person who is an employer in the hotel and catering industry at any time in the twenty-first levy period;

(g) "establishment" (except in sub-paragraphs (i) and (k) of this paragraph) means an establishment comprising catering activities or a hotel and catering establishment;

(h) "establishment comprising catering activities" means an establishment in Great Britain at or from which persons were employed in the twenty-first base period in the supply of food or drink to persons for immediate consumption, but does not include:–

  (i) a hotel and catering establishment; or

  (ii) an establishment in which the employer supplied for immediate consumption light refreshments to persons employed at or from the same where the employer was not otherwise engaged at or from the establishment in any activities to which paragraph 1 of the Schedule to the industrial training order applies or in the manufacture of any chocolate or flour confectionery so supplied as light refreshments;

(i) "exemption certificate" means a certificate issued by the Board under section 14 of the 1982 Act;

(j) "hotel and catering establishment" means an establishment in Great Britain that was engaged in the twenty-first base period wholly or mainly in the hotel and catering industry;

(k) "hotel and catering industry" does not include any activities of an establishment which has been transferred from the industry of the Board to the industry of another industrial training board by one of the transfer orders but save as aforesaid means any one or more of the activities which, subject to the provisions of paragraph 2 of the Schedule to the industrial training order, are specified in paragraph 1 of that Schedule as the activities of the hotel and catering industry or, in relation to an establishment whose activities have been transferred to the industry of the Board by one of the transfer orders, any activities so transferred;

(l) "the industrial training order" means the Industrial Training (Hotel and Catering Board) Order 1966(**b**);

(m) "the levy" means the levy imposed by the Board in respect of the twenty-first levy period;

(n) "notice" means a notice in writing;

(o) "the twenty-first base period" means the period of twelve months that commenced on 6th April 1986;

(p) "the twenty-first levy period" means the period commencing with the day upon which this Order comes into force and ending on 31st March 1988;

(q) "the supply of food or drink to persons for immediate consumption" means such a supply either by way of business or by a person carrying on a business to persons employed in the business;

(r) "the transfer orders" means:–

  (i) the Industrial Training (Transfer of the Activities of Establishments) Order 1980 (**c**);

  (ii) the Industrial Training (Transfer of the Activities of Establishments) (No. 2) Order 1980(**d**);

(**a**) 1970 c. 10.   (**b**) S.I.1966/1347, amended by S.I. 1969/1405.   (**c**) S.I. 1980/586.
(**d**) S.I. 1980/1753.

(s) other expressions have the same meanings as in the industrial training order.

(2) Any reference in this Order to a person who ceases to be an employer shall not be taken to apply where the cessation is of a temporary or seasonal nature, or where the location of the employer's business is changed but the business is continued wholly or mainly at or from the new location.

Imposition of the levy

3.—(1) The levy to be imposed by the Board on employers in respect of the twenty-first levy period shall be assessed in accordance with the provisions of this Article.

(2) Subject to the provisions of this Article the levy on each employer shall be assessed by the Board in respect of the emoluments paid by him to all persons to whom paragraph (3) below applies employed by the employer in the twenty-first base period at relevant establishments of his (that is to say, any hotel and catering establishment or establishments, or any establishment or establishments comprising catering activities other than an establishment of an employer who is exempt from the levy by virtue of paragraph (4) of this Article) and the amount thereof shall be equal to 1 per cent. of the sum of the emoluments where such emoluments are £70,000 or more.

(3) This paragraph applies to:–

    (a) in the case of a hotel and catering establishment, all persons employed;

    (b) in the case of an establishment comprising catering activities, all persons employed wholly or mainly in the supply of food or drink to persons for immediate consumption.

(4) There shall be exempt from the levy:–

    (a) an employer in whose case the sum of the emoluments of all the persons employed by him in the twenty-first base period in the hotel and catering industry at or from the establishment or establishments of the employer was less than £70,000;

    (b) a charity.

(5)(a) Levy shall not be imposed on a person who ceases to be an employer in the hotel and catering industry prior to the commencement of the twenty-first levy period;

    (b) the amount of the levy imposed on a person who ceases to be an employer in the hotel and catering industry during the twenty-first levy period shall be in the same proportion to the amount that would otherwise be due under the foregoing provisions of this Article as the number of days between the commencement of the said levy period and the date on which the person ceases to be an employer in the hotel and catering industry (both dates inclusive) bears to the number of days in the said levy period.

(6) For the purposes of this Article, no regard shall be had to the emoluments of any person employed as follows:–

    (a) wholly in the supply (except at or in connection with a hotel, restaurant, café, snack bar, canteen, mess room or similar place of refreshment) of:–

        (i) ice-cream, chocolate confectionery, sugar confectionery or soft drink;

        (ii) shellfish or eels; or

        (iii) food or drink by means of an automatic vending machine;

    (b) wholly in agriculture;

    (c) otherwise than wholly in the supply of food or drink to persons for immediate consumption, where the employment is at or from an establishment engaged mainly in any activities of an industry specified in column 1 of the Schedule to this Order by virtue of the relevant industrial training order specified in column 2 of that Schedule or in any activities of two or more such industries;

    (d) as a member of the crew of an aircraft, or as the master or a member of the crew of a ship or, in the case of a person ordinarily employed as a seaman, in or about a ship in port by the owner or charterer thereof on work of a kind ordinarily done by a seaman on a ship while it is in port;

    (e) by a local authority in any activities mentioned in sub-paragraph (d) or (e) of paragraph 1 of the Schedule to the industrial training order, not being activities mentioned in head (ii) or head (iv) of paragraph (3)(l) of that Schedule; or

(f) in any activities mentioned in sub-paragraph (b), (c)(ii), (d) or (e) of paragraph 1 of the Schedule to the industrial training order when carried out by:–

    (i) a harbour authority while acting in that capacity;

    (ii) The Electricity Council, the Central Electricity Generating Board or an Area Electricity Board;

    (iii) the North of Scotland Hydro-Electric Board or the South of Scotland Electricity Board;

    (iv) the British Gas Corporation;

    (v) statutory water undertakers within the meaning of the Water Act 1973(**a**) or water authorities within the meaning of the Water (Scotland) Act 1980(**b**) or water development boards within the meaning of the Water (Scotland) Act 1980, being the activities of such undertakers, authorities or boards in the exercise of their powers or duties as such;

    (vi) the British Airports Authority;

    (vii) British Airways Plc or a subsidiary of British Airways Plc;

    (viii) a marketing board; or

    (ix) the United Kingdom Atomic Energy Authority.

Exemption Certificates

4. Exemption Certificates issued by the Board shall not exempt any employer in the industry from that portion of the levy which equals 0.035 per cent. of the sum of the emoluments upon which the levy falls to be assessed under article 3(2) above.

Assessment notices

5.—(1) The Board shall serve an assessment notice on every employer assessed to the levy, but one notice may comprise two or more assessments.

(2) An assessment notice shall state the Board's address for the service of a notice of appeal or of an application for an extension of time for appealing.

(3) An assessment notice may be served on the person assessed to the levy either by delivering it to him personally or by leaving it, or sending it to him by post, at his last known address or place of business in the United Kingdom or, if that person is a corporation, by leaving it, or sending it by post to the corporation, at such address or place of business or at its registered or principal office.

Payment of the levy

6.—(1) Subject to the provisions of this article and of articles 7 and 8, the amount of the levy payable under an assessment notice served by the Board shall be due and payable to the Board in two instalments:–

    (i) the first instalment, being that portion of the levy from which, in accordance with Article 4 above, exemption certificates are not to exempt any employer in the industry, on 1st June 1987, and

    (ii) the second instalment, being the remainder of the levy, on 1st January 1988.

(2) The amount of an assessment shall not be recoverable by the Board until there has expired the time allowed for appealing against the assessment by Article 8(1) of this Order and any further period or periods of time that the Board or an industrial tribunal may have allowed for appealing under paragraph (2) or (3) of that Article or, where an appeal is brought, until the appeal is decided or withdrawn.

Withdrawal of assessment

7.—(1) The Board may, by a notice served on the person assessed to the levy in the same manner as an assessment notice, withdraw an assessment if that person has appealed against that assessment under the provisions of Article 8 of this Order and the appeal has not been entered in the Register of Appeals kept under the appropriate Regulations specified in paragraph (5) of that Article, and such withdrawal may be extended by the Board to any other assessment appearing in the assessment notice.

(2) The withdrawal of an assessment shall be without prejudice:-

(a) to the power of the Board to serve a further assessment notice and, where the withdrawal is made by reason of the fact that a person has ceased to be an employer in the hotel and catering industry in the twentieth levy period, the said notice may provide that the whole amount payable thereunder shall be due one month after the date of the notice; or

(b) to any other assessment included in the original assessment notice and not withdrawn by the Board, and such notice shall thereupon have effect as if any assessment withdrawn by the Board had not been included therein

Appeals

8.—(1) A person assessed to the levy may appeal to an industrial tribunal against the assessment within one month from the date of the service of the assessment notice or within any further period or periods of time that may be allowed by the Board or an industrial tribunal under the following provisions of this Article.

(2) The Board by notice may for good cause allow a person assessed to the levy to appeal to an industrial tribunal against the assessment at any time within the period of four months from the date of the service of the assessment notice or within such further period or periods as the Board may allow before such time as may then be limited for appealing has expired.

(3) If the Board shall not allow an application for extension of time for appealing, an industrial tribunal shall upon application made to the tribunal by the person assessed to the levy have the like powers as the Board under the last foregoing paragraph.

(4) In the case of a person who ceases to be an employer in the hotel and catering industry in the twenty-first levy period on any day after the date of the service of the relevant assessment notice, the foregoing provisions of this Article shall have effect as if for the period of four months from the date of the service of the assessment notice mentioned in paragraph (2) of this Article there were substituted the period of six months from the date on which the person ceased to be an employer.

(5) An appeal or an application to an industrial tribunal under this Article shall be made in accordance with the Industrial Tribunals (England and Wales) Regulations 1965(**a**) except where the establishment to which the relevant assessment relates is wholly in Scotland in which case the appeal or application shall be made in accordance with the Industrial Tribunals (Scotland) Regulations 1965(**b**).

(6) The powers of an industrial tribunal under paragraph (3) of this Article may be exercised by the President of the Industrial Tribunals (England and Wales) or by the President of the Industrial Tribunals (Scotland) as the case may be.

Evidence

9.—(1) Upon the discharge by a person assessed to the levy of his liability under an assessment the Board shall if so requested issue to him a certificate to that effect.

(2) The production in any proceedings of a document purporting to be certified by the Secretary of the Board to be a true copy of an assessment or other notice issued by the Board or purporting to be a certificate such as is mentioned in the foregoing paragraph of this Article shall, unless the contrary is proved, be sufficient evidence of the document and of the facts stated therein.

Signed by order of the Secretary of State

David Trippier
Parliamentary Under Secretary of State,
Department of Employment

14th May 1987

(**a**) S.I. 1965/1101; relevant amending instruments are S.I. 1967/301, 1977/1473.
(**b**) S.I. 1965/1157; relevant amending instruments are S.I. 1967/302, 1977/1474.

Article 3   **SCHEDULE**

THE INDUSTRIES REFERRED TO IN ARTICLE 3(6)(C) OF THIS ORDER

Column 1	Column 2
The construction industry	The Industrial Training (Construction Board) Order 1964(**a**)
The engineering industry	The Industrial Training (Engineering Board) Order 1964(**b**)
The agricultural, horticultural and forestry industry	The Industrial Training (Agricultural, Horticultural and Forestry Board) Order 1966(**c**)
The road transport industry	The Industrial Training (Road Transport Board) Order 1966(**d**)
The offshore petroleum industry	The Industrial Training (Petroleum Board) Order 1967(**e**)
The clothing and allied products industry	The Industrial Training (Clothing and Allied Products Board) Order 1969(**f**)
The plastics processing industry	The Industrial Training (Rubber and Plastics Processing Board) Order 1967(**g**)

EXPLANATORY NOTE

(*This note is not part of the Order*)

This Order, which comes into force on 29th May 1987, gives effect to proposals of the Hotel and Catering Industry Training Board which were submitted to and approved by the Manpower Services Commission, and thereafter submitted by the Manpower Services Commission to the Secretary of State. The proposals are for the imposition of a levy on employers in the hotel and catering industry for the purpose of raising money towards meeting the expenses of the Board.

The levy is to be imposed in respect of the twenty-first levy period commencing with the day upon which this Order comes into force and ending on 31st March 1988. The levy will be assessed by the Board and there will be a right of appeal against an assessment to an industrial tribunal.

(**a**) S.I. 1964/1079, amended by S.I. 1980/1274, 1982/922.   (**b**) S.I. 1964/1086, amended by S.I. 1980/1273.
(**c**) S.I. 1966/969, amended by S.I. 1970/1886.   (**d**) S.I. 1966/1112, amended by S.I. 1982/664.
(**e**) S.I. 1967/648, amended by S.I. 1982/921.   (**f**) S.I. 1969/1375, amended by S.I. 1982/920.
(**g**) S.I. 1967/1062, amended by S.I. 1982/923.

STATUTORY INSTRUMENTS

1987 No. 898

INCOME TAX

The Income Tax (Interest on Unpaid Tax and Repayment Supplement) (No. 2) Order 1987

Made - - - -	*14th May 1987*
Laid before the House of Commons	*14th May 1987*
Coming into force	*6th June 1987*

The Treasury, in exercise of the powers conferred on them by section 40(2) of the Finance Act 1967(**a**), by section 89(2) of the Taxes Management Act 1970(**b**) and by sections 47(7) and 48(6) of the Finance (No. 2) Act 1975(**c**), hereby make the following Order:

1. This Order may be cited as the Income Tax (Interest on Unpaid Tax and Repayment Supplement) (No. 2) Order 1987 and shall come into force on 6th June 1987.

2. The prescribed rate of interest for the purposes of each of the provisions set out in the Table below shall be 8.25 per cent. per annum.

TABLE

Section 8 of the Finance (No. 2) Act 1947 (**d**) (unpaid profits tax, excess profits tax and excess profits levy)

Paragraph 10(1) of Schedule 7 to the Finance Act 1960 (**e**) (unpaid profits tax recovered to make good loss due to taxpayer's fault)

Sections 86 (**f**), 86A (**g**), 87 (**h**) and 88 (**i**) of the Taxes Management Act 1970 (unpaid income tax, surtax, capital gains tax, corporation tax, including

---

(**a**) 1967 c.54.

(**b**) 1970 c.9; section 89(2) was extended to petroleum revenue tax by paragraph 1(1) of Schedule 2 to the Oil Taxation Act 1975 (c.22) and to development land tax by paragraph 23 of Schedule 8 to the Development Land Tax Act 1976 (c.24). The Development Land Tax Act was repealed by section 98(6) of, and Part X of Schedule 27 to, the Finance Act 1985 (c.54) in relation to any disposal of an interest in land on or after 19th March 1985.

(**c**) 1975 c.45.

(**d**) 1947 c.9 (11 & 12 Geo. 6).

(**e**) 1960 c.44.

(**f**) Section 86 was substituted by section 46(1) of the Finance (No. 2) Act 1975 (c.45); the section as substituted was amended by sections 61(3) and 62(1) and (2) of the Finance Act 1980 (c.48), and by section 69(1) of the Finance Act 1982 (c.39). Other modifications of and applications of the section were made by section 46(2) of the Finance (No. 2) Act 1975 (c.45), section 62(6) of the Finance Act 1981 (c.35), and section 26 of, and paragraph 13(9) of Schedule 5 to, the Finance Act 1983 (c.28).

(**g**) Section 86A was inserted by section 41 of, and paragraph 21(2) of Schedule 8 to, the Development Land Tax Act 1976 (c.24) and amended by section 115(2) and section 122(4) of, and Part XIV of Schedule 20 to, the Finance Act 1980 (c.48) and by section 123(4) of the Finance Act 1984 (c.43). The Development Land Tax Act 1976 (c.24) was repealed by section 98(6) of, and Part X of Schedule 27 to, the Finance Act 1985 (c.54).

(**h**) Section 87 was substituted by section 111 of, and paragraph 10 of Schedule 24 to, the Finance Act 1972 (c.41) and amended by section 46(3) of the Finance (No. 2) Act 1975 (c.45) and by section 62(1) and (2) of the Finance Act 1980 (c.48).

(**i**) Section 88 was amended by section 37(1) of, and paragraph 87 of Schedule 6 to, the Finance Act 1971 (c.68), section 111 of, and paragraph 11 of Schedule 24 to, the Finance Act 1972 (c.41), section 46(4) of the Finance (No. 2) Act 1975 (c.45), section 41 of, and paragraph 22(1) of Schedule 8 to, the Development Land Tax Act 1976 (c.24), and by section 61(4) of the Finance Act 1980 (c.48). The amendments made by 1976 c.24 were repealed by section 98(6) of, and Part X of Schedule 27 to, the Finance Act 1985 (c.54).

advance corporation tax, development land tax, and overpaid development land tax)

Paragraph 15(1) of Schedule 2 to the Oil Taxation Act 1975 (a) (unpaid petroleum revenue tax)

3. The prescribed rate of interest for the purposes of sections 47(1) and 48(2) of the Finance (No. 2) Act 1975 (supplement on overpaid income tax, surtax, capital gains tax, and corporation tax, including advance corporation tax) shall be 8.25 per cent. per annum.

Tim Sainsbury
Peter Lloyd

14th May 1987   Two of the Lords Commissioners of Her Majesty's Treasury

---

EXPLANATORY NOTE

(This note is not part of the Order)

On and after 6th June 1987 this Order reduces from 9 per cent. per annum to 8.25 per cent. per annum the rate of interest chargeable on unpaid income tax, surtax, capital gains tax, corporation tax (including advance corporation tax), development land tax, petroleum revenue tax, profits tax, excess profits tax, excess profits levy and on overpaid development land tax. The Order also provides that on and after 6th June 1987 supplement on repayments of income tax, surtax, capital gains tax and corporation tax (including advance corporation tax) will be at the rate of 8.25 per cent. per annum instead of 9 per cent. per annum.

(a)   1975 c.22; paragraph 15(1) was amended by section 2(1) of the Petroleum Revenue Tax Act 1980 (c.1).

STATUTORY INSTRUMENTS

1987 No. 899

REPRESENTATION OF THE PEOPLE

The Returning Officers' Expenses Regulations 1987

Made - - -	*13th May 1987*
Coming into force	*20th May 1987*

The Treasury, in exercise of the powers conferred on them by section 29(3) of the Representation of the People Act 1983(**a**), hereby make the following Regulations:–

1. These Regulations may be cited as the Returning Officers' Expenses Regulations 1987 and shall come into force on 20th May 1987.

2. The maximum charges to which a returning officer at a parliamentary election in England, Wales and Scotland shall be entitled are:–

    (a) in respect of services rendered by him, the amounts specified in Part A of the Schedule to these Regulations; and

    (b) in respect of expenses incurred by him, the amounts specified in Part B of the said Schedule.

3. The Returning Officers' Expenses (England and Wales) Regulations 1984(**b**) and the Returning Officers' Expenses (Scotland) Regulations 1984(**c**) are hereby revoked.

Mark Lennox-Boyd
Peter Lloyd
13th May 1987   Two of the Lords Commissioners of Her Majesty's Treasury

SCHEDULE

SCALE OF MAXIMUM CHARGES IN RESPECT OF SERVICES RENDERED AND EXPENSES INCURRED BY A RETURNING OFFICER FOR THE PURPOSES OF OR IN CONNECTION WITH A PARLIAMENTARY ELECTION

Only the fees and disbursements specified hereunder shall be chargeable and in particular a returning officer shall not be entitled to charge as an expense payments which he makes from his fees (or otherwise) to a deputy acting returning officer or deputy returning officer by way of remuneration for performing functions of the returning officer.

(**a**) 1983 c.2.
(**b**) S.I. 1984/720.
(**c**) S.I. 1984/721.

PART A—FEES	£

I.   In a contested election:

   1. For conducting the election and generally performing duties which a returning officer is required to perform under any enactments relating to parliamentary elections, other than any duties for which separate fees are prescribed herein:

      For each constituency 727.01

      In addition, if the number of entries in the register of electors to be used at the election (as first published) exceeds 50,000 there shall be paid:

         For every 1,000 entries or fraction thereof over 50,000 up to 60,000   4.94

         For every 1,000 entries or fraction thereof over 60,000... ... ...   3.90

         Provided that the amount payable to a returning officer in England and Wales responsible for more than three constituencies or in Scotland responsible for more than three constituences situated wholly or mainly within the same district council area shall be reduced as follows:

            For each constituency exceeding three but not exceeding six, a reduction of 158.44

            For each constituency exceeding six, a reduction of 234.52

   2. For services in connection with the despatch and receipt of the ballot papers of persons entitled to vote by post:

      For each consituency 37.54

      In addition, if the number of persons entitled to vote by post in the constituency exceeds 500, there shall be paid:

         For every 50 or fraction thereof over 500 up to 2,000 ... ...   1.14

         For every 50 or fraction thereof over 2,000 ... ...   0.35

II.   In an uncontested election, for the services specified in paragraph I.1 of this part of the Schedule the amount shall be one-third of the sum prescribed thereunder.

III.   For services in connection with the preparation, maintenance and issue of official poll cards:

      For each constituency:

   (a) For the preparation, the first revision and the issue of the cards on the occasion of an election 225.37

         Provided that the amount payable to a returning officer in England and Wales responsible for more than three constituencies or in Scotland responsible for more than three constituencies situated wholly or mainly within the same district council area shall be reduced as follows:

            For each constituency exceeding three but not exceeding six, a reduction of 71.50

            For each constituency exceeding six, a reduction of 106.96

   (b) For each revision and preparation after the first prior to the issue of the cards 74.93

PART B—DISBURSEMENTS	£

Except as expressly provided in this part of the Schedule, in no case shall a charge exceed the sum actually and necessarily paid or payable by the returning officer. Subject thereto the maximum charges shall be as follows:

I. In a contested election:

1. For the presiding officer at each polling station (to include all expenses, other than any travelling and overnight subsistence expenses specified in this part of the Schedule) **65.00**

In addition, a further sum, not exceeding £4.26 may be paid to one of the presiding officers at a polling place to which there are assigned not less than 3,000 entries in the register of electors to be used at the election (as first published), being a presiding officer who acts as overall presiding officer at that polling place.

                                                       41.64

2. (a) For one clerk at each polling station ... ...

     (b) For additional clerks at a polling station to which there are assigned more than 700 entries in the register of electors to be used at the election (as first published) such additional clerks not to exceed one clerk for every 600 entries or fraction thereof in excess of 700:

        For each additional clerk (whole-time or part-time as the case may require) an amount within a range having a maximum of   **41.64**

3. (1) For the employment of persons in connection with the manual preparation and issue of the official poll cards, including charges for superannuation contributions where payable:

     (a) For the initial preparation of the cards: **2.81**

        For every 100 cards or fraction thereof   ... ...

     (b) For each revision:

        (i) For every 100 cards or fraction thereof prepared on initial preparation **0.46**

        (ii) For every 100 new cards or fraction thereof prepared... ...   **2.81**

        Provided that, if the number of new cards does not exceed 15 per cent of the number prepared on the initial preparation, the total allowance, for the revision shall be increased by 5 per cent.

     (c) For the revision of a particular section of the cards (other than such a revision carried out in the course of a revision of the whole):   **2.81**

        For every 100 new cards or fraction thereof prepared   ... ...

     (d) For the completion and issue of the cards on the occasion of an election:

        For every 100 cards or fraction thereof issued (or withdrawn in respect of votors entitled to vote by post) **1.45**

    (2) For the employment of persons in connection with the issue of poll cards which have not been prepared manually, including charges for superannuation contributions where payable: **0.92**

        For every 100 cards or fraction thereof   ... ...

    Provided that the maximum amount which a returning officer shall be entitled to charge under this paragraph shall be the total of the sums which he would be entitled to charge for such of the stages of work represented by items (1)(a), (b), (c) and (d) and (2) hereunder as he has carried out, notwithstanding that the amount disbursed by him for any particular stage is greater than the amount specified hereunder as the maximum amount for that stage; provided also that the maximum amount which a returning officer shall be entitled to charge under this paragraph shall be increased by any amount by which the maximum amount which he is entitled to charge under paragraph 4 below exceeds the amount disbursed by him for the purposes described in that paragraph.

PART B—DISBURSEMENTS	£

4. For the employment of persons in connection with the count and the ballot papers of electors entitled to vote by post, and for all clerical and other assistance employed by the returning officer, deputy returning officer, acting returning officer or deputy acting returning officer for the purposes of the election, including charges for day subsistence expenses and for superannuation contributions where payable.

(a) If the number of entries in the register of electors to be used at the election (as first published) in the constituency does not exceed 50,000 ... .   **2,305.75**

   For every additional 1,000 entries or fraction thereof over 50,000   **28.77**

(b) For every 100 persons or fraction thereof entitled to vote by post   **26.30**

(c) In the event of a recount of the votes being ordered:
   For each recount **230.58**
   Provided that the maximum amount which a returning officer shall be entitled to charge under this paragraph shall be increased by any amount by which the maximum amount which he is entitled to charge under paragraph 3 above exceeds the amount disbursed by him for the purposes described in that paragraph.

5. Returning officer's, deputy returning officer's, acting returning officer's or deputy acting returning officer's travelling and overnight subsistence expenses where necessary to make arrangements for the poll or otherwise in connection with the conduct of the election.   Actual and necessary cost.

6. Travelling and overnight subsistence expenses of presiding officers and poll clerks (including any expenses incurred in conveying the ballot boxes in those cases in which presiding officers or poll clerks are responsible for the transport of the boxes to or from the polling stations).   Actual and necessary cost.

7. Travelling and overnight subsistence expenses of clerical and other assistants employed by the returning officer, deputy returning officer, acting returning officer or deputy acting returning officer where necessary to make arrangements for the poll or otherwise in connection with the conduct of the election.   Actual and necessary cost.

8. For printing and providing actual ballot papers ... ...   Actual and necessary cost.

9. For printing and providing official poll cards ... ...   Actual and necessary cost.

10. For printing and providing notices and other documents required in and about the election or poll and costs of publishing the same.   Actual and necessary cost.

11. For the renting of any building or room for the purpose of the election and for expenses of heating, lighting and cleaning any building or room for such purpose.   Actual and necessary cost.

12. For adapting and fitting up any building or room for the purpose of the election (including the provision of voting compartments and any necessary furniture) and restoring it to fit condition for its normal use.   Actual and necessary cost

13. For providing ballot boxes, including any repairs ... ...   Actual and necessary cost.

14. For the conveyance of ballot boxes and ballot papers in those cases where the cost of transport is not included in the travelling expenses of presiding officers and poll clerks under paragraph 1.6 of this part of the Schedule.   Actual and necessary cost.

15. For every stamping instrument required to be purchased, hired, altered or repaired.   Actual and necessary cost.

PART B—DISBURSEMENTS	£
16. For copies of the register	Actual and necessary cost.
17. For general stationery, postage, telephone calls, bank charges and miscellaneous expenses.	Actual and necessary cost.

II. In an uncontested election, for all necessary preliminary work the amount shall be the same as the amount specified for corresponding work in a contested election, except that for all clerical and other assistance employed by the returning officer, deputy returning officer, acting returning officer or deputy acting returning officer for the purposes of the election, including charges for day subsistence expenses and for superannuation contributions where payable, the amount shall not be more than one-quarter of the amount specified under paragraph I.4 of this part of the Schedule.

EXPLANATORY NOTE

(This note is not part of the Regulations)

These Regulations revoke and replace the Returning Officers' Expenses (England and Wales) Regulations 1984 and the Returning Officers' Expenses (Scotland) Regulations 1984. They prescribe, in relation to England, Wales and Scotland, a revised scale further increasing the maximum fees in respect of services rendered and the maximum charges in respect of expenses incurred by a returning officer for the purposes of or in connection with a parliamentary election. Separate charges are prescribed in respect of the preparation of poll cards by manual and by non-manual means. The increases over those prescribed in 1984 are between 14 per cent and $18\frac{1}{2}$ per cent save that the maximum charge prescribed for the presiding officer is increased by 30 per cent.

1987 No. 900

REPRESENTATION OF THE PEOPLE

The Returning Officers' Expenses (Northern Ireland) Regulations 1987

Made - - - -	*13th May 1987*
Coming into force	*20th May 1987*

The Treasury, in exercise of the powers conferred on them by section 29(3) of the Representation of the People Act 1983(**a**), hereby make the following Regulations:

1. These Regulations may be cited as the Returning Officers' Expenses (Northern Ireland) Regulations 1987, and shall come into force on 20th May 1987.

2. The maximum charges to which the Chief Electoral Officer for Northern Ireland as the returing officer responsible for the conduct of a parliamentary election in Northern Ireland shall be entitled are, in respect of expenses incurred by him, the amounts specified in the Schedule to these Regulations.

3. The Returning Officer's Expenses (Northern Ireland) Regulations 1984 (**b**) are hereby revoked.

Mark Lennox-Boyd
Peter Lloyd

13th May 1987   Two of the Lords Commissioners of Her Majesty's Treasury

---

(**a**) 1983 c.2.
(**b**) S.I. 1984/722.

SCHEDULE

SCALE OF MAXIMUM EXPENDITURE WHICH MAY BE INCURRED BY THE CHIEF ELECTORAL OFFICER FOR NORTHERN IRELAND AS THE RETURNING OFFICER FOR A PARLIAMENTARY ELECTION IN NORTHERN IRELAND IN RESPECT OF PAYMENT OF FEES AND DISBURSEMENTS TO PERSONS APPOINTED BY THE RETURNING OFFICER TO ASSIST HIM AND HIS DEPUTY ELECTORAL OFFICERS AND ALL OTHER EXPENSES IN CONNECTION WITH A PARLIAMENTARY ELECTION IN A CONSTITUENCY

Except as expressly provided in this Schedule, in no case shall a charge exceed the sum actually and necessarily paid or payable by the returning officer. Subject thereto the maximum charges shall be as follows–

I.   In a contested election–

	£
1. For the presiding officer at each polling station (to include all expenses, other than any travelling and overnight subsistence expenses specified in this part of the Schedule)	65.00
In addition, a further sum, not exceeding £4.26 may be paid to one of the presiding officers at a polling place to which there are assigned not less than 3,000 entries in the register of electors to be used at the election (as first published) being a presiding officer who acts as overall presiding officer at the polling place.	
2. (a) For one clerk at each polling station	41.64
(b) For additional clerks at a polling station to which there are assigned more than 700 entries in the register of electors to be used at the election (as first published), such additional clerks not to exceed one clerk for every 600 entries, or fraction thereof in excess of 700–	
For each additional clerk (whole-time or part-time as the case may require) an amount within a range having a maximum of	41.64
3.—(I) For the employment of persons in connection with the manual preparations and issue of the official poll cards, including charges for superannuation contributions where payable–	
(a) For the initial preparation of the cards–	
For every 100 cards or fraction thereof	2.81
(b) For each revision–	
(i) For every 100 cards or fraction thereof prepared on the initial preparation	0.46
(ii) For every 100 new cards or fraction thereof prepared	2.81
Provided that, if the number of new cards does not exceed 15 per cent of the number prepared on the initial preparation, the total allowances for the revision shall be increased by 5 per cent.	
(c) For the revision of a particular section of the cards (other than such a revision carried out in the course of a revision of the whole)–	
For every 100 new cards or fraction thereof prepared	2.81
(d) For the completion and issue of the cards on the occasion of an election–	
For every 100 cards or fraction thereof issued (or withdrawn in respect of voters entitled to vote by post)	1.45
(II) For the employment of persons in connection with the issue of official poll cards which have not been prepared manually, including charges for superannuation contributions where payable–	
For every 100 cards or fraction thereof	0.92
Provided that the maximum amount which a returning officer shall be entitled to charge under this paragraph shall be the total of the sums which he would be entitled to charge for such of the stages of work represented by items (I)(a), (b),	

(c) and (d) and (II) above as he has carried out, notwithstanding that the amount disbursed by him for any particular stage is greater than the amount specified above as the maximum amount for that stage; provided also that the maximum amount which a returning officer shall be entitled to charge under this paragraph shall be increased by any amount by which the maximum amount which he is entitled to charge under paragraph 4 below exceeds the amount disbursed by him for the purposes described in that paragraph.

4.   For the employment of persons in connection with the count and the ballot papers of electors entitled to vote by post, and for all clerical and other assistance employed by the returning officer or deputy returning officer for the purposes of the election, including charges for day subsistence expenses and for superannuation contributions where payable–

(a) If the number of entries in the register of electors to be used at the election (as first published) in the constituency does not exceed 50,000 — 2305.75
For every additional 1,000 entries or fraction thereof over 50,000 — 28.77

(b) For every 100 persons or fraction thereof entitled to vote by post — 26.30

(c) In the event of a recount of the votes being ordered–
For each recount 230.58

Provided that the maximum amount which a returning officer shall be entitled to charge under this paragraph shall be increased by any amount by which the maximum amount which he is entitled to charge under paragraph 3 above exceeds the amount disbursed by him for the purposes described in that paragraph.

5. Returning or deputy returning officers' travelling and overnight subsistence expenses where necessary to make arrangements for the poll or otherwise in connection with the conduct of the election.	Actual and necessary cost.
6. Travelling and overnight subsistence expenses of presiding officers and poll clerks (including any expenses incurred in conveying the ballot boxes in those cases in which presiding officers or poll clerks are responsible for the transport of the boxes to or from the polling stations).	Actual and necessary cost.
7. Travelling and overnight subsistence expenses of clerical and other assistants employed by the returning officer or deputy returning officer where necessary to make arrangements for the poll or otherwise in connection with the conduct of the election.	Actual and necessary cost.
8. For printing and providing ballot papers.	Actual and necessary cost.
9. For printing and providing official poll cards.	Actual and necessary cost.
10. For printing and providing notices and other documents required in and about the election or poll and costs of publishing the same.	Actual and necessary cost.
11. For the renting of any building or room for the purpose of the election and for expenses of heating, lighting and cleaning any building or room for such purposes.	Actual and necessary cost.
12. For adapting and fitting up any building or room for the purpose of the election (including the provision of voting compartments and any necessary furniture) and restoring it to fit condition for its normal use.	Actual and necessary cost.
13. For providing ballot boxes, including any repairs.	Actual and necessary cost.
14. For the conveyance of ballot boxes and ballot papers in those cases where the cost of transport is not included in the travelling expenses of presiding officers and poll clerks under paragraph **I.6** of this Schedule.	Actual and necessary cost.
15. For every stamping instrument required to be purchased, hired, altered or repaired.	Actual and necessary cost.

| **16.** For copies of the register. | Actual and necessary cost. |
| **17.** For general stationery, postage, telephone calls, bank charges and miscellaneous expenses. | Actual and necessary cost. |

II.   In an uncontested election for all necessary preliminary work the amount shall be the same as the amount specified for corresponding work in a contested election, except that for all clerical and other assistance employed by the returning officer for the purposes of the election, including charges for day subsistence expenses and for superannuation contributions where payable, the amount shall be not more than one-quarter of the amount specified under paragraph **I.4** of this Schedule.

EXPLANATORY NOTE

(This note is not part of the Regulations)

These Regulations revoke and replace the Returning Officers' Expenses (Northern Ireland) Regulations 1984. They prescribe, in relation to Northern Ireland, a revised scale further increasing some of the maximum charges in respect of expenses incurred by the Chief Electoral Officer for Northern Ireland as returning officer for the purposes of or in connection with a parliamentary election. Separate charges are prescribed in respect of the preparation of poll cards by manual and by non-manual means. The increases over those prescribed in 1984 are between 14 per cent and 18½ per cent save that the maximum charge prescribed for the presiding officer is increased by 30 per cent.

STATUTORY INSTRUMENTS

1987 No. 901

ELECTRICITY

The Meters (Determination of Questions) (Expenses) Regulations 1987

Made - - - -	*14th May 1987*
Laid before Parliament	*15th May 1987*
Coming into force	*15th June 1987*

The Secretary of State, in exercise of the powers conferred on him by section 57(5) of the Schedule to the Electric Lighting (Clauses) Act 1899**(a)** as incorporated with the Electricity Act 1947**(b)**, hereby makes the following Regulations:–

Citation and commencement

1. These Regulations may be cited as the Meters (Determination of Questions) (Expenses) Regulations 1987 and shall come into force on 15th June 1987.

Determination of questions

2.—(1) The sums to be paid by the Electricity Boards mentioned in the first column of the Table below to the Secretary of State towards administrative expenses incurred by him in connection with the determination of questions under section 57 shall be the amounts specified in the second column of that Table and shall be paid in advance on the first day of each month.

(2) For the purposes of this Regulation—

a question is determined when a meter examiner signs a certificate that he has determined the question or that he is unable or no longer required to do so; and

"section 57" means section 57 of the Schedule to the Electric Lighting (Clauses) Act 1899 as incorporated with the Electricity Act 1947.

3. The Meters (Determination of Questions) (Expenses) Regulations 1986**(c)** are hereby revoked.

(a) 1899 c.19; section 57 was substituted by the Energy Act 1983 (c.25), Schedule 1, paragraph 13.
(b) 1947 c.54; section 57(2) incorporates the Schedule to the Electric Lighting (Clauses) Act 1899 with adaptations and modifications.
(c) S.I. 1986/1627.

TABLE

Electricity Board	Monthly Payments
Eastern	£1958.67
East Midlands	£941.67
London	£3503.00
Merseyside & North Wales	£941.67
Midland	£4143.33
North Eastern	£226.00
North of Scotland Hydro	£640.33
North Western	£979.33
Southern	£1845.67
South Eastern	£2561.33
South of Scotland	£339.00
South Wales	£1017.00
South Western	£1921.00
Yorkshire	£1243.00

14th May 1987

Alastair Goodlad
Parliamentary Under Secretary of State,
Department of Energy

EXPLANATORY NOTE

(This note is not part of the Regulations)

These Regulations re-enact, with amendments, the Meters (Determination of Questions) (Expenses) Regulations 1986, which provide for Electricity Boards to make monthly payments towards administrative expenses incurred by the Secretary of State in connection with the determination of questions as to the correctness of electricity meters. In addition to drafting amendments, the Regulations alter the amount of the monthly payments.

1987 No. 902

CRIMINAL LAW, ENGLAND AND WALES

The Crown Prosecution Service (Witnesses' Allowances) (Amendment No.4) Regulations 1987

Made - - - -	*13th May 1987*
Laid before Parliament	*15th May 1987*
Coming into force -	*22nd June 1987*

The Attorney General, in exercise of the powers conferred upon him by section 14(1)(b) and (2) of the Prosecution of Offences Act 1985**(a)** and with the approval of the Treasury, hereby makes the following Regulations:

1. These Regulations may be cited as the Crown Prosecution Service (Witnesses' Allowances) (Amendment No.4) Regulations 1987 and shall come into force on 22nd June 1987.

2. In Schedule 1 to the Crown Prosecution Service (Witnesses' Allowances) Regulations 1986**(b)**, in Column 3 of the Table, which sets out relevant amounts in relation to allowances payable under those Regulations–
- (a) for the sums of £49.20 and £98.40 in the entry for Regulation 4(a) (locum allowance payable to a professional witness who attends to give evidence) there shall be substituted £52.50 and £105.00 respectively; and
- (b) for the sums of £33.70, £49.20, £73.90 and £98.40 in the entry for regulation 4(b) (compensatory allowance payable to such witness) there shall be substituted £35.00, £52.50, £78.80 and £105.00 respectively.

3. The Crown Prosecution Service (Witnesses' Allowances) (Amendment No.2) Regulations 1986**(c)** are hereby revoked.

11th May 1987

Michael Havers
Her Majesty's Attorney General

We approve.

13th May 1987

Timothy Sainsbury
Michael Neubert
Two of the Lords Commissioners of Her Majesty's Treasury

(a) 1985 c.23.
(b) S.I. 1986/405, amended by S.I. 1986/842, 1250 and 1818.
(c) S.I. 1986/1250.

EXPLANATORY NOTE

(This note is not part of the Regulations)

These Regulations increase the maximum locum and compensatory allowances payable under regulation 4 of the Crown Prosecution Service (Witnesses' Allowances) Regulations 1986 to a professional witness who, at the instance of the Crown Prosecution Service, attends court to give evidence and thereby incurs certain expenditure or suffers certain loss as described in that regulation.

STATUTORY INSTRUMENTS

1987 No. 903

REPRESENTATION OF THE PEOPLE

The Representation of the People (Variation of Limits of Candidates' Election Expenses) Order 1987

Made	-	-	-	-	*13th May 1987*
Coming into force			-		*14th May 1987*

Whereas a draft of this Order has been approved by resolution of each House of Parliament:

And whereas in my opinion there has been a change in the value of money since 16th July 1985 in the case of the variations made by articles 4 and 7 of this Order and 1st March 1986 in the case of the variations made by articles 2, 3, 5 and 6 of this Order justifying the variations made by this Order:

Now, therefore, in exercise of the powers conferred upon me by sections 76A(1) and 197(3) of the Representation of the People Act 1983(a), I hereby make the following Order:–

1.—(1) This Order may be cited as the Representation of the People (Variation of Limits of Candidates' Election Expenses) Order 1987 and shall come into force on the day after the day on which it is made.

(2) Articles 4, 5, 6 and 7 of this Order do not extend to Northern Ireland.

(3) In this Order "the Act of 1983" means the Representation of the People Act 1983.

2. The maximum amount of a candidate's election expenses at a parliamentary election in a county constituency shall be varied by substituting, for the words "£3,240" and "3.7p" in section 76(2)(a)(i) of the Act of 1983(b), the words "£3,370" and "3.8p", respectively.

3. The maximum amount of a candidate's election expenses at a parliamentary election in a borough constituency shall be varied by substituting, for the words "£3,240" and "2.8p" in section 76(2)(a)(ii) of the Act of 1983(b), the words "£3,370" and "2.9p", respectively.

4. The maximum amount of a candidate's election expenses at an election to the Inner London Education Authority shall be varied by substituting, for the words "£620"

(a) 1983 c.2; section 76A was inserted by section 14(4) of the Representation of the People Act 1985 (c.50) and section 197(3) was amended by paragraph 67(b) of Schedule 4 to that Act.
(b) The sums in section 76(2)(a) are as substituted by S.I. 1986/383.

and "3.7p" in section 76(2)(b)(ia) of the Act of 1983**(a)**, the words "£655" and "3.9p", respectively.

5. The maximum amount of a candidate's election expenses at a local government election to which section 76(2)(b)(ii) of the Act of 1983**(b)** applies shall be varied by substituting, for the words "£144" and "2.9p" in that provision, the words "£150" and "3p" respectively.

6. The maximum amount of a candidate's election expenses at a ward election in the City of London shall be varied by substituting, for the words "£144" and "2.9p" in section 197(1) of the Act of 1983**(c)**, the words "£150" and "3p" respectively.

7. The maximum amount of a candidate's election expenses at an election by liverymen in common hall shall be varied by substituting, for the words "15p" in section 197(2) of the Act of 1983**(d)**, the words "15.8p".

8. The Representation of the People (Variation of Limits of Candidates' Election Expenses) Order 1986**(e)** is hereby revoked.

Home Office
13th May 1987

Douglas Hurd
One of Her Majesty's Principal Secretaries of State

EXPLANATORY NOTE

(This note is not part of the Order)

This Order increases the maximum amounts of candidates' election expenses at parliamentary elections in the United Kingdom (articles 2 and 3), local government elections in Great Britain (articles 4 and 5) and ward elections (article 6) and elections by liverymen in common hall (article 7) in the City of London.

The increases are such as are justified by the change in the value of money since the last occasions on which those maximum amounts were changed or fixed. In the case of elections to the Inner London Education Authority and elections by liverymen in common hall, that last occasion was 16th July 1985 when the Local Government Act 1985 and the Representation of the People Act 1985 (which Acts respectively established and amended the maximum amounts of election expenses for those elections) were enacted. As respects the other elections to which this Order relates, the last occasion was 1st March 1986 when the Representation of the People (Variation of Limits of Candidates' Election Expenses) Order 1986 was made. That Order is revoked by article 8 of this Order.

Except in the case of the election by liverymen in common hall, the maximum amount of a candidate's election expenses is made up of a fixed sum (expressed in pounds) plus a sum expressed in pence (and fractions of pence) for, in the case of parliamentary and

---

(a) Section 76(2)(b)(ia) was inserted by paragraph 1(8) of Schedule 9 to the Local Government Act 1985 (c.51).
(b) The sums in section 76(2)(b)(ii) are as substituted by S.I. 1986/383.
(c) The sums in section 197(1) are as substituted by S.I. 1986/383.
(d) Section 197(2) was amended by paragraph 67(a) of Schedule 4 to the Representation of the People Act 1985 (c.50).
(e) S.I. 1986/383.

local government elections, each entry in the register of electors or, in the case of ward elections in the City of London, each elector. The maximum amount of a candidate's election expenses at the election by liverymen in common hall is calculated by allowing an amount in pence (and fractions of pence) for every elector on the common hall register to be used at the election.

1987 No. 904

AGRICULTURE

LIVESTOCK INDUSTRIES

The Artificial Insemination of Cattle (Advertising Controls etc.) (Great Britain) Regulations 1987

Made - - - -	*14th May 1987*
Laid before Parliament	*15th May 1987*
Coming into force	*30th June 1987*

The Minister of Agriculture, Fisheries and Food in relation to England, the Secretary of State for Scotland in relation to Scotland and the Secretary of State for Wales in relation to Wales, in exercise of the powers conferred on them by section 10 of the Animal Health and Welfare Act 1984(a) and of all other powers enabling them in that behalf, hereby make the following Regulations:

Title and commencement

1. These Regulations may be cited as the Artificial Insemination of Cattle (Advertising Controls etc.) (Great Britain) Regulations 1987 and shall come into force on 30th June 1987.

Interpretation

2.—(1) In these Regulations, unless the context otherwise requires –

"advertisement" includes every form of advertising to the public, whether in a publication, or by the display of any notice, or by means of any catalogue, price list, letter (whether circular or addressed to a particular person) or other document, or by words inscribed on any article, or by the exhibition of a photographic or a cinematograph film, or by way of sound recording, sound broadcasting or television, or in any other way;

"the Animal Health (England and Wales) Regulations" means the Artificial Insemination of Cattle (Animal Health) (England and Wales) Regulations 1985(b);

"the Animal Health (Scotland) Regulations" means the Artificial Insemination of Cattle (Animal Health) (Scotland) Regulations 1985(c);

"dairy breed" means any of the Ayrshire, British Friesian (including Red and White Friesian and Poll Friesian), British Holstein, Jersey or Guernsey breeds or Dairy Shorthorn types of cattle;

"Improved Contemporary Comparison" means predicted transmitting ability for production for bulls of dairy breeds published from time to time jointly by the Milk Marketing Board and the Scottish Milk Marketing Board;

(a) 1984 c. 40.   (b) S.I. 1985/1861.   (c) S.I. 1985/1857.

"licensed artificial insemination organisation or centre" means an organisation or centre authorised for the time being to process, store or supply semen by virtue of a licence issued under the Animal Health (England and Wales) Regulations or under the Animal Health (Scotland) Regulations.

(2) Any reference in these Regulations to a numbered regulation or Schedule shall be construed as a reference to the regulation or Schedule bearing that number in these Regulations.

Advertisement of semen from a bull of a dairy breed

3.—(1) Subject to paragraphs (2) and (3) below, no person shall cause an advertisement relating to any semen from a bull of a dairy breed to be issued unless that advertisement includes –

(a) a statement of the breed and name of the bull from which that semen was taken and the herd book number;

(b) where an Improved Contemporary Comparison has been published for the bull, all the latest information available relating to the matters specified in paragraph 1 of Schedule 1 and a statement that such information is based on progeny testing;

(c) where an Improved Contemporary Comparison has not been published for the bull –

(i) all the latest information available relating to the matters specified in paragraph 2 of Schedule 1 and a statement that such information is based on progeny testing or, as the case may be, sibling testing of the bull and its parents, and

(ii) where the bull was produced under a multiple ovulation and embryo transfer scheme and is being, or has been, sibling tested, all the latest information available relating to the matters specified in paragraph 3 of Schedule 1 and a statement that such information is based on sibling testing; and

(d) all the latest information available relating to any other matters as the appropriate Minister may from time to time require in writing.

(2) Where any information required under paragraph (1)(b) or (1)(c) above is not obtainable in Great Britain in relation to semen from an imported bull of a dairy breed or semen from a bull of a dairy breed in a country other than Great Britain at the time of semen collection, corresponding information from the country of origin shall be given, expressed in terms, so far as is practicable, comparable to the information required under paragraph (1)(b) or (1)(c) above.

(3) Where in relation to any semen any information required under paragraph (1) or (2) above cannot be obtained after reasonable enquiry, a statement to that effect, specifying the information which cannot be so obtained, shall be made in the advertisement.

Form of statements, etc.

4. Any statement or information to be provided under regulation 3 shall be given in a clear manner, and where it is printed it shall be legible, and that which is unfavourable shall be given equal prominence to that which is favourable.

False information

5. No person shall furnish any information under regulation 3 which he knows to be false or does not believe to be true.

Amendment of the Animal Health (England and Wales) Regulations

6. The Animal Health (England and Wales) Regulations shall be amended in accordance with Schedule 2.

Amendment of the Animal Health (Scotland) Regulations

7. The Animal Health (Scotland) Regulations shall be amended in accordance with Schedule 3.

Revocation

8. The Artificial Insemination of Cattle (Livestock Quality) (England and Wales) Regulations 1985(a) and the Artificial Insemination of Cattle (Livestock Quality) (Scotland) Regulations 1985(b) are revoked.

In Witness whereof the Official Seal of the Minister of Agriculture, Fisheries and Food is hereunto affixed on 13th May 1987.

(L.S.)

Michael Jopling
Minister of Agriculture, Fisheries and Food

13th May 1987

John J. MacKay
Parliamentary Under-Secretary of State,
Scottish Office

13th May 1987

Nicholas Edwards
Secretary of State for Wales

SCHEDULE 1

Regulation 3

ADVERTISEMENT OF SEMEN FROM BULLS OF DAIRY BREEDS

1.—(a) The date of publication of, and the following details from, the latest Improved Contemporary Comparison relating to the bull from which the semen was taken, with the appropriate weighting for each Improved Contemporary Comparison, placing the symbol "–" or the word "minus" immediately before negative figures –

(i) number of daughter records in the milk yield Improved Contemporary Comparison,

(ii) number of herds in which the daughters to which those records relate were milked,

(iii) percentage of those daughters in the herd with the largest number of those daughters,

(iv) where the percentage of daughters in the herd with the second largest number of those daughters was more than 10%, that percentage,

(v) kilograms of milk,

(vi) kilograms of butter-fat and butter-fat percentage,

(vii) kilograms of protein and protein percentage.

(b) The number of daughters of the bull from which the semen was taken which have been classified by a breed society or licensed artificial insemination organisation or centre, the associated weighting, classification summary of the ratings of the daughters in respect of the legs, feet and the components of the mammary system, the date on which these summary ratings were last determined and the name of the breed society or licensed artificial insemination organisation or centre from which this information was obtained.

(a) S.I. 1985/1862.   (b) S.I. 1985/1858.

2.—(a) The name of the sire of the bull from which the semen was taken and the details of the latest Improved Contemporary Comparison relating to that sire as set out in paragraph 1(a) above, together with their date of publication.

(b) The number of daughters of the sire of the bull from which the semen was taken which have been classified by a breed society or licensed artificial insemination organisation or centre, classification summary of the ratings of the daughters in respect of the legs, feet and the components of the mammary system, the date on which these summary ratings were last determined and the name of the breed society or licensed artificial insemination organisation or centre from which this information was obtained.

(c) The name of the dam of the bull from which the semen was taken, her breed society type classification, including the source of such classification, and details of the first four authenticated 305 day lactations, including calving dates, and either the current breeding index or the production indices, stating the herd base to which the cow has been compared.

3. The number of records of the dam, full sisters and half sisters on which the evaluation of the bull is based.

Regulation 6

SCHEDULE 2

AMENDMENTS TO THE ANIMAL HEALTH (ENGLAND AND WALES) REGULATIONS

1. In regulation 2(1) (interpretation) the definitions of "extended use" and "supplementarily approved bull" shall be omitted.

2. In regulation 5 (bulls for use in artificial insemination) –
(a) in paragraph (1) the words "subject to paragraph (13) below" shall be omitted; and
(b) paragraph (13) shall be omitted.

Regulation 7

SCHEDULE 3

AMENDMENTS TO THE ANIMAL HEALTH (SCOTLAND) REGULATIONS

1. In regulation 2(1) (interpretation) the definitions of "extended use" and "supplementarily approved bull" shall be omitted.

2. In regulation 5 (bulls for use in artificial insemination) –
(a) in paragraph (1) the words "subject to paragraph (13) below" shall be omitted; and
(b) paragraph (13) shall be omitted.

EXPLANATORY NOTE

(This note is not part of the Regulations)

These Regulations impose controls on the advertisement in Great Britain of semen from bulls of dairy breeds. A person may not cause such an advertisement to be issued unless it includes specified information (regulation 3 and Schedule 1).

Failure to comply with the Regulations is an offence under section 10(6) of the Animal Health and Welfare Act 1984, punishable on summary conviction by imprisonment for a term not exceeding three months or by a fine not exceeding level 3 on the standard scale (currently £400), or both.

The Regulations revoke the Artificial Insemination of Cattle (Livestock Quality) (England and Wales) Regulations 1985 and the Artificial Insemination of Cattle (Livestock Quality) (Scotland) Regulations 1985 (regulation 8). Those Regulations provided for the issue of supplementary approvals by Ministers for bulls for use in artificial insemination that was not restricted to the herds of the owner or co-owners of the bull. Those Regulations also required certain information to be given when advertising or distributing semen from a supplementarily approved bull of a dairy breed.

These Regulations also make consequential amendments to the Artificial Insemination of Cattle (Animal Health) (England and Wales) Regulations 1985 (regulation 6 and Schedule 2) and the Artificial Insemination of Cattle (Animal Health) (Scotland) Regulations 1985 (regulation 7 and Schedule 3).

STATUTORY INSTRUMENTS

1987 No. 905

ANIMALS

ANIMAL HEALTH

The Marek's Disease (Restriction on Vaccination) Order 1987

Made - - - -	*14th May 1987*
Coming into force	*31st May 1987*

The Minister of Agriculture, Fisheries and Food, the Secretary of State for Scotland and the Secretary of State for Wales, acting jointly, in exercise of the powers conferred on them by sections 1, 72 and 88(4)(a) of the Animal Health Act 1981(**a**) and of all other powers enabling them in that behalf, hereby Order as follows:

Title and commencement

1. This Order may be cited as the Marek's Disease (Restriction on Vaccination) Order 1987 and shall come into force on 31st May 1987.

Extension of definition of "disease"

2. For the purposes of the Act in its application to this Order the definition of "disease" in section 88(3) of the Act is hereby extended so as to comprise Marek's disease.

Interpretation

3. In this Order–

"the Act" means the Animal Health Act 1981;

"the appropriate Minister" means, in relation to England, the Minister and in relation to Scotland or to Wales, the Secretary of State;

"inspector" means a person appointed to be an inspector for the purposes of the Act by the Minister or by a local authority and, when used in relation to an officer of the Ministry, includes a veterinary inspector;

"the Minister" and "the Ministry" means respectively the Minister and the Ministry of Agriculture, Fisheries and Food;

"poultry" means live birds of the following species, that is to say domestic fowls, turkeys, geese, ducks, guinea-fowls, pigeons, pheasants and partridges;

"veterinary inspector" means a veterinary inspector appointed by the Minister.

Restriction on vaccination

4. No person shall vaccinate any poultry against Marek's disease with a vaccine consisting of or containing derivatives of the Rispens strain or the SB1 strain except under the authority of a licence issued by the appropriate Minister and in accordance with the conditions subject to which the licence is issued.

(**a**) 1981 c.22.

Production of licences

5. Any person acting under the authority of a licence issued under this Order shall, on demand made by an inspector or by a police officer, produce the licence and allow a copy or extract to be taken, and shall also, on such demand, furnish his name and address.

Offences

6. Any person who, without lawful authority or excuse, proof of which shall lie on him–

(a) contravenes any provision of this order or any provision of a licence issued under it; or

(b) fails to comply with any such provision or with any condition of such a licence; or

(c) knowingly causes or permits any such contravention or non-compliance, commits an offence against the Act.

Local authority to enforce Order

7. The provisions of this Order shall, except where otherwise expressly provided, be executed and enforced by the local authority.

In Witness whereof the Official Seal of the Minister of Agriculture, Fisheries and Food is hereunto affixed on 13th May 1987.

Michael Jopling
Minister of Agriculture, Fisheries and Food

13th May 1987

John J. Mackay
Parliamentary Under-Secretary of State, Scottish Office

14th May 1987

Nicholas Edwards
Secretary of State for Wales

EXPLANATORY NOTE

(This note is not part of the Order)

This Order prohibits the vaccination of any poultry against Marek's disease with a vaccine of the kind specified in the Order (that is to say a vaccine consisting of or containing derivatives of the Rispens strain or the SB1 strain) except under the authority of a licence issued by the appropriate Minister (as defined in the Order) (article 4).

STATUTORY INSTRUMENTS

1987 No. 906

PUBLIC HEALTH, ENGLAND AND WALES
PUBLIC HEALTH, SCOTLAND
PUBLIC HEALTH, NORTHERN IRELAND

CONTAMINATION OF FOOD

The Food Protection (Emergency Prohibitions) (England) (No. 2) Amendment No. 3 Order 1987

Made - - - -	*14th May 1987*
Laid before Parliament	*15th May 1987*
Coming into force	*25th May 1987*

Whereas the Minister of Agriculture, Fisheries and Food is of the opinion, in accordance with section 1(1)(a) of the Food and Environment Protection Act 1985**(a)**, that there has been or may have been an escape of substances of such descriptions and in such quantities and such circumstances as are likely to create a hazard to human health through human consumption of food;

And whereas the said Minister is of the opinion, in accordance with section 1(1)(b) of the said Act, that in consequence of the said escape of substances food which is or may be in the future in the area described in Schedule 1 to the Food Protection (Emergency Prohibitions) (England) (No. 2) Order 1986**(b)**, or which is derived or may be in the future derived from anything in that area, is, or may be, or may become, unsuitable for human consumption;

Now, therefore, the said Minister, in exercise of the powers conferred on him by the said section 1(1) and section 24(3) of the said Act, and of all other powers enabling him in that behalf, hereby makes the following Order:–

Title and commencement

1. This Order may be cited as the Food Protection (Emergency Prohibitions) (England) (No. 2) Amendment No. 3 Order 1987 and shall come into force on 25th May 1987.

Partial revocation and amendment

2. The Food Protection (Emergency Prohibitions) (England) (No. 2) Order 1986 is revoked to the extent that it imposes prohibitions on–
    (a) the slaughter of a sheep which–
        (i) was moved from a place in accordance with a consent given under section 2(1) of the Food and Environment Protection Act 1985 which consent was subject to the condition that the sheep to which it applies should be marked with an apricot mark; and
        (ii) has been examined and marked with an ear-tag by a person authorised in that behalf by one of the Ministers; and

---

(a) 1985 c.48.
(b) S.I. 1986/1689, amended by S.I. 1986/2208, 1987/153 and 249.

(b) the supply or having in possession for supply of meat, or food containing meat, derived from such a sheep,

and accordingly that Order is further amended in accordance with the following provisions of this Order.

3. In article 6, for paragraph (2) there shall be substituted the following paragraph–
"(2) Paragraph (1) above shall not apply in the case of–
    (a) any sheep which was moved to a market in accordance with a consent given under section 2(1) of the Act which consent did not require that the sheep to which it applies should be marked in a manner specified therein;
    (b) any sheep which was moved from any place in accordance with a consent given under the said section 2(1) which consent was subject to the condition that the sheep to which it applies should be marked with a blue mark; or
    (c) any sheep which–
        (i) was moved from any place in accordance with a consent given under the said section 2(1) which consent was subject to the condition that the sheep to which it applies should be marked with a red mark or with an apricot mark; and
        (ii) has been examined and marked with an ear-tag by a person authorised in that behalf by one of the Ministers.".

In witness whereof the Official Seal of the Minister of Agriculture, Fisheries and Food is hereunto affixed on 14th May 1987.

Michael Jopling
Minister of Agriculture, Fisheries and Food

EXPLANATORY NOTE

(This note is not part of the Order)

The Food Protection (Emergency Prohibitions) (England) (No. 2) Order 1986 contains emergency prohibitions restricting various activities in order to prevent human consumption of food which has been or which may have been rendered unsuitable for that purpose in consequence of the escape of radioactive substances from a nuclear reactor situated at Chernobyl in the USSR.

This Order excepts from the prohibition on slaughter throughout the United Kingdom any sheep, and from the prohibition on supply throughout the United Kingdom any meat derived from such sheep, identified by an apricot paint mark which have been examined and subsequently marked with an ear-tag by a person authorised by the Minister of Agriculture, Fisheries and Food or the Secretary of State for Scotland or Wales.

STATUTORY INSTRUMENTS

1987 No. 907 (C.24)

FINANCIAL SERVICES

The Financial Services Act 1986 (Commencement) (No. 5) Order 1987

Made - - - - *14th May 1987*

The Secretary of State, in exercise of his powers under section 211(1) of the Financial Services Act 1986(a), hereby makes the following Order.

1. This Order may be cited as the Financial Services Act 1986 (Commencement) (No. 5) Order 1987.

2. Section 206(4) of the Financial Services Act 1986 shall come into force on 15th May 1987.

3. The provisions of the Financial Services Act 1986 specified in the first column of the Schedule hereto shall come into force on 4th June 1987.

Michael Howard
Parliamentary Under Secretary of State,
Department of Trade and Industry

14th May 1987

Article 3

SCHEDULE

PROVISIONS OF FINANCIAL SERVICES ACT 1986 COMING INTO FORCE ON 4TH JUNE 1987

Provisions of Act	*Subject matter of provisions*
Section 8	Self-regulating organisations.
Section 9	Applications for recognition by self-regulating organisations.
Section 10	Grant and refusal of recognition of self-regulating organisations.
Section 11	Revocation of recognition of self-regulating organisations.
Section 13	Alteration of rules of recognised self-regulating organisations for protection of investors.

(a) 1986 c.60.

SCHEDULE

Article 3

PROVISIONS OF FINANCIAL SERVICES ACT 1986 COMING INTO FORCE ON 4TH JUNE 1987

Provisions of Act	Subject matter of provisions
Section 14	Notification requirements.
Section 15 except insofar as it has the effect of conferring authorisation	Certification by professional bodies.
Section 16	Professional bodies.
Section 17	Applications for recognition by professional bodies.
Section 18	Grant and refusal of recognition of professional bodies.
Section 19	Revocation of recognition of professional bodies.
Section 21	Notification requirements.
Section 36(2) and (3)	Investment exchanges.
Section 37 except insofar as it has effect in relation to a body or association of the kind described in section 40(1) of the Act	Grant and revocation of recognition of investment exchanges other than overseas investment exchanges.
Section 38(2) and (3)	Clearing houses.
Section 39 except insofar as it has effect in relation to a body or association of the kind described in section 40(1) of the Act	Grant and revocation of recognition of clearing houses other than overseas clearing houses.
Section 41	Notification requirements.
Section 46	Power to extend or restrict exemptions.
Section 48	Conduct of business rules.
Section 49	Financial resources rules.
Section 50	Modification of conduct of business and financial resources rules for particular cases.
Section 51	Cancellation rules.
Section 52	Notification regulations.
Section 54	Compensation Fund.
Section 55	Clients money.
Section 56 insofar as it is necessary in order to enable regulations to be made under section 56(1)	Unsolicited calls.
Section 102	Register of authorised persons and recognised organisations etc.
Section 103	Inspection of register.
Section 104(2) and (3)	Power to call for information.
Section 107	Appointment of auditors.
Section 110	Auditors for overseas business.
Section 112(1) to (4)	Application fees for recognition orders under Chapter III or IV of Part I of the Act.
Section 113(1)	Periodical fees – recognised self-regulating organisations, professional bodies, investment exchanges and clearing houses.
Section 119	Prevention of restrictive trade practices – recognised self-regulating organisations, investment exchanges, clearing houses.

Article 3

SCHEDULE

PROVISIONS OF FINANCIAL SERVICES ACT 1986 COMING INTO FORCE ON 4TH JUNE 1987

Provisions of Act	*Subject matter of provisions*
Section 120	Modification of section 119 where recognition function is transferred.
Section 122	Reports by Director-General of Fair Trading.
Section 123	Investigations by Director-General of Fair Trading.
Section 125(1) to (7)	Consequential exemption from competition law – The Restrictive Trade Practices Act 1976(a).
Section 127	Modifications of Restrictive Trade Practices Act 1976 in relation to recognised professional bodies.
Section 129 insofar as is necessary to bring into force paragraphs 3(1), (2) and (4) and 4(1) to (4) of Schedule 10 to the Act, and those paragraphs of that Schedule	Application of investment business provisions to regulated insurance companies.
Section 138(1), (2) and (6)	Insurance brokers.
Section 140 insofar as is necessary to bring into force paragraphs 2 to 5, 7 to 16, 18 to 20, 24, 38 and 42 of Schedule 11 to the Act and those paragraphs of that Schedule	Friendly Societies.
Section 187 insofar as not yet in force	Exemption from liability in damages.
Section 190	Data Protection Act 1984(b).
Section 191	Occupational Pension Schemes.
Section 198(3)(b)	Power to petition for winding-up on information obtained under Act – Northern Ireland.
Section 200(1)(a) insofar as it has effect in relation to an application for a recognition order under Chapter III or IV of Part I of the Act	False and misleading statements in connection with applications.
Section 200(1)(b) insofar as it has effect in relation to a requirement imposed by or under any provision brought into force by this Order	False and misleading statements in purported compliance with requirements imposed by or under Act.
Section 200(3) and (4)	False and misleading statements as to recognised status.
Section 200(5) to (8) insofar as it has effect in relation to any provision brought into force by this Order	False and misleading statements – supplementary provisions.
Section 206(1) to (3)	Publication of information or advice.
Section 211(3) insofar as is necessary to bring into force paragraphs 4, 5, and 6 of Schedule 15 to the Act, and those paragraphs of that Schedule	Transitional provisions.
Section 212(2) insofar as is necessary to bring into force paragraph 27(b) of Schedule 16, and that paragraph of that Schedule	Consequential amendment.
Schedule 2	Requirements for recognition of self-regulating organisations.
Schedule 3	Requirements for recognition of recognised professional body.
Schedule 4	Requirements for recognition of recognised investment exchange.

(a) 1976 c.34.
(b) 1984 c.35.

EXPLANATORY NOTE

(This note is not part of the Order)

This Order brings into force on 15th May 1987 those provisions of the Financial Service Act 1986 which enable the Secretary of State to transfer the function of publishing information and advice to a designated agency.

This Order brings into force on 4th June 1987 those provisions of the Financial Services Act 1986 which are necessary to enable recognition to be granted to self-regulating organisations (including self-regulating organisations for friendly societies), professional bodies and to investment exchanges and clearing houses whose head offices are situated in the United Kingdom. The Order also brings into force on the same date the provisions of the Act relating to withdrawal of recognition from organisations of the kind just described, to information to be supplied by them, to fees payable by them and to their position under competition law and the Data Protection Act 1984. Provisions of the Act concerning immunity from actions in damages and false and misleading statements made in connection with applications for recognition, recognised status and requirements imposed on recognised organisations are also brought into force on that date.

The Order also brings into force on the same date provisions which will enable rules and regulations to be made under Chapter V of Part I of and Schedule 11 to the Act.

The Order also brings into force on the same date the provisions of the Act relating to the maintenance and inspection of the register of authorised persons and recognised organisations etc, to the giving of information and advice, to the appointment of auditors by authorised persons and to communications by auditors with supervisory authorities.

The Order also brings into force on 4th June 1987 provisions concerning rules which may be made under the Insurance Brokers (Registration) Act 1977 (c.46) and the meaning of the expression 'authorised insurer' in that Act. Provisions concerning the position under the Act of managers of occupational pension schemes are also brought into force on that date.

NOTE AS TO EARLIER COMMENCEMENT ORDERS

(This note is not part of the Order)

The following provisions of the Financial Service Act 1986 have been brought into force by commencement orders made before the date of this Order;

Provision	S.I. No
ss.1 and 2	1986/2246
s.5 (partially)	1986/2246
ss.35, 42 and 45 (partially)	1986/2246
s.63	1987/623
ss.105 and 106	1986/2246
ss.114 to 118	1986/2246
s.121	1986/2246

Provision	S.I. No
s.122 and 123 (partially)	1986/2246
ss.124, 126 and 128	1986/2246
ss.129, 132 and 134 (partially)	1986/2246
s.137	1986/2246
s.138, 139 and 140 (partially)	1986/2246
s.141	1986/2246
s.142 to 153	1986/2246
s.154 (partially)	1986/2246
ss.155 to 157	1986/2246
s.172	1986/2246
s.173	1986/2246
s.174 (partially)	1986/2246
s.176	1986/2246
177	1986/1940
s.178 (partially)	1986/1940 1986/2246
s.179	1986/1940 1986/2246
s.180	1986/1940
s.181	1986/2246
s.182	1986/1940 1986/2031
s.183 (partially)	1987/623
s.184 (partially)	1987/623
s.185	1987/623
s.186 (partially)	1987/623
s.187 (partially)	1986/2246
s.188	1986/2246
s.189 (partially)	1986/2246

Provision	S.I. No
s.192	1986/2246
s.198 (partially)	1986/1940
	1986/2246
s.199	1986/1940
	1986/2246
s.200 (partially)	1986/1940
	1986/2246
s.201 (partially)	1986/1940
	1986/2246
	1987/623
ss. 202 and 203	1986/1940
	1986/2246
s.204	1986/2246
ss.205, 207, 209 and 210	1986/1940
	1986/2246
s.211 (partially)	1986/2031
	1986/2246
s.212	1986/2031
	1986/2246
Schedule 1 (partially)	1986/2246
Schedules 7, 8 and 9	1986/2246
Schedules 10 and 11 (partially)	1986/2246
Schedule 12	1986/2246
Schedule 13	1986/1940
	1986/2031
	1986/2246
Schedule 14 (partially)	1986/2246
Schedule 15 (partially)	1986/2031
	1986/2246
Schedule 16 (partially)	1986/2246
Schedule 17 (partially)	1986/2031
	1986/2246

The word ("partially") is used where the provision has been brought into force in part, or for a limited purpose or for a limited area.

1987 No. 908

AGRICULTURE

The Milk (Cessation of Production) (England and Wales) Scheme 1987

Made - - - -	*14th May 1987*
Laid before Parliament	*15th May 1987*
Coming into force -	*10th June 1987*

The Minister of Agriculture, Fisheries and Food and the Secretary of State in exercise of the powers conferred by section 1 of the Milk (Cessation of Production) Act 1985(**a**) and of all other powers enabling them in that behalf, after consultation with the Council on Tribunals under section 10 of the Tribunals and Inquiries Act 1971(**b**), hereby make the following Scheme:–

ARRANGEMENT OF PARAGRAPHS

Paragraph

(**a**) 1985 c.4.
(**b**) 1971 c.62.

Application, title and commencment

1. This Scheme, which applies to England and Wales, may be cited as the Milk (Cessation of Production) (England and Wales) Scheme 1987, and shall come into force on 10th June 1987.

Interpretation

2.—(1) In this Scheme, unless the context otherwise requires–

"the Act" means the Milk (Cessation of Production) Act 1985;

"allocated quota" means registered quota other than transferred quota;

"applicant" means a person who applies for compensation under this Scheme, and "application" shall be construed accordingly;

"appropriate Minister" means, in relation to England, the Minister of Agriculture, Fisheries and Food, and, in relation to Wales, the Secretary of State for Wales;

"authorised officer" means a duly authorised officer of the appropriate Minister;

"base quota" means quota, other than transferred quota, which was allocated under the Dairy Produce Quotas Regulations 1984**(a)** otherwise than in accordance with Article 3(1) (development awards) or Article 4(1)(c) (awards to producers undertaking farming as their main occupation) of Council Regulation (EEC) No. 857/84**(b)**;

"direct sales quota" has the same meaning as in the 1986 Regulations;

"farming press" means any newspaper, journal or similar publication considered by the appropriate Minister to be likely to be read by interested parties;

"Gazette" means the London Gazette;

"holding" has the same meaning as in the 1986 Regulations;

"landlord" means, in relation to the tenant of a holding or part of a holding, any person who either solely or jointly owns, or has a superior tenancy of, that holding, or of that part of that holding, and "landlord's interest" shall be construed accordingly;

"landlord's amount" means an amount calculated in accordance with paragraph 13;

"milk" means cows' milk;

"notice" means notice in writing;

"quota", in relation to a holding, has the meaning ascribed to it in the 1986 Regulations;

"quota year" has the meaning ascribed to it in regulation 2(1) of the 1986 Regulations;

"registered", in relation to quota, means–

    (a) in the case of direct sales quota, registered in the direct sales register maintained under the 1986 Regulations, and

    (b) in the case of wholesale quota, registered in a wholesale register maintained under those Regulations;

"relevant quota" means–

    (a) in a case where a tenant's holding consists only of the land subject to the

(a) S.I. 1984/1047, amended by S.I. 1984/1048, 1538 and 1787 and 1985/509.

(b) O.J. No. L90, 1.4.1984, p.13.

relevant tenancy, the quota registered in relation to that holding under the
1986 Regulations; and

(b) in any other case, such part of that quota as would fall to be apportioned to
land comprised in the relevant tenancy under Regulation 8 of the 1986
Regulations on a change of occupation of that land;

"tenant" means a person who occupies a holding or part of a holding by virtue of a
tenancy or licence to occupy, and "tenancy" shall be construed accordingly;

"the 1986 Regulations" means the Dairy Produce Quotas Regulations 1986(a);

"the Tribunal" means the Dairy Produce Quota Tribunal for England and Wales;

"transferred quota" means quota transferred to a holding by virtue of the transfer to
that holding of the whole or part of another holding;

"wholesale quota" has the same meaning as in the 1986 Regulations.

(2) In this Scheme–

(a) any reference to a numbered paragraph shall be construed as a reference to the
paragraph so numbered in this Scheme; and

(b) any reference in a paragraph to a numbered or lettered sub-paragraph shall be
construed as a reference to the sub-paragraph so numbered or lettered in that
paragraph.

Applications under this Scheme

3.—(1) The appropriate Minister shall, by advertisement published in the Gazette and
the farming press, announce the opening and closing dates of the period during which
applications may be submitted, and the procedural requirements in respect of
applications.

(2) For the purposes of an application under this paragraph, an applicant's quota shall
be taken to be the amount of quota to which he is entitled at the date of the application.

Persons eligible for payments under this Scheme

4.—(1) The appropriate Minister may make payments under this Scheme to any
person who is or has been a registered milk producer and who–

(a) undertakes to cease producing milk for sale or for the manufacture of any milk
product for sale and to surrender all his milk quota to the reserve; or

(b) (i) is entitled to a total milk quota of at least 242,790 litres, and

(ii) undertakes to reduce his production of milk for sale or for the manufacture
of any milk product for sale and to surrender not less than 50% of his milk
quota to the reserve.

(2) The appropriate Minister shall not make any payment under sub-paragraph (1) in
respect of milk quota against which milk has been or will at the date of surrender have
been produced in the 1987/1988 quota year.

(3) The appropriate Minister shall not make a payment under sub-paragraph (1) to a
person who has, at any time, received as applicant a payment under–

(a) Council Regulation (EEC) No. 1353/73(b) and Commission Regulation (EEC)
No. 1821/73(c) (which together lay down a scheme to encourage the reduction
of the production of milk and milk products);

(b) the Farm Structures (Payments to Outgoers) Scheme 1976(d);

(c) Council Regulation (EEC) No. 1078/77(e) and Commission Regulation (EEC)
No. 1307/77(f) (which together lay down schemes to encourage the reduction of
the production of milk and milk products);

(d) a non-statutory Scheme under which a person receiving payments undertook to

---

(a) S.I. 1986/470.
(b) O.J. No. L141, 28.5.73, p.18.
(c) O.J. No. L184, 6.7.73, p.24.
(d) S.I. 1976/2126.
(e) O.J. L131, 26.5.77, p.1.
(f) O.J. L150, 18.6.77, p.24.

give up milk production for the period specified in, and in accordance with the terms of, that Scheme; or

(e) the Milk (Community Outgoers Scheme) (England and Wales) Regulations 1986(a), or any other scheme corresponding with this Scheme which applies in any other part of the United Kingdom.

Basis of claims and rates of compensation under this Scheme

5.—(1) A person may claim compensation under this Scheme in respect of either—

(a) loss or profits in the 7 years immediately following the date on which he ceases to produce milk for sale or for processing into milk products for sale, by reference to the amount of milk quota he surrenders; or

(b) the value of the amount of the milk quota he surrenders.

(2) Payments made by the appropriate Minister under this Scheme shall be calculated—

(a) in a case falling within sub-paragraph (1)(a), at the rate of 3.927 pence per litre on a quantity equal to the amount of milk quota surrendered for each of the 7 years immediately following the date on which the applicant ceases to produce milk for sale or for processing into milk products for sale, in relation to the amount of quota surrendered; and

(b) in a case falling within sub-paragraph (1)(b), at the rate of 27.489 pence per litre on that quantity, payable in 7 equal annual instalments.

Over-subscription

6.—(1) The total amount of quota by reference to which the appropriate Ministers may make payments under this Scheme shall not exceed 34.43 million litres.

(2) In determining whether to accept or reject an application, the appropriate Minister shall give preference to applications in order of their receipt by him.

(3) The appropriate Minister shall give notice of his acceptance or rejection of an application to the applicant.

(4) An applicant may withdraw an application before the end of the period of 14 days beginning with the date of service on the applicant of a notice of acceptance served on him under sub-paragraph (3).

Requirement for landlord's consent

7.—(1) Where an application is made by an applicant who occupies his holding, or any part thereof, as a tenant, he shall, unless the condition specified in sub-paragraph (2) has been fulfilled, serve a copy of the application on his immediate landlord on the day on which he submits it.

(2) The condition referred to in sub-paragraph (1) is that, in respect of each person having a landlord's interest in the holding in relation to which the application is made, or in any part thereof, either—

(a) the consent in writing of that person to the application has been obtained by the tenant; or

(b) that person has unreasonably refused his consent to the application.

(3) Where, within 21 days of the receipt of a copy of an application served in accordance with sub-paragraph (1), or of a notice served in accordance with paragraph 11, a landlord objects to the application by notice served on the tenant and the appropriate Minister on one or more of the grounds specified in paragraph 9, the tenant shall be deemed to have withdrawn his application unless, within 14 days of receipt of that notice of objection, he—

(a) by notice served on that landlord, demands that the question of whether or not that objection should be upheld shall be determined by arbitration; and

(b) by notice served on the appropriate Minister, informs him of that demand.

(a) S.I. 1986/1611, as amended by S.I. 1987/410.

Unreasonable refusal of consent

8.—(1) For the purposes of paragraph 7, a landlord shall have unreasonably refused his consent to an application if–

    (a) having been served with a notice informing him of the tenant's application or intention to make an application, he has not, within 21 days of service on him of that notice, served a notice objecting to that application on one or more of the grounds specified in paragraph 9 on–

        (i) the tenant,

        (ii) his immediate lessee or licensee, where that person is not the tenant, and

        (iii) where the application has already been made, the appropriate Minister; or

    (b) he has so objected, but on arbitration under paragraph 10 an arbitrator has made a determination not to uphold the objection, and the arbitrator's determination has not been reversed, and there is not pending in respect thereof an appeal lodged under paragraph 17.

(2) If a landlord objects to the determination of an arbitrator, he may, within 14 days of the delivery of that determination, lodge an appeal under paragraph 17, and, in that event, he shall serve a notice on–

    (a) the tenant,

    (b) his immediate lessee or licensee, where that person is not the tenant; and

    (c) the appropriate Minister,

informing them of that appeal; and during that period of 14 days, there shall, for the purposes of sub-paragraph (1), be deemed to be pending an appeal lodged under paragraph 16.

Landlord's objections to an application

9.—(1) Subject to sub-paragraph (2), the grounds upon which a landlord may object to a tenant's application in relation to a holding, or part of a holding, for the purposes of paragraph 7 or paragraph 8 are–

    (a) that it appears to him that the compensation which he would receive on arbitration in accordance with this Scheme if that application was successful or the amount which the tenant is prepared to pay (if that amount is greater) would be less than the capital value of the loss of rent which an arbitrator would determine that he would suffer as a result of the surrender of the relevant quota;

    (b) that the tenant, or any landlord, is bound by a covenant (however expressed) entered into with any person holding a superior interest in the relevant land, or with the predecessor of that person, to the effect either that–

        (i) the holding, or any part thereof, will be farmed as a dairy farm, or

        (ii) any quota on that holding or part of that holding will be maintained;

    (c) that the landlord is a smallholdings authority for the purposes of section 38 of the Agriculture Act 1970 (smallholdings authorities)**(a)** which holds the holding, or any part thereof, for the purposes of smallholdings in accordance with Part III of that Act, and which intends, at the end of the current tenancy, to re-let, for the purposes of smallholdings, the holding, or any part thereof, or part of any part of that holding, to be farmed as a dairy farm.

(2) A landlord may not object to a tenant's application on the ground specified in sub-paragraph (1)(b)(ii) if the covenant concerned relates solely to commodities other than milk.

Arbitration of landlord's objection to an application

10.—(1) On a reference under paragraph 7(3) the arbitrator shall determine whether or not the objection should be upheld.

(2) (a) An objection on the ground specified in paragraph 9(1)(a) shall not be upheld unless the arbitrator is satisfied that the landlord's compensation under this

---

(a) 1970 c.40.

Scheme or the amount which the tenant is prepared to pay (if that amount is greater) would be less than the capital value of the loss of rent which the landlord could reasonably be expected to suffer as a result of the surrender of the relevant quota;

(b) where the capital value referred to in sub-paragraph (2)(a) has previously been assessed by an arbitrator for the purposes of paragraph 13(2)(a), the capital value so assessed shall be deemed to be the capital value for the purposes of sub-paragraph (2)(a) but where that capital value has not previously been so assessed, the arbitrator on a reference under paragraph 7(3) shall assess that capital value in accordance with paragraph 13(3)(b).

(3) An objection on the ground specified in paragraph 9(1)(c) shall not be upheld by the arbitrator unless the authority concerned enters into a covenant with the tenant to the effect that–

(a) if any land subject to the tenancy is re-let for any purpose other than dairy farming within 5 years from the date of the covenant, or if any of that land is sold within that period; and

(b) if, but for the authority's refusal of consent, the tenant could have made a valid application,

the authority will pay to the tenant an amount equal to that which he will have lost as a result of the authority's objection.

(4) Any amount due to the tenant by virtue of sub-paragraph (3) may be determined by agreement between the parties, and, in default of agreement, the tenant may, by notice served on the authority, demand that the amount be determined by arbitration; and on a reference under this paragraph, the arbitrator shall determine the amount.

(5) In assessing the amount which the tenant will have lost for the purposes of sub-paragraph (3), the arbitrator shall take into account any payment made to the tenant by any person in respect of the relevant quota.

Service of notices on superior landlords

11. Where a landlord is informed, by the service of a copy of an application under paragraph 7 or a notice under paragraph 8 or this paragraph, of a tenant's application or intention to make an application in respect of a holding, he shall, in respect of any part of that holding in respect of which he has an interest (but in respect of which he is not the owner), within 7 days of the receipt of such copy or notice, serve a notice on his immediate landlord informing him of the tenant's application or intention to make an application; and he shall send a copy of such notice to the tenant and to the appropriate Minister.

Landlord's right to payment

12.—(1) Subject to sub-paragraph (4), where a successful applicant occupies his holding, or any part of that holding, as a tenant, each of his landlords shall be entitled to obtain from the tenant a payment in respect of the relevant quota.

(2) The payment to which a landlord is entitled under sub-paragraph (1) shall be an amount agreed between the tenant and the landlord or, in default of agreement–

(a) where the tenant has only one landlord, the landlord's amount; and

(b) where the tenant has two or more landlords, such proportion of the landlord's amount as shall be agreed or determined in accordance with paragraph 14.

(3) The landlord's amount or, where sub-paragraph (2)(b) applies, the proportion of the landlord's amount to which a landlord is entitled, shall be payable in 7 equal yearly instalments, each instalment being due–

(a) on the day after the day on which the tenant receives his instalment of compensation; or

(b) where, in respect of any quota year, the tenant (by reason of his death or any default of his) does not receive an instalment of compensation, at the end of the period of 3 months after the date on which that instalment would have otherwise become due.

(4) Where–
- (a) a successful applicant who is a tenant dies before he has received all his instalments of compensation, and
- (b) a successor of the deceased tenant enters into that tenant's obligation for the purposes of paragraph 4,

any landlord of the deceased tenant shall be entitled to recover from the successor such instalments of the payment referred to in sub-paragraph (2) as become due to that landlord on or after the date on which that successor entered into those obligations; and from that date, the landlord shall no longer be entitled to recover those instalments from the estate of the deceased tenant.

The landlord's amount

13.—(1) The landlord's amount shall be an amount equal to the full rate of compensation for so much of the relevant quota as is surrendered under this Scheme and consists of–
- (a) standard quota, or, where it is less, allocated quota, multiplied–
  - (i) firstly by the landlord's fraction;
  - (ii) secondly by a fraction of which–
    - –the numerator is the quota surrendered; and
    - –the denominator is the registered quota; and
- (b) transferred quota as follows–
  - (i) where the landlord bore the whole of the cost of the transaction by virtue of which the transferred quota was transferred to the holding, the whole of the transferred quota, multiplied by a fraction of which–
    - –the numerator is the quota surrendered; and
    - –the denominator is the registered quota; and
  - (ii) where the landlord bore only part of that cost, the corresponding part of the transferred quota, multiplied by a fraction of which–
    - –the numerator is the quota surrendered; and
    - –the denominator is the registered quota.

(2) In sub-paragraph (1) "the landlord's fraction" means the fraction of which–
- (a) the numerator is an amount equal to the capital value of the rent which the immediate landlord can reasonably be expected to lose as a consequence of the surrender of the quota; and
- (b) the denominator is the sum of that amount and an amount equal to the capital value of the loss of earnings which can reasonably be expected to be suffered by the tenant as a consequence of the surrender of the quota.

(3) For the purposes of sub-paragraph (2)–
- (a) "rent" includes any other periodic payment;
- (b) the capital value of the rent shall be assessed in accordance with Schedule 2 to the Agricultural Holdings Act 1986(a) (arbitration of rent) on the assumption that the rent will not change until the next rent review; and the said Schedule 2 shall be construed accordingly;
- (c) in assessing loss of earnings, the loss of the annual value of tenant's dairy improvements and fixed equipment shall be included; and the capital value thus calculated shall be reduced by the sale value of any dairy items made redundant but which the tenant can sell.

(4) For the purposes of sub-paragraph (1) and subject to the provisions of sub-paragraph (6), the standard quota for any land shall be calculated by multiplying the relevant number of hectares by the prescribed quota per hectare, and in this sub-paragraph and sub-paragraph (4)–
- (a) "the relevant number of hectares" means the average number of hectares of the land in question used by the applicant during the relevant period for the feeding

---

(a) 1986 c.5.

of dairy cows kept on the land or, if different, the average number of hectares of the land which could reasonably be expected to have been so used (having regard to the number of grazing animals other than dairy cows kept on that land during that period); and

(b) "the prescribed quota per hectare" means such number of litres as the Minister has prescribed for the purposes of sub-paragraph 6(1)(b) of Schedule 1 to the Agriculture Act 1986(a) (calculation of standard quota) by the Milk Quota (Calculation of Standard Quota) Order 1986(b).

(5) Where, by virtue of the quality of the land in question or the climatic conditions in the area, the reasonable amount is greater or less than the prescribed average yield per hectare, sub-paragraph (4) shall not apply, and the standard quota shall be calculated by multiplying the relevant number of hectares by such proportion of the prescribed quota per hectare as the reasonable amount bears to the prescribed average yield per hectare, and for the purposes of this sub-paragraph–

(a) the amount of milk to be taken as the average yield per hectare shall be that taken for the purposes of sub-paragraph 6(2) of Schedule 1 to the Agriculture Act 1986 (calculation of standard quota in exceptional cases) in accordance with the Milk Quota (Calculation of Standard Quota) Order 1986;

(b) "reasonable amount" means the amount of milk which could reasonably be expected to have been produced from one hectare of the land during the relevant period.

(6) In the application of this paragraph–

(a) "dairy cows" means cows kept for milk production (other than uncalved heifers);

(b) "disadvantaged land" and "severely disadvantaged land" means land which has been determined to be disadvantaged land or severely disadvantaged land, as the case may be, in accordance with the definitions of those expressions as they are set out in regulation 2 of the Hill Livestock (Compensatory Allowances) Regulations 1984(c);

(c) "land used for the feeding of dairy cows kept on the land" does not include land used for the growing of cereal crops for feeding to dairy cows in the form of loose grain; and

(d) "the relevant period" means–

(i) the period by reference to which the base quota was determined; or

(ii) where the base quota was determined by reference to more than one period, the period by reference to which the majority was determined or, if equal amounts were determined by reference to different periods, the later of those periods.

Apportionment of landlord's amount

14.—(1) The landlord's amount (or, where one or more landlords have agreed with the tenant the payment to which they are entitled under regulation 12(2), such proportion of the landlord's amount as the remaining landlords shall agree, or in default of agreement as an arbitrator shall determine) shall be apportioned between the landlords who have not made an agreement with the tenant under regulation 12(2) by agreement or, in default of agreement, by arbitration; and on a reference under this paragraph an arbitrator shall take all relevant factors into account in making his award.

(2) Where a reference to arbitration is made under this regulation in conjunction with another regulation, any additional costs of the award caused by the apportionment under this regulation shall be paid by the landlords in such proportions as the arbitrator may determine.

(a) 1986 c.49.
(b) S.I. 1986/1530, amended by S.I. 1987/626.
(c) S.I. 1984/2024.

Settlement of claims

15. Any claim arising under paragraph 12(2)(a) or (b) shall be determined by arbitration.

Arbitrations

16.—(1) Subject to sub-paragraphs (2) to (5), where any matter is, under the provisions of this scheme, to be determined by arbitration, section 84 of the Agricultural Holdings Act 1986 (arbitrations) shall apply as if that matter were required by that Act to be determined by arbitration under that Act.

(2) Paragraph 7 of Schedule 11 to the Agricultural Holdings Act 1986 (time for statement and particulars of case and for amendments thereto) shall apply to arbitrations under this scheme as if, for the words "thirty-five days" in both cases where they occur, there was substituted the words "twenty-one days".

(3) Paragraph 14 of that Schedule (time for making and signing awards) shall apply to arbitrations under this scheme as if, for the words "fifty-six days", there was substituted the words "thirty-five days".

(4) Paragraph 18 of that Schedule (arbitration award to fix a day for payment of money awarded not later than one month after award) shall not apply for the purposes of this Scheme except in relation to any award of costs.

(5) Paragraphs 26 to 28 of that Schedule (special case procedure, setting aside award and remission by the County Court) shall not apply in relation to arbitrations under this Scheme.

Appeals

17.—(1) An appeal shall lie on any question of law arising in the course of an arbitration under this Scheme, or on any question as to the jurisdiction of an arbitrator under this Scheme, to the Tribunal; and for the purpose of determining an appeal under this sub-paragraph, the Tribunal shall consist of a single legally qualified member, approved for the purpose by the Chairman of the Tribunal, assisted, if the Chairman so directs, by such other non-voting member of the Tribunal as the Chairman may appoint.

(2) For the purpose of an appeal under this paragraph, paragraph 2 (quorum for any determination of the Tribunal) and paragraph 3 (determinations by the Tribunal to be by majority) of Schedule 18 to the 1986 Regulations shall not apply.

(3) An appeal under sub-paragraph (1) in relation to an arbitration shall be lodged within 14 days of the delivery of the arbitrator's determination in that arbitration.

Temporarily reallocated quota

18. For the purposes of this Scheme quota which has been temporarily reallocated from one holding to another under regulation 11(2) of the 1986 Regulations (reallocation of wholesale quota) shall be treated as if it had not been temporarily reallocated.

Service of notices or of copies of applications

19.—(1) Any notice under this Scheme shall be duly served on the person on whom it is to be served if it is delivered to him, or left at his proper address, or sent to him by post in a registered letter or by the recorded delivery service.

(2) Any such notice shall be duly served on an incorporated company or body if it is served on the secretary or clerk of the company or body.

(3) For the purposes of this Scheme and of section 7 of the Interpretation Act 1978(a) (service by post), the proper address of any person on whom any such notice is to be served shall be–

    (a) in the case of the secretary or clerk of an incorporated company or body, the address of the registered or principal office of the company or body; and

---

(a) 1978 c.30.

(b) in any other case, the last known address of the person in question.

(4) Unless or until the tenant or a landlord has received–

(a) notice that the original landlord has ceased to be his immediate landlord, and

(b) notice of the name and address of the person who has become his immediate landlord,

any notice served on the original landlord by the tenant or landlord shall be deemed for the purposes of this Scheme to have been properly served; and for the purposes of this sub-paragraph and sub-paragraph (5), "original landlord" means any person who was the tenant's or the landlord's immediate landlord before the person who has become the tenant's or the landlord's immediate landlord.

(5) Where an original landlord receives a notice in the circumstances referred to in sub-paragraph (4), he shall forthwith transmit that notice to the person on whom it should have been served.

(6) In this paragraph, "notice" includes a copy of an application served under paragraph 7.

Loss arising from failure to comply with provisions of this Scheme

20.—(1) Where, in consequence of the failure of any person to comply with the requirements of paragraph 7 or paragraph 11 in relation to a holding or a part of a holding, a landlord suffers loss, the landlord shall be entitled to recover the amount involved as a civil debt from that person.

(2) Where a sum agreed or awarded under the provisions of this Scheme, or an instalment thereof, has not been paid by the person liable to pay that sum within 14 days from the date on which that payment became due, that sum shall, if the County Court so orders, be recoverable from the person in default.

Recovery of compensation

21.—(1) Where any person, with a view to obtaining the payment of compensation to himself or to any other person–

(a) makes any statement which is untrue or misleading in a material respect, or

(b) furnishes to any of the appropriate Ministers any inaccurate information,

that Minister shall be entitled to recover on demand as a civil debt the whole or any part of any compensation paid to that person or to such other person.

(2) Where any person, having undertaken to cease producing milk for sale or having undertaken to reduce milk production in accordance with the provisions of paragraph 4(1), fails in any way to comply with that undertaking, the appropriate Minister shall be entitled to recover from him on demand as a civil debt the whole or any part of any compensation paid to him, or to any other person, in respect of quota registered in his name.

(3) Where any person–

(a) intentionally obstructs an authorised officer in the exercise of the powers conferred on him by section 2(1) of the Act,

(b) fails without reasonable excuse to comply with a requirement of this Scheme, the appropriate Minister shall be entitled to recover on demand as a civil debt the whole or any part of any compensation paid to that person.

Crown land

22.—(1) This scheme shall apply to any holding or part of a holding which belongs to Her Majesty or to the Duchy of Lancaster, the Duchy of Cornwall or a goverment department, or which is held in trust for Her Majesty for the purposes of a government department.

(2) For the purposes of this Scheme–

(a) as respects land belonging to Her Majesty in right of the Crown, the Crown Estate Commissioners or the proper officer or body having charge of the land for the time being or, if there is no such officer or body, such person as Her

Majesty may appoint in writing under the Royal Sign Manual, shall represent Her Majesty, and shall be deemed to be the landlord or tenant, as the case may be;

(b) as respects land belonging to Her Majesty privately, such person as Her Majesty may appoint in writing under the Royal Sign Manual shall represent Her Majesty and shall be deemed to be the landlord;

(c) as respects land belonging to Her Majesty in right of the Duchy of Lancaster, the Chancellor of the Duchy shall represent Her Majesty, and shall be deemed to be the landlord or tenant, as the case may be;

(d) as respects land belonging to the Duchy of Cornwall, such person as the Duke of Cornwall or the possessor for the time being of the Duchy appoints shall represent the Duchy, and shall be deemed to be the landlord or the tenant, as the case may be.

(3) Any sum payable under this Scheme to or by the Duke of Cornwall (or any other possessor for the time being of the Duchy of Cornwall) may be treated, or raised and paid, as if it were a payment made for, or an expense incurred in, as the case may be, permanently improving the possessions of the Duchy as mentioned in section 8 of the Duchy of Cornwall Management Act 1863**(a)**.

(4) Any sum payable under this Scheme to or by the Chancellor of the Duchy of Lancaster may–

(a) be treated, or raised and paid, as if it were a payment made for, or an expense incurred in, as the case may be, the improvement of land belonging to Her Majesty in right of the Duchy within section 25 of the Duchy of Lancaster Act 1817**(b)**; or

(b) be paid in to or out of annual revenues of the Duchy.

Revocation

23. The Milk (Partial Cessation of Production) (England and Wales) Scheme 1986**(c)** is hereby revoked.

In witness whereof the Official Seal of the Minister of Agriculture, Fisheries and Food is hereunto affixed on 14th May 1987.

Michael Jopling
Minister of Agriculture, Fisheries and Food

14th May 1987

Nicholas Edwards
Secretary of State for Wales

EXPLANATORY NOTE

(This note is not part of the Scheme)

Article 1(2)(a) of Council Regulation (EEC) No. 1343/86**(d)** amends Article 4(1)(a) of Council Regulation (EEC) No. 857/84**(e)** by enabling Member States to grant compensation to producers, with a milk quota in excess of a specified level who

---

(a) 1863 c.49.   (b) 1817 c.97.   (c) S.I. 1986/1612.
(d) O.J. No. L119, 8.5.86, p. 34.   (e) O.J. No. L90, 1.4.84, p.13.

undertake to surrender at least 50% of that milk quota. The level of milk quota referred to above is fixed by Article 1(1) of Commission Regulation (EEC) No. 2133/86(a) at 250,000 kilogrammes (242,790 litres).

In exercise of the above powers, the Scheme provides for the payment of compensation by the Minister of Agriculture, Fisheries and Food, in relation to England, and the Secretary of State for Wales, in relation to Wales, to certain holders of milk quota. Recipients must either undertake to surrender their total quota, or have a quota in excess of a specified level and undertake to reduce their milk production and to surrender not less than 50% of their milk quota (paragraph 4).

The Scheme is administered in identical terms to the 1986 Scheme (S.I. 1986/1612).

The time limits and procedural requirements for applications for compensation are to be published in the London Gazette and the farming press (paragraph 3) and it is provided that in the event of over-subscription preference shall be given to applications in order to their receipt by him (paragraph 6).

An applicant for compensation who does not own all of the land which he occupies must attempt to obtain the consent of any person who owns or has a superior tenancy or licence of that holding or any part of it (the "landlords") (paragraph 7). Paragraphs 8 and 9 spell out the criteria for deciding whether or not a landlord's consent has been unreasonably refused and paragraph 10 deals with arbitration on this matter in case of dispute.

Paragraph 12 provides that landlords shall be entitled to obtain from the tenant a payment in respect of the relevant quota and paragraph 13 sets out the amount (the "landlord's amount") to which the landlords as a whole are entitled in the absence of agreement. That amount is to be apportioned among the landlords by agreement or arbitration (paragraph 14).

Arbitrations under the regulations are to be by a single arbitrator in accordance with the provisions of Schedule 11 to the Agricultural Holdings Act 1986. By paragraph 16 two of the provisions of that Schedule are applied for the purposes of this Scheme, with modifications in order to speed up proceedings and other provisions have been disapplied to arbitrators or their awards under this Scheme, in particular, the case stated procedure set out in paragraph 26 of that Schedule (paragraph 16(5)). An appeal to the Dairy Produce Quota Tribunal on any question of law or as to the jurisdiction of an arbitrator has been created by paragraph 17.

Provision is made for recovery from a tenant of any loss suffered by a landlord as a result of an application for compensation by the tenant which fails to comply with paragraph 7 or paragraph 11, and for recovery through the County Court of sums agreed or awarded under the paragraphs (paragraph 20).

Duly authorised officers of the Minister or Secretary of State have power to enter on any land occupied by any person to whom a payment of compensation has been made and to require any person who is engaged in the production of milk to furnish accounts and records in his possession or under his control (section 2 of the Milk (Cessation of Production) Act 1985 (c.4)).

By section 3 of the above Act it is made an offence punishable on summary conviction by a fine not exceeding £2,000 knowingly or recklessly to make a statement which is false in a material particular for the purpose of obtaining compensation, or intentionally to obstruct an authorised officer.

This Scheme applies to Crown land (paragraph 24).

(a) O.J. No. L187, 9.7.86, p.21.

STATUTORY INSTRUMENTS

1987 No. 909

AGRICULTURE

The Milk (Community Outgoers Scheme) (England and Wales) (Amendment) (No.2) Regulations 1987

Made - - - -	*14th May 1987*
Laid before Parliament	*15th May 1987*
Coming into force	*10th June 1987*

The Minister of Agriculture, Fisheries and Food and the Secretary of State, being Ministers designated(**a**) for the purposes of section 2(2) of the European Communities Act 1972(**b**) in relation to the common agricultural policy of the European Economic Community, acting jointly in exercise of the powers conferred on them by that section and of all other powers enabling them in that behalf, hereby make the following Regulations:–

Title and commencement

1. These Regulations may be cited as the Milk (Community Outgoers Scheme) (England and Wales) (Amendment) (No.2) Regulations 1987 and shall come into force on 10th June 1987.

Amendment of principal Regulations

2.—(1) The Milk (Community Outgoers Scheme) (England and Wales) Regulations 1986(**c**) shall have effect with the following amendments.

(2) For regulation 5 there shall be substituted–

"For the purposes of Articles 1 and 3(2) of the Commission Regulation (Member States to make rules for the acceptance of applications) and subject to Article 1(2) second indent of the Council Regulation (Member States authorized to ensure that reductions are spread equally) where the sum of valid applications throughout the United Kingdom together relate to a quantity of eligible quota which exceeds 152,714,910 litres, the appropriate Minister shall give preference to applications in order of their receipt by him."

(3) In regulation 6(2) for the words "13th March 1987" there shall be substituted the words "30th December 1987".

(4) In regulation 7(1) for the words "13th March 1987" there shall be substituted the words "30th December 1987".

(a) S.I. 1972/1811.
(b) 1972 c. 68, to which there are amendments not relevant to these Regulations.
(c) S.I. 1986/1611, amended by S.I. 1987/410.

In Witness whereof the Official Seal of the Minister of Agriculture, Fisheries and Food is hereunto affixed on 14th May 1987.

Michael Jopling
Minister of Agriculture, Fisheries and Food

14th May 1987

Nicholas Edwards
Secretary of State for Wales

EXPLANATORY NOTE

(This note is not part of the Regulations)

These Regulations implement Council Regulation (EEC) No. 1336/86 (O.J. No. L119, 9.5.1986, p. 21) (as amended by Council Regulation (EEC) No. 776/87 (O.J. No. L78, 20.3.1987, p. 8)) fixing compensation for the definitive discontinuation of milk production, and Commission Regulation (EEC) No. 2321/86 (O.J. No. L202, 25.7.1986, p. 13) (as amended by Commission Regulation (EEC) No. 261/87 (O.J. No. L26, 29.1.1987, p. 18)) as regards the submission of applications for compensation for the definitive discontinuation of milk production.

The amendments extend the compensation Scheme to the 1987/88 quota year. Accordingly, the time limit (set by regulation 6 of the principal Regulations) after which an applicant may not withdraw his application is extended to 30th December 1987 (regulation 2(3)).

Where a landlord's consent is required (under regulation 7 of the principal Regulations) an application will only be valid if that consent has been given or unreasonably refused by 30th December 1987 (regulation 2(4)).

The total quantity of eligible quota accepted under the Community Outgoers Scheme throughout the United Kingdom (in accordance with regulation 5 of the principal Regulations) will not exceed 152,714,910 litres and applications in excess of this will be refused by reference to the date of their receipt (regulation 2(2)).

STATUTORY INSTRUMENTS

1987 No. 910

MEDICINES

The Medicines (Products Other Than Veterinary Drugs) (General Sale List) Amendment Order 1987

Made - - - -	*14th May 1987*
Coming into force	*1st June 1987*

The Secretary of State concerned with health in England, the Secretaries of State respectively concerned with health and with agriculture in Wales and in Scotland, the Minister of Agriculture, Fisheries and Food, the Department of Health and Social Services for Northern Ireland and the Department of Agriculture for Northern Ireland, acting jointly, in exercise of powers conferred by sections 51 and 129(4) of the Medicines Act 1968(**a**) and now vested in them(**b**) and of all other powers enabling them in that behalf, after consulting such organisations as appear to them to be representative of interests likely to be substantially affected by this Order pursuant to section 129(6) of that Act, and after consulting and taking into account the advice of the Medicines Commission pursuant to section 129(7) of that Act, hereby make the following Order:

Citation, interpretation and commencement

1.—(1) This Order, which may be cited as the Medicines (Products Other Than Veterinary Drugs) (General Sale List) Amendment Order 1987, amends the Medicines (Products Other Than Veterinary Drugs) (General Sale List) Order 1984(**c**) (hereinafter referred to as "the principal Order") and shall come into force on 1st June 1987.

(2) In this Order, unless the context otherwise requires, a reference to inserting an entry in a column in a Table of a Schedule to the principal Order shall be construed, in the case of an entry to be inserted in column 1, as a reference to inserting that entry at the appropriate point in the alphabetical order of the entries in column 1 of that Table and, in the case of an entry to be inserted, as the case may be, in column 2 or 3, as a reference to inserting that entry so as to appear against the column 1 entry against which it is listed in this Order.

Amendment of Schedule 1 to the principal Order

2.—(1) Schedule 1 to the principal Order (which specifies the class of medicinal products, other than products the subject of a product licence of right, on general sale by virtue of article 2(a) of the principal Order), is amended in accordance with the following paragraphs of this article.

(2) In Table A (internal or external use)–

    (a) there are inserted in column 1 and, as the case may be, columns 2 and 3, those entries set out in columns 1, 2 and 3 respectively of Schedule 1 to this Order, and

---

(**a**) 1968 c. 67.

(**b**) In the case of the Secretaries of State concerned with health in England and in Wales by virtue of article 2(2) of, and Schedule 1 to, the Transfer of Functions (Wales) Order 1969 (S.I. 1969/388), in the case of the Secretary of State concerned with agriculture in Wales by virtue of article 2(3) of, and Schedule 1 to, the Transfer of Functions (Wales) (No. 1) Order 1978 (S.I. 1978/272) and in the case of the Northern Ireland Departments by virtue of section 40 of, and Schedule 5 to, the Northern Ireland Constitution Act 1973 (c. 36), and section 1(3) of, and paragraph 2(1)(b) of Schedule 1 to, the Northern Ireland Act 1974 (c. 28).

(**c**) S.I. 1984/769, amended by S.I. 1985/1540.

(b) for the entries in columns 1, 2 and 3 relating to the substances "Aloxiprin" and "Aspirin" there are respectively substituted the entries set out in Schedule 2 to this Order.

(3) In Table B (external use only)–

    (a) there are inserted in column 1 and, as the case may be, column 2, those entries set out in columns 1 and 2 respectively of Schedule 3 to this Order, and

    (b) there are deleted from column 1 the entries "Dichloroxylenol" and "Sassafras Oil" and from column 2 the entries relating to those substances.

Amendment of Schedule 2 to the principal Order

3.—(1) Schedule 2 to the principal Order (which specifies the class of medicinal products, the subject of a product licence of right, on general sale by virtue of article 2(b) of the principal Order), is amended in accordance with the following paragraphs of this article.

(2) In Table A (internal or external use)–

    (a) for the entries in columns 1, 2 and 3 relating to the substances "Aloxiprin" and "Aspirin" there are respectively substituted the entries set out in Schedule 4 to this Order, and

    (b) there are deleted from column 1 the entries "Birthwort", "Inositol Nicotinate", "Sassafras" and "Serpentary".

(3) In Table B (external use only) there are deleted from column 1 the entries "Safrole" and "Sassafras Oil".

Amendment of Schedule 3 to the principal Order

4. In Schedule 3 to the principal Order (which specifies classes of medicinal products which are not on the general sale list), the word "or" is deleted from paragraph (e) and is inserted at the end of paragraph (f) and after paragraph (f) there is inserted, "(g) for administration wholly or mainly to children being a preparation of Aloxiprin or Aspirin".

Signed by authority of the Secretary of State for Social Services.

Tony Newton
14th May 1987   Minister of State, Department of Health and Social Security

Nicholas Edwards
14th May 1987   Secretary of State for Wales

Glenarthur
14th May 1987   Minister of State for Scotland

In witness whereof the official seal of the Minister of Agriculture, Fisheries and Food is hereunto affixed on 14th May 1987.

Michael Jopling
Minister of Agriculture, Fisheries and Food

Sealed with the official seal of the Department of Health and Social Services for Northern Ireland this 14th day of May 1987.

Maurice N. Hayes
Permanent Secretary

Sealed with the official seal of the Department of Agriculture for Northern Ireland this 14th day of May 1987.

W. H. Jack
Permanent Secretary

Article 2(2)(a)

SCHEDULE 1

ENTRIES INSERTED IN TABLE A OF SCHEDULE 1 TO THE PRINCIPAL ORDER (INTERNAL OR EXTERNAL USE)(a)

(1) *Substance*	(2) *Maximum strength*	(3) *Use, pharmaceutical form or route of administration*	(4) *Maximum dose and maximum daily dose*
Bran			
Celery Seed			
Cetalkonium Chloride	(1) 0.01 per cent	(1) Internal: teething gel (2) External	
Choline Salicylate	(1) 9.0 per cent	(1) Internal: teething gel (2) External	
Hydrotalcite			
Magaldrate			

Article 2(2)(b)

SCHEDULE 2

ENTRIES SUBSTITUTED IN TABLE A OF SCHEDULE 1 TO THE PRINCIPAL ORDER (INTERNAL OR EXTERNAL USE)(a)

(1) *Substance*	(2) *Maximum strength*	(3) *Use, pharmaceutical form or route of administration*	(4) *Maximum dose and maximum daily dose*
Aloxiprin	(1) 400mg (2) 800mg When combined with aspirin, the aspirin limits apply to the combination of aspirin and aspirin equivalent.	(1) Tablet or capsule (2) Powder or granules	
Aspirin	(1) 325mg (2) 650mg	(1) Tablet or capsule (2) Powder or granules	

(a) Note: all columns appearing in Table A of Schedule 1 to the principal Order are set out in this Schedule, although no entries are inserted by this Schedule in column 4 of that Table.

SCHEDULE 3

Article 2(3)(a)

ENTRIES INSERTED IN TABLE B OF SCHEDULE 1 TO THE PRINCIPAL ORDER (EXTERNAL USE ONLY)(a)

(1) *Substance*	(2) *Maximum strength*	(3) *Use, pharmaceutical form or route of administration*
Centella		
Nonivamide	0.1 per cent	
Sodium Hydroxide	12.0 per cent	

SCHEDULE 4

Article 3(2)(a)

ENTRIES SUBSTITUTED IN TABLE A OF SCHEDULE 2 TO THE PRINCIPAL ORDER (INTERNAL OR EXTERNAL USE)(b)

(1) *Substance*	(2) *Maximum strength*	(3) *Use, pharmaceutical form or route of administration*	(4) *Maximum dose and maximum daily dose*
Aloxiprin	(1) 400mg (2) 800mg When combined with aspirin, the aspirin limits apply to the combination of aspirin and aspirin equivalent.	(1) Tablet (2) Powder	
Aspirin	(1) 325mg (2) 650mg	(1) Tablet (2) Powder	

(a) Note: all columns appearing in Table B of Schedule 1 to the principal Order are set out in this Schedule, although no entries are inserted by this Schedule in column 3 of that Table.
(b) Note: all columns appearing in Table A of Schedule 2 to the principal Order are set out in this Schedule, although no entries are inserted by this Schedule in column 4 of that Table.

EXPLANATORY NOTE

(This note is not part of the Order)

This Order amends the Medicines (Products Other Than Veterinary Drugs) (General Sale List) Order 1984 (referred to as "the principal Order") which specifies classes of medicinal products which can with reasonable safety be sold or supplied otherwise than by or under the supervision of a pharmacist (the general sale list) and classes of such products which can with reasonable safety be sold by means of automatic machines (the automatic machines section of the general sale list).

The amendments made by this Order are as follows:

Article 2 amends Schedule 1 to the principal Order (medicinal products, other than products the subject of a product licence of right, on general sale), by inserting certain entries, deleting certain entries and also by substituting new entries in respect of the substances Aloxiprin and Aspirin.

Article 3 amends Schedule 2 to the principal Order (medicinal products, the subject of a product licence of right, on general sale), by deleting certain entries and also by substituting new entries in respect of the substances Aloxiprin and Aspirin.

Article 4 amends Schedule 3 to the principal Order (medicinal products which are not on the general sale list), by excluding from general sale preparations of Aloxiprin or Aspirin promoted, recommended or marketed wholly or mainly for administration to children.

1987 No. 911 (C. 25) (S. 78)

CHRONICALLY SICK AND DISABLED PERSONS

The Disabled Persons (Services, Consultation and Representation) Act 1986 (Commencement No. 3) (Scotland) Order 1987

Made	-	-	-	-	*13th May 1987*

The Secretary of State for Scotland, in exercise of the powers conferred upon him by section 18(2) of the Disabled Persons (Services, Consultation and Representation) Act 1986(**a**), and of all other powers enabling him in that behalf, hereby makes the following Order:

Citation and interpretation

1.—(1) This Order may be cited as the Disabled Persons (Services, Consultation and Representation) Act 1986 (Commencement No. 3) (Scotland) Order 1987.

(2) This Order shall apply only to Scotland.

(3) In this Order "the Act" means the Disabled Persons (Services, Consultation and Representation) Act 1986.

Days specified for the coming into force of certain provisions of the Act

2.—(1) The provisions of the Act specified in column 1 of Schedule 1 to this Order (which relate to the matters specified in column 2 thereof) shall come into force on 1st June 1987.

(2) The provisions of the Act specified in column 1 of Schedule 2 to this Order (which relate to the matters specified in column 2 thereof) shall come into force on 1st October 1987.

New St Andrew's House, Edinburgh
13th May 1987

Glenarthur
Minister of State, Scottish Office

(**a**) 1986 c.33.

Article 2(1)

SCHEDULE 1

PROVISIONS OF THE ACT WHICH COME INTO FORCE ON 1st JUNE 1987

(1) *Provision of the Act*	(2) *Subject matter*
Section 9	Information.
Section 10	Co-option to committees etc. of persons representing interests of disabled persons.
Section 11	Reports to Parliament.
Section 12	Amendment of the Chronically Sick and Disabled Persons Act 1970(**a**) and the Social Work (Scotland) Act 1968(**b**).
Section 14	Assessment and recording of children and young persons.
Section 16	Interpretation.
Section 17	Financial provisions.
Section 18	Short title, commencement, regulations, orders and extent.

Article 2(2)

SCHEDULE 2

PROVISIONS OF THE ACT WHICH COME INTO FORCE ON 1st OCTOBER 1987

(1) *Provision of the Act*	(2) *Subject matter*
Section 4 (except (b))	Services under section 2 of the Chronically Sick and Disabled Persons Act 1970: duty to consider needs of disabled persons.
Section 8(1)	Duty of local authority to take into account abilities of carer.

(**a**) 1970 c.44.
(**b**) 1968 c.49.

EXPLANATORY NOTE

(This note is not part of the Order)

This Order brings into force in Scotland on 1st June 1987 certain sections of the Disabled Persons (Services, Consultation and Representation) Act 1986, namely section 9 (which amends section 1(2) of the Chronically Sick and Disabled Persons Act 1970 in relation to provision of information by local authorities), section 10 (which provides for consultation with organisations of disabled people before making appointments or co-options to certain bodies), section 11 (which provides for reports to be made to Parliament by the Secretary of State), section 12 (which amends section 29(2) of the Chronically Sick and Disabled Persons Act 1970 and section 2 of the Social Work (Scotland) Act 1968), section 14 (which amends the Education (Scotland) Act 1980 (c.44) with regard to assessment and recording of children and young persons), section 16 (which provides for interpretation of the Act), section 17 (which provides for finance) and section 18 (which provides for the short title, commencement and extent of the Act and for procedural requirements for regulations and orders under it).

This Order also brings into force in Scotland on 1st October 1987 sections 4 except paragraph (b) and 8(1) of the 1986 Act (which respectively impose duties on a local authority to consider the needs of disabled persons when requested to do so by certain specified persons, and to take into account the abilities of the carer to continue to provide care to a disabled person).

NOTE AS TO EARLIER COMMENCEMENT ORDERS

(This note is not part of the Order)

The following provisions of the Act have been brought into force by Commencement Order made before the date of this Order.

Provision	Date of Commencement	S.I. No.
ss. 4 (except paragraph (b)), 8(1), 9 and 10 as to England and Wales.	1.4.1987	1987/564
ss. 16, 17 and 18 as to England and Wales.	17.4.1987	1987/729

1987 No. 918

COPYRIGHT

The National Library of Wales (Delivery of Books) (Amendment) Regulations 1987

Made	-	-	-	-	*12th May 1987*
Coming into force					*8th June 1987*

The Lord President of the Council, in exercise of powers conferred by section 15(5) of the Copyright Act 1911**(a)** and now vested in him **(b)**, hereby makes the following Regulations:

Citation and coming into force

1. These Regulations may be cited as the National Library of Wales (Delivery of Books) (Amendment) Regulations 1987, and shall come into force on 8th June 1987.

Revocation

2. The National Library of Wales (Delivery of Books) Regulations 1924**(c)** and the National Library of Wales (Delivery of Books) (Amendment) Regulations 1956**(d)** (which specify classes of books not required to be delivered to the National Library of Wales) are hereby revoked.

Whitelaw
12th May 1987   Lord President of the Council

EXPLANATORY NOTE

(This note is not part of the Regulations)

These Regulations revoke the National Library of Wales (Delivery of Books) Regulations 1924 and the National Library of Wales (Delivery of Books) (Amendment) Regulations 1956 which specified the classes of books not required to be delivered to the National Library of Wales under section 15 of the Copyright Act 1911. They are issued in consequence of a defect in the National Library of Wales (Delivery of Books) (Amendment) Order 1987 which, having been made as an Order and not as Regulations as required by section 15(5) of the Copyright Act 1911, did not take effect.

(a) 1911 c.46.   **(b)** The Transfer of Functions (Arts, Libraries and National Heritage) Order 1986 (S.I. 1986/600).
(c) S.R. & O. 1924/400.   **(d)** S.I. 1956/1978.

STATUTORY INSTRUMENTS

1987 No. 921

RATING AND VALUATION

The New Valuation Lists Order 1987

Approved by both Houses of Parliament

Made - - - -	*31st March 1987*
Laid before Parliament	*7th April 1987*
Coming into force	*15th May 1987*

The Secretary of State for the Environment, in exercise of the powers conferred upon him by section 68(1) of the General Rate Act 1967(a), and of all other powers enabling him in that behalf, hereby makes the following Order:—

1. This Order may be cited as the New Valuation Lists Order 1987 and shall come into force on the day following the day on which it is approved by a resolution of each House of Parliament.

2. 1990 is specified as a year in which new valuation lists are to come into force in each rating area in England and Wales.

Nicholas Ridley
31st March 1987   Secretary of State for the Environment

EXPLANATORY NOTE

(This note is not part of the Order)

This Order specifies 1990 as a year in which new valuation lists are to come into force in rating areas in England and Wales. The new lists have effect from 1st April in that year.

The Secretary of State has power to specify, by Order, a class of hereditaments to be revalued for the purposes of the new valuation lists. An Order was made on the same date as this Order specifying hereditaments other than dwelling houses, private garages and private storage premises as the class of hereditaments which are to be revalued for the purposes of the new lists. It is subject to annulment in pursuance of a resolution of either House of Parliament.

(a) 1967 c.9; section 68(1) was substituted by the Local Government, Planning and Land Act 1980 (c.65), section 28.

1987 No. 925

FINANCIAL SERVICES

The Financial Services (Transfer of Functions Relating to Friendly Societies) Order 1987

Approved by both Houses of Parliament

Made - - - -	*18th May 1987*
Coming into force	*19th May 1987*

Whereas it appears to the Chief Registrar of Friendly Societies that The Securities and Investments Board Limited ("the transferee body") is able and willing to discharge the functions transferred by this Order and that the requirements mentioned in paragraph 28(1)(b) of Schedule 11 to the Financial Services Act 1986 (**a**) ("the Act") are satisfied in the case of the transferee body;

And whereas the Secretary of State and the Chief Registrar of Friendly Societies have been furnished by the transferee body with a copy of the rules and regulations it proposes to make in the exercise of the functions transferred by this Order;

And whereas the Chief Registrar of Friendly Societies has required the transferee body to furnish him and the Secretary of State with a copy of any guidance intended to have continuing effect which it proposes to issue in writing or other legible form;

And whereas the Secretary of State and the Chief Registrar of Friendly Societies are both satisfied that the rules and regulations which the transferee body proposes to make in exercise of the functions transferred by this Order will–

    (i) afford investors an adequate level of protection,

    (ii) in the case of rules and regulations corresponding to those mentioned in Schedule 8 to the Act, comply with the principles set out in that Schedule, and

    (iii) take proper account of the supervision of friendly societies by the Chief Registrar of Friendly Societies under the enactments relating to friendly societies;

And whereas the Secretary of State has sent to the Director General of Fair Trading a copy of the rules and regulations and of any guidance which the Secretary of State is required to consider in making the decision whether he is precluded by paragraph 36(1) of Schedule 11 to the Act from giving his consent to the making of this Order together with such other information as the Secretary of State considered would assist the Director General of Fair Trading in discharging his functions under section 122(2) of the Act as it has effect by virtue of paragraph 36(2) and (5) of Schedule 11 to the Act;

And whereas the Secretary of State has had regard to the report made to him by the Director General of Fair Trading under section 122(2) of the Act, as it has effect by virtue of paragraph 36(2) and (5) of Schedule 11 to the Act, in deciding whether he is precluded by paragraph 36(1) of Schedule 11 to the Act from giving his consent to the making of this Order;

(**a**) 1986 c.60.

And whereas the Secretary of State is satisfied that the rules, regulations and guidance of which copies have been furnished to him under paragraphs 29(a) and 30(1) of Schedule 11 to the Act do not have, and are not intended or likely to have, to any significant extent the effect of restricting, distorting or preventing competition;

And whereas a draft of this Order has been laid before and approved by resolution of each House of Parliament in accordance with paragraph 28(9) of Schedule 11 to the Act;

Now, therefore, the Chief Registrar of Friendly Societies, in exercise of the powers conferred on him by paragraph 28 of Schedule 11 and paragraph 12 of Schedule 15 to the Act and of all other powers enabling him in that behalf and with the consent of the Secretary of State, hereby makes the following Order:

Citation and commencement

1. This Order may be cited as the Financial Services (Transfer of Functions Relating to Friendly Societies) Order 1987 and shall come into force on the day after the day on which it is made.

Transfer of functions

2. Subject to the provisions of article 3, all the functions of the Chief Registrar of Friendly Societies which are transferable in accordance with paragraph 28 of Schedule 11 to the Act (transfer of functions) are transferred to the transferee body.

3. The following functions are not transferred to the transferee body–
  (a) the function under paragraph 17 of Schedule 11 to the Act (power to make rules concerning indemnity); and
  (b) the function of revoking a recognition order in respect of a self-regulating organisation for friendly societies on the ground that the requirement mentioned in paragraph 4(2) of Schedule 11 to the Act (requirement that rules of the organisation should take proper account of friendly societies legislation) is not satisfied.

18th May 1987

J. M. Bridgeman
Chief Registrar of Friendly Societies

I consent to this Order.

18th May 1987

Paul Channon
One of Her Majesty's Principal Secretaries of State

EXPLANATORY NOTE

(This note is not part of the Order)

This Order transfers, with two exceptions, the functions of the Chief Registrar of Friendly Societies under the Financial Services Act 1986 which are capable of being transferred under paragraph 28 of Schedule 11 to that Act to The Securities and Investments Board Limited. These functions include that of making a recognition order in respect of a self-regulating organisation for friendly societies, and that of making rules governing the conduct of business by regulated friendly societies.

The two functions which are not transferred by this Order are–

(a) the function of making rules concerning indemnity against any claim in respect of any description of civil liability incurred by a regulated friendly society (under paragraph 17 of Schedule 11 to the Act); and

(b) the function of revoking a recognition order in respect of a self-regulating organisation for friendly societies on the ground that the organisation's rules do not take proper account of friendly societies legislation (the power to revoke a recognition order is under paragraph 5 of Schedule 11 to the Act).

STATUTORY INSTRUMENTS

1987 No. 926

EUROPEAN COMMUNITIES

The European Communities (Designation) (No.2) Order 1987

Made - - - -	*18th May 1987*
Laid before Parliament	*17th June 1987*
Coming into force	*8th July 1987*

At the Court at Buckingham Palace, the 18th day of May 1987

Present,

The Queen's Most Excellent Majesty in Council

Her Majesty, in exercise of the powers conferred on Her by section 2(2) of the European Communities Act 1972(**a**), is pleased, by and with the advice of Her Privy Council, to order, and it is hereby ordered, as follows:

Citation and commencement

1. This Order may be cited as the European Communities (Designation) (No.2) Order 1987 and shall come into force on 8th July 1987.

Designation of Ministers or departments

2.—(1) For the purposes of section 2(2) of the European Communities Act 1972 the Ministers or government departments specified in column 1 of the Schedule to this Order are hereby designated in relation to the matters respectively specified in column 2 of that Schedule.

(2) Where a Minister or government department is designated in relation to any item in column 2 of the said Schedule, then, for the purposes of the said section 2(2), that Minister or government department is also hereby designated in relation to anything supplemental or incidental to the matters specified in that item.

(3) Where both a Minister and one or more government departments are designated by this Order in relation to any matter, the designation has effect as respects the making of regulations by any of them or by more than one of them acting jointly.

(4) Regulations made by a Northern Ireland department in pursuance of this Order shall form part of the law of Northern Ireland and not of any other part of the United Kingdom.

G.I. de Deney
Clerk of the Privy Council

(**a**) 1972 c. 68.

SCHEDULE

(1) *Ministers or departments*	(2) *Matters in relation to which the Ministers or departments are designated*
The Secretary of State	Measures relating to household appliances which emit noise.
The Secretary of State	Measures in respect of sound pressure level requirements for the marketing of construction plant and equipment and measures in respect of the use of such equipment.
The Secretary of State	Measures and technical requirements in respect of the manufacture, placing on the market, putting into service and use of lifting and mechanical handling appliances and their components.
The Secretary of State	The conferment of preferential treatment in insolvency for debts arising from the application of levies on the production of coal and steel.
Any Northern Ireland Department	The preceding items in this column.
The Secretary of State and the Commissioners of Customs and Excise	Measures relating to the prohibition of the release for free circulation of goods bearing a trade mark without authorisation.
The Secretary of State	Measures to counteract the restriction by countries other than Member States of access to the carriage of passengers or goods by sea.

EXPLANATORY NOTE

(This note is not part of the Order)

This is a further Order in the series of Orders designating the Minister who, and departments which, may exercise powers to make regulations conferred by section 2(2) of the European Communities Act 1972 and specifying the matters in relation to which those powers may be exercised.

STATUTORY INSTRUMENTS

1987 No. 927

DEFENCE

The International Headquarters and Defence Organisations (Designation and Privileges) (Amendment) Order 1987

Made - - - -	*18th May 1987*
Coming into force	*17th June 1987*

At the Court at Buckingham Palace, the 18th day of May 1987

Present,

The Queen's Most Excellent Majesty in Council

Whereas a draft of this Order has in accordance with section 1(4) of the International Headquarters and Defence Organisations Act 1964(**a**) been laid before Parliament and approved by resolution of each House of Parliament:

Now, therefore, Her Majesty, in pursuance of section 1 of that Act, is pleased, by and with the advice of Her Privy Council, to order, and it is hereby ordered, as follows:–

1. This Order may be cited as the International Headquarters and Defence Organisations (Designation and Privileges) (Amendment) Order 1987, and shall come into force at the expiration of thirty days beginning with the day on which it is made.

2. There shall be inserted at the end of Part II of the Schedule to the International Headquarters and Defence Organisations (Designation and Privileges) Order 1965(**b**) the following entries:–

"The Headquarters of the Commander Submarine Forces Eastern Atlantic Area (COMSUBEASTLANT).";

"The Headquarters of the Commander in Chief of UK Air Forces (CINCUKAIR).".

G. I. de Deney
Clerk of the Privy Council

(**a**) 1964 c.5.
(**b**) S.I. 1965/1535; there are no amending instruments.

EXPLANATORY NOTE

(This note is not part of the Order)

This Order adds the Headquarters of the Commander Submarine Forces Eastern Atlantic Area (COMSUBEASTLANT) and the Headquarters of the Commander in Chief of UK Air Forces (CINCUKAIR) to the international headquarters mentioned in Part II of the Schedule to the International Headquarters and Defence Organisations (Designation and Privileges) Order 1965.

The effect is to extend to the two headquarters and certain persons connected with them the Visiting Forces Act 1952 (c.67) as amended by the International Headquarters and Defence Organisations Act 1964. It also confers on the two headquarters the like privileges as respects the inviolability of their official archives as are accorded to diplomats accredited to Her Majesty.

STATUTORY INSTRUMENTS

1987 No. 928

DEFENCE

The Visiting Forces and International Headquarters (Application of Law) (Amendment) Order 1987

Made - - - -	*18th May 1987*
Coming into force	*17th June 1987*

At the Court at Buckingham Palace, the 18th day of May 1987

Present,

The Queen's Most Excellent Majesty in Council

Whereas a draft of this Order has in accordance with section 8(6) of the Visiting Forces Act 1952(**a**) been laid before Parliament and approved by resolution of each House of Parliament:

Now, therefore, Her Majesty, in pursuance of the said section 8, is pleased, by and with the advice of Her Privy Council, to order, and it is hereby ordered, as follows:–

1. This Order may be cited as the Visiting Forces and International Headquarters (Application of Law) (Amendment) Order 1987 and shall come into force at the expiration of thirty days beginning with the day on which it is made.

2. There shall be inserted at the end of article 3(4) of the Visiting Forces and International Headquarters (Application of Law) Order 1965(**b**) (which applies that Order to the headquarters and defence organisations mentioned therein) the following entries:

"The Headquarters of the Commander Submarine Forces Eastern Atlantic Area (COMSUBEASTLANT).";

"The Headquarters of the Commander in Chief of UK Air Forces (CINCUKAIR).".

G. I. de Deney
Clerk of the Privy Council

(**a**) 1952 c.67; section 8 was extended by paragraph 7 of the Schedule to the International Headquarters and Defence Organisations Act 1964 (c.5). (**b**) S.I. 1965/1536; there are no relevant amendments.

EXPLANATORY NOTE

(This note is not part of the Order)

This Order amends the Visiting Forces and International Headquarters (Application of Law) Order 1965, which provides for the application to visiting forces and international headquarters of law applicable to home forces, by adding to the headquarters mentioned in article 3(4) of that Order the Headquarters of the Commander Submarine Forces Eastern Atlantic Area (COMSUBEASTLANT) and the Headquarters of the Commander in Chief of UK Air Forces (CINCUKAIR).

STATUTORY INSTRUMENTS

1987 No. 929

RACE RELATIONS

The Race Relations (Offshore Employment) Order 1987

Made - - - -	*18th May 1987*
Coming into force	*1st November 1987*

At the Court at Buckingham Palace, the 18th day of May 1987

Present,

The Queen's Most Excellent Majesty in Council

Whereas a draft of this Order has been approved by resolution of each House of Parliament:

Now, therefore, Her Majesty, in exercise of the powers conferred on Her by sections 8(5) and 74(3) of the Race Relations Act 1976(a) and of all other powers enabling Her in that behalf, is pleased, by and with the advice of Her Privy Council, to order, and it is hereby ordered, as follows:–

1.—(1) This Order may be cited as the Race Relations (Offshore Employment) Order 1987 and shall come into force on 1st November 1987.

(2) In this Order:–

"the 1976 Act" means the Race Relations Act 1976;

"the Frigg Gas Field" means the naturally occurring gas-bearing sand formations of the lower Eocene age located in the vicinity of the intersection of the line of latitude 59° 53' North and of the dividing line between the sectors of the Continental Shelf of the United Kingdom and the Kingdom of Norway and includes all other gas-bearing strata from which gas at the start of production is capable of flowing into the above-mentioned gas-bearing sand formations;

"oversea company" has the same meaning as in section 744 of the Companies Act 1985(**b**).

(**a**) 1976 c.74; the powers in section 8(5) were extended by section 1(2) of the Employment (Continental Shelf) Act 1978 (c.46).   (**b**) 1985 c.6.

2.—(1) In relation to employment concerned with exploration of the sea bed or sub-soil or the exploitation of their natural resources, but subject to paragraph (2), subsections (1) to (3) of section 8 of the 1976 Act shall have effect as if in both subsection (1) and subsection (3) the last reference to Great Britain included:–

    (a) any area for the time being designated under section 1(7) of the Continental Shelf Act 1964(**a**) except an area or part of an area in which the law of Northern Ireland applies; and

    (b) in relation to employment concerned with the exploration or exploitation of the Frigg Gas Field, the part of the Norwegian sector of the Continental Shelf described in the Schedule to this Order.

(2) This Order shall have no application to employment which is concerned with the exploration or exploitation of the Frigg Gas Field unless the employer is:–

    (a) a company registered under the Companies Act 1985,

    (b) an oversea company which has established a place of business within Great Britain from which it directs the offshore operations in question, or

    (c) any other person who has a place of business within Great Britain from which he directs the offshore operations in question.

G. I. de Deney
Clerk of the Privy Council

(**a**) 1964 c.29.

SCHEDULE

NORWEGIAN PART OF THE FRIGG FIELD

1. The part of the Norwegian sector of the Continental Shelf described in this Schedule is the area defined by–

(a) the sets of lines of latitude and longitude joining the following surface co-ordinates–

Longitude			Latitude		
02°	05'	30"E	60°	00'	45"N
02°	05'	30"E	59°	58'	45"N
02°	06'	00"E	59°	58'	45"N
02°	06'	00"E	59°	57'	45"N
02°	07'	00"E	59°	57'	45"N
02°	07'	00"E	59°	57'	30"N
02°	07'	30"E	59°	57'	30"N
02°	07'	30"E	59°	55'	30"N
02°	10'	30"E	59°	55'	30"N
02°	10'	30"E	59°	54'	45"N
02°	11'	00"E	59°	54'	45"N
02°	11'	00"E	59°	54'	15"N
02°	12'	30"E	59°	54'	15"N
02°	12'	30"E	59°	54'	00"N
02°	13'	30"E	59°	54'	00"N
02°	13'	30"E	59°	54'	30"N
02°	15'	30"E	59°	54'	30"N
02°	15'	30"E	59°	53'	15"N
02°	10'	30"E	59°	53'	15"N
02°	10'	30"E	59°	52'	45"N
02°	09'	30"E	59°	52'	45"N
02°	09'	30"E	59°	52'	15"N
02°	08'	30"E	59°	52'	15"N
02°	08'	30"E	59°	52'	00"N
02°	07'	30"E	59°	52'	00"N
02°	07'	30"E	59°	51'	30"N
02°	05'	30"E	59°	51'	30"N
02°	05'	30"E	59°	51'	00"N
02°	04'	00"E	59°	51'	00"N
02°	04'	00"E	59°	50'	30"N
02°	03'	00"E	59°	50'	30"N
02°	03'	00"E	59°	50'	00"N

(b) a line from the point 02° 03' 00"E 59° 50' 00"N west along the parallel of latitude 59° 50' 00"N until its intersection with the Dividing Line;

(c) a line from the point of intersection specified in paragraph (b) above along the Dividing Line until its intersection with the parallel of latitude 60° 00' 45"N;

(d) a line from the point of intersection specified in paragraph (c) above east along the parallel of latitude 60° 00' 45"N until its intersection with the meridian 02° 05' 30"E.

2. In this Schedule, the "Dividing Line" means the dividing line as defined in an Agreement dated 10th March 1965 and made between the government of the United Kingdom of Great Britain and Northern Ireland and the government of the Kingdom of Norway(a) as supplemented by a Protocol dated 22nd December 1978(b).

(a) Treaty Series No. 71 (1975) Cmd. 2757. (b) Treaty Series No. 31 (1980) Cmnd. 7853.

EXPLANATORY NOTE

(This note is not part of the Order)

This Order brings within the scope of Part II of the Race Relations Act 1976 (which is concerned with discrimination in the employment field) employment concerned with the exploration of the sea bed or subsoil or the exploitation of their natural resources in areas which have been designated under section 1(7) of the Continental Shelf Act 1964. It also brings within scope certain such employment in the Norwegian sector of the Continental Shelf in relation to the Frigg Gas Field. It only has application, however, to employment concerned with the Frigg Gas Field if the employer is a British company or has a place of business in Great Britain from which he directs the offshore operations.

STATUTORY INSTRUMENTS

1987 No. 930

SEX DISCRIMINATION

The Sex Discrimination and Equal Pay (Offshore Employment) Order 1987

Made - - - -	*18th May 1987*
Coming into force	*1st November 1987*

At the Court at Buckingham Palace, the 18th day of May 1987

Present,

The Queen's Most Excellent Majesty in Council

Whereas a draft of this Order has been approved by resolution of each House of Parliament;

Now, therefore, Her Majesty, in exercise of the powers conferred on Her by sections 10(5) and 81(4) of the Sex Discrimination Act 1975 (a) and of all other powers enabling Her in that behalf, is pleased, by and with the advice of Her Privy Council, to order, and it is hereby ordered, as follows:

1.—(1) This Order may be cited as the Sex Discrimination and Equal Pay (Offshore Employment) Order 1987 and shall come into force on 1st November 1987.

(2) In this Order–

"the 1975 Act" means the Sex Discrimination Act 1975;

"the Frigg Gas Field" means the naturally occurring gas-bearing sand formations of the lower Eocene age located in the vicinity of the intersection of the line of latitude 59° 53′ North and of the dividing line between the sectors of the Continental Shelf of the United Kingdom and the Kingdom of Norway and includes all other gas-bearing strata from which gas at the start of production is capable of flowing into the above-mentioned gas-bearing sand formations;

"oversea company" has the same meaning as in section 744 of the Companies Act 1985 (b).

2.—(1) In relation to employment concerned with exploration of the sea bed or subsoil or the exploitation of their natural resources, but subject to paragraph (2), subsections (1) and (2) of section 10 of the 1975 Act shall each have effect as if the last reference to Great Britain in those subsections included–

  (a) any area for the time being designated under section 1(7) of the Continental Shelf Act 1964 (c), except an area or part of an area in which the law of Northern Ireland applies; and

  (b) in relation to employment concerned with the exploration or exploitation of the Frigg Gas Field, the part of the Norwegian sector of the Continental Shelf described in the Schedule to this Order.

(a) 1975 c.65; the powers in section 10(5) were extended by section 1(2) of the Employment (Continental Shelf) Act 1978 (c.46).
(b) 1985 c.6. (c) 1964 c.29.

(2) This Order shall have no application to employment which is concerned with the exploration or exploitation of the Frigg Gas Field unless the employer is–

    (a) a company registered under the Companies Act 1985,

    (b) an oversea company which has established a place of business within Great Britain from which it directs the offshore operations in question, or

    (c) any other person who has a place of business within Great Britain from which he directs the offshore operations in question.

G. I. de Deney
Clerk of the Privy Council

SCHEDULE

NORWEGIAN PART OF THE FRIGG FIELD

1.   The part of the Norwegian sector of the Continental Shelf described in this Schedule is the area defined by–

    (a) the sets of lines of latitude and longitude joining the following surface co-ordinates–

Longitude	Latitude
02° 05′ 30″E	60° 00′ 45″N
02° 05′ 30″E	59° 58′ 45″N
02° 06′ 00″E	59° 58′ 45″N
02° 06′ 00″E	59° 57′ 45″N
02° 07′ 00″E	59° 57′ 45″N
02° 07′ 00″E	59° 57′ 30″N
02° 07′ 30″E	59° 57′ 30″N
02° 07′ 30″E	59° 55′ 30″N
02° 10′ 30″E	59° 55′ 30″N
02° 10′ 30″E	59° 54′ 45″N
02° 11′ 00″E	59° 54′ 45″N
02° 11′ 00″E	59° 54′ 15″N
02° 12′ 30″E	59° 54′ 15″N
02° 12′ 30″E	59° 54′ 00″N
02° 13′ 30″E	59° 54′ 00″N
02° 13′ 30″E	59° 54′ 30″N
02° 15′ 30″E	59° 54′ 30″N
02° 15′ 30″E	59° 53′ 15″N
02° 10′ 30″E	59° 53′ 15″N
02° 10′ 30″E	59° 52′ 45″N
02° 09′ 30″E	59° 52′ 45″N
02° 09′ 30″E	59° 52′ 15″N
02° 08′ 30″E	59° 52′ 15″N
02° 08′ 30″E	59° 52′ 00″N
02° 07′ 30″E	59° 52′ 00″N
02° 07′ 30″E	59° 51′ 30″N
02° 05′ 30″E	59° 51′ 30″N
02° 05′ 30″E	59° 51′ 00″N
02° 04′ 00″E	59° 51′ 00″N
02° 04′ 00″E	59° 50′ 30″N
02° 03′ 00″E	59° 50′ 30″N
02° 03′ 00″E	59° 50′ 00″N

    (b) a line from the point 02° 03′ 00″E 59° 50′ 00″N west along the parallel of latitude 59° 50′ 00″N until its intersection with the Dividing Line;

    (c) a line from the point of intersection specified in paragraph (b) above along the Dividing Line until its intersection with the parallel of latitude 60° 00′ 45″N;

    (d) a line from the point of intersection specified in paragraph (c) above east along the parallel of latitude 60° 00′ 45″N until its intersection with the meridian 02° 05′ 30″E.

2.   In this Schedule, the "Dividing Line" means the dividing line as defined in an Agreement dated 10th March 1965 and made between the government of the United Kingdom of Great Britain and Northern Ireland and the government of the Kingdom of Norway (a) as supplemented by a Protocol dated 22nd December 1978 (b).

(a) Treaty Series No. 71 (1975) Cmd. 2757.
(b) Treaty Series No. 31 (1980) Cmnd. 7853.

EXPLANATORY NOTE

(This note is not part of the Order)

This Order brings within the scope of Part II of the Sex Discrimination Act 1975 (which is concerned with discrimination in the employment field) and within the scope of the Equal Pay Act 1970 (c.41) employment concerned with the exploration of the sea bed or subsoil or the exploitation of their natural resources in areas which have been designated under section 1(7) of the Continental Shelf Act 1964. It also brings within scope certain such employment in the Norwegian sector of the Continental Shelf in relation to the Frigg Gas Field. It only has application, however, to employment concerned with the Frigg Gas Field if the employer is a British company or has a place of business in Great Britain from which he directs the offshore operations.

STATUTORY INSTRUMENTS

1987 No. 931

MERCHANT SHIPPING

The Carriage of Passengers and their Luggage by Sea (Parties to Convention) Order 1987

Made - - - -	*18th May 1987*
Coming into force	*17th June 1987*

At the Court at Buckingham Palace, the 18th day of May 1987

Present,

The Queen's Most Excellent Majesty in Council

Her Majesty, in exercise of the powers conferred on Her by paragraph 10 of Part II of Schedule 3 to the Merchant Shipping Act 1979(**a**) or otherwise in Her Majesty vested, is pleased, by and with the advice of Her Privy Council, to order, and it is hereby ordered, as follows:

1.   This Order may be cited as the Carriage of Passengers and their Luggage by Sea (Parties to Convention) Order 1987 and shall come into force on 17th June 1987.

2.   In this Order, "the Convention" means the Convention relating to the Carriage of Passengers and their Luggage by Sea as set out in Part I of Schedule 3 to the Merchant Shipping Act 1979.

3.   It is hereby declared that, in relation to a State specified in the first column of the Schedule to this Order, the State is a party to the Convention in respect of the country specified opposite thereto in the second column of the Schedule with effect from the date of entry into force of the Convention for that State as specified in the third column of the Schedule.

G.I. de Deney
Clerk of the Privy Council

(**a**) 1979 c. 39.

SCHEDULE

STATES WHICH ARE PARTIES TO THE CONVENTION AND COUNTRIES IN RESPECT OF WHICH THE CONVENTION IS IN FORCE

State	Country	Date of Entry into Force of Convention
The United Kingdom of Great Britain and Northern Ireland	Great Britain and Northern Ireland The Bailiwick of Guernsey The Bailiwick of Jersey The Isle of Man Bermuda British Virgin Islands Cayman Islands Falkland Islands Gibraltar Hong Kong Montserrat Pitcairn Saint Helena and Dependencies	30th April 1987
The Argentine Republic	Argentina	28th April 1987
The Commonwealth of the Bahamas	The Bahamas	28th April 1987
The German Democratic Republic	German Democratic Republic	28th April 1987
The Republic of Liberia	Liberia	28th April 1987
The Polish People's Republic	Poland	28th April 1987
The Kingdom of Spain	Spain	28th April 1987
The Kingdom of Tonga	Tonga	28th April 1987
The Union of Soviet Socialist Republics	All territories comprised within the Soviet Socialist Republics	28th April 1987
The Yemen Arab Republic	Yemen Arab Republic	28th April 1987

EXPLANATORY NOTE

(This note is not part of the Order)

Section 14 of and Schedule 3 to the Merchant Shipping Act 1979 give effect in the United Kingdom to the Convention relating to the Carriage of Passengers and their Luggage by Sea, which was opened for signature at Athens on 13th December 1974 and is set out in Part I of Schedule 3 to the Merchant Shipping Act 1979. This Order declares the States which are parties to the Convention and the countries in respect of which they are parties.

STATUTORY INSTRUMENTS

1987 No. 932

MERCHANT SHIPPING

The Merchant Shipping (Confirmation of Legislation) (Anguilla) Order 1987

Made - - - -	*18th May 1987*
Laid before Parliament	*17th June 1987*
Coming into force	*8th July 1987*

At the Court at Buckingham Palace, the 18th day of May 1987

Present,

The Queen's Most Excellent Majesty in Council

Her Majesty in pursuance of section 735(1) of the Merchant Shipping Act 1894 (**a**) is pleased, by and with the advice of Her Privy Council, to order, and it is hereby ordered, as follows:

1. This Order may be cited as the Merchant Shipping (Confirmation of Legislation) (Anguilla) Order 1987 and shall come into force on 8th July 1987.

2. The Merchant Shipping (Registry) Ordinance, 1986 (**b**) is hereby confirmed.

G. I. de Deney
Clerk of the Privy Council

EXPLANATORY NOTE

(This note is not part of the Order)

This Order, made under section 735(1) of the Merchant Shipping Act 1894, confirms a Law enacted by the House of Assembly of Anguilla which repeals, in relation to the registration of ships in Anguilla, certain provisions of Part I of the Merchant Shipping Act 1894 regarding such registration.

(**a**) 1894 c.60.
(**b**) Ordinance No. 13 of 1986 as amended.

STATUTORY INSTRUMENTS

1987 No. 933

MERCHANT SHIPPING

The Merchant Shipping (Confirmation of Legislation) (Gibraltar) Order 1987

Made - - - -	*18th May 1987*
Laid before Parliament	*17th June 1987*
Coming into force	*8th July 1987*

At the Court at Buckingham Palace, the 18th day of May 1987

Present,

The Queen's Most Excellent Majesty in Council

Her Majesty in pursuance of section 735(1) of the Merchant Shipping Act 1894(**a**), and of all other powers enabling Her in that behalf, is pleased, by and with the advice of Her Privy Council, to order, and it is hereby ordered, as follows:

1. This Order may be cited as the Merchant Shipping (Confirmation of Legislation) (Gibraltar) Order 1987 and shall come into force on 8th July 1987.

2. The Merchant Shipping (Amendment) Ordinance, 1987(**b**) is hereby confirmed.

G. I. de Deney
Clerk of the Privy Council

EXPLANATORY NOTE

(This note is not part of the Order)

By this Order the Queen in Council, in exercise of the powers conferred upon Her by section 735(1) of the Merchant Shipping Act 1894, confirms a Law enacted by the Legislature of Gibraltar by which, *inter alia*, certain provisions of that Act relating to ships registered in the Colony are repealed.

(**a**) 1894 c.60.   (**b**) Ordinance No. 4 of 1987.

STATUTORY INSTRUMENTS

1987 No. 934

CARIBBEAN AND NORTH ATLANTIC TERRITORIES

The Turks and Caicos Islands (Constitution) (Interim Amendment) Order 1987

Made - - - -	*18th May 1987*
Laid before Parliament	*17th June 1987*
Coming into force	*On a day to be appointed under section 1(2)*

At the Court at Buckingham Palace, the 18th day of May 1987

Present,

The Queen's Most Excellent Majesty in Council

Her Majesty, in exercise of the powers conferred upon Her by section 5 of the West Indies Act 1962 (**a**) and of all other powers enabling Her in that behalf, is pleased, by and with the advice of Her Privy Council, to order, and it is hereby ordered, as follows:

Citation, construction and commencement

1.—(1) This Order may be cited as the Turks and Caicos Islands (Constitution) (Interim Amendment) Order 1987 and shall be construed as one with the Turks and Caicos Islands (Constitution) Order 1976(**b**).

(2) This Order shall come into force on such day as the Governor, acting in his discretion, may appoint by proclamation published in the *Gazette*.

Amendment of Turks and Caicos Islands (Constitution) (Interim Amendment) Order 1986

2. Paragraph 3(1)(c) of Schedule 2 to the Turks and Caicos Islands (Constitution) (Interim Amendment) Order 1986(**c**) shall be amended by substituting for the words "up to four persons" the words "up to six persons", and section 5 of the said Order shall have effect accordingly.

G. I. de Deney
Clerk of the Privy Council

(**a**) 1962 c.19.
(**b**) S.I. 1976/1156, amended by S.I. 1979/919, 1982/1075, 1986/1157.
(**c**) S.I. 1986/1157.

EXPLANATORY NOTE

(This note is not part of the Order)

This Order amends the Constitution of the Turks and Caicos Islands, as modified by the Turks and Caicos Islands (Constitution) (Interim Amendment) Order 1986, to increase to a maximum of six the number of persons who may be appointed by the Governor as nominated members of the Executive Council for the Islands.

STATUTORY INSTRUMENTS

1987 No. 935

SOCIAL SECURITY

The Social Security (Australia) Order 1987

Made - - - -	*18th May 1987*
Coming into force	*18th May 1987*

At the Court at Buckingham Palace, the 18th day of May 1987

Present,

The Queen's Most Excellent Majesty in Council

Whereas an agreement was made on 29th January 1958 between the Government of the United Kingdom of Great Britain and Northern Ireland and the Government of the Commonwealth of Australia and effect was given to that agreement by the Family Allowances and National Insurance (Australia) Order 1958(**a**) (hereinafter referred to as "the 1958 Order"):

And Whereas that agreement was modified and extended by a further agreement made on 16th August 1962 between the said Governments and effect was given to that agreement by the Family Allowances and National Insurance (Australia) Order 1962(**b**) (hereinafter referred to as "the 1962 Order"):

And Whereas the said agreement as so modified and extended was further amended by Notes exchanged on 6th March 1975 and effect was given to that amendment by the Social Security (Australia) Order 1975(**c**) (hereinafter referred to as "the 1975 Order"):

And Whereas at London on 31st December 1986 Notes were exchanged on behalf of the said Governments for the purpose of further amending the said agreement and the terms of the Note from the Secretary of State for Foreign and Commonwealth Affairs were reproduced in the Note from the Australian High Commissioner which is set out in the Schedule to this Order:

And Whereas by virtue of section 117(1) of the National Insurance Act 1965(**d**) the 1958 Order and the 1962 Order are deemed to have been made under section 105 of that Act:

And Whereas by virtue of section 2 of, and paragraph 10 of Schedule 3 to, the Social Security (Consequential Provisions) Act 1975(**e**) the 1975 Order provided for the 1958 Order and the 1962 Order to have effect for the purposes of section 143 of the Social Security Act 1975(**f**) with such modifications as are specified therein and to have effect as if any references in the said section 105 and the said section 143 to an agreement included a reference to a proposed agreement:

And Whereas by section 143 of the Social Security Act 1975 it is provided that Her Majesty may by Order in Council make provision for modifying or adapting the said Social Security Act in its application to cases affected by agreements with other governments providing for reciprocity in matters specified in that section:

(**a**) S.I. 1958/422.
(**b**) S.I. 1962/1869.
(**c**) S.I. 1975/812.
(**d**) 1965 c. 51.
(**e**) 1975 c. 18.
(**f**) 1975 c. 14; subsection (1A) of section 143 was inserted by section 6(1) of the Social Security Act 1981 (c. 33).

And Whereas by virtue of section 166(4) of the Social Security Act 1975 any Order in Council made under the said section 143 may be varied by a subsequent Order in Council made under that section:

Now, therefore, Her Majesty, in pursuance of the said section 143 and the said section 2, and of all other powers enabling Her in that behalf, is pleased, by and with the advice of Her Privy Council, to order, and it is hereby ordered, as follows:

Citation and commencement

1.   This Order may be cited as the Social Security (Australia) Order 1987 and shall come into force on 18th May 1987.

Modification of Act and Variation of Orders

2.   The Social Security Act 1975 shall be modified and the Family Allowances and National Insurance (Australia) Order 1958, the Family Allowances and National Insurance (Australia) Order 1962 and the Social Security (Australia) Order 1975 shall be varied so as to give effect to the agreement made on 31st December 1986 the terms of which are contained in the Note from the Australian High Commissioner to the Secretary of State for Foreign and Commonwealth Affairs which is set out in the Schedule to this Order, so far as the same relate to England, Wales and Scotland.

G.I. de Deney
Clerk of the Privy Council

SCHEDULE

Article 2

NOTE FROM THE AUSTRALIAN HIGH COMMISSIONER TO THE SECRETARY OF STATE FOR FOREIGN AND COMMONWEALTH AFFAIRS

31st December 1986

Sir,

I have the honour to acknowledge receipt of your Note of 29th December 1986 which reads as follows:

"I have the honour to refer to the Agreement on Social Security between the Government of the United Kingdom of Great Britain and Northern Ireland and the Government of Australia, which was signed at Canberra on 29th January 1958, as amended by the Agreement signed at Canberra on 16th August 1962, and by an Exchange of Notes at Canberra on 6th March 1975 (which, for the purposes of this Note, are together referred to as "the Agreement"), and to recent discussions between the Department of Health and Social Security of the United Kingdom and the Department of Social Security of Australia, concerning the need further to amend the Agreement so as to preclude working holidaymakers from receiving unemployment benefit under the Agreement and to make other minor modifications.

I now have the honour to propose the following amendments to the Agreement:

(a) Article 3 shall be amended by deleting paragraph (2) and the proviso to paragraph (4).

(b) Article 17 shall be amended by inserting after paragraph (3) the following new paragraph:

"(4) For the purposes of any claim to invalidity pension under the legislation of the United Kingdom, any period in respect of which a person was qualified to receive a sickness benefit or an invalid pension under the legislation of Australia shall be treated as if it were a period of entitlement to sickness benefit or invalidity pension completed under the legislation of the United Kingdom.".

(c) Article 18 shall be amended–

(i) by inserting after paragraph (2) the following new paragraph:

"(3) The provisions of this Article shall not apply to a person–

(a) who is in Australia having been granted an entry permit pursuant to a visa issued on an application for a visa to enter that country for a working holiday; or

(b) who is in the United Kingdom by virtue only of his having obtained leave to enter that country given in accordance with any provision of the immigration rules (as defined in section 33(1) of the Immigration Act 1971 of the United Kingdom) which required him to satisfy an immigration officer at the date upon which that obligation last arose that–

(i) he was seeking permission to enter the United Kingdom for an extended holiday, and

(ii) he intended to take only employment within the United Kingdom which was incidental to that holiday.";

(ii) by renumbering the existing paragraph (3) as paragraph (4), deleting the word and figure "paragraph (2)" and substituting the words and figures "paragraphs (2) and (3)".

(d) Article 22 shall be amended by deleting from paragraph (1) the words:

"unless the dependant is a child for whom child endowment is payable under the legislation of Australia".

If the foregoing proposals are acceptable to the Government of Australia I have the honour to propose that this Note and Your Excellency's reply to that effect shall constitute an Agreement between our two Governments which shall enter into force on 9th February 1987.

I avail myself of this opportunity to renew to Your Excellency the assurance of my highest consideration."

I have the honour to confirm that the foregoing proposals are acceptable to the Government of Australia, who therefore agree that your Note together with this reply, shall constitute an Agreement between our two Governments which shall enter into force on 9th February 1987.

A.R. Parsons

EXPLANATORY NOTE

(This note is not part of the Order)

This Order makes provision for the modification of the Social Security Act 1975 so as to give effect in England, Wales and Scotland to the agreement (set out in the Schedule) contained in Notes exchanged between the Government of the United Kingdom of Great Britain and Northern Ireland and the Government of Australia amending the Agreement contained in the Family Allowances and National Insurance (Australia) Order 1958, the Family Allowances and National Insurance (Australia) Order 1962, and the Social Security (Australia) Order 1975. The principal amendment precludes payment of unemployment benefit under the Agreement to visitors from one country who are on holiday in the other country and who are entitled, under their terms of entry, to work during their stay.

1987 No. 937

REPRESENTATION OF THE PEOPLE

REDISTRIBUTION OF SEATS

The Parliamentary Constituencies (England) (Miscellaneous Changes) (No.2) Order 1987

Made - - - -	*18th May 1987*
Coming into force -	*18th May 1987*

At the Court at Buckingham Palace, the 18th day of May 1987

Present,

The Queen's Most Excellent Majesty in Council

Whereas in pursuance of section 3(3) of the Parliamentary Constituencies Act 1986**(a)** the Boundary Commission for England have submitted to the Secretary of State a report dated 16th April 1987 with respect to the areas comprised in certain constituencies in England and showing the constituencies into which they recommend, in accordance with the Parliamentary Constituencies Act 1986, that the areas should be divided:

And whereas the Secretary of State has laid that report before Parliament together with the draft of this Order in Council to give effect to the recommendations contained in the report and each House of Parliament has by resolution approved the said draft:

Now, therefore, Her Majesty, in pursuance of section 4 of the Parliamentary Constituencies Act 1986, is pleased, by and with the advice of Her Privy Council, to order, and it is hereby ordered, as follows:–

Citation and commencement

1.—(1) This Order may be cited as the Parliamentary Constituencies (England) (Miscellaneous Changes) (No.2) Order 1987.

(2) Subject to section 4(6) of the Parliamentary Constituencies Act 1986, this Order shall come into force forthwith.

Reading East and Wokingham

2. For the county constituencies of Reading East and Wokingham as constituted by the Schedule to the Parliamentary Constituencies (England) Order 1983**(b)** (and described by reference to local government areas referred to in that Order), there shall be substituted the constituencies which are named in the Schedule to this Order and comprise the areas set out in that Schedule, which areas are local government areas

---

(a) 1986 c.56.   **(b)** S.I. 1983/417.

as they existed on 16th April 1987 (and accordingly as altered by the Wokingham (Parishes) Order 1986**(a)**).

Register of electors

3. Each electoral registration officer for the constituencies referred to in article 2 above shall make such re-arrangement or adaptation of the registers of parliamentary electors as may be necessary to give effect to this Order.

G. I. de Deney
Clerk to the Privy Council

SCHEDULE

NEW CONSTITUENCIES

Reading East (county constituency)

(i) The following wards of the Borough of Reading, namely, Abbey, Caversham, Church, Park, Peppard, Redlands, Thames and Whitley; and

(ii) the following wards of the District of Wokingham, namely, Arborfield, Barkham, Finchampstead North, Finchampstead South, Shinfield and Swallowfield.

Wokingham (county constituency)

The following wards of the District of Wokingham, namely Bulmershe, Charvil, Coronation, Emmbrook, Evendons, Hurst, Little Hungerford, Loddon, Norreys, Redhatch, Remenham and Wargrave, Sonning, South Lake, Twyford and Ruscombe, Wescott, Whitegates, Winnersh and Wokingham Without.

EXPLANATORY NOTE

(This note is not part of the Order)

This Order gives effect without modification to the recommendations contained in the report of the Boundary Commission for England dated 16th April 1987. The report contains proposals for changes to the areas of the parliamentary constituencies of Reading East and Wokingham and the new constituencies are set out and described in the Schedule to this Order. By virtue of section 4(6) of the Parliamentary Constituencies Act 1986 the coming into force of this Order does not affect any parliamentary election until a proclamation is issued by Her Majesty summoning a new Parliament.

(a) S.I. 1986/570.

STATUTORY INSTRUMENTS

1987 No. 939

LAND REGISTRATION, ENGLAND AND WALES

The Registration of Title Order 1987

Made - - - -	*18th May 1987*
Coming into force	*1st December 1987*

At the Court at Buckingham Palace, the 18th day of May 1987

Present,

The Queen's Most Excellent Majesty in Council

Her Majesty, in exercise of the powers conferred on Her by section 120(1) and (6) of the Land Registration Act 1925(**a**) and sections 80(2) and 90 of the London Government Act 1963(**b**), is pleased, by and with the advice of Her Privy Council, to order and declare, and it is hereby ordered and declared, as follows:

1.—(1) This Order may be cited as the Registration of Title Order 1987 and shall come into force on 1st December 1987.

(2) In this Order "remainder of the district of Ribble Valley" means that part of the district of Ribble Valley in which registration of land is not declared to be compulsory on sale by article 16 of the Lancashire (District Boundaries) Order 1986(**c**).

2.—(1) In addition to the areas mentioned in column 2 of the Schedule to the Registration of Title Order 1985(**d**) and in article 16 of the Lancashire (District Boundaries) Order 1986 (being the areas in England and Wales in which registration of title to land is already compulsory on sale) registration of title shall be compulsory on sale–

    (a) on and after 1st December 1987, in the districts of Copeland, Derbyshire Dales, Derwentside, Eden, High Peak, South Lakeland, Teesdale and Wear Valley;

    (b) on and after 1st March 1988, in the districts of Brecknock, Colwyn, East Hampshire, Glyndŵr, Hart, Lancaster, Montgomeryshire, Radnor, Rushmoor, Test Valley, Winchester, Wrexham Maelor, Wyre and Ynys Môn—Isle of Anglesey; and

    (c) on and after 1st March 1988, in the remainder of the district of Ribble Valley.

(2) Accordingly, on and after 1st March 1988, registration of title to land shall be compulsory on sale in the areas mentioned in column 2 of the Schedule to this Order.

(3) As from 1st March 1988, the Registration of Title Order 1985 shall cease to have effect.

G.I. de Deney
Clerk of the Privy Council

(**a**) 1925 c. 21.
(**b**) 1963 c. 33.
(**c**) S.I. 1986/1909.
(**d**) S.I. 1985/1999.

Article 2(2)   SCHEDULE

(1) *County (including Greater London)*	(2) *Areas of compulsory registration*
Avon	The whole county
Bedfordshire	The whole county
Berkshire	The whole county
Buckinghamshire	The whole county
Cambridgeshire	The districts of Cambridge, Huntingdonshire, Peterborough and South Cambridgeshire
Cheshire	The whole county
Cleveland	The whole county
Clwyd	The whole county
Cornwall	The districts of Caradon and Restormel
Cumbria	The whole county
Derbyshire	The whole county
Devon	The districts of East Devon, Exeter, Mid Devon, North Devon, Plymouth, South Hams, Teignbridge and Torbay
Dorset	The districts of Bournemouth, Christchurch, Poole, Weymouth and Portland, and Wimborne
Durham	The whole county
Dyfed	The district of Llanelli
East Sussex	The whole county
Essex	The districts of Basildon, Braintree, Brentwood, Chelmsford, Colchester, Epping Forest, Harlow, Southend-on-Sea, Thurrock and Uttlesford
Gloucestershire	The whole county
Greater London	The whole administrative area
Greater Manchester	The whole county
Gwent	The whole county
Gwynedd	The district of Ynys Môn—Isle of Anglesey
Hampshire	The whole county
Hereford and Worcester	The districts of Bromsgrove, Hereford, Redditch and Worcester
Hertfordshire	The whole county
Humberside	The whole county
Isle of Wight	The whole county
Kent	The whole county
Lancashire	The whole county
Leicestershire	The whole county
Lincolnshire	The district of Lincoln
Merseyside	The whole county
Mid Glamorgan	The whole county
Norfolk	The districts of Great Yarmouth and Norwich
Northamptonshire	The whole county
Northumberland	The districts of Blyth Valley, Castle Morpeth and Wansbeck
North Yorkshire	The districts of Craven, Harrogate, Selby and York
Nottinghamshire	The whole county
Oxfordshire	The whole county
Powys	The whole county
Shropshire	The districts of Bridgnorth and The Wrekin
Somerset	The districts of Taunton Deane and West Somerset

SCHEDULE — *continued*

(1) *County (including Greater London)*	(2) *Areas of compulsory registration*
South Glamorgan	The whole county
South Yorkshire	The whole county
Staffordshire	The districts of Cannock Chase, Lichfield, Newcastle-under-Lyme, Stoke-on-Trent and Tamworth
Suffolk	The districts of Ipswich and Waveney
Surrey	The whole county
Tyne and Wear	The whole county
Warwickshire	The whole county
West Glamorgan	The whole county
West Midlands	The whole county
West Sussex	The whole county
West Yorkshire	The whole county
Wiltshire	The districts of Thamesdown and West Wiltshire

EXPLANATORY NOTE

(This note is not part of the Order)

This Order extends the system of compulsory registration of title on sale of land to the districts mentioned in article 2(1)(a) with effect from 1st December 1987 and to those mentioned in article 2(1)(b) with effect from 1st March 1988. In addition, by article 2(1)(c), compulsory registration which, in the district of Ribble Valley, applies only to the parish of Simonstone is extended to the whole of the district with effect from 1st March 1988.

1987 No. 940

COPYRIGHT

The Copyright (Singapore) Order 1987

Made - - - -	*18th May 1987*
Laid before Parliament	*17th June 1987*
Coming into force	*18th June 1987*

At the Court at Buckingham Palace, the 18th day of May 1987

Present,

The Queen's Most Excellent Majesty in Council

Whereas Her Majesty is satisfied that, in respect of the matters provided for in this Order, provision has been made under the laws of Singapore whereby adequate protection will be given to owners of copyright under the Copyright Act 1956(a):

Now, therefore, Her Majesty, by and with the advice of Her Privy Council, and by virtue of the authority conferred on Her by sections 31, 32 and 47 of the said Act, is pleased to order, and it is hereby ordered, as follows:

1.—(1) This Order may be cited as the Copyright (Singapore) Order 1987 and shall come into force on 18th June 1987.

(2) In this Order–

"the Act" means the Copyright Act 1956; and

"material time" means–

(i) in relation to an unpublished work or subject-matter, the time at which such work or subject-matter was made or, if the making thereof extended over a period, a substantial part of that period; and

(ii) in relation to a published work or subject-matter, the time of first publication.

2. Subject to the following provisions of this Order, the provisions of Parts I and II of the Act and all the other provisions of the Act relevant to those Parts shall apply–

(a) in relation to literary, dramatic, musical or artistic works, sound recordings, cinematograph films or published editions first published in Singapore as they apply to such works, recordings, films or editions first published in the United Kingdom;

(b) in relation to persons who at any material time are resident in Singapore as they apply to persons who at such time are resident in the United Kingdom; and

(c) in relation to bodies incorporated under the laws of Singapore as they apply to bodies incorporated under the laws of any part of the United Kingdom.

3. The acts restricted by section 12 of the Act as applied by this Order shall not include causing the recording to be heard in public, broadcasting the recording or including it in a cable programme.

(a) 1956 c.74.

4. Where any person has before the commencement of this Order incurred any expenditure or liability in connection with the reproduction or performance of any work or other subject matter in a manner which at the time was lawful, or for the purpose of or with a view to the reproduction or performance of a work at a time when such reproduction or performance would, but for the making of this Order, have been lawful, nothing in this Order shall diminish or prejudice any right or interest arising from or in connection with such action which is subsisting and valuable immediately before the commencement of this Order unless the person who by virtue of this Order becomes entitled to restrain such reproduction or performance agrees to pay such compensation as, failing agreement, may be determined by arbitration.

5. This Order shall extend to the countries mentioned in the Schedule hereto, subject to the modification that article 2 above shall have effect as part of the law of any of those countries as if for references to the United Kingdom there were substituted references to the country in question.

G. I. de Deney
Clerk of the Privy Council

SCHEDULE   Article 5

COUNTRIES TO WHICH THIS ORDER EXTENDS.

British Indian Ocean Territory
British Virgin Islands
Cayman Islands
Falkland Islands
Falkland Islands Dependencies
Hong Kong
Isle of Man
Montserrat
St Helena
St Helena Dependencies (Ascension, Tristan da Cunha)

EXPLANATORY NOTE

(This note is not part of the Order)

This Order provides for the copyright protection in the United Kingdom of works and other subject-matter originating in Singapore. No provision is made in respect of citizens of Singapore because they are already qualified persons under the Copyright Act 1956 by reason of being British subjects (that is, Commonwealth citizens) within the meaning of that Act. The Order extends to the dependent countries of the Commonwealth to which the 1956 Act has been extended, with the exception of Bermuda and Gibraltar.

STATUTORY INSTRUMENTS

1987 No. 941

PARLIAMENT

The Lord Chancellor's Salary Order 1987

Made - - - -		*18th May 1987*
Coming into force -		*18th May 1987*

At the Court at Buckingham Palace, the 18th day of May 1987

Present,

The Queen's Most Excellent Majesty in Council

Whereas a draft of this Order has been approved by resolution of each House of Parliament:

Now, therefore, Her Majesty, in pursuance of section 1(4) of the Ministerial and other Salaries Act 1975**(a)** and of all other powers enabling Her in that behalf, is pleased, by and with the advice of Her Privy Council, to order, and it is hereby ordered, as follows:–

Citation, commencement and revocation

1.—(1) This Order may be cited as the Lord Chancellor's Salary Order 1987.

(2) This Order shall come into force on 18th May 1987.

(3) The Lord Chancellor's Salary Order 1986**(b)** is hereby revoked.

Increase of Lord Chancellor's salary

2. For the amount specified in subsection (2) of section 1 of the Ministerial and other Salaries Act 1975 as the aggregate annual amount of the salary payable to the Lord Chancellor under that subsection and the salary payable to him as Speaker of the House of Lords there shall be substituted–

> (a) for the period beginning with 18th May 1987 and ending with 30th September 1987, £82,690;

> (b) for any subsequent period, £83,000.

G. I. de Deney
Clerk of the Privy Council

(a) 1975 c.27.
(b) S.I. 1986/1169.

EXPLANATORY NOTE

(This note is not part of the Order)

This Order increases the total salary payable to the Lord Chancellor under the Ministerial and other Salaries Act 1975 and as Speaker of the House of Lords. The Order provides for the Lord Chancellor to receive a £2,000 lead over the Lord Chief Justice. The salary quoted may be not the actual salary claimed.

1987 No. 942

FINANCIAL SERVICES

The Financial Services Act 1986 (Delegation) Order 1987

Made - - - -	*18th May 1987*
Coming into force -	*19th May 1987*

Whereas it appears to the Secretary of State that The Securities and Investments Board Limited is able and willing to discharge the functions transferred by this Order and that the requirements of Schedule 7 to the Financial Services Act 1986**(a)** are satisfied with respect to it, and

Whereas the Secretary of State has been furnished by The Securities and Investments Board Limited with a copy of the rules and regulations it proposes to make in the exercise of the functions transferred by this Order, and

Whereas the Secretary of State is satisfied that the rules and regulations which The Securities and Investments Board Limited proposes to make in the exercise of the functions transferred by this Order will afford investors an adequate level of protection and, in the case of such rules and regulations as are mentioned in Schedule 8 to the Financial Services Act 1986, comply with the principles set out in that Schedule, and

Whereas the Secretary of State has required The Securities and Investments Board Limited to furnish him with a copy of any guidance intended to have continuing effect which it proposes to issue in writing or other legible form, and

Whereas the Secretary of State has sent to the Director-General of Fair Trading a copy of the rules and regulations and of any guidance which the Secretary of State is required to consider in making the decision whether he is precluded by 121(1) of the Financial Services Act 1986 from making this Order together with such other information as the Secretary of State considers will assist the Director-General of Fair Trading in discharging his functions under section 122(2) of that Act, and

Whereas the Secretary of State has had regard to the report made to him by the Director-General of Fair Trading under section 122(2) of the Financial Services Act 1986 in deciding whether he is precluded by section 121(1) of that Act from making this Order, and

Whereas the Secretary of State is satisfied that the rules, regulations and guidance of which copies have been furnished to him under section 114(9) and (10) of the Financial Services Act 1986 do not have, and are not intended or likely to have, to any significant extent the effect of restricting, distorting or preventing competition, and

Whereas the Secretary of State is satisfied that the rules and regulations which The

---

(a) 1986 c.60.

Securities and Investments Board Limited proposes to make under Chapter V of Part I of the Financial Services Act 1986 with respect to regulated insurance companies will take proper account of Part II of the Insurance Companies Act 1982(a) or, as the case may be, of the provisions for corresponding purposes in the law of the member State in which a regulated insurance company is established, and

Whereas a draft of this Order has been approved by a resolution of each House of Parliament pursuant to section 114(11) of the Financial Services Act 1986:

Now, therefore, the Secretary of State in exercise of the powers conferred on him by sections 114, 118, 178(10), 199(7), 201(4) and 206(4) of and paragraph 3(3) of Schedule 10 and paragraph 12 of Schedule 15 to that Act and of all other powers enabling him in that behalf hereby makes the following Order:–

Citation and commencement

1. This Order may be cited as the Financial Services Act 1986 (Delegation) Order 1987 and shall come into force on the day after the day on which it is made.

Interpretation

2. In this Order–

"the Act" means the Financial Services Act 1986;

"designated agency" means the body known as The Securities and Investments Board Limited.

Transfer of functions

3. Except as provided in Schedule 1 to this Order and subject to the provisions of article 4, all those functions of the Secretary of State to which section 114 of the Act applies and which are specified in subsection (4) of that section are hereby transferred to the designated agency.

4. The functions of the Secretary of State specified in Schedule 2 to this Order are transferred to the designated agency subject to a reservation that they are to be exercisable by the Secretary of State concurrently with the designated agency.

5. The functions of the Secretary of State under section 178 of the Act and, to the extent provided in article 6, under section 199 of the Act are hereby transferred to the designated agency subject to a reservation that the functions are to be exercisable by the Secretary of State concurrently with the designated agency and, in the case of functions exercisable by virtue of sections 178 and 199(1)*(a)* of the Act, so as to be exercisable by the designated agency subject to such conditions or restrictions as the Secretary of State may from time to time impose.

6. The function of the Secretary of State under section 199 is transferred–

    (a) where it is exercisable by virtue of section 199(1)*(a)* in any case in which the offence or one of the offences is an offence under section 4 or 57(3) of the Act, and

    (b) where it is exercisable by virtue of section 199(1)*(b)* in any case in which the requirement referred to in that enactment is one which has been imposed by the designated agency or by a person authorised by it under section 106 of the Act.

7. The function of the Secretary of State under section 201(1) of the Act to institute proceedings with respect to any offence specified in Schedule 3 to this Order is hereby transferred to the designated agency subject to a reservation that it is to be exercisable by the Secretary of State concurrently with the designated agency and so as to be exercisable by the designated agency subject to such conditions or restrictions as the Secretary of State may from time to time impose.

(a) 1982 c.50.

8. The functions of the Secretary of State under section 206 of the Act are hereby transferred to the designated agency.

Supplementary provisions

9. Section 102 of the Act shall have effect as if it did not require the designated agency to keep a register containing an entry in respect of each overseas investment exchange, each overseas clearing house and each person in respect of whom a direction under section 59 of the Act is in force, but required it instead to keep a register containing an entry in respect of each body or person who appears to it to be a body or person of the kind described above.

10. Section 109(1) of the Act shall have effect as if–
   (a) the reference to the Secretary of State included a reference to the designated agency, and
   (b) the reference to the functions of the Secretary of State included a reference to the functions of the designated agency transferred to it by this Order.

11. Sections 180(6) and 206(1)(*b*) of the Act, section 19(6) of the Banking Act 1979(**a**), section 449(1A) of the Companies Act 1985(**b**), and article 442(1A) of the Companies (Northern Ireland) Order 1986(**c**) shall have effect as if references to the functions of, or the functions conferred on, the Secretary of State under, or by, the Act included references to the functions transferred by this Order.

Michael Howard
Parliamentary Under Secretary of State,
Department of Trade and Industry

18th May 1987

Article 3

SCHEDULE 1

FUNCTIONS SPECIFIED IN SECTION 114(4) OF THE ACT WHICH ARE NOT TRANSFERRED BY THE ORDER

1. All functions under sections 28, 29, 33, 34, 60, 61, 97, 98, 99, 100 and 101 of the Act in any case in which those functions are exercisable by virtue of a contravention of a partial restriction notice as respects investment business as described in section 184(4) of the Act.

2. The function of giving a direction under section 33(1)(a) of the Act in respect of a regulated insurance company.

3. All functions under sections 37, 39 and 40 of the Act with respect to a body or association of the kind described in section 40(1).

4. All functions under sections 41 and 104 of the Act with respect to an overseas investment exchange or overseas clearing house.

5. All functions under section 53 of the Act.

6. The function of giving a direction under section 59 of the Act and associated functions where the direction would have the effect of prohibiting the employment of an individual in connection with investment business carried on in connection with or for the purpose of insurance business at Lloyd's, being employment by any person who is an exempted person as respects such business.

7. All functions under sections 60 and 61(1) of the Act in any case in which those functions are exercisable by virtue of a contravention of a direction of the kind described in paragraph 6 of this Schedule.

8. All functions under section 61(1) of the Act with respect to a person who is an exempted person by virtue of section 42 of the Act in any case in which the contravention or proposed contravention arises or is likely to arise in the course of investment business as respects which the person is exempt.

9. All functions under section 61 of the Act in relation to a contravention or proposed contravention of section 130 of the Act.

10. All functions under section 61(3) of the Act in relation to a contravention of a provision referred to in section 61(1)(a)(ii) or (iii) by a person who neither is, nor ever has been, an authorised person or an appointed representative.

11. All functions under section 73 of the Act.

12. All functions under Chapter VIII of Part I of the Act.

13. All functions under sections 97, 98, 99, 100 and 101 of the Act in any case in which those functions are exercisable by virtue of the exercise of any function under section 59 or 60 of the Act which, by virtue of paragraph 6 or 7 of this Schedule, is not transferred.

14. All functions under section 112 of the Act with respect to fees in respect of–
  (a) applications under sections 37(1) or 39(1) of the Act by a body or association of the kind described in section 40(1);
  (b) applications under section 77 or 88 of the Act, and
  (c) notices under section 86(2) or 87(3) of the Act.

15. All functions under section 113 of the Act with respect to periodical fees in respect of–
  (a) overseas investment exchanges or overseas clearing houses, and
  (b) managers of authorised unit trust schemes and operators of recognised schemes, but only in so far as those functions are exercisable by virtue of section 113(8) of the Act.

16. The function of revoking a recognition order in respect of a recognised self-regulating organisation whose members include or may include regulated insurance companies on the ground that the requirement specified in paragraph 3(1) of Schedule 10 to the Act is not satisfied.

17. The function of revoking a recognition order in respect of a recognised self-regulating organisation whose members include or may include regulated insurance companies on the ground that the organisation has contravened sub-paragraphs (3) or (4) of paragraph 6 of Schedule 10 to the Act as applied by sub-paragraph (5) of that paragraph.

SCHEDULE 2   Article 4

FUNCTIONS SPECIFIED IN SECTION 114(4) OF THE ACT WHICH ARE TRANSFERRED SUBJECT TO A RESERVATION THAT THEY ARE TO BE EXERCISABLE BY THE SECRETARY OF STATE CONCURRENTLY WITH THE DESIGNATED AGENCY

1. All functions under section 6 of the Act (injunctions and restitution orders relating to contraventions of section 3 of the Act).

2. All functions under section 61(1) of the Act which are exercisable by virtue of section 61(1)(a)(ii) or (iii) (injunctions relating to contraventions of sections 47, 56, 57 or 59 or of requirements imposed under section 58(3)).

3. All functions under section 72 of the Act (winding-up orders (Great Britain)).

4. All functions under sections 105 (investigation powers) and 106 (exercise of investigation powers by officer etc).

Article 7   **SCHEDULE 3**

OFFENCES WITH RESPECT TO WHICH THE POWER TO INSTITUTE PROCEEDINGS IS TRANSFERRED

1. Offences under sections 4 (carrying on or purporting to carry on investment business without authorisation), 32(1) (failure of person authorised under section 31 to give notice of commencement of business), and 111(1) (furnishing of false or misleading information to auditor or second auditor).

2. Offences under section 57(3) (contravention of restrictions on advertising) in any case in which the designated agency institutes proceedings at the same time and against the same person for an offence under section 4 of the Act.

3. Offences under section 59(5) (contravention of disqualification direction) where the direction is issued by the designated agency.

4. Offences under section 105(10) (failure to comply with requirement imposed under section 105 (investigation powers)) where the requirement in question is a requirement imposed by the designated agency or a person authorised by it under section 106.

5. Offences under section 200(1)*(a)* (false and misleading statements for the purposes of or in connection with applications) where the application in question is an application made to the designated agency.

6. Offences under section 200(1)*(b)* (false and misleading statements in purported compliance with requirement imposed by or under Act) where the requirement in question is a requirement imposed by the designated agency or by a person authorised by it under section 106.

7. Offences under section 200(2) and (3).

EXPLANATORY NOTE

(This note is not part of the Order)

This Order transfers certain of the Secretary of State's functions under the Financial Services Act 1986 to the body known as The Securities and Investments Board Limited. The functions transferred are described in articles 3, 5, 6, 7 and 8 of and Schedule 3 to the Order. Schedule 1 to the Order specifies certain functions which are not transferred.

The Order transfers certain functions subject to a reservation that they are to be exercisable by the Secretary of State concurrently with The Securities and Investments Board Limited. These functions are specified in articles 4, 5 and 7 of and Schedules 2 and 3 to the Order. In addition, certain functions specified in articles 5 and 7 and Schedule 3 to the Order are transferred so as to be exercisable by The Securities and Investments Board subject to such conditions or restrictions as the Secretary of State may from time to time impose.

Articles 9, 10 and 11 of the Order make certain supplementary provisions.

STATUTORY INSTRUMENTS

1987 No. 943 (S. 79)

LOCAL GOVERNMENT, SCOTLAND

The Definition of Capital Expenses (Scotland) Order 1987

Approved by both Houses of Parliament

Made - - - -	*25th March 1987*
Laid before Parliament	*1st April 1987*
Coming into force	*1st April 1988*

In exercise of the powers conferred on me by section 94(3) of the Local Government (Scotland) Act 1973(**a**) and of all other powers enabling me in that behalf, I hereby make the following Order:

1.—(1) This Order may be cited as the Definition of Capital Expenses (Scotland) Order 1987 and shall come into force on 1st April 1988.

(2) In this Order "the Act" means the Local Government (Scotland) Act 1973.

2. For the definition of "capital expenses" in section 94(2) of the Act there shall be substituted the following definition:–

""capital expenses" means any expenses which are to be charged to a capital account or which are otherwise of a capital nature irrespective of how they are financed.".

Malcolm Rifkind
New St. Andrew's House, Edinburgh
25th March 1987

One of Her Majesty's Principal
Secretaries of State

(**a**) 1973 c.65; subsection (3) was added by the Local Government (Miscellaneous Provisions) (Scotland) Act 1981 (c.23), section 26.

EXPLANATORY NOTE

(This note is not part of the Order)

This Order amends the definition of capital expenses in section 94 of the Local Government (Scotland) Act 1973. Under that section, it is not lawful for a local authority to incur any liability to meet capital expenses without the consent of the Secretary of State.

Capital expenses is at present defined in section 94(2) of the 1973 Act as meaning–

"any expenses which are to be charged to a capital or borrowing account or which, being of a capital nature, are to be met otherwise than out of current revenue."

This definition is amended in order to include what was formerly excluded, namely any expenses which are of a capital nature which are met out of current revenue. It also removes the reference to expenses which are charged to a borrowing account which has become unnecessary in practice.

STATUTORY INSTRUMENTS

1987 No. 944

NURSES, MIDWIVES AND HEALTH VISITORS

The Nurses, Midwives and Health Visitors (Temporary Registration) Amendment Rules Approval Order 1987

Made - - - -	*15th May 1987*
Coming into force	*5th June 1987*

In exercise of the powers conferred upon me by section 22(4) of the Nurses, Midwives and Health Visitors Act 1979**(a)**, I hereby approve the Rules made by the United Kingdom Central Council for Nursing, Midwifery and Health Visiting and set out in the Schedule hereto.

This Order may be cited as the Nurses, Midwives and Health Visitors (Temporary Registration) Amendment Rules Approval Order 1987 and shall come into force on 5th June 1987.

Norman Fowler
15th May 1987   One of Her Majesty's Principal Secretaries of State

---

(a) 1979 c.36.

SCHEDULE

THE UNITED KINGDOM CENTRAL COUNCIL FOR NURSING, MIDWIFERY AND HEALTH VISITING

THE NURSES, MIDWIVES AND HEALTH VISITORS ACT 1979

The United Kingdom Central Council for Nursing, Midwifery and Health Visiting, in exercise of the powers conferred on it by sections 10(3), 11 and 22(1) of the Nurses, Midwives and Health Visitors Act 1979(a) and of all other powers enabling it in that behalf having, in accordance with section 22(3) of the Act consulted the National Boards and representatives of groups likely to be affected by these Rules, hereby makes the following Rules.

Citation and interpretation

1.—(1) These Rules may be cited as the Nurses, Midwives and Health Visitors (Temporary Registration) Amendment Rules 1987.

(2) In these Rules "the principal Rules" means the Nurses, Midwives and Health Visitors Rules 1983**(b)**.

Amendment of principal Rules

2.—(1) Rule 8 of the principal Rules (Admission to Part or Parts of the register following successful completion of training, as a nurse, a midwife or a health visitor, and original registration outside the United Kingdom) shall be amended in accordance with the following provisions of these Rules.

(2) After paragraph (3)(a) there shall be inserted the following:–

"(aa) be admitted, subject to the provisions of paragraphs (3A) and (3B), to such specific Part or Parts of the register on payment of the required registration fees and for such period, in this rule referred to as a "period of temporary registration", as the Council may specify; or".

(3) Before paragraph (4) there shall be inserted the following:–

"(3A) For the purposes of paragraph (3)(aa) a person shall:–

(a) provide evidence to the Council of acceptance on a course of training approved by a National Board or by the Council, hereinafter referred to as "the approved course", which leads to a qualification which could have been recorded in the register had the person been registered other than for a period of temporary registration; and

(b) not previously have been registered for a period of temporary registration on more than two occasions or have been removed from the register for any reason; and

(c) satisfy the Council that her training and experience are sufficient to enable her to undertake the clinical parts of the approved course without risk to her patients.

(3B) The Council may not specify for the purpose of paragraph (3)(aa) above any period longer than the duration of the approved course; and registration shall lapse at the end of the period specified.".

GIVEN under the Official Seal of the
UNITED KINGDOM CENTRAL COUNCIL
FOR NURSING, MIDWIFERY AND
HEALTH VISITING this 29th day of
April 1987

Audrey Emerton
Chairman.

M. Storey
Registrar.

(a) 1979 c.36.
(b) Approved by S.I. 1983/873; there are no relevant amendments.

EXPLANATORY NOTE

(This note is not part of the Order)

The Rules approved by this Order, and made by the United Kingdom Central Council for Nursing, Midwifery and Health Visiting ("the Council"), amend the Rules approved by the Nurses, Midwives and Health Visitors Rules Approval Order 1983 as they relate to a person who has qualified to practise as a nurse, midwife or health visitor outside the United Kingdom. Provision is made for the Council to admit such a person to the register for a specified period. There is provision for registration to lapse at the end of the period specified.

STATUTORY INSTRUMENTS

1987 No. 949

AGRICULTURE

The Sheep and Goats (Removal to Northern Ireland) (Amendment) Regulations 1987

Made - - - -	*19th May 1987*
Coming into force	*20th May 1987*

The Minister of Agriculture, Fisheries and Food and the Secretary of State, being Ministers designated(a) for the purposes of section 2(2) of the European Communities Act 1972(b) in relation to the common agricultural policy of the European Economic Community, acting jointly in exercise of the powers conferred upon them by that section and of all other powers enabling them in that behalf, hereby make the following Regulations, a draft of which has been approved by resolution of each House of Parliament:–

Title, commencement and interpretation

1.—(1) These Regulations may be cited as the Sheep and Goats (Removal to Northern Ireland) (Amendment) Regulations 1987 and shall come into force on the day after the day on which they are made.

(2) Except where the context otherwise requires any reference in these Regulations to a numbered regulation or schedule refers to the regulation or schedule so numbered in the Sheep and Goats (Removal to Northern Ireland) Regulations 1983(c).

Amendment of definitions

2. In regulation 2 –

    (a) in the definition of "carcase" for the words "salted in brine" there shall be substituted the words "salted, in brine";

    (b) for the definition of "the Commission Regulation", there shall be substituted the following definition:–

(a) S.I. 1972/1811.　　(b) 1972 c.68; section 2 is subject to Schedule 2 to that Act and is to be read, as regards England and Wales, in relation to offences triable only summarily, with sections 37, 40 and 46 of the Criminal Justice Act 1982 (c.48), in relation to offences triable on indictment or summarily, with section 32 of the Magistrates' Courts Act 1980 (c.43), and, in each case, with S.I. 1984/447; as regards Scotland, in relation to offences triable only summarily, with sections 289F and 289G of the Criminal Procedure (Scotland) Act 1975 (c.21), as inserted by section 54 of the Criminal Justice Act 1982, in relation to offences triable on indictment or summarily, with section 289B of the Criminal Procedure (Scotland) Act 1975, as inserted by paragraph 5 of Schedule 11 to the Criminal Law Act 1977 (c.45) and amended by section 55 of the Criminal Justice Act 1982, and, in each case, with S.I. 1984/526; and, as regards Northern Ireland, with S.I. 1984/703 (N.I.3) and S.R. (N.I.) 1984 No. 253.　　(c) S.I. 1983/1158.

" 'the Commission Regulation' means Commission Regulation (EEC) No 1633/84(a) as amended by Commission Regulation (EEC) No 3451/85(b), Commission Regulation (EEC) No 9/86(c) and Commission Regulation (EEC) No 1860/86(d) all of which lay down detailed rules for applying the variable slaughter premium for sheep and the first of which repeals Regulation (EEC) No 2661/80(e);"

(c) after the definition of "the departure charge", there shall be inserted the following definition:–

" 'product' means any product referred to in Article 1(c) of Council Regulation (EEC) No 1837/80 on the common organization of the market in sheepmeat and goatmeat(f);"

(d) for the definition of "removal", there shall be substituted the following definition:–

" 'remove' means remove from Great Britain to Northern Ireland, and 'removal' shall be construed accordingly;";

(e) in the definition of "removal declaration", for the words "animal or carcase", there shall be substituted the words "animal, carcase or product".

Insertion of regulation 2A

3. After regulation 2 there shall be inserted the following regulation:–

"*Application*

2A. These Regulations shall not apply to any animal, carcase or product which –

(a) is brought into, and removed from, Great Britain under the internal or external Community transit procedure(g); or

(b) is not in free circulation in Great Britain.".

Control of prepared and preserved meat

4.—(1) In regulations 3(1), 6 and 13, for the words "animal (other than a pure-bred breeding animal) or carcase", there shall be substituted the words "animal (other than a pure-bred breeding animal), carcase or product".

(2) In regulations 3(1), 4(1), 5, 6, 7 and in regulations 8(1)(a) (as re-numbered by regulation 6(1) below) and 10(4), for the words "animal or carcase", wherever they occur, there shall be substituted the words "animal, carcase or product".

(3) In regulation 6 and in regulation 8(1)(a) (as re-numbered by regulation 6(1) below) and in items 1, 4 and 6 of Schedule 1, for the words "animals or carcases" , there shall be substituted the words "animals, carcases or products".

(4) For items 2 and 3 of Schedule 1 there shall be substituted the following items:–

"2. The numbers, weights and descriptions, including full Common Customs Tariff headings, of the animals, carcases or products to be removed and, for products, an indication as to whether they are bone-in or boneless.

3. The address, if different from that of the consignor, –

(a) of the farm premises from which animals originate;

(b) of the slaughterhouse from which fresh, chilled or frozen carcases originate;

(c) of the packing premises from which carcases which are salted, in brine, dried or smoked originate;

(d) of the packing premises from which products originate.".

(a) OJ No L 154, 9.6.84, p.27.   (b) OJ No L 328, 7.12.85, p.23.   (c) OJ No L 2, 4.1.86, p.14.   (d) OJ No L 161, 17.6.86, p.25.   (e) OJ No L 276, 20.10.80, p.19.   (f) OJ No L 183, 16.7.80, p.1. Article 1(c) was inserted by Article 1(1) of Council Regulation (EEC) No 871/84 (OJ No L 90, 1.4.84, p.35).   (g) The Community transit procedure is established by Council Regulation (EEC) No 222/77 (OJ No L 38, 9.2.77, p.1.)

Time and place of inspection and weighing

5.—(1) At the end of regulation 4(1) the words "before removal" shall be deleted.

(2) In regulation 4(2) for the word "animal" there shall be substituted the words "animal, carcase or product".

Amendment of regulation 8

6.—(1) Regulation 8 shall be re-numbered as regulation 8.—(1) and immediately before the words "A qualified person" there shall be inserted the words "In Great Britain".

(2) In regulation 8 after paragraph (1) there shall be inserted the following paragraphs:—

"(2) In Northern Ireland a qualified person may at any time for the purpose of ascertaining whether the provisions of these Regulations have been or are being complied with –

    (a) enter and examine the contents of any vehicle, vessel or aircraft, or open and examine the contents of any container;

    (b) direct the person in charge of any vehicle to drive it to a place, specified by the qualified person, where it may be unloaded for the purpose of an examination of its contents.

(3) In Northern Ireland a qualified person who reasonably suspects that there has been an offence under these Regulations may, in addition, for the purpose of investigating such an offence –

    (a) enter upon any land on which animals, products or carcases are being held for the time being and inspect any animal, carcase or product found thereon;

    (b) take possession of, or take a copy of, or extract from, any book, account or record appearing to him to be material which is produced pursuant to regulation 6, or which is in the possession or control of a person who he reasonably suspects is guilty of such an offence.

(4) The owner or person in charge of any land on which animals, carcases or products are held for the time being or of any vehicle, vessel or aircraft, or the contents thereof, shall comply with all reasonable requirements of the qualified person in connection with an inspection or examination under this regulation."

Increase of penalties and the insertion of an additional offence

7.—(1) In regulation 10(1), for the words "four hundred pounds", there shall be substituted "£2000".

(2) In regulations 10(2) and 10(3), for the words "two hundred pounds", there shall be substituted "£1000".

(3) In paragraph (a) of regulation 10(3) for the words "regulation 6" there shall be substituted the words "regulation 6 or 8".

(4) In regulation 10(4), for the words "one thousand pounds" there shall be substituted "£2000".

In Witness whereof the Official Seal of the Minister of Agriculture, Fisheries and Food is hereunto affixed on 17th May 1987.

(L.S.)

Michael Jopling
Minister of Agriculture, Fisheries and Food

Tom King
19th May 1987   One of Her Majesty's Principal Secretaries of State

EXPLANATORY NOTE

(This note is not part of the Regulations)

These Regulations amend the Sheep and Goats (Removal to Northern Ireland) Regulations 1983 ("the 1983 Regulations") which, for the protection of arrangements made under the common organization of the market in sheepmeat and goatmeat established by Council Regulation No 1837/80 (OJ No L 183, 16.7.80, p.1.), prohibit the removal of sheep or goats or the carcases of such animals from Great Britain to Northern Ireland unless, inter alia, security for the payment of an amount equivalent to the Sheep Variable Premium paid in Great Britain has been given. The 1983 Regulations are amended as follows:

(a) Their scope of application is extended, in consequence of an amendment to the common organization of the market in sheepmeat and goatmeat made by Council Regulation No 871/84 (OJ No L 90, 1.4.84, p.35), to prepared or preserved meat and offal of sheep or goats by the addition of a reference to "product" (defined by reference to the description set out in Article 1(c) of Council Regulation No. 1837/80 as amended by Council Regulation No 871/84) to the references to "animal" and "carcase" wherever they occur (regulations 2(e), 4 and 5).

(b) Sheep and goats, or the meat of these animals, not originating, and not intended to be placed on the market, in Great Britain are excluded from the scope of application of the 1983 Regulations when transported through Great Britain under appropriate customs arrangements (regulation 3).

(c) The application of the 1983 Regulations to removals from Great Britain to Northern Ireland by air is clarified (regulation 2(d)).

(d) Authorized officers are empowered to inspect and weigh sheep or goats or the meat of those animals after as well as before their removal from Great Britain to Northern Ireland (regulation 5(1)).

(e) The powers of the Intervention Board for Agricultural Produce in relation to the presentation of sheep or goats for inspection pursuant to the 1983 Regulations at premises named by it are extended to the presentation of the meat of those animals (regulation 5(2)).

(f) Additional powers for the enforcement of the 1983 Regulations are conferred on authorized officers in Northern Ireland and in Great Britain (regulation 6 (2)).

(g) The definition of "carcase" is amended to make clear that "salted" meat and meat "in brine" are distinct categories (regulation 2(a)).

(h) Further information in respect of products is required to be given in removal declarations (regulation 4(4)).

(i) A further offence is created and penalties for existing offences are increased (regulation 7).

STATUTORY INSTRUMENTS

1987 No. 964

TRADE MARKS

The Trade Marks and Service Marks (Fees) (Amendment) Rules 1987

Made - - - -	*21st May 1987*
Coming into force	*26th May 1987*

To be laid before Parliament

Whereas in pursuance of the requirements of section 40(3) of the Trade Marks Act 1938(**a**) the Secretary of State has, before making the following Rules under the Act, published notice of his intention to make such Rules and of the place where copies of the draft Rules might be obtained by advertising such notice in the Trade Marks Journal on 13th May 1987, being the manner which he considered most expedient so as to enable persons affected to make representations to him before the Rules were finally settled:

Now, therefore, the Secretary of State, in exercise of the powers conferred by sections 40 and 41 of the Trade Marks Act 1938 and now vested in him(**b**), after consultation with the Council on Tribunals pursuant to section 10(1) of the Tribunals and Inquiries Act 1971(**c**) and with the sanction of the Treasury pursuant to the said section 41, hereby makes the following Rules:

1. These Rules may be cited as the Trade Marks and Service Marks (Fees) (Amendment) Rules 1987 and shall come into force on 26th May 1987.

2. The Trade Marks and Service Marks (Fees) Rules 1987(**d**) shall have effect subject to the amendment that in the third column of the Schedule thereto there shall be substituted for the amount of £79 the amount of £205 as the fee payable in respect of the item specified in the second column of that Schedule opposite the first reference to form TM 11 (renewal of registration of a Trade Mark, etc.).

Lucas of Chilworth
Parliamentary Under Secretary of State,
21st May 1987   Department of Trade and Industry

(**a**) 1938 c.22; the Act was applied, with modifications, to service marks by the Trade Marks (Amendment) Act 1984 (c.19), section 1, as amended by the Patents, Designs and Marks Act 1986 (c.39), section 2(1) and Schedule 3.
(**b**) S.I. 1970/1537.
(**c**) 1971 c.62.   (**d**) S.I. 1987/751.

We sanction the making of these Rules.

Mark Lennox-Boyd
Peter Lloyd
Two of the Lords Commissioners
of Her Majesty's Treasury

21st May 1987

EXPLANATORY NOTE

(This note is not part of the Rules)

These Rules correct an error in the Trade Marks and Service Marks (Fees) Rules 1987. In the draft of those Rules in respect of which notice was published under section 40(3) of the Trade Marks Act 1938 (provision for the making of representations upon draft Rules) it was indicated that the renewal fee payable on form TM 11 would be increased from £198 to £205. Because of an error of transcription, those Rules were made prescribing that fee as only £79. These Rules restore the fee to the intended £205.

STATUTORY INSTRUMENTS

1987 No. 973

CUSTOMS AND EXCISE

The Customs Duties (ECSC) (No. 2) (Amendment No. 6) Order 1987

Made - - - -	*22nd May 1987*
Coming into force	*26th May 1987*

To be laid before the House of Commons

The Treasury, by virtue of the powers conferred on them by section 5(1) and (3) of, and paragraph 4 of Schedule 2 to, the European Communities Act 1972(**a**) and of all other powers enabling them in that behalf, on the recommendation of the Secretary of State, hereby make the following Order:

1. This Order may be cited as the Customs Duties (ECSC) (No. 2) (Amendment No. 6) Order 1987 and shall come into operation on 26th May 1987.

2. Up to and including 31st December 1987, Article 6(1) of the Customs Duties (ECSC) (No. 2) Order 1985(**b**) (which exempts from duty goods to which that Order applies originating in certain countries) shall not apply to goods which fall within heading 73.08 which originate in Yugoslavia.

Michael Neubert
Nigel Lawson
22nd May 1987   Two of the Lords Commissioners of Her Majesty's Treasury

---

(**a**) 1972 c.68; section 5(3) and Schedule 2 were amended by the Customs and Excise Duties (General Reliefs) Act 1979 (c.3), Schedule 2, paragraphs 3 and 5.
(**b**) S.I. 1985/1630, amended by S.I. 1985/2020, 1986/348.

EXPLANATORY NOTE

(This note is not part of the Order)

This Order, which comes into operation on 26th May 1987, amends the Customs Duties (ECSC) (No. 2) Order 1985 ("the main Order") which charges customs duties in accordance with the unified ECSC tariff on certain ECSC products imported into the United Kingdom except from other Member States of the European Coal and Steel Community (ECSC) and from certain other countries named in Schedule 1 to the main Order.

This Order reimposes duties on goods falling within heading 73.08 which originate in Yugoslavia.

This Order implements a reintroduction of duty up to the end of 1987 made pursuant to Article 1, paragraph 3 of a decision 86/642/ECSC of the representatives of the governments of the Member States of the European Coal and Steel Community meeting within the Council on 22nd December 1986 (OJ No. L380, 31.12.1986, p.59). Decision 86/642/ECSC of 22nd December 1986 established ceilings for imports of certain ECSC goods originating in Yugoslavia. These ceilings have now been reached on goods falling within the above headings.

The Commission communication to Member States giving notice of the reintroduction of customs duties is published in OJ No. C138 of 23.5.1987.

STATUTORY INSTRUMENTS

1987 No. 974

OFFSHORE INSTALLATIONS

The Offshore Installations (Safety Zones) (No. 31) Order 1987

Made - - - -	*19th May 1987*
Coming into force	*21st May 1987*

The Secretary of State, in exercise of the powers conferred on him by section 21(1), (2) and (3) of the Oil and Gas (Enterprise) Act 1982(a) (hereinafter referred to as "the Act"), and of all other powers enabling him in that behalf, hereby makes the following Order:–

1. This Order may be cited as the Offshore Installations (Safety Zones) (No. 31) Order 1987 and shall come into force on 21st May 1987.

2.—(1) A safety zone is hereby established around the installation specified in Column 1 of the Schedule hereto (being an installation maintained in waters to which section 21 of the Act(b) applies) having a radius of five hundred metres from the point as respects that installation which has the co-ordinates of latitude and longitude according to European Datum (1950) specified in Columns 2 and 3 of the Schedule.

(2) The prohibition under section 21(3) of the Act on a vessel entering or remaining in a safety zone without the consent of the Secretary of State shall not apply to a vessel entering or remaining in the safety zone established under paragraph (1) above –

- (a) in connection with the laying, inspection, testing, repair, alteration, renewal or removal of any submarine cable or pipe-line in or near that safety zone;
- (b) to provide services for, to transport persons or goods to or from, or under the authority of a government department to inspect, any installation in that safety zone;
- (c) if it is a vessel belonging to a general lighthouse authority performing duties relating to the safety of navigation;
- (d) in connection with the saving or attempted saving of life or property;
- (e) owing to stress of weather; or
- (f) when in distress.

3. The Offshore Installations (Safety Zones) (No. 17) Order 1987(c) is hereby revoked.

Alick Buchanan-Smith
Minister of State, Department of Energy

19th May 1987

(a) 1982 c.23.   (b) *See* section 21(9).   (c) S.I. 1987/201.

SCHEDULE

Article 2(1)

SAFETY ZONE

(1) Name or other designation of the offshore installation	(2) Latitude North	(3) Longitude East
Benvrackie	61° 54′ 36.61″	01° 03′ 45.07″

EXPLANATORY NOTE

(This note is not part of the Order)

This Order establishes, under section 21 of the Oil and Gas (Enterprise) Act 1982, a safety zone, having a radius of 500 metres from a specified point, around the installation specified in the Schedule to this Order and maintained in waters to which the section applies (these include territorial waters and waters in areas designated under section 1(7) of the Continental Shelf Act 1964 (c.29)).

Vessels (which for this purpose include hovercraft, submersible apparatus and installations in transit) are prohibited from entering or remaining in the safety zone except with the consent of the Secretary of State or in the circumstances mentioned in article 2(2) of the Order.

The Order also revokes the Offshore Installations (Safety Zones) Order which created a safety zone around the installation specified in the Schedule to this Order on its previous location

STATUTORY INSTRUMENTS

1987 No. 975

OFFSHORE INSTALLATIONS

The Offshore Installations (Safety Zones) (No. 32) Order 1987

Made - - - -		*19th May 1987*
Coming into force		*21st May 1987*

The Secretary of State, in exercise of the powers conferred on him by section 21(1), (2) and (3) of the Oil and Gas (Enterprise) Act 1982(a) (hereinafter referred to as "the Act"), and of all other powers enabling him in that behalf, hereby makes the following Order:–

1. This Order may be cited as the Offshore Installations (Safety Zones) (No. 32) Order 1987 and shall come into force on 21st May 1987.

2.—(1) A safety zone is hereby established around the installation specified in Column 1 of the Schedule hereto (being an installation maintained in waters to which section 21 of the Act(b) applies) having a radius of five hundred metres from the point as respects that installation which has the co-ordinates of latitude and longitude according to European Datum (1950) specified in Columns 2 and 3 of the Schedule.

(2) The prohibition under section 21(3) of the Act on a vessel entering or remaining in a safety zone without the consent of the Secretary of State shall not apply to a vessel entering or remaining in the safety zone established under paragraph (1) above –

(a) in connection with the laying, inspection, testing, repair, alteration, renewal or removal of any submarine cable or pipe-line in or near that safety zone;

(b) to provide services for, to transport persons or goods to or from, or under the authority of a government department to inspect, any installation in that safety zone;

(c) if it is a vessel belonging to a general lighthouse authority performing duties relating to the safety of navigation;

(d) in connection with the saving or attempted saving of life or property;

(e) owing to stress of weather; or

(f) when in distress.

3. The Offshore Installations (Safety Zones) (No. 53) Order 1986(c) is hereby revoked.

19th May 1987

Alick Buchanan-Smith
Minister of State, Department of Energy

(a) 1982 c.23.   (b) *See* section 21(9).   (c) S.I. 1986/889.

SCHEDULE

Article 2(1)

SAFETY ZONE

(1) *Name or other designation of the offshore installation*	(2) *Latitude North*	(3) *Longitude East*
Britannia	53° 19′ 06.00″	02° 05′ 45.00″

EXPLANATORY NOTE

(This note is not part of the Order)

This Order establishes, under section 21 of the Oil and Gas (Enterprise) Act 1982, a safety zone, having a radius of 500 metres from a specified point, around the installation specified in the Schedule to this Order and maintained in waters to which the section applies (these include territorial waters and waters in areas designated under section 1(7) of the Continental Shelf Act 1964 (c.29)).

Vessels (which for this purpose include hovercraft, submersible apparatus and installations in transit) are prohibited from entering or remaining in the safety zone except with the consent of the Secretary of State or in the circumstances mentioned in article 2(2) of the Order.

The Order also revokes the Offshore Installations (Safety Zones) Order which created a safety zone around the installation specified in the Schedule to this Order on its previous location.

STATUTORY INSTRUMENTS

1987 No. 976

OFFSHORE INSTALLATIONS

The Offshore Installations (Safety Zones) (No. 33) Order 1987

Made - - - -	*19th May 1987*
Coming into force	*21st May 1987*

The Secretary of State, in exercise of the powers conferred on him by section 21(1), (2) and (3) of the Oil and Gas (Enterprise) Act 1982(a) (hereinafter referred to as "the Act"), and of all other powers enabling him in that behalf, hereby makes the following Order:–

1. This Order may be cited as the Offshore Installations (Safety Zones) (No. 33) Order 1987 and shall come into force on 21st May 1987.

2.—(1) A safety zone is hereby established around the installation specified in Column 1 of the Schedule hereto (being an installation maintained in waters to which section 21 of the Act(b) applies) having a radius of five hundred metres from the point as respects that installation which has the co-ordinates of latitude and longitude according to European Datum (1950) specified in Columns 2 and 3 of the Schedule.

(2) The prohibition under section 21(3) of the Act on a vessel entering or remaining in a safety zone without the consent of the Secretary of State shall not apply to a vessel entering or remaining in the safety zone established under paragraph (1) above –

   (a) in connection with the laying, inspection, testing, repair, alteration, renewal or removal of any submarine cable or pipe-line in or near that safety zone;

   (b) to provide services for, to transport persons or goods to or from, or under the authority of a government department to inspect, any installation in that safety zone;

   (c) if it is a vessel belonging to a general lighthouse authority performing duties relating to the safety of navigation;

   (d) in connection with the saving or attempted saving of life or property;

   (e) owing to stress of weather; or

   (f) when in distress.

3. The Offshore Installations (Safety Zones) (No. 11) Order 1987(c) is hereby revoked.

Alick Buchanan-Smith
Minister of State, Department of Energy

19th May 1987

(a) 1982 c.23.   (b) *See* section 21(9).   (c) S.I. 1987/68.

SCHEDULE   Article 2(1)

SAFETY ZONE

(1) *Name or other designation of the offshore installation*	(2) *Latitude North*	(3) *Longitude East*
Drillstar	56° 23′ 36.02″	02° 46′ 45.40″

EXPLANATORY NOTE

(This note is not part of the Order)

This Order establishes, under section 21 of the Oil and Gas (Enterprise) Act 1982, a safety zone, having a radius of 500 metres from a specified point, around the installation specified in the Schedule to this Order and maintained in waters to which the section applies (these include territorial waters and waters in areas designated under section 1(7) of the Continental Shelf Act 1964 (c.29)).

Vessels (which for this purpose include hovercraft, submersible apparatus and installations in transit) are prohibited from entering or remaining in the safety zone except with the consent of the Secretary of State or in the circumstances mentioned in article 2(2) of the Order.

The Order also revokes the Offshore Installations (Safety Zones) Order which created a safety zone around the installation specified in the Schedule to this Order on its previous location.

STATUTORY INSTRUMENTS

1987 No. 977

OFFSHORE INSTALLATIONS

The Offshore Installations (Safety Zones) (No. 34) Order 1987

Made - - - -	*19th May 1987*
Coming into force	*21st May 1987*

The Secretary of State, in exercise of the powers conferred on him by section 21(1), (2) and (3) of the Oil and Gas (Enterprise) Act 1982(**a**) (hereinafter referred to as "the Act"), and of all other powers enabling him in that behalf, hereby makes the following Order:–

1. This Order may be cited as the Offshore Installations (Safety Zones) (No. 34) Order 1987 and shall come into force on 21st May 1987.

2.—(1) A safety zone is hereby established around the installation specified in Column 1 of the Schedule hereto (being an installation maintained in waters to which section 21 of the Act(**b**) applies) having a radius of five hundred metres from the point as respects that installation which has the co-ordinates of latitude and longitude according to European Datum (1950) specified in Columns 2 and 3 of the Schedule.

(2) The prohibition under section 21(3) of the Act on a vessel entering or remaining in a safety zone without the consent of the Secretary of State shall not apply to a vessel entering or remaining in the safety zone established under paragraph (1) above –

    (a) in connection with the laying, inspection, testing, repair, alteration, renewal or removal of any submarine cable or pipe-line in or near that safety zone;

    (b) to provide services for, to transport persons or goods to or from, or under the authority of a government department to inspect, any installation in that safety zone;

    (c) if it is a vessel belonging to a general lighthouse authority performing duties relating to the safety of navigation;

    (d) in connection with the saving or attempted saving of life or property;

    (e) owing to stress of weather; or

    (f) when in distress.

Alick Buchanan-Smith
Minister of State, Department of Energy

19th May 1987

(**a**) 1982 c.23.   (**b**) *See* section 21(9).

SCHEDULE

Article 2(1)

SAFETY ZONE

(1) *Name or other designation* *of the offshore installation*	(2) *Latitude* *North*	(3) *Longitude* *East*
Galveston Key	53° 57′ 34.70″	02° 11′ 30.10″

EXPLANATORY NOTE

(This note is not part of the Order)

This Order establishes, under section 21 of the Oil and Gas (Enterprise) Act 1982, a safety zone, having a radius of 500 metres from a specified point, around the installation specified in the Schedule to this Order and maintained in waters to which the section applies (these include territorial waters and waters in areas designated under section 1(7) of the Continental Shelf Act 1964 (c.29)).

Vessels (which for this purpose include hovercraft, submersible apparatus and installations in transit) are prohibited from entering or remaining in the safety zone except with the consent of the Secretary of State or in the circumstances mentioned in article 2(2) of the Order.

STATUTORY INSTRUMENTS

1987 No. 978

OFFSHORE INSTALLATIONS

The Offshore Installations (Safety Zones) (No. 35) Order 1987

Made - - - -		*19th May 1987*
Coming into force		*21st May 1987*

The Secretary of State, in exercise of the powers conferred on him by section 21(1), (2) and (3) of the Oil and Gas (Enterprise) Act 1982(a) (hereinafter referred to as "the Act"), and of all other powers enabling him in that behalf, hereby makes the following Order:–

1. This Order may be cited as the Offshore Installations (Safety Zones) (No. 35) Order 1987 and shall come into force on 21st May 1987.

2.—(1) A safety zone is hereby established around the installation specified in Column 1 of the Schedule hereto (being an installation maintained in waters to which section 21 of the Act(b) applies) having a radius of five hundred metres from the point as respects that installation which has the co-ordinates of latitude and longitude according to European Datum (1950) specified in Columns 2 and 3 of the Schedule.

(2) The prohibition under section 21(3) of the Act on a vessel entering or remaining in a safety zone without the consent of the Secretary of State shall not apply to a vessel entering or remaining in the safety zone established under paragraph (1) above –

    (a) in connection with the laying, inspection, testing, repair, alteration, renewal or removal of any submarine cable or pipe-line in or near that safety zone;

    (b) to provide services for, to transport persons or goods to or from, or under the authority of a government department to inspect, any installation in that safety zone;

    (c) if it is a vessel belonging to a general lighthouse authority performing duties relating to the safety of navigation;

    (d) in connection with the saving or attempted saving of life or property;

    (e) owing to stress of weather; or

    (f) when in distress.

3. The Offshore Installations (Safety Zone) (No. 19) Order 1987(c) is hereby revoked.

Alick Buchanan-Smith
Minister of State, Department of Energy

19th May 1987

(a) 1982 c.23.   (b) *See* section 21(9).   (c) S.I. 1987/203.

SCHEDULE   Article 2(1)

SAFETY ZONE

(1) Name or other designation of the offshore installation	(2) Latitude North	(3) Longitude East
High Seas Driller	59° 34′ 54.84″	01° 34′ 05.82″

EXPLANATORY NOTE

(This note is not part of the Order)

This Order establishes, under section 21 of the Oil and Gas (Enterprise) Act 1982, a safety zone, having a radius of 500 metres from a specified point, around the installation specified in the Schedule to this Order and maintained in waters to which the section applies (these include territorial waters and waters in areas designated under section 1(7) of the Continental Shelf Act 1964 (c.29)).

Vessels (which for this purpose include hovercraft, submersible apparatus and installations in transit) are prohibited from entering or remaining in the safety zone except with the consent of the Secretary of State or in the circumstances mentioned in article 2(2) of the Order.

The Order also revokes the Offshore Installations (Safety Zones) Order which created a safety zone around the installation specified in the Schedule to this Order on its previous location.

STATUTORY INSTRUMENTS

1987 No. 979

OFFSHORE INSTALLATIONS

The Offshore Installations (Safety Zones) (No. 36) Order 1987

Made - - - -	*19th May 1987*
Coming into force	*21st May 1987*

The Secretary of State, in exercise of the powers conferred on him by section 21(1), (2) and (3) of the Oil and Gas (Enterprise) Act 1982(a) (hereinafter referred to as "the Act"), and of all other powers enabling him in that behalf, hereby makes the following Order:–

1. This Order may be cited as the Offshore Installations (Safety Zones) (No. 36) Order 1987 and shall come into force on 21st May 1987.

2.—(1) A safety zone is hereby established around the installation specified in Column 1 of the Schedule hereto (being an installation maintained in waters to which section 21 of the Act(b) applies) having a radius of five hundred metres from the point as respects that installation which has the co-ordinates of latitude and longitude according to European Datum (1950) specified in Columns 2 and 3 of the Schedule.

(2) The prohibition under section 21(3) of the Act on a vessel entering or remaining in a safety zone without the consent of the Secretary of State shall not apply to a vessel entering or remaining in the safety zone established under paragraph (1) above –

    (a) in connection with the laying, inspection, testing, repair, alteration, renewal or removal of any submarine cable or pipe-line in or near that safety zone;

    (b) to provide services for, to transport persons or goods to or from, or under the authority of a government department to inspect, any installation in that safety zone;

    (c) if it is a vessel belonging to a general lighthouse authority performing duties relating to the safety of navigation;

    (d) in connection with the saving or attempted saving of life or property;

    (e) owing to stress of weather; or

    (f) when in distress.

3. The Offshore Installations (Safety Zones) (No. 20) Order 1987(c) is hereby revoked.

	Alick Buchanan-Smith
19th May 1987	Minister of State, Department of Energy

(a) 1982 c.23.   (b) *See* section 21(9).   (c) S.I. 1987/204.

SCHEDULE

Article 2(1)

SAFETY ZONE

(1) *Name or other designation* *of the offshore installation*	(2) *Latitude* *North*	(3) *Longitude* *East*
Ocean Benarmin	52° 56′ 37.00″	02° 10′ 52.00″

EXPLANATORY NOTE

(This note is not part of the Order)

This Order establishes, under section 21 of the Oil and Gas (Enterprise) Act 1982, a safety zone, having a radius of 500 metres from a specified point, around the installation specified in the Schedule to this Order and maintained in waters to which the section applies (these include territorial waters and waters in areas designated under section 1(7) of the Continental Shelf Act 1964 (c.29)).

Vessels (which for this purpose include hovercraft, submersible apparatus and installations in transit) are prohibited from entering or remaining in the safety zone except with the consent of the Secretary of State or in the circumstances mentioned in article 2(2) of the Order.

The Order also revokes the Offshore Installations (Safety Zones) Order which created a safety zone around the installation specified in the Schedule to this Order on its previous location.

STATUTORY INSTRUMENTS

1987 No. 980

OFFSHORE INSTALLATIONS

The Offshore Installations (Safety Zones) (No. 37) Order 1987

Made - - - -	*19th May 1987*
Coming into force	*21st May 1987*

The Secretary of State, in exercise of the powers conferred on him by section 21(1), (2) and (3) of the Oil and Gas (Enterprise) Act 1982(a) (hereinafter referred to as "the Act"), and of all other powers enabling him in that behalf, hereby makes the following Order:–

1. This Order may be cited as the Offshore Installations (Safety Zones) (No. 37) Order 1987 and shall come into force on 21st May 1987.

2.—(1) A safety zone is hereby established around the installation specified in Column 1 of the Schedule hereto (being an installation maintained in waters to which section 21 of the Act(b) applies) having a radius of five hundred metres from the point as respects that installation which has the co-ordinates of latitude and longitude according to European Datum (1950) specified in Columns 2 and 3 of the Schedule.

(2) The prohibition under section 21(3) of the Act on a vessel entering or remaining in a safety zone without the consent of the Secretary of State shall not apply to a vessel entering or remaining in the safety zone established under paragraph (1) above –

   (a) in connection with the laying, inspection, testing, repair, alteration, renewal or removal of any submarine cable or pipe-line in or near that safety zone;

   (b) to provide services for, to transport persons or goods to or from, or under the authority of a government department to inspect, any installation in that safety zone;

   (c) if it is a vessel belonging to a general lighthouse authority performing duties relating to the safety of navigation;

   (d) in connection with the saving or attempted saving of life or property;

   (e) owing to stress of weather; or

   (f) when in distress.

Alick Buchanan-Smith
Minister of State, Department of Energy

19th May 1987

(a) 1982 c.23.   (b) *See* section 21(9).

SCHEDULE

Article 2(1)

SAFETY ZONE

(1) *Name or other designation of the offshore installation*	(2) *Latitude North*	(3) *Longitude East*
Rowan Gorilla II	57° 18′ 05.58″	01° 35′ 19.94″

EXPLANATORY NOTE

(This note is not part of the Order)

This Order establishes, under section 21 of the Oil and Gas (Enterprise) Act 1982, a safety zone, having a radius of 500 metres from a specified point, around the installation specified in the Schedule to this Order and maintained in waters to which the section applies (these include territorial waters and waters in areas designated under section 1(7) of the Continental Shelf Act 1964 (c.29)).

Vessels (which for this purpose include hovercraft, submersible apparatus and installations in transit) are prohibited from entering or remaining in the safety zone except with the consent of the Secretary of State or in the circumstances mentioned in article 2(2) of the Order.

STATUTORY INSTRUMENTS

1987 No. 981

OFFSHORE INSTALLATIONS

The Offshore Installations (Safety Zones) (No. 38) Order 1987

Made - - - -	*19th May 1987*
Coming into force	*21st May 1987*

The Secretary of State, in exercise of the powers conferred on him by section 21(1), (2) and (3) of the Oil and Gas (Enterprise) Act 1982**(a)** (hereinafter referred to as "the Act"), and of all other powers enabling him in that behalf, hereby makes the following Order:–

1. This Order may be cited as the Offshore Installations (Safety Zones) (No. 38) Order 1987 and shall come into force on 21st May 1987.

2.—(1) A safety zone is hereby established around the installation specified in Column 1 of the Schedule hereto (being an installation maintained in waters to which section 21 of the Act**(b)** applies) having a radius of five hundred metres from the point as respects that installation which has the co-ordinates of latitude and longitude according to European Datum (1950) specified in Columns 2 and 3 of the Schedule.

(2) The prohibition under section 21(3) of the Act on a vessel entering or remaining in a safety zone without the consent of the Secretary of State shall not apply to a vessel entering or remaining in the safety zone established under paragraph (1) above –

- (a) in connection with the laying, inspection, testing, repair, alteration, renewal or removal of any submarine cable or pipe-line in or near that safety zone;
- (b) to provide services for, to transport persons or goods to or from, or under the authority of a government department to inspect, any installation in that safety zone;
- (c) if it is a vessel belonging to a general lighthouse authority performing duties relating to the safety of navigation;
- (d) in connection with the saving or attempted saving of life or property;
- (e) owing to stress of weather; or
- (f) when in distress.

19th May 1987

Alick Buchanan-Smith
Minister of State, Department of Energy

(a) 1982 c.23.   **(b)** *See* section 21(9).

SCHEDULE

Article 2(1)

SAFETY ZONE

(1) *Name or other designation of the offshore installation*	(2) *Latitude North*	(3) *Longitude West*
Santa Fe 140	60° 14′ 21.80″	04° 29′ 44.40″

EXPLANATORY NOTE

(This note is not part of the Order)

This Order establishes, under section 21 of the Oil and Gas (Enterprise) Act 1982, a safety zone, having a radius of 500 metres from a specified point, around the installation specified in the Schedule to this Order and maintained in waters to which the section applies (these include territorial waters and waters in areas designated under section 1(7) of the Continental Shelf Act 1964 (c.29)).

Vessels (which for this purpose include hovercraft, submersible apparatus and installations in transit) are prohibited from entering or remaining in the safety zone except with the consent of the Secretary of State or in the circumstances mentioned in article 2(2) of the Order.

1987 No. 982

OFFSHORE INSTALLATIONS

The Offshore Installations (Safety Zones) (No. 39) Order 1987

Made	-	-	-	*19th May 1987*
Coming into force				*21st May 1987*

The Secretary of State, in exercise of the powers conferred on him by section 21(1), (2) and (3) of the Oil and Gas (Enterprise) Act 1982(a) (hereinafter referred to as "the Act"), and of all other powers enabling him in that behalf, hereby makes the following Order:–

1. This Order may be cited as the Offshore Installations (Safety Zones) (No. 39) Order 1987 and shall come into force on 21st May 1987.

2.—(1) A safety zone is hereby established around the installation specified in Column 1 of the Schedule hereto (being an installation maintained in waters to which section 21 of the Act(b) applies) having a radius of five hundred metres from the point as respects that installation which has the co-ordinates of latitude and longitude according to European Datum (1950) specified in Columns 2 and 3 of the Schedule.

(2) The prohibition under section 21(3) of the Act on a vessel entering or remaining in a safety zone without the consent of the Secretary of State shall not apply to a vessel entering or remaining in the safety zone established under paragraph (1) above –

- (a) in connection with the laying, inspection, testing, repair, alteration, renewal or removal of any submarine cable or pipe-line in or near that safety zone;
- (b) to provide services for, to transport persons or goods to or from, or under the authority of a government department to inspect, any installation in that safety zone;
- (c) if it is a vessel belonging to a general lighthouse authority performing duties relating to the safety of navigation;
- (d) in connection with the saving or attempted saving of life or property;
- (e) owing to stress of weather; or
- (f) when in distress.

Alick Buchanan-Smith
Minister of State, Department of Energy

19th May 1987

(a) 1982 c.23.   (b) *See* section 21(9).

SCHEDULE
Article 2(1)

SAFETY ZONE

(1) *Name or other designation of the offshore installation*	(2) *Latitude North*	(3) *Longitude East*
Sedco 703	59° 30′ 43.36″	01° 31′ 49.87″

EXPLANATORY NOTE

(This note is not part of the Order)

This Order establishes, under section 21 of the Oil and Gas (Enterprise) Act 1982, a safety zone, having a radius of 500 metres from a specified point, around the installation specified in the Schedule to this Order and maintained in waters to which the section applies (these include territorial waters and waters in areas designated under section 1(7) of the Continental Shelf Act 1964 (c.29)).

Vessels (which for this purpose include hovercraft, submersible apparatus and installations in transit) are prohibited from entering or remaining in the safety zone except with the consent of the Secretary of State or in the circumstances mentioned in article 2(2) of the Order.

STATUTORY INSTRUMENTS

1987 No. 983

OFFSHORE INSTALLATIONS

The Offshore Installations (Safety Zones) (No. 40) Order 1987

Made	-	-	-	*19th May 1987*
Coming into force				*21st May 1987*

The Secretary of State, in exercise of the powers conferred on him by section 21(1), (2) and (3) of the Oil and Gas (Enterprise) Act 1982(**a**) (hereinafter referred to as "the Act"), and of all other powers enabling him in that behalf, hereby makes the following Order:–

1. This Order may be cited as the Offshore Installations (Safety Zones) (No. 40) Order 1987 and shall come into force on 21st May 1987.

2.—(1) A safety zone is hereby established around the installation specified in Column 1 of the Schedule hereto (being an installation maintained in waters to which section 21 of the Act(**b**) applies) having a radius of five hundred metres from the point as respects that installation which has the co-ordinates of latitude and longitude according to European Datum (1950) specified in Columns 2 and 3 of the Schedule.

(2) The prohibition under section 21(3) of the Act on a vessel entering or remaining in a safety zone without the consent of the Secretary of State shall not apply to a vessel entering or remaining in the safety zone established under paragraph (1) above –

    (a) in connection with the laying, inspection, testing, repair, alteration, renewal or removal of any submarine cable or pipe-line in or near that safety zone;

    (b) to provide services for, to transport persons or goods to or from, or under the authority of a government department to inspect, any installation in that safety zone;

    (c) if it is a vessel belonging to a general lighthouse authority performing duties relating to the safety of navigation;

    (d) in connection with the saving or attempted saving of life or property;

    (e) owing to stress of weather; or

    (f) when in distress.

19th May 1987

Alick Buchanan-Smith
Minister of State, Department of Energy

(**a**) 1982 c.23.   (**b**) *See* section 21(9).

SCHEDULE   Article 2(1)

SAFETY ZONE

(1) *Name or other designation* *of the offshore installation*	(2) *Latitude* *North*	(3) *Longitude* *East*
Sedco 704	57° 53′ 33.45″	00° 00′ 43.20″

EXPLANATORY NOTE

(This note is not part of the Order)

This Order establishes, under section 21 of the Oil and Gas (Enterprise) Act 1982, a safety zone, having a radius of 500 metres from a specified point, around the installation specified in the Schedule to this Order and maintained in waters to which the section applies (these include territorial waters and waters in areas designated under section 1(7) of the Continental Shelf Act 1964 (c.29)).

Vessels (which for this purpose include hovercraft, submersible apparatus and installations in transit) are prohibited from entering or remaining in the safety zone except with the consent of the Secretary of State or in the circumstances mentioned in article 2(2) of the Order.

1987 No. 984

OFFSHORE INSTALLATIONS

The Offshore Installations (Safety Zones) (No. 41) Order 1987

Made - - - -	*19th May 1987*
Coming into force	*21st May 1987*

The Secretary of State, in exercise of the powers conferred on him by section 21(1), (2) and (3) of the Oil and Gas (Enterprise) Act 1982(**a**) (hereinafter referred to as "the Act"), and of all other powers enabling him in that behalf, hereby makes the following Order:–

1. This Order may be cited as the Offshore Installations (Safety Zones) (No. 41) Order 1987 and shall come into force on 21st May 1987.

2.—(1) A safety zone is hereby established around the installation specified in Column 1 of the Schedule hereto (being an installation maintained in waters to which section 21 of the Act(**b**) applies) having a radius of five hundred metres from the point as respects that installation which has the co-ordinates of latitude and longitude according to European Datum (1950) specified in Columns 2 and 3 of the Schedule.

(2) The prohibition under section 21(3) of the Act on a vessel entering or remaining in a safety zone without the consent of the Secretary of State shall not apply to a vessel entering or remaining in the safety zone established under paragraph (1) above –

    (a) in connection with the laying, inspection, testing, repair, alteration, renewal or removal of any submarine cable or pipe-line in or near that safety zone;

    (b) to provide services for, to transport persons or goods to or from, or under the authority of a government department to inspect, any installation in that safety zone;

    (c) if it is a vessel belonging to a general lighthouse authority performing duties relating to the safety of navigation;

    (d) in connection with the saving or attempted saving of life or property;

    (e) owing to stress of weather; or

    (f) when in distress.

19th May 1987

Alick Buchanan-Smith
Minister of State, Department of Energy

(**a**) 1982 c.23.   (**b**) *See* section 21(9).

SCHEDULE

Article 2(1)

SAFETY ZONE

(1) Name or other designation of the offshore installation	(2) Latitude North	(3) Longitude East
Sedco 707	58° 16' 10.21"	00° 11' 45.24"

EXPLANATORY NOTE

(This note is not part of the Order)

This Order establishes, under section 21 of the Oil and Gas (Enterprise) Act 1982, a safety zone, having a radius of 500 metres from a specified point, around the installation specified in the Schedule to this Order and maintained in waters to which the section applies (these include territorial waters and waters in areas designated under section 1(7) of the Continental Shelf Act 1964 (c.29)).

Vessels (which for this purpose include hovercraft, submersible apparatus and installations in transit) are prohibited from entering or remaining in the safety zone except with the consent of the Secretary of State or in the circumstances mentioned in article 2(2) of the Order.

STATUTORY INSTRUMENTS

1987 No. 985

OFFSHORE INSTALLATIONS

The Offshore Installations (Safety Zones) (No. 42) Order 1987

Made	- - - -		*19th May 1987*
Coming into force			*21st May 1987*

The Secretary of State, in exercise of the powers conferred on him by section 21(1), (2) and (3) of the Oil and Gas (Enterprise) Act 1982(a) (hereinafter referred to as "the Act"), and of all other powers enabling him in that behalf, hereby makes the following Order:–

1. This Order may be cited as the Offshore Installations (Safety Zones) (No. 42) Order 1987 and shall come into force on 21st May 1987.

2.—(1) A safety zone is hereby established around the installation specified in Column 1 of the Schedule hereto (being an installation maintained in waters to which section 21 of the Act(b) applies) having a radius of five hundred metres from the point as respects that installation which has the co-ordinates of latitude and longitude according to European Datum (1950) specified in Columns 2 and 3 of the Schedule.

(2) The prohibition under section 21(3) of the Act on a vessel entering or remaining in a safety zone without the consent of the Secretary of State shall not apply to a vessel entering or remaining in the safety zone established under paragraph (1) above –

(a) in connection with the laying, inspection, testing, repair, alteration, renewal or removal of any submarine cable or pipe-line in or near that safety zone;

(b) to provide services for, to transport persons or goods to or from, or under the authority of a government department to inspect, any installation in that safety zone;

(c) if it is a vessel belonging to a general lighthouse authority performing duties relating to the safety of navigation;

(d) in connection with the saving or attempted saving of life or property;

(e) owing to stress of weather; or

(f) when in distress.

Alick Buchanan-Smith
Minister of State, Department of Energy

19th May 1987

(a) 1982 c.23.   (b) *See* section 21(9).

SCHEDULE

Article 2(1)

SAFETY ZONE

(1) *Name or other designation* *of the offshore installation*	(2) *Latitude* *North*	(3) *Longitude* *East*
Sedco 714	61° 41′ 18.33″	01° 33′ 34.17″

EXPLANATORY NOTE

(This note is not part of the Order)

This Order establishes, under section 21 of the Oil and Gas (Enterprise) Act 1982, a safety zone, having a radius of 500 metres from a specified point, around the installation specified in the Schedule to this Order and maintained in waters to which the section applies (these include territorial waters and waters in areas designated under section 1(7) of the Continental Shelf Act 1964 (c.29)).

Vessels (which for this purpose include hovercraft, submersible apparatus and installations in transit) are prohibited from entering or remaining in the safety zone except with the consent of the Secretary of State or in the circumstances mentioned in article 2(2) of the Order.

STATUTORY INSTRUMENTS

1987 No. 986

OFFSHORE INSTALLATIONS

The Offshore Installations (Safety Zones) (No. 43) Order 1987

Made	-	-	-	-	*19th May 1987*
Coming into force					*21st May 1987*

The Secretary of State, in exercise of the powers conferred on him by section 21(1), (2) and (3) of the Oil and Gas (Enterprise) Act 1982(a) (hereinafter referred to as "the Act"), and of all other powers enabling him in that behalf, hereby makes the following Order:–

1. This Order may be cited as the Offshore Installations (Safety Zones) (No. 43) Order 1987 and shall come into force on 21st May 1987.

2.—(1) A safety zone is hereby established around the installation specified in Column 1 of the Schedule hereto (being an installation maintained in waters to which section 21 of the Act(b) applies) having a radius of five hundred metres from the point as respects that installation which has the co-ordinates of latitude and longitude according to European Datum (1950) specified in Columns 2 and 3 of the Schedule.

(2) The prohibition under section 21(3) of the Act on a vessel entering or remaining in a safety zone without the consent of the Secretary of State shall not apply to a vessel entering or remaining in the safety zone established under paragraph (1) above –

    (a) in connection with the laying, inspection, testing, repair, alteration, renewal or removal of any submarine cable or pipe-line in or near that safety zone;

    (b) to provide services for, to transport persons or goods to or from, or under the authority of a government department to inspect, any installation in that safety zone;

    (c) if it is a vessel belonging to a general lighthouse authority performing duties relating to the safety of navigation;

    (d) in connection with the saving or attempted saving of life or property;

    (e) owing to stress of weather; or

    (f) when in distress.

3. The Offshore Installations (Safety Zones) (No. 21) Order 1987(c) is hereby revoked.

Alick Buchanan-Smith
Minister of State, Department of Energy

19th May 1987

(a) 1982 c.23.   (b) *See* section 21(9).   (c) S.I. 1987/205.

SCHEDULE

Article 2(1)

SAFETY ZONE

(1) *Name or other designation* *of the offshore installation*	(2) *Latitude* *North*	(3) *Longitude* *East*
Sedneth 701	61° 36′ 58.00″	01° 28′ 58.80″

EXPLANATORY NOTE

(This note is not part of the Order)

This Order establishes, under section 21 of the Oil and Gas (Enterprise) Act 1982, a safety zone, having a radius of 500 metres from a specified point, around the installation specified in the Schedule to this Order and maintained in waters to which the section applies (these include territorial waters and waters in areas designated under section 1(7) of the Continental Shelf Act 1964 (c.29)).

Vessels (which for this purpose include hovercraft, submersible apparatus and installations in transit) are prohibited from entering or remaining in the safety zone except with the consent of the Secretary of State or in the circumstances mentioned in article 2(2) of the Order.

The Order also revokes the Offshore Installations (Safety Zones) Order which created a safety zone around the installation specified in the Schedule to this Order on its previous location.

STATUTORY INSTRUMENTS

1987 No. 987

OFFSHORE INSTALLATIONS

The Offshore Installations (Safety Zones) (No. 44) Order 1987

Made - - - -		*19th May 1987*
Coming into force		*21st May 1987*

The Secretary of State, in exercise of the powers conferred on him by section 21(1), (2) and (3) of the Oil and Gas (Enterprise) Act 1982(a) (hereinafter referred to as "the Act"), and of all other powers enabling him in that behalf, hereby makes the following Order:–

1. This Order may be cited as the Offshore Installations (Safety Zones) (No. 44) Order 1987 and shall come into force on 21st May 1987.

2.—(1) A safety zone is hereby established around the installation specified in Column 1 of the Schedule hereto (being an installation maintained in waters to which section 21 of the Act(b) applies) having a radius of five hundred metres from the point as respects that installation which has the co-ordinates of latitude and longitude according to European Datum (1950) specified in Columns 2 and 3 of the Schedule.

(2) The prohibition under section 21(3) of the Act on a vessel entering or remaining in a safety zone without the consent of the Secretary of State shall not apply to a vessel entering or remaining in the safety zone established under paragraph (1) above –

(a) in connection with the laying, inspection, testing, repair, alteration, renewal or removal of any submarine cable or pipe-line in or near that safety zone;

(b) to provide services for, to transport persons or goods to or from, or under the authority of a government department to inspect, any installation in that safety zone;

(c) if it is a vessel belonging to a general lighthouse authority performing duties relating to the safety of navigation;

(d) in connection with the saving or attempted saving of life or property;

(e) owing to stress of weather; or

(f) when in distress.

3. The Offshore Installations (Safety Zones) (No. 22) Order 1987(c) is hereby revoked.

19th May 1987

Alick Buchanan-Smith
Minister of State, Department of Energy

(a) 1982 c.23.   (b) *See* section 21(9).   (c) S.I. 1987/206.

SCHEDULE

Article 2(1)

SAFETY ZONE

(1) *Name or other designation* *of the offshore installation*	(2) *Latitude* *North*	(3) *Longitude* *West*
Treasure Seeker	58° 32' 01.00"	00° 21' 02.50"

EXPLANATORY NOTE

(This note is not part of the Order)

This Order establishes, under section 21 of the Oil and Gas (Enterprise) Act 1982, a safety zone, having a radius of 500 metres from a specified point, around the installation specified in the Schedule to this Order and maintained in waters to which the section applies (these include territorial waters and waters in areas designated under section 1(7) of the Continental Shelf Act 1964 (c.29)).

Vessels (which for this purpose include hovercraft, submersible apparatus and installations in transit) are prohibited from entering or remaining in the safety zone except with the consent of the Secretary of State or in the circumstances mentioned in article 2(2) of the Order.

The Order also revokes the Offshore Installations (Safety Zones) Order which created a safety zone around the installation specified in the Schedule to this Order on its previous location.

STATUTORY INSTRUMENTS

1987 No. 988

OFFSHORE INSTALLATIONS

The Offshore Installations (Safety Zones) (No. 45) Order 1987

Made - - - -	*19th May 1987*
Coming into force	*21st May 1987*

The Secretary of State, in exercise of the powers conferred on him by section 21(1), (2) and (3) of the Oil and Gas (Enterprise) Act 1982(a) (hereinafter referred to as "the Act"), and of all other powers enabling him in that behalf, hereby makes the following Order:–

1. This Order may be cited as the Offshore Installations (Safety Zones) (No. 45) Order 1987 and shall come into force on 21st May 1987.

2.—(1) A safety zone is hereby established around the installation specified in Column 1 of the Schedule hereto (being an installation maintained in waters to which section 21 of the Act(b) applies) having a radius of five hundred metres from the point as respects that installation which has the co-ordinates of latitude and longitude according to European Datum (1950) specified in Columns 2 and 3 of the Schedule.

(2) The prohibition under section 21(3) of the Act on a vessel entering or remaining in a safety zone without the consent of the Secretary of State shall not apply to a vessel entering or remaining in the safety zone established under paragraph (1) above –

(a) in connection with the laying, inspection, testing, repair, alteration, renewal or removal of any submarine cable or pipe-line in or near that safety zone;

(b) to provide services for, to transport persons or goods to or from, or under the authority of a government department to inspect, any installation in that safety zone;

(c) if it is a vessel belonging to a general lighthouse authority performing duties relating to the safety of navigation;

(d) in connection with the saving or attempted saving of life or property;

(e) owing to stress of weather; or

(f) when in distress.

19th May 1987

Alick Buchanan-Smith
Minister of State, Department of Energy

(a) 1982 c.23.   (b) *See* section 21(9).

SCHEDULE

Article 2(1)

SAFETY ZONE

(1) *Name or other designation* *of the offshore installation*	(2) *Latitude* *North*	(3) *Longitude* *East*
Western Pacesetter IV	58° 00′ 28.38″	01° 09′ 11.47″

EXPLANATORY NOTE

(This note is not part of the Order)

This Order establishes, under section 21 of the Oil and Gas (Enterprise) Act 1982, a safety zone, having a radius of 500 metres from a specified point, around the installation specified in the Schedule to this Order and maintained in waters to which the section applies (these include territorial waters and waters in areas designated under section 1(7) of the Continental Shelf Act 1964 (c.29)).

Vessels (which for this purpose include hovercraft, submersible apparatus and installations in transit) are prohibited from entering or remaining in the safety zone except with the consent of the Secretary of State or in the circumstances mentioned in article 2(2) of the Order.

STATUTORY INSTRUMENTS

1987 No. 989

OFFSHORE INSTALLATIONS

The Offshore Installations (Safety Zones) (Revocation) (No. 4) Order 1987

Made - - - -	*19th May 1987*
Coming into force	*21st May 1987*

The Secretary of State, in exercise of the power conferred on him by section 21(1) of the Oil and Gas (Enterprise) Act 1982(**a**), and of all other powers enabling him in that behalf, hereby makes the following Order:

1. This Order may be cited as the Offshore Installations (Safety Zones) (Revocation) (No. 4) Order 1987 and shall come into force on 21st May 1987.

2. The Offshore Installations (Safety Zones) Orders specified in the Schedule hereto are hereby revoked.

Alick Buchanan-Smith
19th May 1987   Minister of State, Department of Energy

(**a**) 1982 c.23.

SCHEDULE

Article 2

OFFSHORE INSTALLATIONS (SAFETY ZONES) ORDERS REVOKED

Order	Reference	Name of installation to which Order relates
The Offshore Installations (Safety Zones) (No. 62) Order 1986	S.I. 1986/1132	Cecil Provine
The Offshore Installations (Safety Zones) (No. 18) Order 1987	S.I. 1987/202	Dan Earl
The Offshore Installations (Safety Zones) (No. 13) Order 1987	S.I. 1987/70	Ocean Bounty
The Offshore Installations (Safety Zones) (No. 105) Order 1986	S.I. 1986/1844	Sedco 700

EXPLANATORY NOTE

(This note is not part of the Order)

This Order revokes the Offshore Installations (Safety Zones) Orders specified in the Schedule. The installations specified in the Schedule which were protected by the safety zones established by those Orders have been removed and accordingly those Orders are no longer required.

1987 No. 999

METROPOLITAN AND CITY POLICE DISTRICTS

CABS

The London Cab Order 1987

Made - - - -	*14th May 1987*
Coming into force -	*21st June 1987*

The Secretary of State for Transport, in exercise of the powers conferred by section 9 of the Metropolitan Public Carriage Act 1869(a), section 1 of the London Cab and Stage Carriage Act 1907(b) and section 1 of the London Cab Act 1968(c), hereby makes the following Order:–

Citation, commencement and introduction

1. This Order may be cited as the London Cab Order 1987 and shall come into force on 21st June 1987.

2. The London Cab Order 1934(d) shall be amended in accordance with the following provisions of this Order.

Scale of fares

3.—(1) For paragraph 40 (scales of fares excluding extras) there shall be substituted the following:

"**40.**—(1) Subject to the following provisions of this paragraph, the fare payable for the hiring of a motor cab shall be according to the following scale:–

    (a) a hiring charge of 40p, and

    (b) in respect of any part of the hiring during which the cab travels at a speed exceeding 9.55 miles an hour, at the rate of 20p for 462 yards or, if the fare shown on the taximeter is £5.20 or more, thereafter at the rate of 20p for 308 yards, and

    (c) in respect of any part of the hiring during which the cab is stationary or travels at a speed not exceeding 9.55 miles an hour, at a rate of 20p for 99

(a) 1869 c.115.
(b) 1907 c.55.
(c) 1968 c.7.
(d) S.R. & O. 1934/1346; the relevant amending instruments are S.I. 1980/588, 1982/610, 1984/707 and 1986/857.

seconds or, if the rate shown on the taximeter is £5.20 or more, thereafter at the rate of 20p for 66 seconds.

(2) In any case where the fare according to the scale prescribed in sub-paragraph (1) above is less than 80p the fare payable shall be 80p, and in any other case where the fare exceeds a multiple of 20p by a sum which is less than 20p the fare payable shall be the next higher multiple of 20p.

(3) At any time during the transitional period specified in Schedule E to this Order when a motor cab is fitted with a taximeter which is not capable of recording and displaying automatically the fare payable according to the scale prescribed in sub-paragraph (1) above, the fare payable—

(a) where the fare shown on the meter does not exceed £10.00 shall, if a notice in the terms set out in that Schedule is kept prominently displayed in the cab in such a manner as to be clearly legible to the hirer, be, as respects a fare shown on the meter, the figure in the column headed "Fare payable" opposite to the figure in the column headed "Shown on meter", and otherwise shall be the fare shown on the meter;

(b) where the fare shown on the meter exceeds £10.00 shall, as respects the amount by which the fare shown exceeds the highest multiple of £10.00 in that fare, be the fare payable under the foregoing provisions of this sub-paragraph and in addition £10.60 shall be payable as respects each multiple of £10.00 in the fare shown on the meter.".

(2) For Schedule E there shall be substituted the Schedule set out in the Schedule to this Order.

Amendment to extra charges

4. For paragraph 41(2)(a)(i) (extra charges for a hiring on certain public holidays) there shall be substituted the following:

"(i) for a hiring which commences or terminates between the hours of 8pm on 24th December and 6am on 27th December or the hours of 8pm on 31st December and 6am on 1st January

.... £2".

Signed by authority of the
Secretary of State
14th May 1987

David B. Mitchell
Minister of State, Department of Transport

SCHEDULE

"SCHEDULE E   Paragraph 40(3)

INCREASE OF FARES

From 21st June 1987 to 20th August 1987 (inclusive) (in this Order referred to as "the transitional period") for all journeys beginning and ending within the Metropolitan and/or City Police Districts the fare shown on the taximeter, excluding extras, is (as authorised by the London Cab Order 1987) increased as shown in the following Table:–

Shown on meter	Fare payable	Shown on meter	Fare payable
£	£	£	£
0.80	0.80	5.80	6.20
1.00	1.00	6.00	6.40
1.20	1.20	6.20	6.60
1.40	1.40	6.40	6.80
1.60	1.60	6.60	7.00
1.80	1.80	6.80	7.20
2.00	2.20	7.00	7.40
2.20	2.40	7.20	7.60
2.40	2.60	7.40	7.80
2.60	2.80	7.60	8.00
2.80	3.00	7.80	8.20
3.00	3.20	8.00	8.40
3.20	3.40	8.20	8.60
3.40	3.60	8.40	8.80
3.60	3.80	8.60	9.00
3.80	4.00	8.80	9.20
4.00	4.20	9.00	9.40
4.20	4.40	9.20	9.80
4.40	4.60	9.40	10.00
4.60	4.80	9.60	10.20
4.80	5.00	9.80	10.40
5.00	5.20	10.00	10.60
5.20	5.40	0.20	0.20
5.40	5.60	0.40	0.40
5.60	6.00	0.60	0.60 ".

EXPLANATORY NOTE

(This note is not part of the Order)

This Order increases the fares payable for the hiring of a motor cab in the Metropolitan Police District and the City of London in respect of all journeys beginning and ending there. This is achieved by substituting a new paragraph 40 (scale of fares for motor cabs) – see article 3. The Schedule to the Order provides a conversion table setting out the new fares for cabs with taximeters which are not capable of recording those fares automatically. The table is required to be kept prominently displayed in the cab and may only be used during the transitional period from 21st June 1987 to 20th August 1987 after which all taximeters must be capable of automatically recording and displaying the increased fare. In addition, the extra charge in relation to hirings over the Christmas period is extended to end at 6am on 27th December (instead of 6am on 26th December) – see article 4.

STATUTORY INSTRUMENTS

1987 No. 1022 (C. 26)

INTERNATIONAL IMMUNITIES AND PRIVILEGES

The Diplomatic and Consular Premises Act 1987 (Commencement No.1) Order 1987

Made - - - -   *8th June 1987*

In exercise of the powers conferred upon me by section 9 of the Diplomatic and Consular Premises Act 1987(a), I hereby make the following Order:

1. This Order may be cited as the Diplomatic and Consular Premises Act 1987 (Commencement No.1) Order 1987.

2. The provisions of the Diplomatic and Consular Premises Act 1987 specified in the Schedule to this Order shall come into force on 11th June 1987.

Foreign and Commonwealth Office
8th June 1987

Geoffrey Howe
One of Her Majesty's Principal
Secretaries of State

SCHEDULE

Article 2

PROVISIONS OF THE DIPLOMATIC AND CONSULAR PREMISES ACT 1987 COMING INTO FORCE ON 11th JUNE 1987

Provisions of the Act	Subject matter of provisions
Section 6	Amendments of Diplomatic Privileges Act 1964(b) and Consular Relations Act 1968(c) concerning protection of diplomatic and consular premises (set out in Schedule 2 to the Act).
Section 7	Amendments of Criminal Law Act 1977(d) concerning trespassing on closed diplomatic and consular premises.
Schedule 2	Amendments of Diplomatic Privileges Act 1964 and Consular Relations Act 1968.

(a) 1987 c.46.   (b) 1964 c.81.   (c) 1968 c.18.   (d) 1977 c.45.

EXPLANATORY NOTE

(This note is not part of the Order)

This Order brings into force on 11th June 1987–

–section 6 of the Diplomatic and Consular Premises Act 1987 (which adds certain provisions of the Vienna Convention on Diplomatic and Consular Relations, relating to diplomatic and consular premises and their protection, to Schedules 1 to the Diplomatic Privileges Act 1964 and the Consular Relations Act 1968 respectively); and

–section 7 of the Act (which adds to section 9 of the Criminal Law Act 1977 provisions concerning trespassing on closed diplomatic and consular premises).

STATUTORY INSTRUMENTS

1987 No. 1028

FOREIGN COMPENSATION

The Foreign Compensation
(Financial Provisions) (No.2) Order 1987

Made - - - -	*10th June 1987*
Laid before Parliament	*18th June 1987*
Coming into force -	*18th July 1987*

At the Court at Buckingham Palace, the 10th day of June 1987

Present,

The Queen's Most Excellent Majesty in Council

Her Majesty, by virtue and in exercise of the powers conferred upon Her in that behalf by section 7(2) of the Foreign Compensation Act 1950(a) or otherwise in Her Majesty vested, is pleased, by and with the advice of Her Privy Council, to order, and it is hereby ordered, as follows:

1. This Order may be cited as the Foreign Compensation (Financial Provisions) (No.2) Order 1987 and shall come into force on 18th July 1987.

2. The Foreign Compensation Commission shall pay into the Consolidated Fund not later than 31st July 1987 out of the Union of Soviet Socialist Republics (Tsarist Assets) Fund the sum of £747,193 which is hereby determined to be the amount of the expenses of the Commission during the period 1st April 1986 to 31st March 1987 attributable to the discharge by the Commission of their functions in relation to the distribution of sums from that compensation fund.

G. I. de Deney
Clerk of the Privy Council

(a) 1950 c.12; the application of section 7(2) was extended by section 3(3) of the Foreign Compensation Act 1962 (c.4 (11 & 12 Eliz. 2)).

EXPLANATORY NOTE

(This note is not part of the Order)

This Order, which is made under section 7(2) of the Foreign Compensation Act 1950, directs the Foreign Compensation Commission to pay into the Consolidated Fund, out of the funds paid to the Commission for the purpose of being distributed under the said Act, an amount in respect of the Commission's expenses during the period 1st April 1986 to 31st March 1987 in relation to the distribution of those funds.

STATUTORY INSTRUMENTS

1987 No. 1029

ARBITRATION

The Arbitration (Foreign Awards) Order 1987

Made - - - -	*10th June 1987*
Coming into force -	*1st July 1987*

At the Court at Buckingham Palace, the 10th day of June 1987

Present,

The Queen's Most Excellent Majesty in Council

Whereas a Convention on the Recognition and Enforcement of Foreign Arbitral Awards (hereinafter called the "New York Convention")(a) adopted on 10th June 1958 entered into force for the United Kingdom of Great Britain and Northern Ireland on 23rd December 1975:

And whereas it is provided by section 7(2) of the Arbitration Act 1975(b) (which Act provides for the enforcement of foreign awards under the New York Convention) that if Her Majesty by Order in Council declares that any State specified in the Order is a party to the New York Convention the Order shall, while in force, be conclusive evidence that that State is a party to that Convention:

Now, therefore, Her Majesty, by and with the advice of Her Privy Council, in pursuance of the powers conferred on Her by section 7(2) of the Arbitration Act 1975 and of all other powers enabling Her in that behalf, is pleased to declare, and it is hereby declared, as follows:

1. This Order may be cited as the Arbitration (Foreign Awards) Order 1987 and shall come into force on 1st July 1987.

2. The People's Republic of China and the Republic of Singapore are parties to the New York Convention.

G. I. de Deney
Clerk to the Privy Council

(a) Cmnd. 6419.
(b) 1975 c.3.

EXPLANATORY NOTE

(This note is not part of the Order)

This Order specifies that the People's Republic of China and the Republic of Singapore are parties to the 1958 New York Convention on the Recognition and Enforcement of Foreign Arbitral Awards. Arbitral awards made in States which are parties to the Convention are enforceable in the United Kingdom under the Arbitration Act 1975.

STATUTORY INSTRUMENTS

1987 No. 1030

COPYRIGHT

The Copyright (Singapore) (Amendment) Order 1987

Made - - - -	*10th June 1987*
Laid before Parliament	*18th June 1987*
Coming into force	*9th July 1987*

At the Court at Buckingham Palace, the 10th day of June 1987

Present,

The Queen's Most Excellent Majesty in Council

Whereas Her Majesty is satisfied that, in respect of the matters provided for in this Order, provision has been made under the laws of Singapore whereby adequate protection will be given to owners of copyright under the Copyright Act 1956(a):

Now, therefore, Her Majesty, by and with the advice of Her Privy Council, and by virtue of the authority conferred on Her by sections 31, 32 and 47 of the said Act, is pleased to order, and it is hereby ordered as follows:

1. This Order may be cited as the Copyright (Singapore) (Amendment) Order 1987 and shall come into force on 9th July 1987.

2. The Copyright (Singapore) Order 1987(b) shall extend to Gibraltar, subject to the modification set out in article 5 of that Order.

3. Article 4 of that Order shall have effect in respect of this Order as it has effect in respect of that Order, references in that article to the commencement of that Order being taken to be references to the commencement of this Order.

G. I. de Deney
Clerk of the Privy Council

EXPLANATORY NOTE

(This note is not part of the Order)

This Order extends to Gibraltar the Copyright (Singapore) Order 1987, which provides for the copyright protection in the United Kingdom and other dependent countries of the Commonwealth of works and other subject-matter originating in Singapore.

(a) 1956 c.74.
(b) S.I. 1987/940.

STATUTORY INSTRUMENTS

1987 No. 1053

CUSTOMS AND EXCISE

The Customs Duties (ECSC) (No. 2) (Amendment No.7) Order 1987

Made - - - -	*13th June 1987*
Coming into force -	*15th June 1987*
Laid before the House of Commons	*17th June 1987*

The Treasury, by virtue of the powers conferred on them by section 5(1) and (3) of, and paragraph 4 of Schedule 2 to, the European Communities Act 1972(a) and of all other powers enabling them in that behalf, on the recommendation of the Secretary of State, hereby make the following Order:

1. This Order may be cited as the Customs Duties (ECSC) (No. 2) (Amendment No.7) Order 1987 and shall come into force on 15th June 1987.

2. Up to and including 31st December 1987, Article 6(1) of the Customs Duties (ECSC) (No. 2) Order 1985(b) (which exempts from duty goods to which that Order applies originating in certain countries) shall not apply to goods which fall within headings 73.11 AI, AIV a) 1 and 73.11B which originate in Yugoslavia.

Nigel Lawson
Michael Neubert
Two of the Lords Commissioners of
Her Majesty's Treasury

13th June 1987

(a) 1972 c.68; section 5(3) and Schedule 2 were amended by the Customs and Excise Duties (General Reliefs) Act 1979 (c.3), Schedule 2, paragraphs 3 and 5.
(b) S.I. 1985/1630, amended by S.I. 1985/2020, 1986/348, 813, 1352, 2179, 1987/973.

EXPLANATORY NOTE

(This note is not part of the Order)

This Order, which comes into force on 15th June 1987, amends the Customs Duties (ECSC) (No. 2) Order 1985 ("the main Order") which charges customs duties in accordance with the unified ECSC tariff on certain ECSC products imported into the United Kingdom except from other Member States of the European Coal and Steel Community (ECSC) and from certain other countries named in Schedule 1 to the main Order.

This Order reimposes duties on goods falling within headings 73.11 AI, AIV a) 1 and 73.11B which originate in Yugoslavia.

This Order implements a reintroduction of duty up to the end of 1987 made pursuant to Article 1, paragraph 3 of a decision 86/642/ECSC of the representatives of the governments of the Member States of the European Coal and Steel Community meeting within the Council on 22nd December 1986 (OJ No. L380, 31.12. 1986, p.59). Decision 86/642/ECSC of 22nd December 1986 established ceilings for imports of certain ECSC goods originating in Yugoslavia. These ceilings have now been reached on goods falling within the above headings.

The Commission communication to Member States giving notice of the reintroduction of customs duties is published in OJ No. C154 of 12.6.1987.

1987 No. 1061 (C.27)

CRIMINAL LAW, ENGLAND AND WALES
CRIMINAL LAW, NORTHERN IRELAND

The Criminal Justice Act 1987 (Commencement No. 1) Order 1987

Made - - - - *17th June 1987*

In exercise of the powers conferred on me by section 16 of the Criminal Justice Act 1987(**a**), I hereby make the following Order:

1. This Order may be cited as the Criminal Justice Act 1987 (Commencement No. 1) Order 1987.

2.—(1) Subject to paragraphs (2) and (3) below, the provisions of the Criminal Justice Act 1987 specified in the Schedule to this Order shall come into force on 20th July 1987.

(2) Section 1 of the said Act of 1987 (including Schedule 1 thereto) shall so come into force for the purposes only of the appointment of a person to be the Director of the Serious Fraud Office, the appointment of staff for the Office and the doing of such other things as may be necessary or expedient for the establishment of the Office.

(3) Nothing in section 12 of the said Act of 1987 shall apply to things done before 20th July 1987.

Home Office
17th June 1987

Douglas Hurd
One of Her Majesty's Principal Secretaries of State

(**a**) 1987 c.38.

SCHEDULE

Article 2

PROVISIONS OF THE CRIMINAL JUSTICE ACT 1987 COMING INTO FORCE ON 20TH JULY 1987

Provisions of the Act	*Subject matter of provisions*
Section 1 and Schedule 1 (for the purposes specified in article 2(2) above).	The Serious Fraud Office.
Section 12.	Charges of and penalty for conspiracy to defraud.
Section 14.	Financial provision.

EXPLANATORY NOTE

(This note is not part of the Order)

This Order brings into force on 20th July 1987 sections 1, 12 and 14 of the Criminal Justice Act 1987 and Schedule 1 to the Act. Section 1 and Schedule 1, which provide for the constitution of the Serious Fraud Office, are by virtue of article 2(2) brought into force for the purposes only of the appointment of the Director of the Office and staff and the doing of other things necessary or expedient for setting up the Office. Section 12 provides for conspiracy to defraud to be charged in circumstances also involving the commission of substantive offences (and conspiracies to commit them) and prescribes a maximum penalty for the offence. Article 2(3) precludes the application of section 12 to conduct occurring before 20th July 1987.

Section 14 makes financial provision consequential upon the enactment of the 1987 Act.

STATUTORY INSTRUMENTS

1987 No. 1062

POLICE

The Police Federation (Amendment) Regulations 1987

Made - - - -	*17th June 1987*
Laid before Parliament	*25th June 1987*
Coming into force	*1st August 1987*

In exercise of the powers conferred on me by section 44 of the Police Act 1964**(a)**, and after consultation with the three Central Committees of the Police Federation for England and Wales sitting together as a Joint Committee, I hereby make the following Regulations:–

1. These Regulations may be cited as the Police Federation (Amendment) Regulations 1987 and shall come into force on 1st August 1987.

2.—(1) In paragraph (4)(h) of regulation 19 of the Police Federation Regulations 1969**(b)**, there shall be substituted for the words from "offence under the Road Traffic Act 1960" to the word "blood" the words "offence under the Road Traffic Act 1972 or any other enactment relating to road traffic, other than offences under sections 5, 6, 7, 8 or 19 of that Act or section 12 of the Licensing Act 1872 (offences of driving or being in charge when impaired by drink or drugs and of driving, etc. with an undue proportion of alcohol in the blood)".

(2) For paragraph (5) of that regulation there shall be substituted the following provisions:–

"(5) Federation funds held by the joint central committee or, with the consent thereof, funds held by a central committee, may, on such terms and conditions as may be specified by the joint central committee in the circumstances of a particular case, and with the prior approval of the joint central committee, be used to defray legal charges incurred by such a person as is mentioned in paragraph (4)(h) in connection with criminal proceedings brought against him for causing the death of or injury to any person, or for any assault, committed as mentioned in paragraph (4)(h).

(5A) In paragraph (5) "injury" includes any impairment of a person's physical or mental condition.".

Douglas Hurd
One of Her Majesty's Principal Secretaries of State

Home Office
17th June 1987

(a) 1964 c.48; section 44 was amended by the Police and Criminal Evidence Act 1984 (c.60), section 109.
(b) S.I. 1969/1787; the relevant amending instrument is S.I. 1971/1498.

EXPLANATORY NOTE

(This note is not part of the Regulations)

These Regulations amend the Police Federation Regulations 1969. Regulation 2(1) brings up to date references in regulation 19(4) of the 1969 Regulations to those driving offences in respect of which central funds of the Federation may be used in paying legal charges incurred by a member or former member of the Federation. Regulation 5(2) permits central funds of the Federation to be used, by or with the consent of the joint central committee, in paying legal charges incurred by a member or former member of the Federation in connection with criminal proceedings brought against him for causing death or injury to any person or for any assault. The joint central committee is empowered to impose terms and conditions on the use of funds for this purpose and its prior approval is required.

The Regulations come into force on 1st August 1987.

1987 No. 1066

ROAD TRAFFIC

The International Carriage of Perishable Foodstuffs (Amendment) Regulations 1987

Made - - - -	*18th June 1987*
Laid before Parliament	*30th June 1987*
Coming into force	*21st July 1987*

The Secretary of State for Transport in exercise of the powers conferred by sections 3(1) and 4(1) of the International Carriage of Perishable Foodstuffs Act 1976**(a)**, and of all other enabling powers, hereby makes the following Regulations:–

1. These Regulations shall come into force on 21st July 1987 and may be cited as the International Carriage of Perishable Foodstuffs (Amendment) Regulations 1987.

2. In Parts I and II of the Schedule to the International Carriage of Perishable Foodstuffs Regulations 1985 **(b)** for "£220" there shall be substituted "£260".

Signed by authority of the
Secretary of State
18th June 1987

Peter Bottomley
Parliamentary Under Secretary of State,
Department of Transport

EXPLANATORY NOTE

(This note is not part of the Regulations)

These Regulations increase the daily fee of £220 prescribed by the International Carriage of Perishable Foodstuffs Regulations 1985 for the use of the facilities of a designated station (as defined in section 2(3) of the International Carriage of Perishable Foodstuffs Act 1976) for the testing of a unit of transport equipment or for the testing of a unit of transport equipment as a type vehicle to £260.

(a) 1976 c.58.
(b) S.I. 1985/1071.

STATUTORY INSTRUMENTS

1987 No. 1072

VALUE ADDED TAX

The Value Added Tax (Construction of Buildings) (No. 2) Order 1987

Approved by the House of Commons

Made - - - -	*22nd June 1987*
Laid before the House of Commons	*24th June 1987*
Coming into force	*25th June 1987*

The Treasury, in exercise of the powers conferred on them by sections 14(10), 16(4) and 48(6) of the Value Added Tax Act 1983(**a**) and of all other powers enabling them in that behalf, hereby make the following Order:

1. This Order may be cited as the Value Added Tax (Construction of Buildings) (No. 2) Order 1987 and shall come into force on 25th June 1987.

2. Group 8(**b**) of Schedule 5 to the Value Added Tax Act 1983 shall be varied–

(a) by substituting for Note (1A) the following Note–

"(1A) Any reference in item 2 or the following Notes to the construction of any building or the construction of any civil engineering work does not include a reference to–

(a) the conversion, reconstruction, alteration or enlargement of any existing building or civil engineering work; or

(b) any extension or annexation to an existing building which provides for internal access to the existing building or of which the separate use, letting or disposal is prevented by the terms of any covenant, statutory planning consent or similar permission;

and the reference in item 1 to a person constructing a building shall be construed accordingly.";

(b) by inserting in Note (2A) after paragraph (c), the following–

"(d) carpets or carpeting materials.".

3. Article 8 of the Value Added Tax (Special Provisions) Order 1981(**c**) shall be varied–

(a) by inserting in paragraph (1) after the words "taxable person constructing a building" and before the words "for the purpose of granting a major interest in it", the following words–

(**a**) 1983 c.55.   (**b**) Group 8 was varied by the Finance Act 1984 (c.43), section 10 and Schedule 6(II).   (**c**) S.I. 1981/1741; article 8 was amended by S.I. 1984/736.

        "or effecting works to any building, in either case";
    (b) by inserting in paragraph (2) after sub-paragraph (c) the following
        sub-paragraph–
        "(d)   carpets or carpeting materials.".

                                                          Tim Sainsbury
                                                         Michael Neubert
22nd June 1987   Two of the Lords Commissioners of Her Majesty's Treasury

---

EXPLANATORY NOTE

(This note is not part of the Order)

This Order replaces, in identical terms, the Value Added Tax (Construction of
Buildings) Order 1987 (S.I. 1987/781) which has expired because it did not get House of
Commons approval in the specified time.

Article 2 of this Order amends Notes (1A) and (2A) of Group 8 of Schedule 5 to the
Value Added Tax Act 1983 (as amended) and article 3 of this Order amends article 8 of
the Value Added Tax (Special Provisions) Order 1981 (as amended).

Group 8 sets out the reliefs available by way of zero-rating for the construction of
buildings etc and Notes (1A) and (2A) have the effect of excluding from zero-rating
supplies that might otherwise fall to be relieved under various items within the Group.
Note (1A) is amended to deny zero-rating to any extension or annexation to an existing
building if it provides for internal access to the existing building, or if separate use,
letting or disposal is prevented by the terms of any convenant, planning consent or
similar permission. Note (2A) is amended to exclude from zero-rating relief carpets
and carpeting materials when installed in the course of the construction of any building.

Article 8 of the Value Added Tax (Special Provisions) Order 1981 prevents the
deduction of input tax on non-standard fixtures and fittings incorporated by a
speculative builder in a dwelling which he is building for supply by sale or long lease.
That article is now further amended to prevent deduction when a person effecting
works to an existing building intends to sell or grant a long lease on any dwelling
resulting from his works. In addition, carpets and carpeting materials are added to the
list of non-standard fixtures and fittings in respect of which input tax deduction is
specifically prevented. This latter change complements and produces the same net
effect for speculative builders as the amendment to Note (2A) does for contract
builders.

The amendments described above came into force on 21st May 1987 under S.I.
1987/781. This Order continues them in force on the expiry of that Instrument.

STATUTORY INSTRUMENTS

1987 No. 1078 (S.82)

SHERIFF COURT, SCOTLAND

Act of Sederunt (Shorthand Writers' Fees) 1987

Made - - - -	*23rd June 1987*
Laid before Parliament	*2nd July 1987*
Coming into force	*27th July 1987*

The Lords of Council and Session, under and by virtue of the powers conferred upon them by section 40 of the Sheriff Courts (Scotland) Act 1907(**a**), and of all other powers enabling them in that behalf, do hereby enact and declare:

Citation and commencement

1.—(1) This Act of Sederunt may be cited as the Act of Sederunt (Shorthand Writers' Fees) 1987 and shall come into force on 27th July 1987.

(2) This Act of Sederunt shall be inserted in the Books of Sederunt.

Amendment of fees

2. In Chapter II of the Schedule to the Act of Sederunt of 7th May 1935(**b**), in the paragraphs specified in column 1 of the following table, for the figures specified in column 2, substitute the figures specified in column 3 of that table:-

TABLE

Column 1	Column 2 (Old fees)	Column 3 (New fees)
1	£11.72	£12.48
1	£28.28	£30.12
1	£34.93	£37.20
2	£ 2.50	£ 2.66
3	£ 0.20	£ 0.21

Edinburgh
23rd June 1987

Emslie
Lord President, I.P.D.

(**a**) 1907 c.51.
(**b**) S.R. & O. 1935/488; the relevant amending Instruments are S.I. 1974/1744 and 1986/1129.

EXPLANATORY NOTE

(This note is not part of the Act of Sederunt)

This Act of Sederunt amends the fees for shorthand writers in the Sheriff Court by increasing certain fees by about 6.5 per cent.

1987 No. 1079 (S.83)

COURT OF SESSION, SCOTLAND

Act of Sederunt (Rules of Court Amendment No.3) (Shorthand Writers' Fees) 1987

Made - - - -		*23rd June 1987*
Coming into force		*27th July 1987*

The Lords of Council and Session, under and by virtue of the powers conferred upon them by section 16 of the Administration of Justice (Scotland) Act 1933(**a**), and of all other powers enabling them in that behalf, do hereby enact and declare:

Citation and commencement

1.—(1) This Act of Sederunt may be cited as the Act of Sederunt (Rules of Court Amendment No.3) (Shorthand Writers' Fees) 1987 and shall come into force on 27th July 1987.

(2) This Act of Sederunt shall be inserted in the Books of Sederunt.

Amendment of fees

2. In Chapter IV of rule 347 of the Rules of Court(**b**), in the paragraphs specified in column 1 of the following table, for the figures specified in column 2, substitute the figures specified in column 3 of that table:–

TABLE

Column 1	Column 2 (Old fees)	Column 3 (New fees)
1	£28.28	£30.12
1	£11.72	£12.48
2	£ 2.50	£ 2.66
2	£ 3.00	£ 3.20
5	£ 0.20	£ 0.21

Edinburgh
23rd June 1987

Emslie
Lord President, I.P.D.

(**a**) 1933 c.41.
(**b**) S.I. 1965/321; the relevant amending Instruments are S.I. 1971/1161 and 1986/1128.

EXPLANATORY NOTE

(This note is not part of the Act of Sederunt)

This Act of Sederunt amends the fees for shorthand writers in the Court of Session by increasing certain fees by about 6.5 per cent.

STATUTORY INSTRUMENTS

1987 No. 1091

SEEDS

The Cereal Seeds (Amendment) Regulations 1987

Made - - - -	*24th June 1987*
Laid before Parliament	*6th July 1987*
Coming into force	
The whole of the Regulations	
except regulation 2(3)(b)(ii)	*27th July 1987*
regulation 2(3)(b)(ii)	*1st July 1988*

The Minister of Agriculture, Fisheries and Food, the Secretary of State for Scotland and the Secretary of State for Wales, acting jointly, in exercise of the powers conferred by sections 16(1), (1A), (2), (3), (4), (5) and (8), 17(1), (2), (3) and (4) and 36 of the Plant Varieties and Seeds Act 1964(a) and now vested in them(b) and of all other powers enabling them in that behalf, after consultation in accordance with the said section 16(1) with representatives of such interests as appear to them to be concerned, hereby make the following Regulations:–

Title and commencement

1.—(1) These Regulations may be cited as the Cereal Seeds (Amendment) Regulations 1987.

(2) These Regulations, except regulation 2(3)(b)(ii) shall come into force on 27th July 1987.

(3) Regulation 2(3)(b)(ii) shall come into force on 1st July 1988.

Amendment

2.—(1) The Cereal Seeds Regulations 1985(c) shall be amended in accordance with the following provisions of this regulation.

(2) In paragraph (3)(a) of regulation 5 (marketing of seeds) for the words "in Schedule 4," there shall be substituted the words "in Schedule 4 or Schedule 5,".

(3) In Schedule 5 (sampling of seed lots)–

    (a) in Part I, in paragraph 9 after the words "an automatic sampling device" there shall be inserted the words "approved by the Minister", and

    (b) in Part II–

        (i) for the words "The maximum weight of a seed lot and minimum weight of a submitted sample shall be as indicated below:–"
there shall be substituted the following words:–
"The maximum weight of a seed lot shall be as indicated below (or a weight which does not exceed that indicated below by more than 5 per

---

(a) 1964 c.14; section 16 was amended by the European Communities Act 1972 (c.68), section 4(1) and paragraph 5(1), (2) and (3) of Schedule 4.
(b) In the case of the Secretary of State for Wales by virtue of S.I. 1978/272.
(c) S.I. 1985/976.

cent) and the minimum weight of a submitted sample shall be as indicated below:–"; and

(ii) in paragraph a. for the words "20 tonnes" in each place in which they appear there shall be substituted the words "25 tonnes"; and

(c) in Part I of Schedule 6 (contents of official labels) in paragraph D (a) 8, the words "For mixtures of varieties" shall be omitted.

In witness whereof the Official Seal of the Minister of Agriculture, Fisheries and Food is hereunto affixed on 22nd June 1987.

John MacGregor
Minister of Agriculture, Fisheries and Food

24th June 1987

Sanderson of Bowden
Minister of State, Scottish Office

24th June 1987

Peter Walker
Secretary of State for Wales

EXPLANATORY NOTE

(This note is not part of the Regulations)

These Regulations, which amend the Cereal Seeds Regulations 1985, implement article 3 of Commission Directive 87/120/EEC (OJ No. L49, 18.2.87, p. 42) in so far as it amends Annex III of Council Directive 66/402/EEC (OJ No. 125, 11.7.66, p. 2309/66) (OJ/SE 1965–66 p. 143) (as amended) on the marketing of cereal seeds by providing (1) that the maximum weight of a seed lot, set out in that Annex, from which a sample is to be drawn for certification shall not be exceeded by more than 5% and (2) that with effect from 1 July 1988 the maximum weight of such a seed lot (other than maize) will be 25 tonnes (regulation 2(3)(b)(i) and (ii)).

The other changes of substance made by these Regulations to the 1985 Regulations are:—

(1) the inclusion of a provision enabling the Minister, by general licence, to authorise a person to market as Breeder's Seed, Pre-Basic Seed, Basic Seed, Certified Seed of the First Generation or Certified Seed of the Second Generation, seeds which have failed in some respect to satisfy the requirements relating to the sampling of such seeds set out in Schedule 5 of the 1985 Regulations (regulation 2(2)): and

(2) the inclusion of a requirement that a sample of seeds taken from a seed stream during processing for the purposes of an official examination shall be taken by an automatic sampling device approved by the Minister (regulation 2(3)(a)).

STATUTORY INSTRUMENTS

1987 No. 1092

SEEDS

The Fodder Plant Seeds (Amendment) Regulations 1987

Made - - - -	*24th June 1987*
Laid before Parliament	*6th July 1987*
Coming into force	*27th July 1987*

The Minister of Agriculture, Fisheries and Food, the Secretary of State for Scotland and the Secretary of State for Wales, acting jointly, in exercise of the powers conferred by sections 16(1), (1A), (2), (3), (4), (5) and (8), 17(1), (2), (3) and (4) and 36 of the Plant Varieties and Seeds Act 1964(**a**) and now vested in them (**b**) and of all other powers enabling them in that behalf, after consultation in accordance with the said section 16(1) with representatives of such interests as appear to them to be concerned, hereby make the following Regulations:

Title and commencement

1. These Regulations may be cited as the Fodder Plant Seeds (Amendment) Regulations 1987 and shall come into force on 27th July 1987.

Amendment

2.—(1) The Fodder Plant Seeds Regulations 1985(**c**) shall be amended in accordance with the following provisions of this regulation.

(2) In regulation 3 (interpretation)–

(a) in paragraph (3)–

    (i) in sub-paragraph (b) of the definitions of "Pre-basic Seed", "Basic Seed" and "Certified Seed of the First Generation" for the words "First, Second or Third Generations" there shall be substituted the words "First or Second Generation",

    (ii) for the definition of "Certified Seed of the Second Generation" there shall be substituted the following definition–

    " "Certified Seed of the Second Generation" means seeds of field peas or field beans–

        (a) which have been produced directly from Basic Seed, Certified Seed of the First Generation or, with the written authority of the maintainer and the Minister, from Pre-basic Seed,

        (b) which are intended for the production of plants, and

        (c) which satisfy the requirements for Certified Seed of the Second Generation set out in Schedule 4 and in respect of which an official certificate has been issued in accordance with Schedule 2;",

---

(**a**) 1964 c.14; section 16 was amended by the European Communities Act 1972 (c.68), section 4(1) and paragraph 5(1), (2) and (3) of Schedule 4.
(**b**) In the case of the Secretary of State for Wales by virtue of S.I. 1978/272.
(**c**) S.I. 1985/975.

(iii) the definition of "Certified Seed of the Third Generation" shall be omitted, and

(iv) in the definition of "Commercial Seed" in the column headed *"Legumes"* the words "Field bean" shall be omitted; and

(b) in paragraph (4) for the words "regulation 5(1)(b)(ii) or (iii) below" there shall be substituted the words "regulation 5(1)(b), (c) or (d) below".

(3) In regulation 5 (marketing of seeds)–

(a) for paragraph (1) there shall be substituted the following paragraph–

"(1) Subject to the provisions of this regulation, no person shall market any seeds unless they are marketed in seed lots or in parts of seed lots and unless they are–

(a) Commercial Seed, or

(b) seeds of plant varieties which may, for the time being, be marketed in accordance with regulation 31 of the Seeds (National Lists of Varieties) Regulations 1982 and which are Breeder's Seed, Pre-basic Seed, Basic Seed, Certified Seed, Certified Seed of the First Generation or Certified Seed of the Second Generation, or

(c) seeds which have been produced and packaged in a Member State other than the United Kingdom, which have been labelled appropriately in accordance with the requirements of regulation 9(1), (2), (3), (4), (5), (6) and (8) and which–

(i) in the case of a small package of seeds, a small EEC A package of seeds or a small EEC B package of seeds, have been sealed in accordance with the requirements of regulation 8(3), or

(ii) in the case of all other seeds, have been officially sealed in a Member State other than the United Kingdom, or

(d) seeds which have been produced elsewhere than in a Member State and which are marketed in accordance with, and subject to, the conditions imposed by a general licence granted by the Ministers under the authority of this sub-paragraph, which licence shall have effect during the period specified in it unless the Ministers earlier revoke it.";

(b) in paragraph (3)(a)–

(i) the words "Certified Seed of the Third Generation" shall be omitted, and

(ii) for the words "in Schedule 4" there shall be substituted the words "in Schedule 4 or Schedule 5,";

(c) in paragraph (3)(e) for the words "or Certified Seed of the Third Generation" there shall be substituted the words "or seeds of any kind as Certified Seed of the Third Generation,";

(d) in paragraph (9) for the words "Basic Seed, Certified Seed of the First Generation or Certified Seed of the Second Generation" there shall be substituted the words "Basic Seed or Certified Seed of the First Generation"; and

(e) after paragraph (13) there shall be inserted the following paragraph–

"(14) In paragraph (3)(e) above "Certified Seed of the Third Generation" means seeds–

(a) which have been produced directly from Basic Seed, Certified Seed, Certified Seed of the First or Second Generation or, with the written authority of the maintainer and the Minister, from Pre-basic Seed, and

(b) which are intended for the production of plants.".

(4) In regulations 6(1) (official certificates), 8(1) (sealing of packages), 9(2)(a) and (3) (labelling of packages) and in paragraph 1 of Schedule 2 (official certificates) the words "Certified Seed of the Third Generation" shall be omitted.

(5) In Schedule 4 (requirements for basic seed, certified seed, certified seed of the first, second and third generations and commercial seed)–

(a) in the heading, for the words "FIRST, SECOND AND THIRD GENERA-TIONS" there shall be substituted the words "FIRST AND SECOND GENERATIONS";

(b) in Part I–

    (i) after paragraph 6 there shall be inserted the following paragraph–

        "**6A.** Field pea crops grown for the production of Pre-basic Seed, Basic Seed, Certified Seed of the First Generation or Certified Seed of the Second Generation shall be isolated by 50 metres, throughout their whole growing period, from all other pea crops not being grown for such production".,

    (ii) for paragraph 7(b) there shall be substituted the following paragraph–

		Crop Area	
"(b) "Field beans. Crops to produce	—	up to 2 hectares	over 2 hectares
Basic Seed and Certified Seed			
1st generation		200m	100m
Certified Seed 2nd generation		100m	50m", and

    (iii) in paragraph 8, in the heading of the table for the words "First, Second and Third Generations" there shall be substituted the words "First and Second Generations";

(c) in Part II–

    (i) in paragraph 1 for the words "First, Second and Third Generations" there shall be substituted the words "First and Second Generations",

    (ii) after paragraph 4 there shall be inserted the following paragraph–
"Pea bacterial blight

        4A. For each seed lot of Breeder's Seed, Pre-basic Seed, Basic Seed and Certified Seed of the First Generation of field peas 1 kg shall be officially examined from a submitted sample of 2 kg thereof for the presence of *Pseudomonas syringae* p.v. *pisi* infection and the level of infection therefrom found to be nil.",

    (iii) in paragraph 5, in the heading of column (6) of the second table for the words "First, Second and Third Generations" there shall be substituted the words "First and Second Generations",

    (iv) in paragraph 5, in column (7) of the second table for the entry "1.5" in relation to Field bean there shall be substituted the entry "e",

    (v) in paragraph 6, in the heading of column (14) of the second table for "1st, 2nd or 3rd Generations" there shall be substituted "1st or 2nd Generations", and

    (vi) in paragraph 6, in column (15) of the second table for the entry "1.3" in relation to Field beans there shall be substituted the entry "t"; and

(d) at the end of Part III there shall be added the following–
"PEA BACTERIAL BLIGHT STANDARDS

    Certified Seed of the Second Generation shall be free from *Pseudomonas syringae* p.v. *pisi* infection".

(6) In Schedule 5 (sampling of seed lots)–

(a) in Part I–

    (i) in paragraph 9, after the words "automatic sampling device" there shall be inserted the words "approved by the Minister", and

    (ii) in paragraph 11(i), in the table after the words "vetches, sainfoin (fruit)" there shall be added the words "ryegrasses, cocksfoot, tall and meadow fescues and tall oatgrass", and

(b) in Part II–

    (i) after the words "The maximum weight of a seed lot and minimum weight of a submitted sample shall be as indicated below" there shall be inserted the words "save that the maximum lot weights in paragraphs a., b. and c. below may be exceeded by not more than 5%:–", and

    (ii) in paragraph a.(ii) for "1st, 2nd and 3rd Generations" there shall be substituted "1st and 2nd Generations".

(7) In Part I of Schedule 6 (official labels)–

   (a) in the heading of paragraph C for the words "FIRST, SECOND AND THIRD GENERATIONS" there shall be substituted the words "FIRST AND SECOND GENERATIONS",

   (b) in paragraphs C(a)11 and (c) for the words "Certified Seed of the Second and Third Generations" there shall be substituted the words "Certified Seed of the Second Generation", and

   (c) in the heading of paragraph F for the word "ON" there shall be substituted the word "IN".

In Witness whereof the Official Seal of the Minister of Agriculture, Fisheries and Food is hereunto affixed on 22nd June 1987.

                                            John MacGregor
               Minister of Agriculture, Fisheries and Food

                                  Sanderson of Bowden

24th June 1987   Minister of State, Scottish Office

                                      Peter Walker
                            Secretary of State for Wales

24th June 1987

EXPLANATORY NOTE

(This note is not part of the Regulations)

These Regulations, which amend the Fodder Plant Seeds Regulations 1985, implement article 2 of Commission Directive 87/120/EEC (OJ No. L49, 18.2.87, p.41) in so far as it amends Annex III of Council Directive 66/401/EEC (OJ No. 125, 11.7.66, p.2298/66) (OJ/SE 1965–66, p.132) (as amended) on the marketing of fodder plant seeds by providing that the maximum weight of a seed lot, set out in that Annex, from which a sample is to be drawn for certification shall not be exceeded by more than 5% (regulation 6(b)(ii)).

These Regulations also implement article 1 of Commission Directive 86/109/EEC (OJ No. L93, 8.4.86, p.21) in so far as it amends Council Directive 66/401/EEC by prohibiting the placing on the market in Member States seed of *Vicia faba* L. (partim) (field bean) of the Commercial seed category (regulation 2(2)(a)(iv)).

The other changes of substance made by these Regulations to the 1985 Regulations are–

(1) the omission of provisions enabling seeds of field peas and field beans to be marketed as Certified Seed of the Third Generation;

(2) the alteration of the isolation distances for field beans grown to produce Certified Seed of the Second Generation (regulation 2(5)(b)(ii);

(3) the inclusion of a requirement that field pea crops must be isolated by 50 metres, throughout the whole of their growing period, from all other kinds of pea crops (regulation 2(5)(b)(i));

(4) the inclusion of a requirement that a sample of field peas must be found to be free from *Pseudomonas syringae* p.v. *pisi* (pea bacterial blight) infection before they can be certified as Breeder's Seed, Pre-basic Seed, Basic Seed or Certified Seed of the First Generation (regulation 2(5)(c)(ii)) and the inclusion of a marketing standard of freedom from pea bacterial blight for Certified Seed of the Second Generation (regulation 2(5)(d)); and

(5) the inclusion of a requirement that a sample of seeds taken from a seed stream during processing for the purposes of an official examination shall be taken by an automatic sampling device approved by the Minister (regulation 2(6)(a)(i)).

STATUTORY INSTRUMENTS

1987 No. 1093

SEEDS

The Vegetable Seeds (Amendment) Regulations 1987

Made - - - -	*24th June 1987*
Laid before Parliament	*6th July 1987*
Coming into force	*27th July 1987*

The Minister of Agriculture, Fisheries and Food, the Secretary of State for Scotland and the Secretary of State for Wales, acting jointly, in exercise of the powers conferred by sections 16(1), (1A), (2), (3), (4), (5) and (8), 17(1), (2), (3) and (4) and 36 of the Plant Varieties and Seeds Act 1964(a) and now vested in them(b) and of all other powers enabling them in that behalf, after consultation in accordance with the said section 16(1) with representatives of such interests as appear to them to be concerned, hereby make the following Regulations:

Title and commencement

1. These Regulations may be cited as the Vegetable Seeds (Amendment) Regulations 1987 and shall come into force on 27th July 1987.

Amendment

2. The Vegetable Seeds Regulations 1985(c) shall be amended as follows–

(a) in paragraph (3)(a) of regulation 5 (marketing of seeds) for the words "in Schedule 4," there shall be substituted the words "in Schedule 4 or Schedule 5,";

(b) in regulation 9(5) (labelling of packages) the words "of at least the minimum size and" shall be omitted;

(c) in Part II of Schedule 4 (requirements for basic seed, certified seed and standard seed), in paragraph 2(a), in the fourth column of the table for the entry "70" in relation to Calabrese and Sprouting broccoli there shall be substituted the entry "75"; and

(d) in Schedule 5 (sampling of seed lots)–

(i) in Part I, in paragraph 9 after the words "an automatic sampling device" there shall be inserted the words "approved by the Minister", and

(ii) in Part II, for the words "The maximum weight of a seed lot and minimum weight of a submitted sample shall be as indicated below:–" there shall be substituted the following words–

"The maximum weight of a seed lot shall be as indicated below (or a weight which does not exceed that indicated below by more than 5%) and the minimum weight of a submitted sample shall be as indicated below:–".

(a) 1964 c.14; section 16 was amended by the European Communities Act 1972 (c.68), section 4(1) and paragraph 5(1), (2) and (3) of Schedule 4.
(b) In the case of the Secretary of State for Wales by virtue of S.I. 1978/272.
(c) S.I. 1985/979.

In Witness whereof the Official Seal of the Minister of Agriculture, Fisheries and Food is hereunto affixed on 22nd June 1987.

John MacGregor
Minister of Agriculture, Fisheries and Food

24th June 1987

Sanderson of Bowden
Minister of State, Scottish Office

24th June 1987

Peter Walker
Secretary of State for Wales

EXPLANATORY NOTE

(This note is not part of the Regulations)

These Regulations, which amend the Vegetable Seeds Regulations 1985, implement article 5 of Commission Directive 87/120/EEC (OJ No. 449, 18.2.87, p.43) in so far as it amends Annex III of Council Directive 70/458/EEC (OJ No. L225, 12.10.70, p.7) (as amended) on the marketing of vegetable seeds by providing that the maximum weight of a seed lot set out in that Annex for which a sample is to be drawn for certification shall not be exceeded by more than 5% (regulation 2(d)(ii)).

The other changes of substance made by these Regulations to the 1985 Regulations are–

(1) the deletion of the minimum size of a supplier label for small packages of Certified or Standard Seed (regulation 2(b)); and

(2) the inclusion of a requirement that a sample of seeds taken from a seed stream during processing for the purposes of an official examination shall be taken by an automatic sampling device approved by the Minister (regulation 2(d)(i)).

STATUTORY INSTRUMENTS

1987 No. 1094

OFFSHORE INSTALLATIONS

The Offshore Installations (Safety Zones) (No. 46) Order 1987

Made	-	-	-	*24th June 1987*
Coming into force				*26th June 1987*

The Secretary of State, in exercise of the powers conferred on him by section 21(1), (2) and (3) of the Oil and Gas (Enterprise) Act 1982(a) (hereinafter referred to as "the Act"), and of all other powers enabling him in that behalf, hereby makes the following Order:–

1. This Order may be cited as the Offshore Installations (Safety Zones) (No. 46) Order 1987 and shall come into force on 26th June 1987.

2.—(1) A safety zone is hereby established around the installation specified in Column 1 of the Schedule hereto (being an installation maintained in waters to which section 21 of the Act(b) applies) having a radius of five hundred metres from the point as respects that installation which has the co-ordinates of latitude and longitude according to European Datum (1950) specified in Columns 2 and 3 of the Schedule.

(2) The prohibition under section 21(3) of the Act on a vessel entering or remaining in a safety zone without the consent of the Secretary of State shall not apply to a vessel entering or remaining in the safety zone established under paragraph (1) above –

- (a) in connection with the laying, inspection, testing, repair, alteration, renewal or removal of any submarine cable or pipe-line in or near that safety zone;
- (b) to provide services for, to transport persons or goods to or from, or under the authority of a government department to inspect, any installation in that safety zone;
- (c) if it is a vessel belonging to a general lighthouse authority performing duties relating to the safety of navigation;
- (d) in connection with the saving or attempted saving of life or property;
- (e) owing to stress of weather; or
- (f) when in distress.

24th June 1987

Peter Morrison
Minister of State, Department of Energy

(a) 1982 c.23.   (b) *See* section 21(9).

SCHEDULE

Article 2(1)

SAFETY ZONE

(1) *Name or other designation* *of the offshore installation*	(2) *Latitude* *North*	(3) *Longitude* *East*
Vulcan I 49/21–PRD	53° 14′ 52.16″	02° 01′ 28.26″

EXPLANATORY NOTE

(This note is not part of the Order)

This Order establishes, under section 21 of the Oil and Gas (Enterprise) Act 1982, a safety zone, having a radius of 500 metres from a specified point, around the installation specified in the Schedule to this Order and maintained in waters to which the section applies (these include territorial waters and waters in areas designated under section 1(7) of the Continental Shelf Act 1964 (c.29)).

Vessels (which for this purpose include hovercraft, submersible apparatus and installations in transit) are prohibited from entering or remaining in the safety zone except with the consent of the Secretary of State or in the circumstances mentioned in article 2(2) of the Order.

STATUTORY INSTRUMENTS

1987 No. 1095

OFFSHORE INSTALLATIONS

The Offshore Installations (Safety Zones) (No. 47) Order 1987

Made - - - -	*24th June 1987*
Coming into force	*26th June 1987*

The Secretary of State, in exercise of the powers conferred on him by section 21(1), (2) and (3) of the Oil and Gas (Enterprise) Act 1982(a) (hereinafter referred to as "the Act"), and of all other powers enabling him in that behalf, hereby makes the following Order:–

1. This Order may be cited as the Offshore Installations (Safety Zones) (No. 47) Order 1987 and shall come into force on 26th June 1987.

2.—(1) A safety zone is hereby established around the installation specified in Column 1 of the Schedule hereto (being an installation maintained in waters to which section 21 of the Act(b) applies) having a radius of five hundred metres from the point as respects that installation which has the co-ordinates of latitude and longitude according to European Datum (1950) specified in Columns 2 and 3 of the Schedule.

(2) The prohibition under section 21(3) of the Act on a vessel entering or remaining in a safety zone without the consent of the Secretary of State shall not apply to a vessel entering or remaining in the safety zone established under paragraph (1) above –

  (a) in connection with the laying, inspection, testing, repair, alteration, renewal or removal of any submarine cable or pipe-line in or near that safety zone;

  (b) to provide services for, to transport persons or goods to or from, or under the authority of a government department to inspect, any installation in that safety zone;

  (c) if it is a vessel belonging to a general lighthouse authority performing duties relating to the safety of navigation;

  (d) in connection with the saving or attempted saving of life or property;

  (e) owing to stress of weather; or

  (f) when in distress.

Peter Morrison
Minister of State, Department of Energy

24th June 1987

(a) 1982 c.23. (b) *See* section 21(9).

SCHEDULE

Article 2(1)

SAFETY ZONE

(1) *Name or other designation* *of the offshore installation*	(2) *Latitude* *North*	(3) *Longitude* *East*
Vanguard 49/16–PQD	53° 22′ 41.77″	02° 06′ 42.26″

EXPLANATORY NOTE

(This note is not part of the Order)

This Order establishes, under section 21 of the Oil and Gas (Enterprise) Act 1982, a safety zone, having a radius of 500 metres from a specified point, around the installation specified in the Schedule to this Order and maintained in waters to which the section applies (these include territorial waters and waters in areas designated under section 1(7) of the Continental Shelf Act 1964 (c.29)).

Vessels (which for this purpose include hovercraft, submersible apparatus and installations in transit) are prohibited from entering or remaining in the safety zone except with the consent of the Secretary of State or in the circumstances mentioned in article 2(2) of the Order.

1987 No. 1096 (C. 28)

SOCIAL SECURITY

The Social Security Act 1986 (Commencement No.7) Order 1987

Made - - - -   *25th June 1987*

The Secretary of State for Social Services, in exercise of the powers conferred on him by section 88(1) of the Social Security Act 1986(a) and of all other powers enabling him in that behalf, hereby makes the following order:–

Citation and interpretation

1.—(1) This Order may be cited as the Social Security Act 1986 (Commencement No.7) Order 1987.

(2) In this Order, unless the context otherwise requires, references to sections and Schedules are references to sections of and Schedules to the Social Security Act 1986.

Appointed days

2.—(1) The day appointed for the coming into force of:–

   (a) Schedule 10, paragraph 94(b) (consultation about regulations) and section 86(1) so far as it relates to it;

   (b) Schedule 10, paragraph 102 (attachment of earnings), and section 86(1) so far as it relates to it;

   (c) the repeal in Schedule 11 and section 86(2) so far as it relates to it, of Schedule 4 of the Attachment of Earnings Act 1971(b) and Schedule 2 paragraph 44 of the Social Security (Consequential Provisions) Act 1975(c) (attachment of earnings); and

   (d) the repeal in Schedule 11 and section 86(2) so far as it relates to it, of the reference to "7 or" in section 45(2)(a) (regulations) of the Social Security and Housing Benefits Act 1982(d),

is 26th June 1987.

(2) The day appointed for the coming into force of Schedule 10, paragraph 96 (child benefit claims and payments) and section 86(1) so far as it relates to it is 6th April 1988.

(3) The day appointed for the coming into force of paragraphs 8, 9 and 10 of Schedule 3 (abolition of industrial death benefit) and section 39 so far as it relates to those paragraphs is 10th April 1988.

(a) 1986 c.50; section 83(1) provides for section 166(1) to (3A) of the Social Security Act 1975 (c.14) (extent of powers) to apply to the powers conferred by section 88(1).
(b) 1971 c.32.
(c) 1975 c.18.
(d) 1982 c.24.

(4) The day appointed for the coming into force of the provisions of the Social Security Act 1986 which are specified in the Schedule to this Order is 11th April 1988.

Signed by authority of the Secretary of State for Social Services.

Nicholas Scott
Minister of State,
Department of Health and Social Security

25th June 1987

SCHEDULE

Article 2(4)

Provisions of the Social Security Act 1986	*Subject Matter*
Section 36	Widowhood
Section 51 for all purposes for which it is not already in force	Claims and payments
Section 65(1) to (3)	Reciprocal arrangements
Section 66 and Schedule 6	Pensioners' Christmas bonus
Section 78	Travelling expenses
Schedule 3 paragraphs 11 and 12 and section 39 so far as it relates to those pargraphs	Industrial death benefit
The following paragraphs of Schedule 10 and section 86(1) so far as it relates to those paragraphs–	Minor and consequential amendments
paragraphs 62 to 66, 67 in so far as it is not already in force, 69 and 70	(benefits under Social Security Act 1975)
paragraphs 85 and 96	(common provisions)
paragraph 101(a) in so far as it is not already in force	(tax)
paragraph 108 except in so far as it substitutes words for the reference in section 4(5) of the Forfeiture Act 1982**(a)** to the Family Income Supplements Act 1970**(b)** and Part I of the Supplementary Benefits Act 1976**(c)**	(forfeiture)
The following repeals in Schedule 11 and section 86(2) so far as it relates to those repeals–	Repeals
Pensioners and Family Income Supplement Payments Act 1972**(d)**, the whole Act except section 3 and section 4 in so far as it refers to expenses attributable to section 3	(pensioners' Christmas bonus)
Pensioners' Payments and National Insurance Contributions Act 1972**(e)**, the whole Act	
Pensioners' Payments and National Insurance Act 1973**(f)**, the whole Act, except section 7 and the Schedule to that Act	
Pensioners' Payments Act 1974**(g)**, the whole Act	
Social Security Act 1975**(h)**–	
(i) in section 12, in subsection (1), paragraph (h) and in subsection (2), the words "and widow's allowance"	(widow's allowance)
(ii) in section 13, in subsection (1) the entry relating to widow's allowance and subsection (5)(a)	

(a) 1982 c.34.
(b) 1970 c.55.
(c) 1976 c.71.
(d) 1972 c.75.
(e) 1972 c.80.
(f) 1973 c.61.
(g) 1974 c.54.
(h) 1975 c.14.

Provisions of the Social Security Act 1986	*Subject Matter*
(iii) in section 25(3), the words "and for which she is not entitled to a widow's allowance"	
(iv) in section 26(3), the words "a widow's allowance or,"	
(v) section 41(2)(e) and (2C)	(child dependants)
(vi) section 50(2)	(industrial injuries benefit)
(vii) sections 67, 68 and 70 to 75	(industrial death benefit)
(viii) sections 79 to 81	(claims and payments)
(ix) in section 82, subsections (3) and (4) and subsection (6)(a)	
(x) in section 84, subsection (3)	(persons maintaining dependants)
(xi) in section 88(a), the words from "or", in the first place where it occurs to "prescribed", in the third place where it occurs	(industrial injuries benefit)
(xii) in section 90, in subsection (2)(a), the words from "(including" to the end and in subsection (3), the references to sections 79 and 81	
(xiii) in section 101(3)(c), the words "or, in relation to industrial death benefit, the deceased"	(death benefit)
(xiv) in Schedule 3, in Part II, in paragraph 8(2), in paragraph (a), the words "other than a widow's allowance" and in paragraphs 9 and 10, the words "(other than a widow's allowance)"	(widow's allowance)
(xv) in Schedule 4, in Part I, paragraph 5, in Part IV, paragraph 4 and in Part V, paragraphs 6, 11, 13 and 15	(widow's allowance and industrial injuries benefit)
(xvi) Schedule 9	(industrial death benefit)
(xvii) in Schedule 20, the definitions of "The deceased" and "Industrial death benefit", in the definition of "Relative", the references to section 66(8) and 72(6), in the definition of "Short-term benefit" the words "and widow's allowance"	(interpretation)
Industrial Injuries and Diseases (Old Cases) Act 1975**(a)**, in section 4(4), paragraph (c)(ii) and the word "or" immediately preceding it	(claims and payments)
Social Security (Consequential Provisions) Act 1975**(b)** in Schedule 3, paragraph 18	(industrial death benefit)
Social Security Pensions Act 1975**(c)**, section 56K(4) and in Schedule 4, paragraph 51	(retirement pensions and occupational pension scheme)
Child Benefit Act 1975**(d)**, section 6(2), (4) and (5), section 8 in so far as it is not already in force, in section 15(1), the words "relating to child benefit", and in Schedule 4, paragraphs 3, 4, 6 and 27	(child benefit claims and payments)
Social Security (Miscellaneous Provisions) Act 1977**(e)**, sections 9, 17(2) and in section 22, in subsection (2), the references to section 24(2) of the Social Security Act 1975	(industrial death benefit)
Pensioners' Payments Act 1977**(f)**, the whole Act	(pensioners' Christmas bonus)
Pensioners' Payments Act 1978**(g)**, the whole Act	

(**a**) 1975 c.16.
(**b**) 1975 c.18.
(**c**) 1975 c.60.
(**d**) 1975 c.61.
(**e**) 1977 c.5.
(**f**) 1977 c.51.
(**g**) 1978 c.58.

Provisions of the Social Security Act 1986	Subject Matter
Pneumoconiosis etc (Workers' Compensation) Act 1979**(a)**, in section 2(3), the words "industrial death benefit under section 76 of the Social Security Act 1975, or"	(industrial death benefit)
Pensioners' Payments and Social Security Act 1979**(b)**, the whole Act	(pensioners' Christmas bonus)
Social Security (No.2) Act 1980**(c)**, in section 4(2), the words "and no earnings-related addition to a widow's allowance"	(widow's allowance)
Social Security and Housing Benefits Act 1982**(d)**, section 44(1)(f) and in Schedule 4, paragraph 14	(pensioners' Christmas bonus and invalidity pension)
Health and Social Security Act 1984**(e)**, section 22, in section 27(2), the words "22 and", in Schedule 4, in paragraph 3 the entry relating to section 79 and paragraph 14, and in Schedule 5, paragraphs 5 and 6	(regulations and miscellaneous other subjects)
Social Security Act 1985**(f)**, section 27(8)(e), in section 32(2), the words "section 15" and in Schedule 5, paragraph 6(a)	(regulations)

EXPLANATORY NOTE

(This note is not part of the Order)

Article 2(1) brings into force on 26th June 1987 the following provisions of the Social Security Act 1986:–
    Schedule 10, paragraph 94(b) (consultation with Occupational Pensions Board)
    Schedule 10, paragraph 102 (attachment of earnings) and
consequential repeals.

Article 2(2) brings into force on 6th April 1988 Schedule 10, paragraph 96 (child benefit claims and payments).

Article 2(3) brings into force on 10th April 1988 Schedule 3, paragraphs 8, 9 and 10 (abolition of industrial death benefit).

Article 2(4) brings into force on 11th April 1988 the provisions of the Social Security Act 1986 which are specified in the Schedule to the Order relating to:–
    section 36 (widowhood)
    section 51 (claims and payments)
    section 65(1) to (3) (reciprocal arrangements)
    section 66 and Schedule 6 (pensioners' Christmas bonus)
    section 78 (travelling expenses)
    Schedule 3, paragraphs 11 and 12 (industrial injuries and death)
and consequential amendments and repeals.

(a) 1979 c.41.
(b) 1979 c.48.
(c) 1980 c.39.
(d) 1982 c.24.
(e) 1984 c.48.
(f) 1985 c.53.

NOTE AS TO EARLIER COMMENCEMENT ORDERS

(This note is not part of the Order)

Provisions	Date of Commencement	S.I. No
s.1	4. 1.88	1987/543
s.2, Sch 1	1. 5.87	1987/543
s.3	4. 1.88	1987/543
s.4	4. 1.88	1987/543
s.5	4. 1.88	1987/543
s.6, Sch 6	6. 4.88	1987/543
s.7	6. 4.88	1987/543
s.8	1.11.86	1986/1719
s.9	6. 4.88	1987/543
s.10	6. 4.88	1987/543
s.11	6. 4.87	1986/1719
s.12 (in certain respects)	4. 1.88	1987/543
(in all other respects)	6. 4.88	1987/543
s.13	1. 5.87	1987/543
s.14	1. 5.87	1987/543
s.15 (in certain respects)	4. 1.88	1987/543
(in all other respects)	6. 4.88	1987/543
s.16	1.11.86	1986/1719
s.17	1. 5.87	1987/543
s.18(1)	6. 4.87	1987/354
s.18(2) to (6)	6. 4.88	1987/543
s.19	6. 4.88	1987/543
s.27 (partially)	6. 4.87	1986/1959
s.32 (partially)	6. 4.87	1986/1959
s.38 (partially)	6. 4.87	1986/1959
s.39, Sch 3 (partially)	1.10.86	1986/1609
(partially)	6. 4.87	1987/354
ss.40 and 41	6. 4.87	1986/1959
s.42 (with saving)	5.10.86	1986/1609
ss.43 and 44	5.10.86	1986/1609
s.46 (partially)	15. 3.87	1986/1959
(partially)	6. 4.87	1986/1959
ss.47 and 48	6. 4.87	1986/1959
s.49, Sch 4 (partially)	15. 3.87	1986/1959
(partially)	6. 4.87	1986/1959
s.50	6. 4.87	1986/1959
s.51 (partially)	1.10.86	1986/1609
(partially)	6. 4.87	1986/1959
s.52, Sch 5 (with saving)	6. 4.87	1986/1958
ss.53 to 60	6. 4.87	1986/1959
s.62	1.10.86	1986/1609
s.67 (partially)	1.10.86	1986/1609
(partially)	6. 4.87	1986/1959
ss.68 and 69	6. 4.87	1986/1959
s.71 (partially)	1.10.86	1986/1609
s.73, Sch 7 (partially)	6. 4.87	1986/1959
s.75, Sch 8	6. 4.87	1986/1959
s.79 (partially)	6. 4.87	1986/1959
(partially)	1. 5.87	1987/543
s.80 (partially)	6. 4.87	1986/1959
(partially)	1. 5.87	1987/543
s.82, Sch 9	6. 4.87	1986/1958
s.86(1), Sch 10 (partially)	1.10.86	1986/1609
(partially)	1.11.86	1986/1719
(partially)	6. 4.87	1986/1719
(partially)	6. 4.87	1986/1959
(partially)	6. 4.87	1987/354
(partially)	1. 5.87	1987/543
(partially)	4. 1.88	1987/543
(partially)	6. 4.88	1987/543

Provisions	Date of Commencement	S.I. No
s.86(2), Sch 11 (partially)	1.10.86	1986/1609
(partially)	5.10.86	1986/1609
(partially)	1.11.86	1986/1719
(partially)	6. 4.87	1986/1959
(partially)	7. 4.87	1986/1959
(partially)	6. 4.87	1987/354
(partially)	4. 1.88	1987/543
(partially)	6. 4.88	1987/543

1987 No. 1097

SEEDS

The Oil and Fibre Plant Seeds (Amendment) Regulations 1987

Made - - - -	*24th June 1987*
Laid before Parliament	*6th July 1987*
Coming into force	*27th July 1987*

The Minister of Agriculture, Fisheries and Food, the Secretary of State for Scotland and the Secretary of State for Wales, acting jointly, in exercise of the powers conferred by sections 16(1), (1A), (2), (3), (4), (5) and (8), 17(1), (2), (3) and (4) and 36 of the Plant Varieties and Seeds Act 1964(**a**) and now vested in them(**b**) and of all other powers enabling them in that behalf, after consultation in accordance with the said section 16(1) with representatives of such interests as appear to them to be concerned, hereby make the following Regulations:

Title and commencement

1. These Regulations may be cited as the Oil and Fibre Plant Seeds (Amendment) Regulations 1987 and shall come into force on 27th July 1987.

Amendment

2.—(1) The Oil and Fibre Plant Seeds Regulations 1985(**c**) shall be amended in accordance with the provisions of this regulation.

(2) In regulation 3 (interpretation)–

(a) in paragraph (3) in the definition of "Commercial Seed" for the words "white mustard or soya bean" there shall be substituted the words "or white mustard", and

(b) in paragraph (4) for the words "regulation 5(1)(b)(ii) or (iii) below" there shall be substituted the words "regulation 5(1)(b), (c) or (d) below".

(3) In regulation 5 (marketing of seeds)–

(a) for paragraph (1) there shall be substituted the following paragraph–

"(1) Subject to the provisions of this regulation, no person shall market any seeds unless they are marketed in seed lots or in parts of seed lots and unless they are–

(a) Commercial Seed, or

(b) seeds of plant varieties which may, for the time being, be marketed in accordance with regulation 31 of the Seeds (National List of Varieties) Regulations 1982 and which are Breeder's Seed, Pre-basic Seed, Basic Seed, Certified Seed, Certified Seed of the First Generation, Certified

---

(**a**) 1964 c.14; section 16 was amended by the European Communities Act 1972 (c.68), section 4(1) and paragraph 5(1), (2) and (3) of Schedule 4.
(**b**) In the case of the Secretary of State for Wales by virtue of S.I. 1978/272.
(**c**) S.I. 1985/977.

Seed of the Second Generation or Certified Seed of the Third Generation, or

(c) seeds which have been produced and packaged in a Member State other than the United Kingdom, which have been labelled appropriately in accordance with the requirements of regulation 9(1), (2), (3), (4), (5), (6) and (8) and which–

    (i) in the case of a small package of seeds, a small EEC A package of seeds or a small EEC B package of seeds, have been sealed in accordance with the requirements of regulation 8(3), or

    (ii) in the case of all other seeds, have been officially sealed in a Member State other than the United Kingdom, or

(d) seeds which have been produced elsewhere than in a Member State and which are marketed in accordance with, and subject to, the conditions imposed by a general licence granted by the Ministers under the authority of this sub-paragraph, which licence shall have effect during the period specified in it, unless the Ministers earlier revoke it."; and

(b) in paragraph (3)(a) for the words "in Schedule 4," there shall be substituted the words "in Schedule 4 or Schedule 5,".

(4) In Schedule 5 (sampling of seed lots)–

(a) in Part I, in paragraph 9 after the words "an automatic sampling device" there shall be inserted the words "approved by the Minister"; and

(b) in Part II for the words "The maximum weight of a seed lot and minimum weight of a submitted sample shall be as indicated below:–" there shall be substituted the following words–

"The maximum weight of a seed lot shall be as indicated below (or a weight which does not exceed that indicated below by more than 5%) and the minimum weight of a submitted sample shall be as indicated below:–".

In Witness whereof the Official Seal of the Minister of Agriculture, Fisheries and Food is hereunto affixed on 22nd June 1987.

John MacGregor
Minister of Agriculture, Fisheries and Food

24th June 1987

Sanderson of Bowden
Minister of State, Scottish Office

24th June 1987

Peter Walker
Secretary of State for Wales

II/1r*

EXPLANATORY NOTE

(This note is not part of the Regulations)

These Regulations, which amend the Oil and Fibre Plant Seeds Regulations 1985, implement article 4 of Commission Directive 87/120/EEC (OJ No. L49, 18.2.87, p.42) in so far as it amends Annex III of Council Directive 66/208/EEC (OJ No. L169, 10.7.69, p.3) (OJ/SE 1969 (ii), p.315) (as amended) on the marketing of oil and fibre plant seeds by providing that the maximum weight of a seed lot, set out in that Annex, from which a sample is to be drawn for certification shall not be exceeded by more than 5% (regulation 2(4)(b)).

These Regulations also implement article 1 of Commission Directive 86/109/EEC (OJ No. L93, 8.4.86, p.21) in so far as it amends Council Directive 66/208/EEC by prohibiting the placing on the market in Member States seed of *Glycine max* (L) Merr. (soya bean) of the Commercial seed category (regulation 2(2)(a)).

The other changes of substance made by these Regulations to the 1985 Regulations are—

(1) the provisions enabling Ministers, to grant equivalence by general licence for seeds produced elsewhere than in a Member State has been extended to seeds of the Commercial seed category (regulation 2(3)(a)); and

(2) the inclusion of a requirement that a sample of seeds taken from a seed stream during processing for the purposes of an official examination shall be taken by an automatic sampling device approved by the Minister (regulation 2(4)(a)).

STATUTORY INSTRUMENTS

1987 No. 1098

SEEDS

The Seeds (Registration, Licensing and Enforcement) (Amendment) Regulations 1987

Made - - - -		*24th June 1987*
Laid before Parliament		*6th July 1987*
Coming into force		*27th July 1987*

The Minister of Agriculture, Fisheries and Food, the Secretary of State for Scotland and the Secretary of State for Wales, acting jointly, in exercise of the powers conferred by sections 16(1), (1A), (3), (4) and (8), 24(5), 26(2) and (3) and 36 of the Plant Varieties and Seeds Act 1964(a) and now vested in them(b) and of all other powers enabling them in that behalf, after consultation in accordance with the said section 16(1) with representatives of such interests as appear to them to be concerned, hereby make the following Regulations:–

Title and commencement

1. These Regulations may be cited as the Seeds (Registration, Licensing and Enforcement) (Amendment) Regulations 1987 and shall come into force on 27th July 1987.

Amendment

2. The Seeds (Registration, Licensing and Enforcement) Regulations 1985(c) shall be amended as follows:–

(a) in regulation 9 (licensing of seed testing stations) after paragraph (1) there shall be inserted the following paragraph:–

"(1A) An establishment licensed under paragraph (1) above shall not derive any private gain in carrying out any tests on seeds for the purposes of seeds regulations (other than any fees payable under such regulations).";

(b) in regulation 10 (licensing of seed samplers and crop inspectors) after paragraph (3) there shall be inserted the following paragraph:–

"(3A) A person licensed under paragraph (1) above to be a seed sampler or a crop inspector shall not derive any private gain (other than any fees payable under seeds regulations) in carrying out the functions of a seed sampler or a crop inspector, as the case may be, specified in the licence."; and

(c) in Part II of Schedule 4 (certificates of the results of tests of seeds) after the table relating to the results of tests for varietal purity there shall be inserted the following–

"Result of test for *Pseudomonas syringae* p.v. *pisi* infection:".

(a) 1964 c.14: section 16 was amended by the European Communities Act 1972 (c.68), section 4(1) and paragraph 5(1), (2) and (3) of Schedule 4.
(b) In the case of the Secretary of State for Wales by virtue of S.I. 1978/272.
(c) S.I. 1985/980.

In Witness whereof the Official Seal of the Minister of Agriculture, Fisheries and Food is hereunto affixed on 22nd June 1987.

John MacGregor
Minister of Agriculture, Fisheries and Food

24th June 1987

Sanderson of Bowden
Minister of State, Scottish Office

24th June 1987

Peter Walker
Secretary of State for Wales

EXPLANATORY NOTE

(This note is not part of the Regulations)

These Regulations amend the Seeds (Registration, Licensing and Enforcement) Regulations 1985 by providing that (1) seed testing stations licensed to test seeds for the purposes of seeds regulations shall not derive any private gain in carrying out such tests (other than any fees payable under seeds regulations) and (2) licensed crop inspectors and seed samplers shall not derive any private gain in carrying out their functions (other than any fees payable under seeds regulations) (regulation 2(a) and (b)).

The Regulations implement in part Council Directive 66/401/EEC (as amended) (OJ No. 125, 11.7.66, p.2298/66) (OJ/SE 1965–66, p.132) on the marking of fodder plant seed, Council Directive 66/402/EEC (as amended) (OJ No. 125, 11.7.66, p.2309/66) (OJ/SE 1965–66, p.143) on the marketing of cereal seed, Council Directive 69/208/EEC (OJ No. L169, 10.7.69, p.3) (OJ/SE 1969 (ii), p.315) on the marketing of seeds of oil and fibre plants, Council Directive 70/458/EEC (OJ No. L225, 12.10.70, p.7) on the marketing of vegetable seeds and Council Directive 66/400/EEC (OJ No. L125, 11.7.66, p.2290/66) (OJ/SE 1965–66, p.143) on the marketing of beet seed, all of which Directives require that a person carrying out the testing, sampling and inspection of seeds for the purposes of those Directives shall not derive any private gain from such activities.

The Regulations also amend the form of certificate prescribed by the 1985 Regulations of the result of a test of a sample of seeds carried out for the enforcement of seeds regulations so as to include reference to the result of a test for pea bacterial blight infection (regulation 2(c)).

STATUTORY INSTRUMENTS

1987 No. 1099

PENSIONS

The Contracting-out (Transfer) Amendment Regulations 1987

Made - - - -	*25th June 1987*
Laid before Parliament	*6th July 1987*
Coming into force	
For the purposes of all the regulations to the extent that they relate to money purchase contracted-out schemes	*6th April 1988*
For all other purposes	*27th July 1987*

The Secretary of State for Social Services, in exercise of the powers conferred upon him by section 168(1) of, and Schedule 20 to, the Social Security Act 1975 (**a**) and sections 38(1) to (1C) and 62(4) of the Social Security Pensions Act 1975 (**b**) and of all other powers enabling him in that behalf, by this instrument, which is made before the end of a period of 12 months from the commencement of the enactment under which it is made, makes the following Regulations:

Citation, commencement and interpretation

1.—(1) These Regulations may be cited as the Contracting-out (Transfer) Amendment Regulations 1987 and shall come into force–

(a) for all purposes in relation to money purchase contracted-out schemes on 6th April 1988, and

(b) for all other purposes on 27th July 1987.

(2) In these Regulations "the principal Regulations" means the Contracting-out (Transfer) Regulations 1985 (**c**).

Amendment of regulation 1(2) of the principal Regulations

2.—(1) Regulation 1(2) of the principal Regulations (interpretation) shall be amended in accordance with the provisions of paragraphs (2) to (10) of this regulation.

(2) After the definition of "the Act" there shall be inserted the following definitions–

" "appropriate personal pension scheme" shall be construed in accordance with Part I of the Social Security Act 1986;

"appropriate policy" means a policy of insurance or an annuity contract such as is described in section 52C(4) of the Act;".

(**a**) 1975 c.14. *See* definitions of "prescribe" and "regulations" in Schedule 20. Section 168(1) applies, by virtue of section 66(2) of the Social Security Pensions Act 1975 (c.60), to the exercise of certain powers conferred by that Act.

(**b**) 1975 c.60; section 38(1) was substituted by the Social Security Act 1986 (c.50), section 86 and paragraph 18 of Schedule 10; section 38(1A) to (1C) was inserted by the Health and Social Security Act 1984 (c.48), section 19.

(**c**) S.I. 1985/1323, amended by S.I. 1986/317, 1716.

(3) After the definition of "the principal regulations" there shall be inserted the following definition–

" "protected rights" has the meaning given by Schedule 1 to the Social Security Act 1986, or where the rights are under a money purchase contracted-out scheme, or a section 49 money purchase scheme, that Schedule as modified by section 32(2B);".

(4) For the definition of "scheme" there shall be substituted the following definition–

" "scheme" means occupational pension scheme or personal pension scheme;".

(5) After the definition of "scheme" there shall be inserted the following definitions–

" "contracted-out salary related scheme" means an occuptional pension scheme which is contracted-out by virtue of section 32(2);

"money purchase contracted-out scheme" has the same meaning as in section 66(1);"(a).

(6) In the definition of "overseas scheme" for "a scheme" there shall be substituted "an occupational pension scheme which is neither one contracted-out by virtue of section 32 nor one which the Board is under a duty to supervise in accordance with section 49, and;"

(7) In the definition of "receiving scheme"–

(a) after "regulation 2" there shall be inserted ", or 2A,";
(b) after "section 44" there shall be inserted ", or to which a transfer payment in respect of rights is made in accordance with regulation 2B".

(8) After the definition of "receiving scheme" there shall be inserted the following definitions–

" "section 49 money purchase scheme" means a scheme which was formerly a money purchase contracted-out scheme and which the Board are under a duty to supervise in accordance with section 49;

"section 49 salary related scheme" means a scheme which was formerly a contracted-out salary related scheme and which the Board are under a duty to supervise in accordance with section 49;".

(9) For the definition of "transferring scheme" there shall be substituted the following definition–

" "transferring scheme" means–

(a) a contracted-out salary related scheme; or
(b) a section 49 salary related scheme,

from which rights are, or liability is, transferred, or from which a transfer payment is made to a receiving scheme;".

(10) After the definition of "transferring scheme" there shall be inserted the following definition–

" "transferring policy" means an appropriate policy from which accrued rights to guaranteed minimum pensions are transferrred, or from which a transfer payment is made, to a receiving scheme;".

Amendment of regulation 2 of the principal Regulations and of the heading to that regulation

3.—(1) In the heading to regulation 2 of the principal Regulations (transfers of accrued rights to and liability for payment of guaranteed minimum pensions from contracted-out schemes) for "*contracted-out schemes*" there shall be substituted "**contracted-out salary related schemes and section 49 salary related schemes**".

(2) Regulation 2 of the principal Regulations shall be amended as follows–

(a) in paragraph (1)–

(i) for "contracted-out scheme" there shall be substituted "contracted-out salary related scheme or a section 49 salary related scheme", and

---

(a) The definition is inserted in section 66(1) of the Social Security Pensions Act 1975 (c.60) by the Social Security Act 1986 (c.50), section 6 and Schedule 2, paragraph 11(b) from the 6th April 1988 (*see* the Social Security Act 1986 (Commencement No.6) Order 1987 (S.I. 1987/543), article 2(3) and Part III of the Schedule).

(ii) for "in paragraphs (2) to (5)" there shall be substituted "in paragraphs (2) to (5A)";

(b) in paragraphs (2), (4) and (5), for "another contracted-out scheme" there shall be substituted "a contracted-out salary related scheme or to a section 49 salary related scheme";

(c) in paragraph (3)–

(i) for "to a scheme which is not a contracted-out scheme" there shall be substituted "to an overseas scheme", and

(ii) there shall be omitted "in either of the paragraphs";

and

(d) after paragraph (5) there shall be inserted the following paragraph–

"(5A) A transfer to a section 49 salary related scheme may be made where it is approved by the Board whether or not subject to conditions;".

Insertion of regulations 2A and 2B into the principal Regulations

4. After regulation 2 of the principal Regulations there shall be inserted the following regulations–

"Transfer of accrued rights to guaranteed minimum pensions from policies of insurance or annuity contracts

2A.—(1) There may be made from an appropriate policy to a contracted-out salary related scheme or to a section 49 salary related scheme a transfer in respect of an earner's accrued rights to guaranteed minimum pensions which are appropriately secured by that policy for the purposes of section 52C, in the circumstances set out in paragraph (2) and subject to the conditions mentioned in paragraphs (3) to (5), and in paragraphs (2) to (5) "a transfer" means a transfer such as is described in this paragraph.

(2) a transfer may be made–

(a) to a contracted-out salary related scheme; or

(b) to a section 49 salary related scheme,

where the earner has consented to it in writing and has entered employment with an employer who is, or in the case of a transfer to a section 49 salary related scheme is or was, a contributor to the scheme.

(3) The receiving scheme must not make provision under section 35(7) (exclusion of guaranteed minimum pension from revaluation under section 21), or any analogous provision, in relation to those rights where the effect would be to increase them at a different rate from that at which they would have been increased had the transfer not have taken place.

(4) Subject to paragraph (3), where the earner has not entered employment which is contracted-out by reference to the receiving scheme, then that scheme must provide for pensions to be paid which are of at least equal value to the annuity which would have been payable by the transferring policy, had the transfer not have taken place, in respect of the earner's accrued rights to guaranteed minimum pensions.

(5) A transfer to a section 49 salary related scheme may be made where it is approved by the Board, whether or not subject to conditions.

Transfer payments in respect of accrued rights to guaranteed minimum pensions made from contracted-out salary related schemes, section 49 salary related schemes and policies of insurance or annuity contracts

2B.—(1) There may be made from a contracted-out salary related scheme, a section 49 salary related scheme or an appropriate policy to a money purchase contracted-out scheme, to a section 49 money purchase scheme or to an appropriate personal pension scheme, a transfer payment in respect of the accrued rights of an earner to–

(a) guaranteed minimum pensions under the transferring scheme; or

(b) guaranteed minimum pensions which are appropriately secured for the purposes of section 52C under the transferring policy, in the circumstances and subject to the conditions mentioned in paragraphs (2) to (4), and in those paragraphs a "transfer payment" means a transfer payment such as is described in this paragraph.

(2) A transfer payment may be made to a money purchase contracted-out scheme–

    (a) in the circumstances described in paragraphs 1 and 2 of Schedule 1A; and

    (b) on the conditions specified in paragraphs 1 and 2 of Schedule 2A.

(3) A transfer payment may be made to a section 49 money purchase scheme–

    (a) in the circumstances described in paragraphs 1 and 3 of Schedule 1A; and

    (b) on the conditions specified in paragraphs 1, 2 and 3 of Schedule 2A.

(4) A transfer payment may be made to an appropriate personal pension scheme–

    (a) in the circumstances described in paragraph 1 of Schedule 1A; and

    (b) on the conditions specified in paragraphs 1 and 2 of Schedule 2A.

(5) References in Schedules 1A and 2A to "the earner" are references to the earner referred to in paragraph (1).".

Amendment of regulation 3 of the principal Regulations

5. Regulation 3 of the principal Regulations shall be amended as follows–

    (a) for "a formerly contracted-out scheme" there shall be substituted, "a formerly contracted-out salary related scheme";

    (b) on the first occasion on which it appears, and in paragraph (d), for "a contracted-out scheme" there shall be substituted "a contracted-out salary related scheme or a section 49 salary related scheme"; and

    (c) in paragraphs (b) and (c), for "to a contracted-out scheme" there shall be substituted "to a contracted-out salary related scheme or to a section 49 salary related scheme".

Insertion of regulation 3A into the principal Regulations

6. After regulation 3 of the principal Regulations, there shall be inserted the following regulation–

"Modifications of Part III of the Act on transfers from policies of insurance or annuity contracts

3A. Where a transfer in respect of an earner's accrued rights to guaranteed minimum pensions has taken place from an appropriate policy in accordance with regulation 2A, Part III of the Act shall have effect subject to the following modifications–

    (a) where the earner has entered employment which is contracted-out by reference to the receiving scheme, the modifications of section 35(1) and (8) specified in paragraphs 2 and 3 of Schedule 3A;

    (b) where the earner has entered employment which is not contracted-out by reference to the receiving scheme, the modifications of sections 26(2), 35(8), 38(3) and 48 specified in paragraphs 1, 3, 4 and 5 of Schedule 3A.".

Amendment of the headings to Part I and Part II of Schedule 1 to the principal Regulations

7. The headings to Part I and II of Schedule 1 to the principal Regulations (circumstances in which a transfer may be made under regulation 2) shall be amended as follows–

    (a) in the heading to Part I, for "ANOTHER CONTRACTED-OUT SCHEME" there shall be substituted "A CONTRACTED-OUT SALARY RELATED SCHEME OR A SECTION 49 SALARY RELATED SCHEME"; and

    (b) in the heading to Part II, for "A SCHEME WHICH IS NOT A CONTRACTED-OUT SCHEME" there shall be substituted "AN OVERSEAS SCHEME".

Amendment of Schedule 1 to the principal Regulations

8.   In paragraph 4 of Schedule 1 to the principal Regulations (circumstances in which a transfer may be made under regulation 2), there shall be omitted "the receiving scheme is an overseas scheme".

Insertion of Schedule 1A into the principal Regulations

9.   After Schedule 1 of the principal Regulations there shall be inserted the following Schedule–

"

SCHEDULE 1A   Regulation 2B

CIRCUMSTANCES IN WHICH A TRANSFER PAYMENT MAY BE MADE UNDER REGULATION 2B

1.   The earner consents to the tansfer payment being made.

2.   The earner has entered employment with an employer who is a contributor to the receiving scheme.

3.   The earner has entered employment with an employer who is or was a contributor to the receiving scheme.".

Insertion of Schedule 2A into the principal Regulations

10.   After Schedule 2 of the principal Regulations there shall be inserted the following Schedule–

"

SCHEDULE 2A   Regulation 2B

CONDITIONS ON WHICH A TRANSFER PAYMENT MAY BE MADE UNDER REGULATION 2B

1.   The transferring scheme or the transferring policy makes a transfer payment (whether or not it forms part of a larger payment in respect of both guaranteed minimum pensions and other accrued rights) of an amount at least equal to the cash value of the earner's accrued rights to guaranteed minimum pensions, as calculated and verified in a manner consistent with Regulations made under paragraph 14 of Schedule 1A to the Act.

2.   The receiving scheme makes provision that the transfer payment will be applied so as to provide money purchase benefits for or in respect of the earner under the scheme.

3.   The transfer payment is approved by the Board whether or not subject to conditions.".

Amendment of Schedule 3 to the principal Regulations

11.   In paragraph 6(a) of Schedule 3 to the principal Regulations (modifications of provisions of Part III of the Act, applying in cases specified in regulation 3), after "the transferring scheme is ceasing" there shall be inserted "or has ceased".

Insertion of Schedule 3A into the principal Regulations

12.   After Schedule 3 of the principal Regulations there shall be inserted the following Schedule–

" SCHEDULE 3A Regulation 3A

MODIFICATIONS OF PROVISIONS OF PART III OF THE ACT, APPLYING IN CASES SPECIFIED IN REGULATION 3A

1. Section 26(2) shall have effect as if–
   (a) after the words "sections 33 and 36 below" there were inserted the words "or in compliance with the condition set out in regulation 2A(4) of the Contracting-out (Transfer) Regulations 1985"; and
   (b) at the end there were added the words "or of that condition".

2. Section 35(1) shall have effect as if the reference to contracted-out employment by reference to the scheme included a reference to employment which falls to be treated as linked qualifying service by reason of section 43(2A)(a)(ii).

3. Section 35(8) shall have effect as if there were added, at the end, the words "so however that separate provision may be made for a member as regards those of his accrued rights transferred in accordance with regulation 2A of the Contracting-out (Transfer) Regulations 1985.".

4. Section 38(3) shall have effect as if, in the definition of "accrued rights", after the words "sections 33 and 36 above", there were inserted the words "or in compliance with the condition set out in regulation 2A(4) of the Contracting-out (Transfer) Regulations 1985".

5. Section 48 shall have effect as if there were omitted–
   (a) In subsection (1), the words "and the person's entitlement is in respect of his or another person's service in employment which was contracted-out by reference to that scheme"; and
   (b) subsection (2).".

Signed by authority of the Secretary of State for Social Services.

Nicholas Scott
Minister of State,
Department of Health and Social Security

25th June 1987

EXPLANATORY NOTE

(This note is not part of the Regulations)

These Regulations are all made under section 38(1) of the Social Security Pensions Act 1975 ("the 1975 Act") inserted by the Social Security Act 1986 ("the 1986 Act"), before the end of a period of 12 months from the commencement of the relevant provision as inserted. Consequently, by virtue of section 61(5) of the 1986 Act, the provisions of section 61(2) and (3) of the 1975 Act (as amended by section 86(1) of, and paragraph 94 of Schedule 10 to, the 1986 Act), which require reference to the Occupational Pensions Board ("the Board") of, and a report by the Board on, proposals to make regulations for certain purposes of both Acts, do not apply to them.

They amend the Contracting-out (Transfer) Regulations 1985 ("the principal Regulations").

Regulations 3, 5 and 11 amend regulations 2 and 3 of, and Schedule 3 to, the principal Regulations so as to provide that salary related occupational pension schemes which retain responsibility for accrued rights to guaranteed minimum pensions after ceasing to be contracted-out, and consequently remain under the supervision on the Board, may make to, or receive from, other salary related occupational pension schemes a transfer of accrued rights to guaranteed minimum pensions or the liability for payment of them. Regulations 7 and 8 make minor and consequential amendments to the principal Regulations for the same purposes.

Regulation 4 inserts regulation 2A into the principal Regulations so as to make provision for the circumstances in which, and the condition subject to which, a transfer of an earner's rights to guaranteed minimum pensions may be made from a policy of insurance or annuity contract to a salary related occupational pension scheme. (Consequential modifications to Part III of the 1975 Act are made by the insertion into the principal Regulations of regulation 3A and Schedule 3A by regulations 6 and 12 respectively).

Regulation 4 also inserts regulation 2B, and regulations 9 and 10 respectively insert Schedules 1A and 2A, into the principal Regulations so as to make provision for the circumstances in which, and the conditions subject to which, a transfer payment may be made in respect of an earner's rights to guaranteed minimum pensions by a salary related occupational pension scheme, or from a policy of insurance or annuity contract, to a money purchase occupational pension scheme or an appropriate personal pension scheme.

The remaining amendments made by these Regulations are minor or consequential.

STATUTORY INSTRUMENTS

1987 No. 1100

PENSIONS

The Contracting-out (Widowers' Guaranteed Minimum Pensions) Regulations 1987

Made - - - -	*25th June 1987*
Laid before Parliament	*6th July 1987*
Coming into force -	*6th April 1988*

The Secretary of State for Social Services, in exercise of the powers conferred upon him by section 168(1) of, and Schedule 20 to, the Social Security Act 1975(a), section 36(7A) of the Social Security Pensions Act 1975(b), and sections 9(6) and 84(1) of the Social Security Act 1986(c), and of all other powers enabling him in that behalf, by this instrument, which is made before the end of a period of 12 months from the commencement of the enactments under which it is made, makes the following Regulations:–

Citation, commencement and interpretation

1.—(1) These Regulations may be cited as the Contracting-out (Widowers' Guaranteed Minimum Pensions) Regulations 1987 and shall come into force on 6th April 1988.

(2) In these Regulations, "the principal Regulations" means the Occupational Pension Schemes (Contracting-out) Regulations 1984(d).

Amendments of the principal Regulations

2.—(1) The principal Regulations shall be amended in accordance with the provisions of this regulation.

(2) After regulation 33A, there shall be inserted the following regulations:–

"Circumstances in which widower's pension is to be payable

33B. For the purposes of section 36(7A) (for a scheme to be contracted-out it must provide for an earner's widower's pension to be payable in prescribed circumstances and for a prescribed period) the prescribed circumstances are that–

    (a) the widower and the earner were both over pensionable age when the earner died; or

    (b) the widower is entitled to child benefit (which expression has in this

---

(a) 1975 c.14. *See* definitions of "prescribe" and "regulations" in Schedule 20. Section 168(1) applies, by virtue of section 66(2) of the Social Security Pensions Act 1975 (c.60), to the exercise of certain powers conferred by that Act.
(b) 1975 c.60. Subsection (7A) was inserted into section 36 by the Social Security Act 1986 (c.50), section 9(3).
(c) 1986 c.50. *See* definitions of "prescribed" and "regulations" in section 84(1).
(d) S.I. 1984/380; the relevant amending instrument is S.I. 1985/1930.

regulation the same meaning as in the Child Benefit Act 1975**(a)**) in respect of a child who is, or residing with a child under 16 who is–

    (i) a son or daughter of the widower and the earner, or

    (ii) a child in respect of whom the earner, immediately before her death, was, or would have been if the child had not been absent from Great Britain, entitled to child benefit, or

    (iii) if the widower and the earner were residing together immediately before the earner's death, a child in respect of whom he then was, or would have been if the child had not been absent from Great Britain, entitled to child benefit;

or

  (c) the widower had attained the age of 45 either–

    (i) when the earner died, or

    (ii) during a period when the circumstances mentioned in paragraph (b) existed.

Period for which widower's pension is to be payable

33C.—(1) For the purposes of section 36(7A) the prescribed period is–

  (a) in a case where the circumstances described in paragraph (a) of regulation 33B exist, the remainder of the widower's life;

  (b) in a case where the circumstances described in paragraph (b), but not either paragraph (a) or paragraph (c), of regulation 33B exist, the period (subject to paragraph (2)) during which the circumstances described in paragraph (b) of regulation 33B continue to exist; and

  (c) in a case where the circumstances described in paragraph (c), but not paragraph (a), of regulation 33B exist, the remainder of the widower's life (subject to paragraph (2)).

(2) There is excluded from the periods prescribed under paragraph (1)(b) and (c) any period–

  (a) after the widower's remarriage under pensionable age;

  (b) during which he is under pensionable age and he and a woman to whom he is not married are living together as husband and wife;

  (c) after he has attained pensionable age if immediately before he attained that age he and a woman to whom he was not married were living together as husband and wife.

Statutory references to persons entitled to guaranteed minimum pensions—application to widowers

33D. The provisions of sections 44(1)(b) and (2)(b), 49(1) and 50(3) shall be construed as if the references to a person entitled to receive a guaranteed minimum pension included references to a person so entitled by virtue of being the widower of an earner only in the case where the earner and the widower were both over pensionable age when the earner died.".

Signed by authority of the Secretary of State for Social Services

Nicholas Scott
Minister of State,
Department of Health and Social Security

25th June 1987

(a) 1975 c.61.

EXPLANATORY NOTE

(This note is not part of the Regulations)

These Regulations are all made under provisions of the Social Security Act 1986 ("the 1986 Act") or provisions inserted into the Social Security Pensions Act 1975 ("the 1975 Act") by the 1986 Act, and are made before the end of a period of 12 months from the commencement of those provisions. Consequently, by virtue of section 61(5) of that Act, the provisions of section 61(2) and (3) of the Social Security Pensions Act 1975 (as amended by section 86(1) of, and paragraph 94 of Schedule 10 to, the 1986 Act), which require reference to the Occupational Pensions Board of, and a report by the Board on, proposals to make regulations for certain purposes of both Acts, do not apply to them.

Section 9(3) of the 1986 Act amends section 36 of the 1975 Act so that, in certain circumstances, an occupational pension scheme has to provide widowers' as well as widows' pensions if it is to be contracted-out.

Regulation 2 of these Regulations inserts into the Occupational Pension Schemes (Contracting-out) Regulations 1984 3 new regulations, 33B to 33D. Regulation 33B sets out the circumstances in which a widower's pension is to be payable: they are related to the ages of the widower and the earner, and to his entitlement (if any) to child benefit. Regulation 33C specifies the period for which a widower's pension is to be payable. Regulation 33D provides that in certain provisions of the 1975 Act, concerning schemes which have ceased to be contracted-out, the references to a person entitled to receive a guaranteed minimum pension include the widower of an earner only in the case where the earner and the widower were both over pensionable age when the earner died.

STATUTORY INSTRUMENTS

1987 No. 1101

PENSIONS

The Money Purchase Contracted-out Schemes Regulations 1987

Made - - - -	*25th June 1987*
Laid before Parliament	*6th July 1987*
Coming into force -	*6th April 1988*

The Secretary of State for Social Services, in exercise of the powers conferred upon him by section 168(1) of, and Schedule 20 to, the Social Security Act 1975(a), sections 30(1C) and 32(2D) of the Social Security Pensions Act 1975(b), and sections 2 and 84(1) of the Social Security Act 1986(c) and paragraphs 3 and 6 of Schedule 1 to that Act as modified by section 32(2B) of the Social Security Pensions Act 1975, and of all other powers enabling him in that behalf, by this instrument, which is made before the end of a period of 12 months from the commencement of the enactments under which it is made, makes the following Regulations:–

Citation, commencement and interpretation

1.—(1) These Regulations may be cited as the Money Purchase Contracted-out Schemes Regulations 1987 and shall come into force on 6th April 1988.

(2) In these Regulations, unless the context otherwise requires–

"the 1975 Act" means the Social Security Pensions Act 1975;

"the 1986 Act" means the Social Security Act 1986;

"earnings period" has the same meaning as in the Social Security (Contributions) Regulations 1979(d);

"emoluments" means so much of a person's remuneration or profit derived from employed earner's employment as constitutes earnings for the purposes of the Social Security Act 1975(a);

"Friendly Society" means a Friendly Society registered under section 7(1)(a) of the Friendly Societies Act 1974(e), or, as the case may be, under section 1(1)(a) of the Friendly Societies Act (Northern Ireland) 1970(f);

(a) 1975 c.14. *See* definitions of "prescribe" and "regulations" in Schedule 20. Section 168(1) applies, by virtue of section 66(2) of the Social Security Pensions Act 1975 (c.60), to the exercise of certain powers conferred by that Act.

(b) 1975 c.60. Sections 30(1C) and 32(2B) and (2D) were inserted by the Social Security Act 1986 (c.50), section 6 and Schedule 2, paragraphs 4 and 5.

(c) 1986 c.50. *See* definitions of "prescribed" and "regulations" in section 84(1).

(d) S.I. 1979/591; the relevant amending instruments are S.I. 1980/1975, 1983/10, 1984/77.

(e) 1974 c.46.

(f) 1970 c.31 (N.I.).

"futures" has the meaning assigned to that word by paragraph 8 of Schedule 1 to the Financial Services Act 1986(a);

"government, local authority or public authority" means—

(a) the government of any member State;

(b) a local authority in any member State; or

(c) any international organisation the members of which comprise any member States;

"income tax month" means the period beginning on the 6th day of any calendar month and ending on the 5th day of the following calendar month;

"investment trust company" means a company which has been approved for the purposes of section 359 of the Income and Corporation Taxes Act 1970(b);

"issuer", in relation to any securities, has the meaning assigned to that word by section 142(7) of the Financial Services Act 1986;

"options" has the meaning assigned to that word by paragraph 7 of Schedule 1 to the Financial Services Act 1986;

"recognised Stock Exchange" has the meaning assigned to that expression by paragraph 13 of Schedule 13 to the Insurance Companies Regulations 1981(c);

"scheme" means occupational pension scheme;

"securities"—

(a) in relation to any government, local authority or public authority, means any investment which would fall within paragraph 3 of Schedule 1 to the Financial Services Act 1986 if "government, local authority or public authority" had the same meaning in that paragraph as in these Regulations; and

(b) otherwise means any investment falling within paragraph 1, 2, 4 or 5 of that Schedule;

"trustees", in relation to a scheme which is not set up or established under a trust, means the managers of the scheme;

and other expressions have the same meaning as in the 1975 Act.

(3) In these Regulations, unless the context otherwise requires, any reference—

(a) to a numbered regulation is to the regulation in these Regulations bearing that number;

(b) in a regulation to a numbered paragraph is to the paragraph of that regulation bearing that number;

(c) in a paragraph to a lettered sub-paragraph is to the sub-paragraph of that paragraph bearing that letter.

Permitted investments

2.—(1) For the purposes of section 32(2A) of the 1975 Act(d) (occupational pension scheme may be contracted-out if among other things the requirements imposed by or by virtue of Schedule 1 to the 1986 Act modified under section 32(2B) of the 1975 Act are satisfied in its case) and of paragraphs 3 and 6 of Schedule 1 to the 1986 Act (schemes to comply with prescribed requirements as regards the investment of their resources, and such other requirements as may be prescribed), the prescribed requirements in relation to an occupational pension scheme are those specified in paragraphs (2) and (3).

(2) The rules of the scheme shall require that the resources of the scheme are not invested in any investments other than those specified in the Schedule to these Regulations.

(3) The rules of the scheme shall require the trustees of the scheme to take all reasonable steps to ensure that—

(a) 1986 c.60.

(b) 1970 c.10; section 359 was amended by the Finance Act 1972 (c.41), section 93(6).

(c) S.I. 1981/1654; the relevant amending instruments are S.I. 1982/675, 1985/1419.

(d) Section 32(2A) was inserted by the Social Security Act 1986 (c.50), section 6 and Schedule 2, paragraph 5.

(a) in relation to the investments specified in paragraphs 5 to 8 of the Schedule, there is not, at any one time, invested in the securities of any one issuer–

   (i) more than 5% of the value of the resouces of the scheme, or

   (ii) more than 10% of that value, where the total of the investments in the securities of any one issuer of more than 5% of that value does not exceed 40% of that value;

(b) not more than 50% of the value of the resources of the scheme is invested, at any one time, in investments specified in paragraph 6 of the Schedule;

(c) not more than 35% of the value of the resources of the scheme is invested, at any one time, in investments of the kinds specified in paragraphs 7 and 8 (read together) of the Schedule;

(d) the aggregate, at any one time, of–

   (i) any sum lent to a person or body associated with the scheme out of the resources of the scheme,

   (ii) any part of the resources of the scheme invested in a person or body or land associated with the scheme, and

   (iii) any part of the resources of the scheme invested in any one or more of the investments specified in paragraphs 8 to 10 of the Schedule,

does not exceed 10% of the value of the resources of the scheme;

(e) not more than 40% of the value of the resources of the scheme is invested, at any one time, in securities issued by any one investment trust company; and

(f) not more than 25% of the value of the resources of the scheme is invested at any one time in land.

Deduction of minimum payments from earnings

3.—(1) Every employer, on making during any tax year to any earner any payment of emoluments in respect of which minimum payments are payable, may deduct minimum payments in accordance with this regulation.

(2) An employer shall not be entitled to recover any minimum payments paid or to be paid by him on behalf of any earner otherwise than by deduction in accordance with this regulation.

(3) Subject to the provisions of paragraph (4), on making any payment of emoluments to the earner the employer may deduct from those emoluments an amount which bears the same ratio to the amount of the minimum payments relating to those emoluments as A does to A plus B, where–

   (a) A is the first percentage mentioned in section 30(1A)(a) of the 1975 Act **(a)**; and

   (b) B is the first percentage mentioned in section 30(1A)(b) of that Act.

(4) Where 2 or more payments of emoluments fall to be aggregated under or by virtue of paragraph 1(1) of Schedule 1 to the Social Security Act 1975, the employer may deduct the amount of the minimum payments based thereon which are payable by the earner either wholly from one such payment or partly from one and partly from the other or any one or more of the others.

(5) In the circumstances specified in paragraph (6), if the employer on making any payment of emoluments to an earner does not deduct therefrom the full amount of minimum payments which by virtue of these regulations he is entitled to deduct, he may recover the amount so underdeducted by deduction from any subsequent payment of emoluments to that earner during the same tax year, so however that any amount deducted under this paragraph may be in addition to but shall not exceed any amount deducted from the same payment of emoluments under paragraph (3) or (4).

(6) Paragraph (5) applies only where–

(a) Section 30(1A) was inserted by the Social Security Act 1986 (c.50), section 6 and Schedule 2, paragraph 4.

(a) the underdeduction occurred by reason of an error made by the employer in good faith; or

(b) the emoluments in respect of which the underdeduction occurred are deemed to be earnings by virtue of regulations made under section 18 of the Social Security (Miscellaneous Provisions) Act 1977(a); or

(c) the underdeduction occurred as a result of the variation of the contracting-out certificate issued in respect of the employment in respect of which the payment of emoluments is made; or

(d) the emoluments in respect of which the underdeduction occurred are, by virtue of regulation 17B of the Social Security (Contributions) Regulations 1979(b), not paid through the secondary contributor in relation to the employment.

Minimum payments to be made by employers to trustees

4.—(1) For the purposes of section 30(1) and (1A) of the 1975 Act, the employer of an earner whose employment is contracted-out by reference to a money purchase contracted-out scheme shall, subject to paragraph (2), make to the trustees of that scheme any minimum payments which fall to be made by him, other than amounts deductible by virtue of regulation 3(4) which he did not deduct, within 14 days of the end of the income tax month in which there arose the liability for Class 1 contributions in respect of the earnings to which those minimum payments relate.

(2) An employer shall for the purposes of paragraph (1) be deemed to have deducted from the last of any number of payments of emoluments which fall to be aggregated under or by virtue of paragraph 1(1) of Schedule 1 to the Social Security Act 1975(c) the amount of minimum payments deductible from those payments which he did not deduct from the earlier payments.

(3) Subject to paragraph (4), if the employer has paid to the trustees on account of minimum payments an amount which he was not liable so to pay, the amounts which he is liable so to pay subsequently, in respect of other payments of emoluments made by him during the same tax year, shall be reduced by the amount so overpaid, so however that if there was a corresponding overdeduction from any payment of emoluments to an earner the provisions of this paragraph shall apply only in so far as the employer has reimbursed the earner therefor.

(4) Paragraph (3) applies only where the overdeduction occurred by reason of an error made by the employer in good faith.

Calculation of minimum payments

5.—(1) Subject to the provisions of paragraphs (3) and (4), minimum payments shall be calculated in accordance with section 30(1A) and (1B) of the 1975 Act, so however that each such calculation shall be to the nearest penny and any amount of half a penny or less shall be disregarded.

(2) In the alternative, but subject to the provisions of paragraphs (3) to (5), minimum payments may be calculated in accordance with a scale prepared for that purpose by the Secretary of State.

(3) Where the amount of the earnings to which the scale is to be applied does not appear in the scale, the amount of the minimum payments shall be calculated by reference to the next smaller amount of earnings in the appropriate column in the scale.

(4) Where the scale would, but for the period to which it relates, be appropriate and the earnings period in question is a multiple of the period in the scale, the scale shall be applied by dividing the earnings in question so as to obtain the equivalent earnings for the period to which the scale relates and by multiplying the amount of minimum payments shown in the scale as appropriate to those equivalent earnings by the same factor as the earnings were divided.

(a) 1977 c.5. Section 18 is amended by the Social Security Act 1986 (c.50), section 86(1) and Schedule 10, paragraph 74, and partially repealed by section 86(2) of and Schedule 11 to that Act. *See* the Social Security (Contributions) (Employment Protection) Regulations 1977 (S.I. 1977/622).
(b) S.I. 1979/591; the relevant amending instrument is S.I. 1983/395.
(c) 1975 c.14.

(5) Unless the Secretary of State agrees to the contrary, all the minimum payments to be made in a tax year in respect of the earnings paid to or for the benefit of an earner in respect of his employed earner's employment or, where he has more than one such employment and the earnings therefrom are aggregated under paragraph 1(1) of Schedule 1 to the Social Security Act 1975, in respect of those employments, shall be calculated either in accordance with paragraph (1) or in accordance with paragraph (2) but not partly in accordance with one and partly in accordance with the other of those paragraphs.

Circumstances in which schemes may change mode of contracting-out

6.—(1) A scheme which has been contracted-out by virtue of section 32(2) of the 1975 Act may become contracted-out by virtue of section 32(2A) of that Act only if its trustees have been discharged of all liability to provide guaranteed minimum pensions.

(2) A scheme which has been contracted-out by virtue of section 32(2A) of that Act may become contracted-out by virtue of section 32(2) of that Act only if its trustees have been discharged of all liability to give effect to protected rights.

Signed by authority of the Secretary of State for Social Services

Nicholas Scott
Minister of State,
Department of Health and Social Security

25th June 1987

SCHEDULE

Regulation 2

1. Insurance policies, or annuity contracts, or both, which are–
  (a) issued by either–
    (i) a person or body (not being a Friendly Society) which is authorised by virtue of Chapter III of Part I of the Financial Services Act 1986; or
    (ii) a Friendly Society which is so authorised and has disclosed in its audited accounts a contributions income of not less than £300,000 in the year 1986 and not less than £400,000 in the year 1987;
    and which are–
  (b) issued under, or in connection with, arrangements which do not permit the trustees of the scheme to direct the way in which the investment of premiums paid or payable to the person or body, specified in sub-paragraphs (a)(i) or (ii), in respect of those policies or contracts, shall be made.

2. The units of any unit trust scheme which has been authorised under section 78(1) of, or by virtue of paragraph 9 of Schedule 15 to, the Financial Services Act 1986.

3. Securities issued by any government, local authority or public authority.

4. An interest-bearing account with–
  (a) a building society as defined in the Building Societies Act 1986**(a)**; or
  (b) a bank recognised under the Banking Act 1979**(b)**; or
  (c) a deposit taker licensed under the Banking Act 1979.

5. Securities listed on a recognised Stock Exchange in a member State, other than those mentioned in paragraphs 3 and 11 of this Schedule.

6. Securities listed on a recognised Stock Exchange in any country other than a member State.

7. Securities which are not listed on a recognised Stock Exchange but which are traded in a second tier market of a recognised Stock Exchange in a member State.

(a) 1986 c.53.
(b) 1979 c.37.

8. Securities which are neither listed on a recognised Stock Exchange nor traded in a second tier market in a member State.

9. The units of any collective investment scheme not authorised under section 78(1) of, or by virtue of paragraph 9 of Schedule 15 to, the Financial Services Act 1986.

10. Futures and options.

11. The securities of any investment trust companies.

12. Land.

EXPLANATORY NOTE

(This note is not part of the Regulations)

These Regulations are all made under section 30(1C) or 32(2D) of the Social Security Pensions Act 1975 ("the 1975 Act") or paragraph 3 or 6 of Schedule 1 to the Social Security Act 1986 ("the 1986 Act"), as modified by section 32(2B) of the 1975 Act, and are made before the end of the period of 12 months from the commencement of those provisions. Consequently, by virtue of section 61(5) of the 1986 Act, the provisions of section 61(2) and (3) of the 1975 Act (as amended by section 86(1) of, and paragraph 94 of Schedule 10 to, the 1986 Act), which require reference to the Occupational Pensions Board of, and a report by the Board on, proposals to make regulations for certain purposes of both Acts do not apply to them.

Section 6 of the 1986 Act, with Schedule 2, introduces the concept of the money purchase contracted-out occupational pension scheme. Regulation 2, with the Schedule, makes provision about the way in which the resources of the scheme must be invested if it is to be a money purchase contracted-out scheme.

For a money purchase scheme to be contracted-out, it is necessary that "minimum payments" should be made to it. Regulations 3, 4 and 5 provide for the calculation of minimum payments; that they should be made by employers to the trustees or managers of schemes; and that parts of them may be deducted by employers from payments of emoluments.

Section 32(2D) of the 1975 Act (inserted by paragraph 5(b) of Schedule 2 to the 1986 Act) provides that a scheme which has been contracted-out by virtue of one of subsections (2) and (2A) of section 32 (schemes which are not, and schemes which are, money purchase contracted-out schemes respectively) may not become contracted-out by virtue of the other, except in prescribed circumstances. Regulation 6 provides that it may do so only if its trustees or managers have been discharged of all their liability, accrued before the change, to provide guaranteed minimum pensions or to give effect to protected rights, as the case may be.

1987 No. 1102

PENSIONS

The Occupational Pension Schemes (Auditors) Regulations 1987

Made - - - -	*25th June 1987*
Laid before Parliament	*6th July 1987*
Coming into force	*27th July 1987*

The Secretary of State for Social Services, in exercise of the powers conferred upon him by section 168(1) of, and Schedule 20 to, the Social Security Act 1975(**a**), section 56P of the Social Security Pensions Act 1975(**b**) and sections 54(1) and 84(1) of the Social Security Act 1986(**c**) and of all other powers enabling him in that behalf, by this instrument, which is made before the end of a period of 12 months from the commencement of the enactments under which it is made, makes the following Regulations:

Citation, commencement and interpretation

1.—(1) These Regulations may be cited as the Occupational Pension Schemes (Auditors) Regulations 1987 and shall come into force on 27th July 1987.

(2) In these Regulations, unless the context otherwise requires–

"the Act" means the Social Security Pensions Act 1975;

"the Appointing Body", in relation to any scheme, means the person or body designated in any document constituting the scheme as the person or body with the function of appointing the auditor of the scheme, or, where there is no such person or body, the trustees of the scheme;

"beneficiary", in relation to any scheme, means a person, other than a member of the scheme, who is entitled to payment of benefits under the scheme;

"the Disclosure Regulations" means the Occupational Pension Schemes (Disclosure of Information) Regulations 1986(**d**);

"employer", in relation to a member or prospective member of a scheme, bears the meaning assigned to it by regulation 2(4) and (5) of the Occupational Pension Schemes (Preservation of Benefit) Regulations 1984(**e**);

"funded", in relation to benefits under a scheme, bears the meaning assigned to it by regulation 1(2) of the Disclosure Regulations;

"member" and "prospective member", in relation to any scheme, bear the meanings respectively assigned to those expressions by regulation 2(2) and (3) of the Disclosure Regulations;

"scheme" means occupational pension scheme;

"scheme year", in relation to any scheme, bears the meaning assigned to it by regulation 1(2) of the Disclosure Regulations;

(**a**) 1975 c. 14. *See* definitions of "prescribe" and "regulations" in Schedule 20. Section 168(1) applies, by virtue of section 66(2) of the Social Security Pensions Act 1975 (c.60), to the exercise of certain powers conferred by that Act.
(**b**) 1975 c.60; section 56P was added by section 11 of the Social Security Act 1986 (c.50).
(**c**) 1986 c.50. *See* definition of "regulations" in section 84(1).
(**d**) S.I. 1986/1046, to which there are amendments not relevant to these Regulations.
(**e**) S.I. 1984/614, to which there are amendments not relevant to these Regulations.

"trustees", in relation to a scheme which is not set up or established under a trust, means the managers of the scheme;

"unfunded scheme" means a scheme whose benefits are not funded;

and other expressions have the same meaning as in the Act.

(3) Except so far as the context otherwise requires, any reference–

(a) in these Regulations to a numbered regulation is to the regulation in these Regulations bearing that number;

(b) in a regulation to a numbered paragraph is to the paragraph of that regulation bearing that number.

Application of Regulations

2. None of the requirements of these Regulations shall apply to any scheme to which regulation 7 of the Disclosure Regulations does not apply.

Appointment, resignation and removal of auditors

3.—(1) The Appointing Body of a scheme shall appoint one or more persons who satisfy the requirements of regulation 7(3) of the Disclosure Regulations to audit the scheme's accounts for each scheme year, or, where the scheme was in operation for only part of a particular scheme year, for that part of that scheme year.

(2) The Appointing Body of a scheme may remove an auditor at any time by serving on him a notice in writing stating the date with effect from which his appointment is terminated.

(3) Subject to the provisions of paragraph (4), an auditor of a scheme may resign at any time by serving on the Appointing Body and the trustees of the scheme a notice in writing, and if he does so his resignation shall be effective from the date (if any) specified in the notice as being that from which he wishes his resignation to be effective, or, if no such date is so specified, the date on which the Appointing Body receives the notice.

(4) An auditor's resignation shall not be effective unless the notice referred to in paragraph (3) contains either–

(a) a statement specifying any circumstances connected with the auditor's proposed resignation which, in his opinion, significantly affect the interests of the members or prospective members of, or beneficiaries under, the scheme; or

(b) a statement that the auditor knows of no such circumstances.

(5) Where an auditor is removed in accordance with paragraph (2), he shall, within 14 days of the removal, serve on the Appointing Body and the trustees of the scheme either–

(a) a statement specifying any circumstances connected with the removal which, in his opinion, significantly affect the interests of the members or prospective members of, or beneficiaries under, the scheme; or

(b) a statement that the auditor knows of no such circumstances.

(6) When the last remaining or only auditor who was appointed to audit the accounts for a scheme–

(a) is removed by the Appointing Body;

(b) resigns; or

(c) dies,

before completing the audit of those accounts for a scheme year or part of a scheme year, the Appointing Body shall either reappoint him with his consent, or appoint one or more other auditors in his place, as soon as reasonably practicable, to audit those accounts.

(7) In a case where a statement has been made under paragraph (4) or (5), the trustees shall–

(a) furnish the next auditor whom the Appointing Body appoints with a copy of that statement on or before the day on which he is appointed, or, if it is later, on or before the fourteenth day after they receive the statement; and

(b) furnish any other auditor who is still in office with a copy of that statement on or before the fourteenth day after they receive it.

Disclosure of information by employers

4.   It shall be the duty of–

(a) any employer who employs any member or prospective member of a scheme in employment to which the scheme applies, and

(b) the auditors (if any) of such an employer,

to furnish the trustees and the auditor of the scheme with such information and explanation as may reasonably be required for the performance of the duties of the auditor of the scheme.

Disclosure of information by trustees

5.   The trustees of a scheme shall–

(a) allow the auditor of the scheme access at all reasonable times to the scheme's books, accounts and vouchers, and

(b) furnish the auditor with such information and explanation as may reasonably be required for the performance of the duties of the auditor.

Statement in auditor's report

6.   In any case where the auditor considers that he has failed to obtain all the information and explanation which, to the best of his knowledge and belief, are necessary for the purposes of his audit, he shall make a statement to that effect in his auditor's report and (so far as he knows them) give the reasons for the failure.

Service of documents

7.   Any–

(a) information or document which these Regulations require any person to furnish or serve; or

(b) request for information or a document to be furnished in pursuance of these Regulations,

may be furnished, served or made by post.

Offences and penalties

8.   Any person who, without reasonable excuse, contravenes or fails to comply with any requirement imposed on him by regulation 3(7), 4 or 5 shall be liable on summary conviction to a penalty not exceeding £400, or where the offence consists of continuing any such contravention or failure after conviction thereof, £40 for each day on which it is so continued.

Signed by authority of the Secretary of State for Social Services

Nicholas Scott
25th June 1987   Minister of State, Department of Health and Social Security

EXPLANATORY NOTE

(This note is not part of the Regulations)

These Regulations are made under either section 56P of the Social Security Pensions Act 1975 ("the 1975 Act") or section 54(1) of the Social Security Act 1986 ("the 1986 Act") before the expiry of the period of 12 months beginning with the bringing into force (on 6th April 1987) of section 11 of the 1986 Act (which inserted section 56P into the 1975 Act) and section 54(1) of the 1986 Act. Consequently, by virtue of section 61(5) of the 1986 Act, the provisions of section 61(2) and (3) of the 1975 Act (which, as amended by section 86(1) of, and paragraph

94 of Schedule 10 to, the 1986 Act, require reference to the Occupational Pensions Board of, and a report by the Board on, proposals to make regulations for the purposes of Part III or IV of the 1975 Act), do not apply to them.

Regulation 2 provides that these Regulations do not apply to any scheme to which Regulation 7 of the Occupational Pension Schemes (Disclosure of Information) Regulations 1986 does not apply.

Regulation 3 provides for the manner of the appointment, resignation and removal of auditors of occupational pension schemes and for the making of a statement, concerning any circumstances of his resignation or removal which affect the interests of members or prospective members of the scheme, by any such auditor when he resigns or is removed. The trustees of a scheme must furnish the next auditor who is appointed, and any remaining auditor, with any such statement.

Regulation 4 provides for the disclosure of information by employers of members and prospective members of a scheme and auditors of such employers, to the trustees or managers of the scheme and to the auditors of it.

Regulation 5 provides for the disclosure of information by trustees of a scheme to the auditors of it.

Regulation 6 provides for the making of a statement by an auditor who considers that he has failed to obtain all the information which is necessary for the purposes of his audit.

Regulation 8 provides for offences and penalties in respect of the contravention of the provisions of regulations 3(7), 4 or 5.

1987 No. 1103

PENSIONS

The Occupational Pension Schemes (Contracted-out Protected Rights Premiums) Regulations 1987

Made - - - -	*25th June 1987*
Laid before Parliament	*6th July 1987*
Coming into force	*6th April 1988*

The Secretary of State for Social Services, in exercise of the powers conferred upon him by section 168(1) of, and Schedule 20 to, the Social Security Act 1975(a), sections 44ZA(4), (6), (7), (9) and (13) and 52 of, and paragraph 6 of Schedule 2 to the Social Security Pensions Act 1975(b), and of all other powers enabling him in that behalf, by this instrument, which is made before the end of a period of 12 months from the commencement of the enactments under which it is made, makes the following Regulations:–

Citation, commencement and interpretation

1.—(1) These Regulations may be cited as the Occupational Pension Schemes (Contracted-out Protected Rights Premiums) Regulations 1987 shall come into force on 6th April 1988.

(2) In these Regulations, "the principal Regulations" means the Occupational Pension Schemes (Contracting-out) Regulations 1984(c).

Manner of calculation and verification of cash equivalents mentioned in section 44ZA(7) and (9)(a)(i) of the Social Security Pensions Act 1975

2.—(1) Except in a case to which paragraph (3) below applies, the cash equivalent mentioned in section 44ZA(7) of the Social Security Pensions Act 1975 of protected rights (being those rights under a scheme, which has ceased to be a money purchase contracted-out scheme, whose cash equivalent is to be the amount of a contracted-out protected rights premium) shall be calculated and verified–

    (a) in such manner as may be approved in particular cases by the trustees or managers of the scheme, and

    (b) by adopting methods consistent with the requirements of Schedule 1 to the

---

(a) 1975 c.14. *See* definitions of "prescribe" and "regulations" in Schedule 20. Section 168(1) applies, by virtue of section 66(2) of the Social Security Pensions Act 1975 (c.60), to the exercise of certain powers conferred by that Act.
(b) 1975 c.60. Section 44ZA was inserted by the Social Security Act 1986 (c.50), section 6 and Schedule 2, paragraph 7. Paragraph 6 of Schedule 2 was amended by the Social Security Act 1980 (c.30), section 3(12), and is modified by the Personal and Occupational Pension Schemes (Modification of Enactments) Regulations 1987 (S.I. 1987/1116), regulation 5(4).
(c) S.I. 1984/380; the relevant amending instrument is S.I. 1985/1928.

Social Security Act 1986 as modified by section 32(2B) of the Social Security Pensions Act 1975**(a)**.

(2) Except in a case to which paragraph (3) below applies, the cash equivalent mentioned in section 44ZA(9)(a)(i) of the Social Security Pensions Act 1975 of a person's rights (being those rights under a scheme, which has ceased to be a money purchase contracted-out scheme, whose cash equivalent is to be used to supplement a contracted-out protected rights premium) shall be calculated and verified in such manner as may be approved in particular cases by the trustees or managers of the scheme.

(3) In a case where the rights under a scheme mentioned in paragraph (1) or (2) above fall, either wholly or in part, to be valued in a manner which involves making estimates of the value of benefits, the cash equivalents of those rights shall be calculated and verified–

(a) in such manner as may be approved in particular cases by–
    (i) a Fellow of the Institute of Actuaries, or
    (ii) a Fellow of the Faculty of Actuaries, or
    (iii) a person with other actuarial qualifications who is approved by the Secretary of State, at the request of the trustees or managers of the scheme in question, as being a proper person to act for the purposes of these regulations in connection with that scheme,
and in this regulation "actuary" means any person such as is referred to in head (i), (ii) or (iii) of this sub-paragraph; and

(b) by adopting methods and making assumptions which–
    (i) if not determined by the trustees or managers of the scheme in question, are notified to them by an actuary, and
    (ii) are certified by an actuary to the trustees or managers of the scheme as being consistent with "Retirement Benefit Schemes—Transfer Values (GN11)" published by the Institute of Actuaries and the Faculty of Actuaries and current at the date of the calculation, and, in the case of protected rights, as being consistent with the requirements of Schedule 1 to the Social Security Act 1986 as modified by section 32(2B) of the Social Security Pensions Act 1975.

Amendment of regulation 1 of the principal Regulations

3.—(1) Regulation 1 of the principal Regulations (interpretation) shall be amended in accordance with the following provisions of this regulation.

(2) In paragraph (2), immediately after the definition of "employer", there shall be inserted the following definition–

" 'qualifying widow or widower' means a widow or widower of the earner who at the date of the earner's death either–

(a) is aged 45 or over; or
(b) is entitled to child benefit in respect of a child under 18 who is, or residing with a child under 16 who is—
    (i) a son or daughter of the widow or widower and the earner, or
    (ii) a child in respect of whom the earner immediately before his death, was, or would have been if the child had not been absent from Great Britain, entitled to child benefit, or
    (iii) if the widow or widower and the earner were residing together immediately before the earner's death, a child in respect of whom the widow or widower then was, or would have been if the child had not been absent from Great Britain, entitled to child benefit;".

Amendment of regulation 18 of the principal Regulations

4.—(1) Regulation 18 of the principal Regulations (liability for payment of state

---

(a) Subsection (2B) was inserted into section 32 by the Social Security Act 1986, section 6 and Schedule 2, paragraph 5.

scheme premiums) shall be amended in accordance with the following provisions of this regulation.

(2) After paragraph (1) there shall be inserted the following paragraph–

"(1ZA) For the purposes of section 44ZA(6) (payment of contracted-out protected rights premiums) the prescribed person is–

(a) in a case where regulation 23A(7)(a) and (c) applies, the person to whom the cash sum mentioned in regulation 23A(7)(c) has been paid; and

(b) in any other case, the trustees of the scheme.".

(3) After paragraph (2) there shall be inserted the following paragraph–

"(2A) A contracted-out protected rights premium shall not be payable–

(a) in a case where the protected rights in question are in respect of an earner who has died and either–

(i) the earner is not survived by a qualifying widow or widower, or

(ii) the earner is survived by a qualifying widower, and the earner or the widower or both were under pensionable age when the earner died;

(b) in a case where the person in respect of whom it otherwise would be payable is not treated, under section 4 of the Social Security Act 1986 or under section 29(2) or (2A) of the Act, as entitled to any guaranteed minimum pension which derives from the minimum contributions, minimum payments, or transfer payment or payments from which the protected rights in question derive, or is treated as entitled to such a guaranteed minimum pension at a nil rate.".

Amendment of regulation 20 of the principal Regulations

5.—(1) Regulation 20 of the principal Regulations (time for payment of state scheme premiums) shall be amended in accordance with the following provisions of this regulation.

(2) In sub-paragraph (b) of paragraph (1), at the end there shall be inserted ", or, in the case of a contracted-out protected rights premium, certifying that the premium is payable".

(3) After paragraph (3) there shall be inserted the following paragraph–

"(3A) In cases where a state scheme premium has become payable by reason of the fact that a contracted-out scheme has ceased to be contracted-out and a person's protected rights are not the subject of approved arrangements under section 44ZA or, having been so subject, have ceased to be so subject, references in paragraph (1)(a) to the date of termination of contracted-out employment shall be read as references to the date on which the Board certify under regulation 18(4) that the protected rights in question are not subject to approved arrangements or have ceased to be so subject.".

(4) After paragraph (4) there shall be inserted the following paragraph–

"(4A) In cases where a state scheme premium has become payable by reason of the fact that a contracted-out scheme has ceased to be contracted-out and a person's protected rights are, in part only, subject to approved arrangements under section 44ZA, references in paragraph (1)(a) to the date of termination of contracted-out employment shall be read as references to the date on which the Board certify under regulation 18(4) that the protected rights in question are, in part only, subject to approved arrangements.".

Addition of regulation 23A to the principal Regulations

6. After regulation 23 of the principal Regulations there shall be inserted the following regulation–

"Miscellaneous provisions affecting contracted-out protected rights premiums

23A.—(1) Subject to paragraphs (3) and (4), where a contracted-out protected rights premium is payable under section 44ZA(4) pursuant to certification by the Board to the Secretary of State under regulation 18(4), the premium shall, for the purpose of extinguishing protected rights and reducing any guaranteed minimum pension to which a person is treated as being entitled, be treated as having been paid, or paid in part in a case to which either paragraphs (6) to (8) apply or paragraph (9) applies, on the date specified in paragraph (2).

(2) The date mentioned in paragraph (1) is whichever is the later of–

(a) the date on which the scheme ceased to be contracted-out; and

(b) any date certified by the Board under regulation 18(4)(c) in relation to the rights mentioned in paragraph (1).

(3) Where a contracted-out protected rights premium has been treated as paid under paragraph (1), the effect of that paragraph shall, except as provided in paragraph (5), be disregarded if–

(a) the Board subsequently approve arrangements for the preservation or transfer of the protected rights, or

(b) the person who is liable to pay the premium fails to do so within the period prescribed by regulation 20(1) or such longer period as the Secretary of State may allow under regulation 20(2).

(4) Where by virtue of the operation of paragraphs (1) and (3) in relation to a person entitled to a benefit specified in section 29(1)(a) an amount of that benefit, as certified by the Secretary of State, was paid to that person which would not otherwise have been paid–

(a) the Secretary of State shall be entitled to recover that amount from the scheme and any amount so recovered shall be paid into the National Insurance Fund; and

(b) the sums payable under the scheme to that person may be reduced by the amount so recovered by the Secretary of State.

(5) Paragraph (3)(b) shall not apply where the Secretary of State is satisfied that the failure to pay was not with the consent or connivance of, or attributable to any negligence on the part of, the person in respect of whom the premium is payable, and where, subject to paragraphs (6) and (8), the scheme, being a scheme which is or has been contracted-out, is being or has been wound up.

(6) In a case where the circumstances specified in paragraph (7)(a) and either (b) or (c) obtain, the contracted-put protected rights premium in question shall be treated as paid under paragraph (1) only in accordance with the provisions of paragraph (8).

(7) The circumstances mentioned in paragraph (6) are that–

(a) a contracted-out protected rights premium has become payable in respect of that person by reason of the withdrawal by the Board of their approval of, or their inability to give their approval to, arrangements for the preservation or transfer of the protected rights in question under section 44ZA;

(b) the scheme is being or has been wound up, its resources are insufficient to meet the cost of that premium, and the Board are satisfied that no arrangements have been made to meet that cost, or, as the case may be, such part of that cost as cannot be met from the resources of the scheme;

(c) the scheme has been wound up and a cash sum in lieu of the protected rights in question has been paid to or for the benefit of the person concerned.

(8) In a case to which paragraph (6) applies, where the Secretary of State is satisfied that the part of the premium that the resources of the scheme are sufficient to meet or the amount of the cash sum referred to in paragraph (7)(c) is less than the value of the protected rights in question, such part of the contracted-out protected rights premium as represents, in the opinion of the Secretary of State, the difference between the lesser and greater amounts shall be treated as having been paid.

(9) Where a person in respect of whom a contracted-out protected rights premium is payable is a person to whom regulation 18(1ZA)(a) applies and that person pays part only of the premium, that part of the premium shall be treated as having been paid under paragraph (1).

(10) Where part of a contracted-out protected rights premium is treated as having been paid under paragraph (1)–

(a) section 44ZA(8) shall be modified so as to have effect as if there were inserted at the end thereof the words 'and payment of part of the premium shall operate to extinguish such part of those rights as corresponds, in the opinion of the Secretary of State, to that part of the premium' and section 44ZA(9)(a) shall have effect as if there were substituted for the words 'the premium' the words 'that part of the premium which has been paid'; and

(b) in a case to which paragraph (6) applies, section 44ZA shall be modified so as to have effect as if–

(i) in subsection (1) there were inserted after the words 'protected rights' the words 'or part thereof',

(ii) in each of paragraphs (a) and (b) of subsection (4) there were inserted after the words 'are not' the words 'or are in part only', and

(iii) in subsection (7) there were inserted after the words 'in question' the words 'to the extent that those rights are not subject to approved arrangements'.".

Addition of regulation 26A to the principal Regulations

7. After regulation 26 of the principal Regulations, there shall be inserted the following regulation–

"Prescribed person and prescribed periods for the purposes of section 44ZA(9)(a)

26A. For the purposes of section 44ZA(9)(a)–

(a) the prescribed person is the Secretary of State; and

(b) the prescribed period–

(i) for the purpose of giving notice to the Secretary of State,

(ii) for the purpose of the payment referred to in section 44ZA(9)(a)(i), and

(iii) for the purpose of the payment referred to in section 44ZA(9)(a)(ii),

is the period allowed for the payment of the premium under paragraphs (1) and (2) to (4) of regulation 20.".

Signed by authority of the Secretary of State for Social Services.

Nicholas Scott
Minister of State,
Department of Health and Social Security

25th June 1987

EXPLANATORY NOTE

(This note is not part of the Regulations)

These Regulations are all made under provisions of the Social Security Act 1986 ("the 1986 Act"), or provisions of the Social Security Pensions Act 1975 ("the 1975 Act") inserted by or modified under the 1986 Act, before the end of a period of 12 months from the commencement of the relevant sections of the 1986 Act. Consequently, by virtue of section 61(5) of the 1986 Act, the provisions of section 61(2) and (3) of the 1975 Act (as amended by section 86(1) of, and paragraph 94 of Schedule 10 to, the 1986 Act), which require reference to the Occupational Pensions Board of, and a report by the Board on, proposals to make regulations for certain purposes of both Acts, do not apply to them.

The amendments made to the 1975 Act by Schedule 2 to the 1986 Act introduced into the 1975 Act the concept of the "money purchase contracted-out scheme". When such a scheme ceases to be a contracted-out scheme, a "contracted-out protected rights premium" may become payable under section 44ZA of the 1975 Act in respect of each person in the categories described in subsection (4) of that section.

Under subsection (7) of that section, the amount of a contracted-out protected rights premium is the cash equivalent of the protected rights of the person concerned, calculated and verified in the prescribed manner.

Regulation 2 provides for the manner in which protected rights, and other rights under the scheme, are to be calculated and verified.

Regulations 3 to 7 make various amendments, in order to deal with the case of contracted-out protected rights premiums, to the Occupational Pension Schemes (Contracting-out) Regulations 1984, and in particular to regulations 18 (liability for payment of state scheme premiums), 20 (time for payment of premiums) and 23 (treating premiums as paid).

The publication "Retirement Benefit Schemes—Transfer Values (GN11)", referred to in regulation 2(3)(b)(ii), may be obtained from the Institute of Actuaries, Staple Inn Hall, High Holborn, London W.C.1N 7QJ, and from the Faculty of Actuaries, 23 St. Andrew Square, Edinburgh EH2 1AQ.

STATUTORY INSTRUMENTS

1987 No. 1104

PENSIONS

The Occupational Pension Schemes (Contracting-out) Amendment Regulations 1987

Made - - - -	*25th June 1987*
Laid before Parliament	*6th July 1987*
Coming into force	*27th July 1987*

The Secretary of State for Social Services, in exercise of the powers conferred upon him by section 168(1) of, and Schedule 20 to, the Social Security Act 1975 (**a**) and sections 31(5) and 52 of, and paragraph 9 of Schedule 2 to, the Social Security Pensions Act 1975(**b**) and of all other powers enabling him in that behalf, after considering the report of the Occupational Pensions Board on the proposals submitted to them (**c**), hereby makes the following Regulations:

Citation, commencement and interpretation

1.—(1) These Regulations may be cited as the Occupational Pension Schemes (Contracting-out) Amendment Regulations 1987 and shall come into force on 27th July 1987.

(2) In these Regulations, "the principal Regulations" means the Occupational Pension Schemes (Contracting-out) Regulations 1984(**d**).

Amendments to the principal Regulations

2.—(1) The principal Regulations shall be amended in accordance with the provisions of this regulation.

(2) In regulation 3 (notices by employers of intended elections for the issue of contracting-out certificates), for paragraph (4) there shall be substituted the following paragraph–

"(4) A notice may specify a date of expiry–
  (a) which is–
    (i) earlier than the date 3 months after, but
    (ii) not earlier than the date one month after,
    that on which the notice is given; and
  (b) which is assented to in writing by all independent trade unions (if any) recognised to any extent for the purpose of collective bargaining in relation to the earners concerned.".

(**a**) 1975 c.14. *See* definitions of "prescribe" and "regulations" in Schedule 20. Section 168(1) applies, by virtue of section 66(2) of the Social Security Pensions Act 1975 (c.60), to the exercise of certain powers conferred by that Act.
(**b**) 1975 c.60.
(**c**) *See* section 61(2) and (3) of the Social Security Pensions Act 1975; section 61(2) is amended in ways not relevant to these Regulations.
(**d**) S.I. 1984/380, to which there are amendments not relevant to these Regulations.

(3) In regulation 6 (information to be included in an election)–

    (a) for paragraph (2)(b) there shall be substituted the following sub-paragraph–

        "(b) a statement by the employer that he has, in accordance with regulation 3(1), given the earners mentioned in regulation 3(1)(a) notice of the intention to make the election;"; and

    (b) in paragraph (2)(c) there shall be added at the end the words "and its date of expiry".

(4) In regulation 10 (making of elections by employers for the variation or surrender of contracting-out certificates), for paragraph (3)(c) there shall be substituted the following sub-paragraph–

    "(c) specify the date of expiry of the notice, which shall be–

        (i)   at least 3 months after the date on which the notice is given, or

        (ii) a shorter period, being at least one month after that date, if that shorter period is assented to in writing by all independent trade unions (if any) recognised to any extent for the purpose of collective bargaining in relation to the earners concerned;".

(5) In regulation 41 (conditions in connection with alteration of rules of contracted-out schemes)–

    (a) in paragraph (4)(c), for the words "approved by the Board and assented to" there shall be substituted "it is a date not earlier than one month from the date of the giving of the notice and it is assented to in writing"; and

    (b) paragraph (4)(d)(i) shall be omitted.

Signed by authority of the Secretary of State for Social Services.

Nicholas Scott
Minister of State,
Department of Health and Social Security

25th June 1987

STATUTORY INSTRUMENTS

1987 No. 1105

PENSIONS

The Occupational Pension Schemes (Disclosure of Information) (Amendment) Regulations 1987

Made - - - -	25th June 1987
Laid before Parliament	6th July 1987
Coming into force	27th July 1987

The Secretary of State for Social Services, in exercise of the powers conferred upon him by section 168(1) of, and Schedule 20 to, the Social Security Act 1975(a) and sections 56A(1) and (3) of the Social Security Pensions Act 1975(b) and of all other powers enabling him in that behalf, after considering the report of the Occupational Pensions Board on the proposals submitted to them(c), hereby makes the following Regulations:

Citation, commencement and interpretation

1.—(1) These Regulations may be cited as the Occupational Pension Schemes (Disclosure of Information) (Amendment) Regulations 1987 and shall come into force on 27th July 1987.

(2) In these Regulations, "the principal Regulations" means the Occupational Pension Schemes (Disclosure of Information) Regulations 1986(d).

(3) Except so far as the context otherwise requires, any reference in these Regulations to a numbered regulation or Schedule is to the regulation in, or, as the case may be, Schedule to, the principal Regulations bearing that number.

Amendments of the principal Regulations

2.—(1) For paragraph (3)(c) of regulation 5, there shall be substituted the following sub-paragraph–

"(c) any independent trade union, in so far as that information is relevant to the rights of members or prospective members of the scheme who are of a class of employee in relation to which that trade union is recognised, to any extent, for the purposes of collective bargaining,".

(2) For paragraph (4) of regulation 6 there shall be substituted the following paragraph–

"(4) Except in relation to money purchase benefits, the information mentioned in paragraph 4 of Schedule 2 shall be furnished to any member whose pensionable service has not terminated before normal pension age, on request (not being a

---

(a) 1975 c.14. *See* definitions of "prescribe" and "regulations" in Schedule 20. Section 168(1) applies, by virtue of section 66(2) of the Social Security Pensions Act 1975 (c.60), to the exercise of certain powers conferred by that Act.
(b) 1975 c.60; section 56A was added by section 3 of, and Schedule 2 to, the Social Security Act 1985 (c.53).
(c) *See* section 61(2) and (3) of the Social Security Pensions Act 1975; section 61(2) is amended in ways not relevant to these Regulations.
(d) S.I. 1986/1046, amended by S.I. 1986/1717.

[SS87/1737]

request made within a year of the last occasion on which any such information as is mentioned in that paragraph was furnished to him) as soon as practicable after he requests it.".

(3) After paragraph (4) of regulation 6 there shall be inserted the following paragraphs–

"(4A) In the case of a scheme which provides only–

(a) money purchase benefits; or

(b) (i) money purchase benefits, and

(ii) salary-related benefits which are payable only in the event of the death of a member who is, immediately before his death, employed in relevant employment,

the information mentioned in paragraphs 4B and 4C of Schedule 2 shall be furnished, as of course, to each member of the scheme, at least once in every period of 12 months after the date of his becoming a member of it.

(4B) Except in the case of a scheme to which paragraph (4A) applies, in relation to money purchase benefits the information mentioned in paragraph 4C of Schedule 2 shall be furnished to any member on request (not being a request made within a year of the last occasion on which any such information as is mentioned in that paragraph was furnished to him) as soon as practicable after he requests it.

(4C) Where a scheme is, or has been, a money purchase contracted-out scheme in relation to one or more members' employments, and that member has or those members have protected rights under it, the information mentioned in paragraph 4D of Schedule 2 shall be sent, as of course, to each member with such rights–

(a) not less than 4 months, but not more than 6 months, before he attains pensionable age, and

(b) not less than 4 months before the member attains the age of 75 years if effect has not been given to his protected rights by the beginning of the sixth month before the member attains the age of 75 years.

(4D) Where a scheme which has been a money purchase contracted-out scheme in relation to one or more members' employments ceases to be such a scheme in relation to any of them, the trustees of the scheme shall inform each member ("the affected member"), in relation to whose employment the scheme has ceased to be such a scheme, as soon as practicable and in any event not more than 4 weeks after the date on which it ceased to be such a scheme that the scheme has so ceased, and furnish the affected member, as soon as practicable and in any event not more than 4 months after the date on which it ceased to be such a scheme with–

(a) the information mentioned in paragraphs 4B, 4C, 4E, 4F and 4G of Schedule 2, and

(b) except where the scheme is able to meet in full its liabilities to the affected member, the information mentioned in paragraph 4H of Schedule 2.".

(4) For paragraph (6) of regulation 6 there shall be substituted the following paragraph–

"(6) The information mentioned in paragraph 7 of Schedule 2 shall be furnished–

(a) as of course to any person as soon as practicable after he or his employer has notified the trustees that his pensionable service has terminated or is about to terminate; and

(b) to any member on request (not being a request made less than 12 months after the last occasion on which such information was furnished to him) as soon as practicable after he requests it.".

(5) In paragraph (11) of regulation 6–

(a) for the words "assets of the scheme have all been realised but before the proceeds", there shall be substituted the words "proceeds of the realisation of the assets of the scheme"; and

(b) in sub-paragraph (a), for "4" there shall be substituted "4A".

(6) In paragraph (10) of regulation 8, after the words "and of the person who" there shall be inserted the words "or trade union which".

2

(7) In paragraph (1)(c) of regulation 9, for "14" there shall be substituted "15".

(8) After paragraph 3 of Schedule 1 there shall be inserted the following paragraphs–

"3A. The period of notice (if any) which a member of the scheme must give to terminate his pensionable service.

3B. Whether, and if so upon what conditions (if any), a member of the scheme, whose pensionable service has terminated before normal pension age, may re-enter pensionable service.".

(9) After paragraph 4 of Schedule 2 there shall be inserted the following paragraphs–

"4A. The amounts of the member's own benefits and of his survivors' benefits which are expected to be payable from normal pension age or death thereafter.

4B. The amount of contributions (before the making of any deductions), credited to the member under the scheme during the 12 months preceding a specified date, and, where the scheme was for the whole or any part of that period, a contracted-out scheme, the amount of those contributions which is attributable to–

   (a) the minimum payments to the scheme made in respect of the member by his employer; and

   (b) the payments (if any) made to the trustees of the scheme by the Secretary of State in accordance with section 7(1) of the Social Security Act 1986 in respect of the member.

4C.(a) As at a specified date–

     (i) the value of the member's protected rights under the scheme, and

     (ii) the value of the member's accrued rights (other than his protected rights) under the scheme.

   (b) Where the cash equivalent (calculated, as at the date specified for the purposes of sub-paragraph (a), in accordance with paragraph 14 of Schedule 1A to the Act, and regulations made thereunder), in respect of the transfer of the member's rights mentioned in sub-paragraph (a)(i) or (ii) or both would be different from the values to be specified under that sub-paragraph, that cash equivalent.

4D. The options available to the member, including those in respect of any accrued rights which are not protected rights.

4E. The date on which the scheme ceased to be a money purchase contracted-out scheme in relation to the member's employment.

4F. Whether arrangements for the preservation or transfer of the member's protected rights have been, or are to be, proposed to the Occupational Pensions Board and an explanation of the intended effects of any such proposed arrangements.

4G. The options available to the member in respect of his protected rights.

4H. An account of the amount by which the member's–

   (a) protected rights; and

   (b) accrued rights other than his protected rights,

have been reduced, and of the arrangements which have been made by the scheme, or are open to the member, to restore the value of his accrued rights under the scheme.".

(10) After paragraph 14 of Schedule 5 there shall be inserted the following paragraph–

"15. A copy of any statement which any auditor of the scheme has made in the year, in accordance with the provisions of regulation 3(4) or (5) of the Occupational Pension Schemes (Auditors) Regulations 1987."(a) .

Signed by authority of the Secretary of State for Social Sevices.

Nicholas Scott
Minister of State,
Department of Health and Social Security

25th June 1987

(a) S.I. 1987/1102.

EXPLANATORY NOTE

(This note is not part of the Regulations)

These Regulations further amend the Occupational Pension Schemes (Disclosure of Information) Regulations 1986 ("the principal Regulations").

Regulation 2(3) inserts further paragraphs into regulation 6 of the principal Regulations providing for the furnishing, in the circumstances specified in those paragraphs, to members of occupational pension schemes of the kinds mentioned in those paragraphs, of the information specified in paragraphs 4B to 4H of Schedule 2 to the principal Regulations (which are all inserted by regulation 2(9) of these Regulations).

Regulation 2(10) inserts a new paragraph 15 into Schedule 5 to the principal Regulations, so that the trustees of an occupational pension scheme are required to furnish the persons specified in regulation 9 of the principal Regulations with a copy of any statement which any auditor of the scheme has made in the scheme year, to which the information relates, in accordance with the provisions of regulation 3(4) or (5) of the Occupational Pension Schemes (Auditors) Regulations 1987.

The remaining provisions of regulation 2 make minor and consequential amendments.

The report of the Occupational Pensions Board on the draft of these Regulations, dated 3rd June 1987, is contained in Command Paper (Cmnd 164) published by Her Majesty's Stationery Office.

85p net

ISBN 0 11 077105 2

Printed in the United Kingdom for Her Majesty's Stationery Office

880/WO 1008 C16 7/87 452/1 9385/9314/1771 PS 7944003

16 JUL 1987

STATUTORY INSTRUMENTS

1987 No. 1106

PENSIONS

The Occupational Pension Schemes (Qualifying Service—Consequential and Other Provisions) Regulations 1987

Made - - - -	*25th June 1987*
Laid before Parliament	*6th July 1987*
Coming into force	*6th April 1988*

The Secretary of State for Social Services, in exercise of the powers conferred upon him by sections 64(1A)(a) and 99(1) and (3) of, and paragraphs 9(2) and (3), 21, 22 and 26 of Schedule 16 to, the Social Security Act 1973**(a)**, section 168(1) of, and Schedule 20 to, the Social Security Act 1975**(b)**, and sections 43(4) and 52C(4) and (5) of, and paragraph 20 of Schedule 1A to, and paragraph 6 of Schedule 2 to, the Social Security Pensions Act 1975**(c)**, and of all other powers enabling him in that behalf, after considering the report of the Occupational Pensions Board on the proposals submitted to them**(d)**, hereby makes the following Regulations:–

Citation, commencement and interpretation

1.—(1) These Regulations may be cited as the Occupational Pension Schemes (Qualifying Service—Consequential and Other Provisions) Regulations 1987 and shall come into force on 6th April 1988.

(2) In these Regulations–

"the Contracting-out Regulations" means the Occupational Pension Schemes (Contracting-out) Regulations 1984**(e)**;

"the Preservation Regulations" means the Occupational Pension Schemes (Preservation of Benefit) Regulations 1984**(f)**;

"the Discharge Regulations" means the Occupational Pension Schemes (Discharge of Liability) Regulations 1985**(g)**; and

"the Revaluation Regulations" means the Occupational Pension Schemes (Revaluation) Regulations 1985**(h)**.

(a) 1973 c.38; subsection (1A) was added to section 64 by section 86(1) of, and paragraph 3 of Schedule 10, to the Social Security Act 1986 (c.50). *See* definition of "prescribe" in section 99(1) and explanation of the meaning of "regulations" in section 99(3).

(b) 1975 c.14. *See* definitions of "prescribe" and "regulations" in Schedule 20. Section 168(1) applies, by virtue of section 66(2) of the Social Security Pensions Act 1975 (c.60), to the exercise of certain powers conferred by that Act.

(c) 1975 c.60. Section 52C and Schedule 1A were inserted by the Social Security Act 1985 (c.53), section 2 and Schedule 1.

(d) *See* section 68(1) and (2) of the Social Security Act 1973 and section 61(2) and (3) of the Social Security Pensions Act 1975; sections 68(1) and 61(2) are amended in ways not relevant to these Regulations.

(e) S.I. 1984/380; the relevant amending instrument is S.I. 1986/317.

(f) S.I. 1984/614, to which there are amendments not relevant to these Regulations.

(g) S.I. 1985/1929, amended by S.I. 1986/2171.

(h) S.I. 1985/1930, amended by S.I. 1986/751.

Amendment of the Contracting-out Regulations

2.—(1) The Contracting-out Regulations shall be amended in accordance with the provisions of this regulation.

(2) In regulation 19(1)(*d*), the words "is under the age of 26 or" shall be omitted and for "5" there shall be substituted "2".

(3) In regulation 24(3)(*e*), for "5" there shall be substituted "2".

Amendment of the Preservation Regulations

3.—(1) The Preservation Regulations shall be amended in accordance with the provisions of this regulation.

(2) In regulation 12(4), after sub-paragraph (*a*), there shall be inserted the following sub-paragraph–

"(aa) for the alternative mentioned in paragraph (1)(e) to be substituted for short service benefit without the member's consent in any case where the conditions specified in paragraph (4A) are satisfied;".

(3) After paragraph (4) of regulation 12 there shall be inserted the following paragraph–

"(4A) The conditions referred to in paragraph (4)(aa) are–

(a) that the short service benefit is not, and does not include, protected rights (within the meaning given to that expression by Schedule 1 to the Social Security Act 1986**(a)**, whether or not as modified under section 32(2B) of the Pensions Act**(b)**);

(b) that the member has at least 2 years' qualifying service but has not 5 years' qualifying service (within the meaning given to that expression by paragraph 7 of Schedule 16 immediately before the coming into force of section 10 of the Social Security Act 1986);

(c) that the insurance policy is taken out or the annuity contract entered into more than 12 months after the member's service in relevant employment is terminated;

(d) that at least 30 days before the insurance policy is taken out or the annuity contract entered into, the trustees or managers of the scheme have sent by post to the member at his last known address, or delivered personally to him, a written notice that it is their intention to take it out or enter into it unless, before the date of expiry of the notice or, if it is later, the first anniversary of the date on which the member's service in relevant employment was terminated, the member has made an application (which he has not subsequently withdrawn) to the trustees or managers of the scheme under paragraph 16 of Schedule 1A to the Pensions Act (transfer values);

(e) that when the trustees or managers of the scheme enter into an agreement with an insurance company to take out the insurance policy or enter into the annuity contract, the member has not made an application in writing to the trustees or managers of the scheme under paragraph 16 of Schedule 1A to the Pensions Act, or if he has made such an application he has withdrawn it under paragraph 17 of that Schedule; and

(f) that the insurance policy or annuity contract is so framed that it may be assigned or surrendered on the conditions set out in regulation 2 of the Occupational Pension Schemes (Discharge of Liability) Regulations 1985.".

(4) In regulations 14(d)(i), 17(3)(b)(iii) and (4) and 21(3)(b), for "5" there shall be substituted "2".

Amendment of the Discharge Regulations

4.—(1) The Discharge Regulations shall be amended in accordance with the provisions of this regulation.

(2) In regulation 4 (c)(ii), for "5" there shall be substituted "2".

(a) 1986 c.50.
(b) Subsection (2B) was inserted into section 32 by the Social Security Act 1986 (c.50), section 6 and Schedule 2, paragraph 5.

(3) In regulation 5(b)(ii), after "12(4)(a)" there shall be inserted "or (aa)".

(4) After paragraph (b) of regulation 5, there shall be inserted the word "or" and the following paragraph–

"(c) (i) the earner died when he had, in relation to the scheme, at least 2 years' qualifying service (within the meaning of paragraph 7 of Schedule 16 to the Social Security Act 1973) but not 5 years' qualifying service (within the meaning given to that expression by paragraph 7 of Schedule 16 to the Social Security Act 1973 immediately before the coming into force of section 10 of the Social Security Act 1986),

(ii) benefit which is or includes a guaranteed minimum pension is payable to the earner's widow or widower,

(iii) the arrangement for securing the benefit by means of the policy or contract was made without the consent of the widow or widower, and

(iv) at least 30 days before the policy is taken out or the contract entered into the trustees or managers of the scheme sent by post to the widow or widower at her or his last known address, or delivered personally to her or him, a written notice of their intention to take it out or enter into it.".

Amendment of the Revaluation Regulations

5.—(1) The Revaluation Regulations shall be amended in accordance with the provisions of this regulation.

(2) In regulations 1(2) and 6, and in the heading to regulation 6, for the words "5 years' qualifying service" (wherever occurring) there shall be substituted the words "2 years' qualifying service".

Purpose prescribed under section 64(1A)(a) of the Social Security Act 1973

6. A purpose prescribed under section 64(1A)(a) of the Social Security Act 1973 (powers of Occupational Pensions Board to authorise modification of occupational pension schemes) is that of enabling the scheme–

(a) to make provision for the alternative mentioned in regulation 12(1)(e) of the Preservation Regulations to be substituted for short service benefit without the member's consent in cases where the conditions specified in regulation 12(4A) of those regulations are satisfied; and

(b) to make provision for a benefit payable to a member's widow or widower to be secured by means of a policy of insurance or annuity contract without the widow's or widower's consent in cases where the conditions specified in regulation 5(c) of the Discharge Regulations are satisfied.

Signed by authority of the Secretary of State for Social Services.

Nicholas Scott
Minister of State,
Department of Health and Social Security

25th June 1987

EXPLANATORY NOTE

(This note is not part of the Regulations)

Section 10 of the Social Security Act 1986 (c.50) makes amendments to Schedule 16 to the Social Security Act 1973 so that members of occupational pension schemes have the benefit of the "preservation requirements" set out in the latter Act after 2, instead of 5, years' qualifying service.

Most of the provisions of these Regulations make amendments of other regulations which are consequential upon section 10, and regulation 2(2) also removes, from the regulation it amends, some wording which refers to the earner's being under the age of 26.

Regulation 3(2) and (3) makes amendments so that where a member's service in employment to which a scheme applies is terminated when he has at least 2, but less than 5, years' qualifying service, and other specified conditions are satisfied, benefits under an insurance policy or annuity contract different from those required to constitute short service benefit (as defined in Schedule 16 to the Social Security Act 1973) may be substituted for his short service benefit without his consent.

Regulation 4(4) makes amendments so that where a member dies when he has at least 2, but less than 5, years' qualifying service, and other specified conditions are satisfied, the trustees or managers of the scheme may be discharged of their liability to provide for the member's widow or widower a benefit which is or includes a guaranteed minimum pension by substituting benefits under an insurance policy or annuity contract.

Regulation 6 enables the Occupational Pensions Board to authorise the modification of an occupational pension scheme to enable it (if its rules would not otherwise allow it) to take advantage of the provisions of regulations 3(2) and (3) and 4(4).

The report of the Occupational Pensions Board on the draft of these Regulations, dated 3rd February 1987, is contained in Command Paper (Cmnd 165) published by Her Majesty's Stationery Office.

85p net

ISBN 0 11 077106 0

Printed in the United Kingdom for Her Majesty's Stationery Office 880 5183 WO 1002 C16 7/87 452/2 3840 PS7944005

STATUTORY INSTRUMENTS

1987 No. 1107

PENSIONS

The Occupational Pension Schemes (Transfer Values) Amendment Regulations 1987

Made - - - -	*25th June 1987*
Laid before Parliament	*6th July 1987*
Coming into force	
For the purposes of regulations 1 and 2(5)	*27th July 1987*
For all other purposes	*6th April 1988*

The Secretary of State for Social Services, in exercise of the powers conferred upon him by section 168(1) of, and Schedule 20 to, the Social Security Act 1975(**a**) , and paragraphs 12(2A) and (2B), 13 and 14 of Schedule 1A to the Social Security Pensions Act 1975(**b**) , and of all other powers enabling him in that behalf, by this instrument, which is made before the end of a period of 12 months from the commencement of the enactments under which it is made, makes the following Regulations:

Citation, commencement and interpretation

1.—(1) These Regulations may be cited as the Occupational Pension Schemes (Transfer Values) Amendment Regulations 1987 and shall come into force–

(a) for the purposes of regulations 1 and 2(5), on 27th July 1987;

(b) for all other purposes on 6th April 1988.

(2) In these Regulations "the principal Regulations" means the Occupational Pension Schemes (Transfer Values) Regulations 1985(**c**) .

Amendments of the principal Regulations

2.—(1) The principal Regulations shall be amended in accordance with the provisions of paragraphs (2) to (5) of this regulation.

(2) In regulation 1(2) (interpretation)–

(a) at the beginning there shall be inserted the following definition–

" "actual service" has the meaning given to that expression by paragraph 3(2) of Schedule 16 to the Social Security Act 1973;";

(b) after the definition of "member" there shall be inserted the following definitions–

(**a**) 1975 c.14. *See* definitions of "prescribe" and "regulations" in Schedule 20. Section 168(1) applies, by virtue of section 66(2) of the Social Security Pensions Act 1975 (c.60), to the exercise of certain powers conferred by that Act.
(**b**) 1975 c.60. Schedule 1A was inserted by the Social Security Act 1985 (c.53), section 2, and Part II of Schedule 1. Paragraph 12(2A) and (2B) of Schedule 1A was inserted, and paragraphs 13 and 14 were amended, by the Social Security Act 1986 (c.50), section 86 and Schedule 10, paragraph 30. Paragraphs 13 and 14 are modified in relation to occupational pension schemes, by the Personal and Occupational Pension Schemes (Modification of Enactments) Regulations 1987 (S.I. 1987/1116), regulation 5(4) and Schedule 6.
(**c**) S.I. 1985/1931, amended by S.I. 1986/1046, 2171.

[SS87/1724]

" "personal pension scheme" has the meaning given to that expression by section 84(1) of the Social Security Act 1986;

"protected rights" has the meaning given to that expression by Schedule 1 to the Social Security Act 1986 as modified by section 32(2B);"; and

(c) for the definition of "scheme", there shall be substituted the following definition–

" "scheme", except in the expression "personal pension scheme", means occupational pension scheme".

(3) In regulation 2(1)–

(a) after "paragraph 13(2)(a)" there shall be inserted "(cash equivalent of member's rights in a scheme to be used for acquiring transfer credits or rights under another scheme or personal pension scheme)";

(b) for sub-paragraph (a) there shall be substituted the following sub-paragraphs–

"(a) if the member's cash equivalent such as is mentioned in paragraph 12(1) (or any portion of it to be used under paragraph 13(2)(a)) is or includes the cash equivalent of his accrued rights to guaranteed minimum pensions under a scheme, then the scheme or personal pension scheme under whose rules transfer credits or rights are acquired is one to which those accrued rights may be transferred, or to which a transfer payment in respect of those accrued rights may be made, in accordance with regulation 2 or 2B, as the case may be, of the Contracting-out (Transfer) Regulations 1985, as amended by the Contracting-out (Transfer) Amendment Regulations 1987;

(aa) if the member's cash equivalent such as is mentioned in paragraph 12(1) (or any portion of it to be used under paragraph 13(2)(a)) is or includes the cash equivalent of his protected rights, then the scheme or personal pension scheme under whose rules transfer credits or rights are to be acquired is one to which a transfer payment in respect of protected rights may be made in accordance with regulations 2 and 3 of the Protected Rights (Transfer Payment) Regulations 1987;"; and

(c) in sub-paragraph (b)–

(i) after "the scheme from which rights are transferred" there shall be inserted "or from which a transfer payment is made", and

(ii) for "the scheme to which rights are transferred" there shall be substituted "the scheme or personal pension scheme to which rights are transferred or to which a transfer payment in respect of rights is made".

(4) After regulation 2 there shall be inserted the following regulations–

"Reduction of the cash equivalent specified in paragraph 12(1)

2A.—(1) For the purposes of paragraph 12(2A), where a member continues in employment to which a scheme applies after his pensionable service in that employment terminates and–

(a) his pensionable service terminated at his request; and

(b) the relevant date is the date when his pensionable service terminated, or where the relevant date is the date of the relevant application his pensionable service, but for that request, would have continued until that date,

he acquires a right to the cash equivalent of only that part of the benefits specified in paragraph 12(1) which is specified in paragraph (2) below.

(2) The part referred to in paragraph (1) above is–

(a) where the benefits are money purchase benefits, such part of them as has accrued to or in respect of him after 5th April 1988; and

(b) in any other case–

(i) where the benefits have accrued to or in respect of him as a result of his actual service, the same proportion of them as his actual service after 5th April 1988 bears to his total actual service,

(ii) where the benefits have accrued to or in respect of him as a result of service notionally attributed to him, or service treated by scheme rules as being longer or shorter than it actually is, such part of them as was credited to him after 5th April 1988, and

(iii) where heads (i) and (ii) above both apply, the aggregate of the benefits derived separately under each of those heads.

Treatment of a number of employments as single employment

2B. For the purposes of paragraph 12(2A), where a member's employment to which a scheme applies terminates but that member enters again into employment to which that scheme applies, then, if there is between those 2 employments–

(a) an interval not exceeding one month; or

(b) an interval of any length if the second of the employments results from the exercise of a right to return to work under section 45(1) of the Employment Protection (Consolidation) Act 1978 (right to return to work following pregnancy or confinement),

they shall be treated as a single employment.".

(5) In regulation 3(2)(b)(ii) for "issued on 18th December 1985", there shall be substituted "current at the date of the calculation".

Signed by authority of the Secretary of State for Social Services.

Nicholas Scott
Minister of State,
Department of Health and Social Security

25th June 1987

EXPLANATORY NOTE

(This note is not part of the Regulations)

These Regulations are all made under provisions of the Social Security Pensions Act 1975 ("the 1975 Act") inserted by, or provisions modified by Regulations made under, the Social Security Act 1986 ("the 1986 Act"), before the end of a period of 12 months from the commencement of the relevant provisions as inserted or modified. Consequently, by virtue of section 61(5) of the 1986 Act, the provisions of section 61(2) and (3) of the 1975 Act (as amended by section 86(1) of, and paragraph 94 of Schedule 10 to, the 1986 Act), which require reference to the Occupational Pensions Board of, and a report by the Board on, proposals to make regulations for certain purposes of both Acts, do not apply to them.

They amend the Occupational Pension Schemes (Transfer Values) Regulations 1985 ("the principal Regulations").

Regulation 2(2) amends regulation 1(2) of the principal Regulations (interpretation).

Regulation 2(3) amends regulation 2(1) of the principal Regulations so that it extends to members of occupational pension schemes who opt to have their transfer value used to acquire transfer credits or rights under the rules of a money purchase contracted-out scheme or a personal pension scheme.

Regulation 2(4) provides for the right to a cash equivalent to be limited in circumstances where a former member of a scheme remains in employment to which that scheme applies after leaving the scheme voluntarily.

Regulation 2(5) amends regulation 3(2)(b)(ii) of the principal Regulations so as to provide that the publication "Retirement Benefit Schemes – Transfer Values (GN11)" referred to in that provision is to be the one current on the date when the calculation of a transfer value is to be made. The current edition of that publication may be obtained from the Institute of Actuaries, Staple Inn Hall, High Holborn, London WC1V 7QJ, and from the Faculty of Actuaries, 23 St Andrew Square, Edinburgh EH2 1AQ.

The remaining amendments made by these Regulations are minor or consequential.

85p net

ISBN 0 11 077107 9

Printed in the United Kingdom for Her Majesty's Stationery Office

880/WO 0994   C16   7/87   452/1   9385/9077/1590   PS 7944003

STATUTORY INSTRUMENTS

1987 No. 1108

PENSIONS

The Pension Schemes (Voluntary Contributions Requirements and Voluntary and Compulsory Membership) Regulations 1987

Made - - - -	25th June 1987
Laid before Parliament	6th July 1987
Coming into force	
For the purposes of personal pension schemes	4th January 1988
For the purposes of occupational pension schemes	6th April 1988

The Secretary of State for Social Services, in exercise of the powers conferred upon him by sections 12(1), 15(1) and 84(1) of the Social Security Act 1986(a), and of all other powers enabling him in that behalf, by this instrument, which is made before the end of a period of 12 months from the commencement of the enactments under which it is made, makes the following Regulations:–

Citation, commencement and interpretation

1.—(1) These Regulations may be cited as the Pension Schemes (Voluntary Contributions Requirements and Voluntary and Compulsory Membership) Regulations 1987 and shall come into force–

(a) for the purposes of personal pension schemes on 4th January 1988; and

(b) for the purposes of occupational pension schemes on 6th April 1988.

(2) In these Regulations, except where the context otherwise requires–

"the Act" means the Social Security Act 1986;

"normal pension age" and "public service pension scheme" shall be construed in accordance with section 66(1) of the Social Security Pensions Act 1975(b);

"pensionable service" and "relevant employment" shall be construed in accordance with Schedule 16 to the Social Security Act 1973(c);

"scheme" means a personal or occupational pension scheme;

"secondary Class 1 contribution" shall be construed in accordance with section 4 of the Social Security Act 1975(d);

and other expressions have the same meaning as in the Act.

(a) 1986 c.50; *see* definitions of "prescribed" and "regulations" in section 84(1).
(b) 1975 c.60.
(c) 1973 c.38.
(d) 1975 c.14.

(3) In these Regulations, except where the context otherwise requires, any reference to a numbered section is to the section of the Act bearing that number.

Exceptions to section 12(1)

2.—(1) Section 12(1) (voluntary contributions requirements) shall not apply to the rules of any public service pension scheme unless it is an exempt approved scheme for the purposes of section 21 of the Finance Act 1970**(a)**.

(2) Section 12(1) shall not apply to the rules of any personal pension scheme in so far as it is comprised in an annuity contract made before 4th January 1988.

(3) Section 12(1)(a) and (b) shall not apply to the rules of any scheme in so far as they relate to the payment by a member of any sum as voluntary contributions where that payment would not qualify for relief from tax in accordance with section 21(4) or 22(2) of the Finance Act 1970**(b)**.

(4) Section 12(1)(a) and (b) shall not apply to the rules of any scheme in so far as they provide that a member of the scheme must give the trustees or managers of the scheme notice, of a period not exceeding 12 months, of his intention to pay voluntary contributions at a specified rate or to vary that rate.

(5) Section 12(1)(a) and (b) shall not apply to the rules of any personal pension scheme in so far as they relate to a member whose rights under the scheme derive only from one or more transfer payments.

(6) Section 12(1)(a) and (b) shall not apply to the rules of any occupational pension scheme ("the first scheme") in so far as they relate to a member–

    (a) in respect of whose current pensionable service the scheme will provide benefit only on his death; or

    (b) whose pensionable service either has not begun or has terminated; or

    (c) who is either within one year of reaching, or has reached, normal pension age; or

    (d) who is, or is eligible to become, a member of at least one other occupational pension scheme which applies to the same employment as the first scheme and which–

        (i) if he is a member of it, complies in relation to him, or, if he is not a member of it, would comply in relation to him if he were, with the voluntary contributions requirements, and

        (ii) is not a scheme which, if he is a member of it, falls in relation to him, or, if he is not a member of it, would fall in relation to him if he were, to be regarded as a scheme excepted from the application of section 12(1)(a) and (b) by virtue of paragraph (1), (2), (5) or (6)(a), (b) or (c) of this regulation.

(7) Section 12(1)(b) shall not apply to the rules of any scheme in so far as they impose, or allow any person to impose, a lower limit on the payment by a member of voluntary contributions in respect of any tax year if that lower limit is not higher than the amount specified in paragraph (8) of this regulation.

(8) The amount last mentioned in paragraph (7) of this regulation is 0.5 per cent. of the member's earnings in that tax year, or, if it is greater, 3 times the lower earnings limit (within the meaning of section 1 of the Social Security Pensions Act 1975**(c)** for that tax year.

(9) In paragraph (8) of this regulation, "member's earnings" means–

    (a) in the case of a member of a personal pension scheme, his earnings attributable to his employment as an employed earner; or

    (b) in the case of a member of an occupational pension scheme, his earnings attributable to his relevant employment,

in respect of which secondary Class 1 contributions are payable.

(a) 1970 c.24; section 21(6) was repealed by the Finance Act 1971 (c.68), sections 56(3) and 69(7) and Schedule 14, Part IV; section 21(10) and (11) was repealed by the Finance Act 1971, section 69(7) and Schedule 14, Part I.
(b) Section 22(2) was amended by the Finance Act 1972 (c.41), section 74(3).
(c) Section 1(2) was amended by section 74(6) of the Social Security Act 1986.

(10) Section 12(1)(b) shall not apply to the rules of any scheme in so far as they impose, or allow any person to impose, an upper limit on the payment by a member of voluntary contributions which is equivalent to the maximum amount which, ignoring any remuneration in kind, could be paid in any period without prejudicing the qualification of the scheme for tax-exemption or tax-approval.

(11) Section 12(1)(c) and (d) shall not apply to the rules of any scheme in relation to a member's voluntary contributions to the extent that those contributions are paid under an agreement–

(a) which was made before the date on which section 12 came into force; and

(b) which has not, since that date, been varied.

(12) Section 12(1)(d)(ii) shall not apply to the rules of any scheme to the extent that the additional benefits provided in accordance with them are money purchase benefits.

Exceptions to section 15(1)(a)

3. Section 15(1)(a) (terms of contracts of service or schemes restricting choice to be void) shall not apply to any term of a contract of service or any rule of an occupational pension scheme to the effect that an employed earner must be a member of a particular occupational pension scheme or one or other of a number of particular occupational pension schemes, during any period when that scheme is, or those schemes are, so framed that in relation to that period–

(a) the earner in question is not required to pay contributions to the scheme, and

(b) the scheme will provide benefit in respect of that earner only on his death.

Signed by authority of the Secretary of State for Social Services.

Nicholas Scott
Minister of State,
Department of Health and Social Security

25th June 1987

EXPLANATORY NOTE

(This note is not part of the Regulations)

These Regulations are made under either section 12(1) or section 15(1) of the Social Security Act 1986 ("the 1986 Act") before the expiry of the period of 12 months beginning with the bringing into force (on 4th January 1988 for the purposes of personal pension schemes and on 6th April 1988 for the purposes of occupational pension schemes) of those sections.

Consequently, by virtue of section 61(5) of the 1986 Act, the provisions of section 61(2) and (3) of the Social Security Pensions Act 1975 (which, as amended by section 86(1) of, and paragraph 94 of Schedule 10 to, the 1986 Act, require reference to the Occupational Pensions Board of, and a report by the Board on, proposals to make regulations for the purposes of Part I of the 1986 Act), do not apply to them.

Regulation 2 provides that section 12(1) of the 1986 Act (voluntary contributions requirements) shall not apply, to the extent specified, to the rules of occupational and personal pension schemes. In particular, regulation 2(1) provides that none of the voluntary contributions requirements shall apply to the rules of any public service pension scheme other than any such scheme which is an exempt approved scheme for the purposes of section 21 of the Finance Act 1970; regulation 2(2) provides that none of the voluntary contributions requirements shall apply to the rules of any personal pension scheme to the extent that it is comprised in an annuity contract made before 4th January 1988; regulation 2(5) provides that a personal pension scheme is not required to accept voluntary contributions from a member whose rights under the scheme derive only from transfer payments; regulation 2(6) provides that an occupational pension scheme need not accept voluntary contributions from a member–

(a) in respect of whom the scheme will pay only death benefits;

(b) who is not in pensionable service;

(c) who is within a year of normal pension age or older; and

(d) who is, or is eligible to become, a member of another occupational pension scheme which meets the voluntary contributions requirements;

and regulation 2(7) provides that a scheme may impose a lower limit, not greater than that specified in regulation 2(8), on the voluntary contributions it will accept from a member in a tax year.

Regulation 3 provides that section 15(1)(a) of the 1986 Act (subject to prescribed exceptions, any term of a contract of service or any rule of an occupational pension scheme to the effect that an employed earner must be a member of a particular scheme or one of a number of particular schemes shall be void) does not apply during any period when that scheme is, or those schemes are, so framed that, in relation to that period–

(a) the earner in question is not required to pay contributions to the scheme, and

(b) the scheme will provide benefit in respect of that earner only on his death.

85p net

ISBN 0 11 077108 7

Printed in the United Kingdom for Her Majesty's Stationery Office

880   WO998   C16   7/87   452/3   4235   PS 7944007   871500C

STATUTORY INSTRUMENTS

1987 No. 1109

PENSIONS

The Personal Pension Schemes (Appropriate Schemes) Regulations 1987

Made - - - -	*25th June 1987*
Laid before Parliament	*6th July 1987*
Coming into force	
regulations 1 to 11, 19 and 20	*27th July 1987*
regulations 12 to 18	*4th January 1988*

The Secretary of State for Social Services, in exercise of the powers conferred upon him by sections 1(1), (2), (4), (5), (9), (10) and (11), 2(1), (2) and (5), 3(1)(b) and (5), 84(1) and 89(1) of, and paragraphs 2 and 6 of Schedule 1 to, the Social Security Act 1986(**a**), and of all other powers enabling him in that behalf, by this instrument, which is made before the end of a period of 12 months from the commencement of the enactments under which it is made, makes the following Regulations:–

Citation, commencement and interpretation

1.—(1) These Regulations may be cited as the Personal Pension Schemes (Appropriate Schemes) Regulations 1987; this regulation and regulations 2 to 11, 19 and 20 shall come into force on 27th July 1987, and regulations 12 to 18 shall come into force on 4th January 1988.

(2) In these Regulations, unless the context otherwise requires–

"the Act" means the Social Security Act 1986;

"administrators", in relation to a personal pension scheme, means the trustees or, if there are no trustees, the managers (except any trustee or manager who is resident outside the United Kingdom, or which, being a company, does not have its registered office in the United Kingdom), and any person who is resident in the United Kingdom, or which, being a company, has its registered office in the United Kingdom, who or which is authorised to act on behalf of the trustees, or, if there are no trustees, on behalf of the managers;

"the Board" means the Occupational Pensions Board;

"contracted-out", "contracted-out scheme" and "money purchase contracted-out scheme" shall be construed in accordance with the Social Security Pensions Act 1975(**b**);

"Friendly Society" means a Friendly Society registered under section 7(1)(a) of the Friendly Societies Act 1974(**c**), or, as the case may be, under section 1(1)(a) of the Friendly Societies Act (Northern Ireland) 1970(**d**);

(**a**) 1986 c.50. *See* definitions of "prescribed" and "regulations" in section 84(1).
(**b**) 1975 c.60. *See* sections 32 and 66, as amended by the Social Security Act 1986 (c.50), Schedule 2, paragraphs 5 and 11.
(**c**) 1974 c.46.
(**d**) 1970 c.31 (N.I.).

"investment business" has the meaning assigned to that expression by the Financial Services Act 1986(a);

"pensionable age" means, in the case of a man, 65, and in the case of a woman, 60;

"scheme" (except in the expressions "contracted-out scheme", "money purchase contracted-out scheme", "occupational pension scheme" and "unit trust scheme") means personal pension scheme;

"tax week" has the same meaning as in the Social Security Act 1975(b);

and other expressions have the same meaning as in the Act.

(3) In these Regulations, unless the context otherwise requires, any reference–

(a) to a numbered regulation is to the regulation in these regulations bearing that number;

(b) in a regulation to a numbered paragraph is to the paragraph of that regulation bearing that number;

(c) in a paragraph to a lettered sub-paragraph is to the sub-paragraph of that paragraph bearing that letter.

Forms of schemes which may be appropriate schemes

2. Without prejudice to any other requirements imposed by the Act or regulations made thereunder, a personal pension scheme can be an appropriate scheme only if it takes the form specified in any one (but not more than one) of paragraphs (a) to (c), namely–

(a) an arrangement for the issue of insurance policies or annuity contracts;

(b) a unit trust scheme which has been authorised under section 78(1) of, or by virtue of paragraph 9 of Schedule 15 to, the Financial Services Act 1986;

(c) an arrangement for the investment of contributions in an interest–bearing account.

Persons who and bodies which may establish schemes

3.—(1) Without prejudice to any other requirements of the Act or regulations made thereunder–

(a) an arrangement such as is described in regulation 2(a) which is established by a Friendly Society can be an appropriate scheme only if paragraph (2) applies to that Friendly Society; and

(b) an arrangement such as is described in regulation 2(c) can be an appropriate scheme only if it is established by a person to whom or a body to which paragraph (3) applies.

(2) This paragraph applies to a Friendly Society which–

(a) is authorised by virtue of Chapter III of Part I of the Financial Services Act 1986; and

(b) has disclosed in its audited accounts a contributions income of not less than £300,000 in the year 1986 and £400,000 in the year 1987.

(3) This paragraph applies to–

(a) a building society as defined in the Building Societies Act 1986(c);

(b) a bank recognised under the Banking Act 1979(d);

(c) a deposit taker licensed under the Banking Act 1979.

(a) 1986 c.60.
(b) 1975 c.14.
(c) 1986 c.53.
(d) 1979 c.37.

Information to be included in an application for an appropriate scheme certificate

4.—(1) Every application for an appropriate scheme certificate shall be made in writing to the Board and shall include the following particulars—

   (a) the name of the scheme and the address where it is administered;

   (b) the names and addresses of the trustees (if any) and administrators of the scheme;

   (c) the name, address and standing (in relation to the scheme) of the person applying for the certificate, if he is not the trustees or administrators, or one or some of them;

   (d) the name and address of the person who or body which has established the scheme (the address in the case of a company being that of its registered office);

   (e) such evidence as the Board may reasonably require that the scheme satisfies such of the requirements of regulation 3 as apply to it;

   (f) which of the forms specified in paragraphs (a) to (c) of regulation 2 the scheme takes;

   (g) the name and address of a bank or building society which accepts payments made by automated direct credit transfer and the name and number of the account at that bank or building society, into which it is desired that minimum contributions should be paid; and

   (h) the date (being a date consistent with the provisions of regulation 5(2)(b)) from which it is desired that the certificate shall have effect.

(2) Every application shall be accompanied by a copy of—

   (a) the documents constituting the scheme; and

   (b) the rules of the scheme, if they are not set out in those documents or any of them,

except where the Board in their discretion dispense wholly or partly with this requirement.

(3) Every person who has made an application shall supply such other documents and information as the Board may reasonably require.

Issue of appropriate scheme certificates

5.—(1) When the Board have determined that a scheme should be treated as an appropriate scheme, they shall issue an appropriate scheme certificate to the person who applied for it.

(2) The appropriate scheme certificate shall specify—

   (a) the name of the scheme and the address where it is administered; and

   (b) the date from which the certificate is to have effect, which shall be 6th April in 1987 or any later year and which may be earlier than the date on which the certificate is issued where the person who applied for the certificate has so requested, but, if the Board receive the application after 5th April 1989, not earlier than 6th April in the tax year in which the Board receive the application.

Further information and change of circumstances

6. The administrators of the scheme shall—

   (a) in such manner and at such times as the Board may reasonably require, furnish to the Board such reports, accounts and other documents and information relating to the scheme to which the certificate relates as the Board may reasonably require; and

   (b) notify the Board in writing of—

      (i) any change in the identity, names or addresses of the trustees (if any) and administrators of the scheme,

      (ii) any change in the name or address of the person who or body which has established the scheme,

      (iii) any change affecting the information given under regulation 4(1)(e) and (f), and

(iv) any such change of circumstances affecting the scheme as the Board may have required them to notify,

as soon as practicable after its occurrence; and the document by which the notification is given may be served by post.

Applications for the variation of, and to surrender, appropriate scheme certificates

7.—(1) Every application for the variation of, or to surrender, an appropriate scheme certificate—

(a) shall be made in writing to the Board by the administrators of the scheme;

(b) shall be made only after notices of intention to make that application have been given by the administrators in accordance with paragraph (2) except where (in the case of an application for the variation of an appropriate scheme certificate) the board dispense with this requirement; and

(c) shall include a statement that all notices required by paragraph (2) to be given in relation to that application have been duly given.

(2) Notices of intention to make an application such as is mentioned in paragraph (1) shall be given in writing to—

(a) any member of the scheme who has protected rights under it; and

(b) any earner who, jointly with the trustees or managers of the scheme, has given in relation to the scheme a notice under section 1(9) of the Act which has not been cancelled,

by sending it to his last known address; and the document comprising the notice may be served by post.

(3) Notices given under this regulation shall specify—

(a) the name of the scheme and the address where it is administered;

(b) the date (being a date consistent with the provisions of regulation 9(5)) from which it is desired that the variation or surrender shall have effect; and

(c) where the application is to surrender an appropriate scheme certificate, any arrangements made or proposed for the preservation or transfer of protected rights under the scheme.

(4) Every person who makes an application under this regulation shall supply such other documents and information as the board may reasonably require.

Determination of question arising on an application for the issue of an appropriate scheme certificate

8.—(1) Subject to the provisions of this regulation, the Board shall treat an application for an appropriate scheme certificate as an application for the determination of the question whether the scheme in question should be an appropriate scheme, and subject to the provisions of paragraph (3), they shall determine the question as soon as practicable.

(2) The Board may refuse to give effect to an application if they are not satisfied that the applicant has complied with the provisions of regulation 4.

(3) The Board may defer making a determination until such documents and information as are mentioned in regulation 4(2) and (3) have been supplied.

(4) Where under this regulation the Board determine that a scheme should be treated as an appropriate scheme they shall issue an appropriate scheme certificate in accordance with regulation 5, and inform the Secretary of State that they have done so.

(5) Where the Board's determination under this regulation does not give effect to the application, the Board shall notify the applicant in writing of the determination and of the reasons for it and shall refer him to the Board's powers of review under section 67 of the Social Security Act 1973**(a)**.

(a) 1973 c.38.

Determination of question arising on an application with a view to the variation or surrender of an appropriate scheme certificate

9.—(1) Subject to the provisions of this regulation, the Board shall treat an application made with a view to the variation or surrender of an appropriate scheme certificate as an application for the determination of the question whether the certificate should be varied or, as the case may be, whether the scheme should cease to be an appropriate scheme; and subject to the provisions of paragraph (3) they shall determine the question as soon as practicable.

(2) The Board may refuse to give effect to an application if they are not satisfied that the applicant has complied with the provisions of regulation 7.

(3) The Board may defer making a determination until such documents and information as are mentioned in regulation 7(4) have been supplied.

(4) When the Board have made a determination under paragraph (1), they shall vary or accept the surrender of the certificate if such action would give effect to the determination, and inform the Secretary of State that they have done so.

(5) The date from which a surrender or variation is to have effect shall be that on which the determination is made, except that, where the person who made the application has requested that it should have effect from a specific date which is earlier or later than the date on which the determination is made, it may have effect from that specific date, so however that that date shall not be earlier than the date on which the Board receive the application, or later than the last day of the tax year in which the Board receive the application.

(6) Where the Board's determination under this regulation does not give effect to the application, the Board shall notify the applicant in writing of the determination and of the reasons for it and shall refer him to the Board's powers of review under section 67 of the Social Security Act 1973; and the applicant shall give notice in writing of the determination and the Board's reasons for it, to—

(a) any member of the scheme who has protected rights under it; and

(b) any earner who, jointly with the trustees or managers of the scheme, has given in relation to the scheme a notice under section 1(9) of the Act which has not been cancelled,

by sending it to his last known address; and the document comprising the notice may be served by post.

Other circumstances in which the Board may cancel an appropriate scheme certificate

10.—(1) Where the Board have reason to suppose that any scheme to which an appropriate scheme certificate applies should not continue to be an appropriate scheme, and the administrators of the scheme have not shown to the satisfaction of the Board that it should so continue, the Board may determine that the scheme should not continue to be treated as an appropriate scheme; where they so determine, they shall cancel the certificate with effect from such date as they may specify (subject to paragraph (2)); the Board shall notify the administrators of the scheme in writing of their determination and the reasons for it and shall refer them to the Board's powers of review under section 67 of the Social Security Act 1973, and shall also notify the Secretary of State of their determination.

(2) The date from which the cancellation is to have effect shall be the date on which the certificate is cancelled, except that, where the Board consider that the scheme has failed to satisfy the requirements for continuing to be an appropriate scheme before that date, they may cancel the certificate with effect from an earlier date, so however that that earlier date—

(a) shall not be a date other than 6th April in any year; and

(b) shall not be earlier than 6th April in the tax year in which the Board consider that the scheme first failed to satisfy those requirements.

Determination of questions

11. Any question—
   (a) whether a scheme is, or at any time was, an appropriate scheme; or
   (b) for what period a scheme is or has been an appropriate scheme,
shall be determined by the Board.

Notice under section 1(9) of the Act

12.—(1) A notice under section 1(9) of the Act (notices to the Secretary of State by an earner and the trustees or managers of a scheme of willingness that that scheme should be his chosen scheme) shall be given in writing in such form as the Secretary of State may in his discretion accept.

(2) Subject to paragraph (3), the date specified in a notice under section 1(9) as the date from which the scheme is to be the earner's chosen scheme shall be one of the following dates, selected by the persons who give the notice, namely—
   (a) 6th April in the tax year in which the Secretary of State receives the notice;
   (b) 6th April in the next tax year; and
   (c) only in a case where the Secretary of State receives the notice before 6th April 1989, 6th April 1987.

(3) In a case where a scheme ("the first scheme") was an earner's chosen scheme on the date with effect from which the first scheme ceased to be an appropriate scheme, the date specified in a notice under section 1(9) as the date from which another scheme ("the second scheme") is to be the earner's chosen scheme may be the date with effect from which the first scheme ceased to be an appropriate scheme (whether or not that date is 6th April), if that date is not earlier than whichever is the earlier of—
   (a) the date 6 months earlier than that on which the Secretary of State receives the notice; and
   (b) 6th April in the tax year in which the Secretary of State receives the notice.

Notice under section 1(10) of the Act

13.—(1) A notice under section 1(10) of the Act (notice cancelling a notice given under section 1(9), in this regulation called "the relevant section 1(9) notice") shall be given in writing and in such form as the Secretary of State may in his discretion accept.

(2) The date specified in a notice under section 1(10) as the date from which the scheme is to cease to be the earner's chosen scheme shall be 6th April in the tax year in which the Secretary of State receives the notice or 6th April in the next tax year, so however that if the notice is given by the earner and not by the trustees or managers of the scheme the date shall be at least a year later than the date specified in the relevant section 1(9) notice.

Circumstances in which minimum contributions are not to be paid to schemes

14.—(1) Minimum contributions shall not be paid in respect of an earner for any part of the tax year in which he attains pensionable age unless they were payable, or would have been payable had his earnings not been taken to be nil under regulation 17, in respect of him for the previous tax year.

(2) After a scheme has ceased to be appropriate, minimum contributions shall not, except as provided by paragraph (11), be paid to the trustees or managers of that scheme for any period during which that scheme was appropriate by virtue of an appropriate scheme certificate which had effect from a date earlier than that on which it ceased to be appropriate.

(3) After effect has been given to protected rights of an earner under a scheme, minimum contributions shall not, except as provided by paragraph (11), be paid to the trustees or managers of that scheme for any period during which that scheme was the earner's chosen scheme by virtue of a notice given under section 1(9) of the Act which had effect from a date earlier than that on which effect was given to those protected rights.

(4) Where–

(a) but for the provisions of paragraph (2), or paragraphs (2) and (3), minimum contributions would have fallen to be paid, to the trustees or managers of a scheme ("the first scheme") which has ceased to be appropriate, for–

(i) any tax year before it ceased to be appropriate, or

(ii) any part of a tax year before it ceased to be appropriate;

(b) no minimum contributions have been paid, except under this paragraph, in respect of that earner for the whole or any part of the period which begins on the first day of –

(i) the tax year mentioned in sub-paragraph (a)(i), or

(ii) the tax year mentioned in sub-paragraph (a)(ii),

and ends on the day before that on which the first scheme ceased to be appropriate; and

(c) with effect from the date on which the first scheme ceased to be appropriate, another scheme ("the second scheme") which is an appropriate scheme has become the chosen scheme of the earner in respect of whom the minimum contributions mentioned in sub-paragraph (a) would have fallen to be paid,

the minimum contributions which would have fallen to be paid to the trustees or managers of the first scheme, except any of them that have been paid in accordance with paragraph (5), shall be paid to the trustees or managers of the second scheme.

(5) Where, but for the provisions of paragraph (3), or paragraphs (2) and (3), minimum contributions would have fallen to be paid to the trustees or managers of a scheme for any period before the end of the tax year in which effect was given to the protected rights in question, those minimum contributions shall, subject to paragraph (6), be paid, in the circumstances described in paragraphs (7), (10) and (13), to the persons described in paragraphs (8), (9), (11), (12) and (14) (and in no other circumstances and to no other persons).

(6) In the case of a scheme which has ceased to be appropriate–

(a) no payment shall be required under paragraph (5) if effect was given to the protected rights in question later than the end of the tax year immediately following the tax year which included the day with effect from which the scheme ceased to be appropriate; and

(b) no payment shall be required under paragraph (5) of any minimum contributions that–

(i) would have fallen to be paid for a period after the end of the tax year immediately preceding the tax year which included the day with effect from which the scheme ceased to be appropriate, or

(ii) are required under paragraph (4) to be paid to the trustees or managers of another scheme.

(7) Paragraphs (8) and (9) apply where effect has been given to the earner's protected rights by the making of a transfer payment to another personal pension scheme or to an occupational pension scheme.

(8) Where the personal pension scheme is an appropriate scheme or the occupational pension scheme is a money purchase contracted-out scheme the minimum contributions shall be paid to the trustees or managers of that scheme.

(9) Where the circumstances described in paragraph (8) do not exist and the minimum contributions are payable for, or for part of, the tax year in which the earner attained pensionable age or died before attaining that age, the minimum contributions shall be paid to the earner or his widow or her widower, or if the earner died unmarried, they may at the Secretary of State's discretion be paid to any person.

(10) Paragraphs (11) and (12) apply where effect has been given to the earner's protected rights by the purchase of an annuity or by the provision by the scheme of a pension.

(11) Where–
  (a) the amount of the minimum contributions in question is at least 10 times as great as the lower earnings limit (within the meaning of section 1 of the Social Security Pensions Act 1975(a)) for the tax year in which the Secretary of State first becomes aware that the minimum contributions are payable, or would be payable but for paragraph (2) or (3); and
  (b) the Secretary of State is satisfied that the minimum contributions will be applied fairly to increase the amount of the annuity or pension,

the minimum contributions shall be paid (in the case of an annuity) to the insurance company from which the annuity has been purchased or (in the case of a pension) to the trustees or managers of the scheme.

(12) Where the circumstances described in paragraph (11) do not exist and the minimum contributions are payable for, or for part of, the tax year in which the earner attained pensionable age or died before attaining that age, the minimum contributions shall be paid to the earner or his widow or her widower, or if the earner died unmarried, they may at the Secretary of State's discretion be paid to any person.

(13) Paragraph (14) applies where effect has been given to the earner's protected rights by the award of a lump sum.

(14) Where the minimum contributions are payable for, or for part of, the tax year in which the earner attained pensionable age or died before attaining that age, the minimum contributions shall be paid to the earner or his widow or her widower, or if the earner died unmarried, they may at the Secretary of State's discretion be paid to any person.

Manner of payment of minimum contributions

15. Minimum contributions shall be paid–
  (a) by automated direct credit transfer into a bank or building society account which relates to the relevant scheme and which accepts payments made by automated direct credit transfer; or
  (b) in such other manner as the Secretary of State may in his discretion approve.

Claim for the purpose of section 3(1)(b) of the Act

16. For the purpose of section 3(1)(b) of the Act, £1.00 shall be substituted for 2 per cent. of the earnings referred to in section 3(1)(a) if 2 per cent. of those earnings is less than £1.00 and the earner or his widow or her widower, or the administrators of the relevant scheme in respect of whom the minimum contributions are to be paid, applies or apply in writing in such form as the Secretary of State may in his discretion accept.

Calculation or estimation of earnings

17.—(1) In relation to any tax year, the earnings of an earner shall be calculated or estimated, for the purposes mentioned in this regulation, on the bases mentioned in this regulation.
  (2) In paragraph (3)–
  "eligible tax week" means any tax week in any part of which the earner in question is at least 16 years of age, and in no part of which he is over pensionable age, and (for the purposes of paragraph (b), but not paragraph (a), of section 3(1) of the Act) which is not a week for which he is entitled to a Class 1 credit, by virtue of regulation 9 of the Social Security (Credits) Regulations 1975(b), by reason of unemployment; and
  "ineligible tax week" means any tax week which is not an eligible tax week.

(3) In relation to any eligible tax week in a tax year the earnings of an earner shall be taken to be the amount calculated or estimated in accordance with paragraph (1) divided by the number of eligible tax weeks in that tax year, and in relation to any ineligible tax week they shall be taken to be nil.

(a) 1975 c.60.
(b) S.I. 1975/556, amended by S.I. 1976/1736, 1977/788, 1978/409, 1981/1501, 1982/96, 1983/197, 1987/414, 687.

(4) For the purposes of section 3(1)(a) of the Act, the formula set out in paragraph (5)(a), or, if it produces a smaller value for X, the formula set out in paragraph (5)(b), shall be applied, so however that if the formula set out in paragraph (5)(a) produces a negative value for X, or if the value of P is nil, the value of X shall be taken to be nil.

(5) The formulae mentioned in paragraph (4) are–

   (a) $X = P + R - S - 52L$; and

   (b) $X = 53U - 52L$.

(6) For the purposes of section 3(1)(b) of the Act, the formula set out in paragraph (7)(a), or, if it produces a smaller value for X, the formula set out in paragraph (7)(b), shall be applied, so however that if the formula set out in paragraph (7)(a) produces a negative value for X, or if the value of $P - Q$ is nil, the value of X shall be taken to be nil.

(7) The formulae mentioned in paragraph (6) are–

   (a) $X = P - Q + R - S - 52L$; and

   (b) $X = 53U - 52L$.

(8) In paragraph (9)–

   (a) "primary Class 1 contributions" does not include contributions which the earner, being a married woman or widow, is liable to make at a reduced rate in accordance with an election which she has made and which is still operative; and

   (b) the reference to contributions as having been paid includes the case of contributions which are treated as having been paid under regulation 39 of the Social Security (Contributions) Regulations 1979(a) but does not include the case of contributions which are treated as not paid under regulation 38(1) and (2)(a) of those regulations.

(9) In this regulation–

   (a) L is the lower earnings limit (within the meaning of section 1 of the Social Security Pensions Act 1975(b)) for the tax year in question;

   (b) P is the total earnings, insofar as the earnings for each week did not exceed U, paid to or for the benefit of the earner in relation to the tax year in question, in relation to which primary Class 1 contributions have been paid with respect to employments that are not contracted-out;

   (c) Q is that part (if any) of P which derives from employments prescribed under section 3(2) of the Act(c) (employments in respect of which incentive payments are not to be made);

   (d) R is the total earnings, insofar as the earnings for each week did not exceed U, paid to or for the benefit of the earner in relation to the tax year in question, in relation to which primary Class 1 contributions have been paid with respect to employments that are contracted-out;

   (e) S is the total earnings, insofar as the earnings for each week equalled or exceeded L but did not exceed U, paid to or for the benefit of the earner in relation to the tax year in question, in relation to which primary Class 1 contributions have been paid with respect to employments that are contracted-out;

   (f) U is the upper earnings limit (within the meaning of section 1 of the Social Security Pensions Act 1975) for the tax year in question; and

   (g) X is so much of the earnings paid to or for the benefit of the earner with respect to any employment which is not contracted-out employment in relation to him as exceeds the lower earnings limit but does not exceed the upper earnings limit.

Adjustment of amount of minimum contributions

18. Where the amount of minimum contributions payable in respect of an earner in relation to a tax year would otherwise not be a whole number of pence, it shall be taken to be the nearest whole number of pence, or, when the 2 nearest whole numbers are equally near, the lower of them.

(a) S.I. 1979/591, to which there are amendments not relevant to these Regulations.
(b) 1975 c.60.
(c) *See* S.I. 1987/1115, regulation 2.

Cancellation of membership of interest-bearing account-funded appropriate personal pension schemes

19.—(1) Without prejudice to any other requirements imposed by the Act or regulations made thereunder, a personal pension scheme which comprises an arrangement of the kind described in regulation 2(c) can be an appropriate scheme only if it satisfies the requirements of paragraph (2).

(2) Without prejudice to any right of a member of the scheme, under section 15(1) of the Act or other rules of the scheme, the rules of the scheme shall include provision—

(a) that, within 7 days of the day on which a person becomes a member of the scheme, he shall be served, personally or by post, with a notice in writing containing the information specified in the Schedule to these Regulations and a form of counter-notice; and

(b) that, if the person signs the form of counter-notice or another document to the same effect and serves it—

(i) by post or otherwise,

(ii) not later than the fourteenth day after the notice referred to in paragraph (2)(a) is served on him,

(iii) on the person nominated, in that notice, to accept service of it,

his membership of the scheme shall be cancelled and the contributions (if any) paid to the scheme by him or for him shall be returned, as soon as reasonably practicable, to the person who paid them.

(3) Where a counter-notice of the kind mentioned in paragraph (2)(b) is properly addressed, pre-paid and served by post, it shall be deemed to have been duly served on the day on which it was posted.

Transitional provisions

20.—(1) During the period beginning on 27th July 1987 and ending on 5th April 1989 the Board may in their discretion issue an appropriate scheme certificate, notwithstanding that they have not satisfied themselves that the scheme in question satisfies the conditions for the issue of such a certificate, on the basis of—

(a) the information specified in paragraph (2) given by the administrators of the scheme; and

(b) an undertaking, given by any person having power to alter any of the rules of the scheme in question, to the effect specified in paragraph (3); and

(c) an undertaking, given by the person who or body which has established the scheme, to the effect specified in paragraph (4).

(2) The information mentioned in paragraph (1)(a) is to the effect that, to the best of the belief of the administrators, the documents submitted with the application satisfy the requirements for the issue of an appropriate scheme certificate in relation to the scheme in question.

(3) The undertaking mentioned in paragraph (1)(b) is to the general effect that the person giving it will—

(a) use his best endeavours to make, within such time as the Board may specify, such alterations to the rules of the scheme (having effect from the date from which the appropriate scheme certificate has effect) as may be necessary to make the scheme satisfy the requirements of Schedule 1 to the Act; and

(b) within such time as the Board may specify lodge with the Board copies of the rules as so altered.

(4) The undertaking mentioned in paragraph (1)(c) above is to the effect that where, as a result of the Board's cancelling the appropriate scheme certificate because alterations as mentioned in paragraph (3)(a) have not been made within the time specified by the Board, any person has incurred financial obligations in respect of personal pension protected rights premiums, the person or body giving the undertaking will provide any additional funds necessary to enable those financial obligations to be met.

(5) For the purposes of section 5(8) of the Act, in a case where –

(a) the Board have issued an appropriate scheme certificate by virtue of paragraph (1) and have subsequently cancelled it with effect from a date which is later than that with effect from which they issued it; and

(b) the rules of the scheme as regards the protected rights of members are not in accordance with Schedule 1 to the Act,

the rules of the scheme shall be deemed to make any such provision as the Board may consider necessary to ensure that its members have protected rights which are in accordance with that Schedule.

Signed by authority of the Secretary of State for Social Services.

25th June 1987

Nicholas Scott
Minister of State,
Department of Health and Social Security

Regulation 19   SCHEDULE

INFORMATION TO BE INCLUDED IN NOTICE

1.   The right of the member to cancel his membership of the scheme.

2.   The provisions of section 15(1) of the Act, the scheme rules and of these regulations which govern the exercise of the right referred to in paragraph 1 of this Schedule.

3.   The name and address of the person on whom the member's counter-notice, mentioned in regulation 19 of these regulations, should be served.

4.   The type of account, or accounts, in which contributions to the scheme are invested.

5.   The rate of interest, at the time when the notice is served, which is accruing to contributions of members of the scheme which are then invested.

6.   The part–
   (a)   of any payment or payments that are made to the scheme by or on behalf of a member;
   (b)   of any income arising from the investment of payments such as are mentioned in sub-paragraph (a) of this paragraph; or
   (c)   of the value of rights under the scheme,
that may be used (otherwise than as an unidentifiable element in the calculation of interest on invested contributions)–
      (i)   to defray the administrative expenses of the scheme;
      (ii)   to pay commission; or
      (iii)   in any other way which does not result in the provision of benefits for or in respect of members.

7.   How tax relief on members' contributions is effected.

8.   How the cessation of the making of contributions to the scheme by a member of it, not less than 21 days after he becomes a member of it, but before the end of the period for which he could continue making such contributions, would affect the member's rights under the scheme.

9.   The address to which enquiries about the scheme generally or about an individual's entitlement to benefit should be sent.

EXPLANATORY NOTE

(This note is not part of the Regulations)

These Regulations are all made under the Social Security Act 1986, and are made before the end of a period of 12 months from the commencement of the relevant sections of that Act. Consequently, by virtue of section 61(5) of that Act, the provisions of section 61(2) and (3) of the Social Security Pensions Act 1975 (as amended by section 86(1) of, and paragraph 94 of Schedule 10 to, the Social Security Act 1986), which require reference to the Occupational Pensions Board of, and a report by the Board on, proposals to make regulations for certain purposes of both Acts, do not apply to them.

If a personal pension scheme is to be an appropriate scheme for the purposes of the Social Security Act 1986, it must, in view of regulation 2, take the form of only one of the following, namely–
   (a)   an arrangement for the issue of insurance policies or annuity contracts;
   (b)   a unit trust scheme which has been authorised under or by virtue of the Financial Services Act 1986; or
   (c)   an arrangement for the investment of contributions in an interest-bearing account.

Regulation 3 provides that a Friendly Society can establish an appropriate scheme only if it is authorised by virtue of Chapter III of Part I of the Financial Services Act 1986 and has disclosed in its audited accounts a contributions income of not less than £300,000 in the year 1986 and £400,000 in the year 1987; and that an appropriate scheme can take the form of an interest-bearing account only if it is established by—

(a) a building society as defined in the Building Societies Act 1986;

(b) a bank recognised under the Banking Act 1979; or

(c) a deposit taker licensed under the Banking Act 1979.

Regulations 4 to 11 set out the procedures for applying to the Occupational Pensions Board for the issue by the Board of an "appropriate scheme certificate" (a certificate that a personal pension scheme is an appropriate scheme for the purposes of the Social Security Act 1986) and for applying to the Board to surrender such a certificate or to have one varied. They make provision for the Board to determine questions whether and for what period a scheme is or was an appropriate scheme, and questions arising on an application concerning the issue, variation or surrender of an appropriate scheme certificate, and they also provide for the cancellation of certificates.

Regulations 12 and 13 set out the procedures for giving notices under section 1(9) and (10) of the Social Security Act 1986 (under which a particular personal pension scheme may become, or cease to be, a particular earner's "chosen scheme").

Regulations 14 to 18 deal with the minimum contributions which the Secretary of State is to pay under section 1(1) of the Social Security Act 1986. Regulation 14 sets out the circumstances in which minimum contributions, otherwise payable to the trustees or managers of a personal pension scheme, are not to be paid, or are to be paid to another scheme or to other persons. Regulation 15 deals with the manner of payment of minimum contributions, and regulation 16 with claims for the purpose of section 3(1)(b) of the Social Security Act 1986, which provides for minimum contributions to be increased for tax weeks ending before 6th April 1993. Regulation 17 sets out the method of calculating or estimating the earnings on which minimum contributions are based, and regulation 18 provides for the rounding of minimum contributions to avoid fractional amounts.

Regulation 19 provides that a personal pension scheme which comprises an arrangement for the investment of contributions in an interest-bearing account or accounts can be an appropriate scheme only if (without prejudice to any right of a member of it which arises otherwise than by virtue of these regulations), the scheme rules include provision—

(a) first, that within 7 days of a member's joining the scheme, he shall be served with a notice which contains the information mentioned in the Schedule to these Regulations; and

(b) secondly, that within 14 days of the service of that notice, the member may cancel his membership of the scheme and receive a refund of any contributions which he has paid to it.

Regulation 20 provides transitionally for the issue (only until 5th April 1989) of an appropriate scheme certificate, even though the Occupational Pensions Board have not satisfied themselves that the scheme satisfies the conditions for the issue of one, on the basis of information given by the administrators of the scheme and undertakings given by any person having power to alter the scheme's rules and by the person who or body which has established the scheme.

STATUTORY INSTRUMENTS

1987 No. 1110

PENSIONS

The Personal Pension Schemes (Disclosure of Information) Regulations 1987

Made - - - -	*25th June 1987*
Laid before Parliament	*6th July 1987*
Coming into force -	*27th July 1987*

The Secretary of State for Social Services, in exercise of the powers conferred upon him by section 168(1) of, and Schedule 20 to, the Social Security Act 1975**(a)**, and section 56A(1) and (3) of the Social Security Pensions Act 1975**(b)**, and of all other powers enabling him in that behalf, by this instrument, which is made before the end of a period of 12 months from the commencement of the enactments under which it is made, makes the following Regulations:

Citation, commencement and interpretation

1.—(1) These Regulations may be cited as the Personal Pension Schemes (Disclosure of Information) Regulations 1987 and shall come into force on 27th July 1987.

(2) In these Regulations, unless the context otherwise requires–

"the 1975 Act" means the Social Security Pensions Act 1975;

"the 1986 Act" means the Social Security Act 1986;

"beneficiary", in relation to a scheme, means a person, other than a member of the scheme, who is entitled to payment of benefits under the scheme;

"linked long-term insurance policy" means any contract under which the benefits payable to the policy holder are wholly or partly to be determined by reference to the value of, or the income from, property of any description (whether or not specified in the contract) or by reference to fluctuations in, or in any index of, the value of property of any description (whether or not so specified);

"member" means a member of a scheme;

"pensionable age" means, in the case of a man, 65, and in the case of a woman, 60;

"scheme" means personal pension scheme;

"scheme year", in relation to a scheme, means whichever of the following periods the trustees of the scheme select–

(a) a year specified for the purposes of the scheme–

(a) 1975 c.14; *see* definitions of "prescribe" and "regulations" in Schedule 20. Section 168(1) applies, by virtue of section 66(2) of the Social Security Pensions Act 1975 (c.60), to the exercise of certain powers conferred by that Act.
(b) 1975 c.60. Section 56A was added by section 3 of, and Schedule 2 to, the Social Security Act 1985 (c.53) and has effect, as modified in relation to personal pension schemes by virtue of the Personal and Occupational Pension Schemes (Modification of Enactments) Regulations 1987 (S.I. 1987/1116), regulation 3(8) and Schedule 3.

(i) in any document comprising the scheme or which is included among the documents comprising it; or

(ii) in the rules of the scheme;

(b) a calendar year;

(c) the 12 months ending with 31st March;

(d) the 12 months ending with 5th April,

and also includes, in a case where the trustees have selected a period ("new scheme year") to replace a previously selected period ("old scheme year"), a period exceeding 12 months but not exceeding 24 months between the last old scheme year and the first new scheme year;

"trustees", in relation to a scheme which is not set up or established under a trust, means the managers of the scheme;

and other expressions have the same meaning as in the 1986 Act.

(3) Except so far as the context otherwise requires, any reference–

(a) in these Regulations to a numbered regulation or Schedule is to the regulation in, or, as the case may be, Schedule to, these Regulations, bearing that number;

(b) in a regulation or Schedule to a numbered paragraph is to the paragraph of that regulation or Schedule bearing that number;

(c) in a paragraph to a lettered sub-paragraph is to the sub-paragraph of that paragraph bearing that letter.

Schemes to which regulations 3 to 6 do not apply

2. None of the requirements of regulations 3 to 6 shall apply to a scheme comprised in an annuity contract or trust scheme which is for the time being approved by the Commissioners Inland Revenue under section 226 or 226A of the Income and Corporation Taxes Act 1970(a).

Constitution of scheme

3.—(1) Subject to the provisions of regulation 2, the trustees of any scheme shall make provision, in the manner specified in paragraphs (2) and (3), for the disclosure to persons in the categories specified in paragraph (4), of–

(a) the contents–

(i) of the trust deed constituting the scheme, if it is constituted by such a deed, and

(ii) of any document constituting the scheme, if it not constituted by a trust deed,

and, if the rules of the scheme are not set out in any trust deed or other document the contents of which fall to be disclosed under head (i) or (ii) above, the contents of the rules; and

(b) the contents of any document which amends or supplements or wholly or partly supersedes a document the contents of which fall to be disclosed under sub-paragraph (a) or this sub-paragraph.

(2) A copy of the contents of any of the documents of which disclosure is required by paragraph (1) shall be made available free of charge for inspection on request (not being a request made by a person within 12 months of the last occasion on which a copy of the contents of the same document was made available for inspection by the same person) by any person in the categories specified in paragraph (4), within a reasonable time after the request is made, at a place which is reasonable having regard to the circumstances of the request.

(3) A copy of any of the documents of which disclosure is required by paragraph (1) shall be furnished, on request, on payment of a reasonable charge, to any person in the categories specified in paragraph (4), within a reasonable time after the request is made, so however that in the case of a document which is publicly available the trustees of the scheme may, instead of furnishing a copy, advise the person who has requested it where copies may be obtained.

(a) 1970 c.10; section 226A was inserted by the Finance Act 1971 (c.68), section 20(4) and Schedule 2.

(4) The categories of persons mentioned in paragraphs (1) to (3) are the following, namely–

  (a) in relation to an appropriate scheme–
      (i) members of the scheme,
      (ii) spouses of members,
      (iii) beneficiaries under the scheme; and
  (b) in relation to any other scheme–
      (i) members of the scheme,
      (ii) beneficiaries under the scheme.

Basic information about the scheme

4.—(1) Subject to the provisions of regulation 2 and paragraph (4), the trustees of any scheme shall furnish in writing the information specified in Schedule 1 to persons in the categories specified in paragraphs (2) and (3).

(2) The information specified in Schedule 1 shall be furnished as of course to every member of the scheme within 13 weeks of his becoming a member.

(3) The information specified in Schedule 1 shall–

  (a) in relation to an appropriate scheme, be given to–
      (i) members of the scheme,
      (ii) spouses of members,
      (iii) beneficiaries under the scheme; and
  (b) in relation to any other scheme, be given to–
      (i) members of the scheme,
      (ii) beneficiaries under the scheme,

on request (not being a request made by a person within 3 years of the last occasion on which the same person was furnished with information in accordance with paragraph (2) or this paragraph) as soon as practicable after he requests it.

(4) Where different information is applicable to different members and beneficiaries, nothing in this regulation shall be construed as requiring the trustees of the scheme to disclose information in relation to a member or beneficiary that is not relevant to his rights under the scheme.

(5) Any member who is entitled to be furnished with information specified in Schedule 1, in relation to any scheme, shall be notified by its trustees of any material alteration in the information specified in paragraph 1, 2, 4 or 8 of Schedule 1 within one month of the occurrence of the alteration.

(6) Any member who is entitled to be furnished with information specified in Schedule 1, in relation to any scheme, shall, except in the circumstances mentioned in paragraph (7), be notified by its trustees of any intended material alteration in the information specified in paragraph 3, 6, 7, 10, 11, 12 or 13 of Schedule 1 not less than 3 months before the alteration is intended to take effect.

(7) Where any intended material alteration in the information specified in those paragraphs of Schedule 1 mentioned in paragraph (6)–

  (a) is consequential on events over which the trustees of the scheme had no control, and
  (b) it is not possible for them to comply with the requirements of paragraph (6) within the 3 month period mentioned in that paragraph,

they shall comply with those requirements as soon as reasonably practicable after the intention is formed to make the alteration.

(8) When any information is provided in accordance with the foregoing provisions of this regulation, it shall be accompanied by a written statement that further information about the scheme is available, giving the address to which enquiries about it should be sent.

Information to be made available to individuals

5.—(1) Subject to the provisions of regulation 2, the trustees of any scheme shall furnish in writing the information specified in Schedule 2, to the persons in the categories and in the circumstances specified in paragraphs (2) to (8).

(2) The information mentioned in paragraphs 1 and 2 of Schedule 2 shall be furnished as of course to each member of the scheme at least once in every period of 12 months after the date of his becoming a member of it.

(3) Where the scheme is not an appropriate scheme, the information mentioned in paragraph 3 of Schedule 2 shall be sent, as of course, to each member who has no protected rights under the scheme, not less than 4 months before the last date on which he may make contributions to the scheme, so however that where—

(a) his expected date of retirement is earlier or later than the last date on which he may make contributions to the scheme, and

(b) he has given the trustees not less than 5 months' prior notice in writing of that expected date,

that information shall be sent not less than 4 months before that expected date.

(4) Where the scheme is, or has been, an appropriate scheme and members have protected rights under it, the information mentioned in paragraph 4 of Schedule 2 shall be sent, as of course, to each member with such rights—

(a) not less than 4 months, but not more than 6 months, before he attains pensionable age, and

(b) not less than 4 months before the member attains the age of 75 years if effect has not been given to his protected rights by the beginning of the sixth month before the member attains the age of 75 years.

(5) Where a member of, or a beneficiary under, a scheme has died and rights or options are available to a person in consequence, the information mentioned in paragraphs 5 and 6 of Schedule 2 shall be furnished—

(a) as of course to that person, if he is at least 18 years old and his address is known to the trustees, as soon as practicable after the trustees receive notification of the death; and

(b) on request (not being a request made within 3 years of the last occasion on which information was furnished under this paragraph to the same person in the same capacity) to any person who is a personal representative of the deceased person or who is authorised to act on behalf of the person to whom rights or options under the scheme are available in consequence of the death, as soon as practicable after he requests it.

(6) Where a member who is an earner gives notice in accordance with section 1(10) of the 1986 Act, the trustees shall, within 3 months of their becoming aware of the giving of the notice, furnish the member who gave it with the information mentioned in paragraphs 1, 2 and 11 of Schedule 2.

(7) Where the trustees of the scheme give notice in accordance with section 1(10) of the 1986 Act, they shall, within 4 weeks of the date of the giving of the notice, furnish the member in respect of whom the notice was given with the information mentioned in paragraphs 1, 2 and 11 of Schedule 2.

(8) Where the scheme is not an appropriate scheme and it has been decided to wind it up or otherwise to cause it to cease accepting contributions or to cause it to cease to manage the contributions already paid to it, the trustees of the scheme shall—

(a) inform each member of that decision as soon as practicable, and in any event not more than 4 weeks after it was made;

(b) furnish each member as soon as practicable, and in any event not more than 4 months after the decision was made, with the information mentioned in paragraphs 1, 2 and 7 of Schedule 2; and

(c) where the scheme is unable to meet in full its liabilities to its members, furnish each member as soon as practicable, and in any event not more than 4 months after the decision was made, with the information mentioned in paragraph 8 of Schedule 2.

(9) Where the Occupational Pensions Board have determined that any scheme should cease to be an appropriate scheme, the trustees of the scheme shall—

(a) inform each member of that determination as soon as practicable, and in any event not more than 4 weeks after it was communicated to the trustees by the Occupational Pensions Board;

(b) furnish each member as soon as practicable, and in any event not more than 4 months after the determination was so communicated to the trustees, with the information mentioned in paragraphs 1, 2, 9, 10 and 11 of Schedule 2; and

(c) where the scheme is unable to meet in full its liabilities to its members, furnish each member as soon as practicable, and in any event not more than 4 months after the decision was made, with the information mentioned in paragraph 8 of Schedule 2.

(10) When any information is provided in accordance with the foregoing provisions of this regulation it shall be accompanied by a written statement that further information about the scheme is available, giving the address to which enquiries about it should be sent.

Availability of other information

6.—(1) Subject to the provisions of regulation 2, the trustees of any scheme shall, in relation to, and not more than one year after the end of, each scheme year which commences on or after 1st October 1987, make available copies of a document or a series of documents which contains information, consisting of or including the information specified in Schedule 3 (so far as it applies to the scheme), to scheme members in the circumstances mentioned in paragraphs (3) and (4).

(2) The trustees shall take reasonable steps to draw to the attention of scheme members the availability of any such document or series of documents as is mentioned in paragraph (1).

(3) A copy of any such document or series of documents as is mentioned in paragraph (1), being neither the latest nor one which relates to a scheme year which ended more than 5 years previously, shall be made available free of charge for inspection on request (not being a request made by a person within 3 years of the last occasion on which a copy of the same document or series of documents was made available for inspection by the same person) by any scheme member within a reasonable time after the request is made, at a place which is reasonable having regard to the circumstances of the request.

(4) A copy of the latest such document or series of documents as is mentioned in paragraph (1) shall be furnished free of charge on request (not being a second or subsequent request by the same person for a copy of the same document or series of documents) to any scheme member as soon as practicable after he requests it.

Service of documents by post

7.—(1) Any information or document, which these Regulations require the trustees of a scheme to furnish to any person, may be furnished by sending it by post to that person to his last address known to the trustees.

(2) Any request for information or a document, or any notification, made by any person to the trustees of a scheme, for the purpose of these Regulations, may be made or given by sending it by post to the trustees, to their last address known to that person.

Signed by authority of the Secretary of State for Social Services.

Nicholas Scott
Minister of State,
Department of Health and Social Security

25th June 1987

SCHEDULE 1

Regulation 4

BASIC INFORMATION ABOUT THE SCHEME

1. The address to which enquiries about the scheme generally, or about an individual's entitlement to benefit, should be sent.

2. The names and addresses of the trustees of the scheme.

3. The conditions of membership.

4. How and where copies of the contents of the documents (relating to the constitution of the scheme) of which disclosure is required by regulation 3(1) may be purchased and inspected.

5. Whether the scheme is an appropriate scheme and, if it is not, whether an application for the scheme to be certified as such a scheme is under consideration by the Occupational Pensions Board.

6. How contributions by members and their employers and (if the scheme is an appropriate scheme) minimum contributions by the Secretary of State, are paid to the scheme.

7. A summary of the conditions of the scheme which govern how a member's accrued rights may be transferred, converted to an annuity or annuities, or commuted to a lump sum.

8. A summary of the scheme's investment policy.

9. Illustrative estimates of the cash equivalents which would be paid on the transfer of protected rights to another scheme at the end of each of the first 5 years of membership, stating the assumptions made, so however that, where a scheme is established by a person to whose business Chapter V of Part I of the Financial Services Act 1986(a) applies, those estimates may be prepared in accordance with rules made under that Chapter of that Part of that Act, and where a scheme is established by a person who is a member of a self-regulating organisation, which is recognised for the purposes of Chapter III of Part I of the Financial Services Act 1986, those estimates may be prepared in accordance with rules which are binding on that person as a member of that organisation.

10. The basis on which any part—
    (a) of any payment or payments that are made to the scheme by or on behalf of a member;
    (b) of any income or capital gain arising from the investment of payments such as are mentioned in sub-paragraph (a); or
    (c) of the value of rights under the scheme,

may be used—
    (i) to defray the administrative expenses of the scheme;
    (ii) to pay commission; or
    (iii) in any other way which does not result in the provision of benefits for or in respect of members,

so however that, where a scheme is established by a person to whose business Chapter V of Part I of the Financial Service Act 1986 applies, the information required to be specified may be specified in accordance with rules made under that Chapter of that Part of that Act, and where a scheme is established by a person who is a member of a self-regulating organisation, which is recognised for the purposes of Chapter III of Part I of the Financial Services Act 1986, the information required to be specified may be specified in accordance with rules which are binding on that person as a member of that organisation.

11. Which of the benefits, if any, are such that fulfilment of the obligation to pay them, to or in respect of particular members, is guaranteed by means of one or more insurance policies which are specifically allocated to the provision of benefits payable to, or in respect of, those members.

12. The arrangements that have been made to enable the scheme to meet its obligations in respect of members' protected rights in the event of the scheme's resources, proving insufficient to do so and the names and addresses of the persons with whom they have been so made.

13. The arrangements that would be made, in accordance with legislation, to enable the scheme to meet its obligations in respect of members' protected rights in the event of the scheme's resources, proving insufficient to do so and the names and addresses of the persons with whom they would be so made.

(a) 1986 c.60.

Regulation 5

SCHEDULE 2

INFORMATION TO BE MADE AVAILABLE TO INDIVIDUALS

1. The amount of contributions (before the making of any deductions), credited to the member under the scheme during the 12 months preceding a specified date, and, where the scheme was for the whole or any part of that period an appropriate scheme, the amount of the minimum contributions paid by the Secretary of State in respect of the member in that period which is attributable to–

    (a) section 3(1)(a) of the 1986 Act; and

    (b) section 3(1)(b) of that Act.

2. (a) As at a specified date–

      (i) the value of the member's protected rights under the scheme, and

      (ii) the value of the member's accrued rights (other than his protected rights) under the scheme.

    (b) Where the cash equivalent (calculated, at the date specified for the purposes of sub-paragraph (a), in accordance with regulations 3 and 4 of the Personal Pension Schemes (Transfer Values) Regulations 1987(**a**)) in respect of the transfer of the member's rights mentioned in sub-paragraph (a)(i) or (ii) or both would be different from the values to be specified under that sub-paragraph, that cash equivalent.

3. The options (if any) available to the member.

4. The options available to the member, including those in respect of any accrued rights which are not protected rights.

5. The rights and options (if any) available on the death of a member or beneficiary, and the procedures for exercising them, including, where the scheme is an appropriate scheme, the contingent option conferred by regulation 10(12) of the Personal and Occupational Pension Schemes (Protected Rights) Regulations 1987(**b**) for the purposes of that regulation.

6. The provisions (or, as the case may be, a statement that there are no provisions) under which any pension payable to a survivor of a member or beneficiary may or will be increased, and the extent to which such increases are dependent on the exercise of a discretion.

7. The options available to a member for preserving, transferring or otherwise disposing of his accrued rights under the scheme.

8. An account of the amount by which the member's–

    (a) protected rights; and

    (b) accrued rights other than his protected rights,

have been reduced, and of the arrangements which have been made by the scheme, or are open to the member, to restore the value of his accrued rights under the scheme.

9. When a scheme has ceased to be an appropriate scheme, the date on which it did so.

10. Whether arrangements for the preservation or transfer of the member's protected rights have been, or are to be, proposed to the Occupational Pensions Board and an explanation of the intended effect of any such proposed arrangements.

11. The options available to the member in respect of his protected rights.

(**a**) S.I. 1987/1112.
(**b**) S.I. 1987/1117.

SCHEDULE 3

Regulation 6

OTHER INFORMATION

1. To the extent that any scheme is comprised in an arrangement for the issue of insurance policies (other than linked long-term insurance policies) or annuity contracts, a statement of the rates of bonus payment declared by the scheme in the scheme year to which the information relates (in this Schedule called "the year") and in each of the 4 scheme years (other than any throughout which the scheme did not exist) immediately preceding the year.

2. To the extent that any scheme is comprised in an arrangement for the issue of linked long-term insurance policies–

    (a) a statement which–

        (i) describes the property to which the scheme is linked, as at a specified date, according to the descriptions specified in Schedule 13 to the Insurance Companies Regulations 1981(a), and

        (ii) specifies the proportion of the scheme's resources invested, on that date, in property of each such description;

    (b) a statement specifying any changes, since the end of the last scheme year (if any), of the descriptions mentioned in sub-paragraph (a), of the property to which the scheme is linked; and

    (c) a statement of the returns on the investment of the scheme's resources during the year and during each of the 4 scheme years (other than any throughout which the scheme did not exist) immediately preceding the year.

3. In the case of any scheme which is comprised in an arrangement to invest the scheme's resources in an interest-bearing account or accounts, a statement of the rates of interest which have accrued to the resources so invested in the year and in each of the 4 scheme years (other than any throughout which the scheme did not exist) immediately preceding the year.

EXPLANATORY NOTE

(This note is not part of the Regulations)

These Regulations are all made under section 56A(1) and (3) of the Social Security Pensions Act 1975 ("the 1975 Act") (as modified in relation to personal pension schemes by the Personal and Occupational Pension Schemes (Modification of Enactments) Regulations 1987) before the expiry of the period of 12 months beginning with the bringing into force (on 23rd July 1987) of those enactments as so modified. Consequently, by virtue of section 61(5) of the 1986 Act, the provisions of section 61(2) and (3) of the 1975 Act (which require reference to the Occupational Pensions Board of, and a report by the Board on, proposals to make regulations for certain purposes of the 1975 Act), do not apply to them. These Regulations specify the information that is to be made available to certain persons, in certain circumstances, by the trustees or managers ("trustees") of personal pension schemes.

Regulation 2 of these Regulations provides for the conditions on which a personal pension scheme is excepted from these regulations.

Regulation 3 provides for the trustees to make available documents containing information about the constitution of the scheme for inspection by specified persons and for copies to be furnished on request on payment of a reasonable charge.

Regulation 4 and Schedule 1 provide for certain basic information about the scheme to be given by the trustees to every member on joining the scheme and to members and

---

(a) S.I. 1981/1654, amended by S.I. 1982/675, 1985/1419.

other specified persons on request, and for material alterations to be drawn to the attention of members.

Regulation 5 and Schedule 2 provide for the trustees to make information about individual benefit entitlement available to specified persons in specified circumstances.

Regulation 6 and Schedule 3 provide for the trustees to make available a document or a series of documents, containing other specified information in relation to the scheme, for inspection by members on request and free of charge (subject to certain exceptions), and for the trustees to furnish the latest such document or series to scheme members on request and free of charge.

Regulation 7 relates to the service of documents by post.

STATUTORY INSTRUMENTS

1987 No. 1111

PENSIONS

The Personal Pension Schemes (Personal Pension Protected Rights Premiums) Regulations 1987

Made - - - -	*25th June 1987*
Laid before Parliament	*6th July 1987*
Coming into force	*4th January 1988*

The Secretary of State for Social Services, in exercise of the powers conferred upon him by section 168(1) of, and Schedule 20 to, the Social Security Act 1975(**a**), section 52 of and paragraph 6 of Schedule 2 to the Social Security Pensions Act 1975(**b**) and sections 5(4), (7), (8), (10) and (14) and 84(1) of the Social Security Act 1986(**c**), and of all other powers enabling him in that behalf, by this instrument, which is made before the end of a period of 12 months from the commencement of the enactments under which it is made, makes the following Regulations:

Citation, commencement and interpretation

1.—(1) These Regulations may be cited as the Personal Pension Schemes (Personal Pension Protected Rights Premiums) Regulations 1987 and shall come into force on 4th January 1988.

(2) In these Regulations, unless the context otherwise requires–

"the Act" means the Social Security Act 1986;

"administrators", in relation to a personal pension scheme, means the trustees or, if there are no trustees, the managers (except any trustee or manager who is resident outside the United Kingdom, or which, being a company, does not have its registered office in the United Kingdom), and any person who is resident in the United Kingdom, or which, being a company, has its registered office in the United Kingdom, who or which is authorised to act on behalf of the trustees, or, if there are no trustees, on behalf of the managers;

"appropriate scheme" shall be construed in accordance with Part I of the Act;

"the Board" means the Occupational Pensions Board;

"child benefit" has the same meaning as in the Child Benefit Act 1975(**d**);

"pensionable age" means, in the case of a man, 65, and in the case of a woman, 60;

"premium" means personal pension protected rights premium;

"scheme" means personal pension scheme;

"trustees", in relation to a scheme which is not set up or established under a trust, means the managers of the scheme;

and other expressions have the same meaning as in the Act.

(**a**) 1975 c. 14. *See* definitions of "prescribe" and "regulations" in Schedule 20. Section 168(1) applies, by virtue of section 66(2) of the Social Security Pensions Act 1975, to the exercise of certain powers conferred by that Act.
(**b**) 1975 c. 60. Paragraph 6 of Schedule 2 was amended by the Social Security Act 1980 (c. 30), section 3(12), and is modified, in relation to personal pension schemes, by the Personal and Occupational Pension Schemes (Modification of Enactments) Regulations 1987 (S.I. 1987/1116), regulation 3(11) and Schedule 5.
(**c**) 1986 c. 50. *See* definitions of "prescribed" and "regulations" in section 84(1).
(**d**) 1975 c. 61.

(3) In these Regulations, except in so far as the context otherwise requires, any reference–

(a) to a numbered regulation is to the regulation in these regulations bearing that number;

(b) in a regulation to a numbered paragraph is to the paragraph of that regulation bearing that number; and

(c) in a paragraph to a lettered sub-paragraph is to the sub-paragraph of that paragraph bearing that letter.

Manner of calculation and verification of cash equivalents mentioned in section 5(8) and (10)(a)(i) of the Act

2.—(1) Except in a case to which paragraph (3) applies, the cash equivalent mentioned in section 5(8) of the Act of protected rights (being those rights under a scheme, which has ceased to be an appropriate scheme, whose cash equivalent is to be the amount of a personal pension protected rights premium) shall be calculated and verified–

(a) in such manner as may be approved in particular cases by the trustees of the scheme, and

(b) by adopting methods consistent with the requirements of Schedule 1 to the Act.

(2) Except in a case to which paragraph (3) applies, the cash equivalent mentioned in section 5(10)(a)(i) of a person's rights (being those rights under a scheme, which has ceased to be an appropriate scheme, whose cash equivalent is to be used to supplement a personal pension protected rights premium) shall be calculated and verified in such manner as may be approved in particular cases by the trustees of the scheme.

(3) In a case where the rights under a scheme mentioned in paragraph (1) or (2) fall, either wholly or in part, to be valued in a manner which involves making estimates of the value of benefits, the cash equivalent of those rights shall be calculated and verified–

(a) in such manner as may be approved in particular cases by–

(i) a Fellow of the Institute of Actuaries, or

(ii) a Fellow of the Faculty of Actuaries, or

(iii) a person with other actuarial qualifications who is approved by the Secretary of State, at the request of the trustees of the scheme in question, as being a proper person to act for the purposes of these regulations in connection with that scheme,

and in this regulation "actuary" means any person such as is referred to in head (i), (ii) or (iii) of this sub-paragraph; and

(b) by adopting methods and making assumptions which–

(i) if not determined by the trustees of the scheme in question, are notified to them by an actuary, and

(ii) are certified by an actuary to the trustees of the scheme as being consistent with "Retirement Benefit Schemes—Transfer Values (GN11)" published by the Institute of Actuaries and the Faculty of Actuaries and current at the date of the calculation, and, in the case of protected rights, as being consistent with the requirements of Schedule 1 to the Act.

Circumstances in which a premium is not payable

3.—(1) A premium shall not be payable–

(a) in a case where the protected rights in question are in respect of an earner who has died and either–

(i) the earner is not survived by a qualifying widow or widower, or

(ii) the earner is survived by a qualifying widower and the earner or the widower or both were under pensionable age when the earner died;

or

(b) in a case where the person in respect of whom it otherwise would be payable is not treated, under section 4 of the Act or under section 29(2) or (2A) of the Social Security Pensions Act 1975, as entitled to any guaranteed minimum pension which derives from the minimum contributions, minimum payments, or transfer payment or payments from which the protected rights in question derive, or is treated as entitled to such a guaranteed minimum pension at a nil rate.

(2) In paragraph (1)(a), "qualifying widow or widower" means a widow or widower of the earner who at the date of the earner's death either–

(a) is aged 45 or over; or

(b) is entitled to child benefit in respect of a child under 18 who is, or residing with a child under 16 who is–

    (i) a son or daughter of the widow or widower and the earner, or

    (ii) a child in respect of whom the earner immediately before his death, was, or would have been if the child had not been absent from Great Britain, entitled to child benefit, or

    (iii) if the widow or widower and the earner were residing together immediately before the earner's death, a child in respect of whom the widow or widower then was, or would have been if the child had not been absent from Great Britain, entitled to child benefit.

Liability for payment of a premium

4.—(1) For the purposes of section 5(7) of the Act (liability to pay a premium to the Secretary of State) the prescribed person is–

(a) in a case where the circumstances specified in regulation 6(7)(a) and (c) obtain, the person to whom the cash sum mentioned in regulation 6(7)(c) has been paid; and

(b) in any other case, the trustees of the scheme.

(2) Where an appropriate scheme ceases to be appropriate, the Board shall certify to the Secretary of State whether or not protected rights under the scheme are subject to approved arrangements as mentioned in section 5 of the Act.

(3) Where protected rights which were subject to approved arrangements as mentioned in section 5 of the Act have ceased to be so subject, the Board shall certify to the Secretary of State the date on which those rights ceased to be so subject.

(4) Any liability for the payment of a premium which is, by any provision of these regulations, imposed on the trustees of a scheme shall be a liability to make that payment out of the resources of the scheme.

Time for payment of a premium

5.—(1) Subject to paragraph (3), any premium which is payable shall be paid on or before whichever is the later of the following days–

(a) the day 6 months after the day on which the Board certify under regulation 4(2) or (3) that the protected rights in question are not subject to approved arrangements or have ceased to be so subject; and

(b) the day one month after the day on which the Secretary of State sends to the person liable to pay the premium a notice certifying that the premium is payable.

(2) Subject to paragraph (3), in cases where a premium has become payable by reason of the fact that a scheme has ceased to be appropriate and an earner's protected rights are, in part only, subject to approved arrangements under section 5 of the Act, the premium shall be paid on or before whichever is the later of the following days–

(a) the day 6 months after the day on which the Board certify under regulation 4(2) or (3) that the protected rights in question are, in part only, subject to approved arrangements; and

(b) the day one month after the day on which the Secretary of State sends to the person liable to pay the premium a notice certifying that the premium is payable.

(3) On application made to him for that purpose the Secretary of State may, in any particular case or class of case, extend the period within which, under paragraph (1) or (2), a premium is required to be paid–

(a) by up to 6 months if he is satisfied that the circumstances are such that payment of the premium could not reasonably be required to be made within that period; and

(b) by such further period as he considers reasonable if he is satisfied that to require earlier payment of the premium would be prejudicial to the interests of the person in respect of whom the premium is payable or of the generality of members of the scheme.

Miscellaneous provisions affecting premiums

6.—(1) Subject to paragraphs (3) and (4), where a premium is payable pursuant to certification by the Board to the Secretary of State under regulation 4(2) or (3) the premium shall, for the purpose of extinguishing protected rights and reducing any guaranteed minimum pension to which a person is treated as being entitled, be treated as having been paid, or paid in part in a case to which either paragraphs (6) to (8) apply or paragraph (9) applies, on the date specified in paragraph (2).

(2) The date mentioned in paragraph (1) is whichever is the later of–

(a) the date on which the scheme ceased to be appropriate; and

(b) any date certified by the Board under regulation 4(3) in relation to the rights mentioned in paragraph (1).

(3) Where a premium has been treated as paid under paragraph (1), the effect of that paragraph shall, except as provided in paragraph (5), be disregarded if–

(a) the Board subsequently approve arrangements for the preservation or transfer of the protected rights; or

(b) the person who is liable to pay the premium fails to do so within the period prescribed by regulation 5(1) or (2), or such longer period as the Secretary of State may allow under regulation 5(3).

(4) Where by virtue of the operation of paragraphs (1) and (3) in relation to a person entitled to a benefit specified in section 29(1)(a) of the Social Security Pensions Act 1975 an amount of that benefit, as certified by the Secretary of State, was paid to that person which would not otherwise have been paid–

(a) the Secretary of State shall be entitled to recover that amount from the scheme and any amount so recovered shall be paid into the National Insurance Fund; and

(b) the sums payable under the scheme to that person may be reduced by the amount so recovered by the Secretary of State.

(5) Paragraph (3)(b) shall not apply where the Secretary of State is satisfied that the failure to pay was not with the consent or connivance of, or attributable to any negligence on the part of, the person in respect of whom the premium is payable, and where, subject to paragraphs (6) and (8), the scheme, being a scheme which is or has been appropriate, is being or has been wound up.

(6) In a case where the circumstances specified in paragraph (7)(a) and either (b) or (c) obtain, the premium in question shall be treated as paid under paragraph (1) only in accordance with the provisions of paragraph (8).

(7) The circumstances mentioned in paragraph (6) are that–

(a) a premium has become payable in respect of the person in question by reason of the withdrawal by the Board of their approval of, or their inability to give their approval to, arrangements for the preservation or transfer of the protected rights in question under section 5;

(b) the scheme is being or has been wound up, its resources are insufficient to meet the cost of that premium, and the Board are satisfied that no arrangements have been made to meet that cost, or, as the case may be, such part of that cost as cannot be met from the resources of the scheme;

(c) the scheme has been wound up, and a cash sum in lieu of the protected rights in question has been paid to or for the benefit of the person concerned.

(8) In a case to which paragraph (6) applies, where the Secretary of State is satisfied that the part of the premium that the resources of the scheme are sufficient to meet or the amount of the cash sum referred to in paragraph (7)(c) is less than the value of the protected rights in question, such part of the premium as represents, in the opinion of the Secretary of State, the difference between the lesser and greater amounts shall be treated as having been paid.

(9) Where a person in respect of whom a premium is payable is a person to whom regulation 4(1)(a) applies and that person pays part only of that premium, that part of the premium shall be treated as having been paid under paragraph (1).

(10) Where part of a premium is treated as having been paid under paragraph (1)–

(a) section 5(9) of the Act shall be modified so as to have effect as if there were inserted at the end thereof the words "and payment of part of the premium shall operate to extinguish such part of those rights as corresponds, in the opinion of the Secretary of State, to that part of the premium" and section 5(10)(a) shall have effect as if there were substituted for the words "the premium" the words "that part of the premium which has been paid"; and

(b) in a case to which paragraph (6) applies, section 5 of the Act shall be modified so as to have effect as if–

    (i) in subsection (1) there were inserted after the words "protected rights" the words "or part thereof",

    (ii) in each of paragraphs (a) and (b) of subsection (4) there were inserted after the words "are not" the words "or are in part only", and

    (iii) in subsection (8) there were inserted after the words "in question" the words "to the extent that those rights are not subject to approved arrangements".

Re-allocation and refund of premium

7.—(1) Where a premium is wrongly paid, or paid as to the wrong amount, the Secretary of State may treat all or part of that premium as paid (wholly or in part) in discharge of a liability for another premium.

(2) Where a premium has been paid in connection with protected rights and another such premium subsequently becomes payable in connection with the same protected rights or protected rights including those rights, the Secretary of State may treat all or part of the first premium as paid (wholly or in part) in discharge of a liability for the second premium.

(3) Subject to paragraphs (1) and (2) the Secretary of State shall refund a premium if–

(a) that premium was paid in error; or

(b) he is satisfied that a transfer of the protected rights will be made in accordance with Schedule 1 to the Act;

and where a premium is refunded under the provisions of this paragraph the protected rights which were extinguished by payment of the premium and the corresponding reduction in any guaranteed minimum pension to which that person or any widow or widower of that person was treated as entitled shall be restored.

(4) A refund under paragraph (3) shall be made only if an application is made in writing, in such form as the Secretary of State may reasonably require for the purpose.

(5) In paragraph (3) "error" means, and means only, an error which–

(a) is made at the time of payment; and

(b) relates to some present or past matter.

(6) The Secretary of State shall refund a premium if he is satisfied that it ought to be refunded where the person in respect of whom it was paid has died without leaving a widow or widower on or before the later of the days first mentioned in sub-paragraphs (a) and (b) respectively of regulation 5(1) or, as the case may be, regulation 5(2).

Prescribed person and prescribed periods for the purposes of section 5(10)(a) of the Act

8. For the purposes of section 5(10)(a) of the Act–

(a) the prescribed person is the Secretary of State;

(b) the prescribed period–

    (i) for the purpose of giving notice to the Secretary of State,

    (ii) for the purpose of the payment referred to in section 5(10)(a)(i), and

    (iii) for the purpose of the payment referred to in section 5(10)(a)(ii),

is the period allowed for the payment of the premium under regulation 5.

Signed by Authority of the Secretary of State for Social Services

Nicholas Scott
25th June 1987   Minister of State, Department of Health and Social Security

EXPLANATORY NOTE

(This note is not part of the Regulations)

These Regulations are all made under provisions of the Social Security Act 1986 ("the 1986 Act"), or provisions of the Social Security Pensions Act 1975 ("the 1975 Act") as modified under powers conferred by the 1986 Act, before the end of the period of 12 months from the commencement of those provisions. Consequently, by virtue of section 61(5) of the 1986 Act, the provisions of section 61(2) and (3) of the 1975 Act (as amended by section 86(1) of, and paragraph 94 of Schedule 10 to, the 1986 Act), which require reference to the Occupational Pensions Board of, and a report by the Board on, proposals to make regulations for certain purposes of both Acts, do not apply to them.

When a personal pension scheme ceases to be an appropriate scheme, within the meaning of the 1986 Act, a "personal pension protected rights premium" may become payable under section 5 of the 1986 Act in respect of each person in the categories described in subsection (4) of that section.

Under subsection (8) of that section, the amount of a personal pension protected rights premium is the cash equivalent of the protected rights of the person concerned, calculated and verified in the prescribed manner.

Regulation 2 provides for the manner in which protected rights, and other rights under the scheme, are to be calculated and verified.

In relation to a personal pension protected rights premium, regulation 3 specifies the circumstances in which it is not payable. Regulation 4 makes provision about the liability to pay it; regulation 5 about the time within which it is to be paid; regulation 6 about treating it as paid; and regulation 7 about re-allocation and refunding. Regulation 8 amplifies section 5(10) of the 1986 Act.

The publication "Retirement Benefit Schemes—Transfer Values (GN11)", referred to in regulation 2(3)(b)(ii), may be obtained from the Institute of Actuaries, Staple Inn Hall, High Holborn, London WC1V 7QJ, and from the Faculty of Actuaries, 23 St. Andrew Square, Edinburgh EH2 1AQ.

1987 No. 1112

PENSIONS

The Personal Pension Schemes (Transfer Values) Regulations 1987

Made - - - -	*25th June 1987*
Laid before Parliament	*6th July 1987*
Coming into force	*27th July 1987*

The Secretary of State for Social Services, in exercise of the powers conferred upon him by section 168(1) of, and Schedule 20 to, the Social Security Act 1975(**a**), and paragraphs 13 and 14 of Schedule 1A to the Social Security Pensions Act 1975(**b**), and of all other powers enabling him in that behalf, by this instrument, which is made before the end of a period of 12 months from the commencement of the enactments under which it is made, makes the following regulations:

Citation, commencement and interpretation

1.—(1) These Regulations may be cited as the Personal Pension Schemes (Transfer Values) Regulations 1987 and shall come into force on 27th July 1987.

(2) In these Regulations, unless the context otherwise requires–

"the Act" means the Social Security Pensions Act 1975;

"cash equivalent" has the same meaning as in Part II of Schedule 1A to the Act as applied to personal pension schemes by the Modification Regulations;

"member" means a member of a personal pension scheme to whom Part II of Schedule 1A to the Act applies by virtue of the Modification Regulations;

"the Modification Regulations" means the Personal and Occupational Pension Schemes (Modification of Enactments) Regulations 1987(**c**) ;

"money purchase benefits" and "personal pension scheme" have the meaning given to those expressions by section 84(1) of the Social Security Act 1986(**d**);

"protected rights" shall be construed in accordance with Schedule 1 to the Social Security Act 1986;

"receiving scheme" means a scheme under whose rules transfer credits or rights are to be acquired by a member in exercise of his choice under paragraph 13(2)(a) of Schedule 1A to the Act as applied to personal pension schemes by the Modification Regulations;

(**a**) 1975 c.14. *See* definitions of "prescribe" and "regulations" in Schedule 20. Section 168(1) applies, by virtue of section 66(2) of the Social Security Pensions Act 1975 (c.60), to the exercise of certain powers conferred by that Act.

(**b**) 1975 c.60. Schedule 1A was inserted by the Social Security Act 1985 (c.53), section 2, and Part II of Schedule 1. Paragraphs 13 and 14 of Schedule 1A were amended by the Social Security Act 1986 (c.50), section 86 and Schedule 10, paragraph 30, and have effect as modified, in relation to personal pension schemes, by virtue of the Personal and Occupational Pension Schemes (Modification of Enactments) Regulations 1987 (S.I. 1987/1116), regulation 3(10) and Schedule 4.

(**c**) S.I. 1987/1116.

(**d**) 1986 c.50.

"scheme" means occupational pension scheme or personal pension scheme;

"trustees", in relation to a scheme which is not set up or established under a trust, means the managers of the scheme;

and other expressions have the same meaning as in Part II of Schedule 1A to the Act as applied to personal pension schemes by the Modification Regulations.

Requirements to be satisfied

2. The prescribed requirements referred to in paragraph 13(2)(a) of Schedule 1A to the Act as applied to personal pension schemes by the Modification Regulations (cash equivalent of member's rights under a personal pension scheme to be used for acquiring transfer credits or rights under another scheme) are that–

    (a) the receiving scheme–

        (i) is approved by the Commissioners of Inland Revenue for the purposes of Chapter II of Part II of the Finance Act 1970 **(a)**, or

        (ii) is a statutory scheme as defined in section 26(1) of the Finance Act 1970, or

        (iii) otherwise satisfies requirements of the Inland Revenue;

    (b) if the member's cash equivalent (or any portion of it to be used under paragraph 13(2)(a) of Schedule 1A to the Act, as applied to personal pension schemes by the Modification Regulations) is or includes the cash equivalent of his protected rights then the receiving scheme is one to which a transfer payment in respect of protected rights may be made in accordance with regulations 2 and 3 of the Protected Rights (Transfer Payment) Regulations 1987 **(b)**.

Manner of calculation and verification of cash equivalents

3.—(1) Except in a case to which paragraph (3) below applies, cash equivalents are to be calculated and verified in such manner as may be approved in particular cases by–

    (a) a Fellow of the Institute of Actuaries; or

    (b) a Fellow of the Faculty of Actuaries; or

    (c) a person with other actuarial qualifications who is approved by the Secretary of State, at the request of the trustees of the personal pension scheme in question, as being a proper person to act for the purposes of these regulations in connection with that scheme,

and in paragraph (2) below "actuary" means any person such as is referred to in sub-paragraph (a), (b) or (c) of this paragraph.

(2) Except in a case to which paragraph (3) below applies, cash equivalents are to be calculated and verified by adopting methods and making assumptions which–

    (a) if not determined by the trustees of the personal pension scheme in question, are notified to them by an actuary; and

    (b) are certified by an actuary to the trustees of the scheme as being consistent–

        (i) with the requirements of Schedule 1A to the Act as applied to personal pension schemes by the Modification Regulations, and

        (ii) with "Retirement Benefit Schemes – Transfer Values (GN11)", published by the Institute of Actuaries and the Faculty of Actuaries and current at the date of the calculation.

(3) Where a member's cash equivalent, or any portion of it–

    (a) represents his rights to money purchase benefits under the personal pension scheme in question; and

    (b) those rights do not fall, either wholly or in part, to be valued in a manner which involves making estimates of the value of benefits,

then that cash equivalent, or that portion of it, shall be calculated and verified in such manner as may be approved in particular cases by the trustees of the scheme, and by adopting methods consistent with the requirements of Schedule 1A to the Act as applied to personal pension schemes by the Modification Regulations.

(a) 1970 c.24.   **(b)** S.I. 1987/1118.

Increases and reductions of cash equivalents

4.—(1) If the whole or any part of the benefits referred to in paragraph 12(1) of Schedule 1A to the Act, as applied to personal pension schemes by the Modification Regulations, is or has been surrendered, commuted or forfeited before the trustees of the personal pension scheme do what is needed to comply with what the member requires, the cash equivalent shall be reduced in proportion to the reduction in the total value of the benefits.

(2) If the trustees of a personal pension scheme fail without reasonable excuse to do what is needed to carry out what a member of the scheme requires within 6 months of the relevant date, that member's cash equivalent shall be increased by–

    (a) the interest on that cash equivalent, calculated on a daily basis over the period from the relevant date to the date on which the trustees carry out what the member requires, at the same rate as that payable for the time being on judgment debts by virtue of section 17 of the Judgment Act 1838(**a**); or, if it is greater,

    (b) the amount, if any, by which that cash equivalent falls short of what it would have been if the relevant date had been the date on which the trustees carry out what the member requires.

(3) In a case where both paragraphs (1) and (2) of this regulation fall to be applied to a calculation, they shall be applied in the order in which they occur in this regulation.

(4) In this regulation "the relevant date" has the same meaning as in paragraph 12(2) of Schedule 1A to the Act as applied to personal pension schemes by the Modification Regulations.

Signed by authority of the Secretary of State for Social Services.

Nicholas Scott
Minister of State,
Department of Health and Social Security

25th June 1987

(**a**) 1 & 2 Vict. c. 110; the rate of interest was amended by S.I. 1985/437.

EXPLANATORY NOTE

(This note is not part of the Regulations)

These Regulations are all made under provisions of the Social Security Pensions Act 1975 ("the 1975 Act") as modified by Regulations made under the Social Security Act 1986 ("the 1986 Act") before the end of 12 months from commencement of the relevant provisions as modified. Consequently, by virtue of section 61(5) of the 1986 Act, the provisions of section 61(2) and (3) of the 1975 Act (as amended by section 86(1) of, and paragraph 94 of Schedule 10 to, the 1986 Act), which require reference to the Occupational Pensions Board of, and a report by the Board on, proposals to make regulations for certain purposes of both Acts, do not apply to them.

They make provision in relation to personal pension schemes for the calculation and verification of cash equivalents (within the meaning of Part II of Schedule 1A to the Social Security Pensions Act 1975, as modified so as to have effect in relation to personal pension schemes by the Personal and Occupational Pension Schemes (Modification of Enactments) Regulations 1987).

Regulation 2 sets out the requirements which an occupational pension scheme, or a personal pension scheme, must satisfy if a cash equivalent is to be used for acquiring transfer credits or rights under it.

Regulation 3 provides for the manner in which a cash equivalent is to be calculated and verified: in particular, except where the calculation or variation does not involve making estimates of the future value of benefits, it must be such manner as may be approved by an actuary.

The publication "Retirement Benefit Schemes – Transfer Values (GN11)", referred to in regulation 3(2)(b)(ii), may be obtained from the Institute of Actuaries, Staple Inn Hall, High Holborn, London WC1V 7QJ, and from the Faculty of Actuaries, 23 St Andrew Square, Edinburgh EH2 1AQ.

Regulation 4 sets out the circumstances in which a cash equivalent is to be increased or reduced to an amount greater or less than the exact equivalent of the benefits in question.

STATUTORY INSTRUMENTS

1987 No. 1113

PENSIONS

The Personal and Occupational Pension Schemes (Abatement of Benefit) Regulations 1987

Made - - - -		*25th June 1987*
Laid before Parliament		*6th July 1987*
Coming into force		
regulations 1 to 3		*4th January 1988*
regulations 4 and 5		*6th April 1988*

The Secretary of State for Social Services, in exercise of the powers conferred upon him by section 168(1) of, and Schedule 20 to, the Social Security Act 1975**(a)**, section 29(2A) and (2C) of the Social Security Pensions Act 1975**(b)** and sections 4 and 84(1) of the Social Security Act 1986**(c)**, and of all other powers enabling him in that behalf, by this instrument, which is made before the end of a period of 12 months from the commencement of the enactments under which it is made, makes the following Regulations:–

Citation, commencement and interpretation

1.—(1) These Regulations may be cited as the Personal and Occupational Pension Schemes (Abatement of Benefit) Regulations 1987, and regulations 2 and 3 and this regulation shall come into force on 4th January 1988, and regulations 4 and 5 on 6th April 1988.

(2) In these Regulations –

"minimum contributions" has the same meaning as in the Social Security Act 1986;

"the Pensions Act" means the Social Security Pensions Act 1975;

"rebate percentage" has the same meaning as in section 3(1) of the Social Security Act 1986;

"relevant year" has the same meaning as in section 35 of the Pensions Act;

"the Transfer Payment Regulations" means the Protected Rights (Transfer Payment) Regulations 1987**(d)**;

and other expressions have the same meaning as in the Pensions Act.

(3) In these Regulations, unless the context otherwise requires, any reference –

(a) to a numbered regulation is to the regulation in these Regulations bearing that number;

(b) in a regulation to a numbered paragraph is to the paragraph of that regulation bearing that number.

(a) 1975 c.14. *See* definitions of "prescribe" and "regulations" in Schedule 20. Section 168(1) applies, by virtue of section 66(2) of the Social Security Pensions Act 1975 (c.60), to the exercise of certain powers conferred by that Act.   **(b)** 1975 c.60. Subsections (2A) and (2C) were inserted into section 29 by the Social Security Act 1986 (c.50), section 6 and Schedule 2, paragraph 5.   **(c)** 1986 c.50. *See* definitions of "prescribed" and "regulations" in section 84(1).   **(d)** S.I. 1987/1118.

Guaranteed minimum pension to which earner is treated as entitled after minimum contributions have been paid

2.—(1) Where, in relation to any tax week, except a tax week such as is mentioned in paragraph (3), minimum contributions have been paid in respect of an earner, sections 16(2B), 28(7A) and 59(1A) of the Social Security Act 1975(a) and section 29 of the Pensions Act shall have effect in relation to him, as from the date on which he reaches pensionable age, as if he were entitled to a guaranteed minimum pension, arising from that tax week –

(a) at the rate described in paragraph (2) if that tax week fell within a tax year which was a relevant year in relation to that earner; and

(b) at a nil rate if it did not.

(2) The rate referred to in paragraph (1)(a) is the same rate as that of the guaranteed minimum pension to which he would have been entitled if –

(a) he had been employed in that tax week in employment which was contracted-out employment by virtue of section 32(2)(a) and (b) of the Pensions Act;

(b) his earnings factor for the relevant year which included that tax week, so far as derived from earnings (being earnings such as are mentioned in section 35(1) of the Pensions Act upon which primary Class 1 contributions have been paid or treated as paid) from that employment in that tax week, had been equal to the amount of which the minimum contributions referred to in paragraph (1) (less any part of them paid under section 3(1)(b) of the Social Security Act 1986) are the rebate percentage; and

(c) the occupational pension scheme by reference to which that employment was contracted-out had made no provision under section 35(7) of the Pensions Act.

(3) In circumstances where, in relation to any tax week –

(a) minimum contributions have been paid in respect of an earner; and

(b) in respect of the protected rights which derived from them a transfer payment has been made in accordance with regulations 2(5) or (6) and 3(b) of the Transfer Payment Regulations,

sections 16(2B), 28(7A) and 59(1A) of the Social Security Act 1975 and section 29 of the Pensions Act shall have effect in relation to him, as from the date on which he reaches pensionable age, as if he were entitled to a guaranteed minimum pension arising from that tax week at a nil rate.

Guaranteed minimum pension to which earner's widow or widower is treated as entitled after minimum contributions have been paid

3.—(1) Where, in relation to any tax week, except a tax week such as is mentioned in paragraph (3), minimum contributions have been paid in respect of an earner, sections 16(2B), 28(7A) and 59(1A) of the Social Security Act 1975 and section 29 of the Pensions Act shall, in the circumstances specified in paragraph (2), have effect in relation to the earner's widow or widower –

(a) if the earner died after reaching pensionable age, as if the widow or widower were entitled to a guaranteed minimum pension at a rate equal to one-half of the rate described in regulation 2(2); and

(b) if the earner died before reaching pensionable age, as if the widow or widower were entitled to a guaranteed minimum pension at the same weekly rate (if any) as that of the guaranteed minimum pension to which she or he would have been entitled if the conditions set out in regulation 2(2) had been satisfied in relation to the earner.

(a) 1975 c.14. Sections 16(2B), 28(7A) and 59(1A) were inserted by the Social Security Act 1985 (c.53), section 9(1)(b), (2)(c) and (4)(b).

(2) The circumstances referred to in paragraph (1) are those in which, if the conditions set out in regulation 2(2) had been satisfied in relation to the earner, a guaranteed minimum pension would have been payable to the widow (by virtue of section 36(6) of the Pensions Act) or to the widower (by virtue of regulations made under section 36(7A) of that Act(**a**)).

(3) In circumstances where, in relation to any tax week –

    (a) minimum contributions have been paid in respect of an earner; and

    (b) in respect of the protected rights which derived from them a transfer payment has been made in accordance with regulations 2(5) or (6) and 3(b) of the Transfer Payment Regulations,

the earner's widow or widower shall not, for the purposes of section 16(2B), 28(7A) and 59(1A) of the Social Security Act 1975 and section 29 of the Pensions Act, be treated as if she or he were entitled to a guaranteed minimum pension arising from that tax week.

Guaranteed minimum pension to which earner is treated as entitled after minimum payments have been made

4.— (1) Where, in relation to any tax week, except a tax week such as is mentioned in paragraph (3), minimum payments have been made in respect of an earner to an occupational pension scheme which in relation to the earner's employment ("the actual employment") is a money purchase contracted-out scheme, then, for the purposes of sections 16(2B), 28(7A) and 59(1A) of the Social Security Act 1975 and section 29 of the Pensions Act, the earner shall be treated, as from the date on which he reaches pensionable age, as if he were entitled to a guaranteed minimum pension, arising from that tax week –

    (a) at the rate described in paragraph (2) if that tax week fell within a tax year which was a relevant year in relation to that earner; and

    (b) at a nil rate if it did not.

(2) The rate referred to in paragraph (1)(a) is the same rate as that of the guaranteed minimum pension to which he would have been entitled if –

    (a) he had been employed in that tax week in employment ("the notional employment") which was contracted-out employment by virtue of section 32(2)(a) and (b) of the Pensions Act;

    (b) his earnings in that tax week from the notional employment had been what his earnings in that tax week from the actual employment in fact were; and

    (c) the occupational pension scheme by reference to which the notional employment was contracted-out had made no provision under section 35(7) of the Pensions Act.

(3) In circumstances where, in relation to any tax week –

    (a) minimum payments have been paid in respect of an earner; and

    (b) in respect of the protected rights which derived from them a transfer payment has been made in accordance with regulations 2(5) or (6) and 3(b) of the Transfer Payment Regulations,

sections 16(2B), 28(7A) and 59(1A) of the Social Security Act 1975 and section 29 of the Pensions Act shall have effect in relation to him, as from the date on which he reaches pensionable age, as if he were entitled to a guaranteed minimum pension arising from that tax week at a nil rate.

(**a**) Subsection (7A) was inserted into section 36 by the Social Security Act 1986 (c.50), section 9(3)(c). *See* the Contracting-out (Widowers' Guaranteed Minimum Pensions) Regulations 1987 (S.I. 1987/1100).

Guaranteed minimum pension to which earner's widow or widower is treated as entitled after minimum payments have been made

5.—(1) Where, in relation to any tax week, except a tax week such as is mentioned in paragraph (3), minimum payments have been made in respect of an earner to an occupational pension scheme which in relation to the earner's employment is a money purchase contracted-out scheme, sections 16(2B), 28(7A) and 59(1A) of the Social Security Act 1975 and section 29 of the Pensions Act shall, in the circumstances specified in paragraph (2), have effect in relation to the earner's widow or widower –

   (a) if the earner died after reaching pensionable age, as if the widow or widower were entitled to a guaranteed minimum pension at a rate equal to one-half of the rate described in regulation 4(2); and

   (b) if the earner died before reaching pensionable age, as if the widow or widower were entitled to a guaranteed minimum pension at the same weekly rate (if any) as that of the guaranteed minimum pension to which she or he would have been entitled if the conditions set out in regulation 4(2) had been satisfied in relation to the earner.

(2) The circumstances referred to in paragraph (1) are those in which, if the conditions set out in regulation 4(2) had been satisfied in relation to the earner, a guaranteed minimum pension would have been payable to the widow (by virtue of section 36(6) of the Pensions Act) or to the widower (by virtue of regulations made under section 36(7A) of that Act).

(3) In circumstances where, in relation to any tax week –

   (a) minimum payments have been paid in respect of an earner; and

   (b) in respect of the protected rights which derived from them a transfer payment has been made in accordance with regulations 2(5) or (6) and 3(b) of the Transfer Payment Regulations,

the earner's widow or widower shall not, for the purposes of section 16(2B), 28(7A) and 59(1A) of the Social Security Act 1975 and section 29 of the Pensions Act, be treated as if she or he were entitled to a guaranteed minimum pension arising from that tax week.

Signed by authority of the Secretary of State for Social Services
Nicholas Scott
Minister of State,
Department of Health and Social Security

25th June 1987

EXPLANATORY NOTE

(This note is not part of the Regulations)

These Regulations are all either made under the Social Security Act 1986 ("the 1986 Act"), or made under provisions inserted into the Social Security Pensions Act 1975 by provisions of the 1986 Act, and are made before the end of a period of 12 months from the commencement of the relevant sections of that Act. Consequently, by virtue of section 61(5) of that Act, the provisions of section 61(2) and (3) of the Social Security Pensions Act 1975 (as amended by section 86(1) of, and paragraph 94 of Schedule 10 to, the 1986 Act), which require reference to the Occupational Pensions Board of, and a report by the Board on, proposals to make regulations for certain purposes of both Acts, do not apply to them.

Section 4 of the 1986 Act provides that where minimum contributions have been paid (by the Secretary of State to a personal pension scheme) in respect of an earner, that earner on reaching pensionable age, or his or her widow or widower in prescribed circumstances, is to be treated as entitled to a guaranteed minimum pension at a prescribed weekly rate for the purposes of certain sections of the Social Security Acts 1975, under which national insurance benefits are abated if the beneficiary is entitled to a guaranteed minimum pension. Regulations 2 and 3 prescribe the rate of the guaranteed minimum pension for the earner and the widow or widower respectively, and regulation 3 also prescribes the circumstances in which the widow or widower is to be treated as entitled to it.

Section 29(2A) of the Social Security Pensions Act 1975 (inserted by Schedule 2 to the 1986 Act) makes provision similar to that of section 4 of the 1986 Act for the case where minimum payments have been made (by an earner's employer to an occupational pension scheme). Regulations 4 and 5 prescribe the rate of the guaranteed minimum pension for the earner and the widow or widower respectively, and regulation 5 also prescribes the circumstances in which the widow or widower is to be treated as entitled to it.

STATUTORY INSTRUMENTS

1987 No. 1114

PENSIONS

The Personal and Occupational Pension Schemes (Consequential Provisions) Regulations 1987

Made - - - -	*25th June 1987*
Laid before Parliament	*6th July 1987*
Coming into force	
regulations 1, 2, 4(1), (14) *and (24)(b) and 7(1) and (2)(a)*	*27th July 1987*
regulations 4(2), (6), *(10), (15), (25) and (26)* *and 7(2)(b)*	*4th January 1988*
remainder	*6th April 1988*

The Secretary of State for Social Services, in exercise of the powers conferred upon him by sections 66(7) and 67(4) of the Social Security Act 1973**(a)**, section 168(1) of, and Schedule 20 to, the Social Security Act 1975**(b)**, and sections 31(1), (2), (5) and (7), 32(2), 38(1), 39(1) and (4), 41B(3), 41C(7), 43(4), 45(1), 51, 52, 52C(4) and (5) and 66(4) of, and paragraphs 1, 6 and 9 of Schedule 2 to, the Social Security Pensions Act 1975**(c)**, and all other powers enabling him in that behalf, by this instrument, which contains only provisions consequential on sections 2, 6, 9(3) and (6) and 86(1) of, and Schedule 2 and paragraph 18 of Schedule 10 to, the Social Security Act 1986**(d)** and is made before the end of a period of 12 months from the commencement of those enactments, makes the following Regulations:–

Citation and commencement

1.—(1) These Regulations may be cited as the Personal and Occupational Pension Schemes (Consequential Provisions) Regulations 1987.

(2) Regulations 2, 4(1), (14) and (24)(b) and 7(1) and (2)(a) and this regulation shall come into force on 27th July 1987, regulations 4(2), (6), (10), (15), (25) and (26) and 7(2)(b) on 4th January 1988 and the remainder of these Regulations on 6th April 1988.

(a) 1973 c.38.
(b) 1975 c.14. *See* definitions of "prescribe" and "regulations" in Schedule 20. Section 168(1) applies, by virtue of section 66(2) of the Social Security Pensions Act 1975 (c.60), to the exercise of certain powers conferred by that Act.
(c) 1975 c.60. Section 38(1) was substituted by the Social Security Act 1986 (c.50), section 86(1) and Schedule 10, paragraph 18. Sections 41B and 41C were inserted by the Health and Social Security Act 1984 (c.48), section 20 and Schedule 6, and section 41B was amended by the Social Security Act 1985 (c.53), sections 6 and 29(1) and Schedule 5, paragraph 24. Section 45(1) was amended by the Social Security (Miscellaneous Provisions) Act 1977 (c.5), section 22(7), and the Social Security Act 1985 (c.53), section 29(1) and Schedule 5, paragraph 25. Section 52C was inserted by the Social Security Act 1985 (c.53), section 2 and Schedule 1, and amended by the Social Security Act 1986 (c.50), section 86(1) and Schedule 10, paragraph 26.
(d) 1986 c.50.

Amendment of the Occupational Pensions Board (Determinations and Review Procedure) Regulations 1973

2.—(1) The Occupational Pensions Board (Determinations and Review Procedure) Regulations 1973(**a**) shall be amended in accordance with the provisions of this regulation.

(2) In regulation 1(2), at the end of the definition of "scheme", there shall be added the words "or personal pension scheme".

Amendments of the Occupational Pensions Board (Determinations and Review Procedure) Regulations 1976

3.—(1) The Occupational Pensions Board (Determinations and Review Procedure) Regulations 1976(**b**) shall be amended in accordance with the provisions of this regulation.

(2) In regulation 1(2), after the definition of "employer", there shall be inserted the following definition–

" 'money purchase contracted-out scheme' has the same meaning as in the Social Security Pensions Act 1975(**c**)".

(3) In regulation 4(2)–

(a) in each of sub-paragraphs (a) and (b), after "where" there shall be inserted "the scheme is not a money purchase contracted-out scheme, and"; and

(b) after sub-paragraph (b) there shall be added "or" and the following sub-paragraph–

"(c) in a case where the scheme is a money purchase contracted-out scheme, and the Board consider that the scheme has ceased to satisfy the requirements for continuing to be a contracted-out scheme, in which case the date may be a date not earlier than the date on which, in the opinion of the Board, it ceased to satisfy those requirements.".

Amendments of the Occupational Pension Schemes (Contracting-out) Regulations 1984

4.—(1) The Occupational Pension Schemes (Contracting-out) Regulations 1984(**d**) shall be amended in accordance with the provisions of this regulation.

(2) In regulation 1–

(a) in paragraph (2), immediately before "other expressions have the same meaning as in the Act", there shall be inserted "subject to paragraph (2A)"; and

(b) after paragraph (2), there shall be inserted the following paragraph–

"(2A) In these regulations, the expression 'state scheme premium' does not include a personal pension protected rights premium under section 5 of the Social Security Act 1986.".

(3) In regulation 8(2)(d), for "6th April 1978" there shall be substituted "6th April 1988 in a case where the scheme whose name is specified under sub-paragraph (b) is a money purchase contracted-out scheme, or 6th April 1978 in any other case".

(4) In regulation 10(1), for the words from "the categories" to "the relevant scheme" there shall be substituted–

"(i) the categories of descriptions of the earners affected by the certificate, or

(ii) in the case of a money purchase contracted-out scheme, the protected rights under, or in the case of any other scheme, the benefits provided by, the relevant scheme, or

(iii) the contributions (if any) payable by those earners to the relevant scheme".

(5) In regulation 11(1)–

(a) in sub-paragraph (a), after "guaranteed minimum pensions" there shall be inserted "or protected rights, as the case may be,"; and

---

(**a**) S.I. 1973/1776, to which there are amendments not relevant to these Regulations.
(**b**) S.I. 1976/185; the relevant amending instruments are S.I. 1981/129, 1986/1716.
(**c**) 1975 c.60. For the definition, *see* section 66(1), as amended by the Social Security Act 1986 (c.50), section 6 and Schedule 2, paragraph 11(b).
(**d**) S.I. 1984/380; the relevant amending instruments are S.I. 1985/1323, 1928, 1986/317, 1716.

(b) in sub-paragraph (b), after "guaranteed minimum pensions" there shall be inserted ", or the protected rights, as the case may be,"

(6) In regulation 18–

(a) in paragraph (1B), for "and 45" there shall be substituted "and, subject to paragraph (1C) below, 45"; and

(b) after paragraph (1B) there shall be inserted the following paragraph–

"(1C) In a case where–

(a) a transfer payment has been made to a scheme in accordance with regulations 2 and 3 of the Protected Rights (Transfer Payment) Regulations 1987; and

(b) the scheme receiving that payment is to exclude one or more of the guaranteed minimum pensions resulting from the payment from full revaluation in accordance with paragraph 2 of Schedule 3 to those regulations,

for the purposes of section 45 (premium where guaranteed minimum pension excluded from full revaluation) the prescribed person is the trustees of the receiving scheme.".

(7) In regulation 18(3), after "state scheme premium", there shall be inserted ", other than a contracted-out protected rights premium,".

(8) In regulation 18(4)–

(a) after "(accrued rights premiums and pensioner's rights premiums)" there shall be inserted ", section 44ZA (contracted-out protected rights premiums)";**(a)**

(b) in sub-paragraph (a), after "section 44" there shall be inserted "or, in the case of a contracted-out protected rights premium, whether or not a person's protected rights are subject to approved arrangements as mentioned in section 44ZA"; and

(c) in sub-paragraph (c), after "section 44" there shall be inserted "or 44ZA, as the case may be,".

(9) In regulation 19(1)(c), there shall be inserted–

(a) after "widow", "or her widower"; and

(b) after "widow's", in both places where it occurs, "or widower's".

(10) In regulation 22(4), after "regulations made thereunder" there shall be inserted "or for members as regards their accrued rights to guaranteed minimum pensions which have arisen under the scheme by reason of a transfer payment made to it in accordance with regulations 2 and 3 of the Protected Rights (Transfer Payment) Regulations 1987".

(11) In regulation 24(1), after "where the premium", there shall be inserted "was not a contracted-out protected rights premium and".

(12) After paragraph (2) of regulation 24 there shall be inserted the following paragraph–

"(2A) Where a contracted-out protected rights premium has been paid in connection with a person's protected rights and another such premium subsequently becomes payable in connection with the same protected rights or protected rights including those rights, the Secretary of State may treat all or part of the first premium as paid (wholly or in part) in discharge of a liability for the second premium.".

(13) In regulation 24(3)–

(a) after sub-paragraph (d) there shall be inserted the following sub-paragraph–

"(dd) in the case of a contracted-out protected rights premium, he is satisfied that a transfer of the protected rights will be made in accordance with Schedule 1 to the Social Security Act 1986 as modified by section 32(2B); or";**(b)**

(b) after the words "and where a premium" (following sub-paragraph (e)) there shall be inserted "other than a contracted-out protected rights premium"; and

---

(a) Section 44ZA was inserted into the Social Security Pensions Act 1975 by the Social Security Act 1986 (c.50), section 6 and Schedule 2, paragraph 7.
(b) Subsection (2B) was inserted into section 32 by the Social Security Act 1986 (c.50), section 6 and Schedule 2, paragraph 5(b).

(c) at the end there shall be inserted ", and where a contracted-out protected rights premium is so refunded, the protected rights which were extinguished by payment of the premium and the corresponding reduction in any guaranteed minimum pension to which any person was treated as entitled shall be restored".

(14) In regulation 24(4), after "regulation 45(d)(iii)," there shall be inserted "or where the earner's rights were appropriately secured for the purposes of section 52C in circumstances analogous to those specified in that provision,"**(a)**.

(15) After regulation 24(4) there shall be inserted the following paragraph–

"(4A) Where a limited revaluation premium has been paid and a transfer payment under regulation 2B of the Contracting-out (Transfer) Regulations 1985 is made thereafter in respect of the accrued rights of the earner in respect of whom that premium was paid, the Secretary of State shall repay the amount of the premium to the trustees of the scheme, or the administrators of the policy, who made the transfer payment.".

(16) In regulation 24(8)(a) and (c), there shall be inserted, after "widow", "or widower".

(17) In regulation 24(8), after sub-paragraph (c) there shall be inserted the following sub-paragraph–

"(d) where it was paid under section 44ZA(4) and the person in respect of whom it was paid has died, without leaving a widow or widower, on or before the later of the days first mentioned in sub-paragraphs (a) and (b) respectively of regulation 20(1).".

(18) For paragraph (1) of regulation 28 there shall be substituted the following paragraph–

"(1) For a scheme to be contracted-out in relation to an earner's employment it must include a specific rule to the effect that if the earner has a guaranteed minimum under section 35–

(a) the weekly rate of his pension under the scheme at pensionable age shall not be less than that guaranteed minimum;

(b) the weekly rate of pension payable to any widow of the earner under the scheme shall be not less than half that guaranteed minimum; and

(c) the weekly rate of pension payable to any widower of the earner under the scheme shall be not less than half of that part of the earner's guaranteed minimum which is attributable to earnings factors for the tax year 1988/89 and subsequent tax years,

that rule to be expressed to override all other provisions of the scheme, except any that are in accordance with the provisions of the Act.".

(19) In regulation 34, there shall be inserted–

(a) after "his widow" in paragraph (1)(c), "or her widower";

(b) after "him" in paragraph (2), "or her"; and

(c) after "widow's", in both places where it occurs in paragraph (2), "or widower's".

(20) In regulation 35, there shall be inserted–

(a) after "widow's", in paragraph (1) and in both places where it occurs in paragraph (2), "or widower's"; and

(b) after "widow" in paragraph (2)(c), "or widower".

(21) In regulation 36–

(a) in each of sub-paragraphs (c), (d) and (e) of paragraph (1), after "guaranteed minimum pensions" there shall be inserted "or his protected rights, as the case may be,";

(b) in paragraph (3)(a)(iii) there shall be inserted, at the end, "or, as the case may be, effect has not been given to protected rights under the scheme arising out of his service in that employment by the making of a transfer payment in accordance with the provisions of the scheme under paragraph 9(1)(b) of

---

(a) Section 52C was inserted into the Social Security Pensions Act 1975 by the Social Security Act 1985 (c.53), section 2 and Schedule 1, paragraph 2.

Schedule 1 to the Social Security Act 1986 as modified by section 32(2B)."**(a)**; and

(c) in paragraph (5)(a)–
  (i) after "guaranteed minimum pensions" there shall be inserted "or protected rights, as the case may be,", and
  (ii) after "benefits" there shall be inserted "or such rights".

(22) In regulation 37(2)(d) there shall be inserted, at the end, "or, as the case may be, effect has been given to protected rights under the scheme arising out of his service in the first employment by the making of a transfer payment in accordance with the provisions of the scheme under paragraph 9(1)(b) of Schedule 1 to the Social Security Act 1986 as modified by section 32(2B).".

(23) In regulation 38(1)(a) and (2)(b), "or widower" shall be inserted after "widow".

(24) In regulation 43–
  (a) in paragraph (3), after "guaranteed minimum pensions" there shall be inserted "(including those to which persons are treated as entitled under section 29(2A))"**(b)**;
  (b) for paragraph (4) there shall be substituted the following paragraph–
    "(4) In any case where a person or body transfers his or its responsibility for, or makes a transfer payment in respect of, a guaranteed minimum pension to another person or body, the first person or body shall, within 5 weeks from the date of the transfer or transfer payment, notify the Secretary of State of its occurrence, giving such particulars as the Secretary of State may reasonably require to enable him to identify the second person or body.";
    and
  (c) in paragraph (5), for "guaranteed minimum pensions and for related purposes" there shall be substituted "guaranteed minimum pensions (including those to which persons are treated as entitled under section 29(2A)), and in order to know for what, if any, protected rights the scheme is responsible, and from what minimum contributions, minimum payments or transfer payments they derive, and for related purposes.".

(25) In regulation 44(e)(ii), after "in such cases" there shall be inserted ", except in such a case to which regulation 18(1C) applies,".

(26) In regulation 49–
  (a) in paragraph (1)–
    (i) after "paragraph (2)", there shall be inserted "and paragraph (3)", and
    (ii) after "another contracted-out scheme", there shall be inserted "or have arisen in such a scheme by reason of a transfer payment giving effect to his protected rights in accordance with regulations 2 and 3 of the Protected Rights (Transfer Payment) Regulations 1987"**(c)**;
  and
  (b) after paragraph (2), there shall be inserted the following paragraph–
    "(3) For the purposes of paragraph (1), where an earner has a guaranteed minimum pension in consequence of a transfer payment made in accordance with regulations 2 and 3 of the Protected Rights (Transfer Payment) Regulations 1987–
      (a) that pension shall be treated as if it had arisen as a result of his service in the employment by reference to which the scheme ceasing to be contracted-out was contracted-out; and
      (b) the reference to earnings factors, to the extent that they relate to that pension, shall be construed so as to include only those which do not fall to be revalued in accordance with section 35(7) as modified by regulation 4(6) of those regulations.".

(a) Subsection (2B) was inserted into section 32 by the Social Security Act 1986 (c.50), section 6 and Schedule 2, paragraph 5(b).
(b) Subsection (2A) was inserted into section 29 by the Social Security Act 1986 (c.50), section 6 and Schedule 2, paragraph 3.
(c) S.I. 1987/1118.

Amendments of the Contracting-out (Protection of Pensions) Regulations 1984

5.—(1) The Contracting-out (Protection of Pensions) Regulations 1984**(a)** shall be amended in accordance with the provisions of this regulation.

(2) The heading to regulation 4 shall be amended by the insertion, after "Widows", of "and widowers"; and regulation 4 shall be amended by–
   (a) the insertion, after "his widow", of "or her widower"; and
   (b) the insertion, after "that widow", of "or widower".

(3) Regulation 6(2) shall be amended by the insertion, after "widow's", in both places where it occurs, of "or widower's".

(4) For the heading to regulation 7 there shall be substituted "Widows' and widowers' pensions increased during initial period of payment"; and regulation 7 shall be amended by the insertion, after "widow", of "or widower".

(5) The heading to regulation 7A shall be amended by the insertion, after "widow's", of "and widower's"; and regulation 7A shall be amended by–
   (a) the insertion, after "wife", of "or husband";
   (b) the insertion, after "he", in both places where it occurs, of "or she"; and
   (c) the insertion, after "his", in both places where it occurs, of "or her".

(6) Regulation 10(2) shall be amended by–
   (a) the insertion, after "he", of "or she";
   (b) the insertion, after "him", in both places where it occurs, of "or her";
   (c) the insertion, after "his", of "or her"; and
   (d) the insertion, at the end, of ", or if he is the widower, to whom a widower's guaranteed minimum pension is payable, of such a person".

Amendment of the Contracting-out (Transfer) Regulations 1985

6.—(1) The Contracting-out (Transfer) Regulations 1985**(b)** shall be amended in accordance with the provisions of this regulation.

(2) In paragraph 5(b) of Schedule 2, after "widow" there shall be inserted "or her widower".

Amendments of the Occupational Pension Schemes (Discharge of Liability) Regulations 1985

7.—(1) The Occupational Pension Schemes (Discharge of Liability) Regulations 1985**(c)** shall be amended in accordance with the provisions of this regulation.

(2) Regulation 2(b)(ii) shall be amended by–
   (a) the substitution, for "in the case only of benefits which are not and do not include guaranteed minimum pensions", of "subject, in the case of benefits which are or include guaranteed minimum pensions, to regulations 2A and 2B of the Contracting-out (Transfer) Regulations 1985"**(d)**; and
   (b) the insertion, at the end, of "or the granting of rights to money purchase benefits under a personal pension scheme".

(3) Regulation 3(1) shall be amended by–
   (a) the insertion, after "widow" in sub-paragraph (a), of "or her widower";
   (b) the insertion, after "widow's" in sub-paragraph (b), of "or her widower's";
   (c) the substitution, for "he" in sub-paragraph (b)(i), of "the earner";
   (d) the substitution, for "his" in sub-paragraph (b)(ii), of "the earner's"; and
   (e) the substitution, for "he" in sub-paragraph (b)(iii), of "the earner".

(a) S.I. 1984/1921; the relevant amending instrument is S.I. 1985/1927.
(b) S.I. 1985/1323, to which there are amendments not relevant to these regulations.
(c) S.I. 1985/1929, to which there are amendments not relevant to these regulations.
(d) S.I. 1985/1323; the relevant amending instrument is S.I. 1987/1099.

(4) Regulation 4 shall be amended by the insertion, at the end of paragraph (b), of the following sub-paragraph–

"(iii) if the earner is a woman, that if she dies or has died leaving a widower the annuity to be paid thereunder to him or for his benefit will be at least equal to the guaranteed minimum due to him, or prospectively due to him in the event of his being left as her widower; and".

(5) Regulation 5 shall be amended by the insertion, after "widow", in both places where it occurs, of "or her widower".

Amendment of the Occupational Pension Schemes (Transfer Values) Regulations 1985

8.—(1) The Occupational Pension Schemes (Transfer Values) Regulations 1985(a)shall be amended in accordance with the provisions of this regulation.

(2) In regulation 3–

(a) at the beginning of paragraphs (1) and (2), there shall be inserted "Except in a case to which paragraph (3) below applies,"; and

(b) after paragraph (2) there shall be inserted the following paragraph–

"(3) Where a member's cash equivalent such as is mentioned in paragraph 12(1), or any portion of it–

(a) represents his rights to money purchase benefits under a scheme which is or was formerly a money purchase contracted-out scheme; and

(b) those rights do not fall, either wholly or in part, to be valued in a manner which involves making estimates of the value of benefits,

then that cash equivalent, or that portion of it, shall be calculated and verified in such manner as may be approved in particular cases by the trustees of the scheme, and by adopting methods consistent with the requirements of Schedule 1A.".

Signed by authority of the Secretary of State for Social Services.

Nicholas Scott
Minister of State,
Department of Health and Social Security

25th June 1987

(a) S.I. 1985/1931; the relevant amending instrument is S.I. 1986/751.

EXPLANATORY NOTE

(This note is not part of the Regulations)

These Regulations contain only provisions which are consequential on enactments contained in the Social Security Act 1986 and are made before the end of a period of 12 months from the commencement of those enactments. Consequently, by virtue of section 61(5) of that Act, the provisions of section 68(1) and (2) of the Social Security Act 1973 and section 61(2) and (3) of the Social Security Pensions Act 1975, which require reference to the Occupational Pensions Board of, and a report by the Board on proposals to make regulations under Part II of the Act of 1973 and proposals to make regulations for the purposes of Part III or IV of the Act of 1975 respectively, do not apply to them.

The Social Security Act 1986 introduces the concepts of personal pension schemes, money purchase contracted-out schemes, and guaranteed minimum pensions for widowers; and these Regulations make amendments, which are consequential on the introduction of those concepts, to the Occupational Pensions Board (Determinations and Review Procedure) Regulations 1973, the Occupational Pensions Board (Determinations and Review Procedure) Regulations 1976, the Occupational Pension Schemes (Contracting-out) Regulations 1984, the Contracting-out (Protection of Pensions) Regulations 1984, the Contracting-out (Transfer) Regulations 1985, the Occupational Pension Schemes (Discharge of Liability) Regulations 1985, and the Occupational Pension Schemes (Transfer Values) Regulations 1985.

STATUTORY INSTRUMENTS

1987 No. 1115

PENSIONS

The Personal and Occupational Pension Schemes (Incentive Payments) Regulations 1987

Made - - - -	*25th June 1987*
Laid before Parliament	*6th July 1987*
Coming into force	
regulations 1 and 2	*4th January 1988*
remainder	*6th April 1988*

The Secretary of State for Social Services, in exercise of the powers conferred upon him by sections 3(2), 7(1), (2), (3), (6) and (7), 14 and 84(1) of the Social Security Act 1986(**a**) and of all other powers enabling him in that behalf, by this instrument, which is made before the end of a period of 12 months from the commencement of the enactments under which it is made, makes the following Regulations:

Citation, commencement and interpretation

1.—(1) These Regulations may be cited as the Personal and Occupational Pension Schemes (Incentive Payments) Regulations 1987, and regulation 2 and this regulation shall come into force on 4th January 1988 and the remainder of these regulations on 6th April 1988.

(2) In these Regulations, unless the context otherwise requires–

"the Act" means the Social Security Act 1986;

"centralised scheme" means an occupational pension scheme for whose benefits earners in employments under different employers qualify by virtue of their respective service in those employments and which is either a money purchase contracted-out scheme or a scheme for which there is a common fund;

"employer" includes a person who, by virtue of regulations 1(4) and (5) and 14 to 16 of the Occupational Pension Schemes (Contracting-out) Regulations 1984(**b**), is treated as an employer for the purpose of those Regulations;

"scheme", except in the expression "personal pension scheme", means occupational pension scheme;

and other expressions have the same meaning as in the Social Security Pensions Act 1975(**c**).

(3) In these Regulations, unless the context otherwise requires, any reference–

(a) to a numbered regulation is to the regulation in these Regulations bearing that number;

(b) in a regulation to a numbered paragraph is to the paragraph of that regulation bearing that number;

(**a**) 1986 c.50. *See* definitions of "prescribed" and "regulations" in section 84(1).
(**b**) S.I. 1984/380, to which there are amendments not relevant to these Regulations.
(**c**) 1975 c.60.

(c) in a paragraph to a lettered sub-paragraph is to the sub-paragraph of that paragraph bearing that letter.

Employments in relation to which payments under section 3(1)(b) of the Act are not to be made

2.—(1) This regulation applies where–

(a) an earner is employed by a person (called in this regulation "the primary employer") in employment (called in this regulation "the primary employment") which is not contracted-out employment; and

(b) the primary employment would be contracted-out employment in relation to the earner by reference to a scheme (called in this regulation "the primary scheme") but for the fact that the earner voluntarily left it.

(2) Where–

(a) the primary scheme is not a centralised scheme; and

(b) there has been a period of at least 2 years, ending after 3rd January 1988, throughout which the earner was employed, whether or not by the primary employer, in employment which was contracted-out by reference to a scheme by reference to which employment by the primary employer was contracted-out,

the primary employer shall notify the Secretary of State of the facts described in sub-paragraphs (a) and (b) of paragraph (1) and sub-paragraph (b) of this paragraph.

(3) Where–

(a) the primary scheme is a centralised scheme; and

(b) there has been a period ending after 3rd January 1988–

  (i) of at least 2 years, throughout which the earner was employed in one employment, or

  (ii) during which the earner was employed in a series of employments with intervals of not more than 6 months between consecutive employments in the series, the total duration of the employments, not including the intervals, being at least 2 years,

and

(c) the one employment referred to in sub-paragraph (b)(i) or each employment in the series referred to in sub-paragraph (b)(ii) is contracted-out by reference to the primary scheme,

the trustees, or, if there are no trustees, the managers of the primary scheme shall notify the Secretary of State of the facts described in sub-paragraphs (a) and (b) of paragraph (1) and sub-paragraphs (a) to (c) of this paragraph.

(4) A notification required to be given under paragraph (2) or (3) shall be given within 6 months after the date on which the employment mentioned in paragraph (1)(a) ceased to be contracted-out employment or, if the Secretary of State is satisfied that the notification could not reasonably have been given within that period, such longer period as he may approve in a particular case or class of case.

(5) A notification required to be given under paragraph (2) or (3) shall be given in writing in such form as the Secretary of State may direct and shall contain such information as the Secretary of State may reasonably require for the purposes of this regulation.

(6) For the purposes of section 3(2) of the Act (no payment under section 3(1)(b) in relation to earnings paid with respect to prescribed employment) the prescribed employment is any employment to which paragraph (7) or (8) applies.

(7) This paragraph applies to the primary employment, where a notification has been given in accordance with paragraph (2) or (3) and the Secretary of State knows of no reason to suppose that the information given to him in the notification is incorrect.

(8) This paragraph applies to any employment (called in this regulation "the secondary employment") which–

(a) is employment of an earner about whom a notification has been given in accordance with paragraph (2) or (3), where the Secretary of State knows of no reason to suppose that the information given to him in the notification is incorrect;

(b) is not contracted-out employment in relation to him; and

(c) is not the primary employment,

except where the Secretary of State is satisfied that the circumstances specified in any one of sub-paragraphs (a), (b) and (c) of paragraph (9) obtain.

(9) The circumstances referred to in paragraph (8) are–

(a) that the earner is employed in the secondary employment by a person other than the primary employer;

(b) that there has been an interval of at least 7 days between the termination of the primary employment and the commencement of the secondary employment; and

(c) that the secondary employment–

(i) is not employment to which the primary scheme applies, and

(ii) commenced before, or while, the earner was employed in employment to which paragraph (10) applies.

(10) This paragraph applies to–

(a) the primary employment;

(b) any employment of the earner by the primary employer which commences immediately after the primary employment terminates; and

(c) any 2 or more employments of the earner by the primary employer of which the first commences immediately after the primary employment terminates and every subsequent one commences immediately after the previous one terminates.

(11) Where a notice under section 1(9) of the Act specifies, as the date from which the personal pension scheme in question is to be the chosen scheme of the earner in question, a date earlier than that on which the Secretary of State receives the notice–

(a) in a case where the Secretary of State receives the notice in the tax year 1988–89 and the date specified by the notice as mentioned above is 6th April 1987, that part (if any) which the Secretary of State is required to pay under section 3(1)(b) of the Act of the minimum contributions which fall due in respect of earnings paid to the earner during the tax years 1987–88 and 1988–89 shall be paid not earlier than October 1989; and

(b) in any other case, that part (if any) which the Secretary of State is required to pay under section 3(1)(b) of the Act of the minimum contributions which fall due in respect of earnings paid to the earner during the tax year in which the Secretary of State receives the notice shall be paid not earlier than October in the tax year following that in which the Secretary of State receives the notice,

unless the Secretary of State has reason to suppose that no notification under paragraph (2) or (3), containing correct information, can or will be served on him in relation to that earner.

Cases in which payments under section 7 of the Act are not to be made, or are to be made to prescribed persons

3.—(1) No payment shall be made under section 7 of the Act (schemes becoming contracted-out between 1st January 1986 and 5th April 1993) in any case to which paragraph (2), (3) or (4) applies.

(2) This paragraph applies to a case where the earner in question, or another earner, has been in employment which–

(a) was contracted-out employment by reference to a scheme other than the scheme in question during part or all of the period beginning on 1st January 1986 and ending on 5th April 1993; and

(b) is indistinguishable from the employment of the earner in question except by reference to the identity of the employer, or the identity of the person employed, or both.

(3) This paragraph applies to a case where the employment in question could have been contracted-out employment by reference to a scheme other than the scheme in

question during part or all of the period beginning on 1st January 1986 and ending on 5th April 1993, but was not, because of a choice made by, or a failure to make a choice on the part of, the earner in question.

(4) This paragraph applies to a case where the earnings in question are either–

(a) earnings in relation to which the earner, being a married woman or widow, is liable to make contributions at a reduced rate in accordance with an election which she has made and which is still operative; or

(b) earnings in relation to which contributions have not been paid or treated as paid, or the earner has paid contributions which are treated as not paid under regulation 38(1) and (2)(a) of the Social Security (Contributions) Regulations 1979(**a**).

(5) In a case where a scheme has ceased, on any date after 31st December 1985, to be a contracted-out scheme, no payment shall be made under section 7 of the Act to the trustees or managers of that scheme.

(6) In a case where–

(a) the scheme in question is a money purchase contracted-out scheme;

(b) a period during which the earner in question has been in an employment which is or was contracted-out by reference to that scheme has terminated; and

(c) effect has been given to that earner's protected rights under that scheme,

no payment shall be made under section 7 of the Act to the trustees or managers of that scheme in respect of that earner in relation to any tax week falling within the period referred to in sub-paragraph (b) of this paragraph, except as provided by paragraph (12).

(7) Where, but for the provisions of paragraph (6), or paragraphs (5) and (6), a payment would have fallen to be made under section 7 of the Act to the trustees or managers of a money purchase contracted-out scheme, a payment of the same amount shall, subject to paragraph (8), be made, in the circumstances described in paragraphs (9) and (11), to the persons described in paragraphs (10) and (12) (and in no other circumstances and to no other persons).

(8) Where a payment would otherwise be required under paragraph (7), it shall not be required if the scheme in question has ceased to be a contracted-out scheme unless effect was given to the protected rights of the earner in question before the end of the tax year following that which included the date with effect from which the scheme ceased to be a contracted-out scheme.

(9) Paragraph (10) applies where effect has been given to the earner's protected rights by the making of a transfer payment to a personal pension scheme or to another occupational pension scheme.

(10) Where the personal pension scheme is an appropriate scheme or the occupational pension scheme is another money purchase contracted-out scheme, the payment shall be made to the trustees or managers of that personal pension scheme or occupational pension scheme.

(11) Paragraph (12) applies where effect has been given to the earner's protected rights by the purchase of an annuity, or, where the scheme is still a contracted-out scheme, by the provision by the scheme of a pension.

(12) Where–

(a) the amount of the payment is at least 10 times as great as the lower earnings limit (within the meaning of section 1 of the Social Security Pensions Act 1975) for the tax year in which the Secretary of State first becomes aware that the relevant payment under section 7 falls to be made, or would fall to be made but for paragraph (5) or (6); and

(b) the Secretary of State is satisfied that the amount paid will be applied fairly to increase the amount of the annuity or pension,

the payment shall be made (in the case of an annuity) to the insurance company from which the annuity has been purchased, or (in the case of a pension) to the trustees or managers of the scheme.

(**a**) S.I. 1979/591, to which there are amendments not relevant to these Regulations.

Claim for payment under section 7 of the Act

4. A payment under section 7 of the Act shall not be made unless a claim is made for it in writing in such form as the Secretary of State may direct, by–

(a) the person who is or was the employer of the earner in question in relation to the employment in question; or

(b) in a case where the Secretary of State is satisfied by information furnished to him by the trustees or managers of the scheme that that person has not made, and does not intend to make, any claim in relation to the scheme in question, the trustees or managers of the scheme.

Manner of payment under section 7 of the Act

5. Payments under section 7 of the Act shall be made–

(a) by automated direct credit transfer into a bank or building society account which relates to the relevant scheme and which accepts payments made by automated direct credit transfer; or

(b) in such other manner as the Secretary of State may in his discretion decide.

Periods to be substituted for a tax week in particular cases

6.—(1) Section 7 of the Act shall have effect–

(a) in the case of an earner whose earnings are paid monthly, as if for any reference to a tax week there were substituted a reference to a month and as if for the references to £1.00 in subsection (4)(b) there were substituted references to £4⅓;

(b) in the case of an earner whose earnings are paid by reference to a period consisting of 2 or more months, as if for any reference to a tax week where were substituted a reference to that period and as if for the references to £1.00 in subsection (4)(b) there were substituted references to £4⅓ multiplied by the number of months in that period; and

(c) in the case of an earner whose earnings are paid by reference to any other period which is not a week or an exact number of weeks or a month or an exact number of months, as if for any reference to a tax week there were substituted a reference to that other period and as if for the references to £1.00 in subsection (4)(b) there were substituted references to a seventh of £1.00 multiplied by the number of days in that period.

(2) Where an amount to be paid under section 7 would otherwise not be a whole number of pence, it shall be taken to be the nearest whole number of pence, or, when the 2 nearest whole numbers are equally near, the lower of them.

State scheme premiums increased by interest on incentive payments

7.—(1) For the purposes of section 7(7)(b) of the Act (state scheme premiums under section 44 or 44A of the Social Security Pensions Act 1975 to be increased by the amount of a payment under section 7 of the Act and interest on that payment) the interest shall be calculated in accordance with paragraph (3).

(2) In this regulation, "the relevant period" means a period beginning on the date on which the payment under section 7 was made, and ending–

(a) where the state scheme premium is an accrued rights premium or a pensioner's rights premium–

(i) on the date (if any) on which arrangements made in relation to the relevant earner and approved by the Occupational Pensions Board under section 44 of the Social Security Pensions Act 1975 ceased to be so approved, or

(ii) if no such arrangements have been so approved, on the date of the determination by the Occupational Pensions Board as a result of which the relevant occupational pension scheme ceased to be contracted-out;

and

(b) where the state scheme premium is a transfer premium, on the date of the election to pay it.

(3) The interest shall be calculated at the rate of 8½ per cent. a year compound, so however that–

(a) if the relevant period is less than a year, no interest shall be paid; and

(b) if the relevant period consists of one or more complete years followed by a part of a year, the interest during that part of a year shall be calculated at the rate, for each day in that part of a year, of 8½ per cent. divided by 366 where that day falls, or 365 where it does not fall, within a period of a year which begins on an anniversary of the first day of the relevant period and includes 29th February.

Signed by authority of the Secretary of State for Social Services.

Nicholas Scott
Minister of State,
25th June 1987   Department of Health and Social Security

EXPLANATORY NOTE

(This note is not part of the Regulations)

These Regulations are all made under the Social Security Act 1986 before the end of a period of 12 months from the commencement of the relevant sections of that Act. Consequently, by virtue of section 61(5) of that Act, the provisions of section 61(2) and (3) of the Social Security Pensions Act 1975 (as amended by section 86(1) of, and paragraph 94 of Schedule 10 to, the Social Security Act 1986), which require reference to the Occupational Pensions Board of, and a report by the Board on, proposals to make regulations for the purposes of Part I of the Social Security Act 1986, do not apply to them.

Regulation 2 provides that where an earner has been employed in contracted-out employment for at least 2 years ending between 4th January 1988 and 5th April 1993 and would still be so employed, but for the fact that he voluntarily left the relevant scheme, the Secretary of State must be notified: in relation to the earnings of the earner in such a case, and in related cases where the earner has more than one employment, the additional minimum contributions otherwise payable by the Secretary of State under section 3(1)(b) of the Social Security Act 1986 to an appropriate pension scheme for tax weeks before 6th April 1993 are not to be paid. There is also provision (in paragraph (11)) for the Secretary of State to defer payment of minimum contributions where he is notified that a personal pension scheme is to be an earner's chosen scheme from a date earlier than the date of the notification.

Regulation 3 provides that, in certain cases, the additional payments otherwise required, under section 7 of the Social Security Act 1986, to be made by the Secretary of State to the trustees or managers of an occupational pension scheme newly contracted-out between 1st January 1986 and 5th April 1993 are not to be made, or are to be paid to another scheme or to other persons.

Regulation 4 deals with claims for payments under section 7; regulation 5 with the manner of making such payments; regulation 6 with adaptations for the case of earners paid otherwise than weekly; and regulation 7 with the addition to certain state scheme premiums of interest on payments under section 7.

STATUTORY INSTRUMENTS

1987 No. 1116

PENSIONS

The Personal and Occupational Pension Schemes (Modification of Enactments) Regulations 1987

Made - - - -	*25th June 1987*
Laid before Parliament	*6th July 1987*
Coming into force	
regulation 5 and	
Schedule 6	*6th April 1988*
remainder	*27th July 1987*

The Secretary of State for Social Services, in exercise of the powers conferred upon him by sections 17(1) and 84(1) of the Social Security Act 1986(a), and of all other powers enabling him in that behalf, by this instrument, which is made before the end of a period of 12 months from the commencement of the enactments under which it is made, makes the following Regulations:–

Citation, commencement and interpretation

1.—(1) These Regulations may be cited as the Personal and Occupational Pension Schemes (Modification of Enactments) Regulations 1987 and shall come into force on 27th July 1987, except regulation 5 and Schedule 6, which shall come into force on 6th April 1988.

(2) In these Regulations, "personal pension scheme" has the same meaning as in the Social Security Act 1986.

Provisions of the Social Security Act 1973 relating to occupational pension schemes to apply, subject to modifications, to personal pension schemes

2. Subsections (1), (1A), (3) (except paragraphs (a), (b), (d), (dd) and (e)), (4), (5) (except paragraph (c)) and (6) to (10) of section 64 of the Social Security Act 1973(b) (modification and winding-up of schemes by order of the Occupational Pensions Board) shall have effect in relation to personal pension schemes subject to the modifications described in Schedule 1.

Provisions of the Social Security Pensions Act 1975 relating to occupational pension schemes to apply, subject to modifications, to personal pension schemes

3.—(1) Section 32(2) of the Social Security Pensions Act 1975(c) (an occupational pension scheme can be contracted-out if specified requirements are satisfied) shall have effect in relation to personal pension schemes as if it provided that, subject to the provisions of section 2 of the Social Security Act 1986 and regulations made thereunder,

---

(a) 1986 c.50. *See* definitions of "prescribed" and "regulations" in section 84(1).

(b) 1973 c.38. Section 64 is amended by the Social Security Pensions Act 1975 (c.60), sections 56(5) and 65(1) and Schedule 4, paragraph 25, and by the Social Security Act 1986, sections 12(11) and 86(1) and Schedule 10, paragraph 3.

(c) 1975 c.60. Section 32(2) is amended by the Social Security Act 1986, sections 6 and 86(1), Schedule 2, paragraph 5 and Schedule 10, paragraph 16.

a personal pension scheme can be an appropriate scheme (for the purposes of the Social Security Act 1986) only if the rules of the scheme applying to protected rights are framed so as to comply with the requirements of any regulations prescribing the form and content of rules of appropriate schemes and with such other requirements as to form and content (not inconsistent with regulations) as may be imposed by the Occupational Pensions Board as a condition of being an appropriate scheme, either generally or in relation to a particular scheme.

(2) Subsections (1), (2), (2A) and (5) of section 49 of the Social Security Pensions Act 1975(a) (supervision by the Occupational Pensions Board of occupational pension schemes which have ceased to be contracted-out) shall have effect in relation to personal pension schemes subject to the modifications described in Schedule 2.

(3) Section 50 of the Social Security Pensions Act 1975(b) (alteration of rules of contracted-out schemes) shall have effect in relation to personal pension schemes subject to the modifications specified in paragraphs (4) to (6) of this regulation.

(4) Subsection (1) shall be so modified as to provide that, where an appropriate scheme certificate has been issued, no alteration of the rules of the relevant appropriate scheme shall be made so as to affect any of the matters dealt with in Schedule 1 to the Social Security Act 1986, or so as to cause the scheme to cease to take one, and thereafter to take another, of the forms specified in paragraphs (a) to (c) of regulation 2 of the Personal Pension Schemes (Appropriate Schemes) Regulations 1987(c), unless it is an alteration to which subsection (1) does not apply or the following conditions are satisfied, namely–

(a) the Board have given their consent to the alteration; and

(b) (except in so far as the Board in their discretion dispense with satisfaction of this condition) notice of intention to apply for that consent was given in accordance with the requirements specified in paragraph (7) of this regulation,

and that, subject to subsection (2), an alteration to which subsection (1) applies but which does not satisfy those conditions shall be void.

(5) Subsection (1A) shall have effect as if paragraph (a) were omitted.

(6) Subsection (3) shall be so modified as to provide that section 50 shall continue in force in relation to a scheme after it has ceased to be appropriate so long as any person has protected rights under the scheme.

(7) The requirements referred to in paragraph (4)(b) are–

(a) that the notice shall be given in writing to–

(i) any member of the scheme who has protected rights under it, and

(ii) any earner who, jointly with the trustees or managers of the scheme, has given in relation to the scheme a notice under section 1(9) of the Social Security Act 1986 which has not been cancelled,

by sending it to his last known address;

(b) that it shall specify the name of the scheme;

(c) that it shall specify the date on which it is desired that the alteration should have effect, being a date which is at least 3 months later than the date on which the notice is given; and

(d) that it shall specify the purport of the intended alteration and give an explanation of the effect on the persons to whom the notice is given.

(8) Sections 56A and 56L of the Social Security Pensions Act 1975(d) shall have effect in relation to personal pension schemes subject to the modifications specified in Schedule 3.

(9) Section 57 of the Social Security Pensions Act 1975 (disclosure of information by the Occupational Pensions Board), except in its application to Northern Ireland, shall have effect in relation to personal pension schemes as if the reference in it to an occupational pension scheme were a reference to a personal pension scheme.

(a) Section 49 is amended by the Social Security Act 1986, sections 6 and 86, Schedule 2, paragraph 9, Schedule 10, paragraph 24, and Schedule 11.
(b) Section 50 is amended by the Social Security Act 1986 (c.50), sections 6 and 86, Schedule 2, paragraph 10, and Schedule 10, paragraph 25.
(c) S.I. 1987/1109.
(d) Sections 56A and 56L were inserted by the Social Security Act 1985 (c.53), section 3 and Schedule 2.

(10) Schedule 1A to the Social Security Pensions Act 1975**(a)** shall have effect in relation to personal pension schemes subject to the modifications specified in Schedule 4.

(11) Paragraph 6 of Schedule 2 to the Social Security Pensions Act 1975 shall have effect in relation to personal pension schemes subject to the modifications specified in Schedule 5.

Modification of provisions of the Social Security Act 1973 in consequence of Part I of the Social Security Act 1986

4.—(1) In consequence of Part I of the Social Security Act 1986, the provisions of the Social Security Act 1973**(b)** specified in paragraphs (2) and (3) of this regulation shall have effect subject to the modifications specified in those paragraphs.

(2) Section 64(3)(c) shall have effect as if, after "another scheme", there were inserted "(whether another occupational pension scheme or a personal pension scheme)".

(3) Paragraph 6 of Schedule 16 shall have effect as if there were added, after paragraph (1)(b)–

"or
(c) a transfer payment in respect of his rights under a personal pension scheme has been made to the scheme,".

Modification of provisions of the Social Security Pensions Act 1975 in consequence of Part I of the Social Security Act 1986

5.—(1) In consequence of Part I of the Social Security Act 1986 the provisions of the Social Security Pensions Act 1975**(c)** specified in paragraphs (2) to (4) of this regulation shall have effect subject to the modifications mentioned in those paragraphs.

(2) Section 49(1) shall have effect as if, after "person" in paragraph (b)(ii) and at the end of the subsection, there were inserted "(not being a person in respect of whom a premium is not payable by virtue of regulation 18(2A) of the Occupational Pension Schemes (Contracting-out) Regulations 1984)"**(d)**.

(3) Schedule 1A shall have effect subject to the modifications described in Schedule 6.

(4) Schedule 2 to the Social Security Pensions Act 1975 shall have effect as if, in paragraph 6(4)(a), after "rights to receive such pensions", there were inserted "or, in the case of a contracted-out protected rights premium, for the purpose of extinguishing protected rights and reducing any guaranteed minimum pension to which a person is treated as entitled,".

Signed by authority of the Secretary of State for Social Services.

Nicholas Scott
Minister of State,
Department of Health and Social Security

25th June 1987

(a) 1975 c.60. Schedule 1A was inserted by the Social Security Act 1985 (c.53), section 2 and Schedule 1.
(b) 1973 c.38.
(c) Sub-paragraph (4) was inserted into paragraph 6 of Schedule 2 by the Social Security Act 1980 (c.30), section 3(12).
(d) Paragraph (2A) was inserted into regulation 18 by the Occupational Pension Schemes (Contracted-out Protected Rights Premiums) Regulations 1987 (S.I. 1987/1103), reg. 4(3).

SCHEDULE 1

MODIFICATIONS SUBJECT TO WHICH SECTION 64 OF THE SOCIAL SECURITY ACT 1973 IS TO HAVE EFFECT IN RELATION TO PERSONAL PENSION SCHEMES

1. In subsection (1), the substitution, for "an occupational pension scheme", of "a personal pension scheme".

2. In subsection (3)(c), the insertion, after "another scheme", of "(whether another personal pension scheme or an occupational pension scheme)".

3. In subsection (7), the omission of "of service".

SCHEDULE 2

MODIFICATIONS SUBJECT TO WHICH SECTION 49 OF THE SOCIAL SECURITY PENSIONS ACT 1975 IS TO HAVE EFFECT IN RELATION TO PERSONAL PENSION SCHEMES

1. In subsection (1)–

   (a) the substitution, for "occupational pension scheme, other than a public service scheme", of "personal pension scheme";

   (b) the substitution, for "a contracted-out scheme", of "an appropriate scheme";

   (c) the substitution, for paragraph (b) (both before and after the coming into force of paragraph 9(a) of Schedule 2 to the Social Security Act 1986), of the following paragraph–

   "(b) there has not been a payment of a premium under section 5 of the Social Security Act 1986 in respect of each person (not being a person in respect of whom a premium is not payable by virtue of regulation 3 of the Personal Pension Schemes (Personal Pension Protected Rights Premiums) Regulations 1987) who has protected rights under it or is entitled to any benefit giving effect to protected rights under it;"; and

   (d) the insertion, at the end, of "(not being a person in respect of whom a premium is not payable by virtue of regulation 3 of the Personal Pension Schemes (Personal Pension Protected Rights Premiums) Regulations 1987"**(a)**.

2. In subsection (2), the substitution, for paragraphs (a) (both before and after the coming into force of paragraph 9(b) of Schedule 2 to the Social Security Act 1986) and (b) and the words following them, of "the matters in respect of which, for the purposes of determining whether a personal pension scheme should be or continue to be an appropriate scheme, they are required to be satisfied under paragraph 10 of Schedule 1 to the Social Security Act 1986".

3. In subsection (2A), the substitution, for the words from "subsection (1C)" to "subsection (3) of that section", of "subsection (2) of section 5 of the Social Security Act 1986 which has not been cancelled under subsection (3) of that section".

4. In subsection (5) (both before and after the coming into force of paragraph 9(c) of Schedule 2 to the Social Security Act 1986), the substitution, for the words from "sections" to "above", of "Schedule 1 to the Social Security Act 1986".

(a) S.I. 1987/1111.

Regulation 3(8)

SCHEDULE 3

MODIFICATIONS SUBJECT TO WHICH SECTIONS 56A AND 56L OF THE SOCIAL SECURITY PENSIONS ACT 1975 ARE TO HAVE EFFECT IN RELATION TO PERSONAL PENSION SCHEMES

1. In section 56A–
    (a) the substitution, for the references to an occupational pension scheme and occupational pension schemes, of references to a personal pension scheme and personal pension schemes respectively;
    (b) the omission of the references to prospective members;
    (c) the omission of subsections (2)(d), (4) and (9);
    (d) the omission, from subsection (7), of "(other than a public service pension scheme)"; and
    (e) the substitution, for paragraphs (a) and (b) of subsection (8), of the following paragraphs–

    "(a) the trustees or managers of the scheme;
    (b) any person other than the trustees or managers who has power to alter any of the rules of the scheme;
    (c) any member of the scheme.".

2. In section 56L(1), the substitution, for the reference to a scheme, of a reference to a personal pension scheme.

Regulation 3(10)

SCHEDULE 4

MODIFICATIONS SUBJECT TO WHICH SCHEDULE 1A TO THE SOCIAL SECURITY PENSIONS ACT 1975 IS TO HAVE EFFECT IN RELATION TO PERSONAL PENSION SCHEMES

1. In paragraph 1–
    (a) the substitution, for sub-paragraph (1), of the following sub-paragraph–

    "(1) This Part of this Schedule applies to any member of a personal pension scheme (other than a member of such a scheme which is comprised in an annuity contract made before 4th January 1988) in respect of whom contributions (which expression includes, where applicable, minimum contributions within the meaning of Part I of the Social Security Act 1986) to the scheme have ceased to be paid and who has accrued rights to benefit under the scheme."; and
    (b) the omission of sub-paragraphs (2) to (4).

2. The omission of paragraphs 2 to 4.

3. In paragraph 5–
    (a) in sub-paragraph (3), the omission of "if the revaluation condition is satisfied,"; and
    (b) the substitution, for sub-paragraph (4), of the following sub-paragraph–

    "(4) The trustees and managers of a personal pension scheme may, when providing a pension or other retirement benefit under sub-paragraph (3) above, deduct a sum which does not exceed–

    (a) the actual administrative expenses of doing so, or, if it is less,
    (b) the amount of the administrative expenses which would have been incurred in providing a money purchase benefit for the same member if contributions had not ceased to be paid to the scheme in respect of him.".

4. The omission of paragraph 6.

5. In paragraph 7–
    (a) in sub-paragraph (1), the omission of "Subject to sub-paragraph (2) below,"; and
    (b) the omission of sub-paragraphs (2) to (4).

6. The omission of paragraphs 8 to 10.

7. In paragraph 11–
   (a) the substitution, for sub-paragraph (1), of the following sub-paragraph–
        "(1) This Part of this Schedule applies to any member of a personal pension scheme (other than a member of such a scheme which is comprised in an annuity contract made before 4th January 1988) who has accrued rights to benefits under that scheme.";
   (b) the omission of sub-paragraph (2); and
   (c) in sub-paragraph (3), the substitution, for "an occupational pension scheme", of "a personal pension scheme".

8. In paragraph 12–
   (a) the substitution, for sub-paragraph (1), of the following sub-paragraph–
        "(1) Subject to the following provisions of this Schedule, a member acquires a right to the cash equivalent at the relevant date of any benefits which have accrued to or in respect of him under the rules of the scheme.";
   (b) in sub-paragraph (2)–
        (i) the omission of the definition of the expression "the applicable rules", and
        (ii) the substitution, for the definition of the expression "the relevant date", of the following definition–
             " 'the relevant date' means the date of the relevant application;";
        and
   (c) the omission of sub-paragraphs (2A), (2B) and (3).

9. In paragraph 13–
   (a) in sub-paragraph (2)(a), the substitution, for "another scheme", of "an occupational pension scheme, or for acquiring rights allowed under the rules of another personal pension scheme", and the insertion, after "whose trustees or managers" and after "which", of ", in either case,";
   (b) the omission of sub-paragraph (2)(b);
   (c) in sub-paragraph (5), the substitution, for paragraphs (a) and (b), of the following paragraphs–
        "(a) the trustees or managers of an occupational pension scheme which is not a contracted-out scheme, or of a personal pension scheme which is not an appropriate scheme, are able or willing to accept a transfer payment only in respect of a member's rights other than his protected rights within the meaning given by Schedule 1 to the Social Security Act 1986; and
        (b) the member has not required the trustees or managers of the scheme from which he is being transferred to use that portion of his cash equivalent that represents protected rights within the meaning given by Schedule 1 to the Social Security Act 1986 in either of the ways specified in sub-paragraph (2) above,";
        and
   (d) in sub-paragraph (6), the substitution, for "his and his widow's guaranteed minimum pensions", of "his protected rights within the meaning given by Schedule 1 to the Social Security Act 1986".

10. In paragraph 14–
   (a) in sub-paragraph (3)(a)(ii), the substitution, for "to provide guaranteed minimum pensions", of "to make provision for protected rights"; and
   (b) the omission of sub-paragraph (4)(a)(i).

11. The substitution, for paragraph 15, of the following paragraph–
        "15.—(1) Where, on or before the relevant date, the whole, or any part, of a member's benefits have become payable under the scheme, the right which he acquires under paragraph 12(1) above is only to the cash equivalent of any of the benefits mentioned in that paragraph which have not become payable.
        (2) A member loses the right to any cash equivalent under this Part of this Schedule if the scheme is wound up.".

12. In paragraph 16–
   (a) in sub-paragraph (2), the substitution, for "to provide such guaranteed minimum pensions", of "to make provision for such protected rights";
   (b) the omission of sub-paragraph (3)(b);
   (c) the omission of sub-paragraph (4);

    (d)   the substitution, for sub-paragraph (5)(a)(ii), of the following–

        "(ii) the scheme is ceasing to be an appropriate personal pension scheme within the meaning of Part I of the Social Security Act 1986,"; and

    (e)   in sub-paragraph (5)(b), the insertion, after "section 49 above", of ", as modified by regulation 3(2) of, and Schedule 2 to, the Personal and Occupational Pension Schemes (Modification of Enactments) Regulations 1987,".

13.   In paragraph 17, the substitution, for "13(2)(a), (b) or (c)" of "13(2)(a) or (c)".

14.   In paragraph 19, the insertion, after "purposes of", of "Part II of".

15.   In paragraph 21–

    (a)   the substitution, for "occupational pension scheme", of "personal pension scheme"; and

    (b)   the omission of sub-paragraph (b).

16.   In paragraph 22–

    (a)   in sub-paragraph (1), the substitution, for "occupational pension scheme (other than a public service pension scheme)", of "personal pension scheme"; and

    (b)   in sub-paragraph (2)(a), the substitution, for "section 41E(2)(a) to (d)", of "section 41E(2)(a), (b) and (d)".

Regulation 3(11)   **SCHEDULE 5**

MODIFICATIONS SUBJECT TO WHICH PARAGRAPH 6 OF SCHEDULE 2 TO THE SOCIAL SECURITY PENSIONS ACT 1975(a) IS TO HAVE EFFECT IN RELATION TO PERSONAL PENSION SCHEMES

   1.   In sub-paragraph (3)(bb), the substitution, for "Part III of this Act", of "Part I of the Social Security Act 1986".

   2.   In sub-paragraph (3)(c), the omission of the words after "another premium".

   3.   In sub-paragraph (4)(a), the substitution, for "extinguishing accrued rights to guaranteed minimum pensions and rights to receive such pensions a state scheme premium", of "extinguishing protected rights and reducing any guaranteed minimum pension to which a person is treated as entitled, a personal pension protected rights premium".

Regulation 5(3)   **SCHEDULE 6**

OTHER MODIFICATIONS OF SCHEDULE 1A TO THE SOCIAL SECURITY PENSIONS ACT 1975 IN CONSEQUENCE OF PART I OF THE SOCIAL SECURITY ACT 1986

   1.   In paragraph 13(2)(a), the substitution, for "another scheme", of "another occupational pension scheme, or for acquiring rights allowed under the rules of a personal pension scheme", and the insertion, after "whose trustees or managers" and after "which", of ", in either case,";

   2.   In paragraph 13(2)(b), the insertion, at the beginning, of "except in respect of the cash equivalent of his protected rights, if any, under a scheme which is, or was formerly, a money purchase contracted-out scheme";

   3.   In paragraph 13(5), the substitution, for paragraphs (a) and (b), of the following paragraphs–

    "(a)   the trustees or managers of an occupational pension scheme which is not a contracted-out scheme, or of a personal pension scheme which is not an appropriate scheme, are

---

(a) 1975 c.60. Sub-paragraphs (3)(bb) and (4) were inserted into paragraph 6 of Schedule 2 by the Social Security Act 1980 (c.30), section 3(12).

able or willing to accept a transfer payment only in respect of a member's rights other than his accrued rights to guaranteed minimum pensions or his protected rights; and

(b) the member has not required the trustees or managers of the scheme from which he is being transferred to use that portion of his cash equivalent that represents guaranteed minimum pensions or protected rights in any of the ways specified in sub-paragraph (2) above,".

4. In paragraph 13(6), the addition, at the end, of "or his protected rights".

5. In paragraph 14(3)(a)(ii), the insertion, after "guaranteed minimum pensions", of "or give effect to protected rights".

6. In paragraph 16(2), the substitution, for "such case as is" and "such guaranteed minimum pensions" of "such cases as are" and "such guaranteed minimum pensions or give effect to such protected rights" respectively.

EXPLANATORY NOTE

(This note is not part of the Regulations)

These Regulations are all made under the Social Security Act 1986 before the end of a period of 12 months from the commencement of the relevant sections of that Act. Consequently, by virtue of section 61(5) of that Act, the provisions of section 61(2) and (3) of the Social Security Pensions Act 1975 (as amended by section 86(1) of, and paragraph 94 of Schedule 10 to, the Social Security Act 1986), which require reference to the Occupational Pensions Board of, and a report by the Board on, proposals to make regulations for certain purposes of both Acts, do not apply to them.

Section 17(1) of the Social Security Act 1986 gives power to make regulations providing that provisions of the Social Security Act 1973 and the Social Security Acts 1975 to 1986 which relate to occupational pension schemes–

(a) shall have effect in relation to personal pension schemes subject to prescribed modifications;

(b) shall have effect subject to such other modifications as the Secretary of State may consider necessary or expedient in consequence of Part I of the Social Security Act 1986.

These Regulations make certain provisions of the Social Security Act 1973 and the Social Security Pensions Act 1975 apply to personal pension schemes, subject to specified modifications, and make other modifications of those Acts in consequence of Part I of the Social Security Act 1986.

1987 No. 1117

PENSIONS

The Personal and Occupational Pension Schemes (Protected Rights) Regulations 1987

Made - - - -	*25th June 1987*
Laid before Parliament	*6th July 1987*
Coming into force	
For the purposes of personal pension schemes	*27th July 1987*
For the purposes of occupational pension schemes	*6th April 1988*

The Secretary of State for Social Services, in exercise of the powers conferred upon him by sections 14 and 84(1) of, and paragraphs 6, 7(2), (4) and (5), 9 (1)(a), (2) to (4) and (7) to (9) and 11 of Schedule 1 to the Social Security Act 1986(a) (including those paragraphs of that Schedule as modified by section 32(2B) of the Social Security Pensions Act 1975(b)), and of all other powers enabling him in that behalf, by this instrument, which is made before the end of a period of 12 months from the commencement of the enactments under which it is made, makes the following Regulations:–

Citation, commencement and interpretation

1.—(1) These Regulations may be cited as the Personal and Occupational Pension Schemes (Protected Rights) Regulations 1987 and shall come into force on 27th July 1987 for the purposes of personal pension schemes and on 6th April 1988 for the purposes of occupational pension schemes.

(2) In these Regulations, unless the context otherwise requires–

"the Act" means the Social Security Act 1986;

"the Board" means the Occupational Pensions Board;

"child benefit" has the same meaning as in the Child Benefit Act 1975(c);

"member" means member of an occupational pension scheme or a personal pension scheme;

"money purchase contracted-out scheme" has the same meaning as in the Social Security Pensions Act 1975;

"pensionable age" means, in the case of a man, 65, and in the case of a woman, 60;

"scheme" means occupational pension scheme or personal pension scheme;

and other expressions have the same meaning as in the Act.

(a) 1986 c.50. *See* definitions of "prescribed" and "regulations" in section 84(1).
(b) 1975 c.60. Subsection (2B) was inserted into section 32 by section 6 of, and Schedule 2 to, the Social Security Act 1986 (c. 50).
(c) 1975 c.61.

(3) In these Regulations, except in so far as the context otherwise requires, any reference–

   (a) to Schedule 1 to the Act includes a reference to that Schedule as modified by section 32(2B) of the Social Security Pensions Act 1975;

   (b) in a regulation to a numbered paragraph is to the paragraph of that regulation bearing that number; and

   (c) in a paragraph to a lettered sub-paragraph is to the sub-paragraph of that paragraph bearing that letter.

Manner of calculation and verification of protected rights mentioned in paragraph 7(2) of Schedule 1 to the Act

2.—(1) Except in a case to which paragraph (2) applies, the value of a member's protected rights (under a scheme which is, or was formerly, an appropriate scheme or a money purchase contracted-out scheme) such as are mentioned in paragraph 7(2) of Schedule 1 to the Act shall be calculated and verified–

   (a) in such manner as may be approved in particular cases by the trustees or managers of the scheme, and

   (b) by adopting methods consistent with the requirements of Schedule 1 to the Act.

(2) In a case where a member's rights (as described in paragraph (1)) fall, either wholly or in part, to be valued in a manner which involves making estimates of the value of benefits, the value of those rights shall be calculated and verified–

   (a) in such manner as may be approved in particular cases by–

      (i) a Fellow of the Institute of Actuaries, or

      (ii) a Fellow of the Faculty of Actuaries, or

      (iii) a person with other actuarial qualifications who is approved by the Secretary of State, at the request of the trustees or managers of the scheme in question, as being a proper person to act for the purposes of these regulations in connection with that scheme,

and in this regulation "actuary" means any person such as is referred to in head (i), (ii) or (iii) of this sub-paragraph; and

   (b) by adopting methods and making assumptions which–

      (i) if not determined by the trustees or managers of the scheme in question, are notified to them by an actuary, and

      (ii) are certified by an actuary to the trustees or managers of the scheme as being consistent with the requirements of Schedule 1 to the Act, and as being consistent with "Retirement Benefit Schemes—Transfer Values (GN11)" published by the Institute of Actuaries and the Faculty of Actuaries and current at the date of the calculation.

Rights which the rules of a scheme may designate as protected rights

3. For the purposes of paragraph 7(2) of Schedule 1 to the Act (scheme rules may provide that a member's protected rights are rights specified in paragraph 7(2) and such other rights as may be prescribed), the prescribed rights are rights to money purchase benefits which derive from–

   (a) guaranteed minimum pensions under an occupational pension scheme, or guaranteed minimum pensions appropriately secured within the meaning of section 52C of the Social Security Pensions Act 1975, which have been the subject of a transfer payment to the trustees or managers of the scheme;

   (b) in the case of a personal pension scheme, a payment made to the trustees or managers of the scheme in accordance with section 7 of the Act and regulation 3(10) of the Personal and Occupational Pension Schemes (Incentive Payments) Regulations 1987**(a)**; and

   (c) in the case of an occupational pension scheme, a payment of minimum contributions made to the trustees or managers of the scheme in accordance with regulation 14(8) of the Personal Pension Schemes (Appropriate Schemes) Regulations 1987**(b)**.

(a) S.I. 1987/1115.
(b) S.I. 1987/1109.

Conditions applying to pensions and annuities which give effect to protected rights

4.—(1) For the purposes of sub-paragraphs (1) (a) (effect may be given to protected rights by the provision by the scheme of a pension which among other things satisfies such conditions as may be prescribed) and (2)(ii) (effect may be given in certain circumstances to protected rights by the purchase by the scheme of an annuity which among other things satisfies such conditions as may be prescribed) of paragraph 9 of Schedule 1 to the Act, the prescribed conditions are that the pension or annuity gives effect to all the protected rights of the member, that in the case of an annuity it is one which is purchased on or after the date on which it commences, and that the terms on which the pension is provided, or the terms of the purchase of the annuity—

    (a) satisfy the requirements of paragraphs (2) to (5) of this regulation; and

    (b) make no provision other than such as—

        (i) is necessary to establish what the initial rate and the method of payment of the pension or annuity are to be, and that it shall continue to be paid at that rate (subject only to paragraphs (3) and (6)) throughout the lifetime of the member,

        (ii) is necessary to satisfy the requirements of paragraphs (2) to (5) and regulation 5, and

        (iii) is permitted by paragraphs (6) to (9).

(2) The rate of the pension or annuity shall be determined without regard to the sex or marital status of the member.

(3) The rate of the pension or annuity shall—

    (a) on a date ("the first date") not later than the first anniversary of the date on which it becomes payable, and

    (b) on each anniversary of the first date,

be increased by the same percentage as that by which parts of guaranteed minimum pensions are increased, by the order (if any) made by the Secretary of State under section 37A of the Social Security Pensions Act 1975**(a)** and coming into operation on the first day of the tax year in which the date of the increase falls.

(4) Except with the written consent of the person to whom the pension or annuity is payable, the pension or annuity, if paid in arrear, shall be paid no less frequently than by monthly instalments.

(5) The pension or annuity shall be paid no less frequently than by annual instalments.

(6) The pension or annuity may be increased, not more frequently than on the first date mentioned in paragraph (3) and on each of its anniversaries, but by larger percentages than paragraph (3) requires, so however that no increase is by more than 3 per cent.

(7) When the member has died, the pension or annuity may continue to be paid, at a rate which satisfies the requirements of paragraph (8), to or for the benefit of other persons if the requirements of paragraph (9) are satisfied.

(8) The requirements first referred to in paragraph (7) are that the rate shall not exceed—

    (a) at any given time during the period which is within 5 years of the date on which the pension or annuity commenced, the rate at which it would have been payable if the member had been living at that time; and

    (b) at any given time during any other period, one-half of the rate at which it would have been payable if the member had been living at that time.

(9) The requirements secondly referred to in paragraph (7) are that the pension or annuity shall be paid only—

    (a) to the member's widow or widower, in a case where immediately after the member's death the pension or annuity is required by virtue of regulation 5 to be paid to her or him;

    (b) to any one person, in a case to which sub-paragraph (a) does not apply;

    (c) for the benefit of any child or children, if—

(a) 1975 c.60; section 37A was inserted by section 9(7) of the Social Security Act 1986 (c.50).

(i) sub-paragraph (a) does not apply,

(ii) the pension or annuity has not been paid in accordance with sub-paragraph (b), and

(iii) immediately before the member's death the member was entitled to child benefit in respect of that child or those children, or would have been so entitled if that child or one, some or all of those children had not been absent from Great Britain;

but only for so long as that child or at least one of those children is under the age of 18; and

(d) to any one person, during any period—

(i) which is within 5 years of the date on which the pension or annuity commenced, and

(ii) which immediately follows the death of a person who died while the pension or annuity was being paid to him in accordance with sub-paragraph (a) or (b) or in accordance with this sub-paragraph, or which begins on the date on which the child or the last of the children in respect of whom the pension or annuity has been paid in accordance with sub-paragraph (c) attained the age of 18 or died under that age.

Circumstances in which and periods for which pension or annuity is to be paid to widow or widower after being paid to member

5.—(1) For the purposes of paragraph 9(7)(b)(i) of Schedule 1 to the Act (pension or annuity to be paid to member's widow or widower in prescribed circumstances and for the prescribed period) the prescribed circumstances are that—

(a) the widow or widower is entitled to child benefit in respect of a child under 18 who is, or residing with a child under 16 who is—

(i) a son or daughter of the widow or widower and the member, or

(ii) a child in respect of whom the member immediately before his or her death, was, or would have been if the child had not been absent from Great Britain, entitled to child benefit, or

(iii) if the widow or widower and the member were residing together immediately before the member's death, a child in respect of whom the widow or widower then was, or would have been if the child had not been absent from Great Britain, entitled to child benefit;

or

(b) the widow or widower had attained the age of 45 either—

(i) when the member died, or

(ii) during a period when the circumstances mentioned in sub-paragraph (a) existed.

(2) For the purposes of paragraph 9(7)(b)(i) of Schedule 1 to the Act the prescribed period is—

(a) in a case to which the circumstances described in sub-paragraph (a), but not sub-paragraph (b) of paragraph (1) exist, the period (subject to paragraph (3)) during which the circumstances described in sub-paragraph (a) of paragraph (1) continue to exist; and

(b) in a case to which the circumstances described in sub-paragraph (b) of paragraph (1) exist, the remainder of the widow's or widower's life (subject to paragraph (3)).

(3) There is excluded from the periods prescribed under paragraph (2) any period after the widow's or widower's remarriage under pensionable age.

Giving effect to protected rights in money purchase contracted-out scheme by providing lump sum

6.—(1) For the purposes of paragraph 9(3)(b) of Schedule 1 to the Act as modified by section 32(2B) of the Social Security Pensions Act 1975 (effect may be given to protected rights in a money purchase contracted-out scheme by the provision of a lump sum where the annual rate of the pension or annuity would not exceed the prescribed amount) the prescribed amount is £104.

(2) For the purposes of paragraph 9(3)(c) of Schedule 1 to the Act as modified by section 32(2B) of the Social Security Pensions Act 1975 (effect may be given to protected rights in a money purchase contracted-out scheme by the provision of a lump sum in prescribed circumstances) the prescribed circumstances are that–

   (a) effect is given to all the member's protected rights by the provision of a lump sum; and

   (b) either–

      (i) the member has no rights under the scheme other than his protected rights; or

      (ii) effect is given to all those of his rights under the scheme which are not protected rights by the provision of a lump sum.

Suspension and forfeiture of payments giving effect to protected rights

7.—(1) For the purposes of paragraph 11 of Schedule 1 to the Act, the circumstances in which the rules of a scheme may provide for payments giving effect to a member's protected rights to be suspended are–

   (a) that the person who is entitled to payments giving effect to those rights is, in the opinion of the trustees or managers of the scheme, unable to act by reason of mental disorder or otherwise, so however that there is provision in the scheme for equivalent sums to be paid or applied, while that person is so unable, for the maintenance of that person or, at the discretion of the trustees or managers, of that person together with his dependants or of his dependants only, and, to the extent that they are not so applied, to be held for that person until he is again able to act or, as the case may be, for his estate;

   (b) that that person is undergoing a period of imprisonment or detention in legal custody, so however that there is provision in the scheme for equivalent sums to be paid or applied during such a period for the maintenance of such one or more of that person's dependants as the trustees or managers of the scheme may in their discretion determine.

(2) For the purposes of paragraph 11 of Schedule 1 to the Act, the circumstances in which the rules of a scheme may provide for a payment giving effect to a member's protected rights to be forfeited are–

   (a) that the trustees or managers of the scheme do not know the address of the person to whom the payment should be made; and

   (b) that a period of at least 6 years has elapsed from the date on which that payment became due.

Choice of insurance company by annuitant

8. For the purposes of paragraph 9(9) of Schedule 1 to the Act (scheme member to be taken to have chosen an insurance company to provide his annuity only if he gives notice in the prescribed manner and within the prescribed period) the prescribed manner is in writing, and the prescribed period is–

   (a) in a case where the trustees or managers of the scheme know of no reason to suppose that the pension or annuity will not commence on the date on which the member will attain pensionable age, a period of 5 months (or such longer period as the rules of the scheme may allow) beginning on the date which is 6 months earlier than that on which he will attain pensionable age; and

   (b) in any other case–

      (i) if the date ("the date of agreement") on which the member agrees, under paragraph 9(7)(a)(ii) of Schedule 1 to the Act, a later date ("the agreed date") for commencement of payment than that on which he will attain pensionable age is more than one month before the agreed date, a period beginning on the date of agreement and ending one month before the agreed date, and

      (ii) if the date of agreement is not more than one month before the agreed date, a period consisting only of the date of agreement,

or such longer period as the rules of the scheme may allow.

Insurance companies that may provide protected rights by way of annuities

9. For the purposes of paragraph 9(8) of Schedule 1 to the Act (annuity complies with paragraph 9 if it is provided by an insurance company which satisfies prescribed conditions) the prescribed conditions are that the insurance company–

(a) is one to which Part II of the Insurance Companies Act 1982(a) applies and which is authorised under section 3 or 4 of that Act to carry on ordinary long-term insurance business as defined in that Act; and

(b) offers annuities, with a view to purchase of those annuities by schemes in order to give effect to the protected rights of their members, without having regard to the sex or marital status of those members either in making the offers or in determining the rates at which the annuities are paid.

Death of scheme member before effect given to his protected rights

10.—(1) In this regulation "qualifying widow or widower" means a widow or widower of the member who immediately after the member's death either–

(a) is aged 45 or over; or

(b) is entitled to child benefit in respect of a child under 18 who is, or residing with a child under 16 who is–

    (i) a son or daughter of the widow or widower and the member, or

    (ii) a child in respect of whom the member, immediately before his death, was, or would have been if the child had not been absent from Great Britain, entitled to child benefit, or

    (iii) if the widow or widower and the member were residing together immediately before the member's death, a child in respect of whom the widow or widower then was, or would have been if the child had not been absent from Great Britain, entitled to child benefit.

(2) For the purposes of paragraph 9(4) of Schedule 1 to the Act (if member has died without effect being given to protected rights effect may be given in prescribed manner), in a case where–

(a) the member is not survived by a qualifying widow or widower; or

(b) the trustees or managers of the scheme, having taken reasonable steps to ascertain whether the member was survived by a qualifying widow or widower, conclude in good faith that he or she was not; or

(c) the member is survived by a qualifying widow or widower who dies before the value of the member's protected rights are paid to or for the benefit of her or him by virtue of paragraphs (3) to (8),

the prescribed manner is by the payment, as soon as practicable, of the value of the member's protected rights to or for the benefit of any person or persons in accordance with directions given by the member in writing, or to the member's estate.

(3) For the purposes of paragraph 9(4) of Schedule 1 to the Act, in a case where the member is survived by a qualifying widow or widower, and the circumstances mentioned in paragraph (2)(b) do not exist, the prescribed manner is–

(a) by the provision, as soon as practicable, of a pension such as is described in paragraph (4); or

(b) by the purchase by the scheme, as soon as practicable, of an annuity such as is described in paragraph (4), which is provided by an insurance company such as is described in paragraph (12); or

(c) in the case only of an occupational pension scheme, by the provision, as soon as practicable, of a lump sum such as is described in paragraph (14).

(4) The pension or annuity referred to in paragraph (3) is one such that it gives effect to all the protected rights of the member, and that the terms on which the pension is provided, or the terms of the purchase of the annuity–

(a) satisfy the requirements of paragraphs (5) to (7); and

(b) make no provision about the payment of the pension or annuity, or about the rate at which, or the categories of persons to whom, it is to be paid, other than such as–

(a) 1982 c.50.

(i) is necessary to establish what the initial rate and method of payment of the pension of annuity are to be, and that it shall continue to be paid to the widow or widower at that rate (subject only to paragraphs (6) and (8)) throughout the period described in paragraph (5),

(ii) is necessary to satisfy the requirements of paragraphs (5) to (7), and

(iii) is permitted by paragraphs (8) to (11).

(5) The pension or annuity shall be paid to the qualifying widow or widower during the period which begins on a date which is as soon as practicable after the member's death and ends when the widow or widower either–

(a) dies; or

(b) remarries while under pensionable age; or

(c) ceases while under the age of 45 to be as described in paragraph (1)(b).

(6) The rate of the pension or annuity shall be increased as described in regulation 4(3).

(7) The pension or annuity shall be paid as described in regulation 4(4) and (5).

(8) The pension or annuity may be increased, not more frequently than on the first date mentioned in regulation 4(3) and on each of its anniversaries, but by larger percentages than paragraph (6) requires, so however that no increase is by more than 3 per cent.

(9) When the qualifying widow or widower has–

(a) died; or

(b) remarried while under pensionable age; or

(c) ceased while under the age of 45 to be as described in paragraph (1)(b),

the pension or annuity may be paid, at a rate which satisfies the requirements of paragraph (10), to or for the benefit of the persons specified in paragraph (11) if the requirements of that paragraph are satisfied.

(10) The requirements first referred to in paragraph (9) are that the rate shall not exceed the rate at which the pension or annuity would have been payable if it had still been payable under paragraph (5).

(11) The requirements secondly referred to in paragraph (9) are that the pension or annuity shall be paid only–

(a) to the person who was the qualifying widow or widower;

(b) for the benefit of any child or children, if a person has died while the pension or annuity was being paid to him in accordance with paragraph (5) or sub-paragraph (a) and immediately before his death he was entitled to child benefit in respect of that child or those children, or would have been so entitled if that child or one, some or all of those children had not been absent from Great Britain, but only for so long as that child or at least one of those children is under the age of 18; and

(c) to any one person during any period–

(i) which is within 5 years of the date on which the pension or annuity commenced, and

(ii) which immediately follows the death of a person who died while the pension or annuity was being paid to him in accordance with paragraph (5) or sub-paragraph (a) or this sub-paragraph, or which begins on the date on which the child or the last of the children in respect of whom the pension or annuity has been paid in accordance with sub-paragraph (b) attained the age of 18 or died under that age.

(12) The insurance company referred to in paragraph (3) is one which satisfies the conditions described in regulation 9(a), and which has, subject to paragraph (13), been chosen by the widow or widower.

(13) A widow or widower is only to be taken to have chosen an insurance company if she or he gives notice in writing of her or his choice to the trustees or managers of the scheme during a period which begins on the date of the member's death and ends on the date which is 3 months after the date on which the trustees or managers notify

her or him of her or his right to choose; and if she or he does not do so, the trustees or managers may themselves choose the insurance company instead.

(14) The lump sum referred to in paragraph (3) is one which is paid to the qualifying widow or widower in the following circumstances, namely where–

    (a) the annual rate of the pension or annuity which would have been provided or purchased for her or him if the lump sum had not been provided does not exceed £104;

    (b) effect is given to all the member's protected rights by the provision of a lump sum; and

    (c) either–

        (i) the member, when he died, had no rights under the scheme other than his protected rights, or

        (ii) effect is given to all those of his rights under the scheme which are not protected rights by the provision of a lump sum.

Enforceable entitlement after death of member

11. Without prejudice to any other requirements, a personal pension scheme can be an appropriate scheme and an occupational pension scheme can be a money purchase contracted-out scheme only if the provision it makes for giving effect to the protected rights of a member who has died is such that any widow, widower or other person who is entitled to any payment giving effect to those rights is able to enforce that entitlement.

Schemes not to discriminate on grounds of sex or marital status

12. Without prejudice to other requirements, a scheme which offers pensions with a view to giving effect, under paragraph 9(1)(a) of Schedule 1 to the Act, to protected rights by means of those pensions, can be (in the case of a personal pension scheme) an appropriate scheme or (in the case of an occupational pension scheme) a money purchase contracted-out scheme only if it offers those pensions without having regard to the sex or marital status of the persons to whom it offers them, both in making those offers and in determining the rates at which those pensions are paid.

Personal pension schemes—notifications to the Secretary of State

13.—(1) Within 5 weeks after effect has been given to the protected rights of a member of a personal pension scheme, the trustees or managers of that scheme shall notify the Secretary of State in writing that effect has been given to those rights, giving such particulars as the Secretary of State may reasonably require to enable him–

    (a) to identify the means by which effect has been given to them;

    (b) where effect has been given to them by means of a pension, annuity or lump sum, to identify the recipient of it;

    (c) where effect has been given to them by means of an annuity, to identify the insurance company responsible for paying the annuity; and

    (d) where effect has been given to them by means of a transfer payment, to identify the personal or occupational pension scheme to which the transfer payment was made.

(2) The trustees or managers of a personal pension scheme which is or has been an appropriate scheme shall, if required to do so by the Secretary of State, in such manner and at such times as he may reasonably require, furnish to him such information relating to members of the scheme as he may reasonably require in order to know for what, if any, protected rights the scheme is responsible, and from what minimum contributions, minimum payments or transfer payments they derive.

Occupational pension schemes—notifications to the Secretary of State

14. Regulation 43 of the Occupational Pension Schemes (Contracting-out) Regulations 1984(a) shall be amended by the insertion, after paragraph (4), of the following paragraph–

(a) S.I. 1984/380, to which there are amendments not relevant to these Regulations.

"(4A) Within 5 weeks after effect has been given to the protected rights of a member of the scheme, the trustees of that scheme shall notify the Secretary of State in writing that effect has been given to those rights, giving such particulars as the Secretary of State may reasonably require to enable him–

(a) to identify the means by which effect has been given to them;

(b) where effect has been given to them by means of a pension, annuity or lump sum, to identify the recipient of it;

(c) where effect has been given to them by means of an annuity, to identify the insurance company responsible for paying the annuity; and

(d) where effect has been given to them by means of a transfer payment, to identify the personal or occupational pension scheme to which the transfer payment was made."

Signed by authority of the Secretary of State for Social Services.

Nicholas Scott
Minister of State,
Department of Health and Social Security

25th June 1987

EXPLANATORY NOTE

(This note is not part of the Regulations)

These Regulations are made under provisions contained in Part I of the Social Security Act 1986, before the end of a period of 12 months from the commencement of those provisions. Consequently, by virtue of section 61(5) of that Act, the provisions of section 61(2) and (3) of the Social Security Pensions Act 1975 (as amended by section 86(1) of, and paragraph 94 of Schedule 10 to, the Social Security Act 1986), which require reference to the Occupational Pensions Board of, and a report by the Board on, proposals to make regulations for the purposes of Part I of the Social Security Act 1986, do not apply to them.

Schedule 1 to the Social Security Act 1986 is concerned with protected rights under an appropriate personal pension scheme, or, where that Schedule is modified by section 32(2B) of the Social Security Pensions Act 1975 (inserted by Schedule 2 to the Social Security Act 1986), protected rights under a money purchase contracted-out occupational pension scheme.

The Regulations prescribe the manner of calculation and verification of protected rights mentioned in paragraph 7(2) of Schedule 1 to the Social Security Act 1986 (regulation 2); the rights which a scheme may designate as protected rights, in addition to those so designated by the Act (regulation 3); the conditions which are to apply to pensions and annuities which give effect to protected rights (regulation 4); the circumstances in which and periods for which a pension or annuity is to be paid to a widow or widower after a scheme member's death (regulation 5); the circumstances in which a lump sum benefit may be provided by a money purchase contracted-out scheme (regulation 6); the circumstances in which protected rights may be surrendered or forfeited (regulation 7); the manner in which and the period within which an insurance company may be chosen by an annuitant (regulation 8); the conditions that an insurance company must satisfy if it is to provide an annuity which is to give effect to protected rights (regulation 9); and the provision that is to be made if a scheme member dies before effect is given to his protected rights (regulation 10). Regulation 11 requires that a scheme's provision for giving effect to the protected rights of a member who has died must be such that the person entitled to any payment giving effect to those rights must be able to enforce that entitlement; and regulation 12 that it should not, in offering pensions which are to give effect to protected rights, discriminate on grounds of sex or marital status.

Regulation 13 provides that, when effect has been given to protected rights under a personal pension scheme, certain information must be given to the Secretary of State, and regulation 14 makes corresponding provision for occupational pension schemes.

The publication "Retirement Benefit Schemes—Transfer Values (GN11)", referred to in regulation 2(2)(b)(ii), may be obtained from the Institute of Actuaries, Staple Inn Hall, High Holborn, London W.C. 1V 7QJ, and from the Faculty of Actuaries, 23 St. Andrew Square, Edinburgh EH2 1AQ.

STATUTORY INSTRUMENTS

1987 No. 1118

PENSIONS

The Protected Rights (Transfer Payment) Regulations 1987

Made - - - -	*25th June 1987*
Laid before Parliament	*6th July 1987*
Coming into force	
For the purposes of all of the regulations to the extent that they relate to personal pension schemes	*27th July 1987*
For all other purposes	*6th April 1988*

The Secretary of State for Social Services, in exercise of the powers conferred upon him by sections 2, 17(1)(b) and 84(1) of, and paragraph 9(1)(b) of Schedule 1 to, the Social Security Act 1986(a), and of all other powers enabling him in that behalf, by this instrument, which is made before the end of a period of 12 months from the commencement of the enactments under which it is made, makes the following Regulations:

Citation, commencement and interpretation

1.—(1) These Regulations may be cited as the Protected Rights (Transfer Payment) Regulations 1987 and shall come into force –

(a) for all purposes in relation to personal pension schemes on 27th July 1987; and

(b) for all other purposes on 6th April 1988.

(2) In these Regulations, unless the context otherwise requires –

"the Act" means the Social Security Act 1986;

"the Pensions Act" means the Social Security Pensions Act 1975(b);

"the Abatement of Benefit Regulations" means the Personal and Occupational Pension Schemes (Abatement of Benefit) Regulations 1987(c);

"appropriate personal pension scheme" shall be construed in accordance with Part I of the Act;

"the Board" means the Occupational Pensions Board;

(a) 1986 c.50. *See* definitions of "prescribed" and "regulations" in section 84(1).   **(b)** 1975 c.60.
(c) S.I. 1987/1113.

"money purchase contracted-out scheme" and "occupational pension scheme" have the meaning given to those expressions by section 66(1) of the Pensions Act;

"overseas scheme" means an occupational pension scheme which is neither one contracted-out by virtue of section 32 of the Pensions Act nor one which the Board is under a duty to supervise in accordance with section 49 of that Act, and which is administered wholly or primarily outside the United Kingdom;

"paying scheme" means a scheme which is, or was formerly –

(a) an appropriate personal pension scheme; or

(b) a money purchase contracted-out scheme,

and which gives effect to the protected rights of a member of it by making a transfer payment in respect of those rights;

"personal pension scheme" has the same meaning as in section 84(1) of the Act;

"protected rights" has the meaning given to that expression by Schedule 1 to the Act, or where the rights are under a money purchase contracted-out scheme, or a section 49 money purchase scheme, that Schedule as modified by section 32(2B) of the Pensions Act(**a**);

"salary related contracted-out scheme" means an occupational pension scheme which is contracted-out by virtue of section 32(2) of the Pensions Act;

"scheme" means occupational pension scheme or personal pension scheme;

"section 49 money purchase scheme" means a scheme, which was formerly a money purchase contracted-out scheme, and which the Board are under a duty to supervise in accordance with section 49 of the Pensions Act(**b**);

"section 49 salary related scheme" means a scheme, which was formerly a salary related contracted-out scheme, and which the Board are under a duty to supervise in accordance with section 49 of the Pensions Act;

"receiving scheme" means a scheme to which a transfer payment is, or is to be, made;

and other expressions have the same meaning as in the Act.

(3) In these Regulations, unless the context otherwise requires, any reference –

(a) to a numbered regulation or Schedule is to the regulation in, or as the case may be, Schedule to, these Regulations bearing that number;

(b) in a regulation to a numbered paragraph is to the paragraph of that regulation bearing that number; and

(c) in a paragraph to a lettered sub-paragraph is to the sub-paragraph of that paragraph bearing that letter.

(**a**) Section 32(2B) is inserted in the Social Security Pensions Act 1975 (c.60) by the Social Security Act 1986 (c.50), section 6 and Schedule 2, paragraph 5(b).   (**b**) Section 49 is amended by the Social Security Act 1986 (c.60), section 6 and Schedule 2, paragraph 9, and *see* section 86 and Schedule 10, paragraph 24.

Transfer payments giving effect to protected rights

2.—(1) Subject to regulation 3 (requirements to be satisfied by certain specified receiving schemes), a paying scheme may give effect to the protected rights of a member by the making of a transfer payment –

(a) to an appropriate personal pension scheme; or

(b) to an occupational pension scheme,

in the circumstances and subject to the conditions mentioned in paragraphs (2) to (7), and in these Regulations a "transfer payment" means a transfer payment such as is described in this paragraph.

(2) A transfer payment may be made to an appropriate personal pension scheme in the circumstances described in paragraph 1 of Schedule 1, and on the condition specified in paragraph 1 of Schedule 2.

(3) A transfer payment may be made to a money purchase contracted-out scheme in the circumstances described in paragraphs 1 and 2 of Schedule 1, and on the condition specified in paragraph 1 of Schedule 2.

(4) A transfer payment may be made to a section 49 money purchase scheme in the circumstances described in paragraphs 1 and 3 of Schedule 1, and on the conditions specified in paragraphs 1 and 2 of Schedule 2.

(5) A transfer payment may be made to a salary related contracted-out scheme in the circumstances described in paragraphs 1, 2 and 5 of Schedule 1, and on the condition specified in paragraph 1 of Schedule 2.

(6) A transfer payment may be made to a section 49 salary related scheme in the circumstances described in paragraphs 1, 3 and 5 of Schedule 1, and on the conditions specified in paragraphs 1 and 2 of Schedule 2.

(7) A transfer payment may be made to an overseas scheme in the circumstances described in paragraphs 1 and 4 of Schedule 1, and on the conditions specified in paragraphs 1 and 2 of Schedule 2.

(8) References in Schedules 1 to 3 to "the member" are references to a member referred to in paragraph (1).

Requirements to be satisfied by receiving scheme

3.   A transfer payment may be made by a paying scheme to –

(a) an appropriate personal pension scheme, a money purchase contracted-out scheme or a section 49 money purchase scheme, where that scheme satisfies the requirement specified in paragraph 1 of Schedule 3; or

(b) a salary related contracted-out scheme or a section 49 salary related scheme, where that scheme satisfies the requirement specified in paragraph 2 of Schedule 3.

Modifications of Part III of the Pensions Act where transfer payments are made to salary related contracted-out schemes or section 49 salary related schemes

4.—(1) Where a transfer payment has been paid by a paying scheme to a salary related contracted-out scheme or to a section 49 salary related scheme in accordance with regulations 2 and 3, Part III of the Pensions Act shall have effect as modified by paragraphs (2) to (9).

(2) Section 26(2) shall have effect as if –

(a) after "sections 33 and 36 below" there were inserted "or in compliance with the requirement set out in paragraph 2 of Schedule 3 to the Protected Rights (Transfer Payment) Regulations 1987"; and

(b) at the end there were added "or, as the case may be, of that requirement.".

(3) Section 29(2) shall have effect as if there were inserted after the words added by paragraph 14(b)(ii) of Schedule 10 to the Act, "unless he is entitled to that guaranteed minimum pension by reason of paragraph 2 of Schedule 3 to the Protected Rights (Transfer Payment) Regulations 1987.".

(4) Section 35(1) shall have effect as if –

   (a) after "guaranteed minimum" there were inserted "both"; and

   (b) at the end there were added "and in relation to any pension provided by a scheme in compliance with the requirement set out in paragraph 2 of Schedule 3 to the Protected Rights (Transfer Payment) Regulations 1987, (guaranteed minimum pension to be paid by a scheme by reason of receiving a transfer payment).".

(5) In a case to which regulation 2(1) of the Abatement of Benefit Regulations applies, section 35(5) shall have effect as if any earnings factor to which regulation 2(2)(b) of those Regulations applies were, before being increased as mentioned in section 35(5), equal to the amount mentioned in regulation 2(2)(b) of them.

(6) Section 35(7) shall have effect –

   (a) if the scheme from which the transfer payment was made was a personal pension scheme –

      (i) in respect only of each relevant year after the year in which minimum contributions, within the meaning given to that expression by section 1 of the Act, were last payable, and

      (ii) in a case to which regulation 2(1) of the Abatement of Benefit Regulations applies, as if any earnings factor to which regulation 2(2)(b) of those Regulations applies were, before being increased as mentioned in section 35(7), equal to the amount mentioned in regulation 2(2)(b) of them; or

   (b) if the scheme from which the transfer payment was made was a money purchase contracted-out scheme or a section 49 money purchase scheme, in respect only of each relevant year after the year in which contracted-out employment by reference to that scheme terminated.

(7) Section 35(8) shall have effect as if there were added at the end ", so however that separate provision may be made for members as regards any guaranteed minimum pensions which have accrued to them by reason of paragraph 2 of Schedule 3 to the Protected Rights (Transfer Payment) Regulations 1987.".

(8) In a case to which regulation 2(1) of the Abatement of Benefit Regulations applies –

   (a) section 44(6)(a) shall have effect as if any earnings factor to which regulation 2(2)(b) of those Regulations applies were, before being increased as mentioned in section 44(6)(a), equal to the amount mentioned in regulation 2(2)(b) of them; and

   (b) section 45(3)(a) shall have effect as if any earnings factor to which regulation 2(2)(b) of those Regulations applies were, before being increased as mentioned in section 45(3)(a), equal to the amount mentioned in regulation 2(2)(b) of them.

(9) Section 45(1) shall have effect as if after "accrued rights" there were inserted ",including any such pensions which have accrued to him by reason of paragraph 2 of Schedule 3 to the Protected Rights (Transfer Payment) Regulations 1987".

Signed by authority of the Secretary of State for Social Services
Nicholas Scott
Minister of State,
Department of Health and Social Security

25th June 1987

Regulation 2

SCHEDULE 1

CIRCUMSTANCES IN WHICH A TRANSFER PAYMENT MAY BE MADE UNDER REGULATION 2

1. The member consents to the transfer payment being made.

2. The member has entered employment with an employer who is a contributor to the receiving scheme.

3. The member has entered employment with an employer who is or was a contributor to the receiving scheme.

4. The member has entered employment to which the receiving scheme applies and that employment is outside the United Kingdom.

5. The transfer payment is made on or after 6th April 1990.

Regulation 2

SCHEDULE 2

CONDITIONS ON WHICH A TRANSFER PAYMENT MAY BE MADE UNDER REGULATION 2

1. The transfer payment made by the paying scheme (whether or not it forms part of a larger payment giving effect to both protected and other rights) is of an amount at least equal to the value of the protected rights of the member to which effect is being given.

2. The transfer payment is approved by the Board, whether or not subject to conditions.

Regulation 3

SCHEDULE 3

REQUIREMENTS TO BE SATISFIED BY THE RECEIVING SCHEME UNDER REGULATION 3 FOR A TRANSFER PAYMENT TO BE MADE

1. The transfer payment is applied by the receiving scheme to provide money purchase benefits for or in respect of the member.

2. In consequence of the transfer payment, and without prejudice to any other rights which the member receives under it, the receiving scheme provides for the member and the member's widow or widower to be entitled to guaranteed minimum pensions equal to those to which they would have been treated as entitled by virtue of section 4 of the Act, or section 29(2) or (2A) of the Pensions Act, as the case may be, if the transfer payment had not been made, except that the receiving scheme may make provision that any earnings factor of the member is to be revalued in accordance with section 35(7) of the Pensions Act, as modified by regulation 4(6).

EXPLANATORY NOTE

(This note is not part of the Regulations)

These Regulations are all made under provisions of the Social Security Act 1986 ("the 1986 Act") before the end of the period of 12 months from the commencement of those provisions. Consequently, by virtue of section 61(5) of the 1986 Act, the provisions of section 61(2) and (3) of the Social Security Pensions Act 1975 (as amended by section 86(1) of, and paragraph 94 of Schedule 10 to, the 1986 Act), which require reference to the Occupational Pensions Board of, and a report by the Board on, proposals to make regulations for certain purposes of both Acts, do not apply to them.

They make provision for the protected rights of a member of a scheme which is or was an appropriate personal pension scheme or a money purchase contracted-out scheme to be given effect to by the making of a transfer payment.

Regulation 2, and Schedules 1 and 2, provide for the circumstances in which, and the conditions subject to which, such a transfer payment may be made.

Regulation 3 and Schedule 3 set out the requirements, if any, to be satisfied by an occupational pension scheme or personal pension scheme for a transfer payment to be made to it.

Regulation 4 provides for Part III of the Social Security Pensions Act 1975 to have effect, subject to modifications, where a transfer payment is made to a scheme which is or was contracted-out under section 32(2) of that Act (a salary related scheme) in order to accommodate the guaranteed minimum pensions to which a member of such a receiving scheme becomes entitled in consequence of that payment.

STATUTORY INSTRUMENTS

1987 No. 1119 (L.4)

COUNTY COURTS

PROCEDURE

The County Court (Forms) (Amendment) Rules 1987

Made - - - -		*26th June 1987*
Coming into force	-	*1st September 1987*

1.—(1) These Rules may be cited as the County Court (Forms) (Amendment) Rules 1987.

(2) In these Rules a form referred to by number means the form so numbered in the Schedule to the County Court (Forms) Rules 1982**(a)** and "the main Schedule" means that Schedule.

2. There shall be substituted in the main Schedule, for forms N.42 and N.49, the forms contained in the Schedule to these Rules.

3. Forms N.43, N.44, N.45 and N.54 shall be omitted.

4. For the heading to Form N.53 there shall be substituted the following heading, "Warrant of Committal to Registrar of a Foreign Court, section 122 County Courts Act 1984".

We, the undersigned members of the Rule Committee appointed by the Lord Chancellor under section 75 of the County Courts Act 1984**(b)**, having by virtue of the powers vested in us in this behalf made the foregoing Rules, do hereby certify the same under our hands and submit them to the Lord Chancellor accordingly.

Norman Francis,	*C.S. Stuart-White,*
Deirdre McKinney,	*R. Lockett,*
R.E. Hammerton,	*A.W. Donaldson,*
P.G. Hebbert,	*Patrick Eccles,*
Timothy Stow,	*Gillian Stuart-Brown.*
Anthony Girling,	

(a) S.I. 1982/586, as amended by S.I. 1982/1141, 1983/1715, 1984/879, 1985/567, 1986/1505.
(b) 1984 c.28.

I allow these Rules, which shall come into force on 1st September 1987.

Dated 26th June 1987   *Havers, C.*

Rule 2

SCHEDULE
WARRANT OF EXECUTION
(Order 26, rule 1(2))

In the ———— County Court

Case no ————
Warrant no ————

To the Registrar and Bailiff

On the
the creditor obtained a judgment
enforceable in this court. Payment has not
been made as ordered and at the creditor's
request this warrant has been issued.
You are now required to levy for the total
shown below in accordance with the
provisions of Sections 85 and 89 of the
County Courts Act 1984.
The creditor applied for the warrant at
                                    o'clock

on

(SEAL)

**To be completed when warrant sent to
another court.**

This warrant has been issued out of this
court for execution at an address within
the jurisdiction of your court.
You are therefore required to execute the
warrant.
Dated

PERFORATION

Debtor(s)

Address(es) to levy at

Creditor

Creditor (solicitor)'s address

Reference

Amount of judgment				
Costs since judgment				
Sub total				
Paid				
Balance				
Amount of warrant				
Fee				
Solicitor's costs				
Land Registry fee				
Total				

Date taken	Amount	Blf	Paid in	Clk

Received on

In the ———— County Court

Case no ————
Warrant no ————

To the Debtor

On the
the creditor obtained a judgment against
you, which is enforceable in this court.
You have not made payment as you were
ordered to do and at the creditor's request
this warrant has been issued.
**The warrant gives the bailiff the power to
seize and sell your goods or to seize your
money unless you pay the total due.**

You should make all payments under the
warrant to the court named below which is
your local county court.
You can make payments either to the
bailiff or at the court office.
You should send any correspondence
concerning this warrant including claims
to the goods to the Chief Clerk at the
address below.

(SEAL)

The Chief Clerk

The court office is open from 10 am to 4
pm Mondays to Fridays

For more information see over

Debtor(s)

Address(es) to levy at

Creditor

Creditor (solicitor)'s address

Reference

Amount of judgment		
Costs since judgment		
Sub total		
Paid		
Balance		
Amount of warrant		
Fee		
Solicitor's costs		
Land Registry fee		
Total		

*The bailiff should give a printed and
numbered receipt from his official receipt
book for every payment made to him under
this warrant. You should not accept any
other form of receipt.*

Returns other than payments

Date of levy

day of   19

Report and details of levy

Date	Date

Walking possession agreement
(Request not to remove goods)

To the Registrar and Bailiff of the court

Please do not remove the goods seized.

Until payment is made or the warrant is withdrawn:

- I will not remove or damage the goods or any part of them or allow any other person to do so without your permission;
- I will show this form to any other person who may call with the intention of levying on the goods and tell you of their visit at once,

and I authorise you to re-enter the premises at any time (and as often as you want) to complete the enforcement of the warrant, or to inspect the goods

Signed   Dated

PERFORATION

Levy Notice

The bailiff has levied on your goods. This means you must not dispose of the goods as the court may have to seize and sell them at public auction to raise money to pay your debt. Certain goods will not be seized by the bailiff; these are clothing and bedding up to a value of £100, and tools of trade up to a total value of £150.

If you pay the total due, which is shown overleaf, your goods will not be removed and you will not have to pay further costs.

Walking Possession agreement

You may request the bailiff not to remove the goods; this is called a walking possession agreement. If you wish to do so you should sign the walking possession agreement and the copy on the bailiff's warrant form.

If your goods are removed

- You will be given a list of the goods removed.
- The goods will not be sold before the 6th day after their removal unless you request an earlier sale or the goods are perishable.
- You will be given at least 4 days notice of the day, time and place of the sale.
- Further fees may be charged which will be listed.

Stopping the sale

If the sale is stopped because the warrant is withdrawn, paid or suspended you will normally have to pay a fee of 10p for every £1 of the assessed value of the goods and any expenses reasonably incurred in removing the goods or advertising the sale.

Auction fees

When your goods have been removed, they may be valued and sold. If they are, you may have to pay the following additional fees:

- **for valuing the goods:** 5p for every £1 of the assessed value.
- **for the sale:** this is normally 15p for every £1 for which the goods were sold.

When the goods are sold

You will be given a detailed account in writing of the sale and distribution of the money.

Walking possession agreement
(Request not to remove goods)

To the Registrar and Bailiff of the court

Please do not remove the goods seized.

Until payment is made or the warrant is withdrawn:

- I will not remove or damage the goods or any part of them or allow any other person to do so without your permission;
- I will show this form to any other person who may call with the intention of levying on the goods and tell you of their visit at once,

and I authorise you to re-enter the premises at any time (and as often as you want) to complete the enforcement of the warrant, or to inspect the goods

Signed   Dated

WARRANT FOR POSSESSION OF LAND
(Order 26, rule 17)

SEAL

To the Registrar and Bailiffs of the Court

ON the   day of   19   , it was adjudged that the plaintiff was entitled to possession of (1)

(1) Describe the land as set out in the judgment

and it was ordered that the defendant should give the plaintiff possession of the said land on or before the

[unless the rent in arrear, amounting to £   and the costs of this action, amounting to £   , were paid into court on or before the   .](2)

(2) Add where judgment was for forfeiture for non-payment of rent.

[AND it was adjudged that the plaintiff should recover against the defendant the sum of £   for rent and mesne profits and £   for costs, making together the sum of £   [and it was ordered that the defendant should pay the last-mentioned sum into the office of this court on or before the

(3) Add where so ordered

(or by instalments of £   for every   ).]](3)

[AND it was ordered that the judgment for possession be not enforced for   days and for so long thereafter as the defendant punctually paid to the plaintiff or his agent the [arrears of rent, mesne profits and] costs by instalments of £   per week in addition to the current rent, the first of such payments to be made on or before the   ]

[AND it was ordered that the judgment for £   [and costs to be taxed] be not enforced for so long as the defendant paid the instalments of £   per week.](4)

(4) Add where judgment suspended under section 36 of A.J. Act 1970.

AND THE DEFENDANT HAVING FAILED TO OBEY THE ORDER THE PLAINTIFF HAS REQUESTED THAT THIS WARRANT SHOULD ISSUE.

YOU ARE THEREFORE required forthwith to give possession of the land to the plaintiff.

[AND YOU ARE THEREFORE REQUIRED forthwith to levy the amount due to the plaintiff under the judgment or order, together with the costs of issue and execution of this warrant by distress and sale of the defendant's goods wherever they may be found within the district of this court (except the wearing apparel and bedding of him or his family to the value of £100 and the tools and implements of his trade to the value of £150), and also by seizing any money, bank notes, bills of exchange, promissory notes, bonds, specialties or securities for money, belonging to him which may be found there or so much thereof as may be sufficient to satisfy this execution, and to bring the proceeds of the levy into court, and immediately thereafter to make a return of what you have done.]

Application was made to this court for this warrant at   minutes past the hour of   o'clock on

NOTICE. The goods are not to be sold until after the end of five days next following the day on which they are seized, unless they are of a perishable nature, or at the request of the defendant.

Form N. 49

PERFORATION

In the   County Court

Case no

Warrant no

Defendant/Debtor(s)

Address(es) to levy at

Plaintiff/Creditor (solicitor)'s address

Plaintiff/Creditor

Reference

Amount of judgment	
Costs since judgment	
Sub total	
Paid	
Balance	
Amount of warrant	
Fee	
Solicitor's costs	
Land Registry fee	
Total	

The bailiff should give a printed and numbered receipt from his official receipt book for every payment made to him under this warrant. You should not accept any other form of receipt. For more information see over

In the _____ County Court

Case no _____

Warrant no ————— ————— —————

Defendant/Debtor(s)

Address(es) to levy at

Plaintiff/Creditor

Plaintiff/Creditor (solicitor)'s address

Reference

Amount of judgment	
Costs since judgment	
Sub total	
Paid	
Balance	

Amount of warrant	
Fee	
Solicitor's costs	
Land Registry fee	

Total

Date taken	Amount	Blf	Paid in	Clk

The name and address of the (Solicitor to the) Plaintiff is:—

Possession obtained and given to the Plaintiff on the

Bailiff

Returns other than payment.

19

I acknowledge having received possession of the land described in this warrant, on the

(For the) Plaintiff.

(For use only when sale or other charges incurred)

Gross amount levied or received .... £

Transport Charges ....

Appraisement Fee on £ ....

Sale Fee on £ ....

Advertising ....

Rent to Landlord ...

Costs of Interpleader ordered to be deducted from the proceeds ....

Net amount paid into Court on

£

PERFORATION

Levy Notice

The bailiff has levied on your goods. This means you must not dispose of the goods as the court may have to seize and sell them at public auction to raise money to pay your debt. Certain goods will not be seized by the bailiff; these are clothing and bedding up to a value of £100, and tools of trade up to a total value of £150. *If you pay the total due, which is shown overleaf, your goods will not be removed and you will not have to pay further costs.*

If your goods are removed
You will be given a list of the goods removed.

The goods will not be sold before the 6th day after their removal unless you request an earlier sale or the goods are perishable.

You will be given at least 4 days notice of the day, time and place of the sale.

Further fees may be charged which will be listed.

Stopping the sale
If the sale is stopped because the warrant is withdrawn, paid or suspended you will normally have to pay a fee of 10p for every £1 of the assessed value of the goods and any expenses reasonably incurred in removing the goods or advertising the sale.

Auction fees
When your goods have been removed, they may be valued and sold. If they are, you may have to pay the following additional fees:

for valuing the goods: 5p for every £1 of the assessed value.

for the sale: this is normally 15p for every £1 for which the goods were sold.

When the goods are sold
You will be given a detailed account in writing of the sale and distribution of the money.

All payments under the warrant should be made to the court named below which is your local county court. Payment can either be made to the bailiff or at the court office.

All notices concerning this warrant or claims to the goods should be given or sent to the Chief Clerk at the address below

(SEAL)

The above court office is open from 10 am to 4 pm Mondays to Fridays

II/1v*

(Page 2)

Form N. 49

EXPLANATORY NOTE

(This note is not part of the Rules)

These Rules amend the County Court (Forms) Rules 1982 so as to substitute a new form of warrant of execution (N.42) and as a consequence (a) to omit forms N.43 (warrant of execution against goods of defendant for part of the amount due), N.44 (warrant of execution against the goods of the plaintiff), N.45 (notice on levy) and N.54 (notice to be endorsed on notice on levy where warrant of execution sent to foreign court) and (b) to amend forms N.49 (warrant for possession of land) and N.53 (warrant of execution or committal to registrar of foreign court).

STATUTORY INSTRUMENTS

1987 No. 1120

MEDICAL PROFESSION

The General Medical Council (Constitution of Fitness to Practise Committees) (Amendment) Rules Order of Council 1987

Made - - - -	*29th June 1987*
Laid before Parliament	*6th July 1987*
Coming into force	*1st August 1987*

At the Council Chamber, Whitehall, the 29th day of June 1987

By the Lords of Her Majesty's Most Honourable Privy Council

Whereas, in pursuance of paragraphs 20, 21 and 22 of Schedule 1 to the Medical Act 1983(**a**) , the General Medical Council have made the General Medical Council (Constitution of Fitness to Practise Committees) (Amendment) Rules 1987;

And whereas, by paragraph 24 of the said Schedule, such Rules shall not come into force until approved by order of the Privy Council;

Now, therefore, Their Lordships, having taken the said Rules into consideration, are pleased to approve the same as set out in the Appendix to this Order.

This Order may be cited as the General Medical Council (Constitution of Fitness to Practise Committees) (Amendment) Rules Order of Council 1987, and shall come into force on 1st August 1987.

G. I. de Deney
Clerk of the Privy Council

(**a**) 1983 c.54.

APPENDIX

THE GENERAL MEDICAL COUNCIL (CONSTITUTION OF FITNESS TO PRACTISE COMMITTEES) (AMENDMENT) RULES 1987

The General Medical Council, in exercise of their powers under paragraphs 20, 21 and 22 of Schedule 1 to the Medical Act 1983, hereby make the following rules:

Citation, commencement and interpretation

1.—(1) These rules may be cited as the General Medical Council (Constitution of Fitness to Practise Committees) (Amendment) Rules 1987 and shall come into force on 1st August 1987.

(2) In these rules "the principal rules" mean the General Medical Council (Constitution of Fitness to Practise Committees) Rules 1986(**a**).

Amendment of the principal rules

2.—(1) The principal rules shall be amended in accordance with the following provisions–

(2) In Rule 4 (composition of the Professional Conduct Committee)–

   (a) in paragraph (1)

      (i) for the number "twenty-nine" there shall be substituted the number "thirty-two";

      (ii) in sub-paragraph (c) for the words "three lay members" there shall be substituted the words "six lay members".

   (b) for paragraphs (4) and (5) there shall be substituted the following–

      "(4) Eleven members of the Committee shall be invited to attend for the hearing of any case, who shall be selected so as to include the Chairman or the Deputy Chairman or both, and such other members so that the eleven members invited include not less than six elected members, not less than two appointed members and two lay members.

      Subject to the foregoing provision the members invited to sit at any meeting shall so far as practicable be chosen in rotation from all the members of the Committee.

      (5) If neither the Chairman nor the Deputy Chairman is able to take the Chair at the hearing of a case the President may temporarily appoint one of the other members of the Committee who has been invited and is available to attend and, if a hearing has begun, has attended, to chair the whole of, or the remaining part of, the hearing.

      (6) The quorum shall be six."

(3) In Rule 5 (composition of the Health Committee) there shall be substituted the following for paragraph (4)–

      "(4) If neither the Chairman nor the Deputy Chairman is able to take the Chair at the hearing of a case, the President may temporarily appoint one of the other members of the Committee who has been invited and is available to attend and, if a hearing has begun, has attended, to chair the whole of, or the remaining part of, the hearing.

      (5) The quorum shall be five."

Given under the official Seal of the General Medical Council this twenty-first day of May, nineteen hundred and eighty-seven.

John N. Walton
  President

(**a**) Approved by S.I. 1986/1390.

EXPLANATORY NOTE

(This note is not part of the Order)

The Rules approved by this Order amend earlier Rules governing the constitution of the General Medical Council's Fitness to Practise Committees. Three additional lay members are being added to the Professional Conduct Committee, and provision is being made, in respect of that Committee and the Health Committee, for the appointment of a temporary chairman of the hearing of a case in the absence of the Chairman or Deputy Chairman of the revelant committee.

1987 No. 1122

CUSTOMS AND EXCISE

The Customs Duties (Quota Relief) Order 1987

Made - - - -	*30th June 1987*
Laid before the House of Commons	*30th June 1987*
Coming into force	*1st July 1987*

The Secretary of State, in exercise of the powers conferred on him by section 4 of the Customs and Excise Duties (General Reliefs) Act 1979(**a**) and of all other powers enabling him in that behalf, hereby makes the following Order:

1. This Order may be cited as the Customs Duties (Quota Relief) Order 1987 and shall come into force on 1st July 1987.

2. In this Order the "relevant quota" means the quantity of goods which are exempt from customs duty on import into the United Kingdom under the provisions of the Council Regulation (EEC) of 25th June 1987 opening, allocating and providing for the administration of a Community tariff quota for rum, arrack and tafia, falling within sub-heading 22.09 CI of the Common Customs Tariff and originating in the African, Caribbean and Pacific States (ACP) (1987–1988)(**b**) ("the EEC Regulation").

3.—(1) For the purposes of the EEC Regulation, subject as provided in Article 4(2) and (3) of the Customs Duties Quota Relief (Administration) Order 1986(**c**) ("the 1986 Order") and subject to paragraph (2) of this Article, goods shall be treated as forming part of the relevant quota in the order in which an entry thereof is accepted on or after 1st July 1987 being an entry for home use under section 37 of the Customs and Excise Management Act 1979(**d**) or under regulation 13 of the Customs Warehousing Regulations 1979(**e**) containing an application for relief from customs duty under the quota, accompanied by such documents as may be required under provisions of Protocol No. 5 to the Third ACP–EEC Convention of Lome(**f**) (relating to the origin of products).

(2) Goods shall not be treated as forming part of the relevant quota if they have been entered for warehousing under the said section 37 in an excise warehouse unless in respect of the goods–

(a) an entry for home use under regulation 13 of the Excise Warehousing (Etc.) Regulations 1982(**g**) ("the 1982 Regulations") is or has been accepted; or

(b) notice of compounding of spirits has been given under regulation 12 of the 1982 Regulations; or

(c) notice of intention to remove for denaturing has been given under regulation 13 of the 1982 Regulations.

(**a**) 1979 c.3.
(**b**) Council Regulation (EEC) No. 1823, O.J. No. L173, 30.6.87.
(**c**) S.I. 1986/2174.
(**d**) 1979 c.2, amended by the Finance Act 1981 (c.35), Schedule 6, para. 1.
(**e**) S.I. 1979/207.
(**f**) O.J. No. L86, 31.3.86.
(**g**) S.I. 1982/612.

(3) The provisions of Article 4(1) of the 1986 Order (which provides for the order in which goods shall be treated as forming part of a quota) shall not apply to the administration of any relief from duty under the EEC Regulation.

30th June 1987

Alan Clark
Minister for Trade, Department of Trade and Industry

EXPLANATORY NOTE

(This note is not part of the Order)

This Order, which comes into force on 1st July 1987, provides for the administration of the United Kingdom's share of the tariff quota opened for the period from 1st July 1987 to 30th June 1988 by the European Economic Community (EEC), under the provisions of the EEC Regulation specified in the Order, providing exemption from customs duty on import into the United Kingdom for home use of rum, arrack and tafia originating in various African, Caribbean and Pacific States (ACP).

1987 No. 1123

MEDICINES

The Medicines (Exemptions from Restrictions on the Retail Sale or Supply of Veterinary Drugs) (Amendment) Order 1987

Made -	-	-	-	*26th June 1987*
Laid before Parliament				*8th July 1987*
Coming into force				*29th July 1987*

The Secretary of State concerned with health in England, the Secretaries of State respectively concerned with health and with agriculture in Scotland and in Wales, the Minister of Agriculture, Fisheries and Food, the Department of Health and Social Services for Northern Ireland and the Department of Agriculture for Northern Ireland, acting jointly, in exercise of the powers conferred by sections 57(1), (2) and (2A) and 129(4) of the Medicines Act 1968**(a)** and now vested in them**(b)**, and of all other powers enabling them in that behalf, after consulting such organisations as appear to them to be representative of interests likely to be substantially affected by the following Order in accordance with section 129(6) of that Act, hereby make the following Order:–

Title, commencement and interpretation

1.—(1) This Order may be cited as the Medicines (Exemptions from Restrictions on the Retail Sale or Supply of Veterinary Drugs) (Amendment) Order 1987 and shall come into force on 29th July 1987.

(2) In this Order "the principal Order" means the Medicines (Exemptions from Restrictions on the Retail Sale or Supply of Veterinary Drugs) Order 1985**(c)**.

Amendment of the principal Order

2. The principal Order shall be amended–

(a) by substituting for Part B of Schedule 1 (veterinary drugs sold by merchants) the provisions set out in Schedule 1 to this Order;

(b) by substituting for Part B of Schedule 2 (veterinary drugs for incorporation in animal feeding stuffs) the provisions set out in Schedule 2 to this Order;

(c) by substituting for Schedule 4 (horse wormers) the provisions set out in Schedule 3 to this Order.

(a) 1968 c.67; section 57(2A) was inserted by the Animal Health and Welfare Act 1984 (c.40), section 14.
(b) In the case of the Secretaries of State concerned with health in England and in Wales by virtue of S.I. 1969/388, in the case of the Secretary of State concerned with agriculture in Wales by virtue of S.I. 1978/272 and in the case of the Northern Ireland Departments by virtue of the Northern Ireland Constitution Act 1973 (c.36), section 40 and Schedule 5, and the Northern Ireland Act 1974 (c.28), section 1(3) and Schedule 1, paragraph 2(1)(b).
(c) S.I. 1985/1823, amended by S.I. 1986/982, 1997.

25th June 1987

John Moore
Secretary of State for Social Services

19th June 1987

Sanderson of Bowden
Minister of State, Scottish Office

22nd June 1987

Peter Walker
Secretary of State for Wales

In Witness whereof the Official Seal of the Minister of Agriculture, Fisheries and Food is hereunto affixed on 26th June 1987.

John MacGregor
Minister of Agriculture, Fisheries and Food

Sealed with the Official Seal of the Department of Health and Social Services for Northern Ireland this 23rd day of June 1987.

M. N. Hayes
Permanent Secretary

Sealed with the Official Seal of the Department of Agriculture for Northern Ireland this 24th day of June 1987.

W. H. Jack
Permanent Secretary

Article 2(a)

SCHEDULE 1

CONTAINING NEW PART B OF SCHEDULE 1 TO THE PRINCIPAL ORDER

"SCHEDULE 1   Article 3

PART B

VETERINARY DRUGS(a)

Product licence No.	Name of Product(b)
1. Growth Promoters	
PL 3405/4030	Avoparcin–20
PL 3405/4019	Avoparcin 50 Premix
PL 0095/4026	Avotan 50
PL 0095/4028	Avotan 50c Avoparcin
PL 0095/4036	{ Avotan Blockmix / Avotan Super
PL 0095/4039	Avotan Farm Mix
PL 3405/4026	Bambermycin–5
PL 0010/4038	Bayo-n-ox 10% Premix
PL 3832/4020	Eskalin 20
PL 3832/4031	Eskalin 100
PL 3832/4017	Eskalin 500
PL 3832/4021	Eskalin S–400
PL 0029/4102	Fedan 10% Premix
PL 0086/4137	Flavomycin 50
PL 4594/4001	FPL 40 "ABCHEM"
PL 5811/4001	Intagen Premix
PL 3405/4022	Monensin–100 Ruminant
PL 3405/4016	Nitrovin
PL 3405/4018	Nitrovin–20
PL 2592/4075	Nitrozone 25
PL 4869/4000 } PL 0777/4002 }	Panazone 250–Nitrovin
PL 0095/4007	Payzone 50 MA Nitrovin Milk Replacer Additive
PL 4188/4008	Pentazone 250
PL 0006/4052	Romensin (Monensin Sodium) Premix
PL 0006/4070	Romensin RDD
PL 0012/4170	SPIRA 200
PL 0012/4182	SPIRA 200L
PL 0006/4055	Tylamix Premix 100 g/kg
PL 0006/4062	Tylamix Premix 250 g/kg
PL 3405/4028	Tylosin–20
PL 3405/4007	Tylosin 100 Premix
PL 4594/4002	Tylosin 250 "ABCHEM" Premix
PL 3405/4027	Virginiamycin–20
PL 4594/4004	Virginiamycin 500 "ABCHEM"
PL 3405/4015	ZB–100
PL 0109/4001	Zinc Bacitracin Premix
2. Coccidiostats	
PL 0025/4035	Arpocox
PL 0031/4011	Avatec Premix
PL 3405/4017	Clopidol
PL 3405/4025	Clopidol 250
PL 0095/4042	*Cygro Premix*
PL 0012/4188	*Deccox Sheep Premix*
PL 4594/4003	Dinitolmide
PL 0109/4000	Dinormix SR 25
PL 4869/4005 } PL 0777/4001 }	D.O.T.
PL 0109/4002	DOT (dinitolmide)
PL 0006/4047	Elancoban Premix
PL 0621/4015	Lerbek

(a) Items shown in italics did not appear in Part B of Schedule 1 as amended by S.I. 1986/1997.
(b) Alternative product names used by specially authorised persons are not shown.

SCHEDULE 1 – *continued*

Product licence No.	Name of Product
PL 3405/4006	Monensin 200
PL 3405/4021	Monensin 100 Poultry
PL 4594/4000	Monensin 200 "ABCHEM" Premix
PL 0006/4061	Monteban 100 Premix
PL 0025/4019	Nicrazin (Premix)
PL 0086/4135	Sacox 60 Premix
PL 1598/4036	Salcostat
PL 1598/4032	Salcostat (DOT) Premix 12.5%
PL 1598/4033	Salcostat (DOT) Premix 25%
PL 0086/4117	Stenorol

3. Anti-Blackhead Preparations

PL 3405/4009	Dazole Premix
PL 4869/4003 PL 0777/4003 }	Dimetridazole BP (Vet.)
PL 3636/4001	Dimetridazole–PML Turkeys
PL 0012/4176	'Emtryl' Premix
PL 0012/4174	'Emtryl' Pure
PL 0012/4175	'Emtryl' Soluble
PL 4188/4014	Unizole T for Poultry
PL 4188/4013	Unizole T Soluble for Poultry

4. Sheep Dips and Ectoparasiticides

PL 1300/4010	Barricade
PL 0676/4089	Battles Improved Organo-Phosphorus Single-Dipping Fluid Dip
PL 0676/4087	Battles Organo-Phosphorus Single-Dipping Fluid Dip
PL 0010/4067	Bayticol Scab & Tick Dip Scab Approved
PL 1300/4011	C Tag 97 Fly Tag/Flectron Fly Tag
PL 1300/4004	Ciodrin Insecticide
PL 5869/4095	*Coopers Border Winter Dip–Scab Approved*
PL 5869/4082	Coopers Dipmaster Dip Scab Approved
PL 5869/4005	Coopers Powerpack Summer Dip
PL 5869/4002	Coopers Powerpack Winter Dip
PL 0003/4149 *PL 5869/4104* }	Coopers Scab Approved Dip (Border Type)
PL 0003/4150 PL 5869/4007 }	Coopers Spoton Insecticide
PL 0003/4124 PL 5869/4003 }	Coopers Summer Dip 400
PL 5869/4006	Coopers Winter Dip 200
PL 4149/4001	Deodorised Malathion Premium Grade
PL 1476/4018	Deosan Dysect
PL 1476/4026	Deosan Flectron
PL 0829/4127	Dermol
PL 1978/4001	Ectoral Tablets No. 1, 2 and 3
PL 4436/4005	Fly Dip
PL 1826/4004	Lice Tick and Mange Dressing (LTM)
PL 2428/4018	Malacide
PL 1826/4001	Northern Fly Dip
PL 1826/4028	*Osmonds Scab Approved Gold Fleece Sheep Dip*
PL 0025/4044	Ovidip Scab Approved Sheep Dip
PL 0676/4097	Paracide Plus
PL 2428/4018	Pharmacide
PL 0038/4068	Porect
PL 0086/4138	Prodip
PL 0038/4093	Ridect
PL 5656/4000	Ridect Fly Tags
PL 2100/4034	Rodgers No. 10 Neu-Fly and Tick Dip
PL 6939/4000	*Rogers No. 11 Scab Dip*
PL 1447/4106	Ryposect
PL 0095/4041	Stockguard Insecticide Cattle Ear Tags
PL 0003/4113	Stomoxin
PL 5869/4013	Stomoxin-CY Fly Tapes

SCHEDULE 1 – *continued*

Product licence No.	Name of Product
PL 0003/4148 } PL 5869/4009 }	Stomoxin Fly Tags
PL 5869/4010	Stomoxin Liquid Concentrate
PL 1300/4005	Supona Sheep Dip
PL 4436/4001	Taktic
PL 1345/4040	Taskill
PL 0086/4140	Tirade Fly Tags
PL 1728/4070	Topclip Parasol
PL 1826/4025	Viper Dip
PL 1447/4052	Young's 200 Liquid Tick Dip
PL 1447/4096	Young's Cypor
PL 1447/4070	Young's Dursban Winter Dip
PL 1447/4073	Young's Iodofenphos Winter Dip
PL 1447/4055	Young's Killtick Liquid Tick Dip
PL 1447/4056	Young's Powder Fly Dip
PL 1447/4058	Young's Scab Approved 200 Liquid Tick Dip
PL 1447/4085	Young's Scab Approved Diazinon Winter Dip
PL 1447/4013	Young's Scab Approved Ectomort Summer Dip
PL 1447/4105	Young's Scab Approved Jason Winter Dip
PL 1447/4080	Young's Scab Approved Summer Dip
PL 1447/4060	Young's Sheep Blowfly Spray
PL 1447/4083	Young's SP Fly Spray
PL 1447/4056	Young's Summer Mycotic Dip
PL 3893/4069	Zeprox

5. Anthelmintics

Product licence No.	Name of Product
PL 0095/4037	Actelmintic Injectable Wormer
PL 0029/4103	'Amatron' Cattle Drench
PL 0029/4105	'Amatron' Sheep Drench
PL 1447/4092	Anthelpor
PL 4318/4003	Ashmintic Drench
PL 4318/4013	Ashmintic Injection
PL 0010/4063	Bayverm Granules 10%
PL 0010/4054	Bayverm L.V. Paste
PL 0010/4058	Bayverm Pellets 1.9%
PL 0010/4049	Bayverm Premix 0.6%
PL 0010/4050	Bayverm Premix 2.4%
PL 0010/4062	Bayverm Roundwormer
PL 0010/4064	Bayverm SC 2.5% Suspension Worm Drench
PL 0010/4065	Bayverm SC 10% Suspension Worm Drench
PL 0010/4047	Bayverm Suspension 2.5%
PL 0010/4048	Bayverm Suspension 10%
PL 3974/4026	Cevasol C Worm Drench
PL 3974/4021	Cevasol Injection
PL 3974/4020	Cevasol Worm Drench
PL 0095/4040	Cyverm 11.5% Gel
PL 0095/4038	Cyverm Levamisole 3.2% Drench
PL 0095/4037	Cyverm Levamisole 7.5% Injection
PL 1861/4055	Day's Worm Drench
PL 3656/4015	*Dio Horse and Pony Wormer Paste*
PL 0010/4046	Droncit
PL 1596/4071	Duphamisole 7.5% Oral
PL 5151/4001	Equidin Paste
PL 3832/4012	Equitac
PL 0829/4044	Equivurm Plus
PL 0829/4058	Equivurm Plus Paste
PL 0025/4027	Equizole Pony Paste
PL 0025/4042	Eqvalan Paste for Horses
PL 0086/4144	Fenbendazole
PL 0829/4131 } PL 0242/4018 }	Flubenol Pellets
PL 0242/4017	Flubenol Premix
PL 0010/4055	Flukombin
PL 3763/4000	Gapex
PL 3832/4038	Helmatac In-Feed Wormer

SCHEDULE 1 – *continued*

Product licence No.	Name of Product
PL 2592/4076	Helminate Sow Wormer Pellets
PL 0025/4041	{ Ivomec Drench { Oramec Drench for Sheep
PL 0025/4040	{ Ivomec Injection { *Ivomec Injection for Cattle*
PL 0025/4043	Ivomec Injection for Pigs
PL 2000/4054	Levacide–C Worm Drench
PL 2000/4049	Levacide Injection
PL 2000/4060	Levacide SC Worm Drench
PL 2000/4050	Levacide Worm Drench
PL 2000/4080	*Levafas Diamond*
PL 2000/4068	Levafas Fluke and Worm Drench
PL 3832/4070	Loditac 20
PL 3832/4069	Loditac 200
PL 3832/4066	Loditac 3% Wormer Pellets
PL 0829/4126 PL 0242/4010	Mebatreat
PL 0829/4113 PL 0242/4016	Mebenvet (1.2%)
PL 0829/4123 PL 0242/4020	Mebenvet (5%)
PL 0829/4114	Multispec
PL 0012/4149	Nemafax 5
PL 0012/4149	Nemafax 14
PL 0012/4151	Nemafax Cattle, Sheep and Goat Wormer Pellets
PL 0012/4003	Nemafax Drench
PL 0012/4151	Nemafax Sow
PL 0012/4153	Nemafax Wettable Powder
PL 0029/4101	Nemicide Cattle Drench
PL 1345/4063 PL 5869/4051	Nilvax
PL 1345/4069 PL 5869/4052	Nilvax under 30Kg
PL 5869/4076 PL 0029/4100	Nilverm C Nilverm C Cattle Drench
PL 0029/4101	Nilverm Cattle Special
PL 5869/4033	Nilverm Cattle Special/Nemicide Cattle Drench
PL 5869/4086	Nilverm Gold
PL 0029/4114 PL 5869/4032	Nilverm Plus Drench
PL 0029/4118 PL 5869/4022	Nilverm Super
PL 0029/4098 PL 5869/4074	Nilzan C
PL 0029/4115 PL 5869/4031	'Nilzan' Drench Plus
PL 0029/4117 PL 5869/4030	'Nilzan' Drench Super
PL 5869/4085	Nilzan Gold
PL 5869/4021	Nilzan SC
PL 0829/4114 PL 0242/4008	Ovitelmin
PL 0829/4162 PL 0242/4007	Ovitelmin Bolus
PL 0829/4163	Ovitelmin SC
PL 0242/4006	Ovitelmin S & C
PL 0086/4121	Panacur 1.5% Pellets
PL 0086/4105	Panacur 2.5% Sheep Wormer
PL 0086/4105	Panacur 2.5% Suspension
PL 0086/4110	Panacur 4% Paste
PL 0086/4106	Panacur 10% Suspension
PL 0086/4107	Panacur 22% Granules
PL 0086/4119	Panacur Paste
PL 0086/4136	Panacur SC Cattle Wormer

SCHEDULE 1 – *continued*

Product licence No.	Name of Product
PL 0086/4130	Panacur SC Sheep Wormer
PL 0057/4075	Paratect Sustained Release Bolus
PL 0025/4031	Porcam
PL 3832/4073	Powacide
PL 0025/4038	Ranizole Paste
PL 0095/4037	Ridaverm Injectable Wormer
PL 0829/4150	Ripercol
PL 0242/4015	Ripercol pour-on
PL 0242/4005	Ripercol 3.2% Drench
PL 0829/4133	Ripercol 3.2% Oral
PL 0242/4004	Ripercol 5% Injection
PL 0829/4140	Ripercol 5% Injectable Solution
PL 0829/4151	Ripercol 7.5% Injectable
PL 0242/4003	Ripercol 7.5% Injection
PL 0242/4000	Ripercol 15% Injection
PL 0829/4132	Ripercol 15% Injectable Solution
PL 0829/4165	Ripercol SC
PL 0086/4115	Rumevite Wormablok with Panacur for Cattle
PL 0086/4114	Rumevite Wormablok with Panacur for Sheep
PL 1447/4094	Rycovet Horse and Pony Wormer
PL 0242/4002	Spartakon
PL 0029/4099	Spectril
PL 5869/4075	
PL 0057/4060	Strongid-P (Granules)
PL 0057/4076	Strongid Paste for Dogs
PL 0057/4062	Strongid-P Paste
PL 0057/4079	Strongid Suspension for Dogs
PL 0057/4063	Suiminth (Morantel Tartrate)
PL 0286/4032	Synanthic
PL 0286/4034	Synanthic DC
PL 0286/4039	Synanthic Horse Paste
PL 0286/4035	Synanthic Horse Pellets
PL 0286/4040	Synanthic I/R
PL 0286/4047	Synanthic Sel/Co
PL 0003/4127	Systamex Paste 18.5% Cattle and Horse Wormer
PL 5869/4061	
PL 0003/4127	Systamex Paste 18.5% Horse and Pony Wormer
PL 5869/4014	Systamex SC
PL 0003/4121	Systamex 906 Concentrated Cattle Wormer
PL 5869/4060	
PL 0003/4112	Systamex Worm Drench for Cattle and Sheep
PL 5869/4059	
PL 0829/4058	Telmin
PL 0242/4013	
PL 0829/4044	Telmin Granules
PL 0829/4112	Telmin KH
PL 0242/4001	
PL 0829/4114	Telmin Liquid
PL 0242/4014	Telmin Paste
PL 4462/4002	Tetramisole Hydrochloride BP (Vet)
PL 0025/4024	Thibenzole Paste
PL 0002/4061	Valbazen 2.5% Total Spectrum Wormer
PL 3832/4022	
PL 0002/4062	Valbazen 10% Total Spectrum Wormer
PL 3832/4023	
PL 3832/4015	Valbazen 40% Paste
PL 3832/4025	Valbazen C 10% Total Spectrum Wormer
PL 3832/4026	Valbazen SC 2.5% Total Spectrum Wormer
PL 3832/4068	Valbazen SC 10% Total Spectrum Wormer
PL 3832/4016	Valbazen Cattle Wormer Pellets
PL 0012/4172	Vermadax
PL 2676/4120	Vermisole Injection
PL 2676/4121	Vermisole Worm Drench
PL 0086/4139	Wormex

SCHEDULE 1 – *continued*

Product licence No.	Name of Product
PL 3832/4076	Wormguard Injection
PL 1447/4091	Young's Anthelpor 20
PL 1447/4090	Young's Anthelworm Feed Pellets
PL 1447/4076	Young's Anthelworm L
PL 1447/4100	Young's Endozal

6. Milk Fever Preparations

PL 0829/4167	Calcitad 50
PL 2324/4077	Calcium Borogluconate 30% and Magnesium Hypophosphite 2.2% Solution CMP 30
PL 0829/4118	Calcium Borogluconate 40% with Magnesium and Phosphorus
PL 2428/4042	*1. Calcium Borogluconate injection 20% Pharmacol 20. 2. Injection of Calcium Borogluconate 20%*
PL 2428/4024	Calcium Borogluconate Injection 25% with Phosphorus Magnesium and Dextrose
PL 2428/4028	Calcium Borogluconate Injection 40%
PL 2428/4027	Calcium Borogluconate Injection 30% with Phosphorus and Magnesium
PL 2324/4076	Calcium Borogluconate Solution CBG 20
PL 2428/4004	Dextrose Injection
PL 2324/4079	Glucose Saline Injection
PL 2324/4078	Injection of Calcium Borogluconate 40% and Magnesium Hypophosphite 2.2% Solution CMP 40
PL 2428/4024	Pharmacal 25 PMD
PL 2428/4027	Pharmacal 30 PM
PL 2428/4028	Pharmacal 40
PL 2428/4004	Pharmadex 50
PL 1345/4007	TVL Calcium Borogluconate "Borocal"

7. Warble Fly Treatments

PL 0003/4115	Cooper Warble Fly Liquid
PL 0095/4024	Cyanamid Systemic Warble Fly Dressing
PL 0829/4127	Dermol
PL 0025/4040	Ivomec Injection
PL 0010/4045	Neguvon Spot-on
PL 0038/4062	Orbisect Warble Fly, Louse and Mange Liquid for Cattle
PL 1447/4074	Young's New Poron
PL 1447/4077	Young's Poron 20

8. Liver Fluke Remedies

PL 0010/4031	Dirian
PL 1728/4065	Fasinex 5%
PL 1728/4067	Fasinex 10%
PL 0025/4036	Flukanide
PL 3832/4073	Powacide
PL 3832/4022	Valbazen 2.5% Total Spectrum Wormer
PL 3832/4023	Valbazen 10% Total Spectrum Wormer
PL 3832/4025	Valbazen C10% Total Spectrum Wormer
PL 3832/4026	Valbazen SC 2.5% Total Spectrum Wormer
PL 1447/4104	Young's Benafox
PL 1447/4101	Young's Flukol

9. Sheep and Cattle Clostridial Vaccines and Antisera

PL 0086/4132	Heptavac P
PL 1345/4063 PL 5869/4051	Nilvax
PL 1345/4069 PL 5869/4052	Nilvax under 30 kg
PL 0086/4129	Ovivac P
PL 1345/4062 *PL 5869/4053*	Tasvax 8
PL 1728/4066	Topclip Ewe Vaccine 8 in 1

SCHEDULE 1 – *continued*

Product licence No.	Name of Product
	10. Poultry Vaccines
PL 5654/4017	AE
PL 3359/4024	Avian Encephalomyelitis Vaccine Delvax AE
PL 1598/4001	Avian Encephalomyelitis Vaccine (Living) Calnek Strain
PL 1708/4133	Avian Encephalomyelitis Vaccine (Living) Nobilis
PL 3832/4041	Combimune
PL 1598/4029	Combined ND (HB1) and IB (Massachusetts MM) Vaccine (Living)
PL 3359/4004	Delvax IB H52
PL 3359/4003	Delvax IB H120
PL 3359/4001	Delvax Marek THV Freeze-dried
PL 3359/4005	Delvax ND HB1
PL 3359/4035	Delvax ND Hitchner
PL 2592/4055	Eavax
PL 1598/4055	Fowl Pox Vaccine (Poxine)
PL 1598/4053	Fowl Pox Vaccine (Poxinet)
PL 1708/4139	Gumboro Disease Vaccine (Living) Nobilis
PL 1598/4076	Ibinac ND
PL 5654/4000	Iblin
PL 5654/4013	Iblin Live
PL 0002/4002 PL 3832/4056	IB Vaccine (Living) Massachusetts H52 Strain
PL 0002/4003 PL 3832/4036	IB Vaccine (Living) Massachusetts H120 Strain
PL 2592/4037	Ibvax
PL 1708/4135	Inactivated ND Vaccine (oil emulsion) Newcavac Nobilis
PL 1598/4056	Infectious Larygotracheitis Vaccine (LT-VAC)
PL 2592/4074	Ivamarek Marek's Disease Vaccine
PL 2592/4044	Lentogen HB1
PL 5654/4018	Marek's
PL 3832/4039	Marek's Disease Vaccine (Living) THV (Strain FC 126) Freeze-dried (Marimune)
PL 3317/4085	Marek's Disease Vaccine (Live) THV
PL 1598/4026	Marek's Disease Vaccine MD–VAC (Living) THV (Witter Strain) Frozen (Wet)
PL 1598/4027	Marek's Disease Vaccine (Lyophilised) MD-VAC
PL 1708/4141	Marexine MD
PL 1708/4169	Marexine THV/CA
PL 5654/4023	Maridin
PL 5654/4001	Maternalin
PL 5654/4012	Maternalin Plus
PL 5654/4002	Myxilin
PL 5654/4021	Myxilin Live
PL 3318/4000	ND Vaccine (Inactivated) Oil Emulsion
PL 5654/4007	Newcadin
PL 5654/4004	Newcadin Day Old
PL 5654/4006	Newcadin 25
PL 5654/4008	Newcadin L
PL 5654/4020	Newcadin Live B–1
PL 2592/4033	Newcastle Disease Vaccine (Inactivated) Oil Emulsion (Layer Plus)
PL 3832/4057	Newcastle Disease Vaccine (Living) Hitchner B1 Strain
PL 1708/4150	Newcavac + EDS '76 Vaccine
PL 1708/4143	Nobi-Vac Egg Drop Syndrome '76 Vaccine BC14 (Inactivated)
PL 1708/4155	Nobi-Vac Gumboro Inactivated
PL 1708/4184	*Nobi-Vac IB + G + ND*
PL 1708/4185	*Nobi-Vac IB + ND*
PL 1708/4187	*Nobi-Vac IB + ND + EDS*
PL 5654/4022	*Paramyxovirus–3 Disease vaccine*
PL 1596/4034	Poulvac AE
PL 1596/4040	Poulvac EDS
PL 1596/4029	Poulvac IB Vaccine H52 (Living)
PL 1596/4030	Poulvac IB Vaccine H120 (Living)
PL 1596/4045	Poulvac Marek HVT Vaccine
PL 1596/4025	Poulvac Marek THV

SCHEDULE 1 – *continued*

Product licence No.	Name of Product
PL 1596/4042	Poulvac ND + EDS
PL 1596/4026	Poulvac ND Vaccine (Living) HB 1
PL 0002/4005 ⎱ PL 3832/4024 ⎰	Tremimune
PL 5654/4019	Ultravac

11. Erysipelas Vaccines

PL 1531/4012	Ferrovac Ery Vaccine
PL 1596/4078	Suvaxyn Erysipelas Vaccine
PL 3317/4110	Swine Erysipelas Vaccine (Inactivated)
PL 1345/4004	Swine Erysipelas Vaccine, Inactivated (Oil Adjuvant) Erysivax

12. Salmonella and E. coli Vaccines

PL 0086/4134	Coliovac
PL 3832/4009	Ecopig
PL 0003/4110	Gletvax K88-Porcine E. coli Vaccine (Polyvalent)
PL 0003/4110	Gletvax-Porcine E. coli Vaccine (Polyvalent)
PL 0003/4110	Gletvax-Porcine E. coli Vaccine (Polyvalent) + K88
PL 0086/4113	Porcovac AT
PL 3832/4004	Scourguard I
PL 1754/4002	Sow Intagen O/I Injectable
PL 1596/4076	Suvaxyn E. coli

13. Other Sheep and Cattle Vaccines

PL 5764/4000	*Footrite*
PL 1345/4070	Footvax
PL 0003/4135	Ovine Enzootic Abortion (Improved) Vaccine
PL 0086/4133	Ovipast

14. Miscellaneous Vaccines

PL 0003/4136 ⎱ *PL 5869/4046* ⎰	Atrovax
PL 3359/4044	Delsuvac RP
PL 1708/4152	Nobi-Vac L.T. K88

15. Local Anaesthetics

PL 3317/4049	Lignavet Plus Injection
PL 2324/4074	Lignocaine Anaesthetic Injection
PL 2000/4029	Lignocaine and Adrenalin Injection
PL 2428/4021	Pharmacaine
PL 1599/4005	Ruby Freezaject

16. Others

PL 4318/4002	Ash-fer 100
PL 2428/4026	Bactasorb Tablets
PL 3832/4034	Bloat Guard
PL 0002/4054 ⎱ PL 3832/4064 ⎰	Bloat Guard Drench
PL 3832/4065	Bloat Guard Liquid
PL 3514/4002	Boar Mate
PL 2428/4023	Brodin
PL 2000/4065	*Calciject 20*
PL 2000/4069	Calciject New Formula 40
PL 1754/4003	Calf Intagen Premix
PL 2545/4009	Codifer 10
PL 0676/4091	Colostrene-Watery Mouth Drench for Young Lambs
PL 3317/4010	Copavet
PL 2987/4003	Copper (Cupric) Carbonate
PL 0038/4088	Copporal 2 g
PL 0038/4089	Copporal 4 g
PL 0038/4090	Copporal 24 g
PL 0038/4078	Copprite 2 g
PL 0038/4084	Copprite 4 g

SCHEDULE 1 – *continued*

Product licence No.	Name of Product
PL 0038/4087	Copprite 24 g
PL 1345/4012	Cujec
PL 5869/4070	
PL 2987/4002	Cupric Oxide
PL 5645/4016	*Deosan Hoofcare*
PL 2676/4127	Dextrose 20%
PL 3656/4012	Dio-Iron
PL 4543/4000	*Ferrodown 10*
PL 4543/4001	*Ferrodown 20*
PL 0113/4005	Fisons Multivitamin Injection
PL 0113/4006	Fisons Vitamin A, D & E Injection
PL 0113/4007	Gleptosil
PL 2324/4079	Glucose Saline Injection
PL 6077/4000	Golden Hoof Zinc Sulphate
PL 0113/4012	Hemofer
PL 1754/4009	HI-FAT Baby Calf Food 'Intagen'
PL 0829/4117	Iron Dextran 10% (Pharmacosmos)
PL 0025/4040	Ivomec Injection
PL 0043/4000	Leodex
PL 0043/4042	Leodex 20%
PL 0043/4036	Leodex Plus
PL 2428/4017	Magnesium Sulphate Injection
PL 2000/4043	Magnesium Sulphate Injection 25% w/v
PL 4127/4000	Micro Anti-Bloat Premix
PL 2592/4059	Microdex
PL 0676/4090	Orfoids-Capsules for Orf
PL 1345/4051	Permasel-C
PL 1345/4052	Permasel-S
PL 2428/4017	Pharmamag 25
PL 2428/4007	Pharmavit AD$_3$E
PL 0829/4133	Ripercol 3.2% Oral
PL 0829/4140	Ripercol 5% Injectable Solution
PL 0829/4132	Ripercol 15% Injectable
PL 1011/4001	Roscofer 10% Vet
PL 1011/4000	Roscoral Vet
PL 4031/4002	Rycovet Cuvine
PL 3317/4077	Sildex
PL 5811/4000	Sow Intagen O/I
PL 2100/4035	Surefoot
PL 1598/4065	Suvaxyn Iron Dextran 20% Injection
PL 1599/4004	Swipoul
PL 0829/4117	Tendex
PL 3317/4128	Tensolvet
PL 5923/4002	Tracerglass C
PL 5923/4001	Tracerglass L
PL 5923/4000	Tracerglass S
PL 3317/4047	Vetrivite Plus
PL 2428/4007	Vitamin ADE Solution
PL 1447/4036	Young's Swaycop
PL 0676/4098	Zincoped"

SCHEDULE 2

Article 2(b)

CONTAINING NEW PART B OF SCHEDULE 2 TO THE PRINCIPAL ORDER

"SCHEDULE 2

Article 4

PART B

VETERINARY DRUGS(a)

Product Licence No.	Name of Product(b)
1. Growth Promoters	
PL 3405/4030	Avoparcin–20
PL 3405/4019	Avoparcin 50 Premix
PL 0095/4026	Avotan 50
PL 0095/4028	Avotan 50c Avoparcin
PL 0095/4036	{ Avotan Super { Avotan Block Mix
PL 0095/4039	Avotan Farm Mix
PL 3405/4026	Bambermycin–5
PL 0010/4043	Bayo-n-ox 10% Premix
PL 3832/4020	Eskalin 20
PL 3832/4031	Eskalin 100
PL 3832/4017	Eskalin 500
PL 3832/4021	Eskalin S–400
PL 0029/4102	Fedan 10% Premix
PL 0086/4137	Flavomycin 50
PL 4594/4001	FPL 40 "ABCHEM"
PL 5811/4001	Intagen Premix
PL 3405/4022	Monensin–100 Ruminant
PL 3405/4016	Nitrovin
PL 3405/4018	Nitrovin–20
PL 2592/4075	Nitrozone 25
PL 4869/4000 } PL 0777/4002 }	Panazone 250 Nitrovin
PL 0095/4007	Payzone 50 MA Nitrovin Milk Replacer Additive
PL 4188/4008	Pentazone 250
PL 0006/4052	Romensin (Monensin Sodium) Premix
PL 0006/4070	Romensin RDD
PL 0012/4170	SPIRA 200
PL 0012/4182	SPIRA 200L
PL 0006/4055	Tylamix Premix 100 g/kg
PL 0006/4062	Tylamix Premix 250 g/kg
PL 3405/4028	Tylosin–20
PL 3405/4007	Tylosin 100 Premix
PL 4594/4002	Tylosin 250 "ABCHEM" Premix
PL 3405/4027	Virginiamycin–20
PL 4594/4004	Virginiamycin 500 "ABCHEM"
PL 3405/4015	ZB–100
PL 0109/4001	Zinc Bacitracin Premix
2. Coccidiostats	
PL 0025/4035	Arpocox
PL 0031/4011	Avatec Premix
PL 3405/4017	Clopidol
PL 3405/4025	Clopidol 250
PL 0095/4042	*Cygro Premix*
PL 0012/4188	*Deccox Sheep Premix*
PL 4594/4003	Dinitolmide
PL 0109/4000	Dinormix SR 25
PL 4869/4005 } PL 0777/4001 }	D.O.T.
PL 0109/4002	DOT (dinitolmide)
PL 0006/4047	Elancoban Premix

(a) Items shown in italics did not appear in Part B of Schedule 2 as amended by S.I. 1986/1997.
(b) Alternative product names used by specially authorised persons are not shown.

SCHEDULE 2 – *continued*

Product Licence No.	Name of Product
PL 3405/4006	{ Elancoban Premix { Monensin 200
PL 0621/4015	Lerbek
PL 3405/4022	Monensin 100 Ruminant
PL 4594/4000	Monensin 200 "ABCHEM" Premix
PL 0006/4061	Monteban 100 Premix
PL 0025/4019	Nicrazin (Premix)
PL 0086/4135	Sacox 60 Premix
PL 1598/4036	Salcostat
PL 1598/4032	Salcostat (DOT) Premix 12.5%
PL 1598/4033	Salcostat (DOT) Premix 25%
PL 0086/4117	Stenorol

3. Anti-Blackhead Preparations

PL 4869/4003 PL 0777/4003	Dimetridazole BP (Vet)
PL 3636/4001	Dimetridazole-PML Turkeys
PL 3405/4009	Dazole Premix
PL 0012/4176	'Emtryl' Premix
PL 0012/4174	'Emtryl' Pure
PL 0012/4175	'Emtryl' Soluble
PL 4188/4014	Unizole T for Poultry
PL 4188/4013	Unizole T Soluble for Poultry

4. Anthelmintics

PL 0010/4049	Bayverm Premix 0.6%
PL 0010/4050	Bayverm Premix 2.4%
PL 0086/4144	Fenbendazole
PL 0829/4131 PL 0242/4018	Flubenol Pellets
PL 0242/4017	Flubenol Premix
PL 0002/4004 PL 3832/4038	Helmatac In-Feed Wormer
PL 3832/4070	Loditac 20
PL 3832/4069	Loditac 200
PL 0829/4113 PL 0242/4016	Mebenvet (1.2%)
PL 0829/4123 PL 0242/4020	Mebenvet (5%)
PL 0012/4149	Nemafax 5
PL 0012/4149	Nemafax 14
PL 0012/4153	Nemafax Wettable Powder

5. Others

PL 3832/4034	Bloat Guard
PL 1754/4003	Calf Intagen Premix
PL 1754/4009	HI-FAT Baby Calf Food 'Intagen'
PL 4127/4000	Micro Anti-Bloat Premix
PL 5811/4000	Sow Intagen O/I"

SCHEDULE 3

Article 2(c)

CONTAINING NEW SCHEDULE 4 TO THE PRINCIPAL ORDER

"SCHEDULE 4

Article 5

HORSE WORMERS(a)

Product licence No.	Name of Product(b)
PL 1732/4059	Astrobot 5
PL 1732/4060	Astrobot 10
PL 0010/4063	Bayverm Granules 10%
PL 0010/4054	Bayverm LV Paste
PL 3636/4015	*Dio Horse and Pony Wormer Paste*
PL 5151/4001	Equidin Paste
PL 1745/4005	Equigard 5
PL 1745/4006	Equigard 10
PL 0829/4043	Equilox
PL 3832/4012	Equitac
PL 0829/4044	Equivurm Plus
PL 0829/4058	Equivurm Plus Paste
PL 0829/4043	Equivurm Syringe
PL 0025/4027	Equizole Pony Paste
PL 0025/4005	Equizole Powder
PL 0025/4042	Eqvalan Paste for Horses
PL 0844/4055	Multiwurma (Horses)
PL 0086/4107	Panacur 22% Granules
PL 0086/4119	Panacur Paste
PL 1599/4001	Ruby Horse Wormer
PL 1447/4094	Rycovet Horse and Pony Wormer Paste
PL 0057/4060	Strongid P (Granules)
PL 0057/4062	Strongid P Paste
PL 0286/4039	Synanthic Horse Paste
PL 0286/4035	Synanthic Horse Pellets
PL 0003/4127	Systamex Paste 18.5% Horse and Pony Wormer
PL 0829/4058 PL 0242/4013 }	Telmin
PL 0829/4044	Telmin Granules
PL 0242/4014	Telmin Paste"

(a) Items shown in italics did not appear in Schedule 4 as amended by S.I. 1986/982.
(b) Alternative product names used by specially authorised persons are not shown.

EXPLANATORY NOTE

(This note is not part of the Order)

This Order further amends the Medicines (Exemptions from Restrictions on the Retail Sale or Supply of Veterinary Drugs) Order 1985.

The Order substitutes updated provisions for Part B of Schedule 1 (veterinary drugs sold by merchants), Part B of Schedule 2 (veterinary drugs for incorporation in animal feeding stuffs) and Schedule 4 (horse wormers) to that Order (article 2). The items shown in italics in the new provisions have been inserted in those Schedules whilst other items have been deleted.

STATUTORY INSTRUMENTS

1987 No. 1124

TERMS AND CONDITIONS OF EMPLOYMENT

The Employment Subsidies Act 1978 (Renewal) (Great Britain) Order 1987

Made - - - -	*26th June 1987*
Coming into force	*1st July 1987*

The Secretary of State, with the consent of the Treasury, in exercise of the powers conferred on him by section 3(2)(a) of the Employment Subsidies Act 1978(**a**) and of all other powers enabling him in that behalf, hereby makes the following Order, a draft of which was laid before the House of Commons and approved by resolution of that House in accordance with section 3(3) of the Employment Subsidies Act 1978:

Citation and commencement

1. This Order may be cited as the Employment Subsidies Act 1978 (Renewal) (Great Britain) Order 1987 and shall come into force on 1st July 1987.

Renewal

2. The powers of section 1 of the Employment Subsidies Act 1978 shall be renewed for Great Britain until the expiration of the period ending with 31st December 1988.

Signed by order of the Secretary of State.

John Lee
Parliamentary Under Secretary of State,
Department of Employment

21st June 1987

We consent,

Michael Neubert
Mark Lennox-Boyd
Two of the Lords Commissioners of Her Majesty's Treasury

26th June 1987

(**a**) 1978 c.6.

EXPLANATORY NOTE

(This note is not part of the Order)

This Order renews for Great Britain until 31st December 1988 the powers of section 1 of the Employment Subsidies Act 1978, which would otherwise not be exercisable after the end of June 1987, the section having been renewed until that date by the Employment Subsidies Act 1978 (Renewal) (Great Britain) Order 1985 (S.I. 1985/1959). Section 1 of the Employment Subsidies Act 1978 authorises the Secretary of State to make payments to employers enabling them to retain in employment persons who might otherwise become unemployed, to take on new employees and generally to maintain or enlarge their labour force.

1987 No. 1125

CUSTOMS AND EXCISE

The Customs Duties (ECSC) (No. 2) (Amendment No. 8) Order 1987

Made - - - -	*30th June 1987*
Laid before the House of Commons	*1st July 1987*
Coming into force	*3rd July 1987*

The Treasury, by virtue of the powers conferred on them by section 5(1) and (3) of, and paragraph 4 of Schedule 2 to, the European Communities Act 1972(**a**) and of all other powers enabling them in that behalf, on the recommendation of the Secretary of State, hereby make the following Order:

1. This Order may be cited as the Customs Duties (ECSC) (No. 2) (Amendment No. 8) Order 1987 and shall come into force on 3rd July 1987.

2. Up to and including 31st December 1987, Article 6(1) of the Customs Duties (ECSC) (No. 2) Order 1985(**b**) (which exempts from duty goods to which that Order applies originating in certain countries) shall not apply to goods which fall within heading 73.13 which originate in Yugoslavia.

Michael Neubert
Tony Durant
30th June 1987   Two of the Lords Commissioners of Her Majesty's Treasury

---

(**a**) 1972 c.68. Section 5(3) and Schedule 2 were amended by the Customs and Excise Duties (General Reliefs) Act 1979 (c.3), Schedule 2, paragraphs 3 and 5.
(**b**) S.I. 1985/1630, amended by S.I. 1985/2020, 1986/348, 813, 1352, 2179, 1987/973, 1053.

EXPLANATORY NOTE

(This note is not part of the Order)

This Order, which comes into force on 3rd July 1987, amends the Customs Duties (ECSC) (No. 2) Order 1985 ("the main Order") which charges customs duties in accordance with the unified ECSC tariff on certain ECSC products imported into the United Kingdom except from other Member States of the European Coal and Steel Community (ECSC) and from certain other countries named in Schedule 1 to the main Order.

This Order reimposes duties on goods falling within heading 73.13 which originate in Yugoslavia.

This Order implements a reintroduction of duty up to the end of 1987 made pursuant to Article 1, paragraph 3 of a decision 86/642/ECSC of the representatives of the governments of Member States of the European Coal and Steel Community meeting within the Council on 22nd December 1986 (OJ No. L380, 31.12.1986, p.59). Decision 86/642/ECSC of 22nd December 1986 established ceilings for imports of certain ECSC goods originating in Yugoslavia. These ceilings have now been reached on goods falling within the above heading.

The Commission communication to Member States giving notice of the reintroduction of customs duties is published in OJ No. C172 of 30.6.1987.

STATUTORY INSTRUMENTS

1987 No. 1126

EDUCATION, ENGLAND AND WALES

The Education (Grant) (Amendment) Regulations 1987

Made - - - -	*24th June 1987*
Laid before Parliament	*8th July 1987*
Coming into force -	*31st July 1987*

The Secretary of State for Education and Science, in exercise of the powers conferred by sections 100(1) and (3) of the Education Act 1944**(a)** and vested in him**(b)**, hereby makes the following Regulations:

1. These Regulations may be cited as the Education (Grant) (Amendment) Regulations 1987 and shall come into force on 31st July 1987.

2. In regulation 10(a) of the Education (Grant) Regulations 1983**(c)** ("the principal Regulations"), there shall be added after the word "profit" the words "except Cranfield Information Technology Institute".

3. In regulation 11 of the principal Regulations, there shall be added–
  (a) in sub-paragraph (*a*) after the word "establishments" the following words
      "or, in the case of Cranfield Information Technology Institute, the persons responsible for the management thereof",
  (b) in sub-paragraph (*b*) after the words "governing bodies" the words "or persons".

4. To the list of establishments mentioned in Schedule 4 to the principal Regulations there shall be added "Cranfield Information Technology Institute".

Kenneth Baker
24th June 1987   Secretary of State for Education and Science

---

(a) 1944 c.31.
(b) S.I. 1964/490.
(c) S.I. 1983/74.

EXPLANATORY NOTE

(This note is not part of the Regulations)

These Regulations amend the Education (Grant) Regulations 1983 by including Cranfield Information Technology Institute as an establishment eligible for grant under those Regulations (regulations 2 and 3).

The Institute is added to those establishments listed in Schedule 4 to the 1983 Regulations to which the conditions as to the payment of grant prescribed in regulation 16 and the provisions for inspection in regulation 24 do not apply (regulation 4). Under regulation 16(6) of the 1983 Regulations the payment of grant to establishments mentioned in Schedule 4 is conditional on such requirements as may be specified by the Secretary of State being satisfied (regulation 4).

STATUTORY INSTRUMENTS

1987 No. 1127

INHERITANCE TAX

The Inheritance Tax (Delivery of Accounts) Regulations 1987

Made - - - -	*30th June 1987*
Laid before the House of Commons	*1st July 1987*
Coming into force -	*1st August 1987*

The Commissioners of Inland Revenue, in exercise of the powers conferred on them by section 256(1) of the Inheritance Tax Act 1984**(a)**, hereby make the following Regulations:

Citation, commencement and extent

1. These Regulations may be cited as the Inheritance Tax (Delivery of Accounts) Regulations 1987 and shall come into force on 1st August 1987.

2. These Regulations do not extend to Scotland or Northern Ireland.

Interpretation

3. In these Regulations "the Principal Regulations" means the Capital Transfer Tax (Delivery of Accounts) Regulations 1981**(b)** as amended by the Capital Transfer Tax (Delivery of Accounts) (No.3) Regulations 1983**(c)**.

Amendments to Principal Regulations

4. In Regulation 3 of the Principal Regulations–
    (a) in paragraph (b) for "£40,000" there shall be substituted "£70,000";
    (b) in paragraph (c) for the words from "10 per cent." to "higher," there shall be substituted "£10,000";
    (c) in paragraph (d) for "1st April 1983" there shall be substituted "1st April 1987".

D. B. Rogers
A. J. G. Isaac
Two of the Commissioners of Inland Revenue

30th June 1987

(a) 1984 c.51. By virtue of section 100(1) and (2) of the Finance Act 1986 (c.41) on and after 25th July 1986 the Capital Transfer Tax Act 1984 may be cited as the Inheritance Tax Act 1984, and any reference in that Act to capital transfer tax is to have effect as a reference to inheritance tax, except where the reference relates to a liability arising before 25th July 1986.
(b) S.I. 1981/880.
(c) S.I. 1983/1039.

EXPLANATORY NOTE

(This note is not part of the Regulations)

The Principal Regulations (S.I. 1981/880, amended by S.I. 1983/1039) dispensed with the need to deliver an account for the purposes of capital transfer tax where (subject to specified exceptions) the value of a deceased's estate did not exceed £40,000 and where the deceased died on or after 1st April 1983. These Regulations increase that limit to £70,000 in respect of deaths on or after 1st April 1987. These Regulations also provide that up to £10,000 of value in respect of property situated outside the United Kingdom may be included in the £70,000 limit without losing "excepted estate" status.

STATUTORY INSTRUMENTS

1987 No. 1128

INHERITANCE TAX

The Inheritance Tax (Delivery of Accounts) (Scotland) Regulations 1987

Made - - - -	*30th June 1987*
Laid before the House of Commons	*1st July 1987*
Coming into force	*1st August 1987*

The Commissioners of Inland Revenue, in exercise of the powers conferred on them by section 256(1) of the Inheritance Tax Act 1984 (**a**), hereby make the following Regulations:

Citation, commencement and extent

1. These Regulations may be cited as the Inheritance Tax (Delivery of Accounts) (Scotland) Regulations 1987 and shall come into force on 1st August 1987.

2. These Regulations extend to Scotland only.

Interpretation

3. In these Regulations "the Principal Regulations" means the Capital Transfer Tax (Delivery of Accounts) (Scotland) Regulations 1981 (**b**) as amended by the Capital Transfer Tax (Delivery of Accounts) (Scotland) (No. 2) Regulations 1983 (**c**).

Amendments to Principal Regulations

4. In Regulation 3 of the Principal Regulations–
  (a) in paragraph (b) for "£40,000" there shall be substituted "£70,000";
  (b) in paragraph (c) for the words from "10 per cent." to "higher," there shall be substituted "£10,000";
  (c) in paragraph (d) for "1st April 1983" there shall be substituted "1st April 1987".

D. B. Rogers
A. J. G. Isaac
30th June 1987   Two of the Commissioners of Inland Revenue

(**a**) 1984 c.51. By virtue of section 100(1) and (2) of the Finance Act 1986 (c.41) on and after 25th July 1986 the Capital Transfer Tax Act 1984 may be cited as the Inheritance Tax Act 1984, and any reference in that Act to capital transfer tax is to have effect as a reference to inheritance tax, except where the reference relates to a liability arising before 25th July 1986.
(**b**) S.I. 1981/881.
(**c**) S.I. 1983/1040.

EXPLANATORY NOTE

(This note is not part of the Regulations)

The Principal Regulations (S.I. 1981/881, as amended by S.I. 1983/1040) dispensed with the need to deliver an account for the purposes of capital transfer tax where (subject to specified exceptions) the value of a deceased's estate did not exceed £40,000 and where the deceased died on or after 1st April 1983. These Regulations increase that limit to £70,000 in respect of deaths on or after 1st April 1987. These Regulations also provide that up to £10,000 of value in respect of property situated outside the United Kingdom may be included in the £70,000 limit without losing "excepted estate" status.

1987 No. 1129

INHERITANCE TAX

The Inheritance Tax (Delivery of Accounts) (Northern Ireland) Regulations 1987

Made - - - -	*30th June 1987*
Laid before the House of Commons	*1st July 1987*
Coming into force	*1st August 1987*

The Commissioners of Inland Revenue, in exercise of the powers conferred on them by section 256(1) of the Inheritance Tax Act 1984(**a**), hereby make the following Regulations:

Citation, commencement and extent

1. These Regulations may be cited as the Inheritance Tax (Delivery of Accounts) (Northern Ireland) Regulations 1987 and shall come into force on 1st August 1987.

2. These Regulations extend to Northern Ireland only.

Interpretation

3. In these Regulations "the Principal Regulations" means the Capital Transfer Tax (Delivery of Accounts) (Northern Ireland) Regulations 1981(**b**) as amended by the Capital Transfer Tax (Delivery of Accounts) (Northern Ireland) (No. 2) Regulations 1983(**c**).

Amendments to Principal Regulations

4. In Regulation 3 of the Principal Regulations–
    (a) in paragraph (b) for "£40,000" there shall be substituted "£70,000";
    (b) in paragraph (c) for the words from "10 per cent." to "higher," there shall be substituted "£10,000";
    (c) in paragraph (d) for "1st April 1983" there shall be substituted "1st April 1987".

D. B. Rogers
A. J. G. Isaac
30th June 1987   Two of the Commissioners of Inland Revenue

(**a**) 1984 c.51. By virtue of section 100(1) and (2) of the Finance Act 1986 (c.41) on and after 25th July 1986 the Capital Transfer Tax Act 1984 may be cited as the Inheritance Tax Act 1984, and any reference in that Act to capital transfer tax is to have effect as a reference to inheritance tax, except where the reference relates to a liability arising before 25th July 1986.
(**b**) S.I. 1981/1441.
(**c**) S.I. 1983/1911.

EXPLANATORY NOTE

(This note is not part of the Regulations)

The Principal Regulations (S.I. 1981/1441, as amended by S.I. 1983/1911) dispensed with the need to deliver an account for the purposes of capital transfer tax where (subject to specified exceptions) the value of a deceased's estate did not exceed £40,000 and where the deceased died on or after 1st April 1983. These Regulations increase that limit to £70,000 in respect of deaths on or after 1st April 1987. These Regulations also provide that up to £10,000 of value in respect of property situated outside the United Kingdom may be included in the £70,000 limit without losing "excepted estate" status.

1987 No. 1130

INHERITANCE TAX

The Inheritance Tax (Double Charges Relief) Regulations 1987

Made - - - -	*30th June 1987*
Laid before the House of Commons	*1st July 1987*
Coming into force	*22nd July 1987*

The Commissioners of Inland Revenue, in exercise of the powers conferred on them by section 104 of the Finance Act 1986(**a**), hereby make the following Regulations.

Citation and commencement

1. These Regulations may be cited as the Inheritance Tax (Double Charges Relief) Regulations 1987 and shall come into force on 22nd July 1987.

Interpretation

2. In these Regulations unless the context otherwise requires–
   "PET" means potentially exempt transfer;
   "property" includes part of any property;
   "the 1984 Act" means the Inheritance Tax Act 1984(**b**);
   "the 1986 Act" means Part V of the Finance Act 1986;
   "section" means section of the 1984 Act.

Introductory

3. These Regulations provide for the avoidance, to the extent specified, of double charges to tax arising with respect to specified transfers of value made, and other events occurring, on or after 18th March 1986.

Double charges—potentially exempt transfers and death

4.—(1) This regulation applies in the circumstances to which paragraph (a) of section 104(1) of the 1986 Act refers where the conditions ("specified conditions") of paragraph (2) are fulfilled.

   (2) The specified conditions to which paragraph (1) refers are–
   (a) an individual ("the deceased") makes a transfer of value to a person ("the transferee") which is a PET,
   (b) the transfer is made on or after 18th March 1986,
   (c) the transfer proves to be a chargeable transfer, and

(**a**) 1986 c. 41.
(**b**) 1984 c. 51; by virtue of section 100(1) and (2) of the Finance Act 1986, on and after 25th July 1986 the Capital Transfer Tax Act 1984 may be cited as the Inheritance Tax Act 1984, and any reference in that Act to capital transfer tax is to have effect as a reference to inheritance tax, except where the reference relates to a liability arising before 25th July 1986.

(d) the deceased immediately before his death was beneficially entitled to property to which paragraph (3) refers.

(3) The property to which paragraph (2)(d) refers is property–

(a) which the deceased, after making the PET to which paragraph (2)(a) refers, acquired from the transferee otherwise than for full consideration in money or money's worth,

(b) which is property which was transferred to the transferee by the PET to which paragraph (2)(a) refers or which is property directly or indirectly representing that property, and

(c) which is property comprised in the estate of the deceased immediately before his death (within the meaning of section 5(1)), value attributable to which is transferred by a chargeable transfer (under section 4).

(4) Where the specified conditions are fulfilled there shall be calculated, separately in accordance with sub-paragraphs (a) and (b), the total tax chargeable as a consequence of the death of the deceased–

(a) disregarding so much of the value transferred by the PET to which paragraph (2)(a) refers as is attributable to the property, value of which is transferred by the chargeable transfer to which paragraph (3)(c) refers, and

(b) disregarding so much of the value transferred by the chargeable transfer to which paragraph (3)(c) refers as is attributable to the property, value of which is transferred by the PET to which paragraph (2)(a) refers.

(5)(a) Whichever of the two amounts of tax calculated under paragraph (4)(a) or (b) is the lower amount shall be treated as reduced to nil but, subject to sub-paragraph (b), the higher amount shall be payable,

(b) where the amount calculated under paragraph (4)(a) is higher than the amount calculated under paragraph (4)(b)–

(i) so much of the tax chargeable on the value transferred by the chargeable transfer to which paragraph (2)(c) refers as is attributable to the amount of that value which falls to be disregarded by virtue of paragraph (ii) shall be treated as a nil amount, and

(ii) for all the purposes of the 1984 Act so much of the value transferred by the PET to which paragraph (2)(a) refers as is attributable to the property to which paragraph (3)(c) refers shall be disregarded.

(6) Part I of the Schedule to these Regulations provides an example of the operation of this regulation.

Double charges—gifts with reservation and death

5.—(1) This regulation applies in the circumstances to which paragraph (b) of section 104(1) of the 1986 Act refers where the conditions ("specified conditions") of paragraph (2) are fulfilled.

(2) The specified conditions to which paragraph (1) refers are–

(a) an individual ("the deceased") makes a transfer of value by way of gift of property,

(b) the transfer is made on or after 18th March 1986,

(c) the transfer is or proves to be a chargeable transfer,

(d) the deceased dies on or after 18th March 1986,

(e) the property in relation to the gift and the deceased is property subject to a reservation (within the meaning of section 102 of the 1986 Act),

(f) (i) the property is by virtue of section 102(3) of the 1986 Act treated for the purposes of the 1984 Act as property to which the deceased was beneficially entitled immediately before his death, or,

(ii) the property ceases to be property subject to a reservation and is the subject of a PET by virtue of section 102(4) of the 1986 Act, and

(g) (i) the property is comprised in the estate of the deceased immediately before his death (within the meaning of section 5(1)) and value attributable to it is transferred by a chargeable transfer (under section 4), or

(ii) the property is property transferred by the PET to which sub-paragraph (f)(ii) refers, value attributable to which is transferred by a chargeable transfer.

(3) Where the specified conditions are fulfilled there shall be calculated, separately in accordance with sub-paragraphs (a) and (b), the total tax chargeable as a consequence of the death of the deceased–

    (a) disregarding so much of the value transferred by the transfer of value to which paragraph (2)(a) refers as is attributable to property to which paragraph (2)(g) refers, and

    (b) disregarding so much of the value of property to which paragraph (2)(g) refers as is attributable to property to which paragraph (2)(a) refers.

(4) Where the amount calculated under paragraph (3)(a) is higher than the amount calculated under paragraph (3)(b)–

    (a) only so much of that higher amount shall be payable as remains after deducting, as a credit, from the amount comprised in that higher amount which is attributable to the value of the property to which paragraph (2)(g) refers, a sum (not exceeding the amount so attributable) equal to so much of the tax paid–

        (i) as became payable before the death of the deceased, and

        (ii) as is attributable to the value disregarded under paragraph (3)(a), and

    (b) so much of the value transferred by the transfer of value to which paragraph (2)(a) refers as is attributable to the property to which paragraph (2)(g) refers shall (except in relation to chargeable transfers which were chargeable to tax, when made by the deceased, for the purposes of an occasion which occurred before the death of the deceased on which tax was chargeable under section 64 or 65) be treated as reduced to a nil amount for all the purposes of the 1984 Act.

(5) Where the amount calculated under paragraph (3)(a) is less than the amount calculated under paragraph (3)(b) the value of the property to which paragraph (2)(g) refers shall be reduced to nil for all the purposes of the 1984 Act.

(6) For the purposes of the interpretation and application of this regulation section 102 of and Schedule 20 to the 1986 Act shall apply.

(7) Part II of the Schedule to these Regulations provides examples of the operation of this regulation.

Double charges—liabilities subject to abatement and death

6.—(1) This regulation applies in the circumstances to which paragraph (c) of section 104(1) of the 1986 Act refers where the conditions ("specified conditions") of paragraph (2) are fulfilled.

(2) The specified conditions to which paragraph (1) refers are–

    (a) a transfer of value which is or proves to be a chargeable transfer ("the transfer") is made on or after 18th March 1986 by an individual ("the deceased") by virtue of which the estate of the transferee is increased or by virtue of which property becomes comprised in a settlement of which the transferee is a trustee, and

    (b) at any time before his death the deceased incurs a liability to the transferee ("the liability") which is a liability subject to abatement under the provisions of section 103 of the 1986 Act in determining the value transferred by a chargeable transfer (under section 4).

(3) Where the specified conditions are fulfilled there shall be calculated, separately in accordance with sub-paragraphs (a) and (b), the total tax chargeable as a consequence of the death of the deceased–

    (a) disregarding so much of the value transferred by the transfer–

        (i) as is attributable to the property by reference to which the liability falls to be abated, and

        (ii) as is equal to the amount of the abatement of the liability, and

    (b) taking account both of the value transferred by the transfer and of the liability.

(4)(a) Whichever of the two amounts of tax calculated under paragraph (3)(a) or (b) is the lower amount shall be treated as reduced to nil but, subject to sub-paragraph (b), the higher amount shall be payable,

    (b) where the amount calculated under paragraph (3)(a) is higher than the amount calculated under paragraph (3)(b)–

(i) only so much of that higher amount shall be payable as remains after deducting, as a credit, from that amount a sum equal to so much of the tax paid–

(a) as became payable before the death of the deceased, and

(b) as is attributable to the value disregarded under paragraph (3)(a), and

(c) as does not exceed the difference between the amount of tax calculated under paragraph (3)(a) and the amount of tax that would have fallen to be calculated under paragraph (3)(b) if the liability had been taken into account, and

(ii) so much of the value transferred by the transfer to which paragraph (2)(a) refers–

(a) as is attributable to property by reference to which the liability is abated, and

(b) as is equal to the amount of the abatement of the liability,

shall (except in relation to chargeable transfers which were chargeable to tax, when made by the deceased, for the purposes of an occasion which occurred before the death of the deceased on which tax was chargeable under section 64 or 65) be treated as reduced to a nil amount for all the purposes of the 1984 Act.

(5) Where there is a number of transfers made by the deceased which are relevant to the liability to which paragraph (2)(b) applies the provisions of this regulation shall apply to those transfers taking them in reverse order of their making, that is to say, taking the latest first and the earliest last, but only to the extent that in aggregate the value of those transfers does not exceed the amount of the abatement to which paragraph (2)(b) refers.

(6) Part III of the Schedule to these Regulations provides examples of the operation of this regulation.

Double Charges—chargeable transfers and death

7.—(1) This regulation applies in the circumstances specified (by this regulation) for the purposes of paragraph (d) of section 104(1) of the 1986 Act (being circumstances which appear to the Board to be similar to those referred to in paragraphs (a) to (c) of that subsection) where the conditions ("specified conditions") of paragraph (2) are fulfilled.

(2) The specified conditions to which paragraph (1) refers are–

(a) an individual ("the deceased") makes a transfer of value to a person ("the transferee") which is a chargeable transfer,

(b) the transfer is made on or after 18th March 1986,

(c) the deceased dies within 7 years after that chargeable transfer is made, and

(d) the deceased immediately before his death was beneficially entitled to property to which paragraph (3) refers.

(3) The property to which paragraph (2)(d) refers is property–

(a) which the deceased, after making the chargeable transfer to which paragraph (2)(a) refers, acquired from the transferee otherwise than for full consideration in money or money's worth,

(b) which was transferred to the transferee by the chargeable transfer to which paragraph (2)(a) refers or which is property directly or indirectly representing that property, and

(c) which is property comprised in the estate of the deceased immediately before his death (within the meaning of section 5(1)), value attributable to which is transferred by a chargeable transfer (under section 4).

(4) Where the specified conditions are fulfilled there shall be calculated, separately in accordance with sub-paragraphs (a) and (b), the total tax chargeable as a consequence of the death of the deceased–

(a) disregarding so much of the value transferred by the chargeable transfer to which paragraph (2)(a) refers as is attributable to the property, value of which is transferred by the chargeable transfer to which paragraph (3)(c) refers, and

(b) disregarding so much of the value transferred by the chargeable transfer to which paragraph (3)(c) refers as is attributable to the property, value of which is transferred by the chargeable transfer to which paragraph (2)(a) refers.

(5)(a) Whichever of the two amounts of tax calculated under paragraph (4)(a) or (b) is the lower amount shall be treated as reduced to nil but, subject to sub-paragraph (b), the higher amount shall be payable,

  (b) where the amount calculated under paragraph (4)(a) is higher than the amount calculated under paragraph (4)(b)–

    (i) only so much of that higher amount shall be payable as remains after deducting, as a credit, from the amount comprised in that higher amount which is attributable to the value of the property to which paragraph (2)(d) refers, a sum (not exceeding the amount so attributable) equal to so much of the tax paid–

      (a) as became payable before the death of the deceased, and

      (b) as is attributable to the value disregarded under paragraph (4)(a), and

    (ii) so much of the value transferred by the chargeable transfer to which paragraph (2)(a) refers as is attributable to the property to which paragraph (3)(c) refers shall (except for the purposes of an occasion which occurred before the death of the deceased on which tax was chargeable under section 64 or 65) be treated as reduced to a nil amount for all the purposes of the 1984 Act.

(6) Part IV of the Schedule to these Regulations provides an example of the operation of this regulation.

Equal calculations of tax—special rule

8. Where the total tax chargeable as a consequence of death under the two separate calculations provided for by any of regulation 4(4), 5(3), 6(3) or 7(4) is equal in amount the first of those calculations shall be treated as producing a higher amount for the purposes of the regulation concerned.

Schedule and saving

9. The Schedule to these Regulations shall have effect only for providing examples of the operation of these Regulations and, in the event of any conflict between the Schedule and the Regulations, the Regulations shall prevail.

D.B. Rogers
A.J.G. Isaac
30th June 1987   Two of the Commissioners of Inland Revenue

SCHEDULE   Regulation 9

INTRODUCTORY

1. This Schedule provides examples of the operation of the Regulations.

2. In this Schedule–

"cumulation" means the inclusion of the total chargeable transfers made by the transferor in the 7 years preceding the current transfer;

"GWR" means gift with reservation;

"taper relief" means the reduction in tax provided under section 7(4) of the 1984 Act, inserted by paragraph 2(4) of Schedule 19 to the 1986 Act.

3. Except where otherwise stated, the examples assume that–

—tax rates and bands remain as at 18 March 1987;

—the transferor has made no other transfers than those shown in the examples;

—no exemptions (including annual exemption) or reliefs apply to the value transferred by the relevant transfer; and

—"grossing up" does not apply in determining any lifetime tax (the tax is not borne by the transferor).

PART I

Regulation 4: Example

Jul 1987	A makes PET of £100,000 to B.	
Jul 1988	A makes gift into discretionary trust of £95,000.	Tax paid £750
Jan 1989	A makes further gift into same trust of £45,000.	Tax paid £6,750
Jan 1990	B dies and the 1987 PET returns to A.	
Apr 1991	A dies. His death estate of £300,000 includes the 1987 PET returned to him in 1990, which is still worth £100,000.	

First calculation under reg. 4 (4)(a)

Charge the returned PET in A's death estate and ignore the PET made in 1987.

		Tax
Jul 1987	PET £100,000 ignored	NIL
Jul 1988	Gift £95,000 Tax £1,500 less £750 already paid	£750
Jan 1989	Gift £45,000 as top slice of £140,000 Tax £13,500 less £6,750 already paid	£6,750
Apr 1991	Death estate £300,000 as top slice of £440,000	£153,000*
	Total tax due as result of A's death	£160,500

* In first calculation the tax of £153,000 on death estate does not allow for any successive charges relief (under S.141 IHTA 1984) that might be due in respect of "the returned PET" by reference to any tax charged on that "PET" in connection with B's death.

Second calculation under reg. 4 (4)(b)

Charge the 1987 PET and ignore the value of the returned PET in A's death estate.

		Tax
Jul 1987	PET £100,000. Tax with taper relief	£2,400
Jul 1988	Gift £95,000 as top slice of £195,000 Tax £34,000 less £750 already paid	£33,250
Jan 1989	Gift £45,000 as top slice of £240,000 Tax £20,000 less £6,750 already paid	£13,250
Apr 1991	Death estate £200,000 as top slice of £440,000	£111,000
	Total tax due as result of A's death	£159,900

Result *

First calculation gives higher amount of tax. So PET reduced to nil and tax on other transfers is as in first calculation.

* If, after allowing any successive charges relief, the second calculation gives higher amount of tax, 1987 PET will be charged and tax on other transfers will be as in second calculation.

PART II

Regulation 5: Example 1

Jan 1988	A makes PET of £150,000 to B.	
March 1992	A makes gift of land worth £200,000 into a discretionary trust of which he is a potential beneficiary. The gift is a "GWR".	Tax paid £19,500
Feb 1995	A dies without having released his interest in the trust. His death estate valued at £400,000, includes the GWR land curently worth £300,000.	

First calculation under reg. 5 (3)(a)

Charge the GWR land in A's death estate and ignore the GWR.

		Tax
Jan 1988	PET (now exempt)	NIL
Mar 1992	GWR ignored	NIL
Feb 1995	Death estate £400,000 Tax £144,000 less £19,500 already paid on GWR*	£124,500
	Total tax due as result of A's death	£124,500

* Credit for the tax already paid cannot exceed the amount of the death tax attributable to the value of the GWR property. In this example the tax so attributable is £108,000 (ie $\frac{144,000}{400,000} \times 300,000$). So credit is given for the full amount of £19,500.

Second calculation under reg. 5 (3)(b)

Charge the GWR and ignore the GWR land in the death estate.

		Tax
Jan 1988	PET (now exempt)	NIL
March 1992	GWR £200,000 Tax £39,000 less £19,500 already paid	£19,500
Feb 1995	Death estate £100,000 (ignoring GWR property) as top slice of £300,000	£48,000
	Total tax due as result of A's death	£67,500

Result

First calculation yields higher amount of tax. So the value of the GWR transfer is reduced to nil and tax on death is charged as in first calculation with credit for the tax already paid.

PART II

Regulation 5: Example 2

Apr 1987	A makes gift into discretionary trust of £150,000.	Tax paid £9,500
Jan 1988	A makes further gift into same trust of £50,000.	Tax paid £10,000
Mar 1993	A makes PET of shares valued at £150,000 to B.	
Feb 1996	A dies. He had continued to enjoy the income of the shares he had given to B (the 1993 PET is a GWR). His death estate, valued at £300,000, includes those shares currently worth £200,000.	

First calculation under reg. 5 (3)(a)

Charge the GWR shares in the death estate and ignore the PET.

		Tax
Apr 1987	Gift £150,000. No adjustment to tax as gift made more than 7 years before death	NIL
Jan 1988	Gift £50,000. No adjustment to tax as gift made more than 7 years before death	NIL
Mar 1993	PET £150,000 now reduced to NIL	NIL
Feb 1996	Death estate including GWR shares £300,000. No previous cumulation	£87,000
	Total tax due as result of A's death	£87,000

Second calculation under reg. 5 (3)(b)

Charge the PET and ignore the value of the GWR shares in the death estate.

		Tax
Apr 1987	Gift £150,000. No adjustment to tax as gift made more than 7 years before death	NIL
Jan 1988	Gift £50,000. No adjustment to tax as gift made more than 7 years before death	NIL
Mar 1993	GWR £150,000 as top slice of £350,000 (ie previous gifts totalling £200,000+£150,000)	£75,000
Feb 1996	Death estate (excluding GWR shares) £100,000 as top slice of £250,000 (the 1987 and 1988 gifts drop out of cumulation)	£43,000
	Total tax due as result of A's death	£118,000

Result

Second calculation yields higher amount of tax. So tax is charged by reference to the PET and the value of the GWR shares in the death estate is reduced to NIL.

PART III

Regulation 6: Example 1

Nov 1987	X makes a PET of cash of £95,000 to Y.
Dec 1987	Y makes a loan to X of £95,000.
May 1988	X makes a gift into discretionary trust of £20,000.
Apr 1993	X dies. His death estate is worth £182,000. A deduction of £95,000 is claimed for the loan from Y.

First calculation under reg. 6 (3)(a)

No charge on November 1987 gift, and no deduction against death estate.

		Tax
Nov 1987	PET ignored	NIL
May 1988	Gift £20,000	NIL
Apr 1993	Death estate £182,000 as top slice of £202,000	£39,800
	Total tax due as result of X's death	£39,800

Second calculation under reg. 6 (3)(b)

Charge the November 1987 PET, and allow the deduction against the death estate.

		Tax
Nov 1987	PET £95,000. Tax with taper relief	£600
May 1988	Gift £20,000 as top slice of £115,000. Tax with taper relief	£3,600
Apr 1993	Death estate (£182,000–loan of £95,000) £87,000 as top slice of £202,000	£32,300
	Total tax due as result of X's death	£36,500

Result

First calculation gives higher amount of tax. So debt is disallowed against death estate, but PET of £95,000 is not charged.

PART III

Regulation 6: Example 2

Aug 1988	P makes a PET of cash of £100,000 to Q.	
Sept 1988	Q makes a loan to P of £100,000.	
Oct 1989	P makes gift into discretionary trust of £98,000.	Tax paid £1,200
Nov 1992	P dies. Death estate £110,000 less allowable liabilities of £80,000 (which do not include the debt of £100,000 owed to Q).	

First calculation under reg. 6 (3)(a)

No charge on August 1988 PET, and no deduction against death estate for the £100,000 owed to Q.

		Tax
Aug 1988	PET ignored	NIL
Oct 1989	Gift £98,000 Tax (with taper relief) £1,920 less £1,200 already paid	£720
Nov 1992	Death estate £30,000 as top slice of £128,000	£9,000
	Total tax due as result of P's death	£9,720

Second calculation under reg. 6 (3)(b)

Charge the August 1988 PET, and allow deduction against death estate for the £100,000 owed to Q.

		Tax
Aug 1988	PET £100,000. Tax with taper relief	£1,800
Oct 1989	Gift £98,000 as top slice of £198,000 Tax (with taper relief) £28,100 less £1,200 already paid	£26,960
Nov 1992	Death estate £30,000–£100,000 (owed to Q)	NIL
	Total tax due as result of P's death	£28,760

Result

Second calculation gives higher amount of tax. So the PET to Q is charged, and deduction is allowed against death estate for the debt to Q.

PART III

Regulation 6: Example 3

1 May 1987	A makes PET to B of £95,000.	
1 Jan 1988	A makes PET to B of £40,000.	
1 Jul 1988	A makes gift into discretionary trust of £100,000.	Tax paid £1,500
1 Jan 1989	A makes PET to B of £30,000.	
1 Jul 1989	B makes a loan to A of £100,000.	
1 Dec 1990	A dies. Death estate £200,000, against which deduction is claimed for debt of £100,000 due to B.	

First calculation under reg. 6 (3)(a)

Disallow the debt and ignore corresponding amounts (£100,000) of PETs from A to B, starting with the latest PET.

		Tax
1 May 1987	PET now reduced to £65,000	NIL
1 Jan 1988	PET now reduced to NIL	NIL
1 Jul 1988	Gift into trust £100,000 as top slice of £165,000 Tax £25,000 less £1,500 already paid	£23,500
1 Jan 1989	PET now reduced to NIL	NIL
1 Dec 1990	Death estate £200,000 as top slice of £365,000	£98,000
	Total tax due as result of A's death	£121,500

Second calculation under reg. 6 (3)(b)

Allow the debt and charge PETs to B in full.

		Tax
1 May 1987	PET £95,000. Tax with taper relief	£1,200
1 Jan 1988	PET £40,000 as top slice of £135,000	£12,000
1 Jul 1988	Gift into trust £100,000 as top slice of £235,000 Tax £41,000 less £1,500 already paid	£39,500
1 Jan1989	PET £30,000 as top slice of £265,000	£15,000
1 Dec 1990	Death estate £100,000 as top slice of £365,000	£53,500
	Total tax due as result of A's death	£121,200

Result

First calculation yields higher amount of tax. So the debt is disallowed and corresponding amounts of PETs to B are ignored in determining the tax due as a result of the death.

PART III

Regulation 6: Example 4

1 Apr 1987	A makes gift into discretionary trust of £100,000.	Tax paid £1,500
1 Jan 1990	A makes PET to B of £60,000.	
1 Jan 1991	A makes further gift into same trust of £50,000.	Tax paid £8,000
1 Jan 1992	Same trust makes a loan to A of £120,000.	
1 Jun 1994	A dies. Death estate is £220,000, against which deduction is claimed for debt of £120,000 due to the trust.	

First calculation under reg. 6 (3)(a)

Disallow the debt and ignore corresponding amounts (£120,000) of gifts from A to trust, starting with the latest gift.

		Tax
1 Apr 1987	Gift now reduced to £30,000. No adjustment to tax already paid as gift made more than 7 years before death	NIL
1 Jan 1990	PET £60,000 as top slice of £90,000	NIL
1 Jan 1991	Gift now reduced to NIL. No adjustment to tax already paid	NIL
1 Jun 1994	Death estate £220,000 as top slice of £280,000 (the 1987 gift at £30,000 drops out of cumulation)	£77,000
		£77,000
	Less credit for tax already paid £1,500+£8,000	£9,500
	Total tax due as result of A's death	£67,500

Second calculation under reg. 6 (3)(b)

Allow the debt and no adjustment to gifts into the trust.

		Tax
1 Apr 1987	Gift £100,000. No adjustment to tax already paid as gift made more than 7 years before death	NIL
1 Jan 1990	PET £60,000 as top slice of £160,000. Tax with taper relief	£12,000
1 Jan 1991	Gift £50,000 as top slice of £210,000 Tax (with taper relief) £16,000 less £8,000 already paid	£8,000
1 June 1994	Death estate £100,000 as top slice of £210,000. (The 1987 gift drops out of cumulation. No credit for tax paid on that gift.)	£37,000
	Total tax due as result of A's death	£57,000

Result

First calculation yields higher amount tax. So the debt is disallowed and corresponding amounts of gifts into trust are ignored in determining the tax due as a result of the death.

PART IV

Regulation 7: Example

May 1986	S transfers into discretionary trust property worth £150,000. Immediate charge at the rates then in force.	Tax paid £13,750
Oct 1986	S gives T a life interest in shares worth £85,000. Immediate charge at the rates then in force.	Tax paid £19,500
Jan 1991	S makes a PET to R of £20,000.	
Dec 1992	T dies, and the settled shares return to S who is the settlor and therefore no tax charge on the shares on T's death.	
Aug 1993	S dies. His death estate includes the shares returned from T which are currently worth £75,000, and other assets worth £144,000.	

First calculation under reg. 7 (4)(a)

Charge the returned shares in the death estate and ignore the October 1986 gift. Tax rates and bands are those in force at the date of S's death.

		Tax
May 1986	Gift into trust made more than 7 years before death. So no adjustment to tax already paid but the gift cumulates in calculating tax on other gifts	NIL
Oct 1986	Gift ignored and no adjustment to tax already paid	NIL
Jan 1991	PET of £20,000 as top slice of (£150,000+£20,000) £170,000	£8,000
Nov 1993	Death estate £219,000 as top slice of £239,000 Tax £56,000 less £19,350 (part of tax already paid)*	£37,150
	Total tax due as result of S's death	£45,150

* £19,350 represents the amount of the death tax attributable to the value of the returned shares, and is lower than the amount of the lifetime tax charged on those shares. So credit against the death charge for the tax already paid is restricted to the lower amount.

Second calculation under reg. 7 (4)(b)

Charge the October 1986 gift and ignore the returned shares in the death estate. Tax rates and bands are those in force at the date of S's death.

		Tax
May 1986	Gift into trust made more than 7 years before death. So no adjustment to tax already paid but the gift is taken into acccount in calculating the tax on the other gifts	NIL
Oct 1986	Gift of £85,000 as top slice of £235,000 Tax (with taper relief) £7,100 less £19,500 already paid	NIL*
Jan 1991	PET of £20,000 as top slice of £255,000	£10,000
Aug 1993	Death estate (excluding the returned shares) £144,000 as top slice of £249,000 (£85,000+£20,000+£144,000)	£57,000
	Total tax due as a result of S's death	£67,000

* Credit for the tax already paid restricted to the (lower) amount of tax payable as result of the death. No repayment of the excess.

Result

Second calculation gives higher amount of tax. So tax is charged as in second calculation by excluding the shares from the death estate.

EXPLANATORY NOTE

(This note is not part of the Regulations)

The Finance Act 1986 by the provisions of section 104 empowered the Board of Inland Revenue to make provision by regulations for avoiding in certain circumstances double charges to inheritance tax in respect of transfers of value and other events occuring on or after 18 March 1986.

These Regulations provide for the avoidance of double charges arising in specified circumstances.

Regulation 1 provides the title and commencement date.

Regulation 2 contains definitions.

Regulation 3 describes the scope of the Regulations.

Regulation 4 provides for the avoidance of a double charge where property given by a potentially exempt transfer (PET) is subsequently returned (otherwise than for full consideration) by the donee to the transferor, and as a result of the transferor's death both that property and the PET become chargeable to tax. If charging the property as part of the death estate produces a higher amount of tax than would be payable if the charge on the PET was taken instead, the value transferred by the original transfer (the PET) is reduced by reference to the amount of the value of that property which is included in the chargeable transfer on the death. Conversely the PET is charged if that produces the higher amount of tax, with a corresponding reduction in the value of that property which is included in the chargeable transfer on the death. To avoid the value of the same property entering twice into the tax calculations this reduction applies for all purposes of the tax.

Regulation 5 provides for the avoidance of a double charge where there is a transfer of value by way of gift of property which is or subsequently becomes a chargeable transfer, and the property is (by virtue of the provisions relating to gifts with reservation) subject to a further transfer which is chargeable as a result of the transferor's death. As under regulation 4, whichever transfer produces the higher amount of tax as a result of the death remains chargeable and the value of the other transfer is reduced by reference to the value of the transfer which produced that amount. However this reduction in value does not apply for the purposes of any discretionary trust charges arising before the transferor's death if the transfer by way of gift was chargeable to tax when it was made. Further, provision is made for credit to be given on account of any tax already paid on the transfer by way of gift against so much of the tax payable on the other transfer as relates to the value of the property in question.

Regulation 6 provides for the avoidance of a double charge where a transfer of value is or subsequently becomes a chargeable transfer, and at the transferor's death his estate owes to the transferee a debt which (under the rules relating to such liabilities) falls to be abated or disallowed in determining the value of the estate chargeable on the death. Two separate calculations of tax payable as a result of the death are made. In the first, the amount of the transfer of value is reduced by the amount of the debt which is disallowed or abated, and in the second, the amount of the transfer of value and of the debt are both taken into account. The higher amount of tax is payable, but relief is given either by reducing the value of the transfer of value or by allowing the debt and charging the transfer of value in full. As under regulation 5, the reduction in value does not apply for the purposes of any charges on discretionary trusts arising before the death if the transfer of value was a chargeable transfer when it was made. Credit is allowed for some or all of the tax already paid on that transfer against the tax payable on the transferor's estate at death.

Regulation 7 provides for the avoidance of a double charge where property given by a transfer of value which is chargeable when made, is returned (otherwise than for full consideration) by the donee to the transferor, and that property is also chargeable as part of the transferor's estate on his death. It provides the same relief as is provided under regulation 4 in the case where the transfer of value was a PET when it was made, but credit is available for tax already paid. The reduction in value does not apply for the purposes of discretionary trust charges arising before the death.

Regulation 8 provides a rule to determine which of two equal amounts under regulation 4(4), 5(3), 6(3) or 7(4) is to be treated as the higher amount for the purposes of each of those regulations.

Regulation 9 introduces the Schedule which provides examples of the operation of these Regulations.

STATUTORY INSTRUMENTS

1987 No. 1131

MONOPOLIES AND MERGERS

The Restriction on Agreements and Conduct (Tour Operators) Order 1987

Made - - - -	*30th June 1987*
Laid before Parliament	*9th July 1987*
Coming into force	
all articles except article 4	*31st July 1987*
article 4	*7th October 1987*

Whereas the Secretary of State, in accordance with section 91(2) of the Fair Trading Act 1973(**a**), published on 10th October 1986 a notice stating his intention to make this Order, indicating the nature of the provisions to be embodied in it and stating that any person whose interests were likely to be affected by it and who was desirous of making representations in respect of it should do so in writing before 14th November 1986;

And whereas the Secretary of State has considered the representations made to him in accordance with that notice;

Now, therefore, the Secretary of State, being the appropriate Minister within the meaning of section 56 of the said Act, in exercise of the powers conferred by sections 56(2) and 90(2) and (4) of, and paragraphs 1, 2, 4 and 7 of Part I of Schedule 8 to, the said Act and for the purpose of remedying or preventing adverse effects specified in a report of the Monopolies and Mergers Commission entitled "A Report on the matter of the existence or the possible existence of a complex monopoly situation in relation to the supply in the United Kingdom of agency services by travel agents for tour operators in relation to the marketing and supply of foreign package holidays"(**b**), hereby makes the following Order:

Citation and Commencement

1. This Order may be cited as the Restriction on Agreements and Conduct (Tour Operators) Order 1987 and shall come into force on 31st July 1987, except article 4 which shall come into force on 7th October 1987.

Definitions

2. In this Order–

"accommodation" means the provision of a place to sleep but includes the provision of sleeping accommodation in a means of transport only where that accommodation represents a substantial proportion of the accommodation for a holiday; and it includes the provision of a site for the erection of a tent or a parking place for a caravan, mobile home or other similar vehicle;

"agency services" means the services of marketing on behalf of a tour operator foreign package holidays provided by that operator;

"foreign package holiday" means services, accommodation and facilities provided, under a contract made within the United Kingdom, by a tour operator in connection

---

(**a**) 1973 c.41.   (**b**) Cmnd 9879.

with a holiday to be taken outside the United Kingdom except where transport to and from the United Kingdom or accommodation outside the United Kingdom (whether or not for the duration of the holiday) is not provided;

"inducement" means a benefit, whether pecuniary or not, offered to a class or classes of persons or to the public at large by a travel agent expressly on his own behalf as an incentive to that class or those classes of persons or the public at large to acquire foreign package holidays through him rather than through another;

"relevant agreement" means an agreement between a tour operator and a travel agent for the supply in the United Kingdom of agency services by the travel agent to the tour operator in relation to the marketing and supply of foreign package holidays;

"tour operator" means a person who provides foreign package holidays to the public or a section of it; and

"travel agent" means a person who markets foreign package holidays under one or more relevant agreements on behalf of a tour operator.

Agreements

3.—(1) Subject to paragraph (3) of this article, it shall be unlawful for a tour operator to make or carry out a relevant agreement to the extent that that agreement contains provisions, express or implied, which prohibit a travel agent from offering inducements or are intended to persuade a travel agent not to offer inducements.

(2) This article shall apply to prohibit the carrying out of a relevant agreement already in existence on the date on which this Order is made.

(3) This article shall not apply to a relevant agreement in so far as it is or would be an agreement to which the Restrictive Trade Practices Act 1976(**a**) applies or, as the case may be, would apply.

4.—(1) Subject to paragraph (2) of this article, any tour operator who is a party to a relevant agreement shall, to the extent that that agreement contains provisions referred to in article 3(1) above terminate it before 5th January 1988.

(2) This article shall not apply to a relevant agreement in so far as it is an agreement to which the Restrictive Trade Practices Act 1976 applies.

Conduct

5. It shall be unlawful for a tour operator to withhold or to agree to withhold or to threaten to withhold orders for agency services from a travel agent who offers or who has offered or who proposes to offer inducements except in circumstances where such orders are withheld, or would be if an agreement or threat to withhold were carried out, for a reason, other than the offering of inducements, which could have led a reasonable tour operator to withhold orders for agency services from a travel agent.

6.—(1) It shall be unlawful for a tour operator to give or agree to give any preference in respect of the giving of orders for agency services to travel agents who do not offer inducements or who offer inducements only to a limited extent or who offer only certain types of inducements or who have not offered or who do not propose to offer inducements.

(2) A tour operator shall be regarded as giving a preference where he treats a travel agent, with regard to the terms or conditions on which orders for services are given or any other matter, in a manner significantly more favourable than that in which he normally treats travel agents who offer inducements.

Francis Maude
Parliamentary Under Secretary of State,
Department of Trade and Industry

30th June 1987

(**a**) 1976 c.34.

EXPLANATORY NOTE

(This note is not part of the Order)

This Order makes it unlawful for a tour operator to make or carry out an agreement (whether existing or future) for agency services with a travel agent to the extent that it prohibits or is intended to dissuade the travel agent from offering inducements to the public to purchase the tour operator's foreign package holidays through him rather than another travel agent. It also requires tour operators to terminate any such existing agreement to that extent. These provisions of the Order do not apply to agreements in so far as they are agreements to which the Restrictive Trade Practices Act 1976 (c.34) applies.

The Order further makes it unlawful for a tour operator to refuse to deal with a travel agent on the grounds that that agent offers inducements, or to give preferential treatment to travel agents who do not offer inducements.

Copies of the report of the Monopolies and Mergers Commission upon which the Order is based (Cmnd 9879) may be obtained from Her Majesty's Stationery Office.

STATUTORY INSTRUMENTS

1987 No. 1132

CIVIL AVIATION

The London City Airport Byelaws (Designation) Order 1987

Made - - - -	*30th June 1987*
Laid before Parliament	*9th July 1987*
Coming into force	*30th July 1987*

The Secretary of State for Transport, in exercise of his powers under section 63(1) of the Airports Act 1986(**a**), hereby makes the following Order:–

1. This Order may be cited as the London City Airport Byelaws (Designation) Order 1987 and shall come into force on 30th July 1987.

2. The London City Airport is hereby designated for the purposes of section 63 of the Airports Act 1986.

Signed by authority of
the Secretary of State
30th June 1987

Peter Bottomley
Parliamentary Under Secretary of State,
Department of Transport

EXPLANATORY NOTE

(This note is not part of the Order)

Section 63(1) of the Airports Act 1986 provides that where an airport is either designated for the purposes of that section or is managed by the Secretary of State, the airport operator (whether the Secretary of State or some other person) may make byelaws for regulating the use and operation of the airport and the conduct of all persons while within the airport. This Order designates the London City Airport for the purposes of section 63.

(**a**) 1986 c.31.

STATUTORY INSTRUMENTS

1987 No. 1133

ROAD TRAFFIC

The Road Vehicles (Construction and Use) (Amendment) (No.2) Regulations 1987

Made - - - -	*30th June 1987*
Laid before Parliament	*10th July 1987*
Coming into force	*31st July 1987*

The Secretary of State for Transport, in exercise of the powers conferred by section 40(1) and (3) of the Road Traffic Act 1972(**a**), now vested in him(**b**), and after consultation with representative organisations in accordance with section 199(2) of that Act, hereby makes the following Regulations:

Citation, commencement and introduction

1. These Regulations may be cited as the Road Vehicles (Construction and Use) (Amendment) (No.2) Regulations 1987 and shall come into force on 31st July 1987.

2. The Road Vehicles (Construction and Use) Regulations 1986(**c**) shall be further amended in accordance with the following provisions of these Regulations.

Amendment of interpretation provisions

3. In the Table in regulation 3(2), the following new definitions shall be inserted in the appropriate places according to alphabetical order–

"coach" means a large bus with a maximum gross weight of more than 7.5 tonnes and with a maximum speed exceeding 60 mph;

"large bus" means a vehicle constructed or adapted to carry more than 16 seated passengers in addition to the driver;

"motor caravan" means a motor vehicle which is constructed or adapted for the carriage of passengers and their effects and which contains, as permanently installed equipment, the facilities which are reasonably necessary for enabling the vehicle to provide mobile living accommodation for its users;

"staircase" means a staircase by means of which passengers on a double-decked vehicle may pass to and from the upper deck of the vehicle.

Additional protective systems

4. After regulation 53 (mascots) there shall be inserted the following new regulations–

"Strength of superstructure

53A.—(1) This regulation applies to every coach which is–

(a) a single decked vehicle;

(**a**) 1972 c. 20.
(**b**) S.I. 1979/571 and 1981/238.
(**c**) S.I. 1986/1078, to which there are no relevant amending instruments.

(b) equipped with a compartment below the deck for the luggage of passengers; and

(c) first used on or after 1st April 1990.

(2) Every vehicle to which this regulation applies shall comply with the requirements of ECE Regulation 66.

Additional exits from double-decked coaches

53B.—(1) This regulation applies to every coach which is–

(a) a double-decked vehicle; and

(b) first used on or after 1st April 1990.

(2) Subject to the following provisions of this regulation, every vehicle to which this regulation applies shall be equipped with two staircases, one of which shall be located in one half of the vehicle and the other in the other half of the vehicle.

(3) Instead of being equipped with two staircases in accordance with paragraph (2), a vehicle to which this regulation applies may be equipped in accordance with the following provisions of this regulation with a hammer or other similar device with which in case of emergency any side window of the vehicle may be broken.

(4) Where a vehicle is equipped with–

(a) a staircase located in one half of the vehicle; and

(b) an emergency exit complying with regulation 21(8) of the Public Service Vehicles (Conditions of Fitness, Equipment, Use and Certification) Regulations 1981(**a**) located in the same half of the upper deck of the vehicle;

the hammer or the similar device shall be located in the other half of that deck.

(5) Any hammer or other similar device with which a vehicle is equipped pursuant to this regulation shall be located in a conspicuous and readily accessible position in the upper deck of the vehicle.

(6) There shall be displayed, in a conspicuous position in close proximity to the hammer or other similar device, a notice which shall contain in clear and indelible lettering–

(a) in letters not less than 25 mm high, the heading "IN EMERGENCY"; and

(b) in letters not less than 10 mm high, instructions that in case of emergency the hammer or device is to be used first to break any side window by striking the glass near the edge of the window and then to clear any remaining glass from the window aperture.

(7) For the purposes of this regulation a staircase, emergency exit, hammer or other similar device (as the case may be) shall be considered to be located in the other half of the vehicle if the shortest distance between any part of that staircase, exit, hammer or device (as the case may be) and any part of any other staircase, emergency exit, hammer or device is not less than one half of the overall length of the vehicle.".

Amendments to regulations relating to seat belts and anchorage points

5. Regulation 46 shall be amended as follows–

(a) in paragraph (1), there shall be added the following new sub-paragraph–

"(c) every heavy motor car first used on or after 1st October 1988.";

(b) in paragraph (2)–

(i) in sub-paragraph (a)(ii), after the words "1st April 1980" there shall be inserted the words "and before 1st October 1988" and the words "in Great Britain (determined in accordance with the provisions of Schedule 11)" shall be omitted;

(ii) for sub-paragraph (b) there shall be substituted the following sub-paragraph–

"(b) a bus, being–

(i) a minibus–

(A) if first used before 1st October 1988, constructed or adapted to carry more than twelve passengers; or

---

(**a**) S.I. 1981/257, to which there are no relevant amending instruments.

(B) if first used on or after 1st October 1988, having a maximum gross weight exceeding 3500 kg; or

(ii) a large bus (other than a coach first used on or after 1st October 1988);";

(iii) in sub-paragraph (d), for the words "an industrial" there shall be substituted the words "a motor";

(iv) in sub-paragraph (f), after the words "goods vehicle" there shall be inserted the words "first used before 1st October 1988";

(v) for sub-paragraph (i) there shall be substituted the following new sub-paragraph–

"(i) a vehicle having a maximum speed not exceeding 16 mph;" and

(vi) after sub-paragraph (j) there shall be inserted the following new sub-paragraph–

"(k) a locomotive.";

(c) in paragraph (4)–

(i) at the beginning there shall be inserted the words "Save as provided in paragraph (4A) or (4B)";

(ii) for sub-paragraph (a)(i) there shall be substituted the following sub-paragraph–

"(i) in the case of a minibus, a motor ambulance or a motor caravan–

(A) if first used before 1st October 1988, the driver's seat and the specified passenger's seat (if any); or

(B) if first used on or after 1st October 1988, the driver's seat and any forward-facing front seat and";

(iii) in sub-paragraph (a)(ii), for the words "in any other case" there shall be substituted the words "in the case of any other passenger or dual-purpose vehicle";

(iv) after sub-paragraph (a)(ii) there shall be inserted the following new paragraph–

"(iii) in any other case, every forward-facing front seat and every non-protected seat, and";

and

(v) in sub-paragraph (b), after the words "comply with" there shall be inserted the words "the technical and installation requirements of";

(d) after paragraph (4) there shall be inserted the following new paragraphs–

"(4A) The requirements specified in paragraph (4) shall not apply to–

(a) a goods vehicle first used on or after 1st October 1988 and having a maximum gross weight exceeding 3500 kg, but any such vehicle shall be equipped with two belt anchorages designed to hold securely in position on the vehicle lap belts for the driver's seat and each forward-facing front seat; or

(b) a coach equipped with anchorage points which are designed to hold securely in position on the vehicle seat belts for all exposed forward-facing seats and which–

(i) comply with the requirements in paragraph (4)(b); or

(ii) in any case where the anchorage points form part of a seat, do not when a forward horizontal force is applied to them become detached from the seat of which they form part before that seat becomes detached from the vehicle.

(4B) Instead of complying with the requirements in paragraph (4), a vehicle may comply with Community Directive 76/115 or 81/575 or 82/318 or ECE Regulation 14.";

(e) for paragraph (5) there shall be substituted the following new paragraphs–

"(5) Save as provided in paragraph (5A), a vehicle of a type mentioned in paragraphs (4), (4A) and (4B) which is fitted with anchorage points other than those required by those paragraphs shall comply with the requirements in paragraph (4)(b) or, in the case of a coach, the requirements in paragraph (4A)(b)(ii) in respect of any additional anchorage points as well as in respect of the anchorage points required by paragraph (4), (4A) or (4B) to be provided.

(5A) The requirements in paragraph (5) shall not apply in respect of any additional anchorage points first fitted before 1st April 1986 in the case of a vehicle of a type mentioned in paragraph (4)(a)(i)(A), or before 1st October 1988 in the case of a vehicle of any other type.";

(f) in sub-paragraph (a) of paragraph (6)–

    (i) after the words "the expressions" there shall be inserted the words '"exposed forward-facing seat"'; and

    (ii) after the words '"forward-facing seat"' there shall be inserted the words '"forward-facing front seat"' and '"lap belt"'; and

(g) for sub-paragraph (b) of paragraph (6) there shall be substituted the following new sub-paragraph–

    "(b) the expression "non-protected seat" means a seat other than a front seat which does not satisfy the requirements of section 4.3.3 of Annex 1 to Community Directive 81/575.".

6. Regulation 47 shall be amended as follows–

(a) in paragraph (2)–

    (i) in sub-paragraph (a), the word "seat" shall be omitted in both places where it appears after the words "body-restraining"; and

    (ii) in sub-paragraph (b), the word "seat" shall be omitted where it appears after the words "three-point";

    (iii) in sub-paragraph (c), after the words "regulation 46(4)(a) (ii)" there shall be inserted the words "or (iii)";

    (iv) after sub-paragraph (c) there shall be inserted the following new sub-paragraphs–

        "(d) regulation 46(4)(a)(i)(B) applies shall be fitted with seat belts as follows–

            (i) for the driver's seat and the specified passenger's seat (if any) a three-point belt; and

            (ii) for any forward-facing front seat which is not a specified passenger's seat, a three-point belt or a lap belt installed in accordance with the provisions of sub-paragraph (c)(i);

        (e) regulation 46(4A)(b) applies shall be equipped with seat belts which shall be three-point belts, lap belts or disabled person's belts."; and

    (v) at the end of the paragraph there shall be inserted the following—

        "Where a lap belt is fitted to a forward-facing front seat of a minibus, a motor ambulance or a motor caravan, or to an exposed forward-facing seat of a coach (other than the driver's seat) either–

            (i) there shall be provided padding to a depth of not less than 50 mm on the surface of any bar or partition which is, or any part of which is, forward of and within 1 metre of the intersection of the back rest and the cushion of the seat in question and such padding shall extend for not less than 150 mm on either side of that point on the bar or partition which would be bisected by a prolongation of the longitudinal centre-line of the seat; or

            (ii) the technical and installation requirements of Annex 4 to ECE Regulation 21 shall be met.";

(b) in paragraph (3), for the words "paragraph (2)(b) or (c)" there shall be substituted the words "paragraph (2)(b), (c), (d) or (e)";

(c) in paragraph (4)–

    (i) in sub-paragraph (c)(ii), after "BS 3254: 1960" there shall be inserted "or BS AU 160c"; and

    (ii) after sub-paragraph (d) there shall be inserted the following new sub-paragraph–

        "(e) to a vehicle to which regulation 46(4A)(a) applies.";

(d) in paragraph (6), there shall be added the following new sub-paragraph–

    "(c) any seat (other than the driver's seat) fitted to a coach.";

(e) in paragraph (8)–

    (i) in the definition of "body-restraining seat belt", the word "seat" shall be omitted where it forms part of the expression "body-restraining seat belt";

(ii) in paragraph (i)(b) of the definition of "British Standard mark", after "BS 3254: 1960" there shall be inserted "or BS 3254: 1960 as amended by Amendment No. 16 published on 31st July 1986 under the number AMD 5210";

(iii) in the definition of "lap belt", at the end there shall be added the words "and which is designed for use by an adult"; and

(iv) there shall be inserted in the appropriate places according to alphabetical order the following new definitions–

"crew seat" has the same meaning as in regulation 3(1) of the Public Service Vehicles (Conditions of Fitness, Equipment, Use and Certification) Regulations 1981(**a**);

"exposed forward-facing seat" means–

(i) a forward-facing front seat (including any crew seat) and the driver's seat; and

(ii) any other forward-facing seat which is not immediately behind and on the same horizontal plane as a forward-facing high-backed seat;

"forward-facing front seat" means–

(i) any forward-facing seat alongside the driver's seat; or

(ii) if the vehicle normally has no seat which is a forward-facing front seat under sub-paragraph (i) of this definition, each forward-facing seat for a passenger which is foremost in the vehicle;

"forward-facing high-backed seat" means a forward-facing seat which is also a high-backed seat;

"high-backed seat" means a seat the highest part of which is at least 1 metre above the deck of the vehicle.

7. In regulation 48, at the end of paragraph (1) there shall be added the words "and also to every anchorage with which a goods vehicle is required to be provided in accordance with regulation 46(4A)(a)".

8. Regulations 46 and 47, as amended by these Regulations, and with consequential adjustments to the punctuation markings and other minor matters, are set out in the Schedule to the Regulations.

Signed by authority of the Secretary of State
30th June 1987

Peter Bottomley
Parliamentary Under Secretary of State,
Department of Transport

(**a**) S.I. 1981/257; the definition of "crew seat" was inserted by S.I. 1982/1058, regulation 3.

THE SCHEDULE

REGULATIONS 46 AND 47 AS AMENDED BY THESE REGULATIONS

Seat belt anchorage points

46.—(1) Save as provided by paragraph (2), this regulation applies to–

(a) every wheeled motor car first used on or after 1st January 1965;

(b) every three-wheeled motor cycle the unladen weight of which exceeds 255 kg and which was first used on or after 1st September 1970; and

(c) every heavy motor car first used on or after 1st October 1988.

(2) This regulation does not apply to–

(a) a goods vehicle (other than a dual-purpose vehicle) which was first used–

    (i) before 1st April 1967; or

    (ii) on or after 1st April 1980 and before 1st October 1988 and has a maximum gross weight exceeding 3500 kg; or

    (iii) before 1st April 1980 or, if the vehicle is of a model manufactured before 1st October 1979, was first used before 1st April 1982 and in either case, has an unladen weight exceeding 1525 kg;

(b) a bus, being–

    (i) a minibus–

        (A) if first used before 1st October 1988, constructed or adapted to carry more than twelve passengers; or

        (B) if first used on or after 1st October 1988, having a maximum gross weight exceeding 3500 kg; or

    (ii) a large bus (other than a coach first used on or after 1st October 1988);

(c) an agricultural motor vehicle;

(d) a motor tractor;

(e) a works truck;

(f) an electrically-propelled goods vehicle first used before 1st October 1988;

(g) a pedestrian-controlled vehicle;

(h) a vehicle which has been used on roads outside Great Britain and has been imported into Great Britain, whilst it is being driven from the place where it has arrived in Great Britain to a place of residence of the owner or driver of the vehicle, or from any such place to a place where, by previous arrangement, it will be provided with such anchorage points as are required by this regulation and such seat belts as are required by regulation 47;

(i) a vehicle having a maximum speed not exceeding 16 mph;

(j) a motor cycle equipped with a driver's seat of a type requiring the driver to sit astride it, and which is constructed or assembled by a person not ordinarily engaged in the trade or business of manufacturing vehicles of that description; or

(k) a locomotive.

(3) A vehicle which was first used before 1st April 1982 shall be equipped with anchorage points which are designed to hold securely in position on the vehicle seat belts for the driver's seat and specified passenger's seat (if any).

(4) Save as provided in paragraph (4A) or (4B) a vehicle which is first used on or after 1st April 1982 shall be equipped with anchorage points which–

(a) are designed to hold securely in position on the vehicle seat belts for–

    (i) in the case of minibus, motor ambulance or a motor caravan–

        (A) if first used before 1st October 1988, the driver's seat and the specified passenger's seat (if any); or

        (B) if first used on or after 1st October 1988, the driver's seat and any forward-facing front seat; and

    (ii) in the case of any other passenger or dual-purpose vehicle, every forward-facing seat constructed or adapted to accommodate one adult;

    (iii) in every other case, every forward-facing front seat and every non-protected seat, and

(b) comply with the technical and installation requirements of Community Directive 76/115 or 81/575 or 82/318 or ECE Regulation 14 whether or not those instruments apply to the vehicle, so however, that the requirements in those instruments which relate to testing shall not apply.

(4A) The requirements specified in paragraph (4) shall not apply to–

(a) a goods vehicle first used on or after 1st October 1988 and having a maximum gross weight exceeding 3500 kg, but any such vehicle shall be equipped with two belt anchorages designed to hold securely in position on the vehicle lap belts for the driver's seat and each forward-facing front seat; or

(b) a coach equipped with anchorage points which are designed to hold securely in position on the vehicle seat belts for all exposed forward-facing seats and which–

    (i) comply with the requirements in paragraph (4)(b); or

    (ii) in any case where the anchorage points form part of a seat, do not when a forward horizontal force is applied to them become detached from the seat of which they form part before that seat becomes detached from the vehicle.

(4B) Instead of complying with the requirements in paragraph (4), a vehicle may comply with Community Directive 76/115 or 81/575 or 82/318 or ECE Regulation 14.

(5) Save as provided in paragraph (5A), a vehicle of a type mentioned in paragraphs (4), (4A) and (4B) which is fitted with anchorage points other than those required by those paragraphs shall comply with the requirements in paragraph (4)(b), or in the case of a coach the requirements in paragraph (4A)(b)(ii), in respect of any additional anchorage points as well as in respect of the anchorage points required by paragraph (4), (4A) or (4B) to be provided.

(5A) The requirements in paragraph (5) shall not apply in respect of any additional anchorage points first fitted before 1st April 1986 in the case of a vehicle of a type mentioned in paragraph (4)(a)(i)(A), or before 1st October 1988 in the case of a vehicle of any other type.

(6) In this regulation—

(a) the expressions "exposed forward-facing seat", "forward-facing seat", "forward-facing front seat", "lap belt", "seat belt" and "specified passenger's seat" have the same meaning as in regulation 47(8); and

(b) the expression "non-protected seat" means a seat other than a front seat which does not satisfy the requirements of section 4.3.3 of Annex 1 to Community Directive 81/575.

Seat belts

47.—(1) This regulation applies to every vehicle to which regulation 46 applies.

(2) Save as provided in paragraph (4) a vehicle to which–

(a) this regulation applies which was first used before 1st April 1981 shall be provided with–

    (i) a body-restraining belt, designed for use by an adult, for the driver's seat; and

    (ii) a body-restraining belt for the specified passenger's seat (if any);

(b) this regulation applies which is first used on or after 1st April 1981 shall be provided with three-point belts for the driver's seat and for the specified passenger's seat (if any);

(c) regulation 46(4)(a)(ii) or (iii) applies which is first used on or after 1st April 1987 shall be fitted with seat belts additional to those required by sub-paragraph (b) as follows–

    (i) for any forward-facing front seat alongside the driver's seat, not being a specified passenger's seat, a seat belt which is a three-point belt, or a lap belt installed in accordance with paragraph 3.1.2.1 of Annex 1 to Community Directive 77/541 or a disabled person's belt;

    (ii) in the case of a passenger or dual-purpose vehicle having not more than two forward-facing seats behind the driver's seat with either–

        (A) an inertia reel belt for at least one of those seats, or

        (B) a three-point belt, a lap belt, a disabled person's belt or a child restraint for each of those seats;

    (iii) in the case of a passenger or dual-purpose vehicle having more than two forward-facing seats behind the driver's seat, with either–

        (A) an inertia reel belt for one of those seats being an outboard seat and a three-point belt, a lap belt, a disabled person's belt or a child restraint for at least one other of those seats;

        (B) a three-point belt for one of those seats and either a child restraint or a disabled person's belt for at least one other of those seats; or

        (C) a three-point belt, a lap belt, a disabled person's belt or a child restraint for each of those seats.

(d) regulation 46(4)(a)(i)(B) applies shall be fitted with seat belts as follows–

    (i) for the driver's seat and the specified passenger's seat (if any) a three-point belt; and

    (ii) for any forward-facing front seat which is not a specified passenger's seat, a three-point belt or a lap belt installed in accordance with the provisions of sub-paragraph (c)(i);

(e) regulation 46(4A)(b) applies shall be equipped with seat belts which shall be three-point belts, lap belts or disabled person's belts.

Where a lap belt is fitted to a forward-facing front seat of a minibus, a motor ambulance or a motor caravan, or to an exposed forward-facing seat of a coach (other than the driver's seat) either–

    (i) there shall be provided padding to a depth of not less than 50 millimetres on the surface of any bar or partition which is, or any part of which is, forward of and within 1 metre of the intersection of the back rest and the cushion of the seat in question and such padding shall extend for not less than 150 mm on either side of that point on the bar or partition which would be bisected by a prolongation of the longitudinal centreline of the seat; or

    (ii) the technical and installation requirements of Annex 4 to ECE Regulation 21 shall be met.

(3) Every seat belt for an adult, other than a disabled person's belt, provided for a vehicle in accordance with paragraph (2)(b), (c), (d) or (e) shall, except as provided in paragraph (6), comply with the installation requirements specified in paragraph 3.2.2 to 3.3.4 of Annex 1 to Community Directive 77/541 whether or not that Directive applies to the vehicle.

(4) The requirements specified in paragraph (2) do not apply–

    (a) to a vehicle while it is being used under a trade licence within the meaning of section 16 of the 1971 Act;

    (b) to a vehicle, not being a vehicle to which the Type Approval (Great Britain) Regulations apply, while it is being driven from premises of the manufacturer by whom it was made, or of a distributor of vehicles or dealer in vehicles–

        (i) to premises of a distributor of or dealer in vehicles or of the purchaser of the vehicle, or

        (ii) to premises of a person obtaining possession of the vehicle under a hiring agreement or hire-purchase agreement;

    (c) in relation to any seat for which there is provided–

        (i) a seat belt which bears a mark including the specification number of the British Standard for Passive Belt Systems, namely BS AU 183:1983 and including the registered certification trade mark of the British Standards Institution; or

        (ii) a seat belt designed for use by an adult which is a harness belt comprising a lap belt and shoulder straps which bears a British Standard mark or a mark including the specification number for the British Standard for Seat Belt Assemblies for Motor Vehicles, namely BS 3254:1960 or BS AU 160c and including the registered certification trade mark of the British Standards Institution, or the marking designated in item 16 in Schedule 2 to the Approval Marks Regulations;

    (d) in relation to the driver's seat or the specified passenger's seat (if any) of a vehicle which has been specially designed and constructed, or specially adapted, for the use of a person suffering from some physical defect or disability, in a case where a disabled person's belt for an adult person is provided for use for that seat;

    (e) to a vehicle to which regulation 46(4A)(a) applies.

(5) Every seat belt provided in pursuance of paragraph (2) shall be properly secured to the anchorage points provided for it in accordance with regulation 46; or, in the case of a child restraint, to anchorages specially provided for it or, in the case of a disabled person's belt, secured to the vehicle or to the seat which is being occupied by the person wearing the belt.

(6) Paragraph (3), in so far as it relates to the second paragraph of paragraph 3.3.2 of the Annex there mentioned (which concerns the locking or releasing of a seat belt by a single movement) does not apply in respect of a seat belt fitted for–

    (a) a seat which is treated as a specified passenger's seat by virtue of the provisions of sub-paragraph (ii) in the definition of "specified passenger's seat" in paragraph (8); or

    (b) any forward-facing seat for a passenger alongside the driver's seat of a goods vehicle which has an unladen weight of more than 915 kg and has more than one such seat, any such seats for passengers being joined together in a single structure; or

    (c) any seat (other than the driver's seat) fitted to a coach.

(7) Every seat belt, other than a disabled person's belt or a seat belt of a kind mentioned in paragraph 4(c)(i) or (ii) above, provided for any person in a vehicle to which this regulation applies shall be legibly and permanently marked–

    (a) if the vehicle was first used before 1st April 1981 or if the belt is a child restraint, with a British Standard mark or a designated approval mark; or

    (b) in any other case, with a designated approval mark.

Provided this paragraph shall not operate so as to invalidate the exception permitted in paragraph (6).

(8) In this regulation–

"body-restraining belt" means a seat belt designed to provide restraint for both the upper and lower parts of the trunk of the wearer in the event of an accident to the vehicle;

"British Standard mark" means a mark consisting of–

    (i) the specification number of one of the following British Standards for Seat Belt Assemblies for Motor Vehicles, namely–

(a) if it is a seat belt for an adult, BS 3254:1960 and BS AU 160a or 160b; or

(b) if it is a child restraint, BS 3254:1960, or BS 3254:1960 as amended by Amendment No. 16 published on 31st July 1986 under the number AMD 5210, BS AU 157 or 157a, BS AU 185, BS AU 186 or 186a, BS AU 202; and, in either case,

   (ii) the registered certification trade mark of the British Standards Institution;

"child restraint" means a seat belt for the use of a young person which is designed either to be fitted directly to a suitable anchorage or to be used in conjunction with a seat belt for an adult and held in place by the restraining action of that belt:

Provided that for the purposes of paragraph (2)(c)(ii)(B) and (2)(c)(iii) it means only such seat belts fitted directly to a suitable anchorage and excludes belts marked with the specification numbers BS AU 185 and BS AU 186 or 186a.

"crew seat" has the same meaning as in regulation 3(1) of the Public Service Vehicles (Conditions of Fitness Equipment, Use and Certification) Regulations 1981;

"designated approval mark" means

(a) if it is a seat belt other than a child restraint, the marking designated as an approval mark by regulation 4 of the Approval Marks Regulations and shown at item 16 of Schedule 2 to those Regulations or the marking designated as an approval mark by regulation 5 of those Regulations and shown at item 23 and 23A in Schedule 4 to those Regulations, and

(b) if it is a child restraint, either of the markings designated as approval marks by regulation 4 of those Regulations and shown at item 44 and 44A in Schedule 2 to those Regulations.

"disabled person's belt" means a seat belt which has been specially designed or adapted for use by an adult or young person suffering from some physical defect or disability and which is intended for use solely by such a person;

"exposed forward-facing seat" means–

   (i) a forward-facing front seat (including any crew seat) and the driver's seat; and

   (ii) any other forward-facing seat which is not immediately behind and on the same horizontal plane as a forward-facing high-backed seat;

"forward-facing seat" means a seat which is attached to a vehicle so that it faces towards the front of the vehicle in such a manner that a line passing through the centre of both the front and the back of the seat is at an angle of 30° or less to the longitudinal axis of the vehicle;

"forward-facing front seat" means–

   (i) any forward-facing seat alongside the driver's seat; or

   (ii) if the vehicle normally has no seat which is a forward-facing front seat under sub-paragraph (i) of this definition, each forward-facing seat for a passenger which is foremost in the vehicle;

"forward-facing high-backed seat" means a forward-facing seat which is also a high-backed seat;

"high-backed seat" means a seat the highest part of which is at least 1 metre above the deck of the vehicle;

"inertia reel belt" means a three-point belt of either of the types required for a front outboard seating position by paragraph 3.1.1 of Annex 1 to Community Directive 77/541;

"lap belt" means a seat belt which passes across the front of the wearer's pelvic region and which is designed for use by an adult;

"seat" includes any part designed for the accommodation of one adult of a continuous seat designed for the accommodation of more than one adult;

"seat belt" means a belt intended to be worn by a person in a vehicle and designed to prevent or lessen injury to its wearer in the event of an accident to the vehicle and includes, in the case of a child restraint, any special chair to which the belt is attached;

"specified passenger's seat" means–

   (i) in the case of a vehicle which has one forward-facing front seat alongside the driver's seat, that seat, and in the case of a vehicle which has more than one such seat, the one furthest from the driver's seat; or

   (ii) if the vehicle normally has no seat which is the specified passenger's seat under sub-paragraph (i) of this definition the forward-facing front seat for a passenger which is the foremost in the vehicle and furthest from the driver's seat, unless there is a fixed partition separating that seat from the space in front of it alongside the driver's seat; and

"three-point belt" means a seat belt which–

   (i) restrains the upper and lower parts of the torso;

   (ii) includes a lap belt;

   (iii) is anchored at not less than three points; and

   (iv) is designed for use by an adult.

EXPLANATORY NOTE

(This note is not part of the Regulations)

These Regulations amend the Road Vehicles (Construction and Use) Regulations 1986 in two main respects. First, there are new requirements as to the strength of the superstructure of single decked coaches (defined as buses weighing more than 7.5 tonnes and having a maximum speed of more than 60 mph and, for the purposes of the new provisions, equipped with under-floor luggage compartments) and as to the emergency exits with which double-decked coaches are to be equipped. Secondly, there are changes in the requirements as to seat belts and their anchorages for goods vehicles, minibuses and coaches.

Regulation 4 introduces into section J (protective systems) two new regulations. New regulation 53A requires single-decked coaches first used on or after 1st April 1990 to comply with ECE Regulation 66: the effect is to require such vehicles to be built with sufficient superstructure and roof strength to provide a survival space for passengers in the event of a roll-over accident. New regulation 53B requires that either a second staircase or a means of breaking the side windows in case of emergency shall be provided in the upper deck of double-decked coaches.

Regulations 5 to 7 amend respectively regulations 46 (seat belt anchorage points), 47 (seat belts) and 48 (maintenance of seat belts and anchorage points).

The principal changes are–
(a) to extend the requirement to fit seat belts and their anchorages to certain seats on coaches, to the front seats of minibuses constructed or adapted to carry more than 12 passengers, and to the centre front seats of minibuses, motor ambulances and motor caravans; and
(b) to extend the requirement to fit seat belt anchorages, capable of taking lap belts, to heavy goods vehicles.

These new requirements will apply to vehicles first used on or after 1st October 1988. The current exemption from fitting a seat belt and its anchorages to the specified front seat, where there is a fixed partition separating that seat from the space alongside the driver's seat, is revoked from that date for new vehicles. Other changes reflect amendments to the British Standards mentioned in the Regulations.

Regulations 46 and 47 as amended by these regulations are set out in the Schedule.

Copies of the British Standards (and amendments thereto) mentioned in the Regulations are available from the British Standards Institution, Linford Wood, Milton Keynes MK14 6LE (telephone number 0908 320060).

1987 No. 1134

FISH FARMING

The Fish Farming (Financial Assistance) Scheme 1987

Approved by both Houses of Parliament

Made - - - -	*1st July 1987*
Laid before Parliament	*3rd July 1987*
Coming into force	*4th July 1987*

The Minister of Agriculture, Fisheries and Food and the Secretaries of State respectively concerned with fisheries in Scotland and Wales, in exercise of the powers conferred on them by section 31(1), (3), (4) and (5) of the Fisheries Act 1981(a) and of all other powers enabling them in that behalf, with the approval of the Treasury in accordance with the said section 31(1), hereby make the following Scheme:

Title, extent and commencement

1. This Scheme, which may be cited as the Fish Farming (Financial Assistance) Scheme 1987, shall apply to Great Britain, and shall come into force on 4th July 1987.

Interpretation

2. In this Scheme, unless the context otherwise requires–

"applicant", in relation to the approval of expenditure for the purposes of a grant, means the person who is making or has made the application for that approval;

"the appropriate Minister" means–

    (a) in relation to England, the Minister of Agriculture, Fisheries and Food,

    (b) in relation to Scotland, the Secretary of State for Scotland,

    (c) in relation to Wales, the Secretary of State for Wales;

"approved" means approved for the purposes of a grant under this Scheme by the appropriate Minister in writing, and "approve" and "approval" shall be construed accordingly;

"the Commission" means the Commission of the European Communities;

"Community aid" means financial aid from European Economic Community funds;

"the Council" means the Council of the European Communities;

"the Council Regulation" means the Council Regulation (EEC) No 4028/86 on Community measures to improve and adapt structures in the fisheries and aquaculture sector(b).

(a) 1981 c.29.
(b) OJ No L376, 31.12.86, p.7.

Grants for fish farming projects

3.—(1) The appropriate Minister may make to any person a grant towards expenditure incurred, or to be incurred, in connection with a project for fish farming, if such grant appears to him–

(a) to be desirable for the purpose of the reorganisation, development or promotion of fish farming in England, Scotland or Wales, as the case may be, and

(b) to be requisite for the purpose of enabling the person to benefit from Community aid for a fish farming project covered by Title IV of the Council Regulation.

(2) The appropriate Minister shall not make such a grant unless–

(a) he has approved the expenditure, and

(b) a decision that the project shall receive Community aid has been taken, and notified to the Unitied Kingdom, under article 35 of the Council Regulation.

(3) The appropriate Minister may approve the expenditure in whole or in part for the purposes of a grant under this Scheme and any such approval may be given subject to such conditions as the appropriate Minister thinks fit.

(4) Any approval of expenditure for the purposes of a grant under this Scheme may be varied or withdrawn by the appropriate Minister with the applicant's written consent.

(5) Any payment by way of a grant under this Scheme may be made at such time, or by such instalments at such intervals or times, as the appropriate Minister may determine.

(6) Any application for approval of expenditure for the purposes of a grant under this Scheme shall be made in such form and manner and at such time as the appropriate Minister may from time to time determine; and the applicant shall furnish all such information relating to the application as the appropriate Minister shall require.

Amount of grant

4.—(1) The amount of grant which may be paid under this Scheme shall not exceed 10 per cent of such expenditure incurred, or to be incurred, for the purposes of the project as is approved by the Commission in deciding the amount of Community aid under the Council Regulation which the project shall receive.

(2) Where the expenditure referred to in sub-paragraph (1) of this paragraph has been approved for the purposes of any grant out of United Kingdom public funds other than a grant under this Scheme, and that other grant is insufficient to enable the project to receive the amount of Community aid decided by the Commission, the amount of grant which may be paid under this Scheme shall not exceed such amount as is sufficient, when added to that other grant, to enable the project to receive that amount of Community aid.

(3) A grant is a grant out of United Kingdom public funds for the purposes of sub-paragraph (2) of this paragraph if, and only if, it constitutes a financial contribution of the United Kingdom to the total investment for the purposes of article 12(1) and annex III of the Council Regulation.

Revocation of approval and recovery of grant

5. If after the appropriate Minister has approved any expenditure for the purposes of a grant under this Scheme it appears to that Minister–

(a) that any condition subject to which the approval was given has not been complied with, or

(b) that any work in respect of expenditure for which the approval was given has been badly done, or has been or is being unreasonably delayed, or is unlikely to be completed, or

(c) that the person by whom the application for that approval or for the making of any payment was made gave information on any matter relevant to the giving of the approval or the making of the payment which was false or misleading in a material respect, or

(d) that the Commission has decided under article 44(1) of the Council Regulation to suspend, reduce or discontinue Community aid and to recover any sums paid,

the appropriate Minister may revoke the approval in respect of the whole or part of the expenditure and, where any payment has been made by way of grant, may, unless a period exceeding six years has elapsed since the payment, on demand recover an amount equal to the payment which has been so made or such part thereof as the appropriate Minister may specify; but before revoking an approval in whole or in part under subparagraph (a), (b) or (c) of this paragraph the appropriate Minister—

    (i) shall give to the person to whom any payment by way of grant would be payable, or from whom any such amount would be recoverable, a written notification of the reasons for the action proposed to be taken by the appropriate Minister,

   (ii) shall afford that person an opportunity of appearing before and being heard by a person appointed for the purpose by the appropriate Minister, and

  (iii) shall consider the report by a person so appointed and supply a copy of the report to the person mentioned in subparagraph (i) above.

Amendment of the Fish Farming (Financial Assistance) Scheme 1984

6. The Fish Farming (Financial Assistance) Scheme 1984(**a**) is hereby amended by substituting for the definition of "the new Council Regulation" in paragraph 2 thereof (interpretation) the following definition—

' "the new Council Regulation" means Council Regulation (EEC) No 2908/83 on a common measure for restructuring, modernising and developing the fishing industry and for developing aquaculture(**b**), as amended by Council Regulation (EEC) No 3733/85(**c**).'.

In Witness whereof the Official Seal of the Minister of Agriculture, Fisheries and Food is hereunto affixed on 24th June 1987.

John MacGregor
Minister of Agriculture, Fisheries and Food

24th June 1987

Sanderson of Bowden
Minister of State, Scottish Office

18th June 1987

Peter Walker
Secretary of State for Wales

We approve,

Tony Durant
Mark Lennox-Boyd
1st July 1987   Two of the Lords Commissioners of Her Majesty's Treasury

---

(**a**) S.I. 1984/341.
(**b**) OJ No L290, 22.10.83, p.1.
(**c**) OJ No L361, 31.12.85, p.78.

EXPLANATORY NOTE

(This note is not part of the Scheme)

This Scheme, which applies to Great Britain, provides for the making of grants for fish farming projects, if such grants appear to Ministers–

(a) to be desirable for the purpose of the reorganisation, development or promotion of fish farming in Great Britain, and

(b) to be requisite for the purpose of enabling a person to qualify for financial aid from the European Economic Community for a fish farming project under Title IV of Council Regulation (EEC) No 4028/86, which relates to the development of aquaculture and structural works in coastal waters (paragraph 3).

Fish Farming is defined in section 31 of the Fisheries Act 1981, under which the Scheme is made, as the breeding, rearing or cultivating of fish (including shellfish) for the purpose of producing food for human consumption.

The maximum amount of grant under this Scheme is 10% of the investment. If the expenditure has been approved for the purpose of any other grant out of United Kingdom public funds, the maximum amount of grant is reduced proportionately (paragraph 4).

In specified circumstances approval of expenditure may be revoked and grant may be recovered (paragraph 5).

Section 31(8) of the Fisheries Act 1981 provides for the application of certain offences in respect of fraudulent applications for grant, for which there is a maximum penalty of £2,000.

The Scheme amends the definition of "the new Council Regulation" in The Fish Farming (Financial Assistance) Scheme 1984 to provide for the inclusion in that definition of Council Regulation (EEC) No 3733/85, which amended Council Regulation (EEC) No 2908/83 (paragraph 6).

1987 No. 1135

SEA FISHERIES

SEA FISH INDUSTRY

The Fishing Vessels (Acquisition and Improvement) (Grants) Scheme 1987

Approved by both Houses of Parliament

Made - - -	*1st July 1987*
Laid before Parliament	*3rd July 1987*
Coming into force	*4th July 1987*

The Minister of Agriculture, Fisheries and Food, and the Secretaries of State respectively concerned with the sea fish industry in Scotland, Wales and Northern Ireland, in exercise of the powers conferred on them by sections 15(1) and (2) and 18(1) of the Fisheries Act 1981(a) and of all their other enabling powers, with the approval of the Treasury in accordance with the said section 15(1), hereby make the following Scheme:

Title and commencement

1. This Scheme may be cited as the Fishing Vessels (Acquisition and Improvement) (Grants) Scheme 1987 and shall come into force on 4th July 1987.

Interpretation

2.—(1) In this Scheme unless the context otherwise requires–
"the control period" means
    (a) in the case of grant paid in respect of any improvement a period of 3 years commencing with the date on which the improvement was completed to the satisfaction of the Ministers, and
    (b) in the case of any other grant paid in respect of or in connection with a vessel, a period of 5 years commencing with the date on which the vessel was first registered in the United Kingdom;
"improvement" has the meaning assigned to it by paragraph 3(1)(b) of this Scheme;
"the Ministers" means the Minister of Agriculture, Fisheries and Food and the Secretaries of State respectively concerned with the sea fish industry in Scotland, Wales and Northern Ireland;
"processing", in relation to sea fish, includes preserving or preparing fish, or producing any substance or article from fish, by any method for human or animal consumption;
"products", in relation to sea fish, means anything produced by processing the fish;
"length", in relation to a fishing vessel, means length between perpendiculars

(a) 1981 c.29.

measured in accordance with Article 2(2) of Council Regulation (EEC) No. 2930/86 defining characteristics for fishing vessels(**a**);

"relevant equipment" means equipment or apparatus of any description constructed or adapted for the purposes of catching or processing sea fish;

"West of Scotland" means the region of Dumfries and Galloway, the islands areas of the Western Isles, Orkney and Shetland, together with the districts of Caithness, Sutherland, Ross and Cromarty, Skye and Lochalsh, Lochaber, Argyll and Bute, Cunninghame, Kyle and Carrick.

(2) Any payment of grant made under this Scheme by the Ministers may be made by any of them and any reference in the Scheme to such payment shall be construed accordingly.

Application for grant

3.—(1) Any person engaged or proposing to be engaged in the sea fish industry by carrying on the business of owning and operating one or more vessels registered in the United Kingdom (of whatever size and in whatever way propelled) for the purpose of catching or processing sea fish may apply to the Ministers for a grant in respect of expenditure incurred–

    (a) in the acquisition of a new vessel, registered or intended to be registered in the United Kingdom to be engaged in the catching or processing of sea fish, including equipment required for the operation of the vessel which is sold with the vessel; or

    (b) subject to sub-paragraph (2) below, in the acquisition, installation, modification, renewal or replacement of any part of a vessel registered in the United Kingdom, engaged in the catching or processing of sea fish, or of an engine or any part of an engine of or for such a vessel, or of any relevant equipment required for, or installed or used on, such a vessel (such acquisition, installation, modification, renewal or replacement being hereinafter referred to as an "improvement"):

(2) No grant shall be payable under sub-paragraph (1)(b) above in respect of–

    (a) expenditure incurred in the acquisition or installation of any second-hand part of a vessel, engine, part of an engine or relevant equipment; or

    (b) expenditure incurred in relation to an improvement in so far as, in the opinion of the Ministers, such expenditure can be regarded as laid out on the routine repair or maintenance of the vessel or of its engine or of any relevant equipment required for the vessel or installed or used thereon.

(3) Applications for grant under this Scheme shall be made in writing in such form as the Ministers may from time to time require, and shall be delivered to them at such address as they may at any time or in any particular case direct.

4.   Applicants for grants under this Scheme in respect of the acquisition of a vessel shall be required to satisfy the Ministers with regard to the prospect of their being able to operate the vessel successfully and that they have the ability to manage, and sufficient financial resources for the purposes of, the business in which the vessel will be employed.

5.   The Ministers may require applicants, in relation to the application made, to make a full statement of their financial position, including their assets, debts and obligations, and to make available for inspection by the Ministers, or their duly authorised agents, such books of account and other records and documents within their possession or control as the Ministers may require.

6.   Where expenditure is shared by two or more persons, applications for grant under this Scheme may be made in respect of either the full expenditure or part of the expenditure incurred and may be made by individual applicants or by two or more applicants jointly.

7.—(1) In considering whether or not to approve an application for the payment of a grant under this Scheme, the Ministers–

(**a**) OJ No. L274, 25.9.1986, p.1.

(a) shall have regard to the needs and interests of the sea fish industry or to that section thereof to which the application relates, but

(b) shall not approve the application so far as it relates to any proportion or item of the proposed expenditure which in their opinion is unnecessary or unwarranted having regard to the benefit likely to be derived from the expenditure in respect of which the application is made; and

(c) in the case of an improvement, shall not approve the application unless they are satisfied that the expenditure in relation to which the grant will be payable is likely to result in an increase in the efficiency or economy of the operation of the vessel in respect of or in connection with which the application is made as regards one or more of the following matters, that is to say–

    (i) the catching of sea fish,

    (ii) the handling, processing or storage of sea fish,

    (iii) the working conditions of the officers or crew,

    (iv) the condition of sea fish or of sea fish products at the time of landing, and

    (v) the safety and seaworthiness of the vessel,

regard being had to the technical and economic standards prevailing in the sea fish industry at the time of the consideration of the application by the Ministers and to the results of any experiments and research which have relation to the subject of the particular expenditure.

(2) No grant shall be paid under this Scheme unless–

(a) the application for the payment of the grant has been approved by the Ministers before 31st December 1991; and

(b) the conditions set out in paragraphs 10 and 11 of the Scheme have been complied with.

Rates of grant

8.—(1) Subject to paragraph 9 of this Scheme (maximum amount of grant), the rates of grant payable under this Scheme shall be as set out in sub-paragraphs (2) to (5) of this paragraph.

(2) The rate of grant in respect of a vessel under 24 metres in length shall be 30 per cent of the expenditure approved by the Ministers.

(3) Subject to sub-paragraph (4) of this paragraph, the rate of grant in respect of a vessel between 24 metres and 33 metres in length inclusive shall be 30 per cent of the expenditure approved by the Ministers.

(4) The rate of grant in respect of a vessel between 24 metres and 33 metres in length inclusive shall be 20 per cent of the expenditure approved by the Ministers where the applicant for grant under this Scheme has received financial assistance from the European Economic Community in respect of that vessel under Title II or III of Council Regulation (EEC) No. 4028/86 on Community measures to improve and adapt structures in the fisheries and aquaculture sector(a) at the rate specified in Annex II to that Regulation in respect of Northern Ireland or the West of Scotland.

(5) The rate of grant in respect of a vessel over 33 metres in length shall be 10 per cent of the expenditure approved by the Ministers.

Maximum amount of grant

9. The maximum amount of grant payable under this Scheme as respects any one vessel in any one ownership shall not exceed £250,000.

Conditions for payment of grant

10.—(1) In a case where the applicant intends to enter into a contract with another person for the carrying out of the whole or any part of the work to which his application for a grant relates, the Ministers shall, before the contract is made, approve–

(a) the plans and specifications of the vessel to which the application for grant relates;

(a) OJ No. L376, 31.12.1986, p.7.

(b) the tender for expenditure to be incurred; and

(c) the form of contract to be entered into between the applicant and the builder, supplier or other contractor.

(2) In a case where the applicant himself intends to undertake the whole or any part of the work to which his application for a grant relates the Ministers shall, before such work is begun, give their approval to the undertaking both as regards the manner in which it is to be carried out and the kind, quantity and cost of the materials to be supplied in the course thereof.

(3) The vessel in respect of or in connection with which an application for a grant is made shall conform to any standards laid down under the Merchant Shipping Acts 1894 to 1986 and shall be constructed or adapted so as to make such provision for the accommodation of officers and crew as, in the opinion of the Ministers, conforms to the best modern practice after making due allowance for the age and kind of vessel concerned, for sleeping and messing accommodation, sanitary accommodation, medical or first-aid facilities, store rooms, catering facilities and other accommodation.

(4) No grant shall be paid in respect of expenditure incurred in the acquisition of a vessel, or part of a vessel, constructed, or the improvement of a vessel carried out, elsewhere than in a member state.

11. Any person authorised in writing by the Ministers shall have the right to inspect the vessel in respect of or in connection with which a grant has been or is to be made under this Scheme at any reasonable time either during its construction and on its completion or during the carrying out of the improvement and on the completion of the improvement, as the case may be, and thereafter at all reasonable times within the control period.

12. No payment of, or on account of, a grant shall be made until the sum to be found by the applicant has been paid towards the expenditure in respect of which the application is made and thereafter payment of, or on account of, the grant may be made by the Ministers direct to the applicant, or on the applicant's behalf to the builder, supplier or other contractor in one sum or by such instalments and at such times as may be required in conformity with the contract, on the receipt of certificates or such further or other evidence that payment is due as may be required by the Ministers.

False statements

13. If any person makes a false statement or furnishes false information in respect of any of the matters required to be disclosed in connection with an application for payment of a grant under this Scheme, any payment of or on account of a grant to that applicant may at any time be refused, and any such payment already made in relation to that application may be recovered as a civil debt by the Ministers.

Undertakings

14.—(1) Any person whose application for a grant under this Scheme is approved by the Ministers may be required to give such undertaking as they may consider appropriate to the case, and in particular (but without prejudice to the generality of the foregoing) shall be required in any case–

(a) during the control period, and as may be appropriate to the case, either to employ the vessel in respect of or in connection with which the application was made (hereinafter in this paragraph referred to as "the vessel") or to take all reasonable steps to ensure its employment in the diligent and vigorous prosecution of the catching or processing of sea fish to the satisfaction of the Ministers;

(b) to insure the vessel and keep it insured against all marine risks and war risks during the control period in a sum approved by the Ministers, which shall be at least sufficient to ensure that in the event of total loss of the vessel there will be made available sufficient monies to meet the repayment of the grant or any part thereof which might be repayable at the date of the loss; and

(c) to keep and make available for inspection by the Ministers at all reasonable times during the control period any books, records or other documents within the applicant's possession or control necessary to enable the Ministers to satisfy themselves that any conditions of the grant have been complied with.

Recovery of grant

15.—(1) The Ministers may recover as a civil debt from any person who receives grant under this Scheme a sum equivalent to the whole or any part of the grant paid to that person if there occurs within the control period–

(a) the total loss of the vessel;

(b) a breach of any undertaking or condition subject to which the grant was made;

(c) a mortgage of the vessel (other than a mortgage created for the raising of money applied towards the cost of construction or improvement of the vessel, being a mortgage approved by the Ministers before it was made), a transfer of registration of the vessel or a charter for any purpose other than the employment of the vessel in the catching or processing of sea fish based on a port in the United Kingdom;

(d) sale or otherwise of the vessel or of any part thereof or of its engine or of any part thereof or of any equipment or apparatus used on or in connection therewith, or of any part of a vessel, engine, part of an engine or relevant equipment which is the subject of the improvement in respect of which the grant or any part of it was made.

(2) If the event which gives rise to the recovery of the grant occurs–

(a) more than 3 years from the commencement of the control period in respect of grant paid towards the acquisition of a vessel, or

(b) more than 2 years from the commencement of the control period in respect of grant paid towards improvements

there shall be repaid to the Ministers a sum equivalent to a proportion of the grant to be calculated by multiplying the total amount of the grant by the fraction which represents the relationship which the un-expired part of the control period bears to the full control period.

Revocation of earlier Schemes

16. The Schemes specified in the Schedule to this Scheme are hereby revoked.

In witness whereof the Official Seal of the Minister of Agriculture, Fisheries and Food is hereunto affixed on 24th June 1987.

John MacGregor
Minister of Agriculture, Fisheries and Food

22nd June 1987

Sanderson of Bowden
Minister of State, Scottish Office

18th June 1987

Peter Walker
Secretary of State for Wales

24th June 1987

Tom King
Secretary of State for Northern Ireland

We approve,

Tony Durant
Mark Lennox-Boyd
Two of the Lords Commissioners of
Her Majesty's Treasury

1st July 1987

Paragraph 16   SCHEDULE

                                    REVOCATIONS

Scheme Revoked	References
The White Fish Industry (Grants for Fishing Vessels and Engines) Scheme 1962	S.I. 1962/1586
The Herring Industry (Grants for Fishing Vessels and Engines) Scheme 1962	S.I. 1962/1616
The White Fish Industry (Grants for Fishing Vessels and Engines) (Amendment) Scheme 1964	S.I. 1964/321
The White Fish Industry (Grants for Improvement of Fishing Vessels) Scheme 1964	S.I. 1964/1173
The Fishing Vessels (Aquisition and Improvement) (Grants) Scheme 1967	S.I. 1967/372
The Fishing Vessels (Acquisition and Improvement) (Grants) (Amendment) Scheme 1967	S.I. 1967/1131
The Fishing Vessels (Acquisition and Improvement) (Grants) (Amendment) Scheme 1971	S.I. 1971/797
The Fishing Vessels (Acquisition and Improvement) (Grants) (Amendment) Scheme 1972	S.I. 1973/116
The Fishing Vessels (Acquisition and Improvement) (Grants) (Amendment) Scheme 1973	S.I. 1974/194
The Fishing Vessels (Acquisition and Improvement) (Grants) (Amendment) Scheme 1975	S.I. 1975/360
The Fishing Vessels (Acquisition and Improvement) (Grants) Scheme 1976	S.I. 1976/304
The Fishing Vessels (Acquisition and Improvement) (Grants) (Variation) Scheme 1976	S.I. 1976/2136
The Fishing Vessels (Acquisition and Improvement) (Grants) (Variation) Scheme 1977	S.I. 1977/2136
The Fishing Vessels (Acquisition and Improvement) (Grants) (Variation) Scheme 1978	S.I. 1978/1820
The Fishing Vessels (Acquisition and Improvement) (Grants) (Variation) Scheme 1979	S.I. 1979/1692
The Fishing Vessels (Acquisition and Improvement) (Grants) (Variation) Scheme 1980	S.I. 1980/1973

EXPLANATORY NOTE

(This note is not part of the Scheme)

This Scheme enables grants to be made by the Minister of Agriculture, Fisheries and Food and the Secretaries of State respectively concerned with the sea fish industry in Scotland, Wales and Northern Ireland being grants towards expenditure incurred in the acquisition or improvement of vessels engaged or to be engaged in catching or processing sea fish (paragraph 3).

No grant may be paid under this Scheme unless the relevant application is approved by Ministers before 31st December 1991 and the conditions set out in paragraphs 9 and 10 of the Scheme have been complied with (paragraph 7). The rates of grant for all vessels, registered or intended to be registered in the United Kingdom, are set out in paragraph 8 of the Scheme.

The Scheme revokes the earlier Schemes listed in the Schedule which have ceased to have effect (paragraph 16).

STATUTORY INSTRUMENTS

1987 No. 1136

SEA FISHERIES

SEA FISH INDUSTRY

The Fishing Vessels (Financial Assistance) Scheme 1987

Approved by both Houses of Parliament

Made - - - -	*1st July 1987*
Laid before Parliament	*3rd July 1987*
Coming into force -	*4th July 1987*

The Minister of Agriculture, Fisheries and Food and the Secretaries of State respectively concerned with the sea fish industry in Scotland, Wales and Northern Ireland, in exercise of the powers conferred on them by sections 15(1) and (2) and 18(1) of the Fisheries Act 1981**(a)** and of all other powers enabling them in that behalf, with the approval of the Treasury in accordance with the said section 15(1), hereby make the following Scheme:

PART I

PRELIMINARY

Title and commencement

1. This Scheme may be cited as the Fishing Vessels (Financial Assistance) Scheme 1987 and shall come into force on 4th July 1987.

Interpretation

2.—(1) In this Scheme unless the context otherwise requires–

"the Commission" means the Commission of the European Communities;

"the Council Regulation" means Council Regulation (EEC) No. 4028/86 on Community measures to improve and adapt structures in the fisheries and aquaculture sector**(b)**;

"exploratory fishing voyage" has the meaning assigned to it by Article 13 of the Council Regulation;

(a) 1981 c.29.
(b) OJ No L376, 31.12.86, p.7.

"joint venture" has the meaning assigned to it by Article 18 of the Council Regulation;

"the Minister" means the Minister of Agriculture, Fisheries and Food;

"registered fishing vessel" means any fishing vessel registered in the United Kingdom under Part IV of the Merchant Shipping Act 1894(b);

"third country" means any country other than a member state and does not include the Isle of Man or any of the Channel Islands.

(2) Any reference in this Scheme to a numbered paragraph shall be construed as a reference to the appropriate paragraph of this Scheme.

(3) Where any document is required by a provision of this Scheme to be submitted to the Minister, the document shall be taken to be submitted to the Minister on date on which it is received at an office of the Minister.

Purpose of Scheme

3. This Scheme provides for the making of the following grants for the purpose of re-organising and developing the sea fish catching industry–

(a) exploratory voyage grants; and

(b) joint venture grants.

PART II

EXPLORATORY VOYAGE GRANTS

Basis of payment

4. An exploratory voyage grant shall be payable, subject to and in accordance with the following provisions of this Part, Part IV of this Scheme and the Council Regulation, to the owner of a registered fishing vessel in respect of an exploratory fishing voyage.

Closing date for applications

5. No application for an exploratory voyage grant shall be submitted after 31st July 1991.

Approval of applications

6.—(1) If the Minister is satisfied that the proposed voyage to which an application for an exploratory voyage grant relates meets the requirements of Title V of the Council Regulation, he may approve the application and submit it to the Commission in accordance with Article 16 of the Council Regulation.

(2) An approval by the Minister under sub-paragraph (1) of this paragraph may be made subject to such conditions as the Minister sees fit.

Voyage not to begin before approval

7. An exploratory voyage grant shall not be paid in respect of an exploratory fishing voyage that is begun before the application relating to that voyage has been approved by the Minister and by the Commission.

Report on completion of voyage

8.—(1) After the completion of an exploratory fishing voyage in respect of which an application for an exploratory voyage grant has been approved by the Minister and by the Commission, the applicant shall submit to the Minister and to the Commission a report in accordance with Article 17 of the Council Regulation.

(b) 1894 c.60.

(2) No such report shall be submitted after 31st May 1992.

Payment

9. On receipt of a report submitted in pursuance of paragraph 8, the Minister may, if he is satisfied–

(a) that the voyage to which the report relates was completed substantially in accordance with the application relating to the voyage,

(b) that the conditions (if any) subject to which his approval or that of the Commission was given have been observed, and

(c) that the foregoing requirements of this Part and the requirements of the Council Regulation have been met in respect of the voyage,

pay an exploratory voyage grant to the applicant.

Amount of grant

10. The amount of grant shall be 10 per cent. of the eligible cost of the voyage calculated in accordance with Article 15 of the Council Regulation.

PART III

JOINT VENTURE GRANTS

Basis of payment

11. A joint venture grant shall be payable, subject to and in acccordance with the following provisions of this Part and Part IV of this Scheme and the Council Regulation, to the owner of a registered fishing vessel in respect of his participation in a joint venture.

Applications

12.—(1) An application for a joint venture grant shall include a description of the proposed joint venture in respect of which the application is made, specifying in particular its expected duration and the area and vessel concerned.

(2) No application for a joint venture grant shall be submitted after 31st July 1991.

Approval of applications

13.—(1) If the Minister is satisfied that the proposed joint venture project to which an application for a joint venture grant relates meets the requirements of Title VI of the Council Regulation, he may approve the application and submit it to the Commission in accordance with Article 21 of the Council Regulation.

(2) An approval by the Minister under sub-paragraph (1) of this paragraph may be made subject to such conditions as the Minister sees fit.

Venture not to begin before approval

14. A joint venture grant shall not be paid in respect of a joint fishing venture that is begun before the application relating to that venture has been approved by the Minister and by the Commission.

Report of completion of joint venture

15.—(1) After the completion of a joint venture in respect of which an application for a joint venture grant has been approved by the Minister and by the Commission, the applicant shall submit to the Minister and to the Commission a report that the venture has been completed.

(2) No such report shall be submitted after 31st May 1992.

(3) For the purposes of this paragraph and paragraph 16, a joint venture which involves the temporary transfer of a vessel to third country waters is completed at the end of the period of transfer.

Payment

16. On receipt of a report submitted in pursuance of paragraph 15(1), the Minister may, if he is satisfied–

    (a) that the venture to which the report relates was completed substantially in accordance with the application relating to the venture,

    (b) that the conditions (if any) subject to which his approval or that of the Commission was given have been observed, and

    (c) that the foregoing requirements of this Part and the requirements of the Council Regulation have been met in respect of the venture,

pay a joint venture grant to the applicant.

Amount of grant

17. The amount of a joint venture grant shall be equal to the amount of the co-operation premium calculated in accordance with Articles 20 and 48 of the Council Regulation.

PART IV
GENERAL

Application to Minister

18. Any application for a grant under this Scheme shall be submitted to the Minister.

Form and manner of applications, etc.

19. Any application, amendment or report submitted in pursuance of or in accordance with any provision of this Scheme shall be made in such form and manner as the Minister may determine.

Furnishing of information

20. Any applicant for a grant under this Scheme shall provide all such information and documentation relating to his application, including any information or documentation or report submitted in pursuance of or in accordance with any provision of this Scheme, as the Minister may require.

Records

21. Any person who has received any payment under this Scheme shall preserve until the end of the third calendar year following the calendar year in which the payment was made all books, documents or other records which relate to any application made by him for payment under the Scheme and shall supply to the Minister such copies of such of those books, documents or other records as the Minister may require.

Recovery where false statement made

22. If any person makes a false statement or furnishes false information in connection with an application for grant under this Scheme, the Minister may recover as a civil debt a sum equivalent to the amount of any grant already made in relation to that application.

In Witness whereof the Official Seal of the Minister of Agriculture, Fisheries and Food is hereunto affixed on 24th June 1987.

John MacGregor
Minister of Agriculture, Fisheries and Food

24th June 1987

Sanderson of Bowden
Minister of State, Scottish Office

18th June 1987

Peter Walker
Secretary of State for Wales

24th June 1987

Tom King
Secretary of State for Northern Ireland

We approve,

1st July 1987

Tony Durant
Mark Lennox-Boyd
Two of the Lords Commissioners of Her Majesty's Treasury

EXPLANATORY NOTE

(This note is not part of the Scheme)

This Scheme provides for the making of grants by the Minister of Agriculture, Fisheries and Food for the purpose of re-organising and developing the sea fish catching industry of the United Kingdom. There are two types of grant, namely exploratory voyage grants and joint venture grants.

Provision for these grants is made in pursuance of Council Regulation (EEC) No 4028/86 on Community measures to improve and adapt structures in the fisheries and aquaculture sector.

An exploratory voyage grant is payable when a registered fishing vessel engages in a fishing operation carried out for commercial purposes in a given area with a view to assessing the profitability of regular, long-term exploitation of the fishery resources in that area (paragraph 4 of the Scheme and Article 13 of the Council Regulation) if certain requirements are met (paragraph 6 of the Scheme and Article 14 of the Council Regulation). The amount of an exploratory voyage grant is 10 per cent. of the eligible cost of the voyage, calculated in accordance with Article 15 of the Council Regulation (paragraph 10).

A joint venture grant is payable when the owner of a registered fishing vessel participates in a contractual association set up for a limited time with natural or legal persons of third countries with which the Community maintains relations on fishing matters for the purpose of the joint exploitation and use of the fishery resources of those countries (paragraph 11 of the Scheme and Article 18 of the Council Regulation) if certain requirements are met (paragraph 13 of the Scheme and Articles 19 and 21 of the Council Regulation). The amount of a joint venture grant varies according to the size of the vessel and the duration of the joint venture (paragraph 17 of the Scheme and Article 20 of the Council Regulation).

Part IV of the Scheme contains general requirements applicable to both types of grant.

Persons receiving grants are required to keep records (paragraph 21) and provision is made for the recovery of grant paid where false information is supplied (paragraph 22).

Offences and penalties in connection with this Scheme are provided by section 17 of the Fisheries Act 1981.

1987 No. 1137 (L.5)

JUSTICES OF THE PEACE, ENGLAND AND WALES

The Justices of the Peace (Size and Chairmanship of Bench) (Amendment) Rules 1987

Made - - - -	*30th June 1987*
Laid before Parliament	*9th July 1987*
Coming into force	*1st August 1987*

The Lord Chancellor, in exercise of the powers conferred on him by section 18 of the Justices of the Peace Act 1979(**a**), after consultation with the Rule Committee appointed under section 144 of the Magistrates' Courts Act 1980(**b**), hereby makes the following Rules:

1.—(1) These Rules may be cited as the Justices of the Peace (Size and Chairmanship of Bench) (Amendment) Rules 1987 and shall come into force on 1st August 1987.

(2) In these Rules, "the principal Rules" means the Justices of the Peace (Size and Chairmanship of Bench) Rules 1986(**c**).

2. For paragraph (2) of rule 6 of the principal Rules there shall be substituted the following paragraph–

"(2) A person who has held office as chairman shall not be eligible for re-election as chairman at an election meeting if on 1st January next after the election meeting he will have held such office for five consecutive years and less than three years will have elapsed from when he last held office unless–

(a) at the time when the election meeting is held he holds office as chairman, and

(b) the justices entitled to vote at the election meeting decide, in accordance with paragraph (3) below, that the restriction on eligibility imposed by this paragraph shall not apply in relation to the election to be held at that meeting."

30th June 1987

Havers, C.

(**a**) 1979 c.55.
(**b**) 1980 c.43.
(**c**) S.I. 1986/923.

EXPLANATORY NOTE

(This note is not part of the Rules)

These Rules provide for a new rule 6(2) in the Justices of the Peace (Size and Chairmanship of Bench) Rules 1986. Rule 6 of the 1986 Rules introduced a restriction on eligibility for election as chairman of the justices where a person has held office for five consecutive years or more and less than three years have elapsed since he last held office unless the justices decide that he should be eligible for re-election.

Under these Rules that restriction on eligibility for re-election may be lifted by such a decision of the justices in the case of a sitting chairman but not otherwise.

STATUTORY INSTRUMENTS

1987 No. 1138

EDUCATION, ENGLAND AND WALES

The Education (Grants) (City Technology Colleges) Regulations 1987

Made - - - -	*1st July 1987*
Laid before Parliament	*13th July 1987*
Coming into force -	*6th August 1987*

In exercise of the powers conferred by section 100(1)(b) and (3) of the Education Act 1944(a) and vested in the Secretary of State(b), the Secretary of State for Education and Science hereby makes the following Regulations:

Citation, commencement and interpretation

1.—(1) These Regulations may be cited as the Education (Grants) (City Technology Colleges) Regulations 1987 and shall come into force on 6th August 1987.

(2) In these Regulations "city technology college" means an independent school situated in England which is for the time being recognised by the Secretary of State as a city technology college or a proposed independent school to be situated in England the proposals for which are, for the time being, recognised by the Secretary of State as proposals for a city technology college as the context may require.

Payments of grant

2.—(1) The Secretary of State may pay grants of such amounts as he may determine to persons other than local education authorities in respect of expenditure incurred or to be incurred by them for the purposes of establishing, altering or maintaining a city technology college, which expenditure is for the time being approved by the Secretary of State.

(2) Payments of grant under these Regulations shall be made at such times and in such instalments as the Secretary of State thinks appropriate.

Conditions of Payment

3. The making of payments of grant under these Regulations shall be dependent on the fulfilment of such conditions as may be specified by the Secretary of State in the case in question.

Requirements to be observed

4. The persons to whom payments of grant are made under these Regulations shall comply with such requirements (including requirements as to the repayment of grant or

---

(a) 1944 c.31.
(b) S.I. 1964/490, 1970/1536, 1978/274.

the payment to the Secretary of State of other sums representing the value of property acquired, altered or maintained with the aid of grant or interest on sums due to him) as may be specified by the Secretary of State in the case in question.

5. Without prejudice to the generality of regulation 4, the persons to whom payments of grant are made under these Regulations shall–

    (a) keep such records and accounts and furnish to the Secretary of State such information, documents, returns and accounts as the Secretary of State may from time to time require;

    (b) open to the inspection of the Comptroller and Auditor General the records and accounts kept pursuant to the requirement imposed under paragraph (a) above;

    (c) where grant has been paid in respect of expenditure to be incurred and the expenditure or part of it is not incurred, repay on application made in that behalf by the Secretary of State the grant paid or the proportionate part thereof;

    (d) open or cause to be opened to inspection by a person authorised for the purposes hereof by the Secretary of State any city technology college or any premises which are the subject of proposals recognised by the Secretary of State as proposals for a city technology college and to afford to any such person all the facilities he requires for inspecting such college or premises.

Kenneth Baker
Secretary of State for Education and Science

1st July 1987

EXPLANATORY NOTE

(This note is not part of the Regulations)

These Regulations authorise the Secretary of State to pay grants to persons to meet or help to meet expenditure incurred or to be incurred by them in establishing, altering or maintaining a city technology college. Grants are payable in respect of expenditure which is approved by the Secretary of State. The Secretary of State may determine the amounts and timing of payments (regulations 1 and 2).

The Secretary of State may specify conditions to be satisfied before grant is payable (regulation 3).

The Secretary of State may also specify requirements to be complied with by recipients of grant. These may include requirements to repay grant or to pay to the Secretary of State sums representing the value of property acquired with grant and to pay interest on overdue sums (regulation 4).

The Regulations require recipients of grant to keep such records and accounts and to furnish such information, documents, returns and accounts to the Secretary of State as he may require, to open their records and accounts to inspection by the Comptroller and Auditor General and to repay on application by the Secretary of State all or part of grant paid in respect of expenditure to be incurred where the expenditure is not, or not wholly, incurred. The Regulations also provide for inspection by an authorised person of any city technology college or premises in which it is proposed to establish such a college (regulation 5).

STATUTORY INSTRUMENTS

1987 No. 1139 (S.84)

LANDS TRIBUNAL

The Lands Tribunal for Scotland (Amendment) (Fees) Rules 1987

Made - - - -	*23rd June 1987*
Coming into force	*1st August 1987*

In exercise of the powers conferred by section 3 of the Lands Tribunal Act 1949(**a**) and now vested in me(**b**) and of all other powers enabling me in that behalf, and with the approval of the Treasury, I hereby make the following Rules:

1. These Rules may be cited as the Lands Tribunal for Scotland (Amendment) (Fees) Rules 1987 and shall come into force on 1st August 1987.

2. For the Table of Fees contained in Schedule 2 to the Lands Tribunal for Scotland Rules 1971(**c**) there shall be substituted the Table of Fees set out in the Schedule to these Rules.

3. The Lands Tribunal for Scotland (Amendment) (Fees) Rules 1983(**d**) are hereby revoked.

Cameron of Lochbroom
Lord Advocate

Lord Advocate's Chambers
8th May 1987

We approve,

Tim Sainsbury
Michael Neubert
Two of the Lords Commissioners of Her Majesty's Treasury

23rd June 1987

(**a**) 1949 c.42; section 3 was amended by the Conveyancing and Feudal Reform (Scotland) Act 1970 (c.35), section 50(2) and by S.I. 1972/2002.
(**b**) S.I. 1972/2002.
(**c**) S.I. 1971/218; relevant amending instrument is S.I. 1983/1428.
(**d**) S.I. 1983/1428.

SCHEDULE

Rule 2

FEES

Item	Fee payable	Fee formerly payable(a)
Applications etc.		
1. On an application under section 1 or 4 of the Conveyancing and Feudal Reform (Scotland) Act 1970(**b**)	£25.00	*£15.00*
2. On an application under Part III of these Rules or where the Tribunal is acting under a reference by consent	£15.00	*£ 8.00*
3. On any other application (not being an appeal under Part IV or Part VA or a reference under Part V or Part VC of these Rules)	£10.00	*£ 8.00*
Hearing Fees, etc.		
4.(a) On the hearing of an application under section 1 of the Conveyancing and Feudal Reform (Scotland) Act 1970	£50.00	*£40.00*
(b) On the making of an order under section 1 of the Conveyancing and Feudal Reform (Scotland) Act 1970	£25.00	–
5. On the hearing of an application under Part III of these Rules or in relation to any dispute relating to the assessment of betterment levy referred to the Tribunal under section 47 of the Land Commission Act 1967(**c**) or where the Tribunal is acting under a reference by consent:–		
(a) Where the amount determined (in terms of a lump sum) –		
(i) is nil or does not exceed £1,000.00	£25.00	*(i) is nil or does not exceed £250.00* *£15.00* *(ii) exceeds £250.00 but does not exceed £500.00* *£20.00* *(iii) exceeds £500.00 but does not exceed £1,000* *£25.00*
(ii) exceeds £1,000.00	£25.00 with an addition of £20.00 in respect of every £1,000.00 or part of £1,000.00 by which the amount determined exceeds £1,000.00 but not exceeding in any case £1,500.00	*£25.00 with an addition of £15.00 in respect of every £1,000.00 or part of £1,000.00 by which the amount determined exceeds £1,000.00 but not exceeding in any case £1,500.00*

(**a**) This column shows the fees which were payable under S.I. 1971/218, as amended by S.I. 1983/1428 before the coming into operation of these Rules.
(**b**) 1970 c.35.
(**c**) 1967 c.1.

Item	Fee payable	Fee formerly payable(**a**)	
(b) Where the amount determined (in terms of rent or other annual payment) –			
(i) does not exceed £25.00 per annum	£25.00	*(i) does not exceed £10.00 per annum*	*£15.00*
		(ii) exceeds £10.00 per annum but does not exceed £25.00 per annum	*£20.00*
(ii) exceeds £25.00 per annum	£25.00 with an addition of £5.00 in respect of every £10.00 or part of £10.00 by which the rent, etc. determined exceeds £25.00 per annum but not exceeding in any case £1,500.00	*£20.00 with an addition of £3.00 in respect of every £10.00 or part of £10.00 by which the rent, etc. determined exceeds £25.00 per annum but not exceeding in any case £1,500.00*	
(c) Where there is a settlement as to amount, for each day on which the Tribunal sits	£50.00	*£40.00*	
6. On the hearing of any other appeal or reference (not being an appeal under Part IV or Part VA or a reference under Part V of these Rules) in which no fee is payable by reference to an amount determined	£50.00	*£40.00*	

Miscellaneous fees

Item	Fee payable	Fee formerly payable(**a**)
7. On supplying and certifying a copy of an order or determination of the Tribunal	£ 1.50	*£ 1.50*
8. For each sheet of a copy of all or part of any document (other than a copy to which item 7 applies)	£ 0.66	*£ 0.66*
9. On a case for the decision of the Court of Session - an application for appeal by way of stated case (to include drafting of case and any necessary copies)	£10.00	*£10.00*

(**a**) This column shows the fees which were payable under S.I. 1971/218, as amended by S.I. 1983/1428 before the coming into operation of these Rules.

EXPLANATORY NOTE

(This note is not part of the Rules)

These Rules amend the Lands Tribunal for Scotland Rules 1971 for two purposes –

  (1) to increase the fees payable to the Tribunal other than for items 5(a)(ii) in part and (b)(ii) in part (hearing fees), and items 7, 8 and 9 (miscellaneous fees) of the Schedule; and

  (2) to impose a fee for the first time on the Tribunal making an order under section 1 of the Conveyancing and Feudal Reform (Scotland) Act 1970 (item 4(b) of the Schedule).

STATUTORY INSTRUMENTS

1987 No. 1140 (S.85)

EDUCATION, SCOTLAND

The Education (Abolition of Corporal Punishment: Prescription of Schools) (Scotland) Order 1987

Made - - - -	*25th June 1987*
Coming into force	*15th August 1987*

The Secretary of State, in exercise of the powers conferred on him by section 48A(8)(a) of the Education (Scotland) Act 1980(**a**), hereby makes the following Order:

Citation and commencement

1. This Order may be cited as the Education (Abolition of Corporal Punishment: Prescription of Schools) (Scotland) Order 1987 and shall come into force on 15th August 1987.

Prescription of school

2. Queen Victoria School, Dunblane, is hereby prescribed for the purposes of subsection (5)(a)(iii) of section 48A of the Education (Scotland) Act 1980.

New St. Andrew's House, Edinburgh
25th June 1987

Michael B. Forsyth
Parliamentary Under Secretary of State,
Scottish Office

EXPLANATORY NOTE

(This note is not part of the Order)

This Order prescribes Queen Victoria School, Dunblane, as a school at which the provisions for abolition of corporal punishment in section 48A of the Education (Scotland) Act 1980 apply to the pupils. Queen Victoria School is an independent school most of the costs of which are paid by the Secretary of State for Defence.

Section 48A of the 1980 Act is inserted into that Act by section 48 of the Education (No. 2) Act 1986 and takes effect on 15th August 1987 by virtue of the Education (No. 2) Act 1986 (Commencement No. 2) Order 1987 (S.I. 1987/344).

(**a**) 1980 c.44; section 48A was inserted by section 48 of the Education (No. 2) Act 1986 (c.61).

HMSO
£28
(2 vol.